LAWYERS AND CLIENTS
CRITICAL ISSUES IN INTERVIEWING AND COUNSELING

■ ■ ■

By

Stephen Ellmann
New York Law School

Robert D. Dinerstein
American University, Washington College of Law

Isabelle R. Gunning
Southwestern Law School

Katherine R. Kruse
William S. Boyd School of Law,
University of Nevada Las Vegas

Ann C. Shalleck
American University, Washington College of Law

AMERICAN CASEBOOK SERIES®

WEST®
A Thomson Reuters business

Mat #16096903

American Casebook Series is a trademark registered in the U.S. Patent and Trademark Office.

© 2009 Thomson Reuters
    610 Opperman Drive
    St. Paul, MN 55123
    1–800–313–9378
Printed in the United States of America

ISBN: 978–0–314–23531–2

To our students, who have inspired us,
To our colleagues, who have encouraged us,
To all those we love, who have supported and cared about us.

*

PREFACE

This book grew out of our hope to write a book that would both instruct students and new lawyers and move the collective enterprise of clinical inquiry further forward. We sought to reflect the insights that have emerged in clinical scholarship over more than a quarter century, to continue the clinical tradition of drawing upon knowledge from other disciplines to inform our understanding of lawyers' work, and to build on these insights with new contributions of our own. We hope we have succeeded.

The book has taken shape over a number of years. It began as a project of writing an interviewing and counseling textbook that would demonstrate variations in the lawyer-client relationship, highlight the importance of context to interviewing and counseling methods, recognize the significance of connection in the lawyer-client relationship, incorporate explicit discussion of legal ethics, and emphasize the need to ground lawyering choices in a theory of lawyering. Although this vision remains in the book we have written, the structure and theme of the book have changed in two significant respects. First, rather than writing a more traditional interviewing and counseling textbook that incorporated the themes of variation, context, connection, ethics and theory-driven lawyering, we have chosen to explore these themes through a series of chapters that focus on critical issues in the lawyer-client relationship. Second, in exploring this series of critical issues, we have found ourselves articulating a common set of values and commitments about connection and engagement in the lawyer-client relationship, which we call "engaged client-centered representation."

We believe that a book on critical issues in interviewing and counseling is a useful addition to the already bountiful field of literature that has developed since clinical scholars first brought serious attention to questions of the lawyering process in the mid–1970s. Our experience as clinical professors has shown us the fertile ground for reflection and analysis that day-to-day interactions between lawyers and clients can provide. Within such interactions, often hidden assumptions—if unpacked—yield deep and interesting questions about the role of lawyers in the lawyer-client relationship as well as in society. By providing lawyer-client dialogues either followed by or interspersed with questions and analysis, we have endeavored to translate some of this richness into material that will make the complexities, indeterminacies, and challenges of lawyering accessible to students. We hope that our book will provide a useful tool for discussing the issues that inevitably arise in live-client clinic seminar classes. We also hope that it will be useful in introducing some of these complexities into simulation-based interviewing and counseling courses, legal ethics or professional responsibility courses, and the growing number of first-year courses designed to introduce law students to lawyers as problem-solvers.

In addition to providing students with challenging and provocative material through which to explore the complexities of lawyering, we also hope that our book advances the scholarly discussion of the critical issues on which we focus. We know that early interviewing and counseling textbooks did more than simply instruct; they also shaped an emerging field of lawyering theory. We have participated in the growth of this field through our own scholarship. This project has been an occasion for us—as like-minded scholars interested in client-centered lawyering theory—to put our minds together on the series of critical issues we discuss. In the course of creating this book, each of us has learned from our fellow authors—the four of us who began this project and Kate Kruse, who joined it later on—through a process of collaborative discussion and reconsideration of each chapter. The final product reflects the impact that our many intense discussions have had on the initial conceptions that each of us brought to the book; as a result, even those portions that were published elsewhere in article form have evolved in argument and sometimes in conclusions from their earlier versions.[1] We hope that the resulting insights and conclusions will provoke further comment and reaction from our colleagues, whether they seek to advance or critique the general vision of engaged client-centered lawyering that we present in these chapters.

Along the way we have benefited from the comments, criticisms, and assistance of many insightful friends and colleagues. These include Jane Aiken, Muneer Ahmad, Annette Appell, Julie Avdeeva, Lenni Benson, Johanna Bond, Camille Broussard, Susan Bryant, Carol Buckler, Ann Cammett, Megan Chaney, Christine Cimini, Teresa Delcorso, Monroe Freedman, Larry Grosberg, Carolyn Grose, Joseph Harbaugh, Randy Hertz, Jon Hyman, Randy Jonakait, John Leubsdorf, Jethro Lieberman, Adrienne Lockie, Rick Marsico, Elliott Milstein, Stephen Pepper, Adeen Postar, Nancy Rosenbloom, Tanina Rostain, Leticia Saucedo, Jim Stark, David Thronson, Anne Traum, Betsy Tsai, Sarah Valentine, Gretchen Viney, Ian Weinstein, Steve Zeidman and Don Zeigler. We are also grateful to the participants at the clinical conferences held at UCLA's Lake Arrowhead Conference Center (generously sponsored by UCLA and at different times by the Institute for Advanced Legal Studies and the University of Warwick), at which we presented a number of the chapters of this book in their initial drafts. For the same reason we thank the participants in the New York Law School Clinical Theory Workshops, in the Albany Law School's Kate Stoneman lecture, and in a session of the Southeastern Association of Law Schools. Some of these chapters were also presented to faculty workshops at our respective schools, and we thank our colleagues at those workshops, too. We are grateful as well for the research support of our respective law schools and the Deans who have served while we have worked on this project: Bryant Garth, Claudio Grossman, Richard

---

1. A very different version of our Introduction (Chapter 1) was published as Robert Dinerstein, Stephen Ellmann, Isabelle Gunning, & Ann Shalleck, *Legal Interviewing and Counseling: An Introduction*, 10 CLIN. L. REV. 281 (2003) . Portions of Chapters 2, 4 and 7 were published together as Robert Dinerstein, Stephen Ellmann, Isabelle Gunning, & Ann Shalleck, *Connection, Capacity, and Morality in Lawyer–Client Relationships: Dialogues and Commentary*, 10 CLIN. L. REV. 755 (2004). Chapter 6 was first published as Stephen Ellmann, *Truth and Consequences*, 69 FORDHAM L. REV. 895 (2000).

Matasar, Richard Morgan, Leigh Taylor, Harry Wellington and John White. We are thankful for the help of students who worked closely with us on this project, and for the steady support for this book that we've received from Thomson West.

We particularly thank our colleagues, past and present, who have worked with us in exploring and bringing to life the ideas and values fundamental to our shared enterprise of teaching our students about the excitement, joy, pain and responsibility of becoming a lawyer. At the end, all of us emerge with renewed respect for the complexity and importance of the task.

As with any difficult and fulfilling project, we thank the people closest to us for their love and patience as we've worked on this book.

Stephen Ellmann
New York Law School

Robert D. Dinerstein
American University, Washington College of Law

Isabelle R. Gunning
Southwestern Law School

Katherine R. Kruse
William S. Boyd School of Law, University of Nevada
Las Vegas

Ann C. Shalleck
American University, Washington College of Law

*

Summary of Contents

*

TABLE OF CONTENTS

*

LAWYERS AND CLIENTS

CRITICAL ISSUES IN INTERVIEWING AND COUNSELING

*

CHAPTER 1

INTRODUCTION: CRITICAL ISSUES IN INTERVIEWING AND COUNSELING

■ ■ ■

If you are picking up this book while studying lawyering skills in a simulation course or in a clinic, you may already have other readings that lay out important elements of the skills of interviewing and counseling. So why another book? The answer is that the skills you are learning are more complex and subtle than your first encounters with them might have suggested. Just as the law, which many lay people assume is a body of clear and precise rules, turns out to be so fraught with ambiguity that the central task of the first year is to learn how to work with that ambiguity, so the encounters between lawyers and clients turn out to have all the nuance and challenge of other human interactions, particularly those in many professional relationships, that deal with important and personal matters. This book is meant to help you go beyond the basic steps of interviewing and counseling—as important as they are, just as the elements of a tort claim or a contract cause of action are important—and to see and learn to work with the shadings of thought and desire that pervade the discussions lawyers and clients have with each other.

The path to this essential lawyering ability is to reflect, fully and thoughtfully, on the kinds of problems that lawyers and clients face with each other. Certainty is not the goal; in fact, recognizing how many different perspectives offer insights, some complementary and some contradictory, leads more reliably to wisdom than a quick search for a single answer. The chapters in this book offer examples of lawyers, generally doing quite good work—yet still encountering difficulties of many sorts, and using techniques which, on close examination, sometimes turn out to have significant flaws as well as important strengths. We view ourselves as in a sense undertaking a dialogue with these lawyers, thinking about how they—we—might work with more sensitivity and skill. In another sense, this book contributes to a dialogue with other authors whose guidance on lawyering techniques you may be studying. In still another, and perhaps the most important, sense, this book is a dialogue with you. As we urge you to seek insight rather than certainty, we also encourage you to consider the arguments we make, but not to assume they are right.

1

Rather, you should address the issues this book presents and formulate your own judgments about them.

That said: why a book about interviewing and counseling in particular? The time lawyers spend and the intellectual energy they bring to their work by no means go mainly to appearances before a tribunal, whether court or agency, or to negotiations and advocacy with others in transactional settings. Instead, lawyers devote much of their work and talent to the development of relationships with their clients. In that task, interviewing and counseling—broadly, learning the client's situation and hopes, and helping the client to formulate objectives for resolving the matter—are central. Interviewing and counseling are not discrete and separable moments that we can easily delineate from each other or from the many other parts of lawyering. These terms do, however, provide useful labels for clusters of activities that lawyers undertake as part of their representation of clients. These clusters of activities occur throughout all parts of the representation and affect the lawyer's ability to conduct other lawyering tasks, such as investigation, negotiation, or direct examination. We approach the complex and fluid activities of interviewing and counseling as interwoven parts of the whole project of creating a lawyer-client relationship. Our exploration of interviewing and counseling helps us understand the constraints and the possibilities that exist within all lawyering activities.

In this book, we explore what we call "critical issues" in interviewing and counseling. The word "critical" means at least three things: it denotes the crucial importance of a matter; it denotes the application of analysis or judgment; and it denotes critique or revisiting of established truths. We choose the word "critical" to convey all three of these meanings. We use it to emphasize the importance of the many choices that lawyers make in the course of interviewing and counseling clients, to convey the need for critical reflection on those choices, and to invite critique of established modes of lawyering.

We begin from a sense of the enormous responsibility and privilege that come with the practice of law. Lawyers are granted access to all kinds of information about their clients' lives, information that is often complex, ambiguous, intimate or emotion-laden. Lawyers constantly make decisions, in consultation with their clients, about how to proceed in light of the parameters, all frequently uncertain, created by the client's desires, by law, and by the information the lawyers obtain. Throughout this process, the lawyer not only formulates and reformulates a theory of the case or of the matter, but also builds a relationship with the client, and that relationship in turn inevitably affects the choices that client and lawyer will make and execute together. Moreover, the choices lawyers make about how to interview or counsel clients in this process are far from simple or mechanical. These choices instead both reflect the particulars of the interaction between lawyer and client, and also grow out of lawyers' (and clients') societal and cultural understandings of the lawyer-client relationship and their visions of what lawyers do or ought to do. In turn, the ways lawyers actually interview and counsel clients shape cultural understandings of that relationship. Critical reflection on these choices helps us both to articulate why we make the choices we make and how we can become the kind of lawyers we want to be.

To illustrate some of the choices that lawyers face in interviewing and counseling clients and the importance of critical reflection on those choices, we proceed throughout this book providing examples of lawyer-client interactions and then carefully analyzing the choices the lawyer made—or could have made. We start here, and offer this scene depicting the opening moments of an initial lawyer-client meeting to help us explore some of the themes that will run throughout the rest of the chapters.

[Karen Davies and Mark Corbett, two students in a clinical program, arrive at 4:00 p.m. at the home of Laura Stevens to meet with Ms. Stevens's sister, Janice Woods]

Laura Stevens: Hello. You must be the students from the law school clinical program. Janice said you would be here about now.

Karen Davies: Yes, I'm Karen Davies and this is my partner, Mark Corbett.

Mark Corbett: Thank you so much for having us.

Laura Stevens: No trouble at all. Janice told me that she didn't feel up to going out—and I agree with her, she shouldn't— and I really wanted her to meet with you. Things are kind of cramped here, with all of us in just these four rooms, but I'm sure we'll manage. I'll go get Janice out of bed. She's still pretty weak.

[Janice Woods enters the living room/dining room area, holding onto her sister's arm.]

Karen Davies: Hello, Ms. Woods. We spoke on the phone. I'm Karen Davies and this is my partner Mark Corbett. I'm glad to meet you.

Mark Corbett: Good afternoon.

Janice Woods: Thanks for coming here. I know it's pretty far for you. I just wasn't up to traveling. Here, have a seat.

[As Karen and Mark sit on the couch, Janice Woods sits in the chair to Mark's right and Laura Stevens sits on the chair to Karen's left. Three children run into the room.]

Janice Woods: Kevin, come here and meet our guests. [Turning to Karen and Mark] This is my son Kevin. He's three. He's been staying here with my sister and her kids since I went into the hospital. That's Raquel and Martin—they're 4 and 7.

Kevin Woods:	Hi. Bye. [Kisses his mother on the cheek]
Mark Corbett:	It looks like he has better things to do than talk to us.
Janice Woods:	He never stops moving. I love to see him so happy.
Karen Davies:	He sure seems to like playing with his cousins.
Laura Stevens:	Yeah. They like to take care of him. Though sometimes they all get carried away.
Karen Davies:	Ms. Woods, Laurence Borders from Memorial Hospital called us to say you might be calling—that he had referred you—but he didn't talk to us about why. He sometimes refers his patients to the law clinic. He seems like a very concerned guy. Not so many people like that in hospitals these days who take the time. You said on the phone that he suggested you call. What can we do for you?
Mark Corbett:	Before we start, Ms. Woods—I know this may seem kind of strange, but it might be important that we talk just to you.
Janice Woods:	Laura can stay. Anyway, she's really the one who pushed me to follow up on Mr. Border's suggestion. Also, she knows a lot of what's been going on.

[Kevin, Raquel and Martin all come over.]

Martin Stevens:	Aunt Janice, Kevin won't listen to me. He says he's allowed to have a cookie in the afternoon, and I said it's almost dinner time. He keeps trying to get into the cabinet where the cookies are.
Janice Woods:	Kevin, listen to Martin. Dinner will be soon.
Kevin Woods:	It's not fair. I get bossed around by Martin just because he's older and it's his house. I want to go home. [Crawls into his mother's lap; Martin and Raquel go into the kitchen]
Karen Davies:	Going back to what we were saying about talking to you—I know it's pretty inconvenient and might seem odd to you, but we need to talk with you about whether anyone else should be present. You see, it has to do with our being able to keep what you tell us private, if you want us to. As your lawyers, we have a duty to keep your secrets. Also, we can't be made to reveal almost anything you don't want us to—but that protection you have can be damaged if other people have heard our conversation.
Janice Woods:	I don't really understand what you're telling me. And there's no place for Laura to go in this apartment—there's just the two bedrooms and the kitchen—and you can hear everything through the walls. And, as I said, she's the one wants me to talk to you anyway.
Laura Stevens:	Janice, I have an idea. These nice people came all the way out here to meet with you, and they say maybe I shouldn't be here when you talk to them. They can talk to me later if they want. I'll take the kids out to the playground for a while. Come on Kevin, Martin, Raquel.

Kevin Woods: I don't want to go to the playground. I want to stay with Mommy.

Laura Stevens: Come on Kevin. Let's see if we can find some ice cream to have for dessert.

[Laura Stevens leaves with the three children]

Mark Corbett: Sorry for all the disruption, Ms. Woods. If you want, we can explain more about why it makes a difference for us to talk to you alone. Or we can talk about how you think we might be able to help you.

Janice Woods: Let's just talk about why everyone wanted me to call. I was in the hospital because my husband beat me up. I got a broken rib and a concussion. And my blood pressure got very high. So they kept me in the hospital for a couple of days. As you know, Kevin stayed with my sister. But I don't know if there's anything you can do to help. Jerome hasn't bothered me or Kevin since I went to the hospital. I haven't heard from him or seen him. Both Mr. Borders and Laura have been pushing me to bring criminal charges or to get a protective order. But I'm really worried about both those things. And my house. I don't know what's right.

Karen Davies: No doubt, you're going to have really hard choices to make. And I don't know if we'll be able to help or not. Here are some of the things we can do. We can get more information from you about what has been happening. We can help you identify things that might be useful in your situation and give you information about those that you find helpful. We can work with you to figure out what you would like to have happen, and then do as much as possible to help make that happen. You can decide at any point what you want our involvement to be.

Janice Woods: Like I said, I don't know if any of this talking is worth much, but I promised Laura I would at least think through what I can do. Ask me whatever you want.

Mark Corbett: Let's begin with the things that happened when you ended up in the hospital. It seems like they were pretty serious.

This depiction of an initial meeting between two students in a clinical program and a client demonstrates the myriad choices that confront lawyers as they develop a lawyer-client relationship. For example, the students have chosen to meet Janice Woods, their client, in the home of Laura Stevens, the client's sister. It appears that the students have had a prior telephone conversation with Ms. Woods in which she has asked them to come to her sister's house because she was not "up to traveling." Their choice to interview her in this setting conveys to Ms. Woods, even before they meet her, that they will travel "far" to help her. During even the brief portion of the encounter depicted here, the students face additional choices, created by their need to learn more about Ms. Woods's situation so that they can help her assess her legal options. They have received a referral from Mr. Borders, who works at a hospital, but he has not provided any further information regarding the subject of the referral. And, as the students learn early in the meeting, Ms. Woods is not sure she wants to be involved with lawyers—she tells the students that her sister "pushed" her "to follow up" on Mr. Borders's suggestion that she call the clinic. The most prominent issue in the students' minds is the need to get Ms. Woods alone so they can have a confidential conversation with her and protect their communication with the attorney-client privilege. The students have to make choices about how far they should challenge Ms. Woods's reluctance to allow them to interview her alone, how to elicit information about her situation that will help them assess her legal options, and how to continue to convey their desire to help her on her own terms.

Throughout this book, we will explore how lawyers can ground the choices they make in interviewing and counseling clients in the fundamental principles that we think should infuse the entire lawyer-client relationship. We use the term "engaged client–centered representation" to describe these principles as a whole. To be **client-centered** is to emphasize the client as the prime decision-maker in the lawyer-client relationship and the person who decides the objectives of the representation. The lawyer's role, then, is a helping one, in which the client ultimately determines the meaning of help. We take as a premise that clients are entitled, within the limits of the law, to choose the steps to be taken on their behalf, both because they probably know their own needs better than anyone else can and because, right or wrong, they are entitled as people to make their own decisions. Correspondingly, we see lawyers' support for client choice as justified, both as a strategy for discerning the best way to proceed and as an expression of respect for clients as people. We see limits on how far to extend these principles, and we will devote a number of chapters to exploring them, but we start with this recognition of the importance of client autonomy.

At the same time, we believe that true client-centeredness must also be **engaged client-centeredness**. The engagement we urge has two fundamental components. First, the lawyer must work with care to build a relationship with the client that will help sustain the client as he or she deals with the questions, sometimes very painful questions, that must be resolved in handling the legal matter. Many scholars have embraced this objective, and have offered guidelines for putting clients at ease and helping them to feel listened to and understood. We take particularly seriously, however, the reality that the many differences between lawyers and clients can divide them and limit how the lawyer can actually help the client. Race, gender, sexual orientation, class, and perhaps most ubiquitously knowledge—the lawyer's expertise about the law—can come between lawyer and client or link them together, and we view the negotiation of difference and connection within the lawyer-client relationship as fundamental to all lawyer-client interactions. In Chapter 2 ("Connection Across Difference and Similarity") we look closely at these lines of difference and similarity and at the ways that lawyers can find productive understanding in the recognition of what differentiates them from and unites them with their clients. Engaged client-centered lawyers work to earn the trust of their clients from the first moment of the first meeting through the conclusion of the representation, even when what the lawyers must say may be hard for their clients to hear. As you'll see, we focus on the value of lawyers' real and active listening and their clear and sensitive speaking, and on techniques for achieving these qualities—and in this chapter we also lay out some basic frameworks for interviewing and counseling overall. Perhaps most important, we emphasize lawyers' ability to find in themselves common ground with their clients, to understand the limitations in themselves that may interfere with doing so, and with these perspectives to respond to their clients with warmth and patience as well as candor.

Second, the lawyer should bring to the relationship all of the insight and wisdom she possesses, while preserving—in fact enhancing—the client's control over his own life choices. Engaged client-centered lawyers listen to clients' accounts of events that are at issue in a matter that a client brings to a lawyer, to clients' perceptions about the relationships and social practices that surround that event, and to clients' often shifting ideas about what they want to achieve in going to a lawyer. Helping the client to articulate her own thinking and to explore what may seem confusing or contradictory can help the client to choose, and the lawyer can and should also help the client to organize and assess the concerns he has voiced. But as we explain in Chapter 3 ("Engaged Client–Centered Counseling About Client Choices"), engaged client-centered lawyers should also seek to assist the client in making choices by entering the process of decision—by offering their own insights, by raising questions about the client's assessments, even, perhaps, by advocating in favor of one choice rather than another. Engaged client-centered lawyers bring to their interactions with clients their knowledge of the law, their understanding of the working of various institutions that the law contributes to structuring, and their own values and moral convictions, yet seek to shape the advice they give to clients in light of the clients' own understandings of themselves, their relationships with others and the world and the clients' evolving desires about what they want. In this broad sense, engaged client-centered lawyers collaborate with their clients in determining how the client's objectives are to be achieved.

All of the rest of the book builds upon, and from, this foundational examination of engagement as connection to and interaction with clients. In Chapter 4 ("Interviewing and Counseling Atypical Clients"), we explore the challenges of working effectively and respectfully with clients who have diminished decision-making capacity: clients with intellectual disabilities, elderly clients, and children. Although we call these clients "atypical" (and they are sometimes labeled "difficult"), we believe there are no "typical" clients. Rather, lawyers typically encounter clients along the entire continuum of capacity, and lawyers must develop strategies for engaging effectively with clients on terms clients can understand. The commitment to engaged client-centeredness offers a framework for shaping the lawyer-client relationship with clients of all sorts—even those clients who may in the end lack the capacity to fully direct their own lives and legal relations.

In Chapter 5 ("Narrative Theory and Narrative Practice"), we return to the interactions between law students Mark Corbett and Karen Davies and their client, Janice Woods, to explore the role of narrative theory in lawyer-client interactions. We use narrative theory not as a guide to advocacy—how to "tell the client's story" in court, for example—but as a framework for lawyers' listening to and questioning their clients. Because the stories lawyers and clients tell each other convey emotion and impart meaning, careful attention to the client's narrative can help a lawyer hear in more nuanced and complex ways of what the client is saying and how the client hears what the lawyer says. A focus on the story as a story may lead the lawyer to ask questions—about the story's setting, for instance, or its moral meaning—that she would not otherwise have asked, and may invite the client to recount, and to reflect on, her own situation differently from how she otherwise would have. Even more profoundly, in hearing how a story evolves over time, the lawyer can understand, even expect, that a client's account will change over the course of the representation. In all these ways, narrative practices for interviewing and counseling offer exciting possibilities for deepening lawyers' engagement with their clients.

In Chapter 6 ("Truth and Consequences") we explore the role of truth-seeking within the lawyer-client relationship. It is almost a truism that the lawyer needs to learn the facts from the client, and it is often assumed that the function of interviewing is to elicit as much information as possible from the client. But the many exceptions to full attorney-client confidentiality that the law recognizes mean that it will not always be to the client's advantage for the lawyer to know "the whole truth," and it may even turn out that the client's candor leads to results that both lawyer and client consider unfair and unjust. Starting from this uncomfortable realization, the chapter explores the dimensions of this aspect of lawyers' engagement with their clients, focusing on whether and in what circumstances lawyers should seek the truth from their clients; what lawyers should tell their clients about the limits of confidentiality and about the law that will apply to the truth the clients reveal; and how lawyers can effectively seek the truth when they believe they should do so.

In Chapter 7 ("Moral Dialogue"), we explore the appropriateness of moral dialogue between lawyers and clients. Our conception of engagement calls on lawyers to interact with their clients about the choices the clients are considering—helping identify relevant considerations, certainly, but also sharing views about what will likely achieve the client's goals and even, perhaps, about what the best choice is in terms of moral considerations. Thus, for us the idea of moral *conversation* between lawyer and client is not a response to a special problem of dealing with an immoral client, but rather an element of connection across difference between lawyer and client, and an integral part of many lawyer-client relationships. This chapter, however, asks whether lawyers should ever go beyond conversation to advocacy—to urging their clients to adopt the lawyers' moral perspectives. We examine the factors lawyers might weigh in deciding whether to intervene in this particularly intimate and particularly intrusive way, and the methods they might employ in such interventions, as an exploration of the uneasy boundary between deep engagement and disregard of client choice, in the context of situations where the lawyer fears profound moral wrong may be done.

In Chapter 8 ("Talking to Clients about the Law"), we explore the choices that lawyers make in explaining and interpreting the law to their clients. The rules of legal ethics tell us that we must represent clients within the bounds of the law, and so it might be thought that the law provides fixed parameters that help define a client's options and the consequences of taking various actions. But we know, as lawyers, that the bounds of the law are themselves often debatable. If we are to engage with our clients about their legal options, then our engagement with them should not deny the ambiguity of what the law says. We view lawyers' explanations of the law as involving interpretive choices with the power to influence client decision-making. We explore how an engaged client-centered lawyer might make interpretive choices that will make the law accessible to the client, so that the client can participate actively in the representation, offer perspectives to the lawyer on the meaning of legal regulation in the context of the client's life and values, and assess the legitimacy of legal regulation.

We end with an exploration, in Chapter 9 ("Fast Talking: Lawyering Expertise and Its Impact on Interviewing and Counseling"), of the question of how lawyers can honor the values of engaged client-centeredness under the constraints of day-to-day practice, where time is almost always short. We emphatically do not suggest abandoning engagement in favor of efficiency, but we do look at what efficient client-centeredness might entail. We find an answer in the study of what expert lawyers (like experts generally) bring to their practice: extensive, well-organized, readily available understanding of the patterns of events that they are likely to encounter. This body of expert knowledge, we suggest, enables experienced attorneys to interview with more focus, more insight and more speed, while still building connection through contacts that may be brief but intense. It also enables them to assist client choice by guiding clients to a clear consideration of the most important choices they face and, in some cases, by offering straightforward guidance about what to do. All of these expert practices, we suggest, can embody client-centeredness—but expert knowledge can also be coercive, as well as mistaken. We end with an exploration of steps expert lawyers may take to limit the dangers that expertise can create—a final instance of our emphasis, throughout the book, on the importance of lawyers' close attention to the implications of the steps they take to interview and counsel their clients.

The importance of lawyers' careful reflection on the choices they are making suggests another way to introduce this book to you. While our chapters set out to explore the particular issues we have just described, we also bring broad perspectives that recur across all our distinct sections, beginning in the dialogue set out earlier in this introduction. Five themes run through this opening dialogue and help define the approach that we bring to our analysis of critical issues in the lawyer-client relationship in other chapters of this book as well: context, connection, the fluidity of client identity, ethics, and the lawyer's openness of mind.

A. CONTEXT

A book on interviewing and counseling must offer general guidelines, but perhaps the most important is that each lawyer-client relationship is different. Context, therefore, is critical. In this book, we return again and again to the impact of the context within which the lawyer and client shape their relationship and the effects that those contextual factors have on creating different sorts of lawyer-client relationships. The scenario with which we introduce this book presents an unusual beginning of a lawyer-client relationship. Even though lawyers may most commonly first meet their clients in a lawyer's office with only the lawyer and client present, lawyers may also encounter, or even wish to generate, alternative ways in which they first meet their prospective clients. When Karen Davies and Mark Corbett meet Janice Woods, there is no receptionist, no desk, no law books on a shelf, no computer. As you think about this interview, we hope you will consider such questions as these: What difference, if any, do these situational factors surrounding the lawyer-client interactions make? How might the students' presence at the client's temporary home make a difference in the lawyer-client relationship? How might the students' presence affect the others in the home? How might the situation look different for a client with more resources, fewer complications, or more certainty of aim? Might there still be reasons that the lawyer meets with the client in the client's home or office? Does the life situation of the client, however, change the meaning of the meeting in the client's home?

The lawyer-client dialogues that occur throughout this book, including this one, do not follow a standard pattern. Rather, we present many of the variable contexts within which the lawyer-client relationship arises and develops, in order to explore the ways those multiple contexts affect our understanding of that relationship: clinic students interviewing a man with intellectual disabilities charged with misdemeanor theft; a divorce lawyer who knows his well-to-do client from golfing at the country club; a legal services attorney interviewing a client in prison about his child support; a white male employment discrimination attorney in his 40's interviewing, from his wheelchair, a younger white man who is also a wheelchair user; an African–American partner at a large law firm working as a pro bono attorney for a civil rights organization. The choices that lawyers make in these various settings may be influenced by a variety of factors, from wanting to allay the fears of a client about dealing with a lawyer, to hoping that conversations during a golf game will lead to the type of interchange that will make the prospective client like and trust the lawyer, to accommodating to the necessity of meeting a criminal defendant in a cell block, to predicting that a meeting at the client's own workplace may help the lawyer understand the activities and problem of the client. We urge you to think flexibly and creatively about how to approach the variety of interactions that can occur within the lawyer-client relationship, rather than taking for granted a standardized vision of the relationship that makes other interactions seem deviant.

Beyond these situational factors, we've already emphasized that our dialogues illustrate how race, class, gender, sexual orientation, disability, culture and other axes of difference and similarity between lawyers and clients create differing contexts for the development of lawyer-client relationships. We do not presume that effective lawyering across differ-ence is impossible, or that sociological and cultural differences automati-cally translate into actual differences between people. Furthermore, we do not assume that individual differences necessarily flow from differences in group membership and identification. Neither, however, do we presume that effective lawyering across difference—or, for that matter, within similarity—can automatically be achieved without conscious, self-critical attention. When lawyers are cognizant of and critical about the assump-tions about difference and similarity that they bring to any lawyer-client interaction, they have a basis for making better judgments about the choices available to them and the actions they take in shaping the relationship. They also may develop a more sophisticated critical vision of both the aspirational value of treating all clients the same, and the causes for divergence between aspiration and reality.

B. CONNECTION

If context frames the challenges the lawyer faces in building a relationship with her client, connection, as we've said, is a major part of the response. But it is important to think carefully about what builds connection between lawyer and client, and this reflection points us as well toward considering the other connections that shape a client's life. Con-nections may form between lawyers and clients concerning almost any aspect of the relationship between lawyer and client. These bonds may be confined to matters directly related to the legal claims or they may extend into all aspects of the representation. It is important that the lawyer be aware of the power of these connections: they give the lawyer insight into the client's thoughts and feelings, and may give her leave to influence the client's choices, and on both counts may assist the lawyer in developing a theory to guide the representation of the client that reflects the client's evolving understanding of himself and his situation. These connections can, however, distort the lawyer's view of the client's situation if the lawyer does not remain aware of her own assumptions about and reactions to the client. We recognize that bonds between lawyer and client can occur across enormous chasms of difference, as well as across sameness. It may be that these bonds grow more easily within sameness. But it may also be that aspects of sameness can cause both lawyers and clients to make assumptions that keep them from working to achieve mutual understanding.

The dialogue that opens this introduction illustrates at least two meanings of connection in the lawyer-client relationship. First, the students face a significant challenge in creating connection with their client. Janice Woods expresses skepticism about meeting with lawyers, as well as distrust of the legal system; the students need to understand the source of both and to be open to the client's feelings concerning what an encounter with the legal system may mean in her life. To do so, the students need empathy, and they need to express it to Ms. Woods. But lawyers may sometimes need to supplement empathy with rigorous self-examination to provide representation that is both caring and, to the degree it must be, dispassionate. For example, the students here may have had their own experiences with violent relationships. Those past experiences may assist them in empathetically understanding Ms. Woods's situation and in seeing potential responses to it. The same experiences, however, may also tempt the students to impose on Ms. Woods their own views of the "solutions" to her problems, and indeed their own definitions of the problems as well. If the problem she sees is primarily that she wants peace and safety for herself and her son, the students need to see what peace and safety mean for her before they focus on how to achieve them. They must also critically examine their own assumptions about the legitimacy and efficacy of the legal system as the vehicle for achieving these goals and not impose these assumptions upon Ms. Woods. If Ms. Woods does not want her husband caught up in that system, the lawyers need to be aware of the values she brings to that decision, as well as the aspects of her life that lead her to that decision.

Students and lawyers need not achieve complete objectivity; that goal is unattainable and, if it could be attained, would be inconsistent with the sympathetic alliance a lawyer should form with her client. Nor should the student, or lawyer, be completely self-effacing and attentive only to the client; that approach would undercut the value the lawyer brings to the relationship as a person with insights and judgments of her own. Rather, the goal is to build connection while also understanding its elements and its potential pitfalls.

Second, the students face the challenge of how to manage the connection of an attorney-client relationship within the context of the many other connections in their client's life. When clients come to lawyers as individuals, they often bring with them, literally and symbolically, other people to whom they have powerful connections. Although the lawyer may see the client as the person whom he or she is representing, the connections that the client feels to others may be powerful determinants in shaping connections between the lawyer and client. Many of the clients in this book are acutely concerned about others in their lives, and in one dialogue, in Chapter 4 ("Interviewing and Counseling Atypical Clients"), lawyer and client agree to bring in a sympathetic member of the client's family to help the client make a painful decision. Here, Laura Stevens, Ms.

Woods's sister, Kevin, her son, and Laurence Borders, the person from Memorial Hospital who made the referral to the clinic students, are all powerful presences in Ms. Woods's life, even though Mr. Borders is not at the meeting at all and the students have excluded the others from the room. Beyond these people directly involved with the situation that has gotten Ms. Woods to her student lawyers, there may be others among her friends and family, in her neighborhood, or in a broader community of which she feels a part who might have a powerful effect on her feelings of trust, on her willingness to be open, on her perceptions of the choices available to her, or on her attitudes toward state power and the judicial system. When the client is a group, the relationships among diverse, yet interconnected, individuals become an explicit part of the complexities of forming and sustaining a lawyer-client relationship.

We believe that the lawyer should respect the client's view of the client's connections to others without favoring the lawyer's own view of those connections. However, the lawyer also must make the client aware of possibilities and choices that may be in conflict with the preferences of those with whom the client feels connection. Otherwise, the lawyer denies the client the opportunity, through the decisions made with the lawyer, to shape his or her own relationship to others within the client's life.

C. THE FLUIDITY OF CLIENT IDENTITY: CLIENTS' EVOLUTION AND LAWYERS' INFLUENCE ON IT

The dialogue foreshadows another theme that runs throughout the chapters in this book: that a client's objectives emerge from and change during the course of the representation and to some extent in light of the relationship between lawyer and client. Here, Ms. Woods has reached out for legal assistance at the urging of others, but remains unclear—and perhaps skeptical—about whether legal intervention can make her situation better. Perhaps her main feeling, right now, is simply a desire for stability to return to her life. But she may find, over the coming weeks and months, that stability isn't achievable, or that it is achievable by some steps, but not others. As she arrives at these conclusions, the specific goals she articulates will change. Her description of her own situation may change too, not out of any kind of dissembling but simply because different aspects of her life grow more, or less, salient to her as the keys to moving forward. The students need to be ready for such evolution, and even to look for it—and certainly not to be shocked by it.

Moreover, the students themselves, and the relationship they develop with Ms. Woods, may be a powerful force in giving shape to the client's own vision of what is desirable in her situation. What the students are able to offer Ms. Woods may affect her view of the possibilities available to her, and that in turn may affect what she decides to seek. For example, Ms. Woods might not understand that a lawyer could help her in ways that have nothing to do with an action to obtain a restraining order against the person who caused her injuries, or with any legal proceedings at all. There might be issues related to housing, medical care or employment that seem more pressing to Ms. Woods. Ms. Woods might have no idea that help with these issues is available from the students unless they make that discussion a part of the relationship—as they should, *if* their clinic (or, later, their law practice) is able to undertake such wide-ranging efforts.

The lawyer's impact on the client, however, goes well beyond widening the range of possible options. The very questions the lawyer asks may encourage the client to reflect on her situation, or constrain her within narrow boundaries of what the client understands the law to care about. Chapter 3 ("Engaged Client–Centered Counseling About Client Choices") explores in detail the extensive, candid interaction that lawyers may have with their clients in counseling them in the course of their work together. Chapter 5 ("Narrative Theory and Narrative Practice") picks up the story of Ms. Woods and further explores how her uncertain objectives might unfold in response to questions that affirm the importance of her story as she is living it. So, too, the ideas the lawyer offers, and of course the positions the lawyer urges, may affect the client's own judgments. In Chapter 8 ("Talking to Clients about the Law"), the lawyer's explanations of the law and its underlying purposes help to move a client away from thinking primarily about the effect of the law on him to expressing continuity between his own values and the values reflected in the law.

In Chapter 7 ("Moral Dialogue"), on the other hand, the lawyer is confronted, in a counseling session in the mid-course of representation, with a client whose previously expressed desire to resolve a divorce amicably has seemingly changed. The lawyer understands the client's new position as a response to the emotional pain of the divorce rather than a fundamental change of heart, and perhaps that is so—but perhaps the lawyer has disregarded the client's own logic and perceptions. And when the lawyer attempts to recall the client to his earlier intentions, his efforts may succeed only in rupturing the attorney-client relationship. The task of responding open-heartedly to a client's changes is not an easy one, but it is no less important for that.

D. ETHICS

Every part of interviewing and counseling is guided and shaped by ethics, because interviewing and counseling are integral parts of performing the lawyer's role of helping her clients. But many elements of what lawyers do in these encounters are directly shaped by specific rules of professional ethics. In pressing hard to meet with their client with no one else literally present, Karen and Mark are, among other things, responding to their duties to protect client confidentiality and the lawyer-client privilege, duties that result from the operation of the ethics rules (and the rules of attorney-client privilege in evidence law). We will examine how lawyers' ethical responsibilities interact with the choices that they and the client must make in deciding how to conduct the representation. Here, for example, the students met Ms. Woods at her sister's apartment; that was an act of consideration for Ms. Woods, and surely facilitated her access to legal services, and yet—because other people lived there and because the walls were thin—it was a decision that potentially undercut the privacy usually required for the protection of attorney-client privilege. The students, obviously troubled by the need to exclude Ms. Woods's sister from her own apartment, try to discuss the question with Ms. Woods herself, only to have her sister intervene to find a graceful solution. Should the students have begun this way? Should they have deferred to Ms. Woods's apparent preference for keeping her sister with her? Was that really Ms. Woods's preference?

More generally, it is fair to say that the rules' demands are sometimes unclear, and that this unclarity reflects, in part, that the values underlying the rules are sometimes complex and even conflicting. Lawyers need to understand the rules, and their underlying values. They also need to understand their own stance on what is ethical, and—since their stance may or may not fit smoothly with what the rules seem to suggest, or command—they need to find ways to reconcile their views and the important, but sometimes limited, guidance that the rules provide. And they need to consider whether the ethical problems they face belong to them alone, or whether they are problems that the client also has a say, even the first say, in resolving.

Throughout the book, we will examine the ways that ethical issues emerge in the dynamics of the lawyer-client relationship. To take just one example, consider some of the ethical issues suggested by the question of whether lawyers should seek the truth from their clients, the subject of Chapter 6 ("Truth and Consequences"). We can start with the familiar observation that lawyers can phrase questions so as to influence clients' answers—by asking, say, "How fast were the cars going when they slammed into each other?" or instead "Could you tell what their rate of speed was at the time of the accident?" Which formulation is better, and why? How does the overall vision of the lawyer-client relationship shape one's answers to those questions? Similarly, it is well understood that lawyers who explain the law to their clients before questioning them may then elicit answers that conform remarkably to the law's necessities—yet it is also acknowledged that clients are entitled to learn the law from their lawyers. How can lawyers provide clients with the legal advice to which they are entitled, while not (unduly) fostering untrue accounts of events? What is the relationship between truthful information and useful information? Should the lawyer be seeking truth? And how far should lawyers press their clients, and by what means, to elicit the truth? Does the lawyer believe that the conception of truth is contested? What does it mean to each lawyer to obtain a truthful account of an event? How can different conceptions of truth affect a lawyer's decisions about whether and how to seek it? Whatever our philosophical views of truth, we all understand that different individuals will experience, understand and remember the same event in different ways. People's perceptions of truth, even the truth about themselves and their reporting of it, are subject to all kinds of pressures and variations. Lawyers constantly struggle with how different accounts of events and different perceptions of truth relate to their actions in working with clients. They also face the question of whether goals of truth and justice come into conflict. If so, how are they to be resolved? Are the answers the same in all contexts? These are only examples of the complex ethical problems that can arise in almost any encounter between lawyer and client and that are critical to the development of the lawyer-client relationship.

E. THE LAWYER'S OPENNESS OF MIND

In sketching these broad perspectives for you to consider as you read this book, we have done something else as well: we have described the considerations that lawyers need to keep in mind as they carry out the tasks of interviewing and counseling. In every interaction, lawyers need to work to understand the part of clients' experiences that the clients bring to the relationship. As lawyers come to know their clients and grasp their legal problems, they need to be able to listen with care and flexibility, shape insightful questions, offer clear explanations, and convey empathy. They need to encounter and take account of difference and sameness; they need to become part of client decisionmaking without taking choice away from the clients; they need to find ways to feel comfortable taking action for a client when much remains uncertain for the client or about the situation the client faces; they may need to wrestle with profound issues of truth, values, emotions and the nature of law; and ultimately they need to learn to do all of this quickly and efficiently as well. And, as if that were not enough, we are also saying that they need to be sensitive to context, to connection, to the fluidity of client identity, and of course to ethics.

To do all this, the lawyer needs a special virtue—openness of mind. The dialogues in this book present some lawyers who do have this virtue, and some who do not. In Chapter 2 ("Connection Across Difference and Similarity"), for example, we look at an attorney, Allen Anderson, who unwittingly offends his client by claiming an "understanding" of the client that the client finds implausible; that might have been a mistake (and good lawyers make mistakes), but the lawyer responds without resentment, saying "I am sorry for my choice of language." In Chapter 3, one law student interviewing a client with an intellectual disability presses the client to demonstrate his understanding of the term "theft," and pushes the client into defensiveness. This student's partner intervenes to rescue the client (and the relationship), saying, "I know you're not stupid—that's obvious to anyone who talks to you. But why don't you tell me what you think the word 'theft' means, just so I can be sure you, Nate [the first student] and I all understand the same thing."

We could multiply these examples, but it will be more valuable for you to look at the lawyers in these pages and ask yourself if they display openness of mind. Are they able to focus on their clients, or are they tripped up by preconceptions or attachments of their own? Are they able to accept their clients not just as the clients first present themselves, but in the different ways the clients may express themselves over time? Are they, the lawyers, able to change too—to reassess a client, a case, or a course of action? Ultimately, this last question may be the most important, for as we will see in Chapter 9 ("Fast Talking: Lawyering Expertise and Its Impact on Interviewing and Counseling"), as lawyers become more expert, they simultaneously become truly masters of the skills of interviewing and counseling—of quickly understanding and connecting with and assisting clients—and they become prey to the danger of jumping too quickly to appraisals that, however expert, are wrong in their judgments about the case and the client. Lawyers who are expert interviewers and counselors have reason to be proud—but perhaps surprisingly, those who are the finest practitioners are probably also people with a humility and interest in others that help them to meet their clients with eyes and mind open.

No one achieves this openness all the time, of course, and we do not suggest that you need superhuman virtues to be a good lawyer. The journey, the aspiration, is as important as the destination. Moreover, we do not suggest that our judgments about the many difficult interviewing and counseling questions we address in this book are necessarily correct. Rather, as you work your way through the critical issues in interviewing and counseling that we explore in these chapters, we invite you to bring your own critical judgment to them. One of the benefits of using lawyer-client dialogues is that they can be critically analyzed in multiple ways. We illustrate this variability by re-analyzing portions of some dialogues or reprising the characters that we have created in these dialogues. For example, attorney Richard Mathiesson and his client, Bill Arnholz—who provide the central characters in Chapter 6 ("Moral Dialogue")—also appear in both Chapter 2 ("Connection Across Difference and Similarity") and Chapter 8 ("Talking to Clients about the Law"). In collaborating on this book, we have found that even as five reflective persons who share the basic values of engaged client-centered representation, we have not always agreed on our critical analysis of the lawyering choices we depict. Our disagreements are perhaps the strongest in Chapter 6 ("Truth and Consequences"), where we disagree about how to balance the importance of truth-seeking in the lawyer-client relationship with the value of client control. However, we view our disagreement as a strength rather than a weakness. We believe that reasonable persons committed to the same set of values often differ in how to resolve situations where those values come into conflict. We invite our readers to similarly re-analyze our dialogues, imagine them differently, re-interpret their meaning, and critique the views we express about how lawyers should balance and resolve the competing values embedded in an engaged client-centered approach.

CHAPTER 2

CONNECTION ACROSS DIFFERENCE AND SIMILARITY

■ ■ ■

For lawyers to do their work effectively, they must make connections of some degree of trust with their clients—whether those clients share similar characteristics and outlooks with the lawyers or have different characteristics and outlooks from the lawyers. Lawyers have always functioned in a "diverse" world. Historically, lawyers have tended to be (and at times been legally required to be) from certain economic, social, racial, religious and gender classes and categories. Yet clients, witnesses and people affected by legal decisions have always included the broad cross section of the society's population. A range of American civil rights movements starting during the middle of the twentieth century had a great impact on invigorating the constitutional mandate and promise of equality for all the peoples of the United States. And changes in immigration policies meant that the peoples of America encompassed an increasingly broader range of cultures and national origins. Civil rights and anti-discrimination legislation has led more segments of the United States' population to have access to the legal system, and consequently, increased their need for lawyers. Lawyers, ourselves, have begun to reflect a wider range of social categories—class, race, ethnicity, religion, national origin, gender, sexual orientation, marital status, language, immigration status, education/training backgrounds and physical abilities to name just some— within our ranks. These visible changes have caused many in legal education and in the legal profession to focus on ensuring that attorneys are prepared to represent a broad range of clients and to work with an equally broad range of witnesses and other participants in the legal system.[1]

This chapter explores some of the challenges and possibilities of connection across difference,[2] as well as the pitfalls and positives of similarity. We explore issues involved in building attorney-client connections in context using engaged client centered representation. How closely aligned with the client as an individual or the issues that arise in the client's case must a lawyer be in order to zealously represent the client's case? Must a lawyer like her client? And related to this but not at all the same—must a client feel like his lawyer likes him? Can a lawyer create

18

connection with her clients and if so, how? Is it possible to be "too close" to a client? How should a lawyer manage the tension between personal connection between herself and her client and the professional distance necessary to provide legal assistance? How do lawyers communicate and translate our legal knowledge into terms that our lay clients can understand so that they can make informed decisions?

A. THE BASIC FRAMEWORK FOR INTERVIEWING AND COUNSELING

We start out with two basic frameworks or outlines for interviewing and counseling. These two outlines are not "models." Other authors have delineated the different steps needed for a good interview or counseling session. Our goal here is not to create some competing model but rather to sketch out the steps most authors would agree are needed so that the issues of connection across difference and similarity can be placed within the frameworks where lawyers will most often encounter such challenges.

An Outline of Interviewing

1. Preparation
2. Introductions and Greetings
3. Construction of the Attorney–Client Relationship
4. Problems and Concerns
5. Fact Exploration
6. Client's Possible Solutions
7. Counseling Preview
8. Closing

As a general matter these "steps" involve the following:

1. <u>Preparation</u> will include both a reflection on the type of attorney-client relationship you as the attorney want as well as the research in the particular area of law within which the client's case is likely to fall if you have that information.

2. <u>Introductions and Greetings</u> will include introductions and whatever "small talk" that can help make a client comfortable. This will typically involve asking directly, How can I help? It may also include a discussion on confidentiality and a preliminary mention of fees. The specific content of what we will call the "Greeting" step constitutes the initial entry or preliminary phase of the interview.[3]

3. <u>Construction of the Attorney–Client Relationship</u> is clearly not a "step" at all but rather a reminder that throughout the life of the attorney-client relationship, you as the attorney should consciously be noticing and acquiring information about your client's feelings, goals and values aside from the factual information about the client's legal problem. The attorney's ability to process this complex of information about the

client is a key factor in the attorney's ability to make the right connection with the client.[4]

4.   Problems and Concerns denotes the fact that, initially, an attorney will allow the client to describe her problem and related concerns at some length. At this early point, the attorney tries not to assume too much about the facts or nature of the legal problem—keeping her questions open. In addition, the lawyer continues "getting to know" the client by (a) consciously creating connection between herself and the client and (b) listening for a range of other factors beyond the facts.

5.   Fact Exploration involves the lawyer asking the client more detailed and directed questions about the facts of the case. Your questioning typically will now be focused on understanding the chronology of the events and be framed in light of your understanding of the possible legal doctrines and theories that may be applicable to the client's problems and concerns.[5] Simultaneously, the questions will be worded and intoned in ways that continue to encourage your client's trust in you.

6.   Client's Proposed or Desired Solutions involves hearing out your client's "wildest dreams" i.e. their goals, values and desires for the resolution of the case both without the constraints of legalistic solutions as well as within those constraints.

7.   Counseling Preview involves providing the client with a preliminary sense of whether the law and you, as the attorney, can help.[6]

8.   Closing You always need a graceful exit. Here may include a full discussion of money and the retainer agreement; confirming the client's personal and contact information; detailing what if anything you need the client to do between this meeting and the next; detailing what the client can expect you will be doing; and setting up a specific time for your next contact or meeting.

An Outline of Counseling

1.   Preparation—Legal Research, Fact Investigation, Legal Theories and Client's Goals

2.   Greeting—More Construction of the Attorney–Client Relationship

3.   Update Your Client

4.   Client Updates You

5.   Discussion of Actions and Options

6.   Consequences

7.   Choosing a Course of Actions and Options

8.   Ethical Issues in Conflicts Between Attorney and Client over Counseling Decisions

As a general matter these "steps" involve the following:

1.   Preparation will include collecting and organizing your legal research and factual investigation. And, even though the situation may be fluid and

somewhat uncertain, preparation will also include a developed legal theory (or legal theories) of your case. In addition, preparation includes reviewing your understanding of your client's goals and desires. What is it that your client wants done in this case to resolve the matter? Are there any political, philosophical, religious/spiritual or moral parameters or constraints within which your client needs his solution to reside?

2.   Greeting and More Construction of the Attorney–Client Relationship In part this is a reminder that it remains your responsibility as the professional to make the client feel comfortable immediately and during the counseling conversation. You will have more information about the client at this point and will bring all this prior knowledge of the client to your greeting and will continue to assess your client's personality, values and feelings.

3.   Update Your Client In many situations, you will have engaged in a good deal of work—legal research and fact investigation—since the last time that you spoke at length with your client. So you want to let the client know that you are, in fact, working hard for the money she is paying you; so you tell her what you have done. This is also a time to report to the client on the status of the evidence in your case given your fact investigation (e.g. did the person the client said would alibi her actually come through?) along with other information (e.g. what settlement offer, if any, has the other side made?)

4.   Client Updates You Your client may well have information for you about new events related to the case or different feelings or concerns that she or other important people in her life (spouse, partner, minister/rabbi/imam) may have about the case or she may be reporting back on some "assignment" you gave her e.g. collecting her employment documents. This is also a time to confirm your understanding of your client's goals and desires. The client's new or different feelings, concerns, information and interactions can and will have an impact on the client's sense of his goals, values and desires.

5.   Discussion of Actions and Options The Actions and Options element of counseling is the point at which attorney and client list and discuss what actions the client would like to see occur in order to accomplish her goals and what legal options or methods exist that could resolve her case. Actions and options are not necessarily the same thing. For example, in some cases clients may ideally want an apology or acknowledgment of wrongdoing as an action that is part of what resolves their situations. Such an action could be included as part of several legal options or methods such as settlement, mediation or even arbitration.

6.   Consequences essentially involves the lawyer and the client assessing the likely outcomes of pursuing each of the listed legal options. "Outcomes" is used broadly here to include both the likely legal result the lawyer assesses will result from each legal option as well as the impact of the process involved in effectuating each of the legal methods on the life of the client. Both such outcomes will be compared with the client's goals

and values. This process will typically include the lawyer recounting the legal theory of the case so that both she and her client agree on what the client's story is, how it relates to the applicable law and what evidence is available and admissible to prove it.[7]

7. Choosing a Course of Action and Options In a general sense, after the attorney and client have defined and discussed the range of legal options as well as the likely legal and personal consequences that will result, the client can now compare the range of legal and personal consequences with her goals and desires along with her moral and personal concerns. Whichever method most closely satisfies all the client's goals and desires and falls within his moral parameters will likely be the chosen method. Sometimes, several options will satisfy the client's goals, in which case her moral concern or other personal preferences will be the deciding factors. Other times all news is bad news, and the client is in the unenviable position of choosing the option that most minimizes the negative consequences to him.

8. Ethical Issues in Conflicts Between Attorney and Client over Counseling Decisions Whether your clients have asked for your counsel or no, there may be times when you may have disagreements with your client over the pragmatic wisdom of one of action over another. Or you will have strong ethical or moral concerns about the choice that the client plans to make. There are a number of thorny issues that arise in this area of counseling, especially those involving moral or ethical disagreements. Some cases involve no ethical rules, per se, but raise moral concerns on client autonomy if you choose to engage your client in a discussion about the wisdom of his choice.[8]

Before exploring selected parts of the interviewing or counseling processes within which to discuss difference and connection between lawyers and clients, there are a few things worth remembering. Interviewing and counseling are parts of an overall "relationship"—a complex interaction between two people (at least) over time. This is most obvious in the attorney-client relationship, which is our primary focus. But it is also true in an attorney's relationship with an expert witness who may be used more than one time or a prosecuting attorney's relationship with a complaining witness or police officers. An attorney's deep understanding of the many aspects of human nature and her ability to "read," through intonations, body language, silence as well as words, what someone is saying are both intangible but essential aspects of interviewing.

Consequently no two interviews or counseling sessions can ever be alike—even if they are between the same lawyer and client. In a real sense the fact that time has passed, during which time both the attorney and the client could have acquired information and insight that have changed their views or emotional outlooks, means that both the lawyer and the client will have experienced a "shift" in their respective "selves;"[9] neither the lawyer nor the client is really the "same."

In addition, context is always important. There are no generic lawyers or clients. Different lawyers will have different kinds of relationships and engage differently with the same client. A deferential client may well react differently to an aggressive lawyer than he would to a lawyer who is also deferential as a personality type. That same client, deferential male, may have a different reaction to an aggressive male lawyer than to an aggressive female lawyer. And race, specifically whether the attorney and client are of the same race, can make a difference as well. For our deferential white male client, an aggressive white male lawyer may remind the client of his father and be seen as domineering but familiar and acceptable. But a similarly aggressive black male attorney may remind the client of every media-perpetuated stereotype of violence and be seen as dangerous and foreign and, consequently, quite unacceptable.

B.   REAL LISTENING FOR MORE THAN JUST FACTS—STARTING THE CONNECTION

Interviewing and counseling both involve a collection of a range of skills. One of the most important is **Listening**. When you are "really" listening to a client, you are in the moment with your client and hearing with empathy (or sympathy) and respect, what he is saying. You are not letting him "blow off steam" or vent and then doing whatever you had already planned without his input.[10] When you listen with empathy/sympathy and respect, you start the process of developing a connection with your client whether that client appears to be similar to you or quite different from you. In addition, you are also "listening for" a number of things or at a number of different layers.[11] The most obvious and the easiest for us as lawyers is to listen for (1) Key Facts and People as well as (2) Chronology of the events relevant to the client's legal case. These involve the kind of information we know from our law school education are essential to apply to the relevant law in the case in order to "solve" the legal problem. But clients need solutions that satisfy both their legal problems as well as an array of nonlegal concerns. And clients and lawyers need a certain level of trust and connection within which to navigate the kinds of conversations and exchange of information necessary for a successful attorney-client relationship. Consequently, in order to start and to continue to make that necessary connection with a client, an attorney needs to also listen for (3) the Client's Feelings—his emotions around the key facts and even his initial reaction to having or wanting to use the legal system; (4) the Client's Goals and Values—both the goals and values that the client presents immediately as well as the long term values that may be different when the client is not in the throes of emotions; (5) the Client's Connection to and Expectations of Others i.e. his relationships with significant others and the key people involved in the events of the client's legal case; and (6) the Client's Expectations of You, the lawyer.

Here is an example of an attorney, Linda Kwak, getting the "basic facts," after appropriate greetings, from her client, John White.

L1:   So Mr. White, I know that you have a criminal matter you want to discuss, how can I help?

C1:   Well, Ms. Kwak, I have been charged with possession of marijuana and I need a lawyer to help me make this go away.

L2:   Well, I certainly have a lot of experience in criminal matters involving drugs and I am happy to help. Can you tell me a little bit about how the police came to arrest you and charge you with possession of marijuana?

C2:   It was ridiculous but ... I was driving home from work and dropped off Letty Thomas at her house. And the cops came up saying something about my broken tail light and then they just went through the car and found the marijuana in the ashtray.

From our narrow legal analysis perspective, we as lawyers look at this set of facts and start building a chronology.[12] We probably want to know what time of day "after work" is for this client; where Letty Thomas lives; and where exactly the client was when the police approached his car. We will want to know how many officers; how exactly they "went through the car" and happened to find the marijuana; and whether Letty Thomas or her neighbors could be witnesses. Lighting, traffic patterns and the specifics of the police officer's action all will tell us something about our ability to "make this go away" through a possible search and seizure violation.

All of these questions are appropriate and necessary, but we are listening for more. For example, Letty Thomas is a key person related to the events involving the client's case, but who is she and is she the only key person involved?

L1:   Hm, the police just went through your car. That is distressing as is having to defend a criminal charge at all of course. Let me ask you some questions so that we can figure out how we can best handle this case. First off, who is Letty Thomas?

C1:   Oh Letty is my boss. Her full name is Leticia. And it is her company, an accounting firm. You don't think I would need to involve her, do you?

L2:   Ah, I can see that is a concern for you as it naturally could be. I don't want to make a determination one way or the other yet. Let me ask—how long have you worked there?

C2:   Well, just 4 years. I had been at another accounting company for almost 20 years but it went out of business and so did my job. So I was lucky to connect with Letty's firm and may be looking at a promotion. I'm trying to be positive about that.

L3:   Absolutely stay positive. And you have family members depending on you?

C3:   Yes I have a wife, Anne. She works too. And we have 3 children.

L4:   Kids, they are something. I have a 4 year old myself. How old are your kids?

C4:   Four. The good old days. Mine are all teens now—13, 15 and 17. And well ... my family does not need to be involved in this, do they?

As the attorney asks more questions, she listens for the other facets of the client's story. Key Facts and People and Chronology are more than what was expressed initially. Thomas is a key person not just as regards the search and arrest; she is clearly key in the client's life as his boss. How this case is handled and resolved will be impacted by the client's concerns related to her. Similarly, the fact that the client has a partner and children also expands the universe of key people who matter to this client's cases.

The lawyer would always be interested in the question, What were you doing before the triggering event in the case?[13]—for this case, What were you doing before you drove Letty Thomas home? But chronology is more than just the time immediately preceding what is understood as the "triggering" event. In cases involving family or business conflicts, the question might involve, What was the relationship during the good times? not just a focus on the specific event that has soured the relationship. In the White case, his status at work and the imminence of a promotion are also a part of the chronology to take into account in how the case will be handled.

The attorney also is listening for the client's feelings. Even in the "best" of circumstances—for example, when transactional attorneys help clients cement and legalize relationships that the clients want—there is still stress and concern along with excitement that the client brings to the attorney-client relationship. In so many of the situations when we as lawyers meet clients, they are in the throes of a range of possible emotions—fear being the biggest but also anger, anxiety, embarrassment, doubt, worry, love as well as hatred and desire.

In the White case, the client reveals a range of emotions. His desire from the very beginning "to make this go away" as opposed to fighting reveals a certain reservation and stress related to the case and, likely, a fear of any publicity involving the matter. Any client's concern for privacy can range from not wanting "the world" or strangers to know to not wanting certain family members or business associates to know. Here, White seems focused on those in his immediate orbit through his questions concerning not wanting Letty or his family to be involved. The addition of the client's feelings has transformed a chronology of events—driving a car at a particular hour when the cops search the car and find marijuana possibly in the presence of witnesses—into a story.[14] A story about driving one's boss home; having illegal activity possibly revealed to the boss thereby undermining one's ability to support one's family.

The client's feelings can lead to information about what the client's connection to and expectation of others is. Here, once White reveals that his passenger is his boss, an attorney could already begin to guess that White will have concerns on how he looks in the eyes of his boss. White's view on how much the boss may have seen of the event will likely run contrary to the attorney's view. White will want the boss to have seen nothing of his interaction with the police, while the attorney is likely to hope for a good witness who has seen the interaction and search in its entirety. White's revelation of his possible promotion and his articulation of his desire to not involve the boss all underscore the attorney's initial assumptions. Similarly, the client's attitude on not involving his family—not even his wife—also hints at the way this client relates to his wife as well as his children.

At some point in an interview (our "step" 6, Client's Possible Solutions) and even in a counseling session, an attorney will directly ask a client how she wants to resolve the matter, what are her goals and concerns. But even before the specific questions, an attorney is listening for information about goals and values.[15] As our previous discussion determined, in the White case one goal that seems quite clear is a resolution that is private and quiet. White's statements about his boss and family also imply a resolution that does not involve the help or testimony of others. You, as the attorney, can already begin to get a sense of preferred methods of resolution based on these preliminary values that have been not so much expressed as revealed by the client's comments so far. These goals or values may or may not remain consistent. An attorney needs to be sensitive to the fact that a client's goals can change even based upon her interaction with the attorney alone. But inconsistent statements or expressions of values or goals by the client are important areas of conversation for the lawyer and client so that the client, in particular, is as clear as he can be about what he truly wants.

The attorney is also listening for the client's expectation of the attorney him- or herself or expectations of the attorney-client relationship. A client's expectation of you is not always something that you can or should satisfy, but awareness of the expectations is helpful in creating a trusting relationship. As young attorneys, you may encounter clients who are much older and have certain expectations of young people you must manage. And young and old attorneys handling juvenile matters will both face expectations from children on dealing with adults. Male attorneys handling rape or domestic abuse cases may encounter a hesitance or lack of trust from rape or abuse survivors.

The White case suggests a more standard expectation that clients have of lawyers and about the attorney-client relationship—that it will be confidential.[16] Clients will typically have concerns on whether what they tell you will be revealed and/or will reveal something about them e.g. that they have behaved badly: Was I stupid to have engaged in this business transaction? Will I appear weak? Will the lawyer think less of me to know that I am guilty? Will the lawyer really keep it quiet? So far, White appears to be comfortably aware of this confidentiality and telling the lawyer all that needs to be told. Kwak is careful to frame supportive statements without any suggestion of her judgment about his involvement with drugs. But, it is always important for an attorney to be aware that a client has to have more than an abstract or intellectual understanding of the confidential nature of the attorney-client relationship. And a client often needs assurances—sometime in statements and often in tone and attitude—that the lawyer is not judging him. He has to feel a connection and trust with the particular lawyer with whom he is involved in order to feel comfortable revealing the fullest range of information, feelings, concerns and values that a lawyer would want in representing the client. And you as the attorney must use a range of listening skills and techniques to develop that trust and connection.

Aside from the specific skills and techniques we will explore later, Attorney Kwak uses a particular tactic, self-promotion, when she asserts in the first conversation at L2, "Well, I certainly have a lot of experience in criminal matters." Providing a client with professional or personal information about yourself that makes you unique and/or might persuade the client to hire you over another attorney—"selling yourself" if you will—is a common practice for most lawyers. The more experienced and expert an attorney, the more information one has to "sell."[17] But even the new attorney can and should use any information about himself, if true, which makes him stand out. For the new attorney who thinks he hasn't much to say beyond I worked hard and graduated from law school, it is important to remember that your skills and knowledge as a law school graduate and member of the bar make you unique to the client at this moment. If you can't draw on a lot of prior experience, you can deliver whatever legal knowledge and capability you do have with confidence. So long as your client is persuaded that you are capable of handling her case well, you have made a significant contribution towards creating trust in your client.

C.   CREATING CONNECTION

There are a number of factors, beyond facts, to "listen for," involved in creating connection between lawyers and clients. Understanding these different and shifting factors or facets of the attorney-client relationship helps a lawyer make the kind connection necessary for a trusting and successful attorney-client relationship across all kinds of differences. In addition, the lawyer needs to be able to communicate to the client that he has in fact "heard" the many different messages the client is relating, both those stated and in some cases, those unstated, in order for this trust and connection to develop between the lawyer and her client. There are a number of techniques to aid the lawyer in doing this.

1.   ACTIVE LISTENING

Another kind of Listening approach that attorneys can use to listen and create connection is **Active Listening (AL)**. Active listening describes a range of approaches through which a lawyer can create connection with her client by withholding judgment and expressly acknowledging facts, emotions and/or positive qualities of character expressed by the client.[18] There are a number of ways to engage in AL. The simplest and the one most commonly employed by lawyers is to summarize the facts as relayed by the client. This ensures that the lawyer has heard what the client has said accurately and conveys this fact to the client—or allows for clarification.

But other forms of AL are equally as important to employ in order to communicate to the client that you have heard more of the client's concerns than just the facts of the matter. One key form is **Reflecting**. This involves the attorney responding to the client by both paraphrasing the factual content of what you have heard and attaching an emotional label to the feelings emanating from the speaker. This allows you both to create clarity on the facts of the matter while also conveying your understanding for the client's emotional state. You can also show your understanding of the client's situation by directly stating your ability to share or understand some portion of her emotions or feelings through **Validation**, i.e., expressing your respect or value for your client or some activity in which he has engaged.

Here are two examples of the use of AL to listen for and acknowledge a client's feelings in the context of the beginning moments of an initial interview—

A.   Harriet Long, a family lawyer, is a divorced African-American woman in her 50's. Her client, Betty Ann Jackson, is also in her 50's, although she is Caucasian, and seeks Long's help for a divorce and custody matter.

L1:   Mrs. Jackson, good to finally meet you in person. Please sit. How may I help you today?

C1:   Hello Ms. Long. Well after 25 years of marriage, of putting him through dental school and raising his children, my husband has found someone younger, thinner and childless and I need to decide how to kill him and get away with it.

L2:   Ah Mrs. Jackson... I see. After all you have done in this marriage, you fear this affair will break it up.

C2:   I guess that is fair. Although he has said that he wants to leave so it seems pretty over.

››››››››››››››››› (a few minutes later in conversation) ›››››››››››››››››

L3:   So Mrs. Jackson.... After many years of marriage where you have been an enormous support and helpmate to your husband and mother to his and your children, your husband has made it clear that this recent affair will break up your marriage and you are hurt and angry at that possibility.

C3:   Yes. I can't believe that this is happening. He was never a cheat... and I guess I thought if he did he would be like my friend's husbands who still stay in the marriage but this.... That he would really leave after all these years!

L4:   OK. So you may well be facing a divorce. And we can talk about the specifics of that. I recognize that this kind of circumstance is bound to cause some very strong feelings in you and I want us to address those. But let's agree to put the killing issue aside shall we? Tell me more about how you are feeling about what your husband said and what you think, now, you would like do about it?

Here Attorney Long immediately learns from her new client that a divorce matter is the likely legal object of this representation *and* that her client is quite bitter and unhappy about this fact. She uses active listening to show her client that she has heard the gist of what the client has said. Long's response at Line L2 both paraphrases some of the facts—"after all she has done"—and names one of the possible emotions involved—fear. It is a judgment call on when an attorney may want to do a summary of all the facts along with a more complete AL response, but you should think in terms of making such a statement to your client. Attorney Long does this at line L3 where she paraphrases all the facts—the marriage has been long, the wife has taken care of the husband in some respects and there are children—and names the emotions—hurt and anger—that underlie the assertion "I need to decide how to kill him and get away with it."

Note several things about the lawyer's restatement of "killing him" as "hurt and anger." First off, her response to that was not a "stupid" or literal paraphrase of the client's statement; Long does not say "Ah Mrs. Jackson, you want to take out a contract on your husband's life and need my help in drawing up the particulars." Secondly, while the phrase "kill him" may be a manner of speech, the lawyer does pick up on the possible ethical issue raised if there is any literal truth to the assertion and puts herself on record immediately as discouraging the client from even thinking about pursuing such a course of action.[19] And thirdly, notice that in lightly discouraging the client from thinking that killing would be appropriate, the attorney is disagreeing with her client. Young lawyers and students sometimes think that AL and the support it conveys means never disagreeing with your client. In truth you will have occasions to disagree with clients; and many of those times clients will expect to hear your differing opinions.[20]

B. Allen Anderson, an employment discrimination attorney, is a white male in his 40's who, due to a shooting accident, cannot walk and uses a wheelchair. His client, Anthony Braxton, is also a white male and in a wheelchair, but in his late 20's.

L1: Mr. Braxton, it is a pleasure to meet you. I see you were given coffee. So ... make yourself comfortable and please tell me what employment matter I can help you with?

C1: Well, Mr. Anderson, where to begin? Well for one thing I just learned this morning that all of my coworkers at the brokerage firm I work at, Burnham and Block, make almost twice as much money as I do and I figured I should talk with a lawyer about my options.

L2: All right, Mr. Braxton. You learned something today that you had not known before, which is that you are apparently the lowest paid employee at your job and you feel that this fact, if true, is unfair and want to know if the law can help.

C2:   Well it's true. And it's not just unfair. I have worked hard, gotten the highest evaluations and gone through ... well just not gotten any kind of support at that office.

L3:   It sounds as if with your work record and evaluations you should be at or near the top of the pay scale and so you are feeling quite angry and maybe even surprised by this revelation.

C3:   Yes but maybe not entirely surprised.

L4:   Please tell me more. How did you discover this and why aren't you surprised?

Here, Attorney Anderson, while given facts, is not given much to work with in the way of emotional content based upon what his client tells him. In an actual situational context, of course, there may be any number of nonverbal cues that convey the client's emotional state, like the tone or intensity of his voice, facial expressions, the color of the eyes or skin, and the movements of different parts of the body.[21] Still, despite the (possible) paucity of information, the attorney forges ahead and both describes the facts he has learned—"you learned something new ... you are the lowest paid ..."—and attaches a likely emotional state—"you feel this is unfair ..." He could be wrong. Indeed in this case, the client does not really feel that "unfair" quite captures it. But as is typically the case, the client does not hold the lawyer's inability to "mind read" (or "heart read") against him. He corrects the lawyer by providing him with more information. That information still tends to be more factual than any direct assertion of his feelings. But the new facts—his hard work and excellent evaluations—lead the lawyer to more confidently identify and label some of the client's feelings of anger and surprise.

As stated earlier, active listening is a critical tool to use to underscore that you are listening to your client. And for the client, "being heard" is a key element in making the necessary connection with his lawyer. AL is generally not seen by the novice as a very natural or comfortable way to respond. The young attorney or law student sometimes feels that it is difficult to come up with true AL responses and that the client will view his awkward attempts as phoniness. True AL responses are difficult to imagine on the spot and so require practice. While the issue of "phoniness" may have some validity, it is our own view and experience that client's *sense* phoniness from the authentic feeling generated by the lawyer regardless of how smoothly or awkwardly she speaks. A sincere attempt to understand the client's factual statement and feelings, no matter how stiff and even off base is generally met with appreciation by clients at the effort made by the attorney—even if the client ends up having to correct you.

Active Listening is just the start of "listening for" the range of issues critical to creating connection. While your client may well clearly state his goals—there may be some goals as well as a range of values that go unstated and yet will be important in his decision making. What the client expects of himself and his relationship to others and how he sees his status changing depending upon the outcome of the legal case will also impact the client's decisionmaking. And his relationship with you, as his attorney, will also affect his decision making especially in terms of his assessment of how many of these other factors he will reveal to you willingly.

2. EMPATHY AND SYMPATHY IN CREATING CONNECTION

Creating the kind of attorney-client relationship that allows for a client to feel open and willing to reveal all the information necessary for the legal solution to her problem to most completely satisfy her is your responsibility as the attorney. To create this kind of connection, you must employ different ways to convey empathy, sympathy and support for your client.

Let's define some terms. By **sympathy**, we mean to suggest that you as the lawyer identify with or understand the thoughts and feelings of your client. Your own self-awareness—or at least your focus on yourself and your own feelings—is reduced as you put yourself in the client's situation and emotional state. Your identification with your client's circumstance and perspective can lend an urgency to your desire to help the client resolve his predicament or task. By **empathy**, we mean to suggest less of an emotional or psychological alignment with the client than sympathy captures but still a sense of your ability as a lawyer to share some of the feelings that the client expresses. Here you do not lose your own sense of self, but try to imagine what it would be like to be in the client's emotional state; to understand, nonjudgmentally, the positive and negative aspects of the client's situation.[22] By **support**, we mean to suggest that however closely or loosely you as a lawyer can identify with the client's particular situation, and regardless of whether you can give out and out **approval**, you are able to empathize or sympathize with the broad feelings that your client conveys and can assert, with some authenticity, that you are willing to help.

Empathy and sympathy raise key and complicated issues around **identification** versus **objectivity** in your relationship as a lawyer with your client. Connection, as we have said, is important in the attorney-client relationship. To sympathize or empathize with a client and self-identify with her circumstances or cause can provide an energy and enthusiasm that can prove invaluable in an attorney-client relationship. One feels the "zeal" in zealously representing one's client. Most of the social justice or civil rights movement attorneys shared (and do share) the passion and perspective of their clients. The attorneys involved in the National Association for the Advancement of Colored People (NAACP) who were instrumental in the landmark desegregation case of *Brown v. Board of Education* were as passionate about equality issues as their clients were, if not more so. That kind of sympathy or empathy can be a benefit to the attorney-client relationship; it can bolster the clients' morale and spirits during long and difficult litigations. But sympathy, in particular, also can have drawbacks. Attorneys can "over-identify" and assume they know exactly what the client wants or needs. And the attorney could be perceived by the client as pushing him to do things that he, the client, may not or no longer wants.[23] The sympathetic attorney must be wary of losing his entire sense of self into that of the client. Some objectivity is necessary for the attorney. You will need to be able to step back from the client's situation, in ways that he may not be able to, in order to provide the critical eye and assessments that are precisely why the client has hired you.

For this reason, we believe that most of the time an attorney is looking to be empathetic rather than sympathetic with his client. This is not to say that being sympathetic can't also be effective if an attorney is aware of the dangers. But because empathy generally allows for more "space" from the emotions of a case or client, empathy generally allows for more of the necessary objectivity than does sympathy.

On the other hand, sometimes an attorney's connection with her client does not come easily. For one thing, there will be a range of client activity with which an attorney may not agree and client values which an attorney may find personally repugnant. And yet, the attorney recognizes that the client deserves representation—significantly the disagreeing attorney accepts that the client deserves *her* representation. The defense of any number of criminal defendants who kill, rape, bomb or embezzle from others as well as the representation of any number of civil defendants who manipulate stocks, massively pollute the environment or manufacture unsafe products all depend upon some attorney's ability to develop an attorney-client relationship with people (as individuals and corporate entities) who have engaged in activity or who hold attitudes with which the attorney cannot closely connect. In some cases, the attorney may find her zeal and passion in some aspect or principle in the client's case—even if she has to work hard to connect at a more personal level with the client himself. In some cases, the attorney will have to stretch to find a loose sympathy with some aspect of the client's circumstances, personal background or personality in order to make some kind of connection. You need to avoid "under identifying" with your client, which can lead to an unconscious unwillingness to do your best and to represent the client zealously as well as undermine your client's confidence and trust in you.

Going back to our examples, Harriet Long as a divorced woman herself may have had an experience so similar to her client's that identification with her feelings of anger and betrayal can come quite easily, and she can empathize with Betty Ann Jackson. Jackson could feel comforted to have an attorney who has "been there" and who resonates with her feelings; it could help her believe that her lawyer is truly a champion for her. On the other hand, Long does have to have enough self-awareness to resist assuming that she knows exactly how Jackson feels and that their divorce situations are exactly alike.

Allen Anderson may have no experience with failure at any job. He may not have had any personal experience of discrimination or unfairness in the employment context. Empathy or identification with Anthony Braxton may be difficult, but by imagining what he might feel like if his hard work had not paid off as it had in his past, Anderson can begin to empathize with Braxton. Braxton's factual situation could turn out to be that Braxton, contrary to his self-portrayal to Anderson, is a lousy worker or maybe even a dishonest one. While this will make him hard to empathize with, your job as an attorney is to stretch your abilities at empathetic understanding to at least be able to appreciate the distress and fear that anyone would feel at finding himself the lowest person on the ladder. This may be a loose connection, but it can be used to convey a support, a willingness to do your best to explore if the client, here Braxton, might still have any case. And assuming that he does not, this kind of empathy can and should be used to craft a nonjudgmental delivery of the bad news i.e. that the law can't help him under these circumstances.

3. TECHNIQUES FOR CONVEYING SUPPORT TO CREATE CONNECTION

Direct assertion is another technique that can be used to make connection and convey empathy and support. You as the attorney can directly assert your own feelings, reactions and intentions. This could be either the direct assertion of the empathy e.g. Attorney Long might say to Mrs. Jackson, "I am sorry to hear about the distressing circumstances of your divorce." (This is also a way of using **apology** even when you are not to blame to convey empathy or support.) Or Anderson could say to Braxton, "I would feel very frustrated to have worked so hard and then not get paid what is my due." Or this could be a direct assertion of what kind of support or help the attorney will give. So Long or Anderson could say: "Mrs. Jackson [Mr. Braxton], you can rest assured that I will work my hardest to help you through this difficult time."

Be careful of making statements like "I can understand how . . . [difficult] [frustrating] etc." especially early on in a relationship. Obviously you are doing your best to understand, but you need to keep that sense of objectivity that allows you to remember that you are not in fact your client and that her circumstances are in fact different from yours. Indeed, sometimes a client's background and circumstances will be quite different from anything to which her attorney has personally been exposed. Especially in these situations, it is additionally important to convey to your client that you are aware that her situation is unique and that you are listening intently to learn her particular facts, feelings and goals.

Another technique to convey empathy or support is **apology**, as was shown above. Most often apology is used as a **recovery technique** reflecting that you, as the attorney, have inadvertently said something that angers or distresses the client and in an attempt to regain or recover the trusting connection and empathy that you had previously established, you apologize for your mistake. However, as shown earlier, to say, "Mrs. Jackson, I am sorry to hear of the distressing circumstances of your divorce," is another way to convey empathy using the apology format when in fact you as the lawyer are not in any way at fault.

Another technique that is also more closely related to a recovery method is **explanation**. As you would expect, explanation is simply telling the client why you have said something or asked a question or suggested a particular course of action. Young attorneys and students especially enjoy asking clients lots of questions. We, as lawyers, are specially trained to ask detailed questions. Typically the questions are all excellent i.e. they directly relate to acquiring information that will allow the attorney to assess which legal doctrines and defenses will or will not be applicable. But clients are often confused about such questions and can experience them all as an indifference to their emotional or nonlegal concerns. Providing them with explanations can alleviate that sense on the clients' part and build (or rebuild) empathy and connection. Explanation is also a good way to convey your respect for the client's dignity and privacy rights.

An additional technique for conveying or maintaining empathy and support is **personal connection or sharing**. An attorney could choose to share some detail in his life as a way of explaining his ability to understand, sympathize or empathize. Attorney Long, being a divorced woman herself, might share that fact or some details of her own history that appear to be similar. Or Attorney Anderson may not have been fairly treated in his previous workplace and could relate his own experiences with inequity.

While the other techniques that we have described are essential and should be used, at appropriate points, by all attorneys, this technique, of course, is a matter of personal choice. Not all individuals will be comfortable sharing personal information with a stranger. This truth is what makes it a powerful tool with clients if you can wield it effectively. Clients typically do not want to have to tell you, a stranger, their personal situation, mistakes, embarrassments and problems. Your willingness to share can make the relationship feel less imbalanced as well as underscoring your ability to empathize with the client's situation. But the technique has its pitfalls as well. When you are acting as someone's attorney—even if the client is, in other circumstances, a personal friend—the focus is not on you and your problems, history or issues; there is no equal time as one would expect with a friend. And you will need to maintain a certain boundary with your client so that you can deliver the critical or negative assessments and information that are a routine part of the lawyer-client relationship. Friends can avoid bad news—rightly or wrongly. Lawyers cannot. Our choice is not whether to deliver it, but how and when.

D. HINDERING CONCERNS IN THE ATTORNEY–CLIENT RELATIONSHIP

In any conversation or relationship, there can and will be factors that can hinder or inhibit the communication and connection between the two parties. In order to develop the virtue of openness of mind, you need to be aware of the general ways in which these hindering concerns can arise so that you can learn to avoid the situation or be able to identify them and employ techniques that create connection to eliminate or at least reduce the force of these issues.

1. WATCH YOUR ATTITUDE— NONRESENTFULNESS

First and foremost in ensuring that communication and connection can flow freely between you and your client is maintaining a calm and positive attitude in all your dealings with your client. But during any particular attorney-client relationship there may arise circumstances where you may find yourself feeling defensive. One wants to maintain an attitude of **nonresentfulness** regardless of the circumstances. If you are in the position of having to apologize as a recovery technique or if you are confronted with a client who, for no discernible reason is angry or accusatory, you may feel defensive. (After all you were only doing your best and you may feel it is your client who was unclear or confusing.) Avoid expressing defensiveness or resentfulness. Be mindful[24] of the fact that your clients are typically in stressful situations; that is why they come to you. Even in transactional work, a client who must close a big contract or deal can be highly stressed and emotional. You can be an easy target for outbursts. While attacks can feel personal (especially to the young attorney who already harbors concerns about his still youthful abilities) and they can certainly be worded in personal terms, be self-aware enough to avoid taking such statements as personal attacks.

As an example, in the Braxton case, it might be that Braxton senses, rightly or wrongly, that since Anderson has a nice office and an apparently successful practice (maybe with posted degrees from schools Braxton recognizes and admires), Anderson has had no experience with injustice at work and so Braxton finds himself resentful of his attorney's success. This might be more likely the case if we were to imagine that Braxton were in his 40's and thus closer in age to Anderson. The age similarity might cause Braxton to see Anderson as a peer and one who had excelled beyond what Braxton had hoped for himself.

L1:   Well, Mr. Braxton it sounds as if with your work record and evaluations you should be at the top of the pay scale. I can certainly understand how being overlooked in the pay and promotion department could make you angry.

C1:   Can you Mr. Anderson? You seem to have done very well for yourself. Probably were Mr. Big Man on Campus starting from kindergarten. Can you really understand what it's like for a guy like me? The kid the jocks bullied until I was halfway through high school and my parents moved to a new town. I don't think so. This was a mistake.

L2:   Wait Mr. Braxton, I am sorry for my choice of language. Neither one of us knows enough about the other to make assumptions. And I shouldn't have assumed too much. I have been successful, yes. And since I came by that success fairly, I believe everybody who works hard should get their just desserts as well. That is why I believe that I can help you. Please, tell me more about your situation so that I can begin to understand.

Here Anderson has used the phrase "I can understand..." and received a very defensive response from this client. We caution against the phrase because of just this kind of response. But clients can get defensive or angry without such a prompt. In Anderson's response to Braxton, he quickly apologizes—"I am sorry for my choice of language." He acknowledges his mistake of "assuming too much" in the context of a gentle rebuke to this client—"neither one of us knows enough. . . ." He uses the technique of explanation to explain what his own values and views are that account for his mistake—since he came by his just desserts fairly he wants that for everyone. And then he uses direct assertion to state that he can help the client and, by implication, that he is willing to help.

Two things are important to flag here. Anderson's successful nonresentful response is highly contextualized, i.e., it is contingent upon his tone and body language. If he in fact is resentful and defensive, no amount of carefully constructed language will prevent the client from hearing the truth. Indeed, if you cannot keep the resentment out of your voice, it may be wise to acknowledge your own feelings directly. To pretend that you are not really angry when you are may only encourage the client to feel that you are not truthful and that may well undermine the client's development of trust in you. Additionally, there is some question as to whether the attorney should say "Neither one of us knows enough about the other to make assumptions." It certainly is a way of saying what many of us would want to say—in essence, "Hey! You are making a lot of assumptions about me and you don't know me!" If the attorney can maintain an appropriately gentle and apologetic tone, this could be successful. On the other hand, right tone or wrong tone, the client could feel criticized and fail to hear anything else the attorney has said.

2. "WHAT'S UP WITH ME?" SELF-REFLECTION BY THE ATTORNEY

It is always important to remember that communication problems are rarely if ever the "fault" of only one party to the conversation. You as the attorney must be willing to engage in rigorous self-examination. You may and will have clients that you experience as "difficult," but you must always engage in a reflection upon yourself, your skills and attitudes as a professional first, before you start a reflection upon and critique of your client.

Hindering concerns that come from the lawyer can be grouped into a few common categories. *Fear* tops the list and is often the foundational emotion for other hindering categories. There are any number of situations that can and should cause fear and anxiety in a lawyer. For example—You are a new attorney. Or an old civil attorney doing criminal law. Anxiety in facing new situations is normal and necessary. A typical aspect of this kind of fear is concerns over time—will I have enough of it to learn all that I do not yet know in order to do a good job for my client? Even an attorney experienced in the area of the law in which he is practicing will feel some fear or anxiety during the course of a representation. If you have no fear or anxiety then you probably do not care enough about what you are doing, about yourself as a professional and person and/or about your client's life, liberty, property or dignity. And then it is time to leave lawyering.

Another common hindering area for lawyers is around *Finances and Reputation*. This can involve getting more concerned with the profits or media attention that a case will bring than being concerned with the client's real interests. For most attorneys lawyering is a business, so it is fair that an attorney should be paid for her work and acquire a positive reputation when she does a job well. But when money, fame or some other personal self-interest becomes more important than the client's interests and case, one cannot do an adequate job. This hindering area could also involve fears about making enough money and taking on too many cases or cases which you are not yet prepared to manage well.

Other hindering concerns go to the heart of difference and connection issues. Sometimes one can feel wonderfully connected with a client, thinking *s/he's just like me!* Typically this is when there are things about the client—generally *similar* economic, racial, cultural, religious, geographic, sexual orientation, physical, or gender characteristics or familiar aspects of the client's circumstances—that make you feel a special affinity for them. This can be a very useful stroke of luck. But do not over identify.[25] You need some distance to provide the client with the bad news that she may need to hear. And, as we noted earlier, you must avoid assuming that because you are so alike you "know" the client's needs, desires and concerns without actually asking him.

The Long and Jackson relationship can, again, serve as an example here.

L1:   . . . . Tell me about your situation. I confess. . . my husband left me for his nurse after I put him through Yale college and med school.

C1:   What an animal! Did you have kids too? I have three to raise and he is arguing about child support!

L2:   I had two to raise. And part of the time he didn't give me a dime. I had to fight him every step of the way. And won.

C2:   You go gal.

L3:   That's why I went to law school, to make sure no woman and her children go through that. We will get that husband of yours. He'll do right in the end. Trust me on that.

Here, Long, rather than having any concern about any differences—for example, race—between herself and her client, has thoroughly identified with the similar divorce situation. She uses personal sharing to reveal circumstances that she shares with her client. As we mentioned earlier and is reflected in the example, while this kind of empathy—or in this case sympathy—and identification can make a client feel like she has a champion, Long needs to be self aware about the possibility of over-identifying with Jackson. Jackson may be angry at this point, but it is not at all clear that she wants (or should want) to "get that husband of hers."

The "flip side" of feeling that the client is just like me is the sense that *we have nothing in common.* Here, you as the attorney, initially, cannot see how you and your client could ever connect. There could be any number of habits, personality or character traits by which a lawyer could be repulsed. Before deciding that it is all the client's fault, an attorney needs to examine his own habits and traits. You could be reacting because of your own issues. As the professional in the relationship, the responsibility is on the lawyer to do the self-analysis to recognize and overcome these kinds of concerns and focus on the client and his problem and concerns.

Identify any and all positive [in the lawyer's view] characteristics in the client. Think through how what appear to be negatives could be viewed as positives.[26] At the least find an explanation for your client's apparently negative behavior. Whether your client is a corporate CEO or a gang leader, both could come off as arrogant and indifferent to others. You don't have to "like" what either is or does to at least recognize that both types of clients could believe that survival demands that no "weakness" or emotion can be shown.

Another aspect of this relates to differences that are not habits, personality or character traits, per se, but larger social or cultural background influences, or socially constructed identity categories, that *could* make your perception of the world quite different from your client's. Here, because you and your client are different because of gender, race, class, cultural, religious, sexual orientation, physical ability, citizenship status or other differences it *seems* like you could never possibly understand her. It is important to consider the old expression "nothing human is alien to me" seriously. We are all related as members of the human race and family. Despite apparently vast differences, the few things in common can make connection a breeze [Irish and Latino but if both Catholic . . .]. And, even if similarities are not immediately evident, generally with enough time and effort, people can find commonalities.

However, do not assume that these connections necessarily can be discovered without work. Good intentions alone may not be enough. Educating yourself about the experiences and lives of homeless people or mentally challenged people or people who are recent immigrants or people from different racial or ethnic groups or whatever is often essential to supplement your well-intentioned attempts to connect with people who are different from you.

We can explore the attorney reactions of *"we have nothing in common"* and *"s/he's just like me"* with some examples that will also explore how the two reactions can be interrelated.

We start with the Long and Jackson relationship which we just discussed and which, as we noted from our earlier description, is one which involves similarities but also possibly significant differences.

L1:   Hello Mrs. Jackson, how can I help you?

C1:   Well, Ms. Long, my husband is about to run off with someone young enough to be our daughter, and I need help especially since here in Connecticut I am so far from my own family.

L2:   Mrs. Jackson, you have come to the right place for help in family matters. And I have some sense of the difficulties of going through hard times without the rest of your family. Connecticut is a long way from my original home too.

C2:   I am guessing Alabama, like me, from the sound of your voice. I am from Birmingham.

L3:   Yes. Birmingham for me too. Most of my family is still there. So tell me more about your situation.

C3:   I just can't believe it. I never thought I would be one of the many people getting divorced. When you think back to when we were kids, marriages stayed together and we all had a much easier life.

L4:   Well, marriages did stay together. And certainly some of us had it easier.

C4:   Oh! Oh, I didn't mean the whole Jim Crow thing. Or the bombing of the Sixteenth Street Baptist church where those little Black girls were killed. I . . .

L5:   I know. Fortunately, some of that has changed. So tell me about your situation. It sounds painful and I confess . . . my own ex-husband left me for his nurse after I put him through Yale College and med school.

Here the fact that the two women are different races could prove an impediment to the attorney-client relationship. While we all hope that these sorts of issues will not matter, too often they do continue to have some significance. The key for an attorney is to be able to examine herself honestly to identify whether she is bringing some hindering issue to the equation. Here, Long does not on the face of it appear to have any racial bias towards whites. But her client's views on what living in Birmingham, Alabama in the 1950's and 1960's was like are drastically different from hers and very reflective of the different experiences that blacks and whites had due to legalized segregation and racial inequality. Here, Long consciously chooses to skirt around their differences and instead focus in on the similarity that she recognizes they share.

Sometimes, it will not be the lawyer's choice to avoid a focus on the differences between herself and her client in favor of their similarities. Clients can bring with them concerns and biases about whether particular differences between themselves and their lawyers will undermine the lawyer's zeal and commitment to their cases. The lawyer needs to be prepared to maintain a nonresentful attitude and to employ all his skills at connection in order to assuage the client's concerns before entertaining the notion that he and his client are so incompatible that the attorney-client relationship should be severed or not pursued.

Assume that the following conversation takes place in the office of attorney Bryan Culbert, a white civil rights and criminal defense attorney in Seattle, Washington. His client, Evelyn Yamashita, has come to his office within a week after several days of massive demonstrations against the World Trade Organization (WTO) in downtown Seattle. Hundreds of people were arrested as a result of the demonstrations which were nationally and internationally publicized. The publicity has generated much debate, locally and elsewhere, over the propriety of the behavior of some demonstrators as well as some police officers.

L1:   Hello. I'm Bryan Culbert ... Ms. Yamashita, how can I help you?

C2:   Well, Mr. Culbert, I was arrested. It is an absolute outrage! And frankly I may want to sue the Seattle police.

L2:   I see. You have been arrested and feel that this was unjust. So you have come to me for the criminal matter. What were you arrested for?

C2:   Destruction of property, assault, resisting arrest. I was arrested near the WTO meetings during the demonstrations downtown. And the cops just went wild! I came to you for the arrest, but I want to sue as well. I mean, what happened to the First Amendment!?

L3:   OK. Well, let's start with the criminal matter first, since that will move faster than any civil matter we might choose to bring and, frankly, the outcome of the criminal case may well affect our civil case.

C3:   What?! You mean I can't sue the cops for beating me because they made up these charges?

L4:   No. But if we don't "beat" the criminal charges, so to speak, while you can sue, a judge or jury may, I stress MAY, feel that whatever injuries you suffered were within the officer's line of duty because you assaulted him or her or were destroying property. So we can sue, but our case is harder. Remember there was a good deal of publicity around the demonstrations. Some people already believe that the Seattle cops lost it with the protestors. And that will help us. But others think that the protestors got out of line. Still even here we can focus on you and your behavior and your right to protest peacefully and be treated with respect and dignity regardless of how others were behaving. So ... let's get back to the criminal situation—you were arrested demonstrating against the WTO....

C4:   No! No! Great! You assume just like those white cops did. What is it with white people! I was not demonstrating! And though black I was not looting! I'm a reporter for the local newspaper and I was trying to cover the demonstrations. And they—the cops—refused to believe that I was downtown after the curfew lawfully because I am black, part black. They just wouldn't listen to me. And when they finally allowed me to pull out my press identification badge and it said 'Yamashita,' my name,

they didn't figure I could be both black and Japanese and ...
American too for heaven's sake! And they hit me! And pepper
sprayed me! I wasn't violent and I didn't do anything wrong!

Here, our lawyer, Culbert, is confronted with a client who is quite
upset about her criminal case and the circumstances of her arrest. Culbert
immediately starts using active listening (line L2); he mirrors his client's
statement of fact by restating the substance ("you were arrested") and he
identifies the feelings she expressed ("and you feel that this was unjust").
His client, Yamashita, is so angry that she is focused on a civil case rather
than the more pressing criminal matter. Culbert, in his attempt to both
calm her down and redirect her attention to the criminal case, makes
some logical assumptions about what happened. If she was arrested
during the recent demonstrations against the World Trade Organization
policies, it's likely that she was *participating* in the demonstrations. But in
fact that doesn't have to be the case.

In this case, the logical but incorrect assumption has managed to
offend the client because, unbeknownst to the lawyer, the client feels that
the crux of her case rests on inappropriate stereotyping and racial assumptions. Culbert has inadvertently triggered concerns and biases Yamashita has regarding what white people believe about black people. Culbert
should have inquired more openly—without assumption or judgment—
about his client's activities at the time of her arrest.[27] Had Culbert been
African–American, he might have been able to ask the same question or
make the same assumption, but not gotten the same reaction of anger and
resentment. Yamashita might take comfort in their racial similarity and
not assume that his logic is analogous to the attitude and behavior of the
police. Context matters. But it is important to note that non-black Culbert
can and does use other skills to regain his client's trust across their
differences.

L5:   Ms. Yamashita, I am sorry. I shouldn't have assumed. You said
        First Amendment and I heard right to protest when you were
        talking about freedom of the press. Both important rights.
        Again I'm sorry. Let's back up. What were you doing that night
        exactly?

C5:   I was downtown at about 8 PM. It was after curfew but it was
        clear there were protestors out and I wanted to ... well, do my
        job. Observe what actions they were engaged in. Maybe inter-
        view people. Some were obviously our own homegrown petty
        criminals out looting, but some people were nonviolent and
        wanted to explain their issues.

L6:   And that means you were doing what... walking or in a car?

C6:   I was walking. I had left my car so that I could really see what
        people were doing. I just talked to people I saw on the street.

L7:   What happened right before the police approached you?

C7:   I was talking with some people who were real protestors, when some other people came and broke a store window. I called to my photographer who was filming. And then I started to shout to the people going in. Saying things like 'What are you doing? Is this part of your protest? How does breaking into a store help your cause?' And then the police came.

L8:   Did you say you were a reporter as soon as you saw them?

C8:   Why? I'm black so I have to identify myself as legitimate?

L9:   No, nothing like that at all. I mean, you mentioned to me you were out past curfew and, as you said, you were near people who had broken into a store; the cops could have made an honest mistake given the heat of the moment.

C9:   Yeah, well.... maybe ... I didn't see them right away. I was trying to stop the looters from going in and the cops came from behind and grabbed me and threw me to the ground. And that is when I said "Hey! I'm a reporter! I'm not with them!

L10:   Did they hear you?

C10:   Of course they heard me! I was screaming as anyone would if your arms were twisted and you had been thrown down. They didn't care!

L11:   OK I'm sorry. I'm just trying to get a sense of what it was like out there. I want to help you. I am not trying to defend and will not defend police officers who beat and arrest innocent civilians—especially if it's racially motivated. That's racial profiling and it's wrong. But if I'm going to help you I need to ask you the kinds of questions—like 'Is it likely the police heard your identification?'—which the prosecutor will raise in the criminal case and even the cops' attorneys will raise if we sue them. I have to ask and know the answer so that we are ready for them in whatever case they come up. OK? So let's keep going so that I can know what you know and help you the best I can. What did they say to you when you said that you were a reporter?

Here, Culbert immediately uses apology—twice—in an effort to calm his client down about his mistaken assumption. (Line L5) He makes no verbal response to his client's remarks about whites. He attempts to avoid exacerbating his client's sense of their difference by proceeding to do his job as a lawyer well by asking the right questions in open-ended form: in line L5 he asks, "what were you doing?" and in line L7 "And what happened right before...." In line L6 when he asks "And that means walking or in a car?", he is prodding and prompting his client but avoiding out and out leading questions ("You were walking; right?").

Culbert then stops asking open questions and begins to ask for specific information about how Yamashita acted towards the police. At line L8 he asks "Did you say you were a reporter as soon as you saw them [the police]?" and at line L10 "Did they hear you [say you were a reporter]?" From the lawyer's perspective, these are excellent questions. He must know the answer to have an understanding of how good any defense of Yamashita or criticism of the police will be in any case—criminal or civil. However, clients are not always clear why their story is being interrupted by such questions. In this case, with a client who is already suspicious and sensitive about whether she can trust her lawyer, Culbert again triggers his client's questions about his commitment to her as a black client.

In each case Culbert uses explanation to regain his client's trust. At line L9, he reminds the client of important facts that she told him—she was out past curfew and near actual looters—to provide an explanation for why under those circumstances it would be important for anyone—regardless of their race—to provide an explanation of their activities to the police. At line L11, he uses explanation imbedded with several other connection skills. He apologizes again. He also directly asserts that he wants to help her. He also directly expresses his personal feelings or values about police officer misconduct and in particular racial profiling by stating "I am not trying to defend and will not defend police officers who beat and arrest innocent civilians . . . ." and "That's racial profiling and it's wrong." He makes a clear statement of what his values are in contrast to the apparent values of the arresting officers and in contrast to his client's assumptions about him.

He continues his separation from the police and his alignment with his client when he starts to explain how the answers to these questions will be important to her case. He frames this explanation by noting that the "other side"—in this case the prosecutor in the criminal case or the police officers' attorneys in the civil suit—will ask these questions and "we" must be ready to answer them. By putting the weight on the "other side" as the "bad guys" who will question her sincerity, Culbert is able to distance himself from these tough questions and, ideally, get answers to them without making the client feel that *he* questions her truthfulness. He underscores his distance from the "other side" and his connection with his client by aligning himself with her—the two of them are a team already—when he says "I have to ask . . . so that *we* are ready. . . ."

Culbert might have been better served in this conversation if he had continued to ask open-ended questions and waited until the client had said all that she wanted to say about what happened on the night in question before beginning to ask specific, direct questions. And especially with a suspicious client, he might want to provide his explanations of his questions before he asked them. Explaining why he is asking the question could reduce—though not always eliminate—the chances of the client assuming an improper motive for the question. In addition, Culbert cannot recover and start to build trust with this client unless the entire conversation is done without resentment and with a willingness to make the extra effort to understand the client. Yamashita appears to have transferred her anger at the police officers on to her lawyer merely because they are the same race. Culbert cannot afford to react to his client based upon his rightful sense of the injustice of his client's attitude towards him. If Culbert can stay calm and open to his client, recognizing that her experiences that night—and perhaps in other situations—are the likely source for her hostility, he will be able to not take his client's attitude personally. The longer Culbert can maintain that attitude and tone, and the longer he continues to use the full panoply of connection skills with his client, the greater the likelihood that the client will become convinced of her lawyer's zeal and commitment. Once she begins to see her lawyer for the individual he is, she and her attorney can re-focus their attention on those characteristics which they share that are similar and can strengthen their connection and trust.

In some cases, both the lawyer and the client may have to determine if each can maintain the focus on similarity over differences in order to sustain a trusting attorney-client relationship. The Anderson–Braxton case can provide a more complicated example of the hindering concerns involving similarity and difference.

L1:   Hello Mr. Braxton. Come in. Ah! I see I don't have to offer you a chair since you like me have brought your own. Get comfortable here.

C1:   Mr Anderson, I hadn't realized when I called to make an appointment that you were in a wheelchair too. Call me Tony.

L2:   Tony it is and I am Al. And yes, I was the victim of a shooting in my teens. Wrong place at the wrong time. But I didn't let that stop me from finishing college and going on to law school.

C2:   I respect that a lot. I was in a car accident. I would have been a pro football player but for it. I had been picked in the draft and everything. But with a lot of prayer and help from friends and family and God, I got through and have recreated my life as a stockbroker. I work for a large company where I have had my troubles.

L3:   My staff told me that this was an employment discrimination case. Does your boss know nothing of the Americans with Disabilities Act?

C3:   It's not that, Al. At least I don't think so. The head of our firm is a very conservative form of 'born again' Christian. He is a member of Harry Halwell's church, and he hates gays and lesbians. He thought I was great, wheelchair and all, when I was hired because he saw me as a church-going former football player. Which, of course is exactly what I am. But I am also gay and when he found that out ... well, everything changed and my work life became hell.

L4:   Uh well ... Mr. Braxton. I think it only fair to tell you that I too am a member of Reverend Halwell's church. My religious views on homosexuality are separate from my job in helping you make sure that your boss follows the law.

Here Al Anderson starts out assuming that he and his client, Tony Braxton, could identify very closely as physically challenged men who, through faith, have overcome difficulties to create successful careers only to discover that other differences—their different sexual orientations and, more significantly, their different moral and religious views on this—may cause them to be quite distant. This alone may make Anderson feel that

Braxton is in the *"we have nothing in common"* category, although clearly as a factual matter that is not true. It may affect whether Anderson feels he can "like" his client. Anderson will have to think carefully and honestly about whether his religious beliefs will allow him to zealously represent this client.

Moreover, even if Attorney Anderson decides he is able and willing to represent Braxton, he must now assess whether his client feels comfortable with him. Even if Anderson cannot fully "like" this client, it will be difficult for him to develop a needed level of trust with Braxton if Braxton feels that Anderson either dislikes or disrespects him. Anderson may wonder if his statement at L4 "My religious views on homosexuality are separate from my job in helping you make sure that your boss follows the law," conveys enough enthusiasm or respect for the client or his situation to engender the trust that Braxton needs to have in Anderson.

Braxton will have to decide how comfortable he is with Anderson as his attorney. On the one hand, Braxton may feel that Anderson will have some greater insight into the defense, since he will have a special understanding of his boss' position and religious views. Braxton could feel that this insight will help his case. On the other hand, he must decide if he will feel comfortable with an attorney whose religious beliefs may cause the attorney to think less of him as a person, and possibly not work as diligently for him. How Anderson portrays his religious attitudes and professional zeal will be a significant factor in Braxton's assessment.

Anderson has not revealed the details of his religiously based moral code other than that it seems to view homosexuality in some kind of negative light. Whether Anderson should politely refuse to represent Braxton is highly contextualized—as we keep saying about the specifics of any attorney-client relationship. If Halwell were a real person one could identify materials that outlined the fundamental tenets of his church. However that would not end the inquiry. The key context is how *Anderson* understands whatever those tenets are. While there may be some tenet that reflects a disapproval of gay and lesbian people or homosexual behavior, there are also tenets on the connection between all people in the eyes of God and the primacy of love as a moving force in one's life. How Anderson understands and balances these two broad moral approaches will be key to his ability to represent Braxton. If Anderson's disapproval of homosexual behavior means that he, personally, dislikes anyone he discovers is gay or lesbian and feels a discomfort with and disrespect for them, then he needs to let Braxton find an attorney who can represent him with zeal. On the other hand, Anderson, who is a civil rights attorney, may find that his religious views are more focused on the overriding power of love. He could decide that their shared physical challenges and the ways in which both men have relied on God and faith to succeed generates a much greater connecting force than their differences around their sexual orientations.

The Anderson–Braxton relationship raises the larger question of when an attorney can in good conscience represent a particular client. Clearly, no attorney can remain in the business and service of lawyering and not represent some clients that he does not like or who have done things with which he does not agree. As we noted earlier, both criminal and civil defense work rests upon the reality that at least some clients will in fact have violated criminal or civil laws or regulations and an attorney need not approve of or like the client personally to provide adequate and even excellent representation. But some clients will raise special moral challenges for any particular attorney based upon the attorney's own moral code. Again, self-awareness and honesty are key.

The Anderson–Braxton dialogue also reveals the complexity of when a lawyer may be ethically obligated and/or practically motivated to disclose some personal belief or attribute. The truth is that everything we are affects everything we do. Still, a lawyer is not obligated to make elaborate self disclosures on a routine matter so that the client can measure all the influences to which her lawyer may be subject. We return to the need for rigorous self-examination and honesty on the part of the lawyer about which attitudes or beliefs need to be revealed to your client.

3. "WHAT'S UP WITH THEM?"

While it is important for a lawyer to always look to himself, first, when connection weakens or breaks down, clients of course do bring an array of issues with them that can impact negatively on their willingness to speak openly and truthfully within the attorney-client relationship. The Culbert–Yamashita dialogue reveals but one example of a client who brings fears and concerns that inhibit her willingness to speak freely with her attorney. As with lawyers, *fear* tops the list and for clients may be much more likely to be the foundational emotion for all others that get expressed. The specifics of their fear and how they show it will vary and be unique to each individual and case. Remember that unless you are working with a longstanding client, the client does not know you so you cannot assume that she or he will be comfortable with you. Although clients know that they *need* an attorney that does not mean that they *want* an attorney. You will often be a stranger to a client, and few people are comfortable revealing personal information to total strangers.

It is also important to remember that fear, stress and concern can be expressed in a range of ways that may not seem logical or appropriate in light of the way you may be comfortable in seeing fear, stress and concern expressed. A client's apparent indifference to a serious legal and personal situation can be very disconcerting to a lawyer working hard to help. It is important to be aware that "indifference" is not always about not caring or trying to be uncooperative. It can be a not irrational defense mechanism.[28] Similarly undue optimism can be both an aspect of denial and also a defense mechanism. People who have endured traumatic situations that have now resulted in some kind of legal case may well have the psychological reaction of depression and find it difficult to provide the kind of energy and help in case preparation that is ideal. Again it is important to bear in mind that, while this reaction has its unhealthy and unhelpful aspects, it is also, often, understandable if you take the time to gather the client's complete story. Clients can also get focused on matters that appear irrelevant to their case. While this can be a defense mechanism, digressions can point to embarrassing facts or situations the client is trying to avoid or concerns for other key people in his life.[29]

Consequently, an attorney should handle all these reflections of fear by continuing to speak with the client with empathy, sincerity and truth. You may have to make clear what is negative to the indifferent or overly optimistic client, to assure yourself that they have at least heard the information. And you may need to encourage some "positivity" in the depressed client, in hope that they will hear that there are possible positive outcomes. You want to assure yourself that clients have heard the necessary information without insisting that they react to it in the way that you might hope. And have some patience. It is called the attorney-client *relationship* because it is something that grows over time.

For some clients, especially severely depressed ones, you may need to encourage the client to obtain professional mental health counseling of one sort or another. Whether you are in private or "public" practice and whether you are on the prosecution, plaintiff or defense sides, it is always a good idea to have some knowledge and ability to refer clients to a range of other services including medical doctors, nurses, naturopaths and other physical health care professionals; psychiatrists, psychologists, counselors and other mental health care professionals; religious and spiritual services; tax, accounting and other related financial services; and public benefits like welfare; social security or medicare.

DISCUSSION QUESTIONS

1.   Think about the Long-Jackson attorney-client relationship. Would it have been appropriate for Attorney Long, in response to Jackson's assertion that she wants to kill her husband, ever to have said, "I can understand perfectly how you might want to kill him. I wanted to kill my ex for a while."? If so, under what circumstances and what else might she need to say?

2.   Should Attorney Long have discussed the limitations of attorney-client confidentiality as soon as her client Betty Ann Jackson stated a desire to "kill" her husband? If not, at what point should an attorney raise the issue?

3.   When Attorney Long asserts that Jackson has in fact been a helpmate for her husband is that approval? Is it an appropriate way to connect with her client and convey her empathy and support? Or if it turns out that Jackson was really not so helpful to her husband, will Jackson feel that she cannot tell Long the truth?

4.   Would it have been all right for Attorney Long to view Jackson's assertion that life in 1950's and 1960's Birmingham, Alabama as one where "we had it so easy" as a racist remark? Would it have been all right for her to be clearer and more negative about the differences in their perspectives e.g. stating that

"Well, marriages did stay together but only you whites had it easy in the South." If not, why not? What if Jackson had not been so easily aware of the racial differences involved and, upon recognizing them, was indifferent or dismissive—if she'd said, "Oh! You were thinking about segregation. Well, sure everyone kind of knew their place then. And you have to admit, people were happier and things were easier." How should Long respond to Jackson's racial attitudes then? Is your answer affected by whether you are a member of a racial minority? An African-American? A person who is or has ever been part of an "out group" and treated with less than full dignity or equality?

5.   Think about the Culbert-Yamashita attorney-client relationship. Should Culbert have addressed his client's racial attitudes and concerns as soon as she said "What is it with white people?" Or was ignoring the remark the appropriate non-response? How would you feel and react if a client of another race made a remark about your race that appeared to be disparaging? Would it make a difference if you were aware, as Culbert was, that the client had had a recent racially discriminatory and disturbing experience that could account for his hostility?

6.   Culbert does give an explanation about his own beliefs on the impropriety of racial profiling. Should he say more about his personal beliefs and history around racial matters or would more sound defensive and possibly false?

7.   Culbert provides an explanation for his challenging questions to his client after he has asked the questions. We suggest that it would be the better practice to provide an explanation before asking the question. Do you agree? How complete an explanation should be provided? When can a full explanation risk telling the client what the "right" answer is regardless of whether that answer is the truth?

8.   Think about the Anderson-Braxton attorney-client relationship. Should Braxton ever say "Neither one of us knows enough about the other to make assumptions"?

9.   Should Anderson discuss his religious views more openly with Braxton as a way to determine not only whether he, Anderson, wants to represent Braxton, but also whether Braxton will be comfortable with Anderson as his attorney? In contrast, should Anderson remain silent about his religious views on the theory that his views are personal and separable from his professional responsibility?

10.   In thinking about Question #9, how much does it matter to you that Anderson was a member of the same church—if not congregation—as the employer? If Anderson were not a member of Halwell's church, but was a member of a church with similarly negative views on homosexuality, would his silence on his religious affiliation be more defensible?

11.   Is Anderson just like a criminal defense attorney who defends a client charged with and guilty of some crime? A criminal defense counsel will normally *not* like the actions which the client is accused of committing (or perhaps has done) and yet defends the client anyway.

It should be noted that while criminal defense attorneys typically disapprove of their client's actions, they are rarely called upon to actually "defend" the actions themselves. Defense counsel normally deny that their client committed the criminal act and demand that the government show that their client did indeed do the deed as is required by our Constitution. Sometimes, they will also present some evidence of who else did the act or evidence to show that their client could not have done the crime. It is rare that defense counsel concedes that the client did an illegal act; yet acts as if the act were not wrong; and then asks jury or judge to ignore the law. The one exception might be in civil disobedience cases.[30]

12. Is Anderson like the African-American or Jewish-American lawyer working for a group like the American Civil Liberties Union who defends the First Amendment rights of a Ku Klux Klan member or other white supremacist client? Assuming Jackson had a racially insensitive or racist attitude about the "benefits" of segregation, is Long like that ACLU attorney even though she practices in the family law context?

13. Are lawyers who are involved in social justice or advocacy work—whether in support of ethnic groups or women, the environment or animals as well as in promoting particular political or religious perspectives—more likely to overly identify with their clients? If so, what are the ways you could imagine to insure that such lawyers maintain a certain measure of objectivity?

14. How do you think you will separate your personal religious and/or moral views from the facts of the case of any particular client? What values or circumstances will be easy for you to "set aside" from your clients' values or actions? Which would be difficult?

E. CONNECTION ACROSS DIFFERENCE IN COUNSELING

Real listening and creating connection start with interviewing—and a solid foundation from the start always benefits the lawyer and her relationship with her client down the road. As the attorney-client relationship unfolds into counseling, the attorney and his client may have more difficult conversations when a decision has to be made on what to do and on which method—trial, administrative hearing, settlement or others—should be chosen to resolve the legal matter. So real listening and creating connection continue through the life of the attorney-client relationship—with opportunities for difference to challenge lawyers and clients as they engage.

In this section, we want to focus on the "steps" that form the heart of counseling: Discussion of Actions and Options, Consequences, and Choosing a Course of Actions and Options. We specifically focus on counseling in the context of dispute resolution rather than the transactional context. And the difference we want to focus on is the Role Difference between lawyer and their clients who are typically laypeople.

The problem of role difference relates to the impact of our education and training as lawyers on how we view and articulate situations; it is the problem of the expert.[31] It is easy, even for the young lawyer/student lawyer, to forget how much you now know that you did not know at one time. In forgetting your former ignorance, you assume that everyone else—including your layperson client—knows these things. And the proliferation of law-related television shows and movies only encourages clients to think that they actually know what you are talking about.

The key to counseling is helping a client choose a legal method of resolution that will best satisfy the client's goals and values. This means the lawyer will need to educate the client about legal methods of resolution. In relating the likely consequences of each legal method, a lawyer will likely compare all "other" legal methods to trial or litigation. In exploring the trial option, the lawyer will likely discuss the "quality of the case" including providing the answers to such questions as: What is the applicable law?[32] What is the story that we would tell at trial and how does it relate to the law and our legal theory? What evidence do we have to prove our theory—and how believable is it? Having answered these questions, the lawyer then assesses what the likely result at trial will be: the lawyer will give her best estimate of what the trier of fact—judge or jury—will decide.[33]

Once the likely result or range of results at trial is assessed, then the outcomes of all the other legal methods are assessed. What will be the likely outcome using other methods where third party neutrals will judge for us?—These include arbitration or some administrative hearings. What is the likely outcome or range of possible solutions using resolution methods over which the attorney and client have more control?—this includes settlement/negotiation and mediation. And with all methods, the attorney needs to explore with the client the question of what will be the impact of the both the *process* of each method as well as the *likely outcome or solution* resulting from each method on the clients' goals and values.

We as lawyers will have our own "expert's view" of the meaning of each dispute resolution method. In the civil context, we are likely to see the options as trial or settlement—although sometimes our own knowledge of how often cases settle may cause us to collapse these two. As alternative dispute resolution methods become more popular, more and more attorneys would add mediation and arbitration. In the criminal context we are likely to just see trial or pleading guilty—with occasionally dismissal as a possibility.

But to really explain to the layperson client what these methods and their resolutions mean we could use a different frame:

Civil Dispute Resolution Options
1. **Trial/Litigation**
2. **Trial/Litigation Leading to Settlement/Negotiation**
3. **Settlement/Negotiation**
4. **Outside Help**
5. **Self-Help**
6. **Alternative Dispute Resolution—Arbitration**
7. **Alternative Dispute Resolution—Mediation.**

Criminal Dispute Resolution Options

1.   **Trial/Litigation**

2.   **Settlement/Negotiation i.e. Plea—includes:**

    A.   **plea + time in jail or prison;**

    B.   **plea + probation;**

    C.   **diversion programs where case or conviction is dropped upon successful completion of probation—including mediation and restorative justice programs**

3.   **Dismissal**

CIVIL OPTIONS

In our list of civil dispute resolution options what the lawyer sees as trial or settlement is "stretched" into three options. Although as lawyers we often speak about trial and settlement in almost the same breath, it is important to explain trial completely before beginning an explanation of settlement options that will likely intersect with different moments in the life of the trial itself. Since clients will often have seen something vaguely resembling a trial on television, it is probably useful to use the television example as a starting point in your explanation of what the process of going to trial means. But it is also important to make clear to the client how the reality is different—especially as regards the impact on the client's life, goals and values. The **process** explanation is different than the **outcome** prediction i.e. your estimate of the decision that the trier of fact is likely to make.

Here is an example involving Richard Mathiesson, a white, 50 year-old divorce lawyer and his client Bill Arnholtz, a white, 35 year-old engineer.[34] Mathiesson already knows the facts of Arnholtz's case which are that Arnholz's wife has initiated divorce proceedings against him so that she can pursue a relationship with someone else. Mathiesson has arranged this meeting specifically as a counseling session to discuss the entire range of legal options available to Arnholtz.

L1:   Bill, How are you? I have not seen you at the golf club in a while. How are you holding up?

C1:   Well, Dick, it's really tough. It's not just that she left me … I mean it is! But the guy she left me for is a world class jerk!

L2:   I know. I understand. These things are never fun and I just respect how you have been handling yourself through it. I want to talk today about the different options we have for getting through this divorce which your wife has filed. There is always trial, of course, although …

C2:   Yes! Why don't we go to trial so that everyone can see what kind of woman she is.

L3: Well, Bill, I know that when you are upset—as you have every right to be under the circumstances—trial can seem like a good way to punish the other side.

C3: Exactly! She hurt me.

L4: Yes, I understand that. What I like to do with clients is give an outline of all the options you have—trial but also settlement and mediation. So that you can have all the information about what each process will be like and what you will likely get out of them. So, let me explain what a trial is.

C4: I know what a trial is. I watch all the lawyer and cop shows. We'll be able to put her on the witness stand and you can cross-examine her about the nervous breakdown she had when our youngest was one and how she was in therapy and drinking. And then, after I stand by her, she leaves with a jerk.

L5: Well, yes, at some point that will happen. It is important for you to remember that it could take years before that moment comes along. From a legal perspective what will happen in those five or six years is that we will have to prepare for trial. This means that you and your wife may have to be deposed. This would occur in my or her lawyer's office with a court reporter present. I would get to ask her all manner of questions that would provide me with fuel for cross-examining her in the way you describe. But you too would be subject to that kind of questioning before-hand as well.

C5: Oh. I didn't realize it would take so long. But as for her attorney questioning me? I know that happens, but I didn't have a nervous breakdown.

L6: This is true. But I want you to look at all the pros and cons here. Depositions are expensive—just one of the reasons along with how much more of my time is needed that going to trial is so expensive. Worse, though, even if I don't verbally go after your wife in the deposition, if I just ask her questions about her nervous breakdown or drinking, you can be assured that she will be defensive and angry. And while you did not have a breakdown, her attorney could frame things to make you *look* bad. For example, her attorney could ask about how much time you spend with your kids given that you are on the road 3 and 4 times a week . . .

C6: Oh, come on! That old complaint that wives come up with. You know how it is, Dick. If we want our families to live at a certain level of comfort we have to work hard.

L7: I know, Bill, I know. But my point is that even at my suggestion you are feeling more stressed. If this happens in a deposition, you will likely be even angrier at the thought that your wife's attorney will try to make you look like an absent father. Now you and your wife are really angry at each other . . . and you still have to spend those five or six years working together to raise your two little ones. How do you think they will be affected by that kind of poisonous tension between you two?

C7: Not so well. They have had it rough through our physical separation really.

L8: Exactly. Once we do get to trial—and this means you are not at work—as you are beginning to see, it will not only be your wife who will be publicly exposed in court but so will you. If I go after her nervous breakdown, her attorney will look for moments when you have been indiscrete. So.... she might look for someone who could testify that while your wife was sick you were at a bar drinking it up. And ...

C8: Drinking it up? I didn't have the drinking problem and if someone said I was drinking it would be part of work or just releasing stress.

L9: Of course. But as you know the point of cross-examination is to make things appear much worse than they are. And it may be that your friends from the club, neighbors, co-workers, even your kids or their teachers, could be called to the stand to testify to any thing they saw or heard to support any allegations of wrongdoing or incompetence as a parent. All these witnesses will take a lot longer than sixty minutes or two hours like a TV show. And the emotional fall out...

C9: Wow. I had not thought that our friends might get dragged in. It's bad enough now wondering whose side they will take. And then my kids! I don't want them involved like that.

L10: Yes. And what would be the point? Once you get beyond your anger at your wife, we have to look at what your goals are in resolving what is not a great situation for you. Do you want custody?

C10: No, not really. I do travel a lot and... really the kids would be better with my ... their mother than a nanny although I could afford that.

L11: Then if you are willing to have your wife keep custody, then after all the dirt is thrown the judge is still likely to divide up the property 50:50 as the law states. I could probably speak with your wife's attorney and negotiate out a settlement agreement with those terms—and there would not be the time, expense or hostility. So let me explain how a negotiation would go and what terms we would like in such a settlement.

Here Attorney Mathiesson lets the client know early on that there are more options than trial even though the client is eager to "choose" trial as his option. He does not assume that because the client has said "Yes" to trial with emphasis (Line C2) that he should start preparing for the deposition. He wants to make sure that the client is aware of what a trial will be like in contrast to what is seen on television, and he wants him to be aware of his other options so he lists them at the beginning (Line L4) and at the end sets the stage for explaining these other options in more detail (Line L11). The attorney lets the client know about how long it will take just to get to the trial (Line L5) and could have included the attorney's estimate of how long the trial itself would take. The attorney notes that trial will be expensive (Line L6) and could have provided some figures on how much it would cost. Indeed, the more seriously a client is considering going to trial, the more important that the financial cost is detailed. Time and expense are the standard negative points about trial. But in addition, Mathiesson speaks about how the types of actions in which lawyers and clients must engage in order to prepare for trial (Lines L6 and L7) and which they will go through at trial (Lines L8 and L9), will affect him as well as the key people in his life i.e. those he loves and others who form part of his social network. The lawyer underscores that the client will not be able to go to work if he is at trial and that his children and friends will also be subject to the "punishment" of testifying and being cross-examined (Lines L8 and L9). The lawyer also asks about the clients goals explicitly (Line L10) and then compares the apparent goal of the client with the likely outcome at trial (Line L11). Mathiesson is clear on how both the process of trial and its outcome will impact the client.

In this dialogue, Attorney Mathiesson uses specific examples from Arnholtz's life—his travel, his activities at the club—to create vivid examples of the negative parts of trial. He is both educating the client on the realities of what the trial process actually means, but also presenting trial in its most negative light. This is a counseling session. So it is likely that their relationship has developed deeply enough so that such persuasive tactics are appropriate. This may be especially true in these circumstances where the two men have a social relationship at their shared club as well. Their prior interactions and relationship may have convinced Mathiesson that Arnholtz's anger has taken over other values that he knows exist in Arnholtz—like being a loving father and a fair man—and that, in the long run, Arnholtz, himself, would be unhappy with himself for a decision made in the heat of anger. Nevertheless, if the attorney is truly going to explain the "pros and cons" (Line L6), which is exactly what he should do, then he must provide some time to acknowledge what the "pros" of trial would be—and the public exposure of the wife's infidelity and sense of vindication for the client are clearly in that category.

If Mathiesson is less certain of the interplay of emotions and values in his client, he still will want to be certain that, even in anger, his client is presented with the full range of options and their consequences. In that conversation, Mathiesson would frame the options differently.

L1:   [After greetings] ... Bill, I want to talk to you today about the different options we have for getting through this divorce. We have trial of course .....

C1:   Yes! Why don't we go to trial so that everyone can see what kind of woman she is.

L2:   Well, Bill, I know that when you are upset—as you have every right to be under the circumstances—trial can seem like a good way to punish the other side.

C2:   Exactly! She hurt me.

L3:   Yes, I understand that. What I like to do with clients is give an outline of all the options you have—trial but also settlement and mediation. So that you can have all the information about what each process will be like and what you will likely get out of them. So, let me explain what a trial is.

C3:   I know what a trial is. I watch all the lawyer and cop shows. We'll be able to put her on the witness stand and you can cross examine her about the nervous breakdown she had when our youngest was one and how she was in therapy and drinking. And then, after I stand by her, she leaves with a jerk.

L4:   Yes that can happen. But let me do this, let me give you a few more details than the TV shows explain on how long a trial will take us and what we'll be doing to prepare for trial. And of course what the costs are. And then let's do a chart on the pros and cons. We'll list the consequences we like—like your wife will be exposed as a cheater—along with the things we don't like—say your kids will feel the stress. List everything. And then.... before you cut in Bill ... and then we'll do the same thing for the other options—settlement and mediation. List the pros and cons for each one of them. And *then* you decide which is best. If it's still trial, fine with me. But I want you clear and educated on all your options.

"Trial/Litigation Leading to Settlement/Negotiation" is separated from "Settlement/Negotiation." This is meant to make explicit two issues which lawyers know but may not necessarily explain to clients. The issues are that *when* you settle may impact the kind of outcome you can get and will definitely impact differently on the client. This distinction is meant to separate out settlements that occur fairly soon after the initiating incident or the filing of a claim ("Settlement/Negotiation") and those that occur close in time to the actual trial ("Trial/Litigation Leading to Settlement/Negotiation"). In Chapter 7 (Engaging in Moral Dialogue), we have a different version of the dialogue between Attorney Mathiesson and Arnholtz discussing settlement.[35] In the Chapter 7 dialogue, the client is suggesting a process that would fit in the category of "Trial/Litigation Leading to Settlement/Negotiation." The client's wife has already filed for divorce so a legal process is started, and more importantly, the client suggests that the lawyer *claim* that the client will try to get custody so that the wife will accept a less than 50:50 settlement offer. One can imagine under these circumstances that the lawyer and client essentially threaten to go to trial in order to prove the seriousness of the custody claim—even though it is not in fact serious. This approach will stretch out the negotiation process and involve some preparation for trial, even though the intention in the long run is to settle. In this case the negative consequences of "Trial/Litigation Leading to a Settlement/Negotiation" are similar to the negative consequences of "Trial/Litigation" itself—hostile feelings between the former spouses, stress on the children and more time and money.

This process is in contrast to a "Settlement/Negotiation" that could have occurred if the couple had negotiated the issues either before the filing or soon after in a more amicable fashion. The client would have fewer visits with his lawyer and no confrontational involvements with his wife or her lawyer. And of course the impact on the children and the couple's social and work communities would be far less.

Additionally the outcome of the settlement is likely to be different in a "Trial/Litigation Leading to a Settlement" compared with a "Settlement/Negotiation." Indeed, Arnholtz suggests the more aggressive settlement approach precisely to alter the outcome i.e. so that he can pay his wife less money. Even if the choice does not raise ethical or moral concerns for lawyer or client, there are any number of reasons to try to settle "early" or "late." That decision will impact the time and stress imposed on the client and may well impact the quality of the settlement that is likely to be reached.

"Outside Help" are entities other than the lawyer himself that the client can use to resolve a part or all of the client's problem. Clearly, these will vary depending upon the case and the area of law in which the legal problem arises. Some options are required by law, but even then how the client approaches them may be influenced by the attorney. For example, in the employment context, the employee client will often be required to file with a state or federal anti-discrimination agency. The agency can do an investigation for the client or the lawyer can file the appropriate papers to allow her to take over the case. It is important for the lawyer to explain *both* processes to the client. It is certainly possible to lose a client who chooses to file on his own. But it is very likely that an explanation of the difference having an attorney can make in maneuvering through a bureaucratic process will be compelling enough for a client to want to prefer to proceed with you by his side rather than to go it alone. In addition, you do not want to have, in effect, made a decision without fully informing your client. Moreover, you risk creating a situation wherein later in the case, the client tells you that he met someone at his job/mosque/church/temple/club who told him about the agency process and now the client wonders why you were not straight with him.

"Self-Help" is a reminder that we often speak with clients about not doing anything legal. In most cases, this means we discuss any sort of grievance procedures that may be available at a job or medical facility or whatever corporate entity is involved in the dispute. Sometimes these processes have gone on before the client comes to us. But if this is not the case, it is important to discuss how the client will handle the process and, possibly, even to help prepare her even if the lawyer will not be present at the hearing or meeting. Some of these processes will have clear legal implications and others may only be persuasive evidence of the client's good faith or intentions at a later formal legal hearing. Sometimes, the conversation about not doing anything legal may really mean doing "something legal" but not something that involves you as the attorney e.g. small claims court. Other times, it may mean both something "not legal" and not using an attorney e.g. using a community mediation program. In some cases, the conversation about not doing anything legal may translate into not doing anything at all. For the client who is contemplating initiating a legal action, it may be that in the final analysis, the nature of the injury is either not legally cognizable or is so financially modest that it makes little sense for the client to go forward with any process that would involve the other party.

Arbitration and Mediation are the two main alternative dispute resolution methods that are contrasted with trial. Because young lawyers often study the two together as part of a course on alternative dispute resolution methods, it can be tempting to describe the two together when explaining them to a client. But it is important to separate the two. Indeed, if a lawyer were to connect or collapse any two of the dispute resolution methods in a way that would make sense to the client, it would be to connect mediation with settlement. The process of mediation is, of course, different than for settlement. The lawyer does most of the work in the typical negotiation process. In the mediation, more time and money may need to be spent to find a mediator and schedule the mediation sessions. In addition, while some mediations only involve the attorneys with the third-party neutral mediator, many others involve the presence of the client. In those that do involve the client's presence, the process has an even greater impact on the client's life as she must prepare herself to be in the presence of the opposing party and possibly to speak to the mediator or the opposing party. As to outcome, mediations and settlements can be very similar since both processes allow for the parties to have control over what the solution will be. Indeed, choosing mediation is often done because parties are having trouble communicating well enough in a negotiation to come to a settlement; the mediator is added to the "negotiation" mix so that the parties agree to a settlement.[36]

Here is an example involving divorce Attorney Harriet Long and her client Betty Ann Jackson.

L1:   Hello, Mrs. Jackson. It is good seeing you again. You look well.

C1:   Hey, Ms. Long. I am doing a lot better. And I have some questions about what's next with our case. In some of the paper work you sent me there is something about going to a meditation? I thought that was where you sit quietly with your legs crossed and say "Ohm." But I looked it up in a law book and it said something … here, I wrote it down, "In mediation, an impartial third party helps others negotiate to resolve a dispute or plan a transaction."[37] What does that mean? I thought we were negotiating ourselves?

L2:   Good question and just what I wanted to talk about. We will have to attend a mediation—not meditation. Although I will tell you *meditation* is a terrific technique for getting relaxed and more open.

C2:   Why do we have to go to a mediation?

L3:   Mediation is always a choice that we could make in a civil case. But in our state it is a requirement in family cases. Family law cases often have a lot of emotions involved. And parents especially have to make some very important decisions about their children at a time when they are so emotional they are not at their best in terms of decision making. So law makers require that we use a process where a third party who is not related to either our side or the other side will help in the communication process.

C3: Is this a good thing?

L4: Generally it is a good thing. Normally we would be left to negotiate out a settlement ourselves. That means that I would talk with your husband's lawyer about all the things that you want, and we two would come up with an agreement that would include all or at least the most important things that you and your husband want to see happen as a way to resolve your divorce. But sometimes, the lawyer can't get the client to see that some of his requests are unreasonable or even the lawyer may get caught up in the client's case. In situations like that, even though it will take more time—and if it were not required but was a choice would cost more money—then having this third person can be helpful. So far we don't have any reason to believe that your husband and his lawyer are trying to short-change you, so, while this required mediation may not be necessary for us, it shouldn't hurt our case.

C4: So this third person will look at what we present in terms of the amount of money I need and that I will have custody of our youngest and decide that it is good?

L5: No. There are mediations where the mediator is hired as an expert in the area and will give feedback on whether each side's' proposed settlement makes sense based upon her experience. Even then she would not be able to decide like a judge. She could only opine about what she thinks is the best solution. The parties would still be able to say they do not want to settle in the mediation on the mediator's terms or decide to not settle on any terms and instead take their chances at trial. But in our state the mediator is likely to spend more time encouraging both sides to present proposals and asking us to really be fair not only to our side but to the other side and especially to think as calmly as we can about the impact on your kids.

C5: OK. That sounds like a good thing then.

L6: Here is the part for you to think about. Like I said, in negotiation it's just me and your husband's attorney talking. You could be there but that is pretty rare in negotiations. But with mediations you will need to be present.

C6: Will you be there? I won't have to go alone, will I?

L7: I will be there. You may hear about mediations where the two clients spoke alone with the mediator but when that happens that is both sides' choice. Mostly lawyers are present although the mediator may ask you questions. It will not be a cross-examination like trial. And I can protect you a lot better in a mediation. I can make sure that only the mediator asks questions of you. And if your husband or his attorney starts up, I can answer. If it gets too difficult for you to be in the same room with your husband, we could also be in separate rooms and just have the mediator move back and forth between us telling us what has been said and offered by them and relaying back to them what we say and feel. Even though these required mediations often take place at the courthouse, we could negotiate having it take place some place else—maybe the mediator's office as neutral ground.

C7:   OK. What will happen once we get there?

Here Attorney Long has a lot more to tell the client about mediation than the standard text book definition. Long is fortunate, in a way, because her client has explicitly asked her to provide an explanation that is understandable by the non-expert. It is important in counseling sessions to provide such understandable explanations as a matter of course. There may be, as in this example, stretches in the counseling session where a lawyer does a lot of talking and defining. That seems to us not to be a problem when the point is to provide, in lay-person's terms, as much information about the processes and outcomes as the client will need to make an informed decision. Here, the attorney explains that the outcome is likely to be similar to negotiation and, in doing this, needs to define negotiation and distinguish it from mediation. (Line L4). She also explains the process; she makes clear that the mediator will not decide even if he gives an opinion on the offers made. (Line L5). And she underscores that the client will need to be present and in the same room as her husband. (Lines L6 and L7). The tone of Attorney Long's explanation suggests that she already has reason to believe that this part of the process will not be easy for Jackson. The attorney's specificity in explaining to the client what a mediation means in terms that allow the client to get a picture of what actually will happen, what the client may or may not have to do, and what role the other side or other parties will have is all significant in helping the client make informed decisions about her options. The attorney's specificity reflects her ability to translate from her expert's language to language that will allow the client to understand.

Arbitration, as an adjudicative process where the third party neutral makes a decision that is binding on the parties, is, of course, very much like trial. Thus it has both process and outcome effects that are more similar to trial. But the ability to have some input into the choice of the decisionmaker as well as its privacy are key differences in the process of arbitration that will have some impact on the client and her goals and values.[38] And the fact that the outcome of the arbitration may differ from trial or any other options will, of course, be an additional factor to compare with the client's goals and values.

CRIMINAL DISPUTE OPTIONS

In the criminal context, again, the main choices are trial or pleading guilty (settlement). And we add to the list dismissal. Dismissal is always, technically, an option for the criminal client. It is important to present this to the client. In many cases, your approach may be fairly brief—a mention to the client that given just a few key pieces of evidence a dismissal is unlikely. Including dismissal, however briefly, is largely a matter of creating trust with the client in the early stages. The issue of at least mentioning dismissal can be especially significant in the public defender arena where clients already assume that the lawyer, since she "works for the government" and not the client, will not work diligently on the client's case. A mention or discussion of dismissal is a way of clearly stating for the client that the lawyer starts from a position of questioning all the evidence presented by the government against her client and is willing to consider the possibility that the evidence is insufficient from the beginning. This can be a key ingredient in developing trust between the lawyer and the client.

In most cases, you will spend much more of your time discussing trial or pleading with your client than you will discussing whether the prosecution will dismiss the case. As in the civil context, the lawyer needs to translate our expert definitions to layperson definitions that elucidate both the process and the outcome to the client. In explaining the trial process, the description of what a trial will be like for the criminal defendant will be similar to what would be said for the civil client. The biggest exception is that the criminal defendant will have a choice on whether to testify or not. If the client goes to trial the stress, time, money and greater public exposure are all aspects of trial to be discussed. If the client also testifies, that will entail additional stress and time as the client will need to be prepared to testify and his time in the witness stand will be more tension-filled than just watching the proceedings. In addition, the decision to testify not only impacts the process effects, it can also impact the outcome. In some cases, when a criminal defendant testifies and loses, the judge will give a more severe sentence than had the defendant not testified, reasoning that the defendant not only committed the act of which he was convicted but also committed the crime of perjury by lying on the witness stand.

In addition to explaining the process of trial, you will also have to provide an explanation of the outcome. Here, the lawyer makes an assessment of the government's evidence, how believable it is and whether the defense has any counter evidence. Winning is generally an acquittal on all charges and losing a conviction. Acquittal as an outcome is easy enough to explain to a client. Not much translation is needed. Convictions can be more challenging if multiple charges exist or "lesser includeds" are involved. Now the attorney must assess the likelihood of an acquittal or conviction for *each* charge. In addition the lawyer will need to relate to the client the maximum (and, if applicable, minimum) amount of time incarcerated that the client *could* get as well as the lawyer's assessment of the amount of time incarcerated the particular judge trying the case is *likely* to give the client. As with plea arrangements, as we will discuss, it is also important to discuss the "quality" of the crimes upon which the jury or judge could convict the client.

Settlement/negotiation or pleading in the criminal context requires more explanation than in the civil context. There will be a part of negotiation in the criminal context where you, the lawyer, speak with the prosecutor about a mutually acceptable plea arrangement; this is analogous to civil settlement negotiations. However, in the criminal context, the client will almost always be required to make a court appearance and respond to some questions from the judge. The process of standing up in court and admitting to facts that constitute one's guilt needs to be explained to the client along with the details of what particular crime is part of the plea deal.

In our outline, we separate out pleading when the result or outcome will be incarceration and when the result will be probation. If a plea arrangement will result in time in prison or jail, not a lot of translation is needed: less is best. But if the outcome involves probation more explanation may be needed. Probation is generally viewed as victory for the defense counsel and client. One of the most salient punishments involved in the criminal case, loss of liberty, has been avoided. Probation arrangements always involve the client refraining from engaging in further criminal conduct but may also require that the client do certain things e.g. keep a job, get tested for drugs frequently, see a probation officer regularly, make restitution to the victim. The client will have his best chance of successfully completing probation if the lawyer takes the time to discuss thoroughly with the client all the requirements of probation and how the client can use his own support network to best insure that he will be able to complete them.[39]

In discussing both trial as well as pleading, the outcome portion also entails discussing the fact that the client will have a criminal record[40] and the quality of the crimes with which the client has been charged or to which he will be required to plead. The main "quality" issue is the difference between a felony and a misdemeanor. Clients can easily understand the main difference that a misdemeanor demands a term of incarceration of one year or less while the felony demands much more. But the lawyer needs to explain other outcome consequences. In many states, a felony conviction will negatively impact an individual's right to vote.[41] Employment opportunities can be affected by whether one has a conviction but in many instances the quality of the conviction is key. Again, the misdemeanor-felony divide is the main one; many employers will tolerate a misdemeanor conviction but not a felony. In addition, within the felony or misdemeanor categories, there are differences that need to be explored with the client. The most obvious example involves comparing misdemeanor sex crimes with other crimes.[42]

Here is an example involving civil rights and criminal defense Attorney Bryan Culbert and his client Evelyn Yamashita discussing a proposed plea offer after the initial "Greeting." Ms. Yamashita faces multiple criminal charges arising out of her actions during a large political protest.

L1:   Ms. Yamashita, I wanted to discuss with you a plea offer that the District Attorney has given us. You'll remember that I mentioned that we were likely to get some kind of offer from the DA where you would stand up in open court and admit guilt to some charges...

C1:   I am not guilty. How can I stand up in a public place like the courtroom and say what is not true?

L2:   I understand that but I am obligated to tell you that we have an offer, and I would like us to discuss the pros and cons of this offer compared to going to trial even though at the end of that discussion you may still feel that, because of your innocence, you cannot take this plea offer. So let's talk it through.

C2:   I don't think I will or can change my mind but ... OK, let's discuss.

L3:   Good. First off, let's remember that they wound up charging you with two felony counts: destruction of property and assault on a police officer (APO). As you may know, when I say that the charges or counts are felonies I mean that a judge could—although she would not have to—but she could lock you up in jail for more than a year if she or a jury found you guilty after a trial or if you admitted guilt by taking a plea offer. In this case the destruction of property carries a maximum possible sentence of five (5) years in prison and the APO carries a maximum of ten (10) years in prison.

C3:   But I did not destroy property and I did not "assault" the two big, male racist cops who arrested me. If anyone was "assaulted" or insulted ..... OK I'll stop for now. You were saying?

L4:   I know. It is frustrating and infuriating to even think about what the government has charged you with given what actually happened that night. But I want to set out some basic points for us to address. In a criminal case we typically have three ways to resolve the matter. The ideal is always to get the government to dismiss some or all of the charges. But most of the time we end up negotiating a plea deal, meaning we agree to admit guilt to charges that are less serious than the ones the government would try to prove at trial. Or we decide to go to trial and make the government prove its case. And when we discuss charges you might admit guilt to or you might get convicted of at trial, we will look at two things: The first is how "bad" a crime it is. I mean, is it a felony so that the judge has the power to give you a lot of jail time. But I also mean, does the crime suggest that you really have a bad moral character. Without even thinking about how much time is involved, if you met someone with a trespass conviction versus someone with a terrorism conviction, you would more likely consider continuing to associate with the first but have a lot more reservations about the other. Second we will discuss what the likelihood is that you will serve time or be set free but under some sort of court-related supervision i.e. probation.

C4:   I like dismissal. All the complications of how "bad" the charge and how much time aren't an issue.

L5:   Me too. And that is something that I discussed with the DA at length. In most criminal cases, an outright dismissal of all charges is unlikely. But it seemed to me that we had a good chance given that your arrest was part of the confusion involved in a mass protest. Yes, some real criminal activity was involved by others, but I told him that you are a reporter and pointed out that the government does not have any witnesses who actually saw you damaging the store where the cops arrested you. That makes our case on the charge of destruction of property very good at trial. We would be very likely to convince a jury of your innocence or put more accurately the *government* will have a hard time carrying its burden of proving you guilty beyond a reasonable doubt. When we have a good argument on a particular charge at trial, that tends to make the government want to either offer an offense that carries less time or to dismiss the charge.

C5:   So did the DA listen to you?

L6:   Yes ... and no. The DA is dismissing the destruction of property count. The problem is the APO count. He wants you to plead guilty to something. I think he wants to tell the cops, who he works with all the time, that he was protecting them in some way by getting a conviction.

C6:   Is the DA actually saying that I hit those guys or hurt them!? I can't believe ....

L7:   No. The problem is how the law defines assault on a police officer. Even though when you say "assault" you would think it means that you hit them or at least threatened to hit them, it doesn't mean that. It includes almost anything that could be considered interfering with an officer while he is performing his duties. So when you started to argue with the police and step in front of them while they were arresting the people that you were interviewing ....

C7:   But they didn't have to handle the people they were arresting as roughly as they did. And they treated me the same way.

L8:   You are right. But the law imagines that you would file charges against the police ....

C8:   After the fact! After the people who were protesting or even breaking in got injured.

L9:   Yes. Not the best solution but that is how the law is written.

C9:   So you are saying that under the legal definition of assault on a police officer, I am guilty.

L10: In effect yes. We could go to trial and you could testify about what you did, why you intervened and then how the police mistreated you afterwards. We will get a jury, and those jury members could feel like we feel—that what you did is not what the law really means by assault on a police officer and they could acquit you. On the other hand, the DA will argue that it is not for the jurors to decide on what they think the law *should be* or what they would like; he will say they have to follow the law as it is. And the judge will give them jury instructions that pretty much say the same thing. They will be encouraged to decide based upon a strict reading of the law and basically be told to hope and trust that the judge will sentence you fairly.

C10:   And will he ... or she?

L11:   Another he ... and I am not so sure. This guy is pretty tough. I have appeared in front of Judge Hangum before and I have heard a lot about him from other attorneys. He was a police officer and a prosecutor before getting on the bench, so he is pretty protective of cops. And he likes to have his cases plead since he assumes that the government was probably right to charge to begin with. So ... he tends to give out jail time if one is convicted after a jury trial—especially if the accused testifies and he thinks he or she has lied under oath. So. If the jury were to convict you at trial on the APO charge, he might sentence you to time in jail. I would not think a lot—it might just be a weekend in jail but some time.

C11:   Jail time!

L12:   Any jail time is too much jail time—I realize that. Unfortunately, I feel pretty confident, given Judge Hangum's past practices, that he will. On the other hand, the DA is offering that you plead to one misdemeanor count of disorderly conduct. When I say a misdemeanor, I mean that the maximum amount of time you could ever get would be one (1) year in jail. And because misdemeanors are not considered especially serious, people who are convicted or plead to misdemeanors often do no jail time at all unless they have a lot of prior convictions. So, if you plead to disorderly conduct, Hangum will almost certainly place you on probation; probably with no conditions—like performing some kind of community service—and no supervision—which means you would not have to call or meet with a probation officer. I feel very confident of this because the DA will agree with me in open court that you should serve no time.

C12:   But I would be saying I'm guilty. I wasn't disorderly. I was being a good reporter.

L13:   I know. And let me throw this in the pot. If we go to trial, I have been discussing the fact that you would be convicted of APO. That is a felony and even if you did not get a lot of time that would mean that you would have a felony criminal conviction on your record. That can have a very negative impact on your current job or on any future job prospects and it might affect your ability to vote.

C13:   What!?

L14:   Now it is possible that at trial we could ask the judge to include what we'd call "lesser includeds" on the jury form—lesser crimes that fall within the definition of more serious crimes. So we could ask the jury to consider convicting you of misdemeanor assault rather than APO. That is a difficult thing for us to do. On the one hand, because this is a protest case and the jurors will hear you testify and know that you have no criminal background, there is a good chance that they will go for the misdemeanor. And that looks a lot better on your record. But for all the same reasons—the circumstances of the demonstration and who you are—if we do NOT ask for the misdemeanor to be considered by the jurors, we stand the best chance of your getting acquitted entirely.

C14:   Because they might really not want to convict me of a felony, even if they think I technically broke the law, but if we give them a misdemeanor it will be like a good compromise for them.

L15:   Exactly.

_____

Here we see Attorney Culbert advising his client, Ms. Yamashita, of a plea offer that the government has presented and placing the offer into one version of our counseling framework. Yamashita is resistant to the idea of a pleading guilty (Line C1) and still feeling that her charges are unjust (Line C3), as she did when she first met Culbert. Culbert persuades his client to allow him to provide her the range of information that he needs to convey to her by letting her know that it is his obligation as a lawyer to convey the plea information to her (Line L2), and by using active listening, when he acknowledges her frustration and anger, (Line L4), to show that he is empathetic to her sense of the injustice of her circumstances. He persists in setting up a framework for how their discussion will unfold, and in Line L4 he lays out the three main options—dismissal, plea or settlement and trial—as well as noting right away that he and his client will explore both "quality" or "badness" of crime issues as well as likelihood of incarceration time issues.

Culbert reminds the client early in the discussion about the specific crimes with which she has been charged. And he immediately explains their seriousness by defining them as felonies and informing her of their maximum possible penalties. (Line L3) His specificity at the beginning sets the stage for the "good news-bad news" he will have to convey to Yamashita. While the government is dismissing one charge—the destruction of property—it is insisting on an admission of guilt on a misdemeanor related to the APO. Culbert makes an assessment of the government's evidence both in discussing the destruction of property charge and in explaining the problems with the APO charge. For the first charge, the evidentiary issue is straightforward—the government lacks significant eyewitness evidence—Line L5—so the government is willing to dismiss.

For the APO count, Culbert needs to explain the law of assault on a police officer in terms that a layperson can understand[43] and then relates the legal definition of APO to the facts in the case that are likely to be elicited at trial, (Line L7). We see Culbert educating the client on the fact that APO includes interference with the police while performing their duties. And he points out that the client has told him that she did attempt to stop the police from arresting some people on the scene. In some cases, an attorney in Culbert's position might have pointed to witnesses who would testify to the client's actions—in this case perhaps the very people she had tried to defend—or to a statement that the client had made to the police. In this case, Yamashita feels justified in the actions she took so that it is likely she would willingly admit the acts on the witness stand. It becomes important for Culbert to convey to her that what she thinks is a perfectly appropriate moral defense is not a recognized legal defense. He does describe for her how he will argue these facts at trial, as well as how the government will counter his arguments. (Line L10). Through his explanation of both the different meanings that can be attached to "the law" and how the facts or evidence can be viewed, he has provided Yamashita with the real uncertainty that exists in trying to foresee how the jury will rule in her case.

Later on, Culbert complicates the issue, by necessity, by explaining both what "lesser includeds" are—"lesser crimes that fall within the definition of more serious crimes" (Line L14)—and by describing the dilemma of requesting that the jurors be instructed on these lesser charges (Lines L13 and L14). In this case, the circumstances of the arrest and the good character/background of Yamashita make her the kind of defendant to whom jurors will be sympathetic. But how sympathetic? Will they so identify with her that they would be willing to acquit her of any charges? And if they are not so sympathetic as to acquit, then wouldn't it be better to give them a conviction option that would be less harmful for the client? Forecasting the degree of juror sympathy is a key issue for trial, and once Culbert has conveyed the dilemma to his client, (See Line C14) now they can both discuss and debate it together.

Culbert also discusses in layperson's terms the quality of the crimes under both conviction-after-trial scenarios i.e. felony APO and misdemeanor assault (Lines L3 and L12 explaining felonies and misdemeanors and L13 explaining the other negative consequences to a felony conviction such as loss of employment opportunities and voting rights) and under the plea offer (Line L12 explaining that the disorderly conduct plea offer is a misdemeanor). He also addresses the likelihood of actually being sentenced to time in jail. (Lines L11 and L12). Culbert relies on both his own personal knowledge of Judge Hangum as well as what others in the legal community have said about the judge's past practices to forecast whether and how much time the judge is likely to mete out to Yamashita after an unsuccessful trial compared to what is likely to happen if Yamashita accepts the plea offer. Culbert explains that his information reveals that if Yamashita accepts this plea offer, she will most likely get probation— especially since the DA will not oppose such a sentence. (Line L12). He gives a practical explanation for what probation can mean—having conditions like community service or reporting to a probation officer—and he predicts what he believes probation will mean in this case for Yamashita— that there will be "no conditions" and that she will not have to report to a probation officer. Culbert also explains that, the judge's past practices strongly signal that Yamashita will face some jail time if she proceeds to trial and does not win an outright acquittal on all charges. While Culbert realizes and notes for Yamashita that the amount of jail time will likely be "not a lot" (Line 11), he is empathetic with the client's perspective by asserting directly that "any jail time is too much jail time." Still he does not back off from his advice (Line L12): this is not what the client wants to hear—it's "unfortunate"—but it is a reality the client must face in order to make a wise choice on how to resolve this case.

DISCUSSION QUESTIONS

1.   How would you explain a trial to a non-lawyer who had never seen one? How would you explain it to someone who had never seen a real trial nor watched a police or lawyer show ostensibly depicting a trial?

2.   What is different about a real trial and what we see on television shows?

3.   How does Attorney Long's explanation of mediation compare with your understanding or experience of it? What else could she or should she explain to her client about what will happen in a mediation?

4.   How would you explain an arbitration to a layperson?

5.   We list seven options to be discussed with the client in the civil context. Should a lawyer discuss all the options with the client even if some appear to the lawyer to be only marginally relevant to the client's case? Should a lawyer omit such "marginally relevant options" entirely or should he at least make a passing reference to them?

6.   How would you explain to a layperson what the client is required to do in accepting a plea?

7.   We have recommended discussing the requirements of probation with your criminal client. How can one discuss such requirements as drug testing, seeing your probation officer and others without being patronizing?

———

Lawyers must always connect with their clients in order to create some trust in the attorney-client relationship. And lawyers will always confront differences as well as similarities with their clients. Some different characteristics will be obvious—such as the client being a non-lawyer or of a different race or gender from your own—while others may only appear over the life of the attorney-client relationship. This chapter has raised the challenges that difference can pose. We have also explored the challenges that similarity can raise. But we have also presented some approaches to create connection across these differences and similarities. While connecting across difference, in particular, can at times seem daunting, we believe that ordinarily by being aware of the impact of different social categories on yourself as well as your clients and employing approaches like those that we suggest and reference, every lawyer can connect with her clients—however similar to or different from her they may be—in ways that allow for zealous and effective interviewing and counseling.

---

1.   *See* Susan Bryant, *The Five Habits: Building Cross Cultural Competence,* 8 CLIN. L. REV. 33, 35 n. 4 (identifying a number of articles by clinical law professors exploring and emphasizing the need to teach about diversity in law school classes and clinics).

2.   Some differences that can exist between lawyers and clients, mental capacity and moral values, are explored in detail in other chapters. *See generally infra* (Chapter 4, "Interviewing and Counseling Atypical Clients") and Chapter 7 ("Engaging in Moral Dialogue").

3.   See *infra* Chapter 5 ("Narrative Theory and Narrative Practices") at 142 and 145.

4.   *Id.* at 145 (discussing the lawyer's and student-lawyer's use of "multiple narratives through which [they] will constitute their relationship, ...").

5.   While chronological order and interviewing by legal elements are typical ways in which lawyers organize and understand clients' stories, they are not the only ways. Narrative theories offer additional ways to understand a client's story. See generally *infra* Chapter 5 ("Narrative Theory and Narrative Practices").

6.   How one explains the "law" that is applicable, at this point and later in a true counseling session, has its own challenges, which we explore in Chapter 8 ("Talking to Clients about the Law").

7.   *Id.*

8.   We explore these complex issues later in Chapter 3 ("Engaged Client-Centered Counseling About Client Choices,") and Chapter 7 ("Engaging in Moral Dialogue").

9.   See generally *infra,* Chapter 5 ("Narrative Theory and Narrative Practices").

10.   *See* Mark Weisberg & Jean Koh Peters, *Experiments in Listening,* 57 J. LEGAL EDUC. 427 (2007). In this article Professors Peters and Weisberg explore various ways of listening. One aspect of their exploration involves the use of a "doubting and believing spectrum." *Id.* at 432. The doubting end of the spectrum is the more familiar to lawyers because it is the companion to critical thinking and focuses on listening in order to evaluate or challenge an idea or factual scenario presented. At the believing end is the ". . . discipline and conscious attempt to believe everything no matter how unlikely or repellent it might seem—to find virtues or strengths we might otherwise miss." *Id.* at 433 (citing PETER ELBOW, EMBRACING CONTRARIES: EXPLORATIONS IN LEARNING AND TEACHING 257 (1986)). The "real" listening described includes an awareness of this kind of spectrum and the ability to move along the spectrum at appropriate moments in the attorney-client relationship. So, as Professors Peters and Weisberg note, in the early portion of the relationship and initial interview, a lawyer will be at the far end of the "believing" portion of the spectrum. *Id.* at 438.

11.   See *infra* Chapter 5 ("Narrative Theory and Narrative Practices)" at 153–157. The idea that in listening a lawyer must listen at different levels or layers is also true when using narrative theory.

12.   Of course, while you will need a chronology eventually for most forms of case presentation in our legal system, it is important to remember that time and space orientations—like ordering events around hours, days, months or years—is one of many culturally determined concepts. Bryant, *supra* note 1, at 44–45. Other culturally formed concepts that lawyers rely on and can misinterpret in clients include body language and credibility. *Id.* at 43–44.

13.   See generally *infra* Chapter 5 ("Narrative Theory and Narrative Practices").

14.   *Id.*

15.   *See* Bryant, *supra* note 1, at 74 n.136 (underscoring the use of exploratory or "narrative mode" questioning around the client's ideal resolution as a tool in gathering culturally sensitive information).

16.   We discuss more fully the range of approaches to presenting the concept of confidentiality to clients in Chapter 6 ("Truth or Consequences").

17.   We discuss more fully the benefits of being "expert" as a lawyer as well as provide some guidance on avoiding pitfalls of expertise in Chapter 9 ("Fast Talking: Lawyering Expertise and Its Impact on Interviewing and Counseling").

18.   The specific approach of restating the assertions made by the client and identifying the client's emotions is articulated in a widely used text on client interviewing and counseling, DAVID A. BINDER, PAUL BERGMAN, SUSAN C. PRICE & PAUL R. TREMBLAY, LAWYERS AS COUNSELORS: A CLIENT-CENTERED APPROACH 52–53 (2nd ed. 2004). In addition, there are other forms of Active Listening that are similarly designed to withhold judgment and create connection using some kind of affirmative statement to the client or speaker. *See* PRUDENCE BOWMAN KENTNER & LARRY RAY, THE CONFLICT RESOLUTION TRAINING PROGRAM: PARTICIPANT'S WORKBOOK 41–45 (2002).

19.   It is also important to note that Attorney Long assumes that "killing him" is a figure of speech and does not launch into a conversation about the limits of attorney-client confidentiality.

20.   *See generally infra* Chapter 3 ("Engaged Client–Centered Counseling About Client Choices"), Chapter 6 ("Truth and Consequences"), Chapter 7 "Engaging in Moral Dialogue," and Chapter 8 ("Talking to Clients about the Law") Each contains several fuller discussions on disagreeing with clients.

21.   *See, e.g.,* Bryant, *supra* note 1, at 43 (citing RICHARD BRISLIN & TOMOKO YOSHIDA, INTERCULTURAL COMMUNICATION TRAINING: AN INTRODUCTION 91 (1994)).

22.   These explanations for empathy and sympathy are simplified working definitions. As you can imagine, scholars have provided far more in depth discussions on these two interrelated ways of connecting with other people. *See e.g.,* Lauren Wispe, *The Distinction Between Sympathy and Empathy: To Call Forth a Concept, A Word is Needed,* 50 JOURNAL OF PERSONALITY AND SOCIAL PSYCHOLOGY 314–321 (1986). Wispe's definitions define empathy and sympathy in the order that we have used in the text. There does not seem to be uniform agreement on where the closest connection should be labeled "empathy" or "sympathy." *See* Stephen Ellmann, *Empathy and Approval,* 43 HASTINGS L.J. 991 (1992) for a review of the various uses of these terms in clinical legal literature. Whatever label is used, the most important issue is to have some sense of the difference. The key aspect for the lawyer is maintaining some sense of one's own self-dentity so that you can perform your job as attorney and counselor properly.

23.   This problem can be especially thorny in the context of Brown-type cases i.e. when attorneys represent groups. From the outset, the issue of who speaks for the group can be a challenge. And as the needs and aspirations of the client group change over time, identifying these shifts can be problematic on top of the lawyer's responsibility to assess her own personal or political goals. *See generally* Stephen Ellmann, *Client–Centeredness Multiplied: Individual Autonomy and Collective Mobilization in Public Interest Lawyers' Representation of Groups,* 78 VA. L. REV. 1103 (1992).

24.   For a longer discussion on mindfulness and its relationship to and cultivation through meditation see generally, Leonard Riskin, *The Contemplative Lawyer: On the Potential Benefits of Mindfulness Meditation to Law Students, Lawyers and their Clients,* 7 HARV. NEGOT. L. REV. 1 (2002).

25.   *See generally* Bryant, *supra* note 1. Professor Bryant and Professor Jean Koh Peters (whom Professor Bryant credits as a collaborator) note that "all lawyering is cross-cultural." *Id.* at 49. They underscore the fact that cultural norms can be based on a broad range of factors— both the legally recognized/debated social categories like race, gender, age or sexual orientation— as well as other categories like role in family, birth order, accent or skin color. *Id.* at 41. More importantly, they note that ". . . . no single characteristic will completely define the lawyer's or the client's culture." *Id.* This leads to an understanding of how the impact of culture is both definite and yet complex because ". . . culture is enough of an abstraction that people can be part of the same culture and yet make different decisions in the particular." *Id.* at 41 (citing RAYMONDE CARROLL, CULTURAL MISUNDERSTANDING: THE FRENCH–AMERICAN EXPERIENCE (1982)). Additionally they observe that "[p]eople can also reject norms and values from their culture." *Id.* at 41. Consequently, it is important to not over-identify with a client who appears to be "just like you" or indeed under-identify with the client who appears terribly dissimilar.

26.   For a discussion of an extensive and systematic approach to exploring similarities and differences, see Bryant, *supra* note 1, at 64–76 (describing the first four Habits); *see also* JEAN KOH PETERS, REPRESENTING CHILDREN IN CHILD PROTECTIVE PROCEEDINGS: ETHICAL AND PRACTICAL DIMENSIONS, Ch. 6 (3d ed. 2007).

27.   In this case, his assumptions have led to racialized assumptions on his client's part, but you could imagine, too, that if Yamashita had not had a legitimate reason for being out past curfew i.e. she was neither lawfully working nor engaged in civil disobedience, the lawyer could have missed an opportunity to learn what she was doing out on the streets. What if Yamashita were a drug dealer and was working, but not lawfully so? Culbert's defense might still focus in on all the confusion of the Seattle demonstrations but if he had not asked his client about her activities in an open and non-judgmental manner, he might have received the expected but incorrect response and would not have been prepared for any "surprises" about his client's history.

28.   *See, e.g.,* Michelle Jacobs, *People from the Footnotes: the Missing Element in Client–Centered Counseling,* 27 GOLDEN GATE U. L. REV. 345 (1997) (discussing how racial differences can affect client actions perceived as difficult).

29.   *See* Chapter 5 ("Narrative Theory and Narrative Practices") at 205–208 (on digressions, silences and elisions in narrative theory).

30. This type of civil disobedience has happened through out American history typically as a way of protesting some aspect of United States domestic or foreign policy. A most recent example involved the arrest on January 11, 2008 of some 75 people for protesting outside and inside the United States Supreme Court. Their call was for the shut down of the American military prison at Guantánamo Bay, Cuba. Michelle Boorstein, *Activists Pose as Guantánamo Prisoners,* THE WASHINGTON POST, Jan. 13, 2008 at C03. The defendant-protestors were part of a group called Witness Against Torture. While part of their defense involved a First Amendment demonstration right to protest—even in parts of the Supreme Court plaza and inside where the law prohibits— most of their defense conceded that they had violated the law and the command by police to disperse. Instead they cited the Nuremberg trials to note that: "The Nuremberg Accords state that individuals have a duty to prevent crimes against humanity . . . and that if people don't act to prevent such, they are actually in complicity in them. We who are on trial today, along with many friends, refuse to be complicit in them." *Activists Found Guilty in D.C.,* WORCESTER TELEGRAM & GAZETTE, May 30, 2008, at B2. *See also* Keith Alexander, *Guantanamo Critics Reiterate Protests as Their Trial Opens,* THE WASHINGTON POST, May 28, 2008, at B03. Thirty-four of the protestors went on trial and all were convicted. *See* Keith Alexander, *34 Convicted in Protest of Guantanamo Bay,* THE WASHINGTON POST, May 30, 2008, at B01.

31. We discuss more fully the issues surrounding experts in Chapter 9 ("Fast Talking: Lawyering Expertise and Its Impact on Interviewing and Counseling").

32. We discuss how explaining "the law" is much more flexible and complicated than is normally acknowledged in Chapter 8 ("Talking to Clients about the Law").

33. Providing one's best estimate of what the trier of fact will decide itself requires that a lawyer analyze a range of information (which increased expertise makes easier) and that the lawyer conveys how certain she is of her estimated outcome. For a more complete discussion of one approach to this process *see generally* BINDER, BERGMAN, PRICE & TREMBLAY, *supra* note 18 at 317–22.

34. See Chapter 7 ("Engaging in Moral Dialogue") where these same characters appear in a conversation about negotiation that raises ethical and moral issues for the lawyer.

35. *Infra* at 280–285.

36. This view of mediation is the most popular view of it. There are other mediation approaches—notably the transformative approach—which view the mediation process as a way to use conflict as a vehicle for the parties involved to grow and transform. Obtaining a solution to the legal problem presented is seen as a welcome but not necessary by-product. *See e.g.,* LEONARD L. RISKIN & JAMES E. WESTBROOK, DISPUTE RESOLUTION AND LAWYERS, 313–36 (2nd ed. 1997).

37. *Id.* at 313.

38. Time and expense are also factors to discuss around arbitration. In the abstract, it is no longer clear how these cut. Typically it is thought that an arbitration will come to fruition faster than a trial. However in some complex corporate cases, there may be fast track possibilities in a state court and long waiting lines for the reputedly "best" arbitrator in the field. And as arbitration has grown as a field, more process has been added to attempt to respect due process rights and concerns and the cost of the best arbitrators has also increased such that it is not clear as a general matter whether arbitration as a process is cheaper than trial in all cases.

39. All jurisdictions will have probation for many crimes. Some jurisdictions are using a more "restorative justice" model. These programs vary from jurisdiction to jurisdiction but typically require more from clients than traditional probation. For example in Los Angeles, California the juvenile justice system has a "teen court" process. It is used in situations where the child is assessed as eligible for probation. But instead of having the child, after consultation with his attorney, admit to the main facts that constitute his guilt and be sentenced by the judge, in teen court, the juvenile testifies in court and is questioned/cross-examined by a panel of his peers, other teenagers. The panel also can call and question the child's parents as well. A juvenile court judge presides and may help the teen panel but most of the questions come from the other teenagers. These same teenagers deliberate and determine what the requirements of the client's probation will entail.

40. It may be more accurate to say that the client will have a criminal record for a period of time. Some plea arrangements build in a set time in which a pending charge or an actual conviction will appear on the client's record but after the set time, the charge will automatically or through some agreed-upon process be expunged. Even in situations where no such arrange- ments are made at the time of the plea arrangement, some states have expungement provisions.

41. In some states, an individual is deprived of the right to vote only for the duration of his incarceration and parole status. Once he is no longer under any state supervision, his voting rights are restored, although an individual may need to learn what the process is to make sure his name is returned to the voting rolls. In other states, the individual is deprived of the right to vote forever.

42.   All of the discussion about the quality of the crimes is made even more complicated if your client is not a United States citizen. What would be considered a minor misdemeanor of little long-term negative consequence for an American citizen could be a deportable offense for a non-citizen, even a permanent resident, who has been in the United States for decades. It is no longer possible to represent the non-citizen criminal defendant without consulting an immigration expert at some point.

43.   The issue of "explaining the law" to a client, while commonly done by lawyers, is actually complex. We address this complexity in detail in Chapter 8 ("Talking to Clients About the Law").

CHAPTER 3

ENGAGED CLIENT–CENTERED COUNSELING ABOUT CLIENT CHOICES

■ ■ ■

In Chapter 2, we set out the basic outline of a counseling session in a dispute-resolution context. The essence of legal counseling is for the lawyer to assist the client in making a decision or set of decisions in the case or matter at hand. Although there are a variety of ways in which a counseling session might be structured, the heart of any good counseling interaction entails the lawyer working with the client to clarify and, if necessary, revise or update the client's goals; identify the choices available to the client to achieve the goals (to whatever extent may be possible); predict the most likely outcomes of those choices; identify the consequences of these options, and work with the client to determine which of these consequences are positive and which are negative; weigh the options against each other, complete with their pros and cons; make a decision; and identify the steps, and the actors, needed to implement the decision.

Of course, these different aspects or stages of client counseling do not occur in linear fashion. The wise and effective legal counselor moves back and forth between and among these portions of the counseling session, revising his or her counseling approach in response to the client's evolving understanding, desire for clarification, need for restatement, and other reasons that might cause someone in the client's situation to approach the decision in question more obliquely. As we noted in Chapter Two, the attorney and client have different roles to play in counseling, and a good counseling session permits both parties to learn enough about the other's perspective—the lawyer's knowledge about the law and the legal system (especially options known to be available within the legal system, such as trial, negotiation and mediation) and the client's knowledge about his or her values, relationships and non-legal concerns—to produce a decision that satisfies the client's goals.

Stating these characteristics of good counseling—and for that matter good client representation—is easy enough. But as with most complex human endeavors, the devil is in the details. How specifically does the lawyer interact with the client to produce a desirable outcome for the client? As the professional in the relationship, should the lawyer tell the client what decision to make, or otherwise be directive toward the client's goals? Conversely, should the lawyer maintain complete neutrality toward the client and simply see his or her role as laying out of options for the client, asking the client to choose, and then implementing the client's decision?[1] If promoting the client's autonomy is one of, if not the most, important goals of the lawyer-client relationship, as we believe it is,[2] does the lawyer's giving of advice to the client on which option the client should choose enhance or detract from the client's autonomy? Should the lawyer seek to collaborate with his or her client in the representation, and, if so, should collaboration extend to the ends of the representation as well as the means? Are the lawyer's moral and political values relevant to the legal representation, and, if so, how far can and should the lawyer go in articulating those values to the client and possibly persuading the client to act consistently with the lawyer's moral and political code?[3]

The answers to these questions may be less important than the process of thinking them through and developing a way of conceptualizing client counseling that can guide your consideration. For us, there are no straightforward one-size-fits-all answers to these inquiries. Rather, because we believe all lawyering is contextual and interactive, the answers will depend very much on, among other things, the characteristics of the particular legal dispute and the system in which it arises; the nature of the legal problem; the temporal context (How much time does the client have to make the decision? How much time does the lawyer have to counsel the client?[4]); the degree of familiarity between lawyer and client (do the lawyer and client have a prior business or social relationship?, for example); the lawyer's level of experience and the client's level of legal sophistication (or put more generally the relative social and economic power of the lawyer and client); and the role of cultural, racial, class, gender or other differences or similarities between lawyer and client. Because these contexts can vary enormously, the appropriateness of any particular approach to the lawyer-client relationship, or the counseling component of it, will need to vary as well.

As we noted in Chapter 1, we believe in an approach to lawyering that we have named engaged client-centeredness. In this Chapter, we apply the principles, underlying attitudes and techniques of engaged client-centeredness to the client counseling process, and, specifically, to that portion of the client counseling session(s) devoted to the client's consideration of choices available in the matter at hand, whether it be litigation, transactional or a combination of the two. Our adoption of a client-centered approach to counseling follows in the footsteps of many commentators, scholars and practitioners who have seen client-centered legal counseling as an important response to traditional models of counseling that tended to stress the centrality of the lawyer rather than the client as the main focus of the counseling session.[5] It developed as an antidote to a lawyer-centered approach that treated clients as passively dependent on powerful lawyers and that presumed lawyers possessed the bulk of the knowledge that would be critical to the client's decision. The traditional model also tended to emphasize legal solutions to problems (perhaps because they would be the easiest ones for lawyers to consider) as opposed to non-legal or creative solutions that clients might suggest.[6] In contrast, client-centered counseling assumes that clients are or can be in the best position to know what they want, and hence make decisions that will effectuate their goals and achieve their desires. Although the lawyer can have important expertise that should be brought to bear (especially in the lawyer's understanding of the law and legal environment in which the client's problem arises), and can provide critical assistance in helping the client clarify his or her goals and choices, the client, as the person who will have to live with the decision, is the appropriate decisionmaker.

Our addition of the word "engaged" as a modifier of "client-centered counseling" is meant to suggest that the lawyer in the relationship is not a passive, detached observer of the client's problem. Insofar as some criticisms of client-centered counseling have suggested that lawyer neutrality or passivity are constitutive of this form of counseling, we reject the inevitability of this view of the lawyer and his or her role.[7] In this Chapter, we will explore some of the ways in which the lawyer can be actively involved in solving the client's problem while remaining respectful of the client's autonomy and the client's right to make his or her own decisions.

The back-and-forth conversation between lawyer and client when participating in engaged client-centered counseling about choices has the following characteristics:[8]

- The lawyer approaches the case, and the counseling session in particular, with an attitude of sympathetic detachment toward the client and the client's problem(s). The lawyer strives for an imaginative and empathetic understanding of the client's situation.

- The lawyer approaches the client, and the client's problem(s), with an open mind and an open heart.

- As part of his or her preparation for the counseling session, the lawyer forms a tentative view of the options available to the client.

- In the session itself, the lawyer and client brainstorm about options, with the lawyer being open to the client's perspective.[9]

- The lawyer uses restatement and clarification to keep the client's focus on vindicating the goals the client has identified. The lawyer understands that a client's goals or circumstances can change over time, and is attentive to the need to re-frame the available choices and their advantages and disadvantages to correspond to the revised goals.

- The lawyer, under the right circumstances, feels able to express disagreement with the client, including about options in which the client seems particularly interested.

- The lawyer, under the right circumstances, is prepared to share his or her own personal feelings with the client.

- The lawyer probes the client's thinking in a critical, thorough fashion.

- The lawyer pays particular heed to the process of counseling, one that focuses closely on identifying options and their perceived advantages and disadvantages. The lawyer will use the power of process to pull the client back from decisions that may appear ill— or insufficiently—considered.

- The lawyer is an active participant in the client's process of weighing the pros and cons of the choices the client and lawyer identify. The lawyer understands the fluidity of the counseling process and is flexible in deploying a counseling structure appropriate to the client and the client's situation.

- Finally, the lawyer thinks very carefully about whether he or she should remain neutral about the client's ultimate decision, and has thought through in advance whether to communicate to the client his or her views on the client's ultimate decision, and, if the lawyer decides to do so, the manner in which that communication should be made.

This last element of engaged client-centered counseling requires some elaboration. Engaged client-centered counseling does not mean that the lawyer should impose his or her views on the client. Nor does it mean that the interactions that constitute the lawyer-client relationship should be characterized by the lawyer offering his or her strong opinions to the client on a broad range of matters, without concern for the client's ability to process the information in an uncoerced manner. It certainly does not mean, as we discuss in Chapter Seven, that the engaged lawyer should impose his or her moral views on the client. But engagement does mean that the lawyer is actively involved in the client's decision-making process, offers his or her perspective on all relevant aspects of the client's problem, and treats the client as a morally serious person. Under circumstances where the lawyer's opinion of the client's choice can help the client make a wise decision (and not just where the lawyer feels the need to talk), offering advice on the "ultimate issue" can promote the interests of the client and contribute to the optimal resolution of the client's problem.[10]

As with much else the lawyer does in the lawyer-client relationship, however, the *manner* in which the lawyer conveys his or her opinion to the client may be as important as the substance of the advice itself. Although we do not believe that the lawyer can ever be completely neutral when thinking about a client's problem, and certainly not when offering an opinion, we do think there are distinctions among the possible approaches.[11] Consider the following alternatives:

- "No question about it—we have to take this case to trial."

- "You really need to litigate this matter. The other side's offer is much too low and I am sure we can obtain more money if we go to trial."

- "If it were me, I'd definitely want to go to trial."
- "Because I am the kind of person who likes to roll the dice, if it were me, I'd definitely go to trial. But it's your decision."
- "You've told me that you feel very strongly that the other side has wronged you. You've also said that while receiving money now through a settlement would be nice, you don't have an immediate need for the money. That is, you are not facing any exorbitant bills or expenses that would cause you to want to take less now rather than wait for the possibility of more money later (as well as achieving a sense of vindication). Is that right? (Client nods in response.) Under the circumstances, and based on what you've told me, my advice to you would be to go to trial."

In all of these examples, the lawyer is offering advice. But only in the last one is the lawyer tying that advice to the client's values (at least as communicated to the lawyer, who, you will note, checks his or her understanding with the client) and providing a full context in which the client can evaluate the value of the opinion.[12] Only the last example comports with our notion of engaged client-centered counseling.

Lawyer advice-giving is only one aspect of engaged client-centered counseling. To provide a fuller understanding of what we mean by the term, and of how to do it, we now consider two dialogues dealing with two very different clients, lawyers and legal scenarios. We believe that the principles and practices of engaged client-centered counseling apply to both.

A. MARTA GONZALEZ AND DENISE WASHINGTON—ENGAGED CLIENT-CENTERED COUNSELING BY A YOUNG LAWYER WITH AN UNSOPHISTICATED CLIENT WHOM SHE DID NOT KNOW PREVIOUSLY

Our description of engaged client-centered counseling about the client's choices in litigation or transactional contexts may seem as if it ought to be limited to situations in which sophisticated lawyers are counseling reasonably sophisticated clients who can articulate their concerns clearly. Yet the benefits of engaged client-centered counseling are not so limited. In fact, it may well be the case that engaged client-centered counseling about choices in litigation or transactions is especially critical for clients who may be less sophisticated, or whose ability to guide the legal representation may be in question (at least in the minds of some).

Marta Gonzalez is a young lawyer who works for a local mental health advocacy organization in Washington, DC. Her cases typically consist of representing individuals in disputes about civil commitment, psychotropic medication, landlord-tenant disputes, guardianship and social security benefits. However, she has done some transactional work on behalf of clients with mental disabilities. Recently, a new client came to her office to discuss the possibility of selling her house to her brother. In the first interview, Ms. Gonzalez learned the following about her client:

Denise Washington is a 44–year–old African–American woman who lives in Washington, DC. She is one of eight adult children (the fifth in age) of Samuel and Marie Washington. Denise Washington has had a difficult life. Although she graduated from high school, she was a marginal student at best. She may have had a mild intellectual disability, but was never diagnosed as such, and did not receive special education services while in school. She has experienced periodic episodes of mental disorder (bipolar disorder), for which she takes medication. She has one child, age 12, who is in foster care. (She is not in contact with the child's father.) Ms. Washington is not employed; she receives social security disability payments and is on food stamps. She controls her own finances (that is, she does not have a representative payee for her social security benefits, nor does she have a guardian or conservator). She is quite independent in her ability to use public transportation. She loves to shop.

Ms. Washington's father died a number of years ago. Denise Washington lived until recently with her mother in the large family house in which she and her siblings grew up. Her other siblings had long since moved out of the house, and all but one, her next younger brother James, had moved out of the city. The house, while spacious, has fallen into disrepair. As Ms. Washington put it in the interview, "it was a lot of house" for Ms. Washington and her aging mother to keep up.

About six months ago, Marie Washington died. She left the house solely to her daughter Denise, reasoning that her other grown children were well-established in life and did not need a home. Denise Washington, while pleased to have the house, has found it to be as much of a burden as a blessing. She has had difficulty remembering to make the utilities payments, which are high because the house is old and large. The upkeep of the house, already a challenge when her mother was alive, has become even more of a problem for her.

Ms. Washington's brother James works for the local public transportation agency. He has helped sister out financially from time to time, especially with utility payments. He is interested in buying the house from her, for a below-market price, and renovating the house for resale. (Even in a depressed housing market, he apparently believes he can make a good profit on the house sale.) He would make sure that Ms. Washington got enough money from the sale to purchase a one-bedroom condominium in town, and perhaps have a little bit extra. The client told Ms. Gonzalez that she agreed with that plan, and that she was willing, and even eager, to sell the house to the brother as long as she could buy a condominium. She and her brother have looked at available condos, and there are several that would appear to be suitable and within her price range.

Ms. Gonzalez told Ms. Washington that she would look into the matter so that she could better advise her about her options. In the several weeks since the first interview, Ms. Gonzalez has done some factual investigation and has talked with a number of people knowledgeable about the local real estate market. She had the house appraised and learned that its fair market value is over $300,000. Ms. Washington's brother has offered her $200,000. The fair market value of the condominiums in which she is interested cluster around a price of $185,000.

Ms. Gonzalez also has consulted with an attorney who represents people with disabilities and senior citizens in estate planning and guardianship matters. This attorney (Phil Hoffman) mentioned that Ms. Gonzalez should be very careful about advising Ms. Washington to go through with the sale. He believes that, if challenged later, the below-market sale might be seen as a wasting of Ms. Washington's assets. If she were later to have a guardian or conservator appointed, that person might argue that the transaction was financially disadvantageous to Ms. Washington and should be rescinded to the extent possible. Hoffman also warned Ms. Gonzalez that someone could later claim that it was malpractice for Ms. Gonzalez to fail to dissuade Ms. Washington from going through with the transaction.

About six weeks have elapsed since Ms. Gonzalez conducted her interview of Ms. Washington. Ms. Gonzalez has asked Ms. Washington to come to her office so that she can counsel her about the choices she faces.

L1:   Ms. Washington, thanks for coming in again today.

C1:   Sure, no problem.

[Small talk omitted]

L2:   I wanted to speak with you again about your desire to sell your house to your brother James.

C2:   OK.

L3:   You told me last time that you felt you needed to sell the house, and that you wanted to sell it to your brother James. Is that right?

C3:   Yes, that's right. That's what I want to do.

L4:   Before we go any further, let me ask you whether anything has changed regarding your situation since we last talked.

C4:   What do you mean, "my situation"?

L5:   I am sorry. I was unclear. Has anything changed regarding your desire to sell the house to James, or your relationship with him, or the condo you might buy, anything like that?

C5:   No, not really. There was that guy who came by to look at the house. He spent a lot of time outside the house, looking around. I forget his name.

L6:   That was a Mr. Henderson. He was the appraiser. An appraiser writes a report and gives an opinion of what the house is worth. It's something that has to be done before a house can be sold. Remember we discussed that the first time you came to the office?

C6:   Yeah, he told me something like that. When he came by the first time, I didn't let him in. I told him to go away.

L7:   Why did you do that?

C7:   I don't know. I wasn't comfortable with his being there. You had told me someone would be coming to the house, but when he came, I don't know. I just didn't feel comfortable. I'm a single woman, and, you know, you can't be too careful.

L8:   OK, I understand that. You didn't feel comfortable, and if you didn't feel comfortable, you did the right thing by not letting him in. But you said "when he came by the first time." Does that mean he came by another time?

C8:   Yes, about a week later he called again and asked if he could come by. He said that all he was doing was to estimate the price of the house. I decided to let him come by and he did.

L9:   Well, that does clear up something. I wasn't sure why it took a little while to get the appraisal. I guess this explains it.

C9:   Did I do something wrong? I don't mean to cause problems.

L10:   Not at all. This is your case, and you get to decide what is to be done. And case or no, if you ever feel unsafe or uncomfortable, it is better to back off than go forward. I apologize if I was not clear enough about why we needed the appraiser—Mr. Henderson—to come by the house. And I should have reminded you he was coming so you wouldn't have had a reason for concern.

C10:   OK. I am glad I didn't mess anything up.

* * *

Ms. Gonzalez has started her counseling session in a standard, if somewhat inartful, manner by asking her client whether anything has changed since they last met. This inquiry is important because legal representation is dynamic. Not only may circumstances change—in this case, Ms. Washington's personal circumstances might have changed, or her brother might have decided not to buy the house after all—but, significantly, a client's goals or objectives might have changed as well. Here, the client has indicated that her goal, to sell the house to her brother, has not changed. But what is Ms. Gonzalez to make of Ms. Washington's having turned away the appraiser the first time he came to the house? Is it an indication that Ms. Washington is reconsidering whether to sell the house to her brother after all? Or is it just that Ms. Washington responds with suspicion to strangers (especially men)? Did Ms. Washington's mild disability play a role here, and, if so, what effect did it have?[13] And even though Ms. Gonzalez had told her client that an appraiser needed to assess the house's value, did she drop the ball by not alerting the client more specifically about when the appraiser would arrive? Should she have been at the house when the appraiser came by?

All of these thoughts, and more, occur to Ms. Gonzalez, who is nothing if not a thoughtful counselor. But as a lawyer intent on pursuing an engaged client-centered approach to counseling her client, she needs to go further and translate her thoughts and doubts into questions of her client:

L11:   Ms. Washington, I want to go through with you the pros and cons of selling the house to your brother. But before we do, I just want to come back to the appraiser for a second. When you didn't let the appraiser in the first time, were you having second thoughts about selling the house?

C11:   Second thoughts? What do you mean?[14]

L12:   Were you thinking that maybe selling the house wasn't such a good idea after all?

C12:   No, it wasn't that.

L13:   Was it something else then?

C13:   Well, I don't know. Maybe I just wasn't ready to go forward right then. Also, the guy was a stranger. He was well-dressed and all but he was just different.

L14:   What do you mean "different"?

C14:   He was a white guy. There aren't that many white guys who come around my neighborhood. I wasn't sure whether to trust him. And, remember, I am a woman living alone.

L15:   So not only didn't you know him, but as a white man in your area you thought he was out of place. You wondered why he was there. And you maybe were a bit scared.

C15:   Yeah. But then I remembered you had told me that someone would be coming by and I thought about it some more. He had good manners. He acted respectful. He didn't push or try to argue. So when he called back a week later, I figured he must not be all bad and I let him come by.

L16:   Thanks for sharing this with me. I think lawyers sometimes forget that clients don't necessarily know all the steps involved in selling a house, or all the people who have a role to play. I will try to be better about giving you all of the information you need. I will also try to remember (when I know) to let you know about when people will be coming around. But at any time, if you have a question, or don't know what is supposed to happen, please ask me and I'll explain it the best that I can.

C16:   OK. I can do that.

* * *

The lawyer's commitment to engaging with her client has generated information that surprised her—the client's initial distrust of the appraiser because of his race, or, more precisely, because he didn't fit in with the neighborhood. (The client's concern as a single woman might have been less surprising to the lawyer, though she did not anticipate the problem.) As we noted in Chapter 2,[15] lawyers need to be aware of the role that difference can play in a client's life. That difference can be a difference between lawyer and client, or, in this case, between a client and another actor in the case.[16] Ms. Gonzalez's acknowledgment (at L15), through active listening, of Ms. Washington's discomfort frees up the client to provide a fuller narrative of the interaction. Ms. Washington's reaction to the appraiser serves to remind Ms. Gonzalez to explain things to the client more fully, and to be aware that seemingly straightforward action steps (such as requesting an appraisal) can seem foreign to an unsophisticated client. The interchange also enables the lawyer to begin to develop a sense of how her client reasons about decisions (it matters to the client that the appraiser was respectful toward her, and was not pushy), which may play a role in how Ms. Gonzalez structures the decisionmaking process for future decisions in the legal matter. Throughout the dialogue so far, and when considered in connection with the initial interview (not shown here), Ms. Gonzalez is developing a sense not only of what the client wants to do (the ostensible point of the representation) but also of what kind of person the client is. That knowledge is surely valuable instrumentally, in that it should help her structure the choices available to the client in a manner that is more accessible to Ms. Washington. But it also is important in assisting the lawyer to fashion a mutually satisfying relationship with the client, a relationship that can reflect engagement and connection.

Ms. Gonzalez proceeds to counsel her client on the primary subject of the representation, whether to sell her house to her brother.

* * *

L17:   Let's talk about what options you have with the house, OK?

C17:   OK.

L18:   One option, of course, the one you came to me for, is to sell the house to your brother. As I understand it, James would buy the house for $200,000 and you would use that money to buy a one-bedroom condo.

C18:   Right, that's what I want to do.

L19:   I know. But if you'll let me, I'd like to run through some other options you have, just to make sure your choice is an informed one. When I say "informed," I mean that you are making this choice while knowing all the information. Is that all right with you? It's what lawyers do to help their clients make good decisions.

C19:   OK, if you say so, I'll listen. What else could I do?

L20:   A second choice is that you could sell the house to someone else, a stranger. If the appraiser is correct, the house is actually worth about $300,000, so you could get more money that way.

C20:   But I don't know how to sell a house. How would I do that?

L21:   We would put you in touch with a real estate agent. You wouldn't have to do anything other than to clean up the house and cooperate with the agent when he or she wanted to show the house.

C21:   I don't know. It sounds complicated.

L22:   Don't worry, I'd be there to explain things to you. But for now, let's just get the choices on the table, OK? [Client nods]. A third choice is that you could stay in the house, and we could try to figure out how to make it more livable for you.

C22:   I don't see how I can do that. I love the house but it's just too damn big. And I don't have the money I would need to keep it fixed up.

L23:   Do you see any other choices?

C23:   Not really.

* * *

Setting out litigation or transactional choices for the client is one of the lawyer's most important tasks, and critical to establishing an engaged client-centered relationship. It would have been very easy for Ms. Gonzalez to do one of two things that did not involve presenting choices to the client: either accept the client's desire to sell the house to her brother without question (what might be called an approach of total deference to the client) or, conversely, follow the advice of the attorney she consulted, Phil Hoffman, and simply refuse to effectuate the transaction (and withdraw from the representation if the client persists in wanting to sell to her brother).[17] The first approach might be thought to maximize client autonomy (though we would consider this particular form of autonomy to be an almost caricatured version of autonomy as isolated individualism). The second approach partakes more of classic professional paternalism: the lawyer knows best and cannot let the client do something that the lawyer believes is unwise. Neither of these approaches, though, reflects the approach of the engaged client-centered counselor. The engaged client-centered lawyer values the process of presenting choices to the client and discussing them with her in depth both because she believes the process can lead to good decisions (as in well-thought-out decisions) and because it permits her to test the rationale of the client's choice and its consistency with the values she has expressed. Ms. Gonzalez's statement, at L19, that making sure her client's choices are informed is "what lawyers do to help their clients make good decisions" might seem a bit didactic, but, in this context and with this client, it can serve to empower the client by reassuring her that the lawyer and client are each doing what they are supposed to do.

There is no magic number to the number of choices the lawyer should present to the client.[18] Indeed, as the number of choices increases, the decision-maker can become overloaded and "choice can be transformed from a blessing into a burden."[19] The lawyer must make some judgments about not only how to present choices to the client but how many variations on a theme the client should consider. Moreover, the lawyer must take into account that few if any decision-makers can engage in perfectly rational decision-making, if that term is defined as accurately defining the problem, identifying all relevant criteria, accurately weighing all of the criteria against one's preferences, knowing all relevant alternative, accurately assessing each alternative against the criteria, and accurately choosing the alternative with the highest perceived value.[20] Rather than seek perfection, the lawyer must work with the client to adopt the decision-making strategy that seems to be the most appropriate for the situation.

In the above dialogue, Ms. Gonzalez identifies three choices for the client: sell to the brother, sell to another, or stay in the house. There are other choices that she might have presented. For example, when the client indicated that she did not have enough money to keep the house in good repair, Ms. Gonzalez might have suggested another option, that Ms. Washington rent out a portion of the house. Or she could have suggested that if Ms. Washington could obtain a loan (perhaps from her brother), she could fix up the house and sell it for an even greater amount (or share with her brother in the appreciated sales price). But Ms. Gonzalez has to judge how many choices the client is prepared to consider. If the client winds up expressing greater interest in versions of the second or third options, the lawyer can explore at a later time these variations on a theme. Throwing a dizzying array of choices at a client may satisfy the lawyer's desire for thoroughness but may ill-serve a client's decision-making process. To engage with the client, and the client's underlying values and concerns, the lawyer must enter into the client's world, be attentive to the client's context, and listen carefully to what the client has told her, both implicitly and explicitly. It is a fair assessment in this case that the client wishes to conduct a straightforward transaction that is no more complicated than it needs to be.

Ms. Gonzalez must take this approach into account in her counseling, and attempts to do so in the excerpt that follows:

L24:   Let's talk about the first option, selling the house to your brother James. From the beginning, this is what you've wanted to do.

C24:   Right.

L25:   But as you know, one thing about selling to James is that you'd get a lot less money from him than you would from someone else. James is willing to pay $200,000 but the house, according to the appraiser, is worth at least $300,000. Does it bother you that you're getting less money than you could?

C25:   Not really. I don't need a lot of money. $200,000 is more than I need to buy any one of the condos that James and I have looked at.

L26:   What about other expenses beyond the house—like clothes, food, and so on? And you also have to remember that even if you buy the condo for cash there are monthly condo fees you'll be responsible for.

C26:   I get by fine on my social security and such. I really don't need a lot. I know about the condo fees. James said he would help me pay the fees if I needed it.

L27:   OK. One thing we might do a little bit later is to work out a budget for you to make sure you have enough money to live on. We could figure out the condo fees and see how much you'd need to cover them. Would that be helpful?

C27:   Sure. I sometimes spend too much on clothes and I bounce a check. Then it costs a lot.

L28:   We can definitely see if there is a way for you to avoid those charges. But anyway, you don't think that getting less money is a problem, right?

C28:   Right, it's not a problem.

L29:   Let me ask you this: why exactly do you want to sell the house to James?

C29:   James has been good to me. More than good to me. He has been there when I needed help. If I run short, he has helped me out with money. My other brothers and sisters don't want to have anything to do with me. Not James—he understands what it means to be family.

L30:   So helping out a family member who has been good to you is important to you.

C30:   Yes it is. I haven't had an easy life. I miss my mom. I miss having my daughter with me. James is really the only one who has been there for me.

L31:   Now I just want to make sure about one thing—you know that if James buys the house he intends to fix it up and then sell it, and to make a profit on that. Is that OK with you?

C31:   Yes, I know that's what he wants to do. I don't expect him to keep the house. It would be too much for him, too. If he makes money, good for him. He's family—more power to him.

L32:   It sounds like you also feel good that you can do something for him, after he's done things for you.

C32:   I'm his big sister. It's the least I can do.

L33:   All right, I have a pretty clear idea now not only of what you want to do but why. Thanks for taking the time to go through this with me.

* * *

How the lawyer and client conceptualize the legal matter here is critical to whether the lawyer has provided appropriate counseling for the client. Looked at from outside the lawyer-client interaction—perhaps as Mr. Hoffman, the lawyer Ms. Gonzalez consulted who warned her of the possibility of her being seen later as having engaged in malpractice, looks at it—it appears that Ms. Gonzalez is about to let a foolhardy and somewhat disabled client make a financially disadvantageous sale to a grasping relative. But looked at from inside the interaction, we see a different scenario. We see a lawyer who listens carefully to her client and who explores with the client her reasons for entering into the transaction with her brother. Those reasons are not only not irrational economically—the transaction will yield enough money for the client to buy her own condo, even if in the future her ability to pay condo fees may be at issue—but, more importantly, are consistent with values such as loyalty to family and the helping role of the older sibling that are important to the client.[21] Her desire to reward her brother for the kindness he has shown her, and the financial assistance he has provided (in marked contrast to her other siblings' neglect), gives her a reason to help him out that makes sense to her. Her choice to help her brother has the consequence of sacrificing financial gain but still yields enough money to permit her to buy her own home and live a reasonably independent life.

This counseling session is ***client-centered*** in that the lawyer has assisted the client in making a decision that plainly is the client's decision. As the session has developed, the decision appears to satisfy the goals the client has identified for herself. We do not know if the lawyer agrees with the decision, because the client does not ask her for her opinion, nor does the lawyer offer it. But the lawyer's opinion does not matter that much here. The client knows what she wants, and the lawyer's job is to help her achieve her goal. Yet the counseling session also reflects ***engagement*** because the lawyer does not just accept the client's choice without probing. She asks questions and seeks the client's articulation of her rationale. She introduces new considerations for the client to evaluate—such as whether it would bother the client that her brother intends to sell the house (L 31). She offers assistance—with budgeting—that is not precisely within the legal problem the client has presented (to help her effectuate a real estate transaction) but that is fairly suggested by the client's lack of financial sophistication. She admits her own mistakes to her client (not providing adequate notice of the appraiser's visit), thereby choosing not to don the professional mask of omniscience that can impede the establishment of a fulfilling relationship between autonomous persons.

Commentators' legitimate concerns about lawyers dominating their poor, unsophisticated clients have provided an important rationale for urging lawyers to remain neutral toward their clients' choices.[22] Here, although the lawyer does not give her opinion about the client's choice, she does engage actively with the client, pressing her on her choice to some extent. That engagement is facilitated by the lawyer taking the time to work with the client, listening carefully to her and assessing the consistency of the client's goals over time. In the absence of these elements, engaged client-centered counseling is difficult to conduct, and may present risks of judgmentalness and domination of some clients. Engaged client-centered counseling is worth the effort, for less sophisticated clients as well as more sophisticated or powerful ones, but the effort, indeed, must be exerted.

B.   FRED JAMISON AND REVEREND JOSEPH MCGILL—ENGAGED CLIENT–CENTERED COUNSELING BY AN EXPERIENCED LAWYER OF A MORE SOPHISTICATED "CLIENT"[23] HE KNOWS

It may have seemed counter-intuitive to you to think of legal services lawyers representing poor clients with disabilities as likely candidates to conduct engaged client-centered counseling. Conversely, it may seem that more experienced lawyers counseling clients with greater sophistication, and with whom they have had a pre-existing professional relationship, would more comfortably adopt such an approach. Of course, just because lawyers and clients might find an engaged client-centered approach more satisfying than a traditional or neutral client-centered focus does not mean that the lawyer will use it. But even where the lawyer wishes to adopt this approach, and the client accepts it, it would be a mistake to think that engaged client-centered counseling is easy or straightforward just because the client is more knowledgeable about the world and the lawyer works in a big law firm. We believe that engaged client-centered counseling is the preferable way to proceed, not because we think it is uncomplicated but because we think the give-and-take between lawyer and client that characterizes this approach is likely to lead to better client decisions both substantively and as a matter of process. That is true even when the counseling session is not conducted in a perfect fashion, as the following extended example demonstrates.

Fred Jamison, an African–American lawyer, is a partner at a large law firm in New York City and provides *pro bono* legal services for a broad-based civil rights organization, Advocacy for Civil Rights ("ACR"). ACR has been in existence for approximately twenty years. About four years ago, the former executive director, Milton Reynolds, engaged in a series of financial arrangements that were, at a minimum, imprudent. The organization, which had expanded significantly under Reynolds's leadership, found itself seriously over-extended and unable to pay its bills. Among the most pressing obligations were a substantial contract with a sister civil rights organization (the Civil Rights Consortium) requiring the performance of services and creation of programs that were no longer feasible, and an unsecured loan and line of credit from a local bank.

The board of directors of ACR was composed of religious leaders from a number of local churches, mosques and synagogues. Once the board (rather belatedly) became aware of the extent of the organization's financial and other problems, it asked for and received the resignation of Reynolds as well as that of the chief financial officer of ACR. The Reverend Joseph McGill, an African–American cleric, and member of the board, agreed to take a leave of absence from his congregation and leave the board to become interim executive director, a post in which he has served for about one year. Almost immediately, Reverend McGill began to put the organization's financial house in order. The organization received a substantial portion of a large settlement in a civil rights case in which it was involved. That settlement permitted ACR to pay off the most of the vendors to which the organization owed money. The remaining significant obligations were to the Civil Rights Consortium and to the bank.

The board, acting on the advice of a law firm partner of Jamison's, negotiated long-term notes with the bank and the Civil Rights Consortium to pay off the debts over time. The organization made about six monthly payments on each loan but soon found itself unable to keep up payments. The bank made no effort to contact ACR once the payments stopped (about six months ago). With interest and penalties, the amount due on the note to the bank is now about $125,000. The sister civil rights organization, which had an interest in seeing ACR stay in business, accepted a revised note that required payments of only $500 per quarter, an amount that ACR has been able to pay. However, there is an unstated agreement with the Civil Rights Consortium that if another big settlement (in the Acme case) comes in to ACR, ACR will use the proceeds to pay off the remaining debt (approximately $200,000).

After filing a series of new cases, the organization received a substantial settlement in the Gem Industries case, and had prospects for more awards in pending cases (though timing of the awards is a significant issue for the organization). The amount received, $350,000, would permit ACR to pay off both the bank and the Civil Rights Consortium and still have some money to spare. But it is not clear that immediate payment of both amounts due is in the best economic interest of ACR.

Fred Jamison has a meeting with the interim executive director to discuss his options regarding the two principal outstanding debts. Jamison and Rev. McGill have known each other since the former started providing *pro bono* services, about six years ago. They do not have a social relationship (Rev. McGill is probably 20 years older than Jamison and they don't live nearby each other) but their business relationship is quite cordial. Since Rev. McGill took over as interim executive director, Jamison and Rev. McGill have worked more closely together. In particular, Jamison has advised Rev. McGill on various litigation matters, and Rev. McGill has appeared to value his advice and counsel.

Tentatively, Jamison has thought that it made sense to pay off the sister civil rights organization immediately to reward it for its faith in ACR and to cement ongoing positive relations with the group. With regard to the bank loan, he thought that while the bank may not technically have written off the loan, it is not expecting complete payment, and he believes that the bank would accept an offer to pay one-half the debt in one lump sum as a resolution of all amounts outstanding.

Finally, Jamison's discussion with Rev. McGill is in the context of the board chair telling him that the board is very happy with the interim executive director's performance, and would like to have Rev. McGill become "permanent director" (with a commitment of at least five years). The board as a whole has not yet acted on this request, but the chair has indicated that there would be a substantial increase in salary for the executive director, and that the chair has reason to think that Rev. McGill is willing to make the commitment and accept the executive director position permanently.

Jamison's meeting is at the offices of Rev. McGill.

L1:   Reverend Joe, how are you today?

C1:   Just great. You have no idea what the excitement level here is like now. I think the staff is highly motivated and I think we're poised to do great things.

L2:   That's great. You must be feeling good about the financial improvement too.

C2:   You bet, and not just for the obvious reasons. The staff and I are much more comfortable in taking risks, and in making some front-end expenditures, knowing that we have a little more wiggle room. We might even be able to have a clean audit one of these days.

L3: Yes, I think we're headed there. Which brings me to what I wanted to talk with you about. Now that we have the big Gem Industries settlement in hand, have you thought about how you want to use the money?

C3: I must say that when I was on the board, the idea that one could even have asked that question, let alone have an answer for it, would have been absurd.

L4: Absolutely. But as you've been telling the board and me, Joe, we need to get used to the organization having turned the corner. It's a new day.

C4: Yes, it is. In fact, I *have* been thinking about what to do with the settlement money. For one thing, I think we need to set aside some money for our new fair employment initiative we've been talking about. I also think it's time to bring some of the staff's salaries up to market levels. But even when we do that, I see us having money left over to deal with our debts. I'd like to pay off Evans Bank immediately.

L5: What about the debt to the Civil Rights Consortium? Have you thought about paying them off?

C5: I am not sure I see the rush there. For one thing, Jane [the executive director of the Civil Rights Consortium] has always said that as long as we can keep paying the $500 per quarter, with full repayment once the Acme Insurance case settles, she and her Board are OK. Second, I've been talking with our litigation consultants in Acme, and they tell me that it might not be bad for there to be a little leverage on the Consortium to settle the case, rather than push the case to a hearing where we might well do a lot worse (or, at the least, not see any money for years). If Jane thinks that settling the case will get her the repayment from us sooner, it might tip the balance toward the settlement.

L6: That's interesting. But wouldn't Jane be annoyed to learn that we were sitting on a six-figure settlement with the ability to pay her off and not using the money to do so? That's assuming, of course, that she even knows about the recent settlement— which of course raises other issues.

C6: Oh, she knows, she knows. Not only did we do a press release, but I made sure to call her directly. I think it's significant that she did not in any way pressure me, or even mention, our debt when I told her about the settlement. She was just happy for us that we had achieved such an important precedent, not to mention a major award.

L7: OK, I can see you've thought some about whether we need to repay the Consortium right away. You have your reasons, and I am glad to hear you've been thinking it through. I do have an additional perspective on this that I'd like to share with you, but before we get to that, I would like to return to the bank for a moment. I must say I was a little surprised to hear that you thought the first priority would be to pay them back in full. I think it is pretty clear that the bank has all but given up on getting any more money from us. Can you tell me what your thinking was there?

C7:   I am surprised you're surprised. We borrowed the money in good faith but we've been unable to pay it back. Now we can. I feel bad that Milton [the former executive director] was able somehow to persuade the inexperienced loan officer to give us the line of credit and loan on an unsecured basis. I think we need to make things right now that we can. For me, it's a moral obligation.

L8:   Don't get me wrong. I am not recommending that we ignore our obligations. But I have been thinking that with the bank, the loan is more of an arms-length transaction. They—or at least the bank officer—must have had their own reasons for giving us the loan and extending the line of credit to us. It didn't work out for the bank (and, by the way, we don't know what happened to the young loan officer—he may be long gone at this point, and if he's not we can assume that it wasn't such a big deal for him to make the unsecured loan). So I was thinking that we could make an offer for some portion of the amount outstanding, say one-half, and that they'd consider that like a gift. Remember that they haven't been in touch with us for months even though we've stopped making payments.

C8:   Well, I'll really have to think about that. If you tell me that the ethic of the marketplace is that offering less than the full amount due would not be seen as bad faith, I am not against negotiating with them. But I think our good name is worth something in the community, and now that we are back in business so to speak, I'd hate for others to see us as engaging in the very kind of sharp practices we are critical of elsewhere.

L9:   Don't you think that's a bit naïve? Banks are in business to make money. They take their lumps like any other entity— sometimes they win, and sometimes they lose.

C9:   (A bit defensively). I don't think I am being naïve at all. When the wolf was at the door—that's an old expression, maybe before your time Fred—I was as willing as anyone to put the bank off, and fully supported the board's decision to pay them back slowly. I just think that the situation has changed. Now we *can* pay them back, and I think we should.

L10:   OK, I see this is a little more complicated than I thought it was going to be. That's fine; it's not a problem. Reverend, let's step back and look more closely at the options I see, and the ones you may see, that we can present to the board. I want to give you my counsel, but I also want to make sure that any decision we come to is your decision, subject to the board's review. How much time do you have for me today?

C10:   I am at your disposal. This is important stuff. I don't know about you, but I could also use a cup of coffee before we proceed. Do you want some?

L11:   That would be great.

* * *

Although Jamison appeared to prepare adequately for the session with regard to the basic choices he saw for the executive director—pay off the civil rights organization in full and come to a work-out agreement with the bank—he seems to have assumed that the choice was an obvious one, and thus seemed surprised (at L7) when the director wanted to approach the problem in the exact opposite manner—pay off the bank and delay repayment to the civil rights organization. It was not a mistake for Jamison to have a tentative view of what choices were available, and even to have a tentative opinion about which choice made the most sense. Indeed, it wouldn't be possible for Jamison to be a good counselor without engaging in some kind of deliberation about choices and which ones made sense for the director. Engaged client-centeredness requires the lawyer to take on the client's problem as his own, even as he remembers that it is the client's problem to solve. A strong commitment to problem-solving is a key aspect of client-centered representation.[24]

Jamison's problem, though, was in truncating the analysis and not going through a process in which he could identify in some systematic fashion the full range of considerations that should inform the director's decision. Perhaps his guard was down. He knew the organization, knew the executive director, and had a good relationship with him. He might even have assumed that despite apparent differences between them—different professions and perhaps different life experiences—their shared commitment to the civil rights organization, and their shared race, would mean they'd see the problem in the same way. We can't read Jamison's mind, but his statements suggest that whatever his assumptions were, and whether or not they were explicit, he needed to approach the problem in a more open-minded way. He needed to engage, not assume.

At two points in the dialogue (L7 and L10), Jamison re-groups and suggests that they try to analyze the situation, and the available choices, in a more systematic fashion. Rev. McGill seems amenable to this suggestion (C10), indicating that there is a good chance the session can get back on track. We will see below how Jamison conducts this part of the counseling session, but for now we would observe that these statements demonstrate his understanding of the nature of the session. Rather than try to persuade the interim director that he is wrong in his apparent choice, he invokes the decisionmaking process itself (L7 and L10) as a mechanism to explore the matter more fully and, if necessary, resolve differences in their approaches once all considerations have been aired.

Jamison and Rev. McGill know each other reasonably well and seem to have an easy relationship with each other, as the beginning and end of this segment of the dialogue suggest. That relationship may give both parties the freedom to express sentiments to each other—such as Jamison's comment about Rev. McGill's apparent "naïveté" (L9) or his admission that he was surprised by McGill's position (L7)—that they would keep to themselves if they did not have an ongoing relationship or if they didn't know each other well. A less experienced lawyer, or a lawyer who did not know the client well, would almost certainly not want to risk rapport with the client by characterizing the client's views in this fashion. (And note the director is not above expressing testiness either, as his "I am surprised you're surprised" comment at C7 indicates.) Interestingly, based on an earlier statement in the dialogue (C5), Jamison's view of Rev. McGill as naïve seems incorrect on its terms. Rev. McGill demonstrates that he is quite capable of making sophisticated arguments and nuanced distinctions. It is just that his calculations differ from Jamison's.

That acquaintances, let alone friends, can have disagreements and speak pointedly to each other is not a novel insight. Part of being engaged in the lawyer-client relationship is to attend to all aspects of the relationship and to understand the role that humor, surprise, anger, and even judgmentalness can sometimes play in the interaction.

So far, the dialogue has set up the opportunity for engagement, and hinted at ways in which the give-and-take between the participants can lend itself to a productive if sometimes painful interaction leading to the director's decision. To demonstrate more concretely the way in which the lawyer's engagement in the actual counseling discussion can facilitate client decision-making and choice we pick up the dialogue as Jamison prepares to discuss options with Rev. McGill.

　　　* * *

L12:　　　Reverend, I see several options for ACR here, and you probably see some as well. First, ACR could pay back both the bank loan and the Civil Rights Consortium loan. Second, ACR could pay back the bank in full and defer payment of at least part of the loan to the Consortium. In this option, ACR would pay nothing to the Consortium until later (perhaps after the Acme settlement). Third, ACR could pay the bank back some portion of the loan after agreement with the bank (say in a range from fifty cents on the dollar up to seventy-five cents on the dollar) and either pay ACR partially or fully. Fourth, ACR could hold on to its cash and pay no one back now or at least wait until either the Consortium or the bank makes a fuss. There are variations on these choices but those are the ones I see. Do you see any others at this point?

C12:　　　That's a pretty good list. I think we should probably think of the bank as one entity and the Consortium as another, and then consider that we have a range of choices for how to deal with the debt we owe to each.

L13:　　　I agree, that's a good way to think of it. Is there any of these options you'd like to discuss first?

C13:　　　Let's talk about paying back the bank. That's the one where I wanted to pay them back in full but you seemed to think that was foolish.

L14:　　　I didn't mean to imply that your suggestion was a foolish one. It certainly is admirable that you want to pay the organization's debts. It's just that I was surprised that you were more concerned about the bank than the Consortium, with whom we have a continuing relationship in the civil rights field.

C14:　　　Well, the relationship is continuing but it's also kind of complicated.

L15:　　　Anyway, let's get back to the bank. Tell me the advantages you see in paying the bank in full.

C15:   Well, one advantage is that it might help us in our continuing effort to re-build our reputation in the community. I am sure the word got around that we were late or in default on some of our obligations. We didn't have much choice at the time. We were basically broke. Now that we're not, and in a position to repay them, we could let the world know that we're the kind of organization that pays its debts when it can.

L16:   So you think paying back the bank can enhance ACR's reputation. All right. What other advantages do you see?

C16:   Well, I don't know what the future holds, but I would like to keep open the possibility that if we repay the bank now that in the future if we need a loan or a line of credit we could go back to them. We are in a much better financial position now than we were, but we continue to depend on settlements and donated attorneys' fees, and as you lawyers keep telling me it is very difficult to predict when that money will come in.

L17:   Do you have any reason to think the bank would want to do business with the ACR in the future even if we pay them back in full? After all, we've been in default for some time and they haven't had the use of the money. This could be a case of once bitten, twice shy, even if we repay them.

C17:   I don't know. It's a question. One thing is for sure: if we don't pay them back at all, they'll never do business with us again.

L18:   I'm sure you're right there. But I have two thoughts. One is that they might not want to do business with us again under any circumstances, so that whether we pay back nothing, one-half or all we cannot expect them to want to work with us in the future. The other issue is that if we did some checking around we might have a sense of whether payment of some significant partial amount would cause them to consider doing business with us in the future. Especially if, in the future, we could provide some meaningful collateral so that they're not left holding the bag.

C18:   Hmmm.

L19:   I don't think we can decide this question definitively now because we need more information. But this discussion has been helpful as a way to clarify some more of what we need to know.

C19:   I agree.

L20:   Are there any other advantages you see?

C20:   Not at this point.

L21:   OK. What about the disadvantages of paying them back in full?

[This discussion is omitted]

        * * *

L22:   Now I'd like to turn to your thought about not paying back the Consortium right now. Earlier you mentioned that you didn't think they were expecting payment now (as opposed to after we settle Acme), and that you believed they would be happy if ACR continued on the payment schedule we had. You also said that keeping the pressure on the Consortium to settle Acme might be a good strategy, and they might be more inclined to settle if they thought that receipt of the settlement would allow ACR to repay the amount due to them. Do you see any other advantages of this approach?

C22:   One advantage is that it allows us to preserve capital and continue the effort to get back on our feet. If we pay the bank back and the Consortium we'll be a little strapped and won't have much margin for operating.

L23:   Any other advantages?

C23:   I don't know if this is an advantage, and it's probably small of me to say this, but I will anyway. It was the Consortium that recommended years ago that we hire Milton Reynolds in the first place. They're not to blame for his financial shenanigans, of course, but part of me thinks it's not the worst thing in the world if they share in the pain. I might feel differently if they were in bad shape financially but I happen to know they're doing great.

L24:   I appreciate your honesty regarding your motivation. I guess it may come down to how important making them share the pain, as you put it, is when put up against some possible disadvantages of putting them off. That might be a good segue to the disadvantages. What ones do you see?

C24:   For one thing, although I have told Jane [the director of the Consortium] about the Gem Industries settlement, and she didn't say anything like "So now you can pay us back," I don't know for certain that she (and her board) wouldn't be annoyed about our accumulating funds and spending them elsewhere while their loan to us remains outstanding.

L25:   Good. Once again, that might be something we would want to strategize about and see what their reaction would be. Consider this: if you told them explicitly what you planned to do—pay back the bank (whether in whole or in part), for some of the reasons you have said, and keep paying the Consortium on the old payment schedule for now as a way to preserve operating income and she said that was all right with her, there might be no problem with this strategy at all. My concerns, that I mentioned earlier, would disappear. Any disadvantage of approaching Jane in that way?

C25:   Only that once we pose this approach to her, we run the risk that she'll react badly and then we'll be stuck. We'd either have to pay her back or really threaten our relationship.

L26:   Okay, so the disadvantage of laying out your rationale to Jane is that she won't agree with us, and you'll either have to pay her back sooner (or in a greater amount) than you planned or risk harming the relationship.

C26:   Yes, that's a good way to put it. That's my worry.

L27:   And how do you think she'd react?

C27:   I don't know. But I have to think—I'd like to think—that, given our long-time relationship, we could have the conversation and take the risk.

L28:   So it might be a potential disadvantage to talk with her, but in the end the downside risk may not be that great.

C28:   Right. That's what I think.

[Additional discussion of pros and cons of delaying full payment to the Consortium omitted]

* * *

The above portion of the lawyer-client interaction between Fred Jamison and Reverend McGill gives you a flavor of the kind of exchange between lawyer and client that demonstrates the lawyer's engagement with the client's problem. Jamison is doing more than simply listing pros and cons on a chart and handing it over to the client. He is engaging in helping the client to solve the problem. Engagement requires the lawyer to demonstrate what Anthony Kronman has called "sympathetic detachment"[25] toward the client. "[T]he wise counselor is one who is able to see his client's situation from within and yet, at the same time, from a distance, and thus to give advice that is at once compassionate and objective."[26]

Jamison brings something else to the table, however. He brings a systematic approach to decision counseling. As he goes through the options with Rev. McGill, he not only demonstrates that he is a good and empathetic listener (e.g., at L24) but also urges the client to think through the problem carefully. First, he makes his own suggestions about how Rev. McGill might address the problem; it is Jamison who raises the possibility of having a direct conversation with the executive director of the Consortium (L25). He is not telling the client what to do (as a traditional lawyer might do, by saying, for example, "I think you need to talk to Jane," or more forcefully "In my professional judgment, you must talk to Jane") nor is he listening passively to the client (as the stick-figure version of the "neutral" lawyer might suggest). He asks questions and probes answers rather than making didactic statements.

Second, Jamison keeps using the language of advantages and disadvantages (or pros and cons) to prevent Rev. McGill from making a decision too quickly or with insufficient analysis. The interactions from L25 on, while not lengthy in total, might be compared to an exchange in which Jamison asks "How would she react?" and Rev. McGill says "Not a problem." In the actual dialogue, we get a fuller sense of the rationale behind the conclusion (in middle school math class terms, we are "showing our work") that the proposed disclosure to Jane would probably make sense. By taking a step-by-step approach the lawyer and client minimize the risk of assuming too much about the situation, and can identify with some precision why the proposed approach might be viable.

Engaged client-centered counseling, in the above context, requires the lawyer to deal with something that he has not so far addressed: the potential distinction between the interests of the interim director and the interests of ACR, which is the client here. Arguably, the director's willingness to see the Consortium "share in the pain" of ACR's financial woes (C 23) expresses not the views or even the interests of the organization but his personal views. Although McGill's desire to exact a kind of retribution from the Consortium probably does not rise to the level of a conflict of interest with the organization or a violation of a legal duty the organization has,[27] which might require Jamison to go over the interim director's head to the Board of Directors,[28] Jamison at least should have explored with McGill the possibility that he was not acting in the organization's best interest. The familiarity between Jamison and McGill is not just a social lubricant; it demands that Jamison raise with McGill tough issues such as potential conflicts of interest.

As noted earlier in this chapter, client counseling does not proceed in a strict linear order, so it would be unrealistic (and probably undesirable) to conceive of a counseling session as proceeding from Option A (pros and cons) to Option B (pros and cons) to Option C (pros and cons), and so on. Frequently, the advantage of one alternative can be seen as a disadvantage of another, and the lawyer-counselor needs to be able to go back and forth between alternatives while making sure that the client gives each alternative its due.[29] Moreover, some aspects of the problem or its potential solutions may not surface until after the systematic examination of advantages and disadvantages (only some of which we have rendered here) has occurred. Assuming that the systematic process of identifying and assessing advantages and disadvantages of each alternative has occurred, we pick up the lawyer-client dialogue once more.

* * *

L29:   Reverend, I think we've done a good job of considering the pros and cons of repaying the bank in full (or not) and deferring payment to the Consortium (or not). We also discussed the flip side [discussion not included above]—the pros and cons of paying back the bank partially and of paying back the Consortium fully.

C29:   Yes, I think you've been pretty thorough in going through this decision. I appreciate your efforts.

L30:   No problem. It's what you pay me to do. Oh, that's right, you're not paying me!

C30:   Thank God. I'd hate to think what it would cost the organization to have to pay your firm's billing rate for the time we've spent here!

L31:   Touché. But we still have more work to do. You have to make a decision of what you are going to recommend to the Board. And to do that, I need to summarize for you what we've discussed.

C31:   Sounds good.

L32:   Although technically it would be possible, it sounds like you don't think it would be in ACR's best interest financially to pay back in full both the bank and the Consortium right now.

That means the organization faces a choice on what amount to pay to which entity. If the ACR pays back the bank in full and holds off paying back the Consortium until the Acme settlement comes in (presumably continuing to pay on the low-level payment plan currently in effect), it will be able to say to both the bank and future creditors that it pays its debts in full when it is able to do so, and may be able to get future assistance from the bank—whether additional loans or a line of credit—by being able to say it met its obligations, at least eventually. ACR also—and perhaps you personally—will be able to say that it has met its moral obligation to repay its debts. However, it is possible that even with paying back the bank in full that it will conclude that we are too risky a customer to be involved with in the future, and, if asked by other banks, will communicate that concern to them. By not paying back the Consortium now, we run the risk that they will be upset with us for not paying them back at the first opportunity, and possibly for giving the bank priority over them. But the Consortium may not react negatively (especially if we tell them what we are doing) because we are maintaining the deal we made with them (we'll pay back the loan when the Acme case settles), they are not hurting for money right now, and they may feel some responsibility for having suggested ACR hire your former director. Are you with me so far?

C32:   Yes, it's a lot to digest, but that's a good summary.

L33:   Well, that's part of the summary. The other part is what happens if we reverse things. If you pay back the bank a percentage of what ACR owes, from what you've said the advantage would be that, of course, ACR would simply have paid out less money (and be in better position to keep doing its important work). Also, you would have avoided paying back some of the penalties and interest the bank added on that compounds the original debt but wasn't really part of it. On the other hand, the bank may distrust us from here on out (it would be even less likely to work with us in the future), it might give us a bad credit reference, and you'd feel like you weren't meeting your moral obligations. As for paying back the Consortium fully, you would clear up the debt, of course, restoring ACR's good name within the civil rights community, though you'd also lose the leverage in the Acme case that you sought. Does that about capture it?

C33:   It comes pretty close. I do want to add one thing, though. I know you think that I am overstating the moral obligation issue with the bank. But I have to tell you as an African American I am particularly sensitive to being seen as not paying my debts.

L34:   Hmm. It's interesting that you are linking your race to the organization. After all, it's not you personally who would not be paying the debt but the organization, which is multi-racial.

C34:   But I'm the face of the organization, at least as long as I'm executive director. And I have to say it would bother me.

L35:   I am not sure I see it. It wouldn't bother me. At my law firm, I don't think of things I do, good or bad, as reflecting on the entire race of African Americans. But it's not about me, it's about you—or at least that's a perspective you might want to bring to the Board. As I said before, I think banks are sophisticated players, and they are unlikely to see partial payment as reflecting badly on people of our race. But that's not something one can prove.

C35:   I just thought of something. What if we made partial payment but asked the bank if it wanted to sponsor the equal employment fair we run each year. We always are looking for corporate sponsors. We could give them a free sponsorship and they might like the publicity.

L36:   That's a very creative idea. I like it. Let's talk a little more about it.

* * *

We have gone into some depth in this part of the counseling session to give you a feel for how complex the conversation between lawyer and client can get. Even as detailed as this discussion was, however, it did not cover all of the considerations that would or might affect Rev. McGill's decision. But note how active a role Fred Jamison has taken in the decision-making process. He has remained neutral as to the ultimate decision (which we've not presented here) but has not simply let the client decide the matter in isolation. He has helped the client weigh the choices he faces by articulating with some clarity, after their discussion, the full dimensions of those choices, and stacking them up against each other.

Moreover, as sometimes happens in real life, the re-statement of the choices and their pros and cons generates an entirely new solution (note it is the client who proposes it), one that might in fact allow Rev. McGill to feel good about a choice he otherwise had serious qualms about. It is perhaps not by chance that Rev. McGill comes up with this idea after disclosing that his identity as an African American affects how he thinks about ACR being seen as not meeting its obligations.[30]

In sum, the above dialogue illustrates many aspects of engaged client-centered counseling about client choices. Although the lawyer has anticipated some of the choices the executive director has before him, he has not anticipated the particular choice that the executive director initially thinks is best. Upon learning of the executive director's predilections, Jamison re-groups—he probes the executive director's reasons, he challenges some of his assumptions, he expresses disagreement, and he moves back and forth in a purposeful manner that suggests his appreciation of the fluid nature of the counseling process. Even though he does not necessarily agree with the executive director's initial instincts here, he does not reject the director's choice out of hand but rather **engages** him and tries to understand his reasoning. He adopts an attitude of sympathetic detachment toward the director.[31] The lawyer is committed to the value of process and if nothing else the systematic exploration of the choices at hand illuminates not only the choices themselves but the values that underlie them. As the lawyer and executive director interact, new options (such as having the bank sponsor the equal employment fair) are identified. One has the sense that this legal matter is in good hands—high praise for any lawyer.

* * *

We do not claim in this chapter that engaged client-centered counseling about the client's choices is a radical break from existing models of legal counseling in general, or even from existing models of client-centered counseling. Critical to our conception of engaged client-centered counseling is the notion that such counseling is highly collaborative between lawyer and client.[32] Not only does the lawyer interact quite fully with the client; in many respects, the lawyer and client negotiate the relationship as relative equals.[33] Engaged client-centered representation is a satisfying way for lawyers to collaborate with clients to help them make decisions.

* * *

C. VARIATIONS ON THE GENERAL APPROACH: WHEN IS ENGAGEMENT TOO MUCH, OR TOO LITTLE?

The two dialogues we have studied in this Chapter reflect our view that in most matters, and with most clients, the lawyer who builds on the personal connection she has established with her client (the subject of Chapter 2), by guiding the client to make decisions after careful thought and with the benefit of the insight the lawyer can provide, is serving her client well. Engaged client-centeredness, as we see it, will usually help a client to make decisions that are both reasonable and freely chosen. It may well be that these choices will not be the same as those that the same client would have made if he had chosen impulsively, and so we do not at all claim that the lawyer following our guidelines is not influencing her client's decisions. She is, but in an appropriate way.

No one approach, however, is always the right one. There are, on the contrary, a variety of circumstances in which a lawyer might question whether "sympathetic detachment" is the kind of engagement she wishes to have. We don't propose here to offer pat solutions for each of these circumstances, nor even to provide an encyclopedic catalogue of what these circumstances are. Rather, we want to identify for you some of the major fields of concern, and to urge you to consider for yourself when you would make exceptions to engaged client-centeredness, and how, concretely, you would go about making such exceptions in terms of the actual approach you would employ instead.

We put aside one possible situation right away. This is the possibility that the lawyer disclaims sympathetic detachment because she feels no sympathy—or more broadly, no disposition to assist the client whatsoever. The lawyer who feels this way simply needs to withdraw from the representation.[34]

Our focus, instead, is on lawyers who feel that "sympathetic detachment" may not be enough. We argued in Chapter 2 that some objectivity is necessary for the attorney, who must be able to step back from the client's situation so as to provide the critical eye and assessment that the client needs. But without departing from this general proposition, we can also say that some lawyers will offer more objectivity and less connection than others, and that some clients and their lawyers may prefer to strike the balance in favor of greater connection. It is hard, for example, to imagine lawyers representing the plaintiffs in a desegregation case without actually holding dear the right to a society free of racial discrimination. Even if that could be imagined, it would be a much greater stretch to argue that lawyers who did hold this right dear were not even among the appropriate counsel for a desegregation case. As a practical matter, moreover, surely identification with clients is a major motivator for lawyers, and if the clients do not have the funds to hire lawyers, they urgently need to find lawyers who will help them out of conviction instead. So we do not believe that complete detachment, even complete yet sympathetic detachment, can be required of lawyers, even if that stance is in general the one most likely to support clients' making choices that are both reasonable and free.

If a lawyer is not fully detached, however, then when she offers her thinking and her advice, what she says will not be fully detached either. We can see just a hint of this in Fred Jamison's answer to Reverend McGill's saying that "I have to tell you as an African American I am particularly sensitive to being seen as not paying my debts." (C33). Jamison's first response is quite detached indeed—he wonders why Reverend McGill is thinking of this as an issue of *his* race, when the debt belongs to the organization, a multi-racial group. But then he briefly becomes more personal: "It wouldn't bother me. At my law firm, I don't think of things I do, good or bad, as reflecting on the entire race of African Americans." (L35). We might imagine that if Jamison's experience at his firm had been more difficult, he might have said something else: "I know. It would bother me too. At my law firm, I sometimes feel like everything I do, good or bad, reflects on the entire race of African Americans." We can even imagine him raising the issue though Reverend McGill had not: "Reverend, have you thought about how not paying the bank back will play into their stereotypes about African Americans, and what that might do to our organization and others like us when we need to borrow money again?"

We do not suggest that any of these responses would have been inappropriate; all of them reflect the attorney's drawing on his experience to help the client think through his options. But consider this possibility instead:

> You can't do that. If the black leader of one of the most prominent civil rights organizations in the city doesn't honor a debt, what do you think banks will say the next time a black civil rights leader asks for their help? This wouldn't just be bad for you and ACR; it would be bad for all of us.

In this comment, Jamison turns from the language of inquiry to the language of persuasion and even command. He also moves from expressing shared understanding to invoking shared responsibility. Given the perspective on banks expressed in the earlier dialogue, he may also have moved from dispassionate, reasonable assessment to impassioned over-reaction. But suppose his assessment is entirely accurate. The question is whether he should have offered the client the benefit of his experience *in this way*. The more lawyer and client agree that they are not detached but rather are comrades, the more appropriate such advice may be—and you will need to decide whether you are in such relationships with your clients, or whether you want to try to make your relationships take on this quality. But when you do, you will still need to beware of the danger that you have truly lost objectivity—as Jamison in this instance might have.

The most common problem of the "sympathetic detachment" stance, however, is probably the possibility that the client will make the wrong decision. Even to state this as a problem, to be sure, assumes a lot. No lawyer can say for sure that a client is making the wrong decision unless the lawyer thinks she knows that some other decision would be better. But the lawyer herself obviously might be mistaken. She does not know (except perhaps in the rarest of circumstances) that the client's decision is the wrong one *for the client*. So the "problem" is not that the client is making a decision the lawyer knows is wrong, but rather that the client is making a decision the client thinks or believes is wrong. Arguably lawyers have no cause, and no authority, to intervene simply because they think their clients are making mistaken decisions.

It might be said that lawyers do have cause, not based on the client's well-being as such but rather based on the lawyer's own, legitimate, self-interest. In this chapter's first dialogue, attorney Gonzalez has been advised by another lawyer, an expert in the relevant field, that she could be sued for malpractice for failing to dissuade the client, Ms. Washington, from going through with the sale of the house to her brother. That is a very good reason for Ms. Gonzalez to practice with care—to send her client a letter confirming their discussion, to record her own reasoning in a file memo, to make sure (as she has) that she knows the market value of the house that's being sold and so can establish what economic costs were being weighed against the noneconomic considerations the client valued so highly. But after all that has been done, it would seem that either the lawyer shouldn't face any malpractice danger, or that, if she still does, she may have a conflict of interest that could mean she cannot continue on the case.

So, too, if the lawyer fears that other lawyers or judges will think poorly of her for doing what she sees as actually her duty on behalf of her client; she must either proceed despite her fear or withdraw. We don't deny, of course, that lawyers' conscientious assessments of what is in clients' interests will be affected by their sense of what others will say about their decisions. Some measure of such influence seems inevitable, and we don't see this human reality as inconsistent with lawyers' meeting their responsibility to exercise independent judgment on their clients' behalf. Moreover, the judgments of peers can be valuable guides as well as distorting pressures. Still, the lawyer who feels she cannot make and act on a reasonably objective judgment needs to let her client find another lawyer.

But let us return to the main issue: does the fact that the lawyer *thinks* that the client is making a bad decision provide a legitimate justification for intervening in the client's decision-making, not to protect the lawyer from consequences down the road but paternalistically to protect the client from his own misjudgment? In a sense, engaged client-centered counseling already offers an answer; the client needs to make his own decision, but it should be an informed decision, and the lawyer engages with the client in the decision-making so that the client will know the relevant considerations and actually consider them. If all this happens, there is no occasion for paternalistic intervention, because the lawyer's non-paternalistic engagement helps the client to avoid the risks that might call for more drastic steps. But in both the dialogues so far, the client quite readily engaged as well, joining in the process of consideration. What if the client isn't so willing?

This question is a profoundly difficult one. We have already considered it once, in connection with the dialogue between attorney Richard Mathiesson and his client Bill Arnholtz in Chapter Two. There it is quite clear that Arnholtz, while saying he wants to take his divorce case to trial in order to expose what his wife has done, really has no grasp on how ferocious and harmful the trial process will be. Mathiesson sets out to educate him, very bluntly and forcefully. As we said, Mathiesson may have reason to believe that Arnholtz's sudden infatuation with going to trial reflects pain rather than considered judgment, and his emphatic language may be compatible with the depth of the relationship the two of them have developed. Even so, we felt that Mathiesson still had work to do, to explain the "pros" as well as the "cons" of trial.

We will encounter Mathiesson and Arnholtz again, in Chapter Seven. There we explore perhaps the most startling case for lawyers' seeking to persuade their clients to adopt one course of action rather than another, namely, that the client should choose as the lawyer urges because that choice is what morality calls for. Chapter Seven examines in detail the factors a lawyer might consider in deciding whether such intervention is appropriate, as well as the techniques a lawyer might properly use in carrying out such a moral dialogue.

But the Mathiesson–Arnholtz dialogues do not quite pose the problem we now face. Arnholtz may be acting out of transient emotion, and perhaps a lawyer should protect a client from the long-term effects of decisions made under such circumstances. Or Arnholtz may be contemplating immoral action, and perhaps a lawyer can speak up on behalf of the third parties whose needs or rights are at stake. But Ms. Washington, considering whether or not to sell her house to her brother for $200,000, does not present either of those problems. She surely is acting in part based on her strong and positive feelings for her brother, but those feelings are not at all transient; her positive relationship with her brother is one of the main components of her life. Similarly, it is certainly possible that her decision to sell at this price will damage her own economic interests, but she is harming no one else, and so she is in no need of moral dialogue on behalf of third parties.

Suppose, however, that the appraiser had come back with a report that the house was worth $500,000—two and one-half times what Ms. Washington's brother is offering her, and enough to raise a real suspicion that the brother is taking gross advantage of her. Let us pick up the dialogue at L20:

L20*:   A second choice is that you could sell the house to someone else, a stranger. If the appraiser is correct, the house is actually worth about $500,000, so you could get more than twice as much money that way.

C20*:   But I don't know how to sell a house. How would I do that?

L21*:   We would put you in touch with a real estate agent. You wouldn't have to do anything other than to clean up the house and cooperate with the agent when he or she wanted to show the house.

C21*:   I don't know. It sounds complicated.

L22*:   Don't worry, I'd be there to explain things to you.

C22*:   I don't really care how much the house is worth exactly. I have a house that's too much for me, and my brother will make sure that when this is over I have a condo that I'll be able to be happy in.

Attorney Gonzalez might respond at this point with the following:

L23*:   You know, sometimes people make decisions that they wish later they'd made differently. I don't think we should make a final decision today; I'd like you to go home and think about it for a week and then we'll get together and discuss it again.

This response, of putting off the final decision, is in some measure paternalistic. But the measure of the paternalism is brief—one week's delay, in this case—and many lawyers might feel that this kind of intervention with a client contemplating a seriously questionable choice is quite appropriate.

Ms. Gonzalez might choose a different response, however. She might say:

L23†:   You know, lots of people haven't ever sold a house, and it can certainly be difficult. I'm not really suggesting you should go through all that. What I think is this: what if we have a meeting, you, your brother and me, to talk about the price of the house? I can explain to him how much the appraisal says the house is worth, and why it makes more sense for you and him if he gives you more like $350,000 for it.

This response is not precisely a paternalistic intervention, in the sense of pushing the client to make a choice she otherwise might not make. Here the lawyer has instead offered the client a new option, one that she likely has not considered before. It's not clear that the client will welcome the lawyer's direct encounter with her brother (or that it would work), and it's also not clear that the client's desire to sell to her brother has much to do with the difficulty of selling the house on the market. But the lawyer hasn't overridden the client's concerns or feelings, even if she is pushing the client to a degree; instead, the lawyer has offered the client an option and it may turn out that this option does appeal to the client after all.

Or, instead, Ms. Gonzalez might say the following:

L23‡:   You know, I understand how you feel. But $300,000—that's the difference between what your brother wants to pay and what the house is really worth—is a lot of money. I know you and your brother are close, but you never know what might happen to his finances down the road, or to yours. You might find yourself needing money that he couldn't give you. But if you tell him that the house is worth $500,000 and that you need him to give you more than the $200,000, you can have more security for the future whatever happens. That's what I'd advise.

C23*:   I don't know; I already told my brother the $200,000 was fine.

L24*:   I think you're going to really regret it later on if you stick with that price.

C24*:   I just don't feel right about it.

L25*:   I know you don't want to disappoint your brother. But right now you're talking about something that's going to hurt you. Your mom left you the house, not him. She wouldn't want you to lose the security she was giving you. Wouldn't she be sad if she knew you were doing this?

Now the lawyer is explicitly urging the client to give up her stated preference in favor of what the lawyer thinks would be a better choice. In her first intervention, L23‡, the lawyer provides the client with new information to consider (the possibility of changes in her brother's, or her own, circumstances). That in itself can't be questionable, and even her explicit statement of her advice is not beyond the bounds of engagement as we've described it (though we believe it is open to debate whether explicitly offering advice about the bottom line is wise or not). Here, however, the lawyer is not just offering advice; rather, she offers her view as part of an argument against the client's view. In L24*, she adds another level of argument, and not an entirely logical one—the fear of future regret. But we cannot say that this in itself is clearly improper, because human beings are emotional creatures, and a discussion of a major decision that was somehow devoid of emotion would be incomplete. Indeed, here the client is acting on emotion; the lawyer has tried to bring another emotion into her judgment.

Finally, in L25*, she in effect tells the client that she is disappointing her dead mother by making this deal. To this point, it seems to us that the lawyer might be seen as still within the bounds of engaged client-centeredness—in roughly the way that, as we elaborate in detail in Chapter Seven, a lawyer might engage in moral persuasion and still remain within the bounds of fundamental respect for client choice. But in L25*, it seems to us, the lawyer has gone beyond engagement as we would ordinarily understand it. Perhaps what she has done can still be justified, but if so that justification must lie in a belief that this client, at this moment, lacks capacity to make a reasoned decision. That could be true—but it is a conclusion we would in most cases be loath to reach.

CONCLUSION

Engaged client-centered counseling of a client regarding the choices he or she faces in a litigation or transactional context is not a formula for generating perfect or ideal decisions. Rather, it reflects an approach toward clients that recognizes the importance of the client as decision-maker yet also embraces the active role of the lawyer in helping the client make the choice that is right for the client. The lawyer who is able to implement this approach will be well on the way toward earning the sobriquet of "wise counselor."

QUESTIONS

1. In the examples of lawyer advice-giving presented on pp. 75–76 of this Chapter, how would you characterize the differences among them? Do you agree that only the last example is consistent with the principles of engaged client-centered counseling? Do you disagree with us that the last example *is* consistent with engaged client-centered counseling? Why or why not?

2. In the Gonzalez–Washington dialogue, does Gonzalez do an adequate job of counseling Washington on how much money the latter will need to pay her condominium fees (L 26 through L 27)? Shouldn't she have worked out in advance the amount of the condo fees before implicitly suggesting that the $200,000 sales price would permit her client to buy and live in her condominium? Should the lawyer have insisted on James Washington committing in writing to pay her client's condo fees if the client had insufficient money to do so? How might the client have reacted to such a suggestion?

3. As noted above, in the Jamison–McGill dialogue, Jamison represents the organization ACR, and not the interim director individually. In light of this distinction, was it appropriate for Jamison, at L32, to observe that paying the bank would allow McGill "perhaps … personally" to be able to say he has met his moral obligation to pay his debts? Doesn't reference to the director's personal interests confuse the question of who the client is? Does Rev. McGill's later comment that he is the "face of the organization" (C34) also

complicate the matter, or is it just a recognition of the reality that the organization can only act through individuals such as its director? Should the board president have been at the meeting, either with the director or in lieu of him? If Rev. McGill is not the client, is engaged client-centeredness, with its focus on deference to client choice and goal-setting, appropriate? Is there an alternative approach that would be more appropriate?

4. Note that in the second Jamison–McGill dialogue segment (L12 through C28) the lawyer first addresses the "pay the bank back in full option" (the client's seemingly preferred choice) and later addresses the "pay back the Consortium partially" option, which is also part of the client's initial preferred choice. Not presented in this part of the dialogue are the other possible ways of thinking about the bank and the Consortium: paying back the bank some percentage of the debt owed, or paying back the Consortium in full. If you were counseling this client, would you discuss these options in this order, or would you first look at the two bank options (pay back in full or partially) and then the two Consortium options (pay back partially or in full)? What would be the advantages or disadvantages of each approach? Does one or the other approach seem more consistent with "engaged client-centered representation"? Why or why not?

5. In the last segment of the Jamison–McGill dialogue, the issue of race becomes prominent. Do you think someone in Rev. McGill's position would have raised this issue if the lawyer were white or some other race besides African American? Do you think a white lawyer would have made the responsive comment he did here? How important is it here that the two men know each other reasonably well, though are not close friends? What other factors would go into your assessment of whether this question would have arose?

6. With regard to the last section of the Chapter, in which we discuss some circumstances in which engaged client-centered counseling might be inapplicable (or would at least need to be modified), consider the case of a client who tells the lawyer that he will do whatever the lawyer says. Is it possible for the lawyer to comply with this request and still practice engaged client-centered counseling? How would the lawyer do it?

---

1. Implicit in any discussion of implementation of a client's decision is the recognition of legal requirements that may preclude a particular choice, or ethical considerations that may prevent the lawyer from advocating a certain course of action.

2. *See* Katherine R. Kruse, *Fortress in the Sand: The Plural Values of Client–Centered Representation,* 12 CLIN. L. REV. 369 (2006); Robert D. Dinerstein, *Client–Centered Counseling: Reappraisal and Refinement,* 32 ARIZ. L. REV. 501 (1990); Stephen J. Ellmann, *Lawyers and Clients,* 34 UCLA L. REV. 717 (1987). Not all commentators agree. *See* William Simon, *Lawyer Advice and Client Autonomy: Mrs. Jones's Case,* 50 MD. L. REV. 213 (1991). According to Kim O'Leary,

Designing a counseling model that pays particular attention to issues of client autonomy might be especially important in two very different lawyering settings: settings in which the client has very little power, is capable of making reasoned choices, and the client does not want a more directive response from the lawyer, and settings in which a powerful client dictates an autonomous model. By contrast, lawyering settings in which client has power equal to or greater than the attorney, but chooses a less autonomous model, settings in which the client is not powerful but is unable to make reasoned choices, or situations where a less powerful client expresses a well considered desire for more direction do not lend themselves to such an approach.

Kimberly E. O'Leary, *When Context Matters: How to Choose an Appropriate Client Counseling Model*, 4 T. M. COOLEY J. PRAC. & CLINICAL L. 103, 107 (2001).

3. We address some of the specific questions raised by moral counseling in Chapters 7 ("Engaging in Moral Dialogue") & 8 ("Talking to Clients about the Law"), *infra*.

4. See Chapter 9 ("Fast Talking: Lawyering Expertise and Its Impact on Interviewing and Counseling") for discussion of how expert lawyers interview and counsel their clients.

5. The earliest textbook to articulate a client-centered approach to lawyering was DAVID A. BINDER & SUSAN C. PRICE, LEGAL INTERVIEWING AND COUNSELING: A CLIENT-CENTERED APPROACH (1977). Binder & Price, with co-authors Paul Bergman and Paul Tremblay, have produced two subsequent editions refining their approach to client-centered representation: DAVID A. BINDER, PAUL BERGMAN & SUSAN C. PRICE, LAWYERS AS COUNSELORS: A CLIENT-CENTERED APPROACH (1991) and DAVID A. BINDER, PAUL BERGMAN, SUSAN C. PRICE & PAUL R. TREMBLAY, LAWYERS AS COUNSELORS: A CLIENT-CENTERED APPROACH (2d ed. 2004). Other clinical textbooks also adopt this approach. *See, e.g.* ROBERT M. BASTRESS & JOSEPH D. HARBAUGH, INTERVIEWING, COUNSELING AND NEGOTIATING: SKILLS FOR EFFECTIVE REPRESENTATION (1990); STEFAN H. KRIEGER & RICHARD K. NEUMANN, JR., ESSENTIAL LAWYERING SKILLS: INTERVIEWING, COUNSELING, NEGOTIATION, AND PERSUASIVE FACT ANALYSIS (3d ed. 2007) (and previous editions); DAVID F. CHAVKIN, CLINICAL LEGAL EDUCATION: A TEXTBOOK FOR LAW SCHOOL CLINICAL PROGRAMS (2002). Our own previous scholarly work also has adopted the client-centered framework, while offering suggestions for how to refine its meaning. *See, e.g.*, Kruse, *supra* note 2; Dinerstein, *supra* note 2; Stephen Ellmann, *Client–Centeredness Multiplied: Individual Autonomy and Collective Mobilization in Public Interest Lawyers' Representation of Groups*, 78 VA. L. REV. 1103 (1992); Ann Shalleck, *Theory and Experience in Constructing the Relationship Between Lawyer and Client: Representing Women Who Have Been Abused*, 64 TENN. L. REV. 1019 (1997).

6. For a descriptions of the traditional model, *see, e.g.,* Dinerstein, *supra* note 2, at 506.

7. As Kate Kruse points out in Kruse, *supra* note 2, at 385–98, lawyer neutrality within client-centered theory is problematic from a number of perspectives. Her conception of client-centered representation is one of plural approaches, comprising holistic, narrative integrity, client-empowerment, partisan, and client-directed lawyering approaches. *Id.* at 419–26. These approaches do not require lawyer neutrality in the sense that the original Binder & Price version of client-centeredness did. *See, e.g., id.* at 422 (narrative integrity approach to client-centered representation "may impel a lawyer past neutrality into a more interactive and collaborative process of legal representation.").

8. There are no bright lines among the following attributes, attitudes, or approaches of the engaged client-centered counselor, nor do we mean to suggest that these elements should constitute a checklist against which an engaged client-centered counselor should be measured. Rather, this list should be seen as, in its totality, suggesting an approach to client counseling that values the client and his or her legal problem and recognizes that the lawyer must be an active participant in assisting the client in solving the client's problem.

9. *See* Dinerstein, *supra* note 2, at 596.

10. *See, e.g.,* Ellmann, *supra* note 2, at 767–68 (lawyer advice appropriate for clients who are "vigilant decisionmakers"); Dinerstein, *supra* note 2, at 587 (lawyer advice is appropriate for clients who are independent decision-makers; the lawyer can make the judgment about whether the client is such a decision-maker without having to wait to see if the client asks for the lawyer's opinion). For strong statements of the importance of lawyer advice-giving, *see,* Simon, *supra* note 2 (lawyers should be required in most cases to make judgments about the client's best interests and then influence the client to accept such judgments) and Abbe Smith, *'I Ain't Takin' No Plea': The Challenges in Counseling Young People Facing Serious Time*, 60 RUTGERS L. REV. 11, 16 & n.15 (2007) ("I believe that lawyers should give advice, sometimes forcefully" and citing sources).

11. *See* Robert D. Dinerstein, *Clinical Texts and Contexts*, 39 UCLA L. REV. 697, 728 n.123 (1992) & Dinerstein, *supra* note 2, at 581. For criticisms of lawyer neutrality in client-centered representation, *see, e.g.,* Kruse, *supra* note 2, at 385–98; Michelle S. Jacobs, *People from the Footnotes: The Missing Element in Client–Centered Counseling*, 27 GOLDEN GATE UNIV. L. REV. 345 (1997); and Ellmann, *supra* note 2.

12. Note that if the client has withheld information from the lawyer about the client's goals (consciously or otherwise), the lawyer's grounding of the opinion in what the lawyer has learned from the client allows the client to reject the advice if there are other matters driving the decision that the lawyer does not know about.

13. See Chapter 4 ("Interviewing and Counseling Atypical Clients"), concerning interviewing and counseling techniques for clients with disabilities.

14. As we note in Chapter 4 ("Interviewing and Counseling Atypical Clients") *infra*, lawyers for atypical clients need to be careful about using phrases the meaning of which may not be obvious to their clients. Although the phrase "second thoughts" is not a highly technical one, it may be a bit colloquial for this client. Fortunately, she felt comfortable enough with Ms. Gonzalez to ask her what she meant by the term.

15. See Chapter 2 ("Connection Across Difference and Similarity").

16. There are other potential differences operating here, most notably those between lawyer and client. The lawyer is a Latina woman who presumably is middle-class. Without knowing more, we can assume she is highly intelligent when compared to the general population. In contrast, Ms. Washington is an economically lower-class African–American woman with minimal education, possibly limited life experiences (especially with people of other races, or at least white people), and a mild disability of unclear origin and nature. Connection also exists; Ms. Gonzalez and Ms. Washington are both women of color, and Ms. Washington may have an easier time relating to her lawyer than she would to a white male lawyer (or may well have felt uncomfortable telling a white male lawyer that the presence of the white male appraiser made her uneasy).

17. The applicable rules of professional responsibility in your jurisdiction may limit the circumstances in which the lawyer can withdraw from the representation, although since this matter is not in litigation and it seems unlikely that Ms. Washington would be prejudiced (in a legal sense) by her lawyer's withdrawal, Ms. Gonzalez probably would be able to withdraw if she chose to do so.

18. Though consider the observations of Janis and Mann that people can usually only process seven plus or minus two categories of information at one time. I. Janis & L. Mann, Decision Making: A Psychological Analysis of Conflict, Choice and Commitment 11 (1977), cited in Stephen Ellmann, *Lawyers and Clients*, 34 UCLA L. Rev. 717, 730 (1987).

19. Barry Schwartz, The Paradox of Choice: Why More Is Less 2, 48 (2004). *See* Jean R. Sternlight & Jennifer Robbennolt, *Good Lawyers Should Be Good Psychologists: Insights for Interviewing and Counseling Clients,* 23 Ohio St. J. on Disp. Res. 437, 522 & n.370 (2008) ("having more options to consider is not necessarily or always a good thing") (citations omitted).

20. *See id.* at 521 (citations omitted).

21. It may be especially important to this client, who has a mild disability, to be able to assist her brother, a person of typical intelligence, rather than always being the recipient of his assistance. People with disabilities are often in circumstances (which to a great extent can be socially constructed or the result of factors, such as poverty, that are not inherently a part of disability), in which they are dependent on others and not in a position to be helpful to them. Ms. Washington seems comfortable with accepting help from her brother, and interested in participating in a relationship with him that reflects mutuality rather than one-sided largesse.

22. *See* Dinerstein, *supra* note 2, at 517–24; Paul R. Tremblay, *Critical Legal Ethics: Review of* Lawyer's Ethics and the Pursuit of Social Justice: A Critical Reader, 20 Geo. J. Legal Ethics 133 (2007).

23. As we explain more fully below, the client in the following dialogue is actually the civil rights organization and not the interim executive director who participates in the interchange. This distinction can have important implications for the determining the lawyer's ethical obligations, *see* Model Rule of Prof'l Conduct R. 1.13 (a), Organization as Client ("A lawyer employed or retained by an organization represents the organization acting through its duly authorized constituents") & cmt. [1], but for our purposes that the director is authorized to speak and act for the organizational client permits us to explore the lawyer's counseling relationship with him as an example of engaged client-centered counseling.

24. *See* Kruse, *supra* note 2, at 375; Alex J. Hurder, *The Lawyer's Dilemma: To Be or Not to be a Problem–Solving Negotiator,* 14 Clin. L. Rev. 253, 284–88 (2007). The MacCrate Report Statement of Fundamental Lawyering Skills and Values identifies problem-solving as the first skill that lawyers should develop. A.B.A. Sect. of Legal Educ. & Admissions to the Bar, Legal Education and Professional Development–An Educational continuum (Report of the Task Force on Law Schools and the Profession: Narrowing the Gap) 138 (1992) *See also* Roy Stuckey, et al., Best Practices for Legal Education: A Vision and A Road Map 62 (Clinical Legal Education Association 2007) ("The core function of practicing lawyers is to help people and institutions resolve legal problems.").

25. Anthony T. Kronman, The Lost Lawyer: Failing Ideals of the Legal Profession 66–74 (1993).

26. Dinerstein, *supra* note 5, at 502 (quoting Anthony Kronman, *Living in the Law,* 54 U. Chi. L. Rev. 835, 866 (1987)).

27. *See* Model Rules of Prof'l Conduct R. 1. 13 (b).

28. *Id.* (circumstances under which the lawyer shall refer the matter to "higher authority in the organization.") Because Rev. McGill is the CEO of the organization, Jamison would presumably need to go to the Board of Directors if this situation were one in which he had a duty to seek out a higher authority.

29. *See* Sternlight & Robbennolt, *supra* note 19, at 523–24, describing a series of alternative decisionmaking strategies in which people engage, including satisficing (finding a minimally acceptable solution), elimination by aspects (eliminating options that do not meet a pre-determined standard on a relevant criterion), choosing the option that is best on the most important attribute, choosing the option that is the best on the most attributes, choosing the first option that comes to mind, and so on. Clearly, some of these strategies are more useful than others. It is the lawyer's job to be sensitive to the client's decision-making style and deploy a decision-making method that is the best suited for the particular client and the choice that is to be made.

30. The discussion between Jamison and Rev. McGill and the latter's belief that he or ACR has a moral obligation to repay the debt implicates as aspect of moral counseling, which we discuss in Chapter 7.

31. It helps, of course, that the lawyer and executive director know each other, and it may help that they are of the same race, though their differences in professional orientation (lawyer vs. clergyman/CEO) are also salient.

32. *See, e.g.,* Kruse, *supra* note 2. Some critics have viewed collaborative lawyering (also variously called political lawyering, critical lawyering or, most recently, democratic lawyering), as distinct from, and, in some ways, a response to client-centered lawyering). *See, e.g.,* Ascanio Piomelli, *The Challenge of Democratic Lawyering*, 77 FORDHAM L. REV. 1383 (2009) (citing numerous authors; *see also* a series of earlier works by Piomelli); Tremblay, *supra* note 22; Laura Cohen & Randi Mandelbaum, *Kids Will Be Kids: Creating a Framework for Interviewing and Counseling Adolescent Clients*, 79 TEMP. L. REV. 357 (2006); Kristin Henning, *Loyalty, Paternalism, and Rights: Client Counseling Theory and the Role of Child's Counsel in Delinquency Cases*, 81 NOTRE DAME L. REV. 245 (2005). Kate Kruse notes that these critical approaches have their intellectual roots in client-centered lawyering approaches. Kruse, *supra* note 2, at 395. Some interviewing and counseling texts also distinguish collaborative lawyering from client-centered lawyering, though less based on the political lawyering model. *See* THOMAS L. SHAFFER & ROBERT F. COCHRAN, JR., LAWYERS, CLIENTS AND MORAL RESPONSIBILITY (2002) (viewing client-centered lawyer as "lawyer as hired gun" and urging "lawyer as friend" model); ROBERT F. COCHRAN, JR., JOHN M.A. DIPIPPA & MARTHA M. PETERS, THE COUNSELOR-AT-LAW: A COLLABORATIVE APPROACH TO CLIENT INTERVIEWING AND COUNSELING (2d ed. 2006), Chapter 1 (distinguishing among "The Authoritarian Model," "The Client–Centered Counseling Model," and "The Collaborative Decision–Making Model") and 112 (describing collaborative approach, which authors advocate, as adopting some of the techniques of client-centered counseling as well as short-term counseling). Although there are a number of differences among these collaborative models, and between them and our notion of engaged client-centered representation, it is critical to our approach that the lawyer collaborate with the client in the decision-making process and make self-conscious choices about when and how to shed neutrality toward the client's ends.

33. *See* Alex J. Hurder, *Negotiating the Lawyer–Client Relationship: A Search for Equality and Collaboration*, 44 BUFF. L. REV. 71 (1996). While we like Prof. Hurder's concept of negotiation between lawyer and client, we disagree with his view that client-centered representation, at least as we conceive of it, prevents such negotiation and collaboration. *See id.* at 75–76.

34. Note that it is important for the lawyer to make this determination as soon as possible, and preferably before a lawyer-client relationship has been established. A lawyer who becomes unsympathetic toward the client during the course of the representation may be limited in his or her ability to withdraw from the case depending on the effect of the withdrawal on the client's case. *See* MODEL RULES OF PROF'L CONDUCT R. 1.16(b), (c) (2009).

CHAPTER 4

INTERVIEWING AND COUNSELING ATYPICAL CLIENTS

■ ■ ■

It is a truism that no two clients are exactly the same, just as no two lawyers are the same. Interviewing and counseling are quintessentially human interactions, and thus subject to all of the vagaries that characterize human relationships, vagaries that make some relationships easier and more productive than others.

For a variety of reasons, not all clients will be easy for you to work with. But although it can be difficult to work with some clients, a central implication of the lessons we hope to teach about building connection in context is that there are few "difficult clients."[1] In general, the challenges clients present to you are the challenges of finding ways to work effectively and respectfully with people who, whatever their differences, are no more imperfect than you. Conveying empathy and support, identifying your own hesitations and attractions, engaging in careful planning for the overall goals and individual questions you seek to pose in interviews and counseling sessions, and providing needed (and perhaps extensive) guidance without overriding the client's decision are all important to forming relationships with your clients. When these skills are well practiced the result, we expect, is that many seemingly difficult clients will turn out to be both less difficult and more receptive to your representational efforts. Contexts, however, vary widely, and the skills or approaches that are effective with most clients may not be adequate for some others.

In this chapter, we do not purport to identify all of the kinds of clients who might present challenges to the lawyer.[2] Rather, we focus on certain kinds of clients who, because of intellectual ability, maturity level or cognitive limitations, may require the lawyer to vary the techniques or approaches he or she deploys in the interview or counseling session. The examples we discuss should not be interpreted to describe all of the clients in a particular category; there is no generic "client with an intellectual disability" or "adolescent client," any more than there is a generic "middle-aged female client of typical intelligence."[3] Rather, these examples are meant to be suggestive of some of the kinds of issues that might arise with clients whose characteristics place them outside the central portion of the continuum of client variety.

Yet as important as the skill dimension is, the underlying approach to the representation of atypical clients may be the most important consideration of all. Too often, lawyers, when faced with clients who are "different" intellectually or from the standpoint of age, believe that they must act so as to do what is best for the client rather than what the client says he or she wants. Such a protective or paternalistic approach to one's client is problematic from a number of perspectives, not the least of which is the denial of the client's capacity to make his or her own decisions (with, it should be added, the ability to choose whether to consult with others, and with whom, before making the decision in question).[4] Client capacity is contextual, and is not an all-or-nothing proposition.[5] Importantly, lawyers should presume that their clients have capacity.[6] Lawyers can enhance client capacity by starting out with a healthy respect for the client's point of view, aided by techniques designed to build on the client's existing capacity, or help the client develop additional capacity. A client treated in this manner is more likely to be aided in making decisions that respond more fully to his or her individuality.

The model of engaged client-centered representation that we advocate in this book, and the engaged client-centered counseling that was the subject of the preceding chapter, are, in our judgment, fully applicable to the types of atypical clients we discuss in this chapter. Indeed, it may well be that this engagement is even more necessary with clients who may articulate their concerns, or recount their stories, in a less-straightforward way than would so-called typical clients. The dialogues presented here demonstrate the importance of the lawyer's respect for the client's sense of autonomy—the desire to be self-determined, to be the author of one's life.[7] But they also demonstrate the connections that matter to clients—friendships and family relationships—and how the lawyers must consider those in interviewing and counseling their clients.

In the end, thinking about representing "atypical clients" is both a recognition of the true complexity of lawyers' roles, and a reminder of the importance of attention to the techniques of building connection in *every* case.

A. INTERVIEWING A CLIENT WITH AN INTELLECTUAL DISABILITY

The scene is in a law school clinic. Two third-year law students, Nate Goldstein and Mary Thompson (both in their early 20's), are handling their first case in a criminal defense clinic. Their client, Roger Martinez, is a 35–year–old person with a mild intellectual disability.[8] He is charged with misdemeanor theft (theft of property that has a value of less than $300) based on an incident in which Mr. Martinez and a co-defendant, Michael Gregg, allegedly stole several items of fruit from a Safeway supermarket. Other than these basic facts, the students know very little about the case, which they have received on referral from the local public defender's office. After receiving the case, Nate Goldstein called the telephone number they had for Mr. Martinez, which turned out to be that of a group home for people with intellectual disabilities. Goldstein spoke to

Mr. Martinez and they agreed that the client would come in for an interview today. He asked Mr. Martinez if he would be able to get to the law clinic offices, and the client said he would get a ride from the group home house manager.

The law students wanted to meet with their clinical supervisor before the interview, as was standard practice in their program, but the supervisor was unavailable and told them to go ahead without him. Part of the supervisor's rationale was that he knew Mary Thompson had had some experience in working with people with intellectual disabilities prior to attending law school. When the students discussed who would conduct the interview, however, Goldstein said he'd like to try his hand with beginning the interview, and Thompson agreed to let him do so.

Mr. Martinez has now arrived and the interview begins:

L1 (Goldstein):	Good morning, Roger. My name is Nate Goldstein and this is my partner Mary Thompson. As you know, we asked you to come in today to speak with us about your criminal case. Did you have any trouble getting here?
C1:	No, the house manager gave me a ride. He knew where your office was.
L2 (Thompson):	Great. That's terrific. We know this must be a little scary for you.
C2:	Uh-huh.
L3 (G):	We also want to reassure you that if there's anything you don't understand, we will try to explain it to you. Have you ever been charged with a crime before?
C3:	I don't know.
L4 (G):	You don't know if you've been charged with a crime?
C4:	Well, I don't think I have.
L5 (G):	OK, well let's just talk about this incident. Can you tell us what happened?
C5:	Well, Mike and I were hanging out near the Safeway on 70th Avenue like we do a lot. Mike said that Safeway were cheaters. They stole some money from him. He was mad about it. Um . . . [Martinez trails off].
L6 (G):	Roger, you're doing great. Just keep going. What happened next?
C6:	Mike said he was going to get back at Safeway. He asked me if I was willing to help him. I said yeah, I

would. So we went into the store and went to where the fruit is. He put some apples in his jacket. I did too. Mike then said, "Quick, let's go," so we ran out of the store.

L7 (G):   Okay. So what happened after you left the store?

C7:   I don't remember.

L8 (G):   Did you go anywhere? Did the police stop you?

C8:   We just ran real fast. We went to the group home. I went in the house and Mike went home, I guess. Man, it was cool!

L9 (G):   Did someone then arrest you?

C9:   I don't know.

L10 (G):   How did you know you were in trouble with the police?

C10:   What do you mean trouble with the police? I didn't do anything wrong. (Mr. Martinez becomes somewhat agitated.)

L11 (G):   [With a somewhat frustrated tone] Look, Roger, I didn't say you did anything wrong. But you've been charged with theft and we need to ask you these questions so we can defend you in the best way possible.

L12 (T):   [To Goldstein] Let me try something.

L13 (T):   Mr. Martinez, do you know what "theft" is?

C11:   Sure I do. I'm not stupid!

L14 (T):   I know you're not stupid—that's obvious to anyone who talks to you. But why don't you tell me what you think the word "theft" means, just so I can be sure you, Nate and I all understand the same thing.

C12:   I don't know how to say it exactly.

L15 (G):   So you really don't know what "theft" means.

C13:   I *told* you, I'm not stupid.

L16 (T):   Actually, Mr. Martinez, a lot of people don't know what that word means. Do you know what "stealing" means?

C14:   [Brightening] Sure! That's when you take something from someone.

L17 (T):	Has that ever happened to you, that someone took something from you when you didn't want them to?
C15:	Uh-huh. Like when Mary Kay stole my Beatles CD at the group home. She said she didn't take it but I knew she did. Larry helped me get it back from her. I really like that CD.
L18 (T):	That's exactly right. You really know your stuff. Theft is just a fancy word for stealing. So in your case, it's just like what happened with your CD, only you are like Mary Kay and Safeway is like you. And the fruit is the CD. Safeway is saying that you took the fruit without their permission. Just like you said Mary Kay took your CD without your permission.
C16:	But Mike said they were cheaters!
L19 (T):	Let's talk a little more about that . . .

* * *

Interviewing clients who are atypical in some way—such as Roger Martinez, who is a person with mild intellectual disabilities—can present particular challenges for both inexperienced and experienced attorneys alike. While there is no such thing as the normal client (a term we specifically eschew) or typical client,[9] it is undeniably true that some kinds of clients require law students and lawyers to vary the techniques they would usually employ in consideration of their clients' special circumstances.[10] Those circumstances can reflect cognitive limitations (such as with Roger Martinez), age limitations (*e.g.*, child clients or elderly clients), or emotional or psychological limitations (such as with clients with psychosocial disorders such as schizophrenia). Being an effective interviewer in such cases requires consideration of approaches that must be adapted to the client's context.

In cases like this one, it is critical that you not assume that the client lacks capacity to tell his story or make decisions merely because he is labeled as having an intellectual disability. Not only is the presumption of client capacity required by a decent respect for the client's autonomy,[11] but the ethical rules require it as well. Model Rule of Professional Conduct, Rule 1.14 (a): Client With Diminished Capacity, states:

> When a client's capacity to make adequately considered decisions in connection with a representation is diminished, whether because of minority, mental impairment or for some other reason, the lawyer shall, as far as reasonably possible, maintain a normal client-lawyer relationship with the client.[12]

To be sure, this formulation of the lawyer's responsibilities begs a number of questions[13] (including what is meant by a normal client-lawyer relationship), but it at least requires you as a lawyer to justify deviations from what you would consider the usual or standard lawyer-client relationship that you generally adopt. Moreover, the Commentary to the Rule points out, quite correctly, that capacity is not an all-or-nothing concept but rather exists on a continuum, and that even a client with diminished capacity "often has the ability to understand, deliberate upon, and reach conclusions about matters affecting the client's own well-being."[14]

In the law students' interview of Roger Martinez, there are a number of contextual elements that come into play, and the law students demonstrate their appreciation of some of these and their lack of understanding of others. For example, at L1, Nate Goldstein's somewhat standard opening icebreaker of "Did you have trouble getting here?" may be an especially useful inquiry in the context of a client who might be expected to have more than the usual difficulty in following directions and getting to the law clinic office. Even though Mr. Martinez had told Goldstein over the telephone that he would get a ride from his house manager, making even such a seemingly easy arrangement could have created difficulties for this client. This seemingly straightforward colloquy with the client thus has the potential to identify important ways in which the client may have, or lack, capacity. Mary Thompson's follow-up at L2 with an active listening response is also well-timed to put the client at ease, even if it does not apparently elicit a significant response. Goldstein's reassurance to the client, at L3, that he will explain anything the client does not understand, and his open-ended question at L5, are, again, standard things to say to a client but particularly important here.

But if the interview starts well in some respects, it clearly breaks down in others. Goldstein chooses to start the interview by addressing the client by his first name. Would he have done so if his 35–year–old client (who was older than both of the students) had typical intelligence, or is the familiarity a subtle form of infantilizing the client? At the least, Goldstein might have asked the client's permission to address him by his first name. Note that when Thompson addresses the client (at L13), she refers to him as Mr. Martinez. Goldstein's use of Mr. Martinez's first name may also be problematic to the extent it suggests, or at the least plays into, stereotypical interactions between white people and people of color, in which the former refer to the latter by first names even when age difference would suggest a more deferential form of address.[15]

As the interview proceeds, a dynamic develops in which the client seems not to understand what Goldstein is getting at, or the terms that he is using. Mr. Martinez reacts sharply to Goldstein's imputation of his wrongdoing, at C10, and Goldstein's reaction at L11 reflects his frustration with the client's inability to help him with the factual background of the case. Nate Goldstein plainly is not demonstrating the openness of mind that is critical to understanding and working with all clients, not just atypical ones. (Moreover, it's not so clear that Mr. Martinez's recitation of events, including those portions where his understanding is vague, is really very different from the knowledge of many clients charged with similar low-level crimes.) Thompson's intervention, at L13, is clearly crucial. Rather than assuming Mr. Martinez's knowledge, she asks him to explain what he knows. She then skillfully handles Mr. Martinez's anger at being called, implicitly, "stupid," by reassuring him that many people do not understand legal terms (after overcoming Goldstein's boorish interjection) and, most importantly, substituting a term ("stealing" for "theft") that the client might be more likely to understand. Mr. Martinez's reaction reflects his sense of empowerment, if not outright joy, at being able to demonstrate his knowledge to his attorneys.[16]

But Thompson goes further, at L17 and L18, by asking him to analogize his crime to his prior experiences. In this way, she is asking the client to engage in higher-order thinking than he has so far exhibited. That thinking may well lead to understanding that will make further interaction in the case much smoother. Indeed, it could inform later decisions about Mr. Martinez's capacity to understand the case and take the stand if the case is tried. The best way for the law students to gauge the client's capacity-in-context is to test it out, and not to assume that the client's diagnostic label means that his apparent limitations in understanding necessarily reflect a fixed characteristic of his decision-making that cannot, with the right kind of interventions, develop over time. This process of probing the client's situated capacity for decision-making takes time, sensitivity, and skill, but, if done well, can reassure the lawyers about the legitimacy of the steps to be taken (and the client's understanding of them) during the course of the legal representation.

The law students' partial interview of Mr. Martinez, with its positive and negative aspects, does demonstrate some important characteristics of clients with mild cognitive impairments. First, research has shown that such individuals respond well to open-ended questions or "open, free recall questions."[17] Closed questions elicit more details from these clients, but the level of inaccuracy is higher than it would be for people without cognitive limitations. Leading questions, especially when designed to be confusing (as they might well be in cross-examination), are especially likely to lead to inaccurate recall. The reasons why people with intellectual disabilities in particular are more susceptible than others to suggestive questioning are complex,[18] but appear related to lower mental capacity, a heightened desire to please the interviewer/questioner, and the phenomenon of "passing"—trying to hide one's mental retardation (intellectual disability) by feigning knowledge so as to avoid admitting not knowing something one thinks one should know.[19] Mr. Martinez's reactions in the above dialogue at C11 and C13 reflect his sensitivity about appearing not to know something he thinks he should.

That Mr. Martinez's case arises in a criminal context raises other important issues. In addition to the inevitable concern with whether the client "did anything wrong," which certainly was an issue for Mr. Martinez (C10), the client arguably finds himself in trouble criminally because of his too-ready willingness to follow the lead of his friend Michael Gregg. That suggestibility and lack of judgment, often constitutive of mild intellectual disabilities, may play a salient role in the ultimate defense or negotiation of this case.[20] Moreover, though not apparent in the excerpt presented here, defendants with cognitive limitations may present issues of competency to stand trial of which the attorney will need to be aware.

Some of the most interesting work on interviewing focuses on the difficulties of, and techniques for enhancing, eyewitness testimony. Investigators have developed the concept of the "cognitive interview" to assist people with questionable capacity (and others) in recalling events they have observed.[21] Although the earliest use of the cognitive interview was in the context of police interviews of adult eyewitnesses to crimes, experts have adapted it for use with children (including children who may have been abused) and people with cognitive limitations.[22] The cognitive interview focuses on the importance of concentrating the interviewee's limited mental resources on the task at hand; re-creating the context of the events sought to be recalled; encouraging the interviewee to engage in "extensive and varied retrieval" of memories; using "multiple coding and guided imagery" in remembering events in different ways; and using witness-compatible questioning.[23] The cognitive interview proceeds in stages that look very much like those of an interview of a conventional or typical client: "(a) the introduction; (b) open-ended narration; (c) the probing stage, during which the interviewer guides the witness [interviewee] to exhaust the contents of memory; (d) a review stage, during which the interviewer checks the accuracy of notes about the interview and provides additional opportunities to recall; and (e) the closing."[24] The principles of cognitive interviewing bear on all interviewing,[25] and careful application of this approach—or of analogous ones such as the "structured interview"[26]—may be particularly fruitful with clients of limited capacity.

To see how the portion of the cognitive interview involving the probing stage,[27] and, in particular, "re-creating the context of the events sought to be recalled" might work, let's pick up the Martinez interview at a later time, when Mary Thompson seeks to get more information about the circumstances under which her client met up with Mike Gregg before going to the Safeway:

L20 (T):   OK, Mr. Martinez, you have given us a good sense of what happened at the day you were at the Safeway. I need a few more details, though. Do you mind if I ask you a few more questions?

C20:   No, that's fine.

L21 (T):   Let's take you back to when Mike picked you up at the group home on that day. Are you with me?

C21:   Sure.

L22 (T):   OK. Now tell me exactly what you were doing when Mike came by.

C22:   I was watching TV.

L23 (T):   Do you remember what show it was?

C23:   Gee, I can't remember.

L24 (T):   Think back. Try to remember what shows you like to watch.

C24:   Hmmm. Let me see, let me see. Oh yeah, I remember now. It was a rerun of "Everybody Loves Raymond."

L25 (T):   Great. That was a great job of remembering. Did you go to the door when Mike arrived?

C25:   No. I was watching TV, and he just came over to me.

L26 (T):   OK. What did Mike say to you?

C26:   He said hi and I said hi to him. He asked me what I was watching and I told him I was watching "Everybody Loves Raymond."

L27 (T):   OK. And what did he say to that?

C27:   He said, "Oh, that's a rerun. Haven't you seen it already?"

L28 (T):   Go on. And what did you say?

C28:   I don't know. I think I said, "So what. I like watching the show. What else should I do?"

L29 (T):   And what did he say?

C29:   He said, "Wouldn't you like to do something fun and go with me to the Safeway?"

L30 (T):   And what did you say?

C30:   I said, "Sure. That sounds like fun. Can we get some ice cream?" He said, "Yeah, we can. But let's first just go there and hang out." So I said, "OK" and we went to the Safeway to hang out.

L31 (T):   How did you get there?

C31:   Mike drove his car. I got to sit in the front seat.

L32(T):   About how long did it take Mike to drive to the Safeway?

C32:   Oh, I don't know. I am not good with time. It could have been an hour or maybe 20 minutes.

L33 (G):   Roger, could it have been 30 minutes?

C33:   Yeah, it could have been. I don't know.

L33 (T):   OK, it's not that important. We may be able to figure it out in a different way. But let's move up to when you actually got to the Safeway. What's the first thing that happened?

C34:   Mike parked the car and we just sat for awhile and talked.

L34 (T):   About what?

C35:   I don't know. Stuff.

L35 (T):   I know this is hard, and you've been doing amazingly so far. But it's really important to think about what Mike and you talked about. Can you think back and picture yourself in the car? You were in the passenger seat and Mike was in the driver's seat, right?

C36:   Right. We talked about his girlfriend. I told him what I had for dinner the night before. It was spaghetti. I love spaghetti.

L36 (T):   OK. And what did you talk about after that.

C37:   Let me see, let me see (thinking). Oh yeah, that's when he said that Safeway were cheaters . . .

* * *

This segment of the dialogue demonstrates the law student's painstaking efforts to establish the context for the trip to Safeway. During the earlier portion of the interview, the client gave only a brief overview (certainly appropriate in context) for how he and his friend Mike came to take fruit from Safeway. In the above segment, the law student probes specific details about the circumstances of the client and Mike getting together that day. One might question why (at L23 (T)) the student presses the client about what show he was watching. It is a detail that surely is not important to the theory of the case. But its importance may lie elsewhere. Recalling the television show may stimulate a sharper memory of the day in question, and make it more likely that the client will remember events later in the day that will be important for the case. It also may give the client a sense of competence, in that he was able to remember the show after thinking about it. Had the law student moved on too soon, it might have contributed to the client's frustration and lack of self-esteem, as he might have thought he did not have a good memory and would not be able to remember other important things.

Of course, had the client not remembered the television show after awhile, it would have been important for the law student to move on, so as not to get stuck on a matter that, after all, is not important for its own sake. Later in this segment (from L32 (T) through L33 (T)), the law student does move on, when the client is unable to remember how long the car ride was from the group home to the Safeway. This fact certainly was potentially more important than correctly identifying the television show, so one might ask why didn't the law student probe more fully on the time issue? The answer, we think, lies in closely examining the client's answer at C32. Not only does he announce that he is not good with time, the two estimates he gives are quite discrepant, and, moreover, are not the kind of linked estimates a person of typical intelligence would likely give.[28] It is not at all unusual for a client with an intellectual disability to be very capable in some areas (such as Mr. Martinez's ability to recall the television show) and much less so in other areas (such as telling time or estimating distances). Not only did Mary Thompson recognize that she might be able to get the information in another way, she also realized that Mr. Martinez probably would not be able to provide a more accurate time estimate no matter how much she probed. Continued questioning would likely have frustrated Mr. Martinez, as he might well have recognized that accurately estimating time and distance is the kind of thing "normal" people should be able to do.

Mary Thompson's sound decision to move on from the issue of the elapsed time of the car ride was almost undone by the intervention of her partner Nate Goldstein. The desire to push the client to recall a fact that might be important, while an understandable one, can raise particular problems when interviewing a client with an intellectual disability. Nate Goldstein, who had been absent from this portion of the interview, intervenes at L33 (G) to ask a leading question, designed to nail down the time period of the car ride. But Mr. Martinez's answer, assenting to the leading question, hardly gives one confidence in the accuracy of the information he provides. Mary Thompson wisely moves on, recognizing that the information is not critical, or that even if somewhat important is not the kind of information that Mr. Martinez will be able to provide. Discretion is sometimes the better part of interviewing.

* * *

Now assume, in the following brief excerpt, that the law students wanted to use the cognitive interview techniques of "extensive and varied retrieval" and "multiple coding and guided imagery" mentioned above. After the above segment, they might have done the following:

L37 (T):   Mr. Martinez, this has been very helpful. I'd like you to do one more thing for me if you can.

C38:   Sure.

L38 (T):   I'd like you to close your eyes and imagine yourself when you first went into the Safeway. Think about everything and everyone you saw, no matter how unimportant you think it might be. Describe everything as best as you can. Can you do that?

C39:   I think so.

L39 (T):   OK, now open your eyes. You're in the Safeway. What's the first thing, or who's the first person, you see?

C40:   Well, I see Mike, who's with me. I see the guy from the store who is in the produce section. He's got an apron on. I see a lady; she's buying lettuce. [continues]

* * *

In this brief segment, Mary Thompson tries to get Roger Martinez to use a different way to remember the scene—to have him picture it in his mind's eye and then report everything without editing himself regarding what might or might not be important. Although Mr. Martinez had shown himself to have a reasonably good memory, if he had not, the technique of varying the mode of retrieval might have yielded important information that otherwise would have been inaccessible to the client, and, of course, to the lawyers. Or, if Mr. Martinez did not have a good visual memory, the law students might have asked him to report on everything he heard (multiple coding). If the students thought the start-to-finish chronology they used earlier had not yielded sufficient information, they might have started with the end (being stopped in the store, or even being booked at the police station) and worked backwards (varied retrieval). Although the lawyer must be careful not to confuse the client with too many ways of recalling information, knowing that there can be many ways of getting this information can help the lawyer develop needed flexibility in the approach to the client.

* * *

Throughout the segments of the Martinez interview, Mary Thompson, in particular, moves the dialogue along by simple questions and the occasional comment of praise for Mr. Martinez's efforts. He rewards her patience and attentiveness with a reasonably coherent narrative of the beginning portion of the story, with relatively few tangential comments. This technique, of course, is not just one that a lawyer would use with a client with an intellectual disability. Indeed, what may be most remarkable is how similar these questions (and answers) might look when compared to a similar colloquy conducted with a client of typical intelligence. Interviewing clients with intellectual disabilities, in the end, may not be that different from interviewing clients with typical intelligence after all.[29]

B.   COUNSELING OTHER "ATYPICAL" CLIENTS—AN ADOLESCENT CLIENT

While the interview of Roger Martinez raises issues regarding the capacity of people with mild intellectual disabilities, other kinds of clients—children, adolescents, elders, clients with psychosocial disorders (mental illness) or emotional disturbance—may present special considerations as well. It is critical for you to recognize the role that these clients' "differences" may play in how you conduct the client interview or counsel the client without assuming that there is a bright line between "atypical" and "typical" client interviewing. Nor should you assume that a "one size fits all" approach will work for all clients within the same category of difference. As we've said, these categories of difference or atypicality themselves contain wide variations within, as well as between, categories.

Kareem Glenn is a young lawyer in a suburban public defender office assigned to the juvenile delinquency division. His client, Marie Lee, is a 16–year–old Asian–American girl who has been charged as a juvenile with theft of a motor vehicle, which would be a felony if the client were an adult. The client has had several prior arrests, for simple drug possession and misdemeanor theft (shoplifting), which have been handled through informal diversion. She has no prior findings of delinquent involvement, equivalent to a finding of guilt in the adult criminal justice system.

Glenn's investigation of the case revealed that Ms. Lee was a passenger in a car (a late-model Toyota Camry) along with three male friends, ages 17–18. One of the other friends was the driver. The three friends picked up Ms. Lee outside of a local fast food restaurant. Ms. Lee got into the back seat and the car drove away. A few minutes later, a police officer pulled over the car and asked the occupants to get out. The police officer told the teenagers that the car was listed on his computer as stolen. He arrested all of the juveniles and charged them each with one count of felony theft. All of the juveniles, including Ms. Lee, were released into the custody of their parent or parents. Each of the juveniles has his or her own lawyer. No one gave a statement to the police.

When Kareem Glenn interviewed Marie Lee shortly after being assigned to the case (and about one week after her arrest), she told him that she did not know the boys that well and that she did not know the car was stolen. She said she hung out somewhat with the boys at school but was not close to them. She said that she met the boys that night because one of them text-messaged her that they were going to a party and asked her to come along. Although she insisted that she did not *know* the car was stolen, she did admit to Glenn that she did suspect the boys didn't have permission to use the car. (This admission did not come easily, especially because the client needed to be reassured that the lawyer had a duty of confidentiality toward her, and would not disclose this information to the court or the prosecutor.) But she didn't think she could get in trouble if she was not the driver and did not know for certain the car was stolen.

Trial is scheduled in the case for one week from now. Because it is not the client's first offense, the prosecutor has indicated to Glenn that she will not drop the charges. The prosecutor is interested in having a finding of delinquency on the client's record and imposing fairly stringent conditions of probation (one year of probation, community service, drug testing, frequent meetings with a probation officer). The prosecutor might be willing to consider a more lenient disposition—withholding the finding of delinquency pending the client's performance on probation and her ability to stay out of trouble—if she were willing to testify against the other occupants of the car. If the case were to go to trial and the juvenile court were to find Ms. Lee delinquent, it is likely that the client would receive at least the more stringent probation conditions, and might be sent to a juvenile training school (a locked institution for juvenile delinquents). Although juvenile sentences are indeterminate (until, in most cases, age 18), Ms. Lee would most likely serve about six (6) months in the training school and be placed on probation for 12 months thereafter.[30]

Glenn has asked Ms. Lee to come to his office so that he can counsel her about the choices she faces. After going over preliminary matters, Glenn indicates that he sees three choices for Ms. Lee: (1) plead not involved and go to trial; (2) plead involved but refuse to testify against her co-respondents; and (3) plead involved and offer to testify against her co-respondents. We pick up the counseling session at the point at which Glenn is discussing these choices with Ms. Lee:

L1:   Let's first talk about the trial option. Is it OK to start with that one?

C1:   I guess so.

L2:   If you go to trial, the state will put on witnesses who will testify that the car was stolen and that you and the others did not have the permission of the owner to drive the car. The state will put the owner of the car on the stand and then have the police officers testify that you were all in the car. Proving the car is stolen is relatively straightforward from the state's point of view. As we discussed, our theory of the case is that you did not know the car was stolen, and you had no reason to know it was stolen.

C2:   I still don't get it. How can they say I stole the car when I was a passenger in the back seat?

L3:   Remember that we discussed that question last time? Under the law, you can be considered in possession of the car if you were a passenger and you knew it was stolen.

C3:   But I told you I didn't know it was stolen!

L4:   Well, it all comes down to whether the judge believes your version of what happened. He might think that you really knew, or must have known, that your friends couldn't have owned a relatively new Toyota Camry.

C4:   That is so unfair! This is really terrible. I just can't deal.

L5:   I know it is upsetting for you. But my job is to help you think through your options. Work with me here, OK?

C5:   All right, I'll try.... So you think I will lose at trial?

L6:   Not necessarily. I actually think we have a pretty good chance of winning. And if we do win, you will be found not involved and you will have no record (other than the arrest). But if we lose, it is possible that the judge would lock you up in Mortonville [the local juvenile training school] and you'd spend about six months there.

C6:   Six months! No way. No damn way can I do six months in juvie jail. That's so unfair! I was already kinda scared of going to trial and just makes it worse. What if I take the plea—what happens then? I think that's the way to go.

L7:   There are two possibilities with a plea. If you agree to testify against the others—

C7:   Forget that—I could never do that! I wouldn't be able to show my face at school or in the neighborhood if I ratted them out.

L8:   I understand your concern but just hear me out and let me finish describing the offer.

C8:   All right, but you're really freaking me out.

L9:   I am certainly not trying to do that. Again, I am just trying to explain things to you. The decision is going to be yours but I am not going to leave you to hang out to dry. I am going to help you with this decision.

C9:   I'm sorry. I'm just not used to dealing with this stuff.

L10:   No need to be sorry. It's natural for you to be concerned. In fact, it's a good thing, because it tells me you are treating this as the serious matter it is.

Listen, I am not saying you should take the plea, but here's the thing. If you agree to testify, the prosecutor would agree to withhold the finding of delinquency. If you stayed out of trouble for about six months, the case would be dropped and it would no longer appear on your record. I am pretty sure the judge would go along with the prosecutor's recommendation here. Or, you could plead involved and not testify. In that case, you wouldn't do time but you'd be on probation for one year and the judge would impose some pretty stiff conditions—community service, drug tests, and probably a longer period of probation.

C10:   I think I like the plea, but the one where I don't have to rat on my friends.

L11:   I do want you to understand, though, that you'd have to plead involved—you know, plead guilty—to the charge of car theft.

C11:   But I didn't know it was stolen! How can I say I did something when I didn't?

L12:   That's a real issue. I understand your frustration. But remember you did tell me that you thought that the guys probably didn't have permission to drive the car.

C12:   It just seems that the system is stacked against people like me. But I am scared of going to trial and taking the stand. And if I say that I *thought* the car was stolen, wouldn't I be lying if I went to trial? Seems I'm damned if I do and damned if I don't.

L13:   Actually, that's something I should have mentioned earlier. You can go to trial and not take the stand. In our system, the defendant (in this case, you) in a juvenile or criminal trial has an absolute right not have to testify and the judge cannot hold it against you. The state has to prove the theft beyond a reasonable doubt. Even if you are actually guilty, you could still force the state to go to trial and no one would think you were doing anything improper.

C13:   This is all pretty confusing ... I don't know what to do. Can't we get a delay or something? Anything but having to deal with it now.

L14:   You mean a continuance? [Ms. Lee nods her head.] Not with this judge. She's pretty strict and we don't really have grounds for a continuance.

C14:   What if I just don't feel like going to court that day? What could they do to me?

L15:   That's not a good idea. It gets you into more trouble, because by missing a court appearance, the Court would issue a bench warrant and the cops could pick you up anytime. And it also shows the Court that you are not a good risk to be in the community, which might make probation more difficult to get if we get that far.

C15:   I just don't know what to do.

L16:   I know it is a difficult decision. Is there any one you'd want to talk it over with? Like your parents?

C16:   My parents are very traditional. If they thought I was guilty they'd say I should admit it to the judge. They'd say that I should have known something was up when they came by in the car, and I should have refused to get into the car.

L17:   Parents are like that sometimes. I do want to say again what I said at our first interview. My role is to represent you and advocate the position you want. Whether to plead involved is your decision and no one else's—not mine, not your parents', not anyone else's. Is there anyone else you might want to talk with?

C17:   I could talk to my friends.

L18:   You mean the other kids in the car?

C18:   Yeah.

L19:   I don't think that's such a good idea. I am not sure they showed the best judgment in this case.

C19:   Well, *you* could talk to them.

L20:   Actually, I can't, at least I can't without going through their attorneys.[31] By the way, the same thing holds true for your friends' lawyers. They can't talk with you unless I give my permission. I will probably talk to their lawyers at some point to see what they plan to do, but what I am talking about here is whether there is any person you trust, who has good judgment, who you'd want to talk to.

C20:   Hmm.... Well, there *is* my Aunt Mary. She is my mother's younger sister and she's a lot cooler than my parents. I can really talk to her about stuff.

L21:   So maybe it would be good for you to talk with her.

C21:   I don't know. She doesn't know anything about this car thing. Could you talk to her for me?

L22:   How about we talk to her together? That way we both can get a direct sense of what she thinks.

C22:   I guess that could work. This is a lot to think about. When do I have to decide?

L23:   We have a little time—probably about 3 or 4 days before the prosecutor is going to want to know our answer.

C23:   OK. Let's call my Aunt Mary.

* * *

Counseling adolescents presents some particular challenges for lawyers. Insofar as models of client counseling assume that clients are autonomous decision-makers who can weigh choices and make decisions in a rational, dispassionate manner, there are characteristics of adolescence that may cause us to question whether young people fit this profile. As compared to adults, adolescents, among other things, are more likely to value short-term thinking over long-term thinking; are more likely to be subject to peer pressure and influence; are likely to evaluate risk (and risky behavior) differently from adults; are likely to consider fewer options available to them; are likely to be less good at predicting future outcomes; and are used to having adults make decisions for them.[32] "Research suggests that youth rely on their cognitive reasoning skills with even less dependability and uniformity than adults in stressful settings."[33] Moreover, children and adolescents may not understand the role of the lawyer, may not understand the concept of confidentiality, and may have difficulty in developing a trusting relationship with counsel.[34] An approach to client counseling that does not take into account these and other differences is unlikely to be a successful one—at least if one defines success as counseling designed to help people make decisions their own decisions in their own way.

Context matters in all areas of legal representation. The context of legal representation is especially important when representing adolescents and children because of the situatedness of children within families and other social structures.[35] Context also requires that the lawyer spend sufficient time with the adolescent client to understand his or her circumstances as well as possible, and to assist in developing a trusting relationship with the client. This requirement can be challenging for lawyers with busy caseloads to cover.[36]

The context of adolescence suggests that the effective lawyer take some steps that, while not irrelevant for "typical" (here, adult) clients, may be particularly important when representing young people. Lawyers sometimes assume too readily that lay clients understand terms or situations that in fact they do not. So, for example, the lawyer in the dialogue appears to assume that the client understands that going to trial need not entail the client testifying. It is only when the client indicates (at C12) that she is afraid of having to testify that the lawyer clarifies that the client need not testify at trial.[37] It would have been preferable for the lawyer to have provided to his client a fuller explanation of the trial option because the client might not articulate her concerns as this one did. The client also (at C7) reacts quickly and negatively to the plea option that would require her to testify against her co-respondents. Wisely, the lawyer does not attempt to dissuade her from valuing this consideration as highly as she does, though he does ask her to permit him to describe the option completely. The lawyer might well want to probe this client preference more fully, helping the client see the possible trade-offs. But what would not work would be for the lawyer to assert to the client that this concern of hers is unimportant.

At various points in the dialogue, Ms. Lee exercises what might be considered poor judgment, though in fact her concerns and proposed actions are not so far out of the mainstream of those a typical adult client might express. For example, her suggestion of a continuance (which she calls a delay) at C13, although perhaps reflective of an immature desire to avoid dealing with her problems, is neither an outrageous suggestion nor one that an adult of typical intelligence might not make, even if her lawyer quickly rejects the possibility. Less sensible is her suggestion that she just not show up that day. But the lawyer is able to explain, in a seemingly calm manner, why this proposal is not a good one, and the client appears able to accept that advice. Indeed, in the context of this dialogue, it is possible that the client is not really serious about skipping court but is simply expressing her frustration at what appear to be her limited options.

Moreover, the lawyer may have been too quick too reject Ms. Lee's suggestion of a continuance. Although it would be improper to seek a continuance without having adequate grounds, in many courts the first unopposed continuance request is often granted. It is possible that Glenn rejects the continuance option because he does not want to incur the judge's displeasure, but such a concern about professional image or reputation would likely be outweighed by the client's legitimate substantive or strategic interests. Assuming adequate grounds for a continuance could be developed, a by-product of a delay in some criminal or juvenile cases is an increase in the likelihood that some prosecution witnesses would experience a loss or reduction of memory, or become unavailable.[38] In any event, it would have been better here if the lawyer had discussed the pros and cons of seeking a continuance rather than dismissing it out of hand. Among other things, he might have discovered that even though the client's stated reason for seeking a continuance would not pass muster, there might have been other grounds that would have done so.

Given the lawyer's sense that Ms. Lee is having some difficulty in making a decision, and that it might be helpful for her to talk with someone else about it, the lawyer's explicit suggestion (at L16) that the client consider talking to trusted others about her situation is a good one. This suggestion is appropriate for any client, but may be particularly useful for young people who may have family members and others who are closely connected to them, and who will influence their decision outside of the specific location of the client counseling session. That the client's first response—to talk with the very friends who got her into trouble in the first place (at C17)—is unwise (and may suggest that she continues to be subject to unhealthy peer pressure) does not mean that the lawyer's suggestion that she seek the help of others is not a good one. By continuing to probe this possibility, the client is encouraged to identify a seemingly more appropriate confidante. To be sure, after considering that her Aunt Mary might be a good person with whom to consult, the client still seeks to have an adult solve her problems—"could you talk to her for me?"(C21) The lawyer's suggestion that they talk with her together is a nice win-win proposal that blunts the potential of increasing the likelihood that the client will engage in oppositional behavior that can be characteristic of adolescence. This interchange also allows the lawyer to state (or restate, assuming, as would be good practice, that the lawyer discussed this issue with the client in the initial client interview) that the lawyer represents the adolescent client, not the parents or anyone else, and that it is for the client to make the decision, even if the decision differs from what her parents would want her to do.[39]

A final thought about this dialogue and its reflection of the behavior of some adolescents. At various points, the client expresses frustration with her apparently inadequate options and with the enormity of the problem she faces (see, e.g., C4, C6, and the colloquy regarding not showing up for trial). Public defender Glenn responds with brief active listening responses (at L5, L8, L12 and elsewhere) as well as with an expression of emotional support (L10) and a normalizing response ("Parents are like that sometimes." L17). A normalizing response is one that places the person's statement in context by linking it to the common reactions of other people.[40] By keeping the client focused on the decision to be made, but acknowledging (in a non-judgmental manner) the client's emotional outbursts, the lawyer is able to move the client closer to making a decision, or at least a process (consulting with her aunt) that might lead her closer to making one. In the end, the use of active listening, support and other techniques,[41] as well as openness of mind, can assist the lawyer to understand the adolescent client and provide wise counsel to him or her.[42]

* * *

C. OTHER TYPES OF ATYPICAL CLIENTS

We have chosen to go into some depth regarding two kinds of so-called atypical clients—a client with an intellectual disability and an adolescent client—to give you a sense of the extent to which the standard techniques and attitudes of engaged client-centered interviewing and counseling apply, and how and why one might want to vary the techniques (if not the attitudes) for these kinds of clients. There are other kinds of atypical clients, of course, who can raise related but distinct issues. Without attempting to be exhaustive, either with respect to the kinds of clients or the nature of the issues involved, we offer the following observations about some other client groups who are sometimes thought to raise particular challenges for the lawyer-client relationship.

1. PRE-ADOLESCENT CHILDREN

Pre-adolescent children present issues distinct from those that exist for adolescents.[43] Depending on the age of the child and the nature of the proceeding, children are likely to have less capacity for decision-making (independent or otherwise) and more need for someone else (parent, lawyer, other) to provide guidance and advice. In child protection contexts, for example, children may find themselves caught between their love for a parent and the state child abuse agency seeking to remove the child from the parent's custody because of the parent's failure to protect the child from abuse committed by the parent's partner.[44] A lawyer for the child may be required to adopt a "best interest" approach to representing her child client,[45] which may call for different techniques from those used with "typical" clients who direct the goals of their representation. But here, as elsewhere, context matters. Lawyers for children "have extraordinary power to either promote or undermine the norms that determine how their clients' interests will be defined and met."[46]

Professor Jean Koh Peters argues, and we agree, that it is critical that lawyers for children to adopt a "child-in-context" approach to representation, one that requires the lawyer to enter into the child's world and make decisions with—and not just for—the client.[47] Her child-in-context approach, as its name suggests, emphasizes not only understanding the context in which the child exists but also the context in which the decision in question must be made. She urges the lawyer to enter into the child's world and use images and constructs the child will understand in order to counsel the child effectively. Her techniques are an excellent example of the kind of engaged client-centered counseling we advocate.[48]

Again, these issues are complex. The critical thing is for the lawyer to understand that he or she must take special care, and make special efforts to educate him or herself, regarding the representation of child clients and their interests.[49]

2.   ELDERLY CLIENTS

At the other end of the age spectrum, elderly clients can present their own set of complications for lawyers. Unlike young children or people with significant intellectual disabilities who may never have had the capacity for independent decision-making, some elderly clients had capacity at one time only to no longer have it because of such diseases as dementia or Alzheimer's disease. Other elderly clients suffer from physical losses that can affect their ability to participate fully in a lawyer-client relationship.[50] It is critical not to equate "old age" with "incapacity" in some reductionist manner; many people in their 80s and 90s remain intellectually sharp and quite capable of making decisions about their lives, including legal decisions. But as medical interventions and technology have increased the average life span of individuals, there are undeniably some people who no longer have the capacity to make considered decisions, and who require the lawyer to adopt special techniques to provide meaningful and respectful representation.

The tendency of some lawyers—in some sense the same tendency that some lawyers exhibit when dealing with the very young or people with disabilities—is to assume older clients are incompetent and therefore adopt techniques and strategies that are overly protective of the individual, failing to take account of the client's residual interests in autonomy. As Erica Wood has observed:

> Attorneys must recognize that their older clients are adults experiencing increasing limits on their autonomy as they age. Physical and financial independence may increasingly be threatened. Their social and family world may be shrinking at a frightening rate. Because of this, the attorney must give particular attention to avoiding overly protective and intrusive responses.[51]

The task for the lawyer, in interviewing and counseling an elderly client, is to take account of the relevant context of age-related diminution of capacity while not using that diminution to justify "overly protective and intrusive responses."[52] A rich, contextual assessment of the capacity of an elderly client can and should inform the lawyer's sensitive representation of elderly clients.[53]

As elderly persons confront changes in life circumstances that may call for adjustments in their residential, financial, and health care options, it is incumbent on their lawyers to be sensitive to the lawyer's tendency toward overprotection, paternalism, and devaluation of client autonomy.

An elderly client may have reached the stage in life where he or she needs someone to assist the client in making health care decisions, handling financial arrangements, or deciding whether it is still possible to live alone in the family home or continue to drive an automobile. Too many lawyers, faced with these set of concerns, may believe that intrusive legal options, such as general or plenary guardianship or conservatorship, are the most efficient means of addressing these issues. But less restrictive options— such as a durable power of attorney, health care proxy, or appointment of a representative payee—may provide as much if not more legal protection for the elderly client and yet preserve significant decision-making autonomy for him or her.

Beyond these substantive concerns, lawyers for elderly clients need to adapt their interviewing and counseling techniques to the context of aging. So, for example, lawyers may well want to interview elderly clients with questionable capacity early in the day, when the client is likely to be more alert. If they suspect that the client is having difficulty hearing (whether or not the client will admit it), they can take care to speak more slowly and a little louder than they might with younger clients. They might ask clients to restate their understanding of what the lawyer has said as a way of confirming the client's ability to integrate the information the lawyer has conveyed. If faced with a client who appears to want to act in a manner inconsistent with the client's lifelong commitments and relationships—such as a recently expressed desire to disinherit a caring adult child—the lawyer can assist the client in thinking back over the arc of the client's life (reinstating the context) with the goal of asking the client to reconsider this seemingly unwise course of conduct. As with any client, there are no easy fixes here, and, at some point, the lawyer may need to confront the difficult question of whether to engage in more self-conscious moral counseling, or paternalistic intervention, designed to dissuade the client from the client's desired action.[54]

3. CLIENTS WITH PSYCHOSOCIAL OR MENTAL DISORDERS

Clients with mental disorders (psychosocial disorders or mental illnesses, as opposed to intellectual disability), provide additional challenges for lawyers trying to maximize client capacity and loyalty to client choice. Unlike clients with intellectual disabilities, but perhaps more like elderly clients, many people with mental disorders will demonstrate fluid capacity, and will have periods, perhaps of substantial length, in which they are quite lucid and can provide adequate guidance to the lawyer. In other circumstances, the lawyer may take the position that the client's interest in avoiding involuntary commitment, given the massive curtailment of liberty it represents, should be presented to a court, even if the client does not specifically articulate a desire to oppose commitment.[55] In the end, the same considerations we have tried to apply to the kinds of clients discussed in this chapter would, in our judgment, apply to clients with mental disorders.[56]

We have one final observation to make about so-called atypical clients. One of the greatest challenges the less experienced lawyer faces with such clients is the seemingly large distance between the nascent lawyer and the much younger, much older, or much less cognitively capable client. You may feel that it is particularly difficult for you to identify with an elderly client, or with a person with an intellectual disability. You may think it is easier to identify with a child or adolescent, having been one yourself, though other differences—of race, ethnicity, class—may serve to distance you from these clients as well.[57] But even if your own situation differs from that of these clients more so than it might differ from clients of similar age, race, intelligence, and social class, it is critical to make the effort to understand and empathize with these clients. You may not be able to know what it is like to be elderly, but you may well have (or have had) people and family members in your life who are or were closer in age to your client, and you can call upon your interactions with these persons to imagine the client's situation. You may not have an intellectual disability, but you may have a physical disability (or know someone who does) and be able to identify with the desire of the client to be treated with dignity and respect. You can, finally, develop and nurture an attitude of respectful inquisitiveness, careful listening and openness of mind[58] that leaves you open to the client's experience and perspective and just might enrich your own understanding of life's vicissitudes.

D. WHAT TO DO WHEN YOUR CLIENT MAY NOT HAVE CAPACITY

Notwithstanding the presumption of client capacity, and the lawyer's desire to establish a normal or typical client-lawyer relationship with the client, there will be some atypical clients who will not have capacity to enter into a client-lawyer relationship with the lawyer. The Model Rules of Professional Conduct, Rule 1.14, Client with Diminished Capacity, directs the lawyer to maintain a "normal" client-lawyer relationship "as far as reasonably possible."[59] In appropriate and limited circumstances—where the lawyer reasonably believes that the client has diminished capacity, is at risk of substantial physical, financial or other harm cases, and is unable to act—the lawyer can seek protective action, which can include consulting with outside entities or seeking the appointment of a surrogate decision-maker, such as a guardian, a guardian ad litem, or a conservator.[60] If a court appoints one of these surrogate decision-makers to act for the client,[61] whether or not at the lawyer's urging, "the lawyer should *ordinarily* look to the representative [surrogate decision-maker] for decisions on behalf of the client."[62] Yet, the lawyer is further admonished "as far as possible to accord the represented person the status of client, particularly in maintaining communication."[63] Especially in cases in which the incapacitated person (the represented person or ward) and the guardian do not see eye to eye,[64] it is not obvious how the lawyer can both look to the surrogate for guidance and yet also accord the incapacitated person the status of client.

Legal ethics commentators have struggled with how to give meaning to these seemingly contradictory requirements.[65] For our purposes, it is enough to observe that even when a client is not able to function as a typical client (in the sense of guiding the representation), the thoughtful lawyer will maximize the client's level of participation in the legal matter, seek interventions that are no more restrictive than necessary to protect the client's interests,[66] and urge any surrogate decision-maker to use a substitute judgment standard for client decision-making—that is, to make the decision that the client would make if the client could make the decision.[67] As a group of legal educators put it when analyzing the role of lawyers for children with diminished capacity or incapacity:

> When the client lacks capacity to decide, the attorney may be required to interpose other viewpoints or even to substitute her judgment for that of the client. This important step involves gathering information from a wide range of sources as well as familiarizing oneself with the child's family, community and culture in order to arrive at or to advocate for a decision the child would make if she or he were capable.[68]

The desirability of the surrogate decision-maker using a substituted judgment standard in decision-making[69] is premised on the importance of client autonomy and preservation of as much capacity as possible for the affected individual. In contrast, the best interest standard is more pater-nalistic, focused as it is on what is best for the individual rather than on what he or she may desire. Substituted judgment, by being closer to the decision-making goals, interests and processes of the individual, is more consistent with the kind of engaged client-centered lawyering that we espouse. Do you agree?

    * * *

Many of the concerns that drive the approach to legal interviewing and counseling that we present in this book—the importance of context and difference, the value of the lawyer-client relationship, the significance of engaged client-centeredness—are just as valid for atypical clients as for others. The differences may lie more in the need for you to make some adjustments in technique, or in the recognition that many atypical clients have multiple people in their lives (family members, other professionals) who may seek to play a role in the lawyer-client relationship you set out to establish. These other people can be helpful, even essential, to the client's well-being and full participation in the lawyer-client relationship, but you must always remember that it is the person with cognitive limitations (or other aspects of atypicality) who is the client and who gets to decide (if he or she can) the role that these other people play in his or her life.

DISCUSSION QUESTIONS

1. What are the downsides for the lawyer or the client of presuming client capacity too easily? What is the lawyer to do when he or she genuinely

believes the client is making a poor decision because of questionable capacity? How does the lawyer distinguish between a poor decision based on incapacity and one that merely seems wrong because it is different from what the lawyer would choose to do?

2.   In those cases in which the lawyer consults with others regarding the client with questionable capacity—such as family members, friends, or professional staff members—how can the lawyer be sure that those individuals are acting in good faith toward the client, or are not exercising undue influence over the client? What if the surrogate decision-maker appears to be using not a substitute judgment standard but a best interest standard—how, if at all, should the lawyer intervene with the surrogate?

3.   If the lawyer uses some number of leading questions in an interview with an atypical client, even if only to clarify specific factual events or circumstances, how can the lawyer be sure that he or she does not receive an answer designed to please the lawyer rather than reflect a genuine recollection?

4.   When, and by what criteria, should a lawyer decide that he or she is "over his or her head" in representing a client with a mental disability and needs to make a referral to a mental health professional? What risks, if any, are involved in making such a referral?

---

1.   *Compare* DAVID A. BINDER ET AL., LAWYERS AS COUNSELORS: A CLIENT-CENTERED APPROACH (2d ed. 2004), Chapter 12, Gathering Information from Atypical and Difficult Clients (discussing techniques for interviewing "problem clients," including "aging and infirm clients").

2.   *See id.* (identifying client reluctance to discuss particular topics; client reluctance to start an interview; communicating with aged and infirm clients; rambling clients; clients who are hostile, angry and explosive; and clients who fabricate as comprising "atypical and difficult clients."). *See also, id.,* Ch. 21, Referring Clients to Mental Health Professionals.

3.   *See, e.g., City of Cleburne v. Cleburne Living Center,* 473 U.S. 432, 442 (1985) (people with mental retardation are "a large and diversified group").

4.   Recognition of the increasing importance of the concept of capacity in disability law is reflected in the recently adopted United Nations Convention on the Rights of Persons with Disabilities. Convention on the Rights of Persons with Disabilities, G.A. Res. 61/106, 76th plen. mtg., U.N. Doc A/RES/61/106 (Dec. 13, 2006). (The Convention entered into force on May 3, 2008.) Article 12, Equal Recognition Before the Law, provides in paragraph 2 that "States Parties shall recognize that persons with disabilities enjoy legal capacity on an equal basis with others in all aspects of life." Acknowledging that sometimes people with disabilities need assistance in exercising their capacity, paragraph 3 of Article 12 provides that, "States Parties shall take appropriate measures to provide access by persons with disabilities to the support they may require in exercising their legal capacity." *See generally* Arlene S. Kanter, *Symposium: The United Nations Convention on the Rights of Persons with Disabilities: Introduction: The Promise and Challenge of the United Nations Convention on the Rights of Persons with Disabilities,* 34 SYRACUSE J. INT'L L. & COM. 287 (2007).

5.   *See* Robert D. Dinerstein, *Guardianship and Its Alternatives,* Chapter 23 in ADULTS WITH DOWN SYNDROME 235, 239 (Siegfried M. Pueschel, ed., 2006).

6.   *See* Peter Margulies, *The Lawyer as Caregiver: Child Client's Competence in Context,* 64 FORDHAM L. REV. 1473, 1474 & n.4 (1996).

7.   *See* Katherine R. Kruse, *Fortress in the Sand: The Plural Values of Client–Centered Representation,* 12 CLIN. L. REV. 369, 404 (2006); Robert D. Dinerstein, *Client–Centered Counseling: Reappraisal and Refinement,* 32 ARIZ. L. REV. 501, 512–13 (1990).

8.   We use the term "mild intellectual disability" instead of the more conventional "mild mental retardation" because, increasingly, people with mental retardation, their families and their allies object to the latter term, which they associate with societal stigma. In part, the stigma comes from the increasingly prolific use of the word "retard," which the Associated Press describes as "a casual insult that derives from an out-of-favor medical term [that] has long been considered inappropriate." Associated Press, "Special Olympics Fights Use of Word 'Retard'," March 31, 2009 (available at http://www.msnbc.msn.com/id/29981699/). While no one alternative has replaced the term "mental retardation," some professional groups have adopted "person with intellectual disabilities" as the best alternative, and we adopt that convention here. *See, e.g.,* 68 Fed. Reg. 52,401 (Sept. 3, 2003) (noting Executive Order changing name of President's Committee on Mental Retardation to President's Committee for People with Intellectual Disabilities, "reflect[ing] efforts to promote equality for people with intellectual disabilities.") Another term sometimes used, "person with developmental disabilities," is both over-inclusive (there are many developmental disabilities, such as cerebral palsy or autism, that are not mental retardation), and under-inclusive (in that people with mild mental retardation may not actually be considered to have a developmental disability). *See* Developmentally Disabled Assistance and Bill of Rights Act of 2000, 42 U.S.C. § 15002 (8) (2003) (defining "developmental disability" as meaning, *inter alia,* a "severe, chronic disability of an individual that—... (iv) results in substantial functional limitations in 3 or more of the following areas of major life activity: (I) Self-care. (II) Receptive and expressive language. (II) Learning. (IV) Mobility. (V) Self-direction. (VI) Capacity for independent living. (VII) Economic self-sufficiency.")

9. *Compare* D.C. Rules of Prof'l Conduct R. 1.14 (a), Client with diminished capacity, and cmt. [1] (using terminology "typical client-lawyer relationship") *with* Model Rules of Prof'l Conduct ("Model Rules") R. 1.14 (a), Client with diminished capacity (using terminology "normal client-lawyer relationship"). Most states have adopted the ABA Model Rules terminology.

10. For an extensive critique of society's construction of difference with respect to disability, see Martha Minow, Making All the Difference: Inclusion, Exclusion and American Law (1990).

11. *See* Stanley S. Herr, Chapter 6, "Capacity for and Consent to Legal Representation," in A Guide to Consent (R. Dinerstein, S. Herr & J. O'Sullivan, eds., 1999). *See also,* UN Convention on the Rights of Persons with Disabilities, *supra* note 4, Art. 12, Equal Recognition Before the Law.

12. Model Rules of Prof'l Conduct R. 1.14 (a) (2000). The revised Rule 1.14, part of the Ethics 2000 Commission revisions to the Model Rules, substituted the term "diminished capacity" for disability, disorder, or competence, terms which appeared in the original Rule 1.14. The Reporter explained that the change in terminology was meant to reflect more accurately the notion of capacity existing on a continuum. It is unfortunate, however, that the term "diminished capacity" has a different meaning in a criminal law context that might sow confusion when used in Rule 1.14. *See, e.g., Washington v. Gough,* 768 P.2d 1028, 1029–30 (Wash. 1989) ("diminished capacity arises out of a mental disorder, usually not amounting to insanity, that is demonstrated to have a specific effect on one's capacity to achieve the level of culpability required for a given crime") (citation omitted).

13. *See* Paul R. Tremblay, *On Persuasion and Paternalism: Lawyer Decisionmaking and the Questionably Competent Client,* 1987 Utah L. Rev. 515; Stanley S. Herr, *Representation of Clients with Disabilities: Issues of Ethics and Control,* 17 NYU Rev. L. & Soc. Chge. 609 (1989–1990). For a discussion (and criticism) of the role of counsel for clients with mental disabilities, *see* Michael L. Perlin, *Fatal Assumption: A Critical Evaluation of the Role of Counsel in Mental Disability Cases,* 16 Law & Hum. Behav. 37 (1992).

14. Model Rules, *supra* note 9, R.1.14 cmt. [1].

15. Of course, we have not told you what race or ethnicity Nate Goldstein and Mary Thompson are. Nate's last name would probably suggest he is Jewish (at least ethnically if not religiously), though Mary's last name provides fewer clues.

16. Mary Thompson's comment at L14 that it is "obvious to anyone" that Mr. Martinez is not stupid may be stretching the truth, of course, regarding how others might perceive the client as a person with cognitive limitations. But in this context, it seems not only to be a supportive intervention designed to create (or re-establish) rapport, but also one calculated to elicit additional factual information. It also puts the law student on the side of the client by depicting her as one who does not accept the stigma that attaches to people with intellectual limitations.

17. The discussion in this paragraph is based on several sources, including Nitza B. Perlman, et al., *The Developmentally Handicapped Witness: Competency as a Function of Question Format,* 18 Law & Hum. Beh. 171 (1994) and Mark R. Kebbell & Chris Hatton, *People with Mental Retardation as Witnesses in Court: A Review,* 37 Mental Retardation 179 (June 1999).

18. *See, e.g.,* W.M.L. Finlay & E. Lyons, *Acquiescence in Interviews with People Who Have Mental Retardation,* 40 Mental Retardation 14 (2002) (while acquiescence by people with mental retardation to yes-no questions is a function of a desire to please or submissiveness, it also may be a product of questions that are overly complex either in grammatical structure or the type of judgments they seek).

19. *See* Robert B. Edgerton, Cloak of Competence: Stigma in the Lives of the Mentally Retarded (1967; rev. ed. 1993).

20. For a general discussion of the lawyer-client relationship with a client with an intellectual disability in a criminal case, see Robert D. Dinerstein & Michelle Buescher, Chapter 7, "Capacity and the Courts," in A GUIDE TO CONSENT, *supra* note 11.

21. *See, e.g.,* RONALD FISHER & R. EDWARD GEISELMAN, MEMORY ENHANCING TECHNIQUES FOR INVESTIGATIVE INTERVIEWING: THE COGNITIVE INTERVIEW (1992).

22. *See* DEBRA A. POOLE & MICHAEL E. LAMB, INVESTIGATIVE INTERVIEWS OF CHILDREN: A GUIDE FOR HELPING PROFESSIONALS 83–84 (1998); Kebbell & Hatton, *supra* note 17, at 181–82.

23. POOLE & LAMB, *supra* note 22, at 84–86.

24. *Id.* at 87. *See also* FISHER & GEISELMAN, *supra* note 21, at 145–57 (on the "Sequence of the Cognitive Interview").

25. *See* STEFAN H. KRIEGER & RICHARD K. NEUMANN, JR., ESSENTIAL LAWYERING SKILLS: INTERVIEWING, COUNSELING, NEGOTIATION, AND PERSUASIVE FACT ANALYSIS 77–80, 87–91 (3d ed. 2007).

26. *See* POOLE & LAMB, *supra* note 22, at 92–94. Poole and Lamb note that the cognitive interview may not be appropriate for young children of 7 or 8 years old, who may interpret the repeated probing and multiple requests for recall as indicating that somehow they have not given the correct answer and need to change it. *Id.* at 89. They write that the structured interview, developed by researchers in Germany and the United Kingdom, "mimics the Cognitive Interview in all but a few special respects." *Id.* at 92. For example, the structured interview may dispense with context reinstatement, "report everything" instructions, image probing, and "recalling in reverse order." *Id.* (reporting on study). Despite these differences, however, "the Structured Interview thus parallels the Cognitive Interview by emphasizing rapport, allowing witnesses to guide interactions, recommending open-ended rather than specific or leading questions, and encouraging multiple recall attempts." *Id.* at 93.

27. See Chapter 2 ("Connection Across Difference and Similarity") (in the outline of Interviewing, this probing would occur in the fifth stage, fact exploration).

28. That is to say, a person of typical intelligence would be more likely to say something like, "Oh, I don't know it was probably 20–30 minutes," rather than selecting two time periods, twenty minutes and one hour, that are relatively far apart.

29. *See* Linda F. Smith, *'Maybe we can change the rule'—Case Study of An Interview*, ExpressO, available at http://works.bepress.com/linda_smith/4 (paper presented at New York Law School Clinical Theory Workshop, Sept. 12, 2008; revised Feb. 2009) (analyzing lawyer's interview of author's son, a young man with Down syndrome).

30. One thing for Kareem Glenn to consider here is the extent to which, after trial, a prosecutor might seek a harsher disposition, such as institutionalization, than she would have agreed to in a plea offer (because, for example, she had to prepare for and conduct the trial, which even in a simple case would take more time than proffering a plea agreement). The court as well might be more inclined to impose a sentence of institutionalization than she would have imposed pursuant to a proffered plea agreement as a way to "punish" a client for going to trial (especially if the client testifies and the court concludes that the client was lying). *See* Robert D. Dinerstein, *A Meditation on the Theoretics of Practice*, 43 HASTINGS L.J. 971, 974 n.10 (1992) (describing phenomenon in adult criminal case). *See also* the discussion in Chapter 2 ("Connection Across Difference and Similarity"), in the section on Criminal Dispute Options.

31. *See* MODEL RULES, supra note 9, R. 4.2, Communication with Person Represented by Counsel ("In representing a client, a lawyer shall not communicate about the subject of the representation with a person the lawyer knows to be represented by another lawyer in the matter, unless the lawyer has the consent of the other lawyer or is authorized to do so by law or a court order.").

32. *See, e.g.,* Abbe Smith, *'I Ain't Takin' No Plea': The Challenges in Counseling Young People Facing Serious Time*, 60 RUTGERS L. REV. 11, 18–21 (2007); Laura Cohen & Randi Mandelbaum, *Kids Will Be Kids: Creating a Framework for Interviewing and Counseling Adolescent Clients*, 79 TEMP. L. REV. 357 (2006); Kristin Henning, *Loyalty, Paternalism, and Rights: Client Counseling Theory and the Role of Child's Counsel in Delinquency Cases*, 81 NOTRE DAME L. REV. 245, 270–74 (2005); Elizabeth S. Scott, et al., *Evaluating Adolescent Decision Making in Legal Contexts*, 19 L. & HUM. BEH. 221 (1995). See *Roper v. Simmons*, 543 U.S. 551, 569–70 (2005) (banning the death penalty for juveniles under the age of 18, based on juveniles' lack of maturity and underdeveloped sense of responsibility (leading to a greater propensity to engage in impetuous actions); when compared to adults, their greater susceptibility to "negative influences and outside pressures, especially peer pressure"; and that their characters are not fully formed and their personality traits are less fixed).

33. Henning, *supra* note 32, at 272.

34. *Id.,* 272–73; *see* Emily Buss, *"You're My What?" The Problems of Children's Misperceptions of Their Lawyers' Roles,* 64 FORDHAM L. REV. 1699 (1996).

35. *See Special Issue on Legal Representation of Children: Proceedings of the UNLV Conference on Representing Children in Families: Children's Advocacy and Justice Ten Years After Fordham: Recommendations of the Conference,* 6 NEV. L.J. 592, 592–93 (2006) ("Effective representation requires attorneys to be self-aware and respectful of the full context in which the client lives.").

36. *Id.,* 593–94. *See also* Smith, *supra* note 32, at 25; Cohen & Mandelbaum, *supra* note 32, at 411.

37. See Chapter 2 ("Connection Across Difference and Similarity"), Criminal Dispute Options, discussing the decision whether to testify. Not covered in this dialogue is whether, as a practical matter, the client might need to testify in order to present her story to the trier of fact. That would depend, of course, on the nature of the other evidence likely to be submitted in the case.

38. Moreover, as Abbe Smith points out, in Smith, *supra* note 32, at 23 n.43, gaining additional time might be important in the lawyer's efforts to get her client to consider her options fully (and to see the wisdom of the lawyer's advice), especially if the decisions are "weighty ones."

39. In juvenile delinquency proceedings, the vast majority of commentators (not to mention professional standards, statutory and case law) argue that the lawyer's role is to represent the client's expressed interests, and not the adolescent client's best interest. However, in practice, many lawyers for juveniles continue to act paternalistically toward their clients and use more of a best interest model of representation. *See* Henning, *supra* n.32, at 246, 255–56. *See also,* Annette Ruth Appell, *Representing Children Representing What?: Critical Reflections on Lawyering for Children,* 39 COLUM. HUMAN RIGHTS L. REV. 573, 634 (2008) (many attorneys continue to use best interest approach, especially in child welfare and custody proceedings).

40. *See, e.g.,* BINDER ET AL., *supra* note 1, at 250, 262.

41. *See* Katherine Hunt Federle, *The Ethics of Empowerment: Rethinking the Role of Lawyers in Interviewing and Counseling the Child Client,* 64 FORDHAM L. REV. 1655, 1689 (1996) (suggesting that lawyers for adolescents provide clear explanations, use concrete language, explain confidentiality, and use active listening and empathy). *See also,* the extensive discussion of various aspects of legal representation of children in two symposia: *Proceedings of the Conference on Ethical Issues in the Legal Representation of Children: Recommendations of the Conference,* 64 FORDHAM L. REV. 1301 (1996) (Fordham Conference) and *Special Issue on Legal Representation of Children: Proceedings of the UNLV Conference on Representing Children in Families: Children's Advocacy and Justice Ten Years After Fordham: Recommendations of the Conference,* 6 NEV. L.J. 592 (2006) (UNLV CONFERENCE). The Fordham Conference attendees adopted a series of recommendations, including ones related to "The Obligations of Lawyers for Children in Interviewing and Counseling." Fordham Conference, at 1302–08. Among other things, the conferees urged the lawyer to use developmentally appropriate language; establish rapport with the client; use concrete examples when discussing the case and provide a roadmap to the client for how the interview and case will likely proceed; use appropriate, culturally competent listening techniques and provide nonjudgmental support; explain the role of the lawyer, confidentiality, and the court process; explain the options and their consequences available to the client; and provide the client with ample time to make the decision.

42. This counseling dialogue also reflects some aspects of engaged client-centered counseling, as discussed in the previous chapter. In particular, the lawyer here does not simply throw the problem into the client's lap but rather offers both emotional support and a structure designed to help the client make a decision.

43. Representation of children in legal proceedings is a complex subject that raises a range of considerations that go beyond the scope of this chapter. For a very thorough exploration of representation of children in child protective settings, *see* JEAN KOH PETERS, REPRESENTING CHILDREN IN CHILD PROTECTIVE PROCEEDINGS: ETHICAL AND PRACTICAL DIMENSIONS (3d ed. 2007). Our goal here is simply to alert you to the need to examine relevant differences when considering how to interview and counsel clients who vary, perhaps significantly, from the adult client of average cognitive capacity and emotional maturity.

44. As noted in Comment 1 to MODEL RULE 1.14, Client with Diminished Capacity, even if there is a question of whether a child can be considered a "normal client" for purposes of guiding the lawyer, "a client with diminished capacity often has the ability to understand, deliberate upon, and reach conclusions about matters affecting the client's own well-being. For example, children as young as five or six years of age, and certainly those of ten or twelve, are regarded as having opinions that are entitled to weight in legal proceedings concerning their custody." R.1.14 cmt. [1]. Nevertheless, scholars have noted the less-than-helpful nature of the guidance Rule 1.14

provides for lawyers for children. *See* KOH PETERS, *supra* note 38, at 28–30 (citing numerous sources).

45.   *See* KOH PETERS, *supra* note 43, at Appendix B, 663 et seq. ("best interests" model in general continues to dominate in U.S. jurisdictions). When such a best interest role is not compelled, many commentators recommend that the lawyer represent the client's expressed interests, the traditional role of the lawyer. *See* Fordham Conference, *supra* n.37, at 1301 ("The lawyer for a child who is not impaired ... must allow the child to set the goals of the representation as would an adult client."); UNLV Conference, *supra* note 41, at 609 ("Children's attorneys should take their direction from the client and should not substitute for the child's wishes the attorney's own judgment of what is best for children or for that child.").

46.   Appell, *supra* note 39, at 595.

47.   KOH PETERS, *supra* note 43. *See* Cohen & Mandelbaum, *supra* note 32, at 378 et seq. (discussing Jean Koh Peters's work). Martin Guggenheim, *Counseling Counsel for Children*, 97 MICH. L. REV. 1488 (1999) (book review of JEAN KOH PETERS, REPRESENTING CHILDREN IN CHILD CUSTODY PROCEEDINGS: ETHICAL AND PRACTICAL DIMENSIONS (1st ed. 1997)).

48.   Koh Peters advocates five principles of action planning when counseling child clients about their available options and their choices: action planning should begin where the child is and should lead in the direction the child wants to go; the counseling process should concretely link legal requirements with the client's available options; the counseling process should incorporate methods that are meaningful and also constructive for the client; be as clear as you can possibly be, but no clearer; counsel the child about her own best interests. *Id.* at 368–85. Koh Peters goes on to identify additional steps lawyers should take when statutorily required to use a best interests approach, when the client cannot formulate an informed wish, or when the client cannot act in her own interests. These involve having the lawyer engage in interdisciplinary learning through a variety of possible means, return to the child to explain her remaining options; argue for all remaining and against all rejected options, and inform the decision-maker of the child's wishes. *Id.* at 385–96.

49.   *See* UNLV Conference, *supra* note 41, at 598 (importance for lawyers for children of engaging in multidisciplinary practice); Koh Peters, *supra* n.43, at 132 (importance of interdisciplinary learning).

50.   *See, e.g.,* Erica Wood, *Effective Counseling of Older Clients: The Attorney–Client Relationship* 6 (Comm'n on Legal Probs. of the Elderly of the ABA and Legal Counsel for the Elderly, Inc.1995) (estimating that 60% of Americans over 65, and 90% of Americans over 80, have some degree of hearing impairment); *see also* Lawrence A. Frolik & Melissa C. Brown, ADVISING THE ELDERLY OR DISABLED CLIENT (1997), Ch. 3., Overview of Common Mental and Physical Impairments.

51.   Wood, *supra* note 50, at 2.

52.   *Id.*

53.   *See* Peter Margulies, *Access, Connection, and Voice: A Contextual Approach to Representing Senior Citizens of Questionable Capacity*, 62 FORDHAM L. REV. 1073, 1085 (1994) (arguing for assessment of following elements in determining capacity: ability to articulate reasoning behind decision; variability of state of mind; appreciation of consequences of decision; irreversibility of decision; substantive fairness of transaction; and consistency with lifetime commitments).

54.   *See* Chapter 7 ("Engaging in Moral Dialogue").

55.   Michael Perlin has written extensively about the importance of zealous advocacy for clients in the civil commitment context. *See, e.g.,* Perlin, *supra* note 13.

56.   *See generally,* MICHAEL L. PERLIN ET AL., LAWYERING SKILLS IN THE REPRESENTATION OF PERSONS WITH MENTAL DISABILITIES (2006), esp. Ch. 2, "Interviewing and Counseling Your Client." Perlin, in a series of articles, has coined the term "sanism" for the prevalence of irrational prejudice against people with disabilities, a prejudice similar to racism, sexism and homophobia, but which often is not recognized. *See id.* at 54 & n.35 (citing articles).

57.   *See, e.g.,* UNLV Conference, *supra* note 41, at 593–94.

58.   See the discussion of real listening in Section B. of Chapter 2 ("Connection Across Difference and Similarity"). *See also,* Section D.2, of Chapter 2, Hindering Concerns in the Attorney–Client Relationship, Whats up with me? Self reflection by the attorney (discussing the need to connect with clients across apparent differences).

59.   MODEL RULE R. 1.14 (a), *supra* note 9.

60.   *Id.*, R. 1.14 (b).

61.   The appointment of a guardian, guardian ad litem, or conservator is a matter of state law, and a lawyer would need to consult the relevant state statutes and regulations in determining how to proceed with seeking such an appointment. *See* Nancy J. Knauer, *Defining Capacity: Balancing the Competing Interests of Autonomy and Need*, 12 TEMP. POL. & CIV. RTS. L. REV. 321, 334–35 (2003). The National Conference of Commissioners on Uniform State Laws has adopted a Uniform Guardianship and Protective Proceedings Act (first adopted in 1982 and significantly revised in 1997), which as of June 2009 six states had adopted. *See generally,* Rebecca C. Morgan, *Introduction: The Uniform Guardianship and Protective Proceedings Act of 1997—Ten Years of Developments*, 37 STETSON L. REV. 1 (2007).

62. MODEL RULE R. 1.14, *supra* note 9, cmt. [4] (emphasis added).

63. *Id.*, R. 1.14, cmt. [2].

64. Such as, for example, if an individual with an intellectual disability who lives in an institution seeks to move into a community residence, and the guardian objects.

65. *See generally* Laurence Frolik, *Is a Guardian the Alter Ego of the Ward?*, 37 STETSON L. REV. 53 (2007); Rebecca C. Morgan, *Who is the Client? Ethical Issues in an Elder Law* Practice, 16 J. AM. ACAD. MATRIM. LAW 463 (2000); *Ethical Issues in Representing Older Clients*, 62 FORDHAM L. REV. 961 (1994); Margulies, *supra* note 53; Mark Falk, *Ethical Considerations in Representing the Elderly*, 36 S.D. L. REV. 54 (1991); Tremblay, *supra* note 13.

66. See *supra* note 55 and accompanying text. A lawyer might seek such "rights-maximizing" solutions in other areas as well, especially where important liberty interests are at stake. *See, e.g.,* UNLV Conference, *supra* note 41, at 610 ("When the child has diminished capacity, the child's attorney should promote client-directed representation by: i. Adopting a position requiring the least intrusive state intervention.").

67. *See* MODEL RULE R. 1.14, *supra* note 9, cmt. [5]. THE RESTATEMENT (THIRD) OF THE LAW GOVERNING LAWYERS adopts the substituted judgment standard as well. In Section 24 (2), it states: "A lawyer representing a client with diminished capacity as described in Subsection (1) and for whom no guardian or other representative is available to act, must, with respect to a matter within the scope of the representation, pursue the lawyer's reasonable view of the client's objectives or interests as the client would define them if able to make adequately considered decisions on the matter, even if the client expresses no wishes or gives contrary instructions."

68. UNLV Conference, *supra* note 41, at 609.

69. The National Conference of Commissioners on Uniform State Laws, in the prefatory note to its Uniform Guardianship and Protective Proceedings Act (1997), at iii, emphasizes that general or plenary guardianship should be the last resort for an individual, and that, when a guardian is appropriately appointed, the guardian must consider the incapacitated person's "expressed desires and personal values when making decisions."

CHAPTER 5

NARRATIVE THEORY AND NARRATIVE PRACTICES

■ ■ ■

A. INTRODUCTION: WHY NARRATIVE?

Throughout their relationships, lawyers and clients tell stories to each other. In the activities we know as interviewing and counseling, lawyers and clients create evolving narratives, often rooted in or beginning from particular events, moments in the clients' relationships, or the clients' participation in activities and organizations.[1] Clients usually come to lawyers for help: they have identified a problem; been subjected to legal action or state intrusion; or want to structure a relationship or further an activity or enterprise that is part of their lives. They have stories to tell that express their reasons for, hesitation or excitement about, and fear of whatever prompted their need for legal help. Lawyers devote time, energy, and thought to listening carefully to their clients, trying to understand what has happened to them, what they want, how they approach the decisions they face, and the possibilities for achieving their desires.[2] In the course of clients' narratives, lawyers hear how particular experiences and choices relate to complicated and diverse aspects of clients' lives and the worlds they inhabit. As they listen and work to understand a client's world, lawyers cannot help but interpret that world as they connect events and evaluate meaning. With their own understanding, they engage with clients who are situated in relationships, communities, organizations, and institutions—with people who identify themselves in shifting and over-lapping ways. Lawyers react emotionally and cognitively to what they hear, ask questions, respond to clients' behaviors and stories, consult with clients, and take action.[3]

Lawyers also tell stories to clients—about themselves; about lawyers, judges, legal institutions and other actors in the legal system; about the law and multiple interpretations of it;[4] about the context within which the law operates; about consequences that may flow from invocation or application of law and the operation of institutions; and about the parameters of the relationship between lawyers and clients. As lawyers listen to and help construct narratives within the lawyer-client relationship, they also consider and formulate the variety of narratives that they will present to others through all aspects of the representation.[5] Like clients, lawyers, too, are situated in relationships, communities, organizations and institutions and identify themselves in shifting and overlapping ways. Unlike most clients, however, lawyers also react to and shape their identities as legal professionals, subject to norms and rules embedded in the complexity of multiple aspects of legal culture. Clients listen to these law stories and work to understand them and the meaning of the law for their lives, trying to make sense of how their own problems relate to the world of the law and lawyers. As they try to comprehend this world, clients inevitably interpret law and lawyers, organizing the information they hear, bringing their own understanding to the evolving narrative.

In each interaction between lawyers and clients, the stories of both intersect, each penetrating and shaping the story of the other.[6] The narratives that develop out of the interactions not only reflect what each brings to the relationship, but also shape the understanding each has as they move forward.[7] These narratives of lawyers and clients may coincide or diverge during the representation in different ways at different points, some explicit and others implicit. Depending upon the needs of a legal matter, the dynamics of the representation, the impact of others on the lawyer-client relationship, or events in the world, the congruence between the narratives of lawyers and clients shifts and the divergence may or may not be of consequence.[8] As clients and lawyers engage through reciprocal and interconnected narratives, they create the lawyer-client relationship.

Throughout this book, we approach the lawyer-client relationship mostly through an understanding of interviewing and counseling. These frameworks help to differentiate stages or aspects of a lawyer's work. Theories about the lawyering process also create useful concepts for identifying and analyzing practices and developing skills that contribute to good legal practice. We scrutinize throughout the book critical issues raised by these lawyering concepts and practices. In this chapter, we consider how narrative understanding of the relationship between lawyers and clients contributes new insights that expand our theories about lawyering. This parallel framework derived from narrative theory helps us shape new practices that contribute to engaged client-centered lawyering.[9] In approaching the representation as stories told back and forth, lawyers can create new ways, grounded in narrative theory, to explore and understand the substance of the problem with which a client seeks help.[10] Narrative practices, when carefully attentive to the principles of narrative theory that guide considering the accounts of another, can help lawyers find entry points into the complex process of constructing and reconstructing their understanding of the world of another. By entering that world with narrative understanding, lawyers may better grasp the substance of a client's problem. Thus, using narrative theory, lawyers can draw upon an enlarged repertoire of practices, ones that in particular highlight the complexities of the content of clients' stories, to complement practices developed from the more traditional constructs based in our theories of interviewing and counseling.

Examining client narratives that grow within and extend throughout the lawyer-client relationship can yield insight into clients' experiences, identities, values, and modes of reaching decisions, as well as the context of clients' lives.[11] With narrative understanding, lawyers can develop varied and imaginative ways to decipher the stories they hear. Using the practices derived from narrative theory, lawyers can think in new ways about the trajectories that bring clients to them and the accounts of what has happened. They can delve into the scenarios that shape what clients want to communicate and the dynamics driving the reasons that communication matters. They can explore differently clients' wishes for their interactions with lawyers and their encounters with the legal system. As lawyers inquire about how clients imagine achieving their desires, they free their own imaginative understanding about the matters at stake as clients face and make decisions.[12] With this understanding, lawyers can gain new insight into the worlds of their clients as they encounter those worlds through their connections to and involvement in their clients' stories. Similarly, as lawyers acknowledge that clients assimilate lawyers' narratives, they can appreciate clients' efforts to incorporate the often new and strange stories of the world of the law.

In addition, by seeing their own participation in the creation of narratives within the lawyer-client relationship, lawyers have new ways to attend to their own reconstructions of clients' narratives—their role, through their interactions with clients, in the construction of clients' narratives. They gain new ways to approach the narratives of law, lawyers and legal institutions that they and their clients shape throughout the representation.[13] As these multiple narratives unfold, lawyers can assess how their contributions to the evolving narratives reveal their own assumptions and judgments, evaluate the impact on their clients of their own reframing of the narratives, and consider how their encounters with their clients' stories reshape their own stories about themselves, about the law and legal institutions, and about the world.[14]

Recasting the relationship between lawyers and clients in terms of reciprocal storytelling proceeds through the analysis and development of an interaction of two student lawyers with their client, Janice Woods. Through the evolution of this relationship, we elucidate some basic concepts of narrative theory, we identify practices for lawyers rooted in that theory, and we suggest some implications of a narrative approach for thinking broadly about the lawyer-client relationship.

To lay the groundwork for these narrative practices, we begin with two important aspects of a narrative approach to relationships between lawyers and clients. First, we examine the implications of narrative thinking for shaping how lawyers structure and approach interactions with clients. Second, we highlight three basic components of lawyers' narrative listening: listening for stories rather than facts; listening for the reasons clients and lawyers tell their stories; and remaining aware of expectations in listening to each other. With that foundation, we proceed to identify two types of narrative practices by expanding upon and varying the dialogue between the students and Ms. Woods. In each moment of the evolving dialogue, we examine a narrative concept and show how it can inform particular inquiries and responses. The first set of practices draws upon the elements and structure of clients' stories as a basis for disassembling a client's account to develop a deep and nuanced understanding of it. The second set singles out recurring practices lawyers can use as they engage in the process of interpreting and ascribing tentative meanings to clients' evolving stories. Finally, we look back on that interaction as narratively understood to explore some implications for understanding relationships between lawyers and clients.

B. REVISITING THE STORY OF JANICE WOODS: NARRATIVE POSSIBILITIES AND NARRATIVE PRACTICES

In the chapter introducing the themes of the book, a dialogue illustrates the beginning of a lawyer-client relationship. Two students, Karen Davies and Mark Corbett, have come to meet with Janice Woods, who is living temporarily with her young son in her sister Laura Stevens's apartment. Through examining that beginning of a lawyer-client relationship in our own beginning of this book, we announced the themes we find that continue throughout relationships between lawyers and clients: context, connection, the fluidity of client identity, ethics, and the lawyer's openness of mind.[15] We now revisit through narrative theory this dialogue, an account of a brief and early piece of a relationship, to explore how this different way to frame our understanding of the lawyer-client relationship yields possibilities that further the development of that relationship. With this expansion of our theories through which lawyers approach and interpret the lawyer-client relationship and our identification of new practices, we identify new ways of practicing engaged client-centered lawyering.

From the perspective of frameworks for interviewing and counseling, this interaction between clinical students, inevitably novice lawyers, and a possible new client presents what we think of as the preliminaries of an interview: the introductions, the greetings, and the initial entry into the matter.[16] While lawyering theory highlights how these interactions matter because they signal important characteristics of lawyers' attitudes toward clients and can set a tone or give a feel to the relationship before the participants have begun to discuss the subject matter of the visit,[17] narrative theory reveals how the process of narrative construction has already begun. Through the evolving narratives of lawyer and client, the student lawyers begin constructing their relationship with their client and discovering the contours and meaning of the matter that brings them together. We start our exploration of narrative theory by revisiting this dialogue and using it to demonstrate alternative narrative possibilities for developing the relationship.

Karen Davies and Mark Corbett, two students in a clinical program, arrive at 4:00 p.m. at the home of Laura Stevens to meet with Ms. Stevens's sister, Janice Woods.

Laura Stevens:	Hello. You must be the students from the law school. Janice said you would be here about now.
Karen Davies (L1):	Yes, I'm Karen Davies and this is my partner, Mark Corbett.
Mark Corbett (L2):	Thank you so much for having us.
Laura Stevens:	No trouble at all. Janice told me that she didn't feel up to going out—and I agree with her, she shouldn't—and I really wanted her to meet with you. Things are kind of cramped here, with all of us in just these four rooms, but I'm sure we'll manage. I'll go get Janice out of bed. She's still pretty weak.

[Janice Woods enters the living room/dining room
area, holding onto her sister's arm.]

Karen Davies (L3):	Hello, Ms. Woods. We spoke on the phone. I'm Karen Davies and this is my partner Mark Corbett. I'm glad to meet you.
Mark Corbett (L4):	Good afternoon.
Janice Woods (C1):	Thanks for coming here. I know it's pretty far for you. I just wasn't up to traveling. Here, have a seat.

[As Karen Davies and Mark Corbett sit on the couch, Janice Woods sits in the chair to Mark Corbett's right and Laura Stevens sits on the chair to Karen Davies's left. Three children run into the room.]

Janice Woods (C2):	Kevin, come here and meet our guests. [Turning to Karen Davies and Mark Corbett] This is my son, Kevin. He's three. He's been staying here with my sister and her kids since I went into the hospital. That's Raquel and Martin—they're 4 and 7.
Kevin Woods:	Hi. Bye. [Kisses his mother on the cheek]
Mark Corbett (L5):	It looks like he has better things to do than talk to us.
Janice Woods (C3):	He never stops moving. I love to see him so happy.
Karen Davies (L6):	He sure seems to like playing with his cousins.
Laura Stevens:	Yeah. They like to take care of him. Though sometimes they all get carried away.
Karen Davies (L7):	Ms. Woods, Laurence Borders from Memorial Hospital called us to say you might be calling—that he had referred you—but he didn't talk to us about why. He sometimes refers his patients to the law clinic. He seems like a very concerned guy. Not so many people like that in hospitals these days—who take the time. You said on the phone that he suggested you call. What can we do for you?
Mark Corbett (L8):	Before we start, Ms. Woods—I know this may seem kind of strange, but it might be important that we talk just to you.

Janice Woods (C4):   Laura can stay. Anyway, she's really the one who pushed me to follow up on Mr. Borders's suggestion. Also, she knows a lot of what's been going on.

[Kevin, Raquel and Martin all come over.]

Martin Stevens: Aunt Janice, Kevin won't listen to me. He says he's allowed to have a cookie in the afternoon, and I said it's almost dinner time. He keeps trying to get into the cabinet where the cookies are.

Janice Woods (C5):   Kevin, listen to Martin. Dinner will be soon.

Kevin Woods: It's not fair. I get bossed around by Martin just because he's older and it's his house. I want to go home. [Crawls into his mother's lap; Martin and Raquel go into the kitchen.]

Karen Davies (L9):   Going back to what we were saying about talking to you—I know it's pretty inconvenient and might seem odd to you, but we need to talk with you about whether anyone else should be present. You see, it has to do with our being able to keep what you tell us private, if you want us to. As your lawyers, we have a duty to keep your secrets. Also, we can't be made to reveal almost anything you don't want us to—but that protection can be damaged if other people have heard our conversation.

Janice Woods (C6):   I don't really understand what you're telling me. And there's no place for Laura to go in this apartment—there's just the two bedrooms and the kitchen—and you can hear everything through the walls. And, as I said, she's the one who wants me to talk to you anyway.

Laura Stevens: Janice, I have an idea. These nice people came all the way out here to meet with you, and they say maybe I shouldn't be here when you talk to them. They can talk to me later if they want. I'll take the kids to the playground for a while. Come on, Kevin, Martin, Raquel.

Kevin Woods: I don't want to go to the playground. I want to stay with Mommy.

Laura Stevens: Come on, Kevin. Let's see if we can find some ice cream to have for dessert.

[Laura Stevens leaves with the three children.]

Mark Corbett (L10):   Sorry for all the disruption, Ms. Woods. If you want, we can explain more about why it makes a difference for us to talk to you alone. Or we can talk about how you think we might be able to help you.

Janice Woods (C7):   Let's just talk about why everyone wanted me to call. I was in the hospital because my husband beat me up. I got a broken rib and a concussion. And my blood pressure got very high. So they kept me in the hospital for a couple days. As you know, Kevin stayed with

	my sister. But I don't know if there's anything you can do to help. Jerome hasn't bothered me or Kevin since I went to the hospital. I haven't heard from him or seen him. Both Mr. Borders and Laura have been pushing me to bring criminal charges or to get a protective order. But I'm really worried about both those things. And my house. I don't know what's right.
Karen Davies (L11):	No doubt, you're going to have really hard choices to make. And I don't know if we'll be able to help or not. Here are some of the things we can do. We can get more information from you about what has been happening. We can help you identify things that might be useful in your situation and give you information about those that you find helpful. We can work with you to figure out what you would like to have happen, and then do as much as possible to help make that happen. You can decide at any point what you want our involvement to be.
Janice Woods (C8):	Like I said, I don't know if any of this talking is worth much, but I promised Laura I would at least think through what I can do. Ask me whatever you want.
Mark Corbett (L12):	Let's begin with the things that happened when you ended up in the hospital. It seems like they were pretty serious.

While much more will happen in this meeting, we approach these early moments not just as a preliminary stage to the real business of the meeting, but as the beginning of the creation of multiple narratives through which Ms. Woods, Karen Davies and Mark Corbett will constitute their relationship and shape their understanding of the legal problem that is the subject of their relationship. Therefore, we analyze this slice of the developing relationship between the student lawyers and their client through the concepts of narrative theory. This narrative frame suggests several practices that may help Karen Davies and Mark Corbett in their quest to help Ms. Woods find her way through the situation she faces and to learn if and how their work as lawyers with access to the law and legal institutions might make a difference in Ms. Woods's efforts to move her life forward in the way she wants.[18]

C. NARRATIVE AND THE STRUCTURE OF THE CONVERSATION

In lawyering theories of interviewing, this dialogue portrays the preliminary phase of an interview, including attention to ethical issues implicated by the presence of others within the interview space. Karen Davies and Mark Corbett meet their potential client, her son, and other important members of her family at the home of their client's sister. They interact with her around her family, her living situation, the meeting site and the events that led her to call them. They also prominently and mysteriously, from the perspective of the other people in the apartment, address ethical issues, which loom large for them, generated by the complexities of other people being in the apartment during their meeting. By reaching out to Ms. Woods to respond to the difficulties of her situation, Mark Corbett and Karen Davies, who are novice lawyers, now confront a setting that diverges from the paradigm of the lawyer's office and find themselves somewhat flustered about how to deal with the awkwardness of the situation and how to interpret and apply the rules governing their ethical obligations.[19]

Laura Stevens saves them from having to wend their way through the ethical terrain and Mark Corbett and Karen Davies have an interview setting that comports with their default understanding of the ethical regime. They recover, attempting to reestablish the rapport engendered by their coming to the apartment, by acknowledging that their concerns may seem odd and that they have caused a "disruption."[20] Mark Corbett asks Ms. Woods if she wants to understand what all the fuss was about or wants to get to the reason she had them come. Mark Corbett and Karen Davies have taken upon themselves to raise the issues about who should be present. Realizing that their decision has created problems, they ask whether Ms. Woods wants to know more about an issue that, for the students, implicates their professional role. While Mark Corbett and Karen Davies's worries have dominated the dynamics, they now seek to let Ms. Woods shape the direction of the interview.[21]

Narrative theory suggests still another dimension of Mark Corbett and Karen Davies's interaction. They have established a structure for listening and talking to the client. While this structure emerges for them from both a set of ethical rules regarding confidences and privileges and common professional practices, the resulting interview setting also defines a space in which the only story teller is Ms. Woods, the client, and the only listeners are Mark Corbett and Karen Davies, the lawyers.[22] While the legal rules realize a set of policies about who are the correct participants in the legally-bounded discussion, narrative theory alerts lawyers that they must attend to how this structure may have consequences for their relationship with their client and for the story that emerges. This structure may promote intimacy or engender distrust; it may foster the communication of certain information and expression of emotion while submerging other material.[23] Narrative theory reveals how, from the very beginning, the story that emerges is bound up with the structure within which narratives unfold. Unlike the ethical rules, narrative theory does not have a default preference for a dialogue between lawyer and client, which lawyers can work around when needed and appropriate; instead, it alerts lawyers to the consequences for the narrative of having different participants in it.[24]

Narrative theory presents the possibility of a somewhat different intervention. When Mark Corbett first introduces the subject of talking just to Ms. Woods alone and Karen Davies follows up with a brief explanation of the concepts of confidentiality and privilege, they are, quite appropriately, thinking about their ethical obligations. They might, with their client's story in mind, have proceeded this way:

Mark Corbett (L1): I know this may be hard to work out here, but we'd like to understand if you'd like us to help by listening first just to you.

Ms Woods might have responded just as she did:

Janice Woods (C1): Laura can stay. Anyway, she's really the one who pushed me to follow up on Mr. Borders's suggestion. Also, she knows a lot of what's been going on.

After Laura Stevens's interaction with the children, Karen Davies could then follow up with Ms. Woods's story at the forefront.

Karen Davies (L2): Your sister might have important information for us to hear and Laurence Borders, too; but, if it's ok with you, we'd like to hear everything first as you experienced it. Also, what you tell your lawyer gets special protection and things get more complicated if other people are there. But, if you want to tell us while your sister's here, we can figure out how to deal with the rules. It's up to you.

While the reframing of the need to structure the dialogue around listening to the client ends in the same place and the ethical rules still matter, Mark Corbett and Karen Davies have introduced the idea that they want to hear how the client tells her story, not just to follow rules for lawyers. The more Ms. Woods asserts that her sister has prompted the meeting, Mark Corbett and Karen Davies become more attentive to a dynamic that might be influencing the request for the meeting, as well as the story itself. They do not use the ethical rules as a surrogate for their early sense that hearing the story from Ms. Woods matters. Instead, they single her out for their attention.

D. NARRATIVE LISTENING

Having created a structure for the conversation, Karen Davies and Mark Corbett now need to listen. This initial scene with Janice Woods reveals the complexity of that process. While lawyering theory provides one way to approach listening, narrative theory reveals other ways to hear what clients recount.[25] We will revisit Karen Davies and Mark Corbett's discussion with Ms. Woods to see how they might have listened differently and been able to frame questions based on that listening, but first we identify some basic narrative concepts and practices that create an alternative framework.

1. HEARING STORIES NOT FACTS

Narrative theory directs lawyers to attend to stories as distinct from collecting facts. Rather than approaching a client's account as presenting discrete pieces of information, lawyers can listen for the different components of a story, arranged in different ways. These arrangements give meaning to the discrete facts through their placement in the overall story, their relationship to other facts, their salience to the overall thrust of the story, or their emotional resonance. Lawyers always listen to client stories but usually define this activity as learning the facts, or, for certain purposes, the client's understanding of the facts. Narrative concepts provide a different and more self-consciously differentiated way of listening. Narratives have essential features—elements and structure—that provide a framework for listening.[26] From the very beginning of representation, most obviously throughout interviewing but also in the many accounts that emerge in all stages of counseling, lawyers can listen to and interpret the accounts they hear in light of the elements of narrative and the structure that connects the elements to form a story. By identifying the elements and structure of a client's story, lawyers have additional ways to explore its meaning for the teller and the listener and to suggest questions about its construction and dynamics. With this narrative framework, lawyers learn about the substance of the matter that is the focus of the representation, as well as the meaning for the client of the representation itself.

a. Elements of Narrative

Narrative theory, within its multiple strands, points to basic elements of narrative that recur throughout storytelling. While this list is hardly exhaustive, we take some narrative elements to craft devices for lawyers both to listen better and question more astutely. 1) Client stories have a setting or multiple settings that may ground the account or reveal the context within which a client's problem develops. 2) Characters, whether they be human or human-like, who hold beliefs, have feelings and are in relationships with each other, make appearances, both major and minor.[27] 3) These characters proceed with motives or purposes, sometimes in conflict, that may drive the story. 4) Perhaps most comfortably, lawyers pay attention to the acts that the characters perform. 5) Focusing on acts, however, can obscure another element of stories—agency. The instruments through which action occurs (what or who makes things happen in a story) can matter as much or more than the sequence of acts or the presence of actors. 6) Clients' emotions, whether proclaimed or suppressed, often convey a mood or sensibility to a story and shape a client's understanding of experience.

b. Structures to Narratives

Narratives also cohere. Each has its structure rooted in plot or relationships. Plot provides one organizing force.[28] Characters pursue their purposes within the temporal framework of a scene, with a beginning, middle and end. These beginnings, middles and ends, however, get their definition from the meaning of the story the client intends to convey rather than from chronological time.[29] Events unfold within this relatively stable plot structure constructed by the client.[30] While plot may provide the unifying dynamic of narrative, relationships may, too. The role of relationships in narrative is often more than as an aspect of the characters. Along with the trajectory of events that constitute a plot, relationships can exert a unifying force with an analogous structure that drives the unfolding of the story. As they listen for the elements of narrative, lawyers can also listen for its structure, in terms of both plot and relationships rather than relying solely or even primarily on the legal elements of potential claims to guide them in listening for salient information.

The stories of problems that clients bring to lawyers have a steady state that expresses the client's sense of the legitimacy and ordinariness of the situation.[31] While that background state of things may not be pleasant or desirable, or even stable, it reflects the status quo, the accepted way that things are, that the client takes for granted.[32] The disruption of that state often brings a client to a lawyer. Usually some trouble has caused the disruption. Sometimes, a client has already attempted to redress or transform the disruption, usually not completely satisfactorily or else the client would not have come to a lawyer. The client's narrative may contain within it an explicit or implicit vision of whether the client would like restoration of the old steady state or transformation into a new one. And, often, a client's narrative carries with it a coda—a message, a theme, a moral, a meaning that the client attaches to the narrative, that makes the story seem relevant to the present and the future[33] and that may connect the client's own story to others in the world.

c.   Deciphering Narratives

Identifying the elements and seeing how they get combined to structure clients' narratives, lawyers can expand their capacity to listen differently and find new ways to respond. These essential features of narrative—the elements and the structure—along with the ways to explore and interpret them, provide both a tentative framework to re-conceive the activities in the relationship between lawyers and clients and actual practices for engagement between lawyer and client. Each element and the relationships among them, as well as each aspect of the unfolding narrative structure, present possibilities for listening to clients' accounts in a different way. They also yield possibilities for shaping inquiries, guiding imagination, and pursuing interpretations. Lawyers would never have the time nor inclination to pursue every element nor every aspect of a story's structure.[34] Presumably because stories do cohere, these essential components of narrative offer not checklists for analyzing accounts, but multiple entry points for listening and questioning that likely lead back to similar places. Thus, these features of narrative give lawyers a kind of tiered listening prompting them not to gather facts but to use multiple features of narrative simultaneously to identify how a client's account reveals (or perhaps disguises) what problem the client has and what the client wants.

d. Re–Conceiving Facts

The differences between learning the facts and listening for narrative matter. When we describe what we hear from a client as the facts, we are in danger of giving the client's account too much fixity.[35] Every new piece of information that is added, every new individual who appears, every new event that is recounted can seem like a change in the facts. The deletion of information, people, and events can have the same effect. No matter how much the lawyer knows and anticipates these changes, the notion of the facts of the case carries with it a kind of solidity or boundedness. Replacing the concept of learning the facts with narrative listening builds the idea of change into the process. In everyday life, every time anyone tells a story, it is a little different.[36] We find it remarkable, and perhaps even a little suspicious or troubling, when someone tells a story in exactly the same way, every time, to every person.[37] Thus, a narrative framework normalizes changes in a client's accounts.

Also, when lawyers identify, either orally or in writing, the facts of the case within the confines of the lawyer-client relationship, as in a memo to the file about a client interview, they engage inevitably in multiple forms of interpretation, conscious and unconscious, intentional and unintentional, of the client's account. They interpret the client's interpretation of the client's experience as recounted to the lawyer. Again, no matter how conscious the lawyer is of the inevitability of this layered interpretive process, he or she constantly runs up against the supposed solidity of facts. No matter how schooled in the indeterminacy and uncertainty of facts, lawyers must self-consciously evaluate urges, both in themselves and within the legal world, to have relatively stable definitions of the facts of the case, even if those accounts are in competition or tension with each other.[38]

Operating in a legal world in which the relative determinacy, as opposed to the indeterminacy, can matter enormously, lawyers' desire for certainty is often particularly strong. Something happened and they need to find reasonably stable places within an account in order to make innumerable decisions about how to proceed.[39] The process of interpretation of the facts is not only inevitable but a major advocacy tool of the lawyer in constructing a case theory, writing a pleading, making an argument, developing a negotiation strategy or in countless other settings. However, it may feel more problematic in the setting of the lawyer-client relationship, when changes in or recastings of accounts can carry many meanings, sometimes attached to complicated feelings between lawyer and client.

Narrative listening provides a construct for a lawyer's own framing of a client's account that can incorporate the interpretive process and also provide lawyers a vantage point from which to examine the emotions generated in the lawyer by changing narratives. Lawyers who self-consciously discriminate between recording the facts and re-telling a story are more likely to be aware of the futility, if not the danger, of being a mere recorder of a client's narrative.[40] Thus, they are more likely to recognize their own choices in doing the retelling, perhaps be more aware of their gap-filling based on their own assumptions about the narrative, and perhaps more conscious that the client is engaged in a process of giving meaning to his or her own experience and observation. This awareness coupled with an attentiveness to the elements and structures of narratives can help lawyers develop ways to listen to and record, in a more cautious and tentative way, their understanding of the what happened, who is involved, what problems trouble the client, how the client's life has been disrupted, why the problem matters to the client, what the client desires, and what the client seeks from the lawyer.[41]

2. HEARING STORIES: THE REASON FOR TELLING

In addition to listening for the elements of narrative, lawyers need to listen for a client's reason for bringing the account to a lawyer, as these reasons may shape overtly or subtly the material within the narrative.[42] People almost always tell stories for reasons—conscious or unconscious, explicit or hidden. For lawyers, why clients bring their stories to them may matter in understanding what the client wants and what the client says. Mark Corbett and Karen Davies's encounter with Ms. Woods shows how her reasons for seeking out lawyers might shape her narrative. She has given multiple conversational clues that she did not initially feel a need for the meeting—she called at the request or instigation or insistence of her sister and Mr. Borders. Even as she responds to Mark Corbett's classic open-ended question, basic to lawyering theory, about what she thinks might help her, she defines the subject as "why everyone wanted me to call." Only after locating the subject of the discussion in the motivations or promptings of others, Ms. Woods states that her husband beat her up and describes that event in terms of her injuries and hospitalization. Most of the rest of her initial account reveals her confusion about doing anything at all and her concern about others' "pushing" her to take some action. She is "worried," but not about what her husband has done, is doing just then, or might do in the future. Rather, her articulated worries center on the legal actions others think she should take.

Caught in the cross-currents of interpreting what they are hearing, Mark Corbett and Karen Davies, as novice lawyers, have trouble identifying both Ms. Woods's account of what happened to her and her announcement that others are responsible for the discussion. They jump right to what they assume the narrative to be about—the events leading up to the hospitalization, leaving aside the reasons for the narrative. Ms. Woods, however, seems to be distancing herself from the narrative of her husband's assault. Others want her to tell that story and she does: she was beat up, injured, and hospitalized. But the reasons for the spare recitation remain unclear. What does it mean that she seems to be speaking in response to the urgings of others?

She may be responding in a hesitating way to the urgings of concerned people, one in an institutional role, the other a close family member, to get help with a difficult problem. This interpretation is certainly plausible, in light of the other details that Karen Davies and Mark Corbett know about the situation and a general understanding about barriers women who have been abused face in seeking help. It may also reflect a seriously distorted or only partially correct understanding of the situation. What if Laura[43] seriously dislikes Jerome? What if Laura shaped Mr. Borders's view of Ms. Woods's injuries? What if they each have made their own assumptions about what happened? What if Ms. Woods would have liked to seek help but didn't want her sister involved? What if other aspects of Ms. Woods's relationship with Jerome, in addition to the beating, cause her great distress? If Laura Davies and Mark Corbett perceive these ambiguities in her reason for talking to them, they can move in a different direction to learn more about these possibilities. We revisit the dialogue from the point where Ms. Woods responds to Mark Corbett's invitation to talk about how they "might be able to help" with the following account:

Janice Woods (C1):	Let's just talk about why everyone wanted me to call. I was in the hospital because my husband beat me up. I got a broken rib and a concussion. And my blood pressure got very high. So they kept me in the hospital for a couple days. As you know, Kevin stayed with my sister. But I don't know if there's anything you can do to help. Jerome hasn't bothered me or Kevin since I went to the hospital. I haven't heard from him or seen him. Both Mr. Borders and Laura have been pushing me to bring criminal charges or to get a protective order. But I'm really worried about both those things. And my house. I don't know what's right.
Karen Davies (L1):	Ms. Woods, before we hear about what happened, you keep mentioning Mr. Borders and your sister. It seems they've each played some role in your calling us. Mr. Borders even called us himself. We're here to help you in whatever way you want—not anyone else, whatever their motives might be.
Janice Woods (C2):	Oh, I don't mean to be saying anything bad about either one of them. They're both just concerned about me. But they have their own views of the situation. And maybe they're right. But.... it's all more complicated. And I just don't know what's right for me or for Kevin.
Karen Davies (L2):	For now, rather than trying to figure out who's right or what's right, do you want to tell us about all these things that seem to be weighing on you?
Janice Woods (C3):	I promised Laura I'd talk to you about the beating.
Karen Davies (L3):	Don't worry, we can get to that. Start wherever you want.
Janice Woods (C4):	It goes back to the house....

This narrative alternative repositions the story in Ms. Woods's own account—not in the one she is giving for someone else. By explicitly asking about the roles of other recurring characters in Ms. Woods's story, Karen Davies has freed Ms. Woods to start her narrative where she wants and to include within it the material that matters to her, partly by reassuring her that she will still be able to fulfill her promise to her sister and partly by deferring judgments about who's "right" until later. If Janice Woods has reasons for talking with lawyers in addition to satisfying her sister, Mark Corbett and Karen Davies have laid the groundwork for hearing them. As they engage with the client about her narrative, they can then better assess the meaning of Laura and Mr. Borders's roles in Ms. Woods's call, and more broadly, in the situation for which Ms. Woods seeks help.

3. HEARING STORIES: THE EXPECTATIONS OF LISTENING

In establishing their framework for hearing their client's narrative, Mark Corbett and Karen Davies have yet another task. They also need to be aware of their own expectations about the story they will be hearing.[44] In the initial narrative, after Karen Davies reflects back Ms. Woods's confusion,[45] shows that she can foresee "hard choices," and foreshadows some standard aspects of client counseling,[46] Mark Corbett directs Ms. Woods to the events leading up to her hospitalization. He is poised to hear details about how Jerome, her husband, beat her up; he has implicitly framed the problem that will be the subject of their representation.[47] Having heard about injuries that sound "serious," he anticipates an interaction with Ms. Woods about whether to bring a legal action for a protection order, maybe even about seeking criminal charges.[48] They, like others in Ms. Woods's life, might already have defined her problem as domestic violence, involving choices about remedies, and now want to find out the facts that provide a full account of the schematic summary she gave.[49]

While lawyering theory tells us that Karen Davies and Mark Corbett might have moved too quickly through the process of "problem identification,"[50] narrative theory also alerts us to how the law and legal actors have their own reasons for creating standard narratives[51] providing linkages among events in the world: when a woman is beaten up by her husband, she can seek a legal remedy in a civil protection order.[52] These standard legal narratives can prove particularly attractive to novice lawyers encountering a troubling, complicated, or emotion-laden situation.[53] They sound familiar and serve as useful templates for proceeding competently and efficiently. Even when steeped in lawyering theory—which demands attention to legal and non-legal aspects of a client's problems,[54] requires attention to alternative solutions,[55] and has at its core respect for client-centered decision-making about whether to pursue legal remedies[56] —lawyers may find that the linkages created by the standard stories provide a reasonably comfortable role for them. In role, they are to proceed through various lawyering activities clustered around whether and, if the client wants, how to pursue the relief that legal action provides. They may even feel relieved that the standard story helps them feel competent in what they imagine their role to be. These standard narratives can prove particularly efficient and effective, when they reasonably accurately reflect a particular client's experience and desire, as lawyers do not have to rediscover and recreate the stages in the story.

These standard narratives, however, pose dangers, beyond inadequate attention to the multiple dimensions of clients' lives, because of their capacity easily to distort how lawyers hear a client's narrative constructions[57] and to divert them from the material that the client most wants to pursue.[58] Developing judgment about how and when to distinguish standard narratives from distinctive ones and recognizing subtle differences within a range of standard stories are critical aspects of expert knowledge.[59] Resisting too easy acceptance of the standard script is necessary for novice lawyers.[60] For lawyers such as Mark Corbett and Karen Davies, careful attention to their own expectations provides one check on too-ready adoption of a framework built around a standard narrative. Once the lawyer moves to the standard account, moving back from it to uncover whether and how the client's experiences relate to that paradigmatic story will often be hard. Lawyers and clients will have already done much work in constructing a client's narrative against the background of the standard narrative. A client who feels some connection to the standard story may not easily or clearly identify the points of tension, finding the template of some comfort, too.[61]

However reluctantly Ms. Woods may be talking to Karen Davies and Mark Corbett in the initial dialogue, she may still want or even appreciate the opportunity to consult with them. She might not have articulated for herself her hopes, both precise and ill-formed, for the conversation, other than to placate her sister or comply with a social worker's request. While confused and skeptical, she might, like those who have prompted her to consult a lawyer, be worried about her husband's behavior and the harm to herself. She might want information about how the law and the legal system would deal with the injuries her husband inflicted on her, for possible use now or later in a legal action. She might want validation in not pursuing legal action. While all these aspects of her life might connect her to the standard narrative of domestic violence, she might want strongly or at least initially to describe other things going on with her husband, with her family, or in other aspects of her life for which legal help may be useful.[62] When she seemingly out of nowhere identifies "her house" among her worries,[63] she injects into the conversation an element without an easy fit, one that eluded Mark Corbett and Karen Davies's notice. Lawyers may discover only later that the standard story rubs against a client as the client backs away from the lawyer. At the least, the lawyer will then have to back-track. Not uncommonly, lawyers may find clients not returning phone calls or missing meetings. These actions may indicate that the standard narrative feels increasingly constraining or uncomfortable because it conflicts with some aspect of a client's under-standing of her experience. While clients' signs of withdrawal from the relationship can reflect many other dynamics, a story that may not fit their experience can generate this result.[64]

Thus, the open-ended questions basic to the beginning of getting a client's account reflect more than lawyering technique.[65] From the per-spective of narrative theory, they also reflect openness to multiple possible stories, not necessarily contained within the standard narratives of the law.[66] Mark Corbett's initial invitation to "talk about how you think we might be able to help you" is just the sort designed to prompt a response shaped by a client, one that enables a client to give her own unencum-bered account of the problem and lets lawyers elicit an account as the client wishes to convey it.[67] The problem comes in the listening to Ms. Woods's brief response which contains a jumbled mixture of the beating, the injuries, her medical condition, the hospitalization, her son, possible legal action, the entreaties of hospital staff and family, her house and, perhaps most powerfully, her confusion.

In the face of their own probable confusion at what to do with this account or with Ms. Woods's need to accommodate her sister, Karen Davies first tries an abstract outline of the interviewing and counseling process. When Ms. Woods, who can't yet grasp that process or see herself within it, reiterates her sister's role, Mark Corbett focuses her on the part of her account related to the beating. His prompt will likely trigger a response framed around a narrative of domestic violence.[68] Instead, by resisting the standard script and anticipating possible other stories, Mark Corbett and Karen Davies could have immediately signaled continued openness to other narratives beyond the legal that could weave together the incipient elements in the spare story they have already heard. We revisit again the point in the dialogue following Mark Corbett's inquiry in order to see another narrative possibility presented by attentiveness to alternative stories:

Janice Woods (C1):	Like I said, I don't know if any of this talking is worth much, but I promised Laura I would at least think through what I can do. Ask me whatever you want.
Mark Corbett (L1):	There's a lot in what you said a minute ago and there's so much you're worrying about. I have a suggestion. If it's OK, let's put aside for a few min-utes what you want to do. We'll be able to help you more with that process if you give us a fuller sense of what is troubling you so now. Try to tell us from your own perspective. We can get to how Laura sees things later. And, we'll certainly come back to identifying and thinking through choices about what to do.
Janice Woods (C2):	It's all so complicated. Laura's so upset about Je-rome's hitting me and hurting me so. And I am, too. She says there's no excuse. But so much more is

	involved and it feels like Laura just blocks that all out.
Mark Corbett (L2):	It must be hard to sort through all the pieces. They don't need to be neatly put together for us. Just tell us, in whatever way you want, what's so complicated.
Janice Woods (C3):	Well, we can start with the house. Jerome and I bought a little bungalow about three years ago. We got a VA mortgage—Jerome had been in the Army. Kevin was just a baby and we wanted a house with a yard in a neighborhood we knew to raise him. Also, I'd never lived in a house I owned and it meant a lot to me. I'm getting off track....
Karen Davies (L3):	It's OK. Go on however you want.
Janice Woods (C4):	Anyway, last month I found out that Jerome had refinanced the house about a year ago—without my knowing. I don't know how he did it. I found out almost by mistake—he makes the mortgage payments. His check got returned and the envelope was addressed to both of us so I opened it. I called the company and learned that a different company had the mortgage. Anyway, after lots of calls, I found out that we owed lots more than I thought and that we were behind on payments—way behind. I was panicked and upset. When Jerome came home, I was beside myself—really angry. Anyway, that was the beginning of an enormous set of fights ... which ended in his hitting me and pushing me down.

Mark Corbett here communicates clearly their openness to multiple narratives and holds off resort to the legal structure. He begins by telling Ms. Woods that he has heard many parts to her narrative—there's a lot in what she's said. He then sets aside temporarily her need to figure out what to do by reassuring her that they will come back to decisions; he sees that her choices, now all framed around her sister's plea for legal action regarding domestic violence, are constricting her telling a story grounded in her own experience. He prompts her to speak from her own perspective, contrasting it with "how Laura sees things," and to think about what is "troubling" her. When Ms. Woods still seems stymied by inhabiting her own story, Mark Corbett reflects back the complexity that seems to be overwhelming her, reassuring her that she doesn't need to structure her account for them—"It must be hard to sort through all the pieces. They don't need to be neatly put together for us." And then he prompts her to tell her story however she wants—"Just tell us, in whatever way you want, what's so complicated." When Ms. Woods gets momentarily stuck in telling her story, Karen Davies gently encourages her to go on as she wants. By soliciting narratives beyond the dominant one of domestic violence, Mark Corbett and Karen Davies have begun both to get a fuller account of Ms. Woods's situation and, perhaps ironically, have gotten an initial sense of how her husband's violence might connect to other dynamics in her life.[69] In addition, they are likely to discover more easily and quickly why Ms. Woods called them and what Ms. Woods wants to come from talking with them.[70]

E. NARRATIVE PRACTICES: USING THE ELEMENTS AND STRUCTURE OF NARRATIVE TO UNDERSTAND AND ENGAGE CLIENTS

While narrative listening provides an overall approach to hearing a client's account as a construction of elements to form a story rather than a collection of discrete facts, it also suggests specific practices of listening and questioning that complement the practices that emerge from lawyering theory. Narrative theory does not leave Karen Davies and Mark Corbett in paralyzing chaos having abandoned the seeming solidity of facts for the fluidity of stories. Rather, the essential features of narratives described above—their elements and their structures—yield practices for listening and questioning that aid lawyers in engaging in productive and helpful conversations with their clients—most obviously in interviewing, but also in counseling.

These practices contain three intertwined dynamics for lawyers to master. First, they all require two-layered listening. Lawyers must attend to narratives as they get created in the process of telling and listening as unified accounts that carry the listener forward through connection to the narrator. But they must simultaneously listen critically, disaggregating the essential features of the narrative, to identify its elements and structure.[71] Second, as they identify the features of a narrative, lawyers must decide whether to turn insights into questions that direct a client's account toward that aspect of the narrative or to note them, filing them away as part of their ongoing interpretation of their client's developing narrative. Third, they must recognize that, in this process of disaggregation, they will make choices about which features to pursue.[72]

No one could listen to a story with awareness of all its elements and structural components. Some entry points may resonate more with different clients' approach to their experiences; some may foster easier or more animated conversations; each may draw upon different capacities and responses in the lawyer, including the lawyer's own intuitions and imagination. With multiple routes to understanding clients, among which they can choose, lawyers have nuanced and differentiated ways of learning about clients' experiences, as well as several contexts for connecting to clients and gaining their trust. While some clients may respond easily to a lawyer's inquiries about plot—about all the details of what happened, in what order, for how long—others may feel inadequate in or uncomfortable about providing that part of the narrative. The lawyer may come across as one more official seeking to obtain an explanation of an event, making the client recount material already communicated to others. Furthermore, the client brings all those previous tellings to this particular interaction with the lawyer. By moving the conversation to relationships, to the setting, or to the situation prior to the event at the center of the controversy, the lawyer may establish important bonds with the client that may subsequently make learning about the plot far easier.[73]

In addition, the usefulness of narrative practices comes from deploying them selectively, not exhaustively. Choice also involves awareness of the impact of the story: Do the characters, plot, or setting seem to drive the story? Is the account laden with symbolic meaning? Are the timeframes of the story striking? Disorienting? The lawyer's own reaction, curiosity, and judgment can provide, at least initially, a useful guide to some core aspects of a narrative. While the lawyer's reaction or judgment may be flawed, the process has the self-correcting feature of redundancy.

A question about the characters may lead to the same place as one about setting. Noting and exploring who exercises agency in a story may uncover similar dynamics as those identified in examining the trajectory of a client's account. This redundancy provides important protections in narrative analysis and is hardly surprising. Because the features of narrative are woven together in a story, only disassembled as an analytic device, the multiple routes to insight about a narrative will often converge, and distinctive or compelling aspects of each individual narrative may yield particularly promising entry points. Thus, as lawyers draw upon narrative elements and structure to engage in two-layered listening and to frame questions at different moments in the conversation or over the course of the relationship, the components of the narrative are likely to come together to produce for the lawyer similar or overlapping insights.

1. ATTENDING TO THE ELEMENTS OF CLIENT NARRATIVES

To illustrate how attending to the elements of client narratives can produce practices of multi-layered listening and of framing questions, we revisit again Janice Woods's meeting with Mark Corbett and Karen Davies, drawing upon elements of narratives to suggest ways to use them as multiple points of entry for further inquiry and analysis.[74]

a. The Setting

In thinking about the different scenes for Ms. Woods's story, what do they convey about the client's situation? When she describes her troubles, where are they situated? When she moves from what others want to what she wants, what is the setting in which her desire will be realized? In her initial narrative, Ms. Woods interjects her house, without further explanation. Kevin, in the interactions at the beginning of the meeting, declares that he wants to go home. In the narrative possibilities developed up to now, Ms. Woods begins her story at her house. Is that the primary site around which the narrative will unfold? What about the hospital? Ms. Woods mentions it three times in her initial account responding to Mark Corbett's question about how he and Karen Davies might help. Does the hospital convey the seriousness of the situation? An alien or frightening intrusion? Or, perhaps, a clinical and neutral setting for otherwise terrifying and uncontrollable events? And then Laura's apartment, the site of the meeting: as the place Ms. Woods has come after her hospitalization, is it an important setting in Ms. Woods's narrative?

Thinking about these different locations, their role in the story, the feelings connected to them, and what they convey about the client's situation can provide an indirect entry point for exploring the dynamics of a narrative. Unlike an author, a client may not think self-consciously about where to situate events; but the client's choices might reveal aspects of how a client understands what happened and what she wants. Identifying these settings can get Karen Davies and Mark Corbett's minds wondering and can help them frame questions.

Returning to the last narrative segment in which Ms. Woods begins to talk about how her house figures in her account, we can see how setting might inform further inquiry.

Janice Woods (C1):	Anyway, last month I found out that Jerome had refinanced the house about a year ago—without my knowing. I don't know how he did it. I found out almost by mistake—he makes the mortgage payments. His check got returned and the envelope was addressed to both of us so I opened it. I called the company and learned that a different company had the mortgage. Anyway, after lots of calls, I found out that we owed lots more than I thought and that we were behind on payments—way behind. I was panicked and upset. When Jerome came home, I was beside myself—really angry. Anyway, that was the beginning of an enormous set of fights ... which ended in his hitting me and pushing me down.
Karen Davies (L1):	Ms. Woods, do you want to go through more slowly what happened from when you discovered the refinancing or do you want to tell us more about the ways that this information about your house is so distressing?
Janice Woods (C2):	It will take me a while to get straight exactly what happened when—it upsets me now just to think about each step and there were so many. I can explain, though, why the house set everything off. Like I said, this is the first home I've owned and I don't want to lose it. I always had to move from place to place when I was growing up and I want things to be different for Kevin. Also, from the beginning, Jerome and I didn't see buying the house the same way. We had saved up a few thousand dollars—I wanted to use it for a down payment. He wanted it to expand the hardware store he had started a few years earlier. Our savings came mostly from my income—I was a computer programmer. His profits at the store mostly got plowed back into the store to get it established. After I lost my job and my health insurance, I got high blood pressure. We worried a lot about money. I got a new job but it

didn't have health insurance; Jerome felt a lot of
pressure about the business. When things got tight,
he went to one of these fly-by-night operations to
refinance the mortgage and they let him do it without
my signature. All this came out in our first fight.

Had Karen Davies proceeded differently by taking the steps of the
fight one by one—for example, by saying "Ms. Woods, let's go through
more slowly what happened from when the fighting started"—she might
have gotten this same background information that puts both the fights
and the worries about the house in the broader context of Ms. Woods's
life. It's possible that the chronological account, typical of traditional
interviewing approaches, would have veered off intermittently into this
background material or it's equally possible that Ms. Woods would have
censored herself, thinking that she needed to stick with the chronology.
While none of these possibilities presents significant danger to the lawyer-
client relationship, framing a question around the setting of the house
provides Ms. Woods a chance to express her strong feelings connected to
that setting, as well as her reasons for them. It also gives Karen Davies
and Mark Corbett much information through which to understand the
dynamics and meaning of the fights—information about the house, even
Ms. Woods's health, subjects they can explore now or later. Perhaps, with
this background, they will be able to proceed more effectively—and
efficiently—through the complexities of both the fight and the mortgage
situation.

b.   Characters and Motives

Similarly, lawyers can identify each character in a client's narratives.
Along many axes, what kinds of characters are they?[75] Are they figure-
heads, put in the story to fill a stock role in a plot, for example, the boss.
Are they fully developed individuals with motivations, beliefs, feelings,
conflicts, or self-concepts? Are they major or minor players in the action?
Are they agents in the story; that is, do they move the action forward?
What are their relationships to the client and to each other? How have the
relationships changed over time? Do the same characters appear in the
same way when the lawyer and client explore different alternatives for
approaching the legal matter?

Mark Corbett and Karen Davies have already met or talked to many
people who inhabit Ms. Woods's narrative and have heard about others.
The cast may be incomplete. Other characters as yet unknown may
appear. Splintering the story into its characters may help to open lawyers,
from the beginning, to hearing how those who are part of this episode of a
client's life reveal the multiple, shifting pieces that are part of the world in
which a client experiences the disruption of the fabric of life.[76] Since Mark
Corbett and Karen Davies don't yet know why Ms. Woods has sought their
help, how she understands her problems, or what she wants to achieve,
they can't yet assess whether these characters play major roles, whether
they serve as agents moving the events forward, whether they appear

primarily in an abstract role or as individuals whose particular characteristics and feelings matter in the development of the narrative, or how
their relationships to Ms. Woods and to each other shape and are shaped
by the narrative.[77]

We return to the Janice Woods excerpt to see how Karen Davies and
Mark Corbett might have used character as they used setting in the
narrative excerpt above as the entry point to elicit a story expressing Ms.
Woods's understanding of her situation:

Karen Davies (L1):   Ms. Woods, do you want to go through more slowly
                       what happened from when you discovered the refi-
                       nancing or do you want to tell us about how you see
                       your husband's role in all this?

Janice Woods (C1):   It will take me a while to get straight exactly what
                       happened when—it upsets me now just to think about
                       each step and there were so many. I can explain,
                       though, about Jerome and the house. From the begin-
                       ning, Jerome and I didn't see buying the house the
                       same way. Like I said, this is the first home I've
                       owned and I don't want to lose it. I always had to
                       move from place to place when I was growing up and I
                       want things to be different for Kevin. Jerome's life
                       was more stable. We had saved up a few thousand
                       dollars—I wanted to use it for a down payment. He
                       wanted it to expand the hardware store he had start-
                       ed a few years earlier. Our savings came mostly from
                       my income—I was a computer programmer. His prof-
                       its at the store mostly got plowed back into the store
                       to get it established. After I lost my job and my health
                       insurance, I got high blood pressure. We worried a lot
                       about money. I got a new job but it didn't have health
                       insurance. Jerome felt a lot of pressure about the
                       business and about supporting the family. When
                       things got tight, he went to one of these fly-by-night
                       operations to refinance the mortgage and they let him
                       do it without my signature. All this came out in our
                       first fight.

While the account emerges in a somewhat different order with a slightly
different emphasis than when Mark Corbett and Karen Davies framed a
question around the house, much of the material is the same. Thus, using
either scene or character as narrative entry points and framing questions
around those narrative elements can elicit more about Ms. Woods's
understanding of her situation.

In addition to using narrative elements in interviewing, the practices
can serve the counseling process, too. Mark Corbett and Karen Davies
know that Laura has played a significant role as an agent in Ms. Woods's
narrative of how this meeting came to be and as a source of support and
care for Ms. Woods and Kevin around the hospitalization. We have seen,
too, that, in listening to Ms. Woods's narrative about the help she wants,

Karen Davies and Mark Corbett must take care not to assume what role Ms. Woods wants her sister to play in the future or how the dynamics between the sisters will affect Ms. Woods's decision-making.

Exploration of the characters, of the people who inhabit clients' narratives, acts as a lens through which to view clients' desires as well as their experiences—how they want the narrative to end and how they see different trajectories it might follow. Through the characters, lawyers can examine how others have contributed to the disruption in a client's life and how they affect a client's desires about reconstituting life and give meaning to possibilities for realizing their desires.[78] When it comes time for client decision-making, lawyers may then grasp better how a client's situation and those who are part of a client's life enter into the process of making decisions and the substantive decisions that the client reaches.

A word here about motivation. Motive is, of course, an aspect of character. Understanding who the characters are in a client's narrative often involves learning about their motives. But attending to motivation apart from its attachment to particular characters can also provide insight into a client's view of or feeling about the situation. For example, if a client presents everyone in the narrative as either benevolent or malevolent, or a lawyer sees other patterns in a client's attribution of motives, the lawyer may get a clue to some dynamic in the client's view of the world, personality, or approach to this problem or problems in general. These insights may prove helpful when counseling a client about alternative ways to proceed.[79]

While Karen Davies and Mark Corbett do not yet know much about Ms. Woods's attribution of motives, they have seen quite quickly and starkly her lumping together of her sister with a hospital social worker in their desire for her to take legal action. While Karen Davies and Mark Corbett don't know what motive Ms. Woods thinks these two people have or whether they share the same motive, she does seem to be folding together the motives of two people in very different relationships with her. Discovering more about how Ms. Woods characterizes each of their motives might help Karen Davies and Mark Corbett shape their own approach to Ms. Woods. If Ms. Woods sees them both as meddling in her private affairs or as misunderstanding the real problems in her life or as demonizing her husband, Mark Corbett and Karen Davies can take care not to step into an analogous position.

We revisit Karen Davies and Mark Corbett's relationship with Ms. Woods, picking up at a later time when they have begun to engage more directly in counseling. Assume that in the interim they have heard much about a mortgage crisis, in which Ms. Woods is in danger of losing her house, although foreclosure action has not started. And assume that they have also learned much about the fighting between Ms. Woods and her husband, as well as details about her injuries and hospitalization. Assume, too, that Ms. Woods seems to respond to them easily in expanding her narrative, although she tends to begin with abbreviated accounts that compress many events, and elaborates only upon further probing. Now, Karen Davies and Mark Corbett want to tease out from the motivations of others at least an initial sense of what Ms. Woods wants from the lawyer-client relationship and how her view of being involved with lawyers relates to what she wants.

Mark Corbett (L1):	Just like you said back at the beginning, things are really complicated. And there's still much we'll need to get clearer about. But, for now, could we shift to what you want? You began by saying you don't know what's right and we told you we'd get back to these issues.
Janice Woods (C1):	Yes, Laura and the social worker both want me to get an order against Jerome. Or even get the police involved.
Mark Corbett (L2):	These are both possibilities—and there are lots of others—regarding both the house and the beating. But before we go through figuring out all these, can you tell us, at least for now, what you think you want to happen?
Janice Woods (C2):	I want to go back to my house with Kevin. I don't know about Jerome. He really hurt me—scared me—I didn't know he could get so angry. And I'm so upset about how he refinanced the house. But we really are in a mess—over our heads.... (long silence). Maybe Laura and Mr. Borders are right—if I don't do something about the beating, Jerome will never understand.
Mark Corbett (L3):	You keep coming back to your sister and the social worker—since the beginning and even now. Can you tell us more why they're so important in your thinking about what you want?
Janice Woods (C3):	It's different for each of them—but maybe because they agree, it's hard not to do what they want.
Mark Corbett (L4):	Tell me more about each of them.
Janice Woods (C4):	Laura—she's my big sister—she's always been there for me. All those moves—she always took care of me. And now she's still taking care of me. And she thinks my wanting the house so much is a little crazy—she told me to be careful when we bought it. She says Jerome's refinancing the house is just the same as his beating me up—he doesn't think about how he hurts me.
	Mr. Borders—he's different. He's nice and concerned and all that. But I get the sense he's giving me the same speech he's given a thousand times. Or else, Laura has given him her opinion. I don't think he knows anything about the house—unless Laura told him. He says I need to go after Jerome for my self-image. They're each a little right. But, I don't know, they both miss a lot.

Mark Corbett (L5):	I can see both their opinions matter to you. But since they're each missing something and they each seem to have their own reasons for giving the advice they did, can you tell me what you want to happen? I know you said you want to be back in your house. Tell me more about what that could be like.
Janice Woods (C5):	I'd like Jerome to work with me on dealing with the mortgage mess. Maybe we could save the house—working together. And maybe that would help me see about his violence. Can I get a protection order later if I want?

Getting Ms. Woods to talk about characters and motives here, rather than a diversion, provides a way to push her to think about what she wants, a task that is hard for her. Mark Corbett, using active listening techniques, reflects back prior thoughts Ms. Woods has expressed about complexity and about her sister and the social worker.[80] He characterizes for her the pattern he sees of "coming back to your sister and the social worker." Then, rather than immediately redirecting her to focus on herself—a technique that he tried and that failed—he gives her the opportunity to speak directly about the importance to her of these other characters. Perhaps Ms. Woods is articulating for herself for the first time how large Laura and Mr. Borders loom. Perhaps she has mulled over these ideas a lot. Whatever the situation, listening to her own narrative about these two people, told to her lawyers, can free her to speak about what she wants, rather than remain stuck in an internal or external argument with them. While this description of their roles may not decrease their power, at least Mark Corbett and Karen Davies now have some sense of how these characters might reappear in the decision-making process. Ms. Woods's account provides a point of reference to which they can return as they work with their client through her decisions.

c. Actions/Events

Perhaps lawyers most readily seek out and listen for actions in what they hear: "Tell me what happened." Lawyering theory provides many techniques for moving clients through reconstructing what happened to them. Narrative theory offers complementary insight into the complexities of the process of hearing a client's own narrative of events, while also directing the client to describe actions that lawyers think are of legal or persuasive significance.[81] In both approaches, at least initially,[82] lawyers give primacy to listening for a client's depiction of the acts, taking care not to fill in missing pieces.[83] Other accounts and other perspectives will matter for other purposes. But at least early in interviewing and at other important moments within the relationship, listening for a client's naming, ordering, elaboration of detail, and characterization of actions not only helps lawyers get close to a client's experience and understanding of the events as they unfolded in his or her world, but also constitutes part of honoring the dignity of that client by respecting the integrity of the client's account.[84]

We can use narrative theory to see how the dynamic between lawyers and clients can affect the description of an incident.[85] Clients recount life events in the context of their relationship with a lawyer. Therefore, clients shape what they say in light of expectations about and understandings of this context.[86] For example, embarrassment, lack of trust, misunderstanding about the aspects of experience encompassed by a legal matter, shielding another from a problem, or cultural gulfs may make clients reluctant to include parts of an experience in talking to lawyers.[87] Also, because a client may be unfamiliar with lawyers and law or perhaps base expectations and understandings on other encounters with lawyers different from the present one, a client may give an account that differs from one about those same events given in a different context to a different audience.

Clients may be quite willing to broaden their presentation of an experience or describe actions in greater detail or with more precision if they understand that these subjects interest the lawyer or matter in the legal world.[88] In interviewing and counseling, lawyers face the delicate task of giving primacy to clients' own accounts of events and also letting clients know that various aspects of experience matter more than others in the world of law.[89] Since there is no one authentic description of actions, but only accounts that emerge contextually, lawyers operate in difficult terrain.[90] To elicit full accounts that may help clients, lawyers need clients to understand the parameters of their experiences that may be of legal significance,[91] At the same time, lawyers must avoid either imposing on clients' narratives a legal framework that makes their account of events conform to standard legal stories or valuing stories that fit into the legal world over other aspects of clients' experiences.[92]

In attending to the actions in clients' narratives, lawyers can differentiate among at least three ways that clients identify and describe acts: 1) spontaneous accounts; 2) accounts that emerge with lawyer prompting, for example, to clarify a description of events or to direct attention to aspects of actions that a client did not address or addressed only briefly; and 3) accounts resulting from lawyer probing, for example, to confront inconsistencies or to explore difficult material.[93] By noting how clients' depictions of actions vary depending upon the nature of the lawyer's role in the evolving narrative, lawyers can be aware of how their interventions might be affecting a client's narrative.[94]

Listening for how clients' accounts of events emerge in relationship to lawyers' interventions, while a delicate task, can be guided by several principles. First, as explained above, lawyers must give primacy, at least initially, to non-judgmental listening for a client's spontaneous narrative. Second, in framing their subsequent promptings or questions, lawyers must decide how to direct the emerging narrative so that a client can continue or expand the story based upon his or her own experience, perceptions and needs.[95] Third, lawyers should expect that client accounts will change with deeper inquiry, with development of trust, with time, and with changing circumstances in a client's life.[96]

In the initial narrative excerpt, Karen Davies and Mark Corbett hear about acts related to Ms. Woods's request for the meeting, her hospitalization, and her husband's behavior since the hospitalization. All emerge in response to a classic open-ended question without further prompting or probing. In subsequent excerpts, after narrative prompting, Ms. Woods elaborates on the role of her sister and the social worker in instigating the meeting and her husband's refinancing of their house. Each prompt leads Ms. Woods's account toward descriptions of different events. As the narrative has developed, Mark Corbett and Karen Davies's interactions demonstrate the first two principles: they have listened non-judgmentally to Ms. Woods's spontaneous narrative and they have framed subsequent inquiries to help her create a story based on her own experience of the world. They need to recognize, however, that they have intervened in her spontaneous framing by moving her away from the promptings of her sister and the social worker. While their decision may be a good and important one, made to foster hearing her story at least partially detached from others or to further the autonomy of their client,[97] they need to recognize their decision, understand their assumptions,[98] note the consequences in the account they elicit, and remain willing to question its effectiveness as they see how their interventions affect the client's narrative.[99]

Now, they need to examine how their client's narrative develops with further probing of events. Returning to Ms. Woods's introduction of events related to her husband's refinancing, Karen Davies and Mark Corbett want to find out much more about what happened—both in terms of their emerging concern about protecting the house from foreclosure and in terms of the connection between the refinancing and the fights. Assume that, after some further discussion of the meaning of the house in Ms. Woods's relationship with her husband, she is now ready to return to the events connected to the refinancing.

Janice Woods (C1):	Anyway, last month I found out that Jerome had refinanced the house about a year ago—without my knowing. I don't know how he did it. I found out almost by mistake—he makes the mortgage payments. His check got returned and the envelope was addressed to both of us so I opened it. I called the company and learned that a different company had the mortgage. Anyway, after lots of calls, I found out that we owed lots more than I thought and that we were behind on payments—way behind. I was panicked and upset. When Jerome came home, I was beside myself—really angry. Anyway, that was the beginning of an enormous set of fights ... which ended in his hitting me and pushing me down.
Karen Davies (L1):	Ms. Woods, do you want to go through more slowly what happened from when you discovered the refinancing or do you want to tell us about how you see your husband's role in all this?

Janice Woods (C2):   It will take me a while to get straight exactly what happened when—it upsets me now just to think about each step and there were so many. I can explain, though, about Jerome and the house. From the beginning, Jerome and I didn't see buying the house the same way. Like I said, this is the first home I've owned and I don't want to lose it. I always had to move from place to place when I was growing up and I want things to be different for Kevin. Jerome's life was more stable. We had saved up a few thousand dollars—I wanted to use it for a down payment. He wanted it to expand the hardware store he had started a few years earlier. Our savings came mostly from my income—I was a computer programmer. His profits at the store mostly got plowed back into the store to get it established. After I lost my job and my health insurance, I got high blood pressure. We worried a lot about money. I got a new job but it didn't have health insurance. Jerome felt a lot of pressure about the business and about supporting the family. When things got tight, he went to one of these fly-by-night operations to refinance the mortgage and they let him do it without my signature. All this came out in our first fight.

* * *

Karen Davies (L2):   I know you said that it will be hard to reconstruct all the events related to the refinancing—and we probably won't be able to get clear on them all today—but could we start with the day you accidentally found out about the refinancing—when you first saw the letter that alerted you to the problem?

Janice Woods (C3):   Actually, it wasn't a complete accident. When I saw that envelope, I kind of knew that something bad was in it. I didn't know it would be a returned check. Jerome had been fretting about the mortgage. But I felt so bad about losing my job and making things harder that I didn't ask him about it. I just left it to him.

Karen Davies (L3):   I can see all this was scary for you. What did you know about the state of your mortgage?

Janice Woods (C4):   I knew that Jerome was having trouble with each payment. We had a VA mortgage—fixed rate—about $6\frac{1}{2}$ percent. There were lower ones around when we got it, but it was a sure thing because of Jerome's military service.

Karen Davies (L4):   Were there any problems with making the payments?

Janice Woods (C5):   When I had my programming job, the payments were big for us, but we could make them—just had to be careful. Things changed after I lost the job. Jerome had never liked taking on such high payments.

Karen Davies (L5):   What changes happened?

Janice Woods (C6): There sometimes wasn't enough money in our checking account—so we had to figure out different ways to put together enough for the payment.

In this interaction, Karen Davies and Mark Corbett might note Ms. Woods's re-characterization of just how accidental her discovery was. They might also see how Ms. Woods was more involved in the payment of the mortgage than she initially indicated, an involvement that only incrementally emerges. At this point, they have no reason for concern about these developments in her account. Many possible explanations exist and they have no reason for thinking that Ms. Woods is hiding something, particularly something nefarious.[100] Elaboration and recasting of accounts occur commonly as people recount events in their lives. At the same time, the nature of her precise involvement might matter in both a mortgage matter and a domestic violence matter.

While further probing of or sometimes challenging a client's account of events will be necessary and require the use of appropriate practices from both lawyering theory and narrative theory, attending to how the narrative evolves in response to lawyer questioning will help the lawyer decide when and how to probe or challenge in an engaged, client-centered way.[101] Listening for accounts as clients present them spontaneously and with different kinds of lawyer interventions may assist lawyers to remain engaged with their client in difficult moments—for example, when they think they need to call into question clients' own understanding of actions or they think clients must confront, explain or even accept accounts at odds with their own understanding of what happened in the world.[102] By listening carefully to whether their interventions in client narratives further the development of the account of events, lawyers are in a better position, on one side, to avoid harmful distortion of client accounts, on a second side, to make self-conscious and careful choices about ways to elicit further narrative important to some aspect of a client's problem that the client might overlook or find difficult to pursue,[103] or, on a third side, to challenge or dispute a client's account.[104]

For example, Karen Davies and Mark Corbett can tentatively identify patterns of response to their inquiries about specific events. Ms. Woods may harbor bad feelings about her contribution to the financial stress or may be hesitant to discuss her precise involvement, but she does not completely withdraw and remains willing to proceed, although haltingly, with an account of actions regarding mortgage payments. These patterns provide Mark Corbett and Karen Davies with at least two clues to further action. First, proceeding with a strict chronological account of the payment history filled with detail is likely to go slowly or get stuck, requiring many careful follow-up questions. Devising other ways to elicit the dynamics around the payment history is perhaps in order—maybe getting all the papers, reviewing them, and then using Ms. Woods's account to describe things that papers would not reveal. Or perhaps, proceeding through other narrative entry points may yield more information.[105]

Questioning based on the other elements of narrative might be easier for Ms. Woods to incorporate; the narrative excerpts based on setting and character show how these inquiries can be productive. If Karen Davies proceeds further on her quest concerning the dynamics around the payment history and gets similar limited answers, she might switch entry points.

Karen Davies (L1):	It seems that in the period before you saw the returned check and found out how far behind things were, you and your husband had difficulty when the mortgage was due. Tell me about what would happen when he was writing the checks.
Janice Woods (C1):	I wasn't always there—maybe three or four times. He'd always ask me if I had anything coming in that could contribute to the payment. If I'd just gotten my paycheck, I'd sign it over to the mortgage company. Also, I do quilting and sometimes I'd have a check for a quilt that I'd sign over. I knew that other expenses would be hard, but giving him the money right then would avoid more conflict—and I'd deal with other expenses later.

Karen Davies moves from directing Ms. Woods to each step in the history of mortgage payments to the setting for the interactions with her husband.[106] Because Karen Davies diverts from the task of getting from Ms. Woods right then the sequence and details of each event, she and Mark Corbett do not have their chronology of acts. But they have gotten important details of interactions between Ms. Woods and her husband when paying the mortgage. They have other techniques for putting together the chronology that do not force Ms. Woods into this event-based mode of storytelling.[107] For example, if they develop their own chart of mortgage payments, they can insert pieces as Ms. Woods reveals them through an approach more comfortable for her.

Expecting the history of mortgage payments to emerge not from a linear account but from diverse conversations, Karen Davies and Mark Corbett may be more inclined to devise alternative strategies for creating the chronological, event-focused story they will need for their legal work. Many legal matters demand careful and precise development of the events and other acts that mark the progression of a narrative; eliciting that aspect of the narrative requires the honing of many practices basic to interviewing. Deploying these practices, lawyers may still find as they press harder and harder for the details of legally significant acts a client who resists—directly or indirectly, intentionally or unintentionally. Lawyers may become frustrated or angered by this resistance. With these feelings, they may interpret a client's behavior as hiding something or even lying. While they might be right, it helps neither the client nor the case to jump quickly or easily to these interpretations. Narrative theory contributes additional practices to lawyers' methods for obtaining sufficiently precise and detailed accounts of acts. One practice of listening for patterns of client response to act-focused inquiry and another of framing interventions not focused around acts might in the end produce the necessary event-focused chronology, without producing so much resistance.

d. Agency: Listening for Who Moves the Story Forward

With the setting, the characters and the actions identified, lawyers must also pay attention to agency. Who or what provides the dynamic force in the action? In a client's narrative, agency might rest in a person or persons, an institution (the welfare department, the court, the bank), an abstraction (the market, the legal system), a supernatural force (a god, luck) or a complicated mixture of them all. Agency is also not linear, unidirectional, unilateral, or static. For example, while one person may seem to be moving events forward, another might be pushing in a different direction, and others might be resisting, loudly or silently, directly or subversively. Thus, agency provides an entry point into understanding the operation of power and control in a client's view of a situation.[108] Equally important, it alerts lawyers to clients' views of their own power in a situation and their capacity or willingness to assert control. As a closely related matter, it cautions lawyers to be wary of taking actions that may undermine a client's emerging sense of agency.[109] Also, understanding how a client sees actions progressing or stalling, both in the past and in the future, offers insight into the possibility that legal representation may create its own force in a client's narrative. Attentive to how clients might feel about a lawyer or the law reshaping the dynamics of the client's situation, lawyers can better help clients see and evaluate how using the law might distribute power and therefore affect the development of the story.

Listening for agency can be particularly valuable to Mark Corbett and Karen Davies's grasp of how Ms. Woods both understands what has happened and wants to proceed with the representation. In Ms. Woods's narrative about her husband, her house and the violence, a story still in its early development, it is unclear how each person has moved the action forward, from the decision to buy the house through her beating. Attending to if, how, and to what extent Ms. Woods, in these interactions, has exercised power or has resisted her husband's power will help Mark Corbett and Karen Davies understand and empathize with Ms. Woods's decisions about how to proceed.

Also, as several of the excerpts reveal, her sister and the social worker have played a critical role as agents in getting Ms. Woods to a lawyer and in framing her problem. Karen Davies and Mark Corbett, in paying attention to the structure of the interview, see that Ms. Woods contests others' framing yet feels deeply conflicted over how to deal with their views. Karen Davies and Mark Corbett also know from the counseling excerpt concerning her desires in which they question Ms. Woods about the role of her sister and social worker that these two people will continue to exert force in Ms. Woods's decisions about how to proceed. By listening for agency in the story as Ms. Woods weaves it together and as they disassemble it into its narrative components, Karen Davies and Mark Corbett can more intentionally remain aware of the dynamics of power and influence that are likely to course through the representation. With this two-layered listening, they can track Ms. Woods's view of her own agency in shaping her approach to her problems. Attentive to changes in Ms. Woods's position amidst these forces, they can anticipate the ambivalence that may result from competing forces and shape their role so as to help Ms. Woods in the way that she ultimately defines for herself.

Mark Corbett and Karen Davies may also decide to use their insights about agency as a source for further questioning about what Ms. Woods would like to see happen. We return to the excerpt in which Mark Corbett and Karen Davies seek to get Ms. Woods to move from what others want to articulate what she wants. Assume that after Ms. Woods's question about getting a protection order in the future, Mark Corbett and Karen Davies discuss with her the various ways the mortgage and the violence problems could both be addressed. In the middle of the discussion, Ms. Woods again invokes her sister.

Mark Corbett (L1):	Tell me more about each of them.
Janice Woods (C1):	Laura—she's my big sister—she's always been there for me. All those moves—she always took care of me. And now she's still taking care of me. And she thinks my wanting the house so much is a little crazy—she told me to be careful when we bought it. She says Jerome's refinancing the house is just the same as his beating me up—he doesn't think about how he hurts me.
	Now, Mr. Borders—he's different. He's nice and concerned and all that. But I get the sense he's giving me the same speech he's given a thousand times. Or else, Laura has given him her opinion. I don't think he knows anything about the house—unless Laura told him. He says I need to go after Jerome for my self-image. They're each a little right. But, I don't know, they both miss a lot.
Mark Corbett (L2):	Since they're each missing something and they each seem to have their own reasons for giving the advice they did, can you tell me what you want to happen. I know you said you want to be back in your house. Tell me more about what that could be like.
Janice Woods (C2):	I'd like Jerome to work with me on dealing with the mortgage mess. Maybe we could save the house—working together. And maybe that would help me see about his violence. Can I get a protection order later if I want?

* * *

Mark Corbett (L3):	So, you see, you could start with either or do both at the same time.

Janice Woods (C3):	It seems that maybe the mortgage should come first. You've given me hope that maybe I won't lose the house. Any maybe even Jerome could be involved.... But, you know if I do this Laura will be really angry. She's helped me in some bad times with the payments. And she can't even afford a house herself.
Mark Corbett (L4):	These dynamics with your sister seem incredibly complicated—so much involved going back so long. It must be hard to make a decision now with all that affecting you.
Janice Woods (C4):	That's only a fraction of what I'm feeling—she's so important to me. I can't lose her.
Mark Corbett (L4):	Maybe that wouldn't have to happen. We can keep working on ways to keep your house and not lose your sister.

As with other narrative elements, Mark Corbett uses his insights about agency to frame responses to move the discussion forward. In addition, his identifying and naming the pattern of her sister's influence may help Ms. Woods state what she feels is at stake in her relationship with her sister. Seeing Ms. Woods's struggle, Mark Corbett identifies himself with her dual projects, even if they turn out to be irreconcilable.

e. Emotional Texture

Stories come with emotion, sometimes tied directly to other elements of the narrative—the characters, particular events, a location—and sometimes running beneath or pervading them. This element of emotion may exert great power on both the teller and the listener. Lawyers in even the most technical and arcane areas of practice know that clients may have a deep emotional orientation toward a problem they bring to a lawyer.

Our lawyering theory enhances understanding of the lawyer-client relationship by acknowledging the role of client feelings as lawyers seek to understand the client's problem, develop solutions, and achieve what the client wants. Drawing on practices derived from lawyering theory,[110] lawyers have techniques for grappling with the challenge of putting client emotions in the service of client decision-making, while guarding against emotion overwhelming either their clients or themselves.[111] Karen Davies and Mark Corbett can see ways that emotions will figure in Ms. Woods's decisions. For example, Ms. Woods states repeatedly that her feelings for her sister are prominent in thinking about what is "right." Mark Corbett and Karen Davies, even at this early stage of the relationship, deploy standard lawyering techniques such as active listening for both honoring the importance and impact of these feelings and creating space for Ms. Woods to feel less constrained by them.

We can use narrative theory to shape a different and complementary approach to emotion. It shifts the focus from how a lawyer addresses a client's concern with emotional aspects of a problem to how a lawyer understands the operation of emotion in the client's situation.[112] Through attention to narrative, this analysis helps lawyers identify the emotional texture of a client's account apart from a client's invocation of emotional concerns in facing and making decisions. Mark Corbett and Karen Davies can attend to the emotional texture of Ms. Woods's narrative to help them understand the meaning the account has for her, whether or not she sees these emotions as significant in her decision-making. For example, Ms. Woods's desire to prevent foreclosure of her house cannot be separated from her feelings about the instability of her childhood, her hopes to save Kevin from the same fate, and her embarrassment or even her depression about loss of her job. As Mark Corbett and Karen Davies identify how these and other feelings shape her story, they remain aware of how the cross-currents of powerful feelings might create shifting views of her situation and of what she wants to do.[113]

In addition, as with other narrative elements, Mark Corbett and Karen Davies might use their sense of Ms. Woods's emotions to frame questions. We return to the dialogue about the history of the mortgage payments to see how Karen Davies might proceed after Ms. Woods describes the interactions with her husband as he makes each payment.

Karen Davies (L1):	It seems that in the period before you saw the returned check and found out how far behind things were, you and your husband had difficulty when the mortgage was due. Tell me about what would happen when he was writing the checks.
Janice Woods (C1):	I wasn't always there—maybe four or five times. He'd ask me if I had anything coming in that could contribute to the payment. If I'd just gotten my paycheck, I'd sign it over to the mortgage company. Also, I do quilting and sometimes I'd have a check for a quilt that I'd sign over. I knew that other expenses would be hard, but giving him the money right then would avoid more conflict—and I'd deal with other expenses later.
Karen Davies (L2):	It seems that you contributed more than a little to the mortgage, even when you'd lost your job, and felt bad about the size of your contribution and that buying the house was your idea.
Janice Woods (C2):	I felt so responsible and so scared. And things just got harder and harder with Jerome—I couldn't talk to him about these things. He was so angry and stressed—and, I guess, scared, too.

Here Karen Davies draws upon the emotions seeming to animate Ms. Woods's understanding of her experience around the financial pressures generated by buying the house. Bringing the emotional meaning to the surface, she elicits from Ms. Woods insight about the emotions inhabiting her account—she feels "responsible." As in other moments in the dialogue, Ms. Woods may have had this thought before or she may be articulating it for the first time. In either case, the shared understanding of the emotional terrain will help Karen Davies and Mark Corbett as they help Ms. Woods figure out what she wants to do.

2. ATTENDING TO THE STRUCTURE AND DYNAMICS OF CLIENT NARRATIVES

Just as the elements of a narrative yield practices of listening and questioning, so do the components of a narrative's structure—whether that structure comes from plot or character. We continue with Janice Woods's narrative, disaggregating its structural components to explore more entry points for analysis and inquiry.

a. The Steady State

The problems that clients bring to lawyers often deviate from a situation that has some ordinary character. A problem emerges from or intrudes into the regularity of life. Those problems might reflect opportunities as well as difficulties, but they present challenges that depart from the way things are. The disruption of the normal course of clients' lives—the steady state—prompts visits with lawyers. In seeing how a client's experience makes that background situation seem ordinary, the lawyer may better fathom the meaning and consequences of the disruption for the client and ways the client might want to put life back together. In addition, the dynamics of everyday life may feel not just ordinary but also legitimate or at least acceptable. If clients have accepted a situation enough to continue in it, how have they understood that acceptance or why do they now consider rejecting it? Did the state of affairs seem right, comfortable, inevitable, or as good as possible? Does the client see the ordinariness and legitimacy of the background situation as the same or do they depart in the narrative? Do others who matter in the situation share the client's sense?

Listening for what clients take as ordinary and legitimate may not be in the forefront of lawyers' minds.[114] For lawyers, just as clients, the trouble prompting the visit with the lawyer may easily dominate. If the narrative has no explicit steady state, as a client' narrative may all be about trouble, a client might nevertheless assume an implicit steady state without describing it because of its very ordinariness. The regular way life proceeds for clients, however stable or chaotic, may help lawyers both understand the trajectories of clients' stories and also provide a context for interpreting what clients want to happen. The steady state may be one that a client wants to reestablish, if possible; it may be one from which a client wants to escape; or it may be one that a client wants to transform. Whatever a client's attitude toward that steady state, understanding it may help the lawyer decipher and appreciate what the client desires now and in the future and the actions that the client can imagine taking.[115]

Karen Davies and Mark Corbett enter Ms. Woods's life, as do many lawyers, at the point of disruption. But already, from the pieces of the interview that we have, we can tentatively identify some elements of the situation that preceded the trouble generating the meeting. Ms. Woods has a young son embedded in an extended family. Her marriage has had some conflict—certainly around the house, going back to the decision to purchase it. Both Ms. Woods and her husband have worked to support the family—he started his own business, a hardware store, and she was a computer programmer. Ms. Woods's sister, a regular presence and steady source of support, has her own feelings about the house and about Jerome.

For Mark Corbett and Karen Davies, knowing more about how Ms. Woods thinks about the situation prior to her current problems will help them both see what is most troubling to her now and what from the past she wants to recreate or salvage. While they know her house has long been important to her, how did it figure in what her life was like? While her sister has been a constant presence in Ms. Woods's life, how did she shape the contours of Ms. Woods's experience? Understanding Ms. Woods's view of the past will help Karen Davies and Mark Corbett place the present difficulties in context, shape with their client possibilities for the future, and assist her in deciding among them.

We return to the excerpt in which Ms. Woods, in thinking about what she wants to do, both reveals that Laura has actually helped with making payments on the mortgage and worries that, if she tries to work with Jerome on saving the house, her sister will be angry. In that segment, Mark Corbett pursues directly the complexity of Laura's role in Ms. Woods's decision-making concerning both the mortgage and the violence. While that discussion proceeds productively to help Ms. Woods sort out the important role of her sister in deciding what to do in the future, he could also have taken the discussion into the past to learn about Laura's involvement in the dynamics around the house before the current problems erupted.

Mark Corbett (L1):	So, you see, you could start with either or do both at the same time.
Janice Woods (C1):	It seems that maybe the mortgage should come first. You've given me hope that maybe I won't lose the house. And maybe even Jerome could be involved.... But, you know if I do this Laura will be really angry. She's helped me in some bad times with the payments. And she can't even afford a house herself.
Mark Corbett (L2):	Help me understand the dynamics surrounding the house before the trouble started.
Janice Woods (C2):	When I had my programming job, things around the mortgage weren't so stressful because we had enough money coming in. I was really happy in the house. There are lots of little kids on the street so things are really nice for Kevin. From the time we moved in right after Kevin was born, Laura came over often with Raquel and Martin and they just fit right in. Jerome has never been around much because he works so hard at the store. I started worrying when they did a restructuring at work—my skills weren't as up-to-date as others.

Mark Corbett (L3):   So how did you handle it?

Janice Woods (C3):   With Kevin, I couldn't go to courses and training like lots of my co-workers—or spend hours at home on the internet. Laura pushed me to take a course at the Community College at night, but what with Jerome's being so tired when he got home, I needed to take care of Kevin. Laura knew I was worried, but, especially since she had warned me about taking on the payments, she was careful not to get involved in things with Jerome.

Mark Corbett (L4):   You were juggling a lot.

Janice Woods (C4):   Yeah. I wasn't so surprised when I got fired. And then juggling just got harder and harder. And my blood pressure went up even higher just when I lost my insurance. So we all lost our insurance. Jerome didn't have any at work because it was so expensive.

Mark Corbett and Karen Davies have developed an initial sense of how Ms. Woods views a place in her life that, while filled with much instability, nonetheless felt manageable or ordinary to her. They can, therefore, better understand the dynamics among the different characters in relationship to the problems she now faces and the connections among different parts of her life. Knowing these interwoven strands in her life— her job, her house, her health, her relationships—and hearing of them as they functioned in a more regular if not completely satisfactory way may help them as they proceed to address her troubles.

b.   Client Narratives and Stock Stories

Stock stories reflect normal expectations and practices, whatever those are in a particular situation, community or culture. They often organize much background knowledge in comprehensible form as people experience those expectations and practices.[116] These standard accounts often create background structures to individual stories. Law develops its own stock stories, customary ways that a story gets framed both through legal rules and processes and through repeated retellings of distinctive narratives in standard form in legal tribunals, lawyers' offices, and other settings that draw upon the law.[117] Within those regularized scripts, law both provides for alternative accounts and presents porous boundaries that lawyers test as to whether a particular situation falls within or outside the customary narrative. In this process, the standard legal narrative constantly changes.

We have already seen how standard legal narratives of domestic violence can affect both client and lawyer. When Janice Woods first talked with Mark Corbett and Karen Davies, the urgings of her sister and social worker to pursue a typical court action regarding domestic violence seemed to shape her initial account. Concurrently, as Mark Corbett and Karen Davies listened to that story, their own expectations of hearing an account of domestic violence shaped their initial prompt to learn more about the events leading up to the hospitalization. All involved responded to the standard narrative of the law, whether taking it for granted, invoking its power, trying to fit within it, or feeling constrained by it. As Karen Davies and Mark Corbett went on to deploy techniques of narrative listening in developing their relationship with their client, we have seen how Janice Woods's narrative has departed from this standard script of the law as her lawyers have signaled that she could deviate from that script. Thus, the principles of narrative listening and questioning highlight the importance of resisting the unexamined pull of standard stories—whether situated in a client, others in the client's life, or the lawyer.

Although identifying the influence of a customary script in a particular situation may be difficult, awareness of its presence will help lawyers make more intentional decisions about how it may prove both useful and distorting.[118] When a client seems to be reciting a standard script, that is, a narrative about what happened or what a client wants that mimics what seems to be the normal way things are done[119]—as when Ms. Woods first recounts a beating, injuries and hospitalization leading up to court action—lawyers need to exercise caution. While everything may be true, she perhaps structures the narrative around the stock story of domestic violence that others expect her to tell, making decisions about what to include and exclude based upon this template.[120]

Four types of responses may help lawyers explore the significance of the standard script. First, lawyers can check for a client's stance toward that stock story to see how the client thinks and feels about following it, as when Ms. Woods initially expresses her worries about court action. When Ms. Woods proclaims her apprehension and confusion, she seems to fight against the script. Not knowing how to proceed, she looks to her lawyers. Their response to her resistance can influence the development of a client's affirmation of her doubts about the standard legal narrative. Second, in addition to looking for a client's stance toward the stock story, lawyers can also listen for ways a client declares something as out of the ordinary,[121] as in Ms. Woods's seemingly irrelevant mention of her house as she concludes her first account. This statement might signal a major departure from a set of ordinary expectations that have a sense of legitimacy,[122] or she might be reshaping the standard script within the basic contours of a standard legal narrative to make it better reflect her own experience. For example, if doing the latter, Ms. Woods may be recasting the standard narrative of domestic violence as one in which the violence is caused by conflict over money. While the reason for the deviation may be unclear, the departure alerts the lawyers to exploring the possibilities. Third, lawyers can wonder what has generated the standard script—a prior experience, another person, background information in the environment—as when Mark Corbett and Karen Davies seek to learn the role of Mr. Borders and Ms. Woods's sister. Fourth, lawyers can assess the effect of the standard script upon themselves.[123] Remaining aware of how the script operates as a kind of background template, they more effectively seek out how a client's narrative describes a breach of that script and also note how the stock story affects their own openness to hearing other accounts.

When a client, rather than reciting a standard script, appears to be uncertain or concerned about the regular way things are done, lawyers can explore what generates that anxiety. A client may look to the lawyer for direction or reassurance in a confusing situation by searching out the standard legal narrative.[124] In this situation, lawyers must remain attentive to the meaning clients take from the lawyer's account of the customary story since the lawyer's response can shape the developing narrative. Clients may seek out the standard story in order to conform their account to what they think a lawyer or the legal system expects. Thus, lawyers need to take care not to endorse the stock story or otherwise push clients toward that account without understanding how that regular approach relates to the client's own needs and desires.[125]

We revisit a moment in Ms. Woods's narrative when she identifies how stock stories may be affecting her own understanding of the situation. In response to Mark Corbett's question about why she keeps returning to Mr. Borders and her sister in thinking about what she wants, Ms. Woods describes how Laura, who has cared for her throughout her life, believes that Jerome "doesn't think about" the ways he hurts her. But, as for Laurence Borders, he's "giving ... the same speech he's given a thousand times." Ms. Woods concludes that while each is "a little right," they both "miss a lot." While Mark Corbett proceeds by directing Ms. Woods to think more about what she wants, Karen Davies and Mark Corbett could have used their client's insight about the background stories of others to engage her directly in a dialogue about how her experience deviates from a stock story.

Janice Woods (C1):	Laura—she's my big sister—she's always been there for me. All those moves—she always took care of me. And now she's still taking care of me. And she thinks my wanting the house so much is a little crazy—she told me to be careful when we bought it. She says Jerome's refinancing the house is just the same as his beating me up—he doesn't think about how he hurts me.
	Now, Mr. Borders—he's different. He's nice and concerned and all that. But I get the sense he's giving me the same speech he's given a thousand times. Or else, Laura has given him her opinion. I don't think he knows anything about the house—unless Laura told him. He says I need to go after Jerome for my self-image. They're each a little right. But, I don't know, they both miss a lot.
Karen Davies (L1):	What are they missing about you?
Janice Woods (C2):	Mr. Borders, he thinks the stuff about my self image has to do with what he calls the abuse. But, it really has to do with my job. It was my own fault I lost it—I should have listened to Laura about keeping up my skills. And then I couldn't make the mortgage payments—so I left everything on Jerome, who already was feeling so much pressure about the store. And

didn't want the house in the first place. So, even though Laura also thought I wasn't responsible about buying the house, she doesn't get it that Jerome bore the brunt of my mistakes. And Mr. Borders thinks about just the time he grabbed me and shook me and pushed me down.

Karen Davies (L2):   It seems there's something about both of their linking everything to the violence that doesn't fit for you.

Janice Woods (C3):   No, it doesn't. He shouldn't have grabbed me and pushed me so hard that I cracked my rib when I hit the arm of the chair and then banged my head on the floor. But Jerome had never touched me before. Never threatened me. He scared me during this period because he was so panicked and withdrawn. I never thought he would do something so stupid as threaten our survival by going to some scam artists. Or not even talk to me about it. At the hospital, I got so tired of all those questions about prior abuse. It seemed Mr. Borders thought I was hiding something. Trying to protect Jerome. But he was right about my feeling bad about myself. But getting a court order against Jerome won't help that.

Karen Davies (L3):   I can see that Mr. Borders's assumptions about what happened don't work for you, and I'd like to talk about the story Laura had in her mind, too. But, first I'm concerned that you're taking on so much responsibility for all that happened—blaming yourself. It seems to me that you had lots of limits on what you could do and lots out of your control.

Karen Davies's pushing on how Ms. Woods herself thinks she differs from either her sister's or Mr. Borders's views of her lets Ms. Woods reject what she thinks are stock stories and, in differentiating herself from these stories, she reveals a lot, including much detail, about what matters to her. Thus, Karen Davies and Mark Corbett get some of the clearest statements so far about how Ms. Woods sees the violence. She thinks it was wrong, but not at the center of her problems or a solution. Her views, while they might change, also start to reveal the nature of her anger at Jerome, which does not rest on his being a stock character of an abuser. Once Ms. Woods moves on to Laura's story of an uncaring husband willing to do damage, including physical violence, Karen Davies and Mark Corbett will probably find out more. By creating an opportunity for Ms. Woods to claim her deviation from another's story, however that story connects to the standard legal story of domestic violence, Karen Davies and Mark Corbett have shifted the focus to the particulars of her narrative. Their later job in counseling will partially entail helping Ms. Woods see whether and how her narrative coincides with available legal narratives (including challenging their boundaries) or is susceptible to other ways to solve her problems—within or outside law.

At the same time, however, Karen Davies sees in Ms. Woods's narrative a different stock story that makes her nervous. While Ms. Woods has no ambivalence about who's responsible for the violence, Karen Davies sees her taking on what seems excessive responsibility for the loss of her job and the well-being of her family. Karen Davies may have her own reasons for interpreting Ms. Woods's account in this way, and may be right, but perhaps she replicates a process of relying too easily on her own standard narratives of a suffering wife. To not impose her own narrative upon Ms. Woods, Karen Davies might have concluded the segment without injecting her own assumptions.

Karen Davies (L4):   I can see that Mr. Borders's assumptions about what happened don't work for you, and I'd like to talk next about the story Janice had in her mind. But, I also see that you're taking on a lot of responsibility for all that happened—saying things were your fault. We'll be sure to get your own account. First, tell me what's wrong with your sister's assumptions?

Instead of creating yet another narrative about the source or nature of Ms. Woods's problems, Karen Davies here sticks to Ms. Woods's own words, continuing to create space for Ms. Woods's own interpretation. While Karen Davies does not retreat from interjecting her own perspective about responsibility, she now does so in a way to engage Ms. Woods in a dialogue to help her develop understanding of her own perspective on her problems.[126]

c. Narrative Time

As lawyers listen narratively, they focus on the temporal construction of clients' accounts rather than the units of chronological time. Aspects of a story that matter to a client tend to consume time; others may virtually disappear. The marking of beginnings and endings and the ordering of the middle may signal clients' understandings of the source and meaning of their troubles. Therefore, how clients account for time in their narratives can alert lawyers to how they understand their problems. Beginnings often reveal much. When does the story start?[127] Is there a preamble that sets the stage for events to follow?[128] Does the client start telling the story from the beginning?[129] The client's presentation of the beginning of the story often announces in conversation with the lawyer how the client looks back and marks the onset of problems. That beginning may change as a client's telling or understanding of the problem shifts. That beginning may have a clear definition, reflecting often a sharp break with the steady state. Or it may have a preamble, an introductory framing that serves as the context out of which a problem emerges, a kind of bridge between a steady state and a problem.

Within the middle of the narrative, lawyers must listen to whether and how segments connect to each other, as well as the transitions among them. As clients assemble, self-consciously or not, the segments of their narrative for a lawyer, they pick and order various aspects of their lives that they think matter to understanding their problem. In each telling, they may choose and reorder differently. The transitions that connect one segment to another often convey clients' feelings about what dynamics drive the unfolding of events and the development of relationships. As a narrative progresses, periods where it slows down, taking on more detail and greater elaboration of characteristics of the events and characters, may reveal issues or themes of importance or concern.[130] Perhaps para-doxically, periods when it speeds up, becoming vague and ambiguous, may also signal themes or issues that, although significant, spark discomfort or embarrassment. As the narrative progresses toward its ending, lawyers need to pay particular attention as this aspect of the story may help in discovering what clients desire. We return to issues of endings in later sections.

Listening for narrative time provides a supplement to the chronologi-cal frame sometimes adopted by lawyers.[131] Narrative time as deployed by the client is useful for the lawyer, not primarily as a tool for constructing a narrative for the outside world (although it might serve that purpose), but as a way to grasp a client's concerns, worries, or preoccupations. As the pace and feel of time[132] alert the lawyer to what matters to the client, they also provide insight into how the client thinks about those areas where the action slows down or speeds up. In the construction of the moments, the listener may hear what is upsetting, feared, or desired.[133] Thus, narrative time may suggest possibilities for and feelings about alternative courses of action. As the temporal fabric of the narrative may communicate emotions about different situations or people, the lawyer might gain knowledge about how different possibilities for handling a problem would work for a client.

Ms. Woods's initial narrative has a straightforward chronological order with a constricted time frame.[134] That story begins with her hus-band's beating her up and ends with her recovering at her sister's apartment having no further contact with her husband. Some details about her injuries and hospitalization consume most of the story. We have seen how this temporal structure most likely reflects Ms. Woods's desire at this early point in her relationship with Karen Davies and Mark Corbett to comply minimally with the entreaties of her sister and Mr. Borders and to conform to the bare essentials of a standard narrative. While the temporal structure might have expressed her desire to keep the subject of the representation confined, further inquiries from Karen Davies and Mark Corbett show other reasons for the constriction. While Mark Corbett and Karen Davies could not yet know how to interpret the narrative time of Ms. Woods's account, the temporal construction, in combination with other aspects of her narrative, indicates deeper reasons for restricting her initial narrative.

In their further interactions with Ms. Woods, Karen Davies and Mark Corbett enable Ms. Woods to expand the time frame of her narrative. In different moments of dialogue, Ms. Woods evokes important times—her unstable childhood, the decision to buy the house, life in the house, the loss of her job, trouble paying the mortgage, the discovery of the refinancing, her husband's grabbing and pushing her down with resulting injuries, her time in the hospital—but not in this chronological order. Some emerge spontaneously, others in response to inquiries from Mark Corbett and Karen Davies. Through Ms. Woods's choice of these segments, Mark Corbett and Karen Davies have gotten a pretty good sense of the issues of importance to their client as she faces this moment of deciding what to do. Returning to Ms. Woods's description of the steady state, of how things were in the house before her trouble, in which she makes the transition into her getting fired, Mark Corbett and Karen Davies explore how she sees the beginning of her trouble.

Mark Corbett (L1):	You were juggling a lot.
Janice Woods (C1):	Yeah. I wasn't so surprised when I got fired. And then juggling just got harder and harder. And my blood pressure went up even higher just when I lost my insurance. So we all lost our insurance. Jerome didn't have any at work because it was so expensive.
Mark Corbett (L2):	There's so much that happened to you to get you to this current situation with your house and with your husband. Where did it all start for you?
Janice Woods (C2):	That's a hard question. It depends on why you ask.
Mark Corbett (L3):	We want to help you deal with the problems you face in the way that's best for you. So, we want to take account of what you see as causing the problems you have—well, the ones we can help with.
Janice Woods (C3):	Like I said before, I'm pretty sure I want to start by trying to save the house—stop any foreclosure—and put off deciding what to do about Jerome. So maybe things started with my losing my job and our not being able to pay for health insurance and medical bills and not having enough money to make mortgage payments. But, you can't fix my job.
Mark Corbett (L4):	There might be some parts of the health insurance piece we can help with—programs you might not know about. But that's probably important for reasons other than being able to get out of the refinancing and then make the mortgage payments. As to the job, we can check to make sure the firing didn't violate any laws. We can't tell if there's anything there or not. As to your programming skills, we might be able to refer you to some programs, if you're interested. Now to the mortgage, which seems to be where you're most immediately concerned—we can begin to work on that. But, at the same time, we need to pay attention to whether you'll be able to make the payments if we can prevent foreclosure. I think you want to stay in your house, not just stop it from being foreclosed. And at some point, those efforts will probably involve Jerome since he got the refinancing—in whatever way you decide—and maybe your sister—again in whatever way you decide. But we'll need to figure out a lot more as we move on preventing foreclosure.

Janice Woods (C4):   That plan makes lots of sense to me. What next?

By going back to discover how Ms. Woods sees the beginning of her story, Mark Corbett and Karen Davies learn immediately that the beginning is not a fixed point. For the purposes of the representation, Ms. Woods sees the beginning in terms of problems with which the lawyers can help. The rest, while not irrelevant, is preamble, the situation out of which the trouble arose. Mark Corbett, while reassuring Ms. Woods that they will focus on the foreclosure, also engages her in discussing ways that earlier events relate to the central aspect of the representation—assuming they can save the house, she needs to be able to make the mortgage payments, which probably requires addressing different sorts of threats to her security. While respecting Ms. Woods's definition of the start of her story, Mark Corbett and Karen Davies, use their narrative understanding to place her beginning within the whole story. They look forward to what she wants and backward to what has happened, while bringing in other characters they expect to be involved in ongoing developments. With this attentiveness to narrative time, they can identify alternative ways of marking the beginning of the narrative and challenge what they fear may be Ms. Woods's too narrow interpretation of the problem. Therefore, they can engage with Ms. Woods over the significance of what she presents as preamble in a way that she can not only accept but seemingly welcomes.

d.   Trouble

Because clients commonly come to lawyers for help with a problem, whether actual or potential, and many legal matters revolve around trouble, the concept of trouble often provides a pivot point for lawyers' narrative analysis.[135] Sometimes seeing a lawyer may be prompted less by trouble than by pursuing some possible activity in the future—the conveyance of a house, the formation of a business, the creation of a partnership, the establishment of a trust. Often these activities, while filled with opportunities, also present problems, and clients or lawyers may anticipate possible trouble. Clients can experience, communicate, and frame trouble in many ways. A problem endemic to or acceptable in one client's life may be shocking or unbearable in another's. A problem may appear random or capricious in one account or made comprehensible in another.[136]

Also, clients often confront multiple, cascading, or intersecting problems that may, throughout the relationship with the lawyer, come together into different accounts in a client's construction of the narrative. Therefore, lawyers must listen for the connections among many trouble points. The relationships among the financial issues, the medical issues and the employment issues can take different forms. Because troubles and opportunities are rarely static, clients' experiences of both will also change. As clients recount their problems, hear the connections they make themselves, and experience the reactions of lawyers, their understanding of trouble and opportunity will inevitably shift. Understanding the changing connections among troubles and opportunities in a client's life, lawyers can better anticipate how actions taken in pursuing any alternative can disrupt another aspect of the client's life. Finding a solution to one problem can easily exacerbate another existing one, generate a new one, or open up unanticipated possibilities regarding another.[137] In addition, in clients' experiences with lawyers, the trust engendered or the information conveyed may contribute to new ways of viewing troubles and opportunities and to seeing new paths through a thicket of problems.

The multiple ways to understand and approach disruption in clients' lives—and disruption can come from opportunities as well as troubles—can prove overwhelming for both clients and lawyers. Jumping too quickly to one understanding of or approach to the disruption can yield unproductive activity and frustration for both lawyers and clients. Lawyers' early work of figuring out the relationship among the different aspects of disruption and a client's inclinations about which ones to pursue, in what order, and in what ways can help create a more stable grounding for future actions in the matter. The elements of narrative discussed above offer useful entry points for lawyers to see the shifting dimensions of the client's problem as they help clients identify the parameters of the disruption at the heart of the representation. From Ms. Woods's narrative so far, beginning with the relationship of characters to her problems holds promise as a way to work with her to frame her approach to the trouble points in her life.

Who is in trouble? While clients have a privileged relationship with their lawyers regarding the interests to be protected, clients' narratives of trouble often embody their concern about and connection to other people and about values of significance in their lives. Clients' accounts of the relationship of various characters to their problems can reveal the extent and nature of the disruption in a client's life, as well as the values implicated by the problems. Ms. Woods would be unable to disentangle the meaning to her and to Kevin of her worries about the loss of the house. Saving the house involves preserving her vision of life for Kevin, as well as for herself. Perhaps she even worries about the trouble that losing the house would cause for Jerome, too, especially any potential financial consequences for the hardware store. Thus, Ms. Woods's understanding of the significance for others of her troubles may figure significantly in her decisions about how to proceed. With a nuanced sense of Ms. Woods's feelings about the meaning of the disruption for herself and others, Mark Corbett and Karen Davies can better engage her in developing and testing approaches to framing and resolving the trouble.

Also, knowing the other characters' feelings, intentions, and beliefs regarding the disruption can help lawyers begin to assess how others are likely to act with respect to the trouble. Karen Davies and Mark Corbett saw in their contact with Kevin how, when feeling overpowered by his older cousin, he asserted his desire to go home. While Karen Davies and Mark Corbett know nothing about Kevin's awareness of the threat to the house or how Ms. Woods has presented or will present it to her young child, they can anticipate that his sense of stability will matter. Karen Davies and Mark Corbett also need to know more about Jerome's stance toward the house, as well as toward his violent behavior. As far as Karen Davies and Mark Corbett know, he has disappeared from events since he caused Ms. Woods's injuries. Ms. Woods has suggested involving him in preventing foreclosure and has little confidence in a court order as a way to address his violence. Figuring out how he is situated within and toward the different trouble points matters in decisions about moving forward. As to Laura's stance toward Ms. Woods's intersecting problems, Karen Davies and Mark Corbett know a lot already, but need to discover whether she will be a resource, a source of emotional support, or a dispenser of judgment in Ms. Woods's framing of her trouble.

Karen Davies and Mark Corbett can also help Ms. Woods by drawing upon their understanding of how she portrays the protagonist regarding the trouble.[138] Ms. Woods presents herself largely as an agent, sometimes even a protagonist, in the trouble she faces, even to the dismay of Karen Davies who worries that she takes on too much blame. In describing her desperate fear of foreclosure and loss, she creates narrative links among her responsibility for the problems she faces. Her failure to keep up her skills led to her loss of her job, which led to loss of income and insurance, which led to financial stress on herself and her husband, and so on. Even regarding those aspects of her trouble for which she adamantly disclaims responsibility—notably her husband's resort to shady mortgage brokers and his physical violence—she does not take on the mantle of victim. She sees her husband as stupid in refinancing and, at the very least, withdrawn and scared in not consulting with her. She sees his violence toward her as wrong, whatever the circumstances. Only with regard to her sister does she express hesitancy about her own role. She thinks about how her sister has cared for her in times of trouble, how her sister has judged her actions that are part of her trouble, and how her sister will react to her approach to her trouble.

In returning to the discussion about the beginning of Ms. Woods's trouble, Karen Davies and Mark Corbett now pursue further her framing of the content of the trouble—first in terms of the role of her husband.

Mark Corbett (L1):	.... Now to the mortgage, which seems to be where you're most immediately concerned—we can begin to work on that. But, at the same time, we need to pay attention to whether you'll be able to make the payments if we can prevent foreclosure. I think you want to stay in your house, not just stop it from being foreclosed. And at some point, those efforts will probably involve Jerome since he got the refinancing—in whatever way you decide—and maybe your sister—again in whatever way you decide. We'll need to figure out a lot more as we move on preventing foreclosure.
Janice Woods (C1):	That plan makes sense to me. What next?
Karen Davies (L2):	However you decide to proceed, we'll need to figure out just what the current state of the new mortgage is

	and what happened in the refinancing. Whatever papers about any of this that you have or could get would be very useful—notices, letters, checks, notes you made yourself, anything with any information could help.
Janice Woods (C2):	I'll get together the things I brought with me to the hospital—I took the papers I'd kept together once I saw the letter that scared me so. I was going to call the company anyway after the weekend to see about making a payment.
Karen Davies (L3):	What about the actual refinancing papers—did you see them, are they at the house, does your husband have them?
Janice Woods (C3):	I don't even know if he's at the house.
Karen Davies (L4):	So, let's talk about ways you see your husband's being involved in all this—or not. It affects even your getting the papers we need. You mentioned way back how confused you are about what you want Jerome's involvement to be. You seem scared of and angry at him—but also you mentioned that you might want him to work with you on the refinancing. How do you see his connection to the troubles you're having?
Janice Woods (C4):	He's to blame for these high mortgage payments we now have. I know he was under lots of pressure—and I was responsible for lots of that—but he shouldn't have gone behind my back that way. And then pushing me so hard that I got hurt so badly. And I'll be out of work a little longer. I'm so relieved that they're being good about my taking time off—but I'm not getting paid. I guess I want him to help fix the mess he made.
Karen Davies (L5):	Why do you want him to fix the mess?
Janice Woods (C5):	He owes it to me—and to Kevin.
Karen Davies (L6):	Do you think he wants to fix the mess or is at least willing to?
Janice Woods (C6):	I bet he can't even tell—I think he's panicked—otherwise he wouldn't have been so stupid. He's normally got good sense about financial things. The store was kind of making it. I don't know if something happened there—if there wasn't something more than the loss of my income. And even if he's angry at me, he cares about Kevin. And even if he were just selfish, foreclosure couldn't help him financially.
Karen Davies (L7):	You seem concerned about him—despite everything. Do you think he's a resource for you?
Janice Woods (C7):	I don't know. I don't know . . . . . But at least he'd give me the refinancing papers. I could call him to get them. I haven't wanted to call him—there are all kinds of things I could say, but I don't know what I want to say.
Karen Davies (L8):	There are alternatives—one of us could call him. Or we could send an email.
Janice Woods (C8):	No, I'll call him. A lawyer's calling him would just make things worse.

As Ms. Woods talks about her husband's role in the disruption of her life, the narrative has a different feel from her account of the beginning of the trouble. In the earlier dialogue, she focused more on her own role in the development of financial stress leading to problems paying the mortgage. Now, Jerome's feelings and actions emerge from the background to create links in the narrative. He has the major role in causing the immediate crisis by not confronting financial problems responsibly and in doing additional harm by so losing control and giving in to panic that he injures her. Hearing this change in Ms. Woods's construction, Karen Davies pushes a little by first using active listening to reflect back Ms. Woods's concern and then asking directly if Ms. Woods actually sees him as a resource.

This interchange about Jerome's connection to the disruption in Ms. Woods's life begins a long process of Ms. Woods's sorting out how she defines the trouble in her life and what his and others' involvement will be in moving forward. While she has consistently placed the danger to her house at the center of her concern, her job, the violence, and her health continue to swirl around her strong desire to protect against that danger. By focusing on her husband's role in disrupting Ms. Woods's life, Karen Davies and Mark Corbett refine their own understanding of how defining the problem as saving the house from foreclosure must take account of others in her life, an inquiry that reveals the connections to his violence, to her work, and to her health. As Mark Corbett signals at the beginning of this segment, an analogous dialogue concerning her sister will probably need to occur.

In the earlier segment of the discussion with Ms. Woods concerning the beginning of the trouble and this segment concerning Jerome's role in the trouble, Karen Davies and Mark Corbett have respected yet challenged Ms. Woods's framing of the narrative of trouble. They demonstrate respect by putting immediate action regarding foreclosure at the forefront of their representation. But Mark Corbett also engages her on the need to think beyond stopping foreclosure to being able to stay in the house. Karen Davies engages her on Jerome as a resource. This engagement will need to continue on the other critical parts of her narrative of trouble if they are to move effectively to address her problems.

e.   Redress and Transformation

Clients rarely arrive at a lawyer without having tried to deal with the problems they face. Understanding the contours and meaning for clients of the disruption in their lives, lawyers can more readily identify efforts to redress the harms or transform the troubled situation, as well as clients' feelings about and interpretation of these attempts. Listening to those accounts of redress and transformation as part of clients' efforts to regain or reshape their lives can prevent lawyers from imposing too early their own legal narratives of redress on a client's narrative. Narratives of efforts to fix the problem, cope with the crisis, adapt to some hardship, or escape from the situation—among many other responses—offer a beginning point for seeing what resources, capacities, and inclinations a client has for approaching the trouble.[139] For lawyers to devise ways to work with clients on identifying new possibilities for addressing the trouble—a critical component of client counseling—they need to understand how the efforts already made or imagined and new possibilities molded with the lawyer relate to clients' emerging understanding of what they can do.[140]

Even though Janice Woods presents herself in her narrative as having brought about the financial stress from which her husband's seemingly desperate refinancing action emerged, Karen Davies and Mark Corbett can listen to her account with alternative interpretations of her actions in mind. They can identify ways Ms. Woods, who demonstrated energy and perseverance in dealing with her many troubles, has approached her own problem-solving. When she lost one job, she found another. She used her skills to supplement her income. While her direct financial contribution to the mortgage decreased, she found ways to adapt the other needs of the household to making the mortgage payment. She sought help from another resource, her sister, around mortgage payments and her husband's violence. While each of these actions contains ambiguities and complexities for Ms. Woods, they also signal her openness to confronting vigorously and flexibly the multiple obstacles she faces. Seeing Ms. Woods's efforts, Mark Corbett and Karen Davies can identify other ways to approach discussions with her about addressing her problems.

As they move forward with developing approaches to clients' troubles, lawyers also need to look back to the steady state to understand the dynamics likely to affect each possible approach. Seeing how multiple trouble points created disruption to important parts of the ordinary functioning of life yields insight into which aspects of the trouble create most problems and which ones clients can and want to address in what ways. Karen Davies and Mark Corbett can tentatively identify some critical elements of the situation that preceded Ms. Woods's troubles that reappear in her efforts to cope. Ms. Woods has kept Kevin embedded in his extended family. She has adapted her own efforts to manage the long-standing conflict in her marriage around the house, going back to the decision to purchase it, by trying to contribute as much as possible to the mortgage, even with less income. While both Ms. Woods and her husband have worked to support the family—he in his own business, she as a computer programmer—the tensions over their different views of the meaning of that work for the family have erupted under financial pressure. Ms. Woods, who supported, even subsidized, her husband in his efforts to start a new business by caring for virtually all the needs of the household, has, under great stress, been unable through her own efforts to meet both his desire to build a business and her desire to keep the house. He has responded to increasing conflict with violence. Ms. Woods's sister, a regular presence and steady source of support, has remained a resource for her sister and nephew.

Efforts to cope with disruption, however limited, partial or problematic, can also reveal a client's desires—the ways a client wants to restore the steady state or transform the pre-existing situation[141]—as well as possible ways to achieve a result that fits with a client's situation and capacities. By helping clients see and evaluate ways they have dealt with the rupture they feel, lawyers may simultaneously generate new endings to clients' stories.[142] Because these conversations happen in the midst of trouble, clients' changing sense of possibilities dynamically interacts with their desires about whether to try to restore, as much as possible, the steady state prior to their trouble or to transform their situation, in ways from the marginal to the profound. Prompting clients' narratives about actual or possible ways to remedy the disruption in their lives can yield insight into the often complex and dynamic nature of the resolution a client desires.

Proceeding from their discussion with Ms. Woods about framing her trouble, Mark Corbett and Karen Davies move on to see how Ms. Woods's past efforts to solve her problems might generate new ways to approach the complex problems she now faces. Assume that Mark Corbett and Karen Davies have continued to explore Jerome's role in Ms. Woods's view of her situation and, after discussion about her sister's role in her trouble, seek to learn more about how Laura might be a resource in Ms. Woods's resolution of her problems.

Mark Corbett (L1):	From so many things you've said, it seems that even though your sister may see the situation differently from you, she's always been there for you. And you want her to stay in your life.
Janice Woods (C1):	I can't imagine anything different.
Mark Corbett (L2):	I know she's sometimes helped make mortgage payments. Assume for a minute that we'll be able to get rid of this refinancing deal and either get back to your old mortgage or some arrangement not so different from it. But it might take a while and things could be pretty chaotic until we get there. And then, from what I understand about your current job, you still won't be able to make the payments.
Janice Woods (C2):	That's right.
Mark Corbett (L3):	Could your sister play any role?
Janice Woods (C3):	She doesn't have much money. Her husband died right after Raquel was born so there's no money from him. His life insurance is all used up. She barely makes ends meet from her salary and the Social Security survivor's benefits—with rent, day care, and just living. She'd give me whatever she had, but it wouldn't be enough.
Mark Corbett (L4):	Could you see living together?
Janice Woods (C4):	Her apartment wouldn't work—except for a short time in crisis. You see how small it is.

Mark Corbett (L5):	How about your house?
Janice Woods (C5):	I'd never even thought of that. She's at my house a lot, but she and Jerome—there was tension before—but now.... I was about to say impossible, but I don't know about Jerome. I don't want to go to court, but I don't know what's going to happen to us. Like I said before, I don't even know if he's at the house. He might have gone to his brother's—or his partner, Shawn's. I don't know what I want.... and I don't know what he wants. And I don't know if we can talk about everything that's happened. Maybe, when I talk to him about the refinancing papers, I'll get a little clearer. But, if Jerome and I aren't together—even for a while—.... Maybe. I'd love to have her with me.
Mark Corbett (L6):	I know there must be lots of issues—for her, for all the kids, for you.
Janice Woods (C6):	I'll think about it.

In asking Ms. Woods to talk about her sister as a resource, Mark Corbett has moved Ms. Woods from ways Laura has helped in the past to possibilities for the future. As Ms. Woods projects a possible solution into the future, she immediately confronts Jerome again. Describing having Laura live with her as a way to pay the mortgage brings her immediately to her confusion about Jerome. But this time, Ms. Woods can move forward a little, grounding her account of facing the problems with Jerome in the details of life—she can describe where Jerome might be, what might happen in talking to him—and she can articulate the possibility that they might not be together. Narration has helped move her from abstraction. In addition, Ms. Woods's narrative has revealed that, whatever the problems with her sister, she can see Laura as more than a resource for the future, but as a welcome part of a new vision of daily life.

f. Teleology[143]

As with the beginning of a story, the end frames the account and, therefore, reveals much about the meaning of the story to the client. Within that frame, the story has a trajectory, or a telos, that drives the narrative forward toward its conclusion. The necessity or logic of the account comes from the dynamic of the narrative itself. Lawyers usually enter clients' narratives in the middle when the story remains incomplete. As lawyers listen for how a story proceeds from the past, through the point of seeking a lawyer, toward possible endings, lawyers can attend to whether and how clients' desires drive the story forward. The unfolding of the narrative may not reflect the ending a client would like, may express a constrained vision of what the client believes is possible, may echo the influence of another, or may even express a client's hopelessness or resignation. Yet, the trajectory can reveal connections between story and desire.[144]

When clients come to lawyers, whatever the disruption in their lives—whether from pursuing an opportunity that may generate problems or from troubles that plague them—they have reached at least a temporary resting place that has prompted the involvement of a lawyer. Often the client or someone else in the situation finds that resting place unacceptable. Thus, lawyers confront two stories with two endings—the temporary or partial stopping place that clients bring and the conclusion looming in the future that clients form throughout the representation. For lawyers, both endings reveal aspects of the trajectory of a client's narrative as it moves toward its conclusion—its telos. From the moment lawyers become involved, they work to understand and communicate to clients how the law, the legal system, and their own actions can affect the development of possibilities available to clients—enlarging, limiting, or changing their potential directions. As lawyers engage with clients about these possibilities, the trajectory of the story is likely to vary as clients see and understand ways that they and their lawyers may be able to affect, even within limiting parameters, their situations. Thus clients' stories about what they want to happen in the future help lawyers shape their counseling of clients about the decisions they face.[145]

Within the trajectories leading to both partial and anticipated endings, lawyers can explore the nature and object of client striving, as it initially appears and develops during the representation. If, at the point of the meeting, the trouble has reached some temporary resolution, the client's view of that state may help the lawyer understand what the client wants. In the ways that clients like aspects of the situation as it appears to them, however filled with trouble, lawyers may find something that a client has been striving toward, something comfortable or pleasing. They may see how those aspects of the partial resolution matter to the client. In the ways clients find the situation unsatisfactory, lawyers can identify violations of clients' desires. However, while clients' discontents with the state of things sometimes reveal aspects of clients' underlying desires, clients do not always want primarily to be rid of what is making them unhappy; their desire may be for more fundamental change or for some broader resolution.

In describing a future end point, a conclusion to the story in which the lawyer is now enmeshed, clients may reveal the nature of their striving, what they want to happen to life as it was prior to the disruption and life as it is at the point of seeking representation. Perhaps a client wants to get back to ordinary life prior to the disturbance, or at least certain aspects of it. The story may reveal what about that steady state feels compelling and meaningful or what its loss means for the client. That loss may have changed the client's life, relationships, or sense of self. The client may be trying to figure out if regaining that prior state is possible or if the disruption has done irreparable damage. If the harm cannot be fixed, the lawyer's understanding of the nature and extent of a client's loss may help in seeing what the client might want in the future. A client's dissatisfaction with the life that had come to feel ordinary may provide hints about how the client wants the situation transformed in the future or the reasons propelling the client to seek change.

As lawyers derive insights about what clients want from their accounts about the past and the present, lawyers can also use narrative in helping clients imagine how to get from the midst of trouble to some other, better place. Asking a client to describe what a desired future looks and feels like may provide specificity and context to inquiries about aspirations. A client who has trouble articulating a goal as an abstract ending point may be able to tell a story about a situation that brings comfort, security, or pleasure. In developing that account, the client may choose characters, imagine a setting, identify obstacles, or even speculate on how difficulties might be avoided or overcome, all of which provide entry points for further exploration by the lawyer—the same sort of entry points that we have seen lawyers use to help clients recount stories of the past.

In their interactions with Ms. Woods, Mark Corbett and Karen Davies might discern some teleology to her story. She and her son have come to rest at her sister's house, a temporary place with some comfort. But Ms. Woods's desire for her own home seems to have been a driving force in the development of the story up to this point and remains critical as she thinks about the future. Mark Corbett and Karen Davies can now use the knowledge they have developed about her desires, built into the beginning of the story and fundamental to her sense of the trouble in her life, in helping her figure out what she wants to happen. While they know that preserving her house and returning to it matter enormously to her, they still know little about how returning home relates to how she sees resolution of the other aspects of trouble in her life.

As Mark Corbett and Karen Davies used Ms. Woods's past efforts at coping with her problems to move her to consider new ways her sister might help her remain in the house, Karen Davies and Mark Corbett can also help Ms. Woods imagine what a future in her house means. Building upon their exploration of how her sister might be a new kind of resource, Mark Corbett and Karen Davies can shift the focus of the discussion to how the house involves a restoration or transformation of her life.

Karen Davies (L1):	Our discussion about the possibility of your sister's moving into the house with you to help you keep it raised lots of questions about Jerome. I know that you need some time to think about all these changes, but let's just start talking a little about where you'd like all of this to end up. I don't mean to suggest that you have any answers. And I guess you'll go through lots of stages. But, what do you imagine if it turns out we're able to keep the house out of foreclosure?
Janice Woods (C1):	With my ribs and my arm aching and still dizzy from hitting my head, it's hard to think about the future. My first thought, as crazy as it seems, is to be back in the house with Kevin and Jerome—as if nothing had happened. But lots has happened and I can't forget it.

	Kevin doesn't understand. He knows about the hospital and that his father's not around, but I haven't told him that Jerome did this. He hasn't asked a lot of questions about how I got hurt. He just wants to make sure that I'm OK and to go home. Laura brought him to the hospital right away so that he could see I was OK and could climb in bed with me. I'm going to have to figure out soon how to talk to him about all this. I can tell he keeps looking for Jerome to come and I know Jerome wants to see him but is too ashamed to contact me.
Karen Davies (L2):	It seems that Kevin's a big part of how you see the future—and Kevin's relationship with Jerome is part of that.
Janice Woods (C2):	I hadn't really said it to myself, but whatever happens, whether Jerome's in the house or not, Jerome's going to be part of my life because he has to be part of Kevin's. I can't really focus beyond that.
Karen Davies (L3):	We'll keep at this. I know that what this means for Kevin is a big part of your thinking about the future. And figuring out about Jerome is filled with complicated emotions. I'd like to come back to what you mean that you can't forget. But, we don't have to do that now—little by little, if that's what's best for you. Mark and I will have a much better idea about what to do and how to do it if we keep talking about how you want this all to be at the end.

In this scenario, Mark Corbett and Karen Davies have begun to work with Ms. Woods on getting an account of how she wants things to be in the future. Rooting the questions within Ms. Woods's own imagination, placing her within a picture in her mind, helps her see herself in the future—in a particular situation, with particular people. Her picture involves aspects of restoration of the past as well as transformation into a different future, with much ambivalence about the mixture. Keeping the house seems to represent continuity with an important stability that she established and maintained at great cost. With that stability now threatened by her husband's actions, she wants fervently to retain it for herself and her son. While wary of recovering life with her husband, with including him in her vision of being in her house, she also sees that a relationship between her son and her husband will be part of life. Ms. Woods is open to transformation.

Having tentatively identified some elements of Ms. Woods's picture of the future, even as that depiction expands and changes, Karen Davies and Mark Corbett have a beginning point for understanding how Ms. Woods might see including Jerome within the situation that represents security and continuity for her. By eliciting this account, by making the development of this scene part of the counseling dialogue, Mark Corbett and Karen Davies also can ground in Ms. Woods's account their further inquiries about what to do. Realizing that in questioning Ms. Woods about the difficult choices she faces they affect how she sees possibilities, Mark

Corbett and Karen Davies can keep returning to her own changing picture of her future. While this picture does not save Mark Corbett and Karen Davies from imposing their own image or interpreting her narrative about that picture from their own perspectives, they have a specifically delineated account about the future that they can test out and explore using the techniques they have deployed in eliciting her narrative of the past.

Karen Davies might have gotten to a similar place by asking Ms. Woods about her goals, but a goal question can be difficult for people who do not easily abstract from their own experiences or who, in crisis, find this kind of discussion hard. While others might like the distance that a goal conversation gives them and might feel freed up by the abstraction, using narrative imagination about the end of the story may, with some clients in some situations, elicit fuller, more nuanced, and more elastic accounts of the elements of the state that they seek to establish as they move toward resolution of their troubles.

g. Alternative Trajectories

As part of lawyers' counseling of clients, we have seen lawyers use narrative to explore clients' own efforts at redress and transformation as a source for potential solutions and to draw out clients' visions of the ending of a story. Lawyers can also think narratively in approaching the decisions clients face. As lawyers engage clients in exploring and assessing alternative ways to deal with problems and make decisions, narrative can help clients see how the situations they face can develop in the future and understand how each alternative approach to their problems will affect the dynamics of their lives.[146] Thus, as clients work on alternative resolutions of the disruptions they feel, the trajectories of their stories are likely to change, sometimes slowly and subtly, sometimes abruptly and intensely, as clients encounter in their various accounts of approaches to their problems the consequences generated by each alternative.

During their conversations with Ms. Woods, Mark Corbett and Karen Davies have up until now heard an evolving story of financial and family stress, housing foreclosure, illness, and domestic violence, one that has eclipsed the initial narrative of domestic violence that seemed at the beginning to define the story. They have developed through careful listening and questioning some initial understanding of how Ms. Woods's connection to her house gives a unifying and driving force to her narrative, one that seems to join together the other elements of her story and around which the other problems seem to swirl. They have started to get a sense of how maintaining her home connects to caring for her son. They are beginning to get Ms. Woods to examine whether and how her husband will inhabit her future. They have also embarked on helping her explore how she may bring the resources of her life, such as her sister, to bear on potential resolution of her problems. They will continue to work with her on identifying other possibilities.

As Karen Davies, Mark Corbett, and Ms. Woods generate and evaluate these possibilities through narrative, each account will involve both obstacles that may intrude and pathways that can be created. Often the stories will reveal consequences that Ms. Woods may not have foreseen and new material that Karen Davies and Mark Corbett have not heard. The accounts that flow from examination of alternatives may clarify or alter the end of her story.[147] As active participants in generating possibilities that elicit alternative stories, Karen Davies and Mark Corbett must exercise care that the accounts they provoke attend to Ms. Woods's sense of openness to different ways of approaching the future.

In this inquiry so far, Ms. Woods imagines new possibilities and sees potential endings that previously seemed unattainable. But, as the relationship is still new, Karen Davies and Mark Corbett have proceeded slowly, giving Ms. Woods the chance to go only so far as she is ready. Other clients may feel a stronger need to stay connected to what is known and familiar. While options might feel exciting or liberating to some, they may feel dissonant, distorting, or alien to others. Thus, the development of alternative stories about possible ways of approaching the future requires care that the imagined stories are helpful in making decisions, not frightening or paralyzing.

As Karen Davies has already initiated the process of thinking about the end of the story, even at this early stage of the relationship, Mark Corbett and Karen Davies might also begin the process of generating alternative stories about how Ms. Woods may want to resolve the disruption in her life. In a sense, they already started this process when Mark Corbett got Ms. Woods to consider how her sister Laura could be a new kind of resource for her in keeping the house. Drawing upon this part of their conversation, as well as the discussion of imagining the future, Mark Corbett and Karen Davies might now move toward bringing their meeting to a close by engaging Ms. Woods briefly in the ongoing project of developing alternative accounts of how she might proceed.

Mark Corbett (L1):	I know we've covered a lot today and you must be tired.
Janice Woods (C1):	Yes, I am. But I know there's a lot to do, probably pretty quickly. And I know I'm still pretty confused about a lot.
Mark Corbett (L2):	Why shouldn't you be confused by all you've gone through and all the decisions you'll need to make? You've been incredibly helpful to us in understanding lots of what's going on for you. Do you have the energy for one more thing that might help with getting clearer about what you'd like to do?
Janice Woods (C2):	I'll do my best.
Mark Corbett (L3):	When we talked about Laura's living in the house as a way of continuing to help you out, that presented some new possibilities and some new problems.
Janice Woods (C3):	Yeah. I'll think about that more.

Mark Corbett (L4):	But it's useful to think about other possibilities, too. For example, your job. We haven't talked about that much. Having a lower salary has made things hard. What would it be like to get back to the kind of information technology job you had before?
Janice Woods (C4):	I was so discouraged—and embarrassed—when I lost my job that I haven't thought about it in a long time. But I loved working with organizations making their systems work. I just couldn't figure out how to keep up with all the technology involved. Other people were just better at learning the new skills than I was.
Mark Corbett (L5):	How would you go about getting up to speed? Are there ways to do it quickly?
Janice Woods (C5):	There are lots of intensive courses, seminars—I always saw notices about them, but I couldn't do them. I'd need day care—or a way to take care of Kevin in the evening.
Mark Corbett (L6):	What if we could figure out something for day care, is this something you'd like to do?
Janice Woods (C6):	I'd be nervous, I think. I'm not feeling so sure of my skills. But I think I could get back into it. And it might be fun. I'll think about it.
Karen Davies (L7):	Like the possibility of Laura's moving in with you, we'll talk about this more when you've had some time to consider what it would look like and what it might mean for you. But, perhaps more importantly, keep thinking about other possibilities—even if they seem far-fetched. We'll spend time soon talking about the ideas you have and other ones we may have. But for now, let's go over what we'll all do before we meet again.

Ms. Woods might have responded differently. Her discouragement and embarrassment might have ended this thread of the conversation. Mark Corbett has also shifted the frame of Ms. Woods's story, which may not be helpful to or welcomed by some clients. Ms. Woods may have found focusing upon her job, which is not at the center of her concerns, disconcerting. But the rhythm that Mark Corbett and Karen Davies have established of inviting Ms. Woods to explore the terrain of her problems helps her move on, even with some tentativeness, toward further exploration of routes to resolution. In her account of her work, she encounters the sense of pleasure it brought her, a feeling that got squelched by her inadequate skills. By going back to an aspect of the steady state that preceded the disruption in Ms. Woods's life, Mark Corbett encourages her to see that part of her narrative about the past could be altered in her construction of the future. While Ms. Woods has not identified the loss of her job as the problem she wants to solve, she has marked it as the event that set off a cascade of other events creating the trouble she now faces. Mark Corbett has used this event to investigate another possibility that could contribute to resolution.

Each of these possibilities presents other possible plots, comprised of other actions, perhaps involving other characters—stories that have the potential to lead to an ending the client desires. Pursuing these possible stories in later conversations, Karen Davies and Mark Corbett will use their narrative techniques to examine whether other plot lines or relational dynamics present dangerous or insurmountable obstacles as well as interesting or attractive opportunities. As lawyers, they will bring their particular knowledge to exploring and explaining the role that law and lawyers could play in these stories. They will need to get a sense of how the uncertainties that accompany legal action relate to Ms. Woods's desired endings, to learn whether the ambiguities of the legal aspects of possible plots create unmanageable anxiety for her. They will need to learn more about how participation in the legal system comports with Ms. Woods's view of herself. While she does not want legal action regarding Jerome's violence, she seems very receptive to using law to stop a foreclosure, if that result is possible, and even to participating in furthering the legal action by getting papers from Jerome. Thus, Karen Davies and Mark Corbett will need to learn not just whether Ms. Woods wants the result that a legal action might produce, but whether she feels comfortable in the role that comes along with a particular legal action and whether that role confers a sense of control or power or validation or vindication.

In thinking about client decision-making as developing and choosing among alternative stories, lawyers do not abandon the instrumental or strategic thinking more commonly associated with development and evaluation of options or attainment of goals.[148] Rather, through narrative, lawyers have a complementary way to listen and talk to clients that may give clients another way to participate fully and meaningfully in decision-making. The information gained and insights suggested by this type of exchange can help lawyers know more about what matters to their clients, what clients see as possible, what actions clients are able and willing to take, and what ways lawyers can expand the possibilities available to clients without distorting the structure of clients' narratives of desire.[149]

While lawyers engage, often intensely, with their clients in this process of developing, framing, and assessing alternatives, they must simultaneously remain aware that clients may develop for themselves alternatives that bypass or dispense with the lawyer and that generate narratives with trajectories entirely unanticipated by the lawyer. Even after this meeting with Ms. Woods in which Karen Davies and Mark Corbett found many ways to engage productively with a hesitant and wary client, they may want to proceed cautiously in making sure that Ms. Woods wants their representation. They may discover that she seeks out her own way to resolve her problems. They have had access to a slice of a client's life, but that life is filled with other experiences and relationships of which they have no knowledge. Lawyers may connect very strongly to a client's narrative, particularly one that they have helped to develop with such care, and they may find deep meaning and fulfillment in the process. But, however important lawyers and clients might be to each other, clients' lives involve far more than the aspect of their experiences implicated by the representation. Lawyers, like Karen Davies and Mark Corbett here, are wise to remain ready to pull back when clients find ways to proceed outside the lawyer-client relationship.[150]

h. Themes and Morals

In clients' stories about harm or possibility, about obstacles encountered or opportunities sought, lawyers can often hear a client's theme or moral. Clients' stories often take on meaning for them within some larger view of the world and what matters in it—stories of good and evil, trust and betrayal, love and hate, justice and tyranny, selfishness and sacrifice, greed and denial, striving and failure, respect and denigration, care and abandonment.[151] While clients may or may not express these judgments, lawyers can listen for the message or the moral seeming to animate or emerge from the account. These themes in clients' narratives may infuse each aspect of the story, shaping setting, character and plot, intertwined with the ending. Or they may seem like an external message that a client takes from a single event or person, or from the client's own way of dealing with whatever has happened. These apparent or implicit codas to client stories provide another entry point for understanding how clients see the world working or how they wish it to be and how clients' values operate as they face multiple decisions about disruption to their lives.[152]

As her narrative develops, Ms. Woods offers her judgments of herself and others. At this early moment in the creation of her story, Karen Davies and Mark Corbett could hardly know the themes that will ultimately emerge or the moral that Ms. Woods takes or wants others to take from her experience. But, however tentatively, they can hear themes emerging that may help them situate Ms. Woods's actions and decisions in a broader meaning that this narrative has in her life. So far, Mark Corbett and Karen Davies might hear her story as her quest for stability against the fragility of life. They might hear it as her efforts to keep together a household buffeted by external and internal forces threatening to tear it apart. They might hear it as a woman struggling to work and raise a child without the aid or support of her husband who allows himself to act violently when overcome by stress. Their tentative interpretations may be wrong in that they miss, only partly grasp, or even sometimes distort Ms. Woods's intended meaning.

Efforts to identify her themes and moral offer ways for Mark Corbett and Karen Davies to explore with Ms. Woods the meaning for her of her account, as well as the meaning that she may want to communicate to them or to others. Their attempts to understand the meaning for Ms. Woods also increase their self-consciousness of the meaning that they attribute to her story. That understanding can help Karen Davies and Mark Corbett engage with Ms. Woods about the larger values that infuse her life and the place of this experience within it, should any of them choose to pursue these issues. It may also provide them a foundation for a discussion about values, probably later in the representation, in which they may probe or even challenge her decisions, a conversation in which their understanding helps them not impose or ascribe to her themes or a moral that distorts her desires or derails the representation.[153]

F. PRACTICES FOR ENGAGING WITH CLIENT NARRATIVES

Deploying the essential features of narrative—the elements and structure of client stories—to work with clients creates the foundation for a narrative approach to engaged client-centered representation. Each feature of element and structure creates its own entry point for listening, shaping inquiries, and guiding conversation in ways that take account of and respond to how clients present themselves, their problems, and their desires within their relationships with lawyers. We have seen how this process of disaggregation yields useful insight, promising inquiries, and productive conversation. Mark Corbett and Karen Davies in their meeting with Ms. Woods disassembled the features of her narrative to help them listen, inquire, and respond. They can continue to rely upon this process to approach the ongoing storytelling within the representation.

Mark Corbett and Karen Davies drew upon an additional set of narrative practices as they disaggregated Ms. Woods's narrative. These practices run through and extend beyond disaggregation; lawyers use them as they inquire into, reflect upon, maneuver among, and recombine the disassembled pieces of narrative. Narrative probing,[154] narrative charting,[155] narrative projection, valuing narrative digression, and hearing narrative silence provide ways to connect insights and conversational exchanges resulting from inquiry grounded in the essential features of narrative. Lawyers use these practices within the process of disaggregating narrative features but also as they explore and expand upon interpretations of a client's story as it develops and changes over time. With these practices, lawyers execute an intentional process that builds understanding of the narratives clients construct through the process of reciprocal storytelling and engages clients in using their stories to achieve what is important to them.

1. PROBING THE NARRATIVE

Narrative probing has two critical aspects. It is a process by which lawyers identify, organize, and pursue lines of questions that arise out of the disaggregation of the client's narrative into its elements and structure. It also entails lawyers' maneuvering among and recombining the elements to explore how the features come together to create a story. Lawyers—attentive to setting, characters, events, emotion, steady state, trouble, resolution, and themes, and aware of the trajectory of a story as framed by a client's sense of time and directed towards an end with particular meaning—develop not just new ways to listen to and inquire about those features, but also ways to pursue the dynamics among these features that produce the stories told by clients.[156] Throughout relationships with their clients, lawyers can both repeatedly examine how narrative features interact to give particular shape and meaning to their clients' stories and re-evaluate how their understanding of these evolving and dynamic stories informs their approach to their clients.

For example, as lawyers listen for the characters in a story, note the roles they play, their relationships among each other and to the client, and their centrality in moving the story forward, they can inquire about this aspect of a client's narrative. While these inquiries might divert lawyers from understanding the development of the plot—often the central focus of the lawyer—they may also provide indirect ways to understand parts of clients' stories that may be difficult to describe in terms of specific actions. These inquiries may also reveal clients' fears, hopes, connections, and capacities, as well as clients' understanding of the meaning of an experience within the relationships of their lives. Thus, once attentive to the elements and structure of narrative, lawyers not only have multiple entry points into a client's experience and different ways of pursuing dialogue, but also a framework for investigating how the different features of the narrative come together and change over time.

In probing the narrative's shape and development, lawyers see how particular features interact and evolve to create complex stories underlying the legal terrain on which lawyers and clients meet. Lawyers can then make more self-conscious decisions about how some aspects of a story seem to relate to others and which aspects of the narrative seem promising to pursue. Lawyers can also gain awareness of their own ways of understanding and interpreting clients' narratives. Recognizing their understanding as tentative and limited, lawyers can then inquire further about the questions they have, the confusion they feel, or the problems they identify by engaging with the client around the narrative as the client seeks to construct it. When they think that a narrative seems to miss some essential feature or be stuck on another, they can probe to find out why. When they can see how one feature seems in tension with or fails to fit with another, they can inquire about the limitations of their own sense of how the pieces cohere.

For example, when Karen Davies asks Ms. Woods to imagine the future, Ms. Woods focuses her attention on Jerome and his relationship to Kevin. While Jerome has been present in her stories, he has rarely been at the center and never linked so closely to Kevin. In addition, in the context of discussing her own efforts at resolving the situation, Ms. Woods has just considered with some excitement the possibility of sharing the house with her sister. As Mark Corbett and Karen Davies contemplate how these different features of Ms. Woods's narrative relate to each other, as they wonder what tensions or ambivalence may underlie these differing emphases or urges when asked about different parts of the narrative structure, Karen Davies and Mark Corbett will decide whether, when, and how to probe further, not just about the narrative features themselves, but about Ms. Woods's process of constructing her narrative. In the segments above, Karen Davies and Mark Corbett chose, during this initial interview, to narrate back to Ms. Woods her concern about Kevin and her confusion about Jerome, to continue inquiring about different possibilities for addressing her problems, and to stress that they are at the beginning of a process of imagining endings and developing alternative approaches to her troubles. They have, in these ways, chosen not to probe further now to get more clarity about the multiplicity and ambiguity of her stories. Instead, they have alerted Ms. Woods that their representation will involve an ongoing process of exploring through reciprocal storytelling the fluidity of her narrative to create possibilities and to help her come to resolution.

By probing the relationships among the different features of clients' narratives, lawyers have a way of proceeding when they have an intuition that something about the story seems striking or odd or just not right. They are better able then to examine the entire narrative to see if they need to inquire further into that dissonant, submerged, or missing part of the story. Lawyers must also remain aware that, as clients construct their narratives within the lawyer-client relationship, they respond to lawyers' inquiries and probing about the components of their narrative.[157] The components lawyers choose to pursue can create a narrative within the relationship that may bypass, minimize, or even conceal aspects of a client's experience.[158] While lawyers never probe all components of a narrative, their choices must reflect their discussions with their client about whether and how to explore the connections among particular features of the client's narrative. Thus, when lawyers assess whether to probe further on a particular topic, their decisions rest within the framework of engaged client-centeredness.[159]

As an explicit lawyer practice, narrative probing of how the features of narrative combine to form a story underscores one way that a narrative approach views a client as constructing a story that gives meaning to facts. Approached from different entry points, all essential to the narrative, the client's story emerges somewhat differently each time. Probing the construction of the narrative as a whole helps lawyers see that facts are not fixed and static but take shape and get meaning through a client's ongoing process of narrative construction.[160] That construction resists linear organization, draws upon divergent aspects of experience, and develops as clients engage with lawyers about the various features of a narrative that have meaning in their lives.

2.   CHARTING THE NARRATIVE

Clients' narratives inevitably evolve in response to lawyers' questions. They also vary with changes in a client's life, as well as attitudes and feelings toward the subject of the representation. Narrative charting is the practice of recording and following the changes in the accounts of a client, a practice running parallel to but informing the client's formal case file. As a lawyer notes shifts in any element—such as setting, character, or events—or in the structural components—such as steady state, trouble, narrative time, or redress—of the narrative, these shifts suggest further areas for probing. The shifts can result from or signal dynamics that exist within or outside the lawyer-client relationship and can range from memory lapse[161] to change of heart.

Attending to and reflecting on these multiple shifts in a systematic way may help lawyers see how a client's narrative evolves. The charting may reveal changes that would otherwise escape the notice of a lawyer but reveal important dynamics in a client's life. A narrative frame for this practice of charting the development of the narratives created between lawyers and clients[162] may help further probing feel integral to the lawyer-client dialogue, instead of challenging of the client's truthfulness. Asking why a character of prominence in an earlier account has disappeared may feel less accusatory than asking more directly why a client's story has changed. Similarly, a later question from Karen Davies and Mark Corbett about how Ms. Woods's picture of the future differs if Jerome or Laura lives in the house with her may feel less threatening than one asking which person she prefers. As charting increases lawyers' awareness of shifts in the features of client narrative, they may better resist their own tendencies to judge clients for changing stories.[163]

Lawyers can develop many ways to chart a narrative, from the informal to the highly structured. As lawyers experiment with their own ways of recording their narrative understanding, they can create different sorts of devices arranged around both the disaggregated features of narrative, as well as ongoing reflection about the process of development and change in the narrative. For example, they might create a separate file with categories for all the essential features of narrative, set up at the beginning of the representation. After each client contact, they might record any changes in each essential feature of the narrative, such as the appearance of a new character, or an unexpected plot twist. Taking a different approach, they might create a file in which they consciously try to record each encounter with the client as a story told by the client—in the order, with the details and chronology, and expressing the emotional texture as recounted by the client. These narratives about the client reveal how the lawyer has heard the story and may help the lawyer attend carefully to the account as the client expressed it.[164] As a third approach, lawyers might try keeping a file of their own reflections on the features of the client's narrative.[165] By recording in some systematic way their observations and thoughts about the features of client narratives as they evolve and by noting their own reactions to and further reflection about the ongoing reconfigurations of narrative as a matter proceeds, lawyers give themselves unconventional material from which to assess what is happening with a client and how they can be most helpful.

3. NARRATIVE PROJECTION

While narrative probing and narrative charting provide ways for lawyers to focus on how clients construct their evolving narratives across time, narrative projection focuses on wishes about and actions in the future. In narrative projection, a lawyer asks a client, through imagination, to extend the existing narrative into the future, beyond the point of the temporary ending that exists at the time of the representation. Lawyers can use narrative projection in different ways. Narrative projection can help clients explore alternatives that they already see within their situation or enrich their understanding of how different approaches to their problems relate to their wishes for achieving resolution. We saw Mark Corbett and Karen Davies repeatedly urge Ms. Woods to extend her narrative into the future. As clients project their own sense of potential alternatives through imaginative storytelling, they create accounts that may amplify and give specificity to the ways that pursuing a course of action will affect their lives. They may see possibilities or assess consequences in terms that feel less abstract, in ways that seem built into a context they know.

Using narrative projection, clients can vary an existing narrative as a way to generate alternatives from within their own stories. For example, a lawyer may intervene in a client's narrative by suggesting an alteration in a feature of a client's narrative about the past and asking the client to imagine and narrate how that change could affect possible routes to resolution. A character may be removed from or added to the story. A setting might be altered. Mark Corbett used narrative projection this way when he suggested Ms. Woods's sister as a possible inhabitant of the house. While Laura had been very present as a resource for Ms. Woods— she had contributed to mortgage payments and was now providing a temporary home—Mark Corbett's suggestion turned Ms. Woods's household from one comprised of Ms. Woods, Jerome, and Kevin into one including her sister and her children. He then asked Ms. Woods to begin describing what that arrangement would look like and then to think more about what it might mean to her and others. While these sorts of lawyer interventions present risks of diverting the evolving narrative in ways uncomfortable to a client, they also may reveal unseen possibilities for the future.

Similarly, narrative projection can help lawyers engage with clients in developing alternatives in a way that keeps lawyer-generated options connected to the client's own experience and view of the world. When lawyers identify alternatives from within or outside a client's narrative, they can prompt the client to imagine and narrate how that possibility may work in the client's life. Mark Corbett used narrative projection in this way when he asked Ms. Woods to imagine and describe getting the skills to resume her prior work. Although Ms. Woods had indicated earlier that she felt bad about losing her job and had not identified her work situation as a source of possibilities for remaining in the house, Mark

Corbett chose nonetheless to enter difficult territory by drawing upon narrative projection. By introducing through the vehicle of narrative a problematic possibility that presented dangers but also opportunities, he gave Ms. Woods a way to navigate that terrain within the context of her own story as she wanted to tell it.[166] While these stories might feel painful, frightening, or disorienting, the familiar activity of telling a story about one's own life in the future may make consideration of difficult options more manageable.

Lawyers' knowledge of substantive law or their own strategic analysis may also suggest or even demand that they identify alternatives for clients to consider. Narrative projection may help lawyers present legal options or legally significant questions in a context that does not overwhelm clients or helps prevent a legal framework from dominating client decision-making. For example, when a lawyer knows of a statutory or regulatory framework that could be of consequence in addressing a client's problem, but the client's story provides little or no information about whether this law may prove helpful to the client, narrative offers a way to make the law feel less intimidating or alien to clients' experiences. Mark Corbett and Karen Davies could use this practice to present to Ms. Woods her husband's child support obligation by introducing it within the context of exploring how Jerome could be a financial resource even if she decides not to live with him.[167] They know she has some hesitancy to pursue Jerome through the legal system. And she might not realize that he has a legal obligation to provide child support for Kevin. Therefore, they could ask her to imagine ways Jerome might devote some of his income to Kevin and how he would feel about providing that support. Within the framework of her story, they could then explain how the law regarding child support could be integrated into her projection into the future.

Presenting alternatives to clients as part of questioning about clients' narratives can be useful in maintaining the focus of the representation upon a client's experience. This practice can provide a check on lawyers' imposing a legal structure on the dialogue between lawyer and client, while enabling them to offer possibilities from the legal system. By expanding the scope of a client's narrative to an area affected by law, lawyers can help clients situate discussion of the law within their own experience, rather than situate discussion of their experience within legal categories. Ms. Woods likely has information about the income from the hardware store and has insight into her husband's sense of responsibility toward Kevin. By drawing on Ms. Woods's experience and prompting her to project herself into this new territory, Karen Davies and Mark Corbett connect the discussion of the legal requirements and parameters of child support to the problem Ms. Woods presented to them. They are then able to discuss with her the possibilities and obstacles in pursuing this alternative, as they would any other. With this stance and through this process, they may be better able to situate consideration of legal possibilities, particularly those that generate conflicts or other difficulties for clients, within the framework of their lives.

4. VALUING NARRATIVE DIGRESSIONS

While narration creates ways to approach and understand the interaction between lawyers and clients, it exists within the boundaries of the representation. Clients come to lawyers seeking representation for help with problems and lawyers take care in the formation of the relationship for particular purposes.[168] While a narrative frame invites a broad understanding of the ways lawyers can understand a client's problem, decisions, and desires, the importance of working within the boundaries of the matter of the representation remains. Therefore, when lawyers draw upon narrative practices, they may need to think through the meaning of their approach to client digressions from the matter of the representation.

While client digressions from the main trajectory of the story are time-consuming and can be annoying, narrative theory alerts lawyers to the possible value of those digressions as the source of hints to things the client may be worried about or consumed with.[169] Seemingly unrelated parts of an account may not be digressions at all within the client's narrative. The connection between the digression and the main thrust of the story may be important. While listening to all digressions with the hope that they may yield something valuable to the representation would extend the boundaries of the relationship beyond what either lawyer or client wanted, noting and marking the digressions before bringing a client back to what seems salient to the main story may alert the lawyer to some part of the client's narrative that actually matters a lot. These markings might be useful later, might alert lawyers to potential areas of concern to a client, or create ways to not dismiss the parts of the client's narrative that might reveal how the problem matters in the client's life.

5. HEARING NARRATIVE SILENCE AND NARRATIVE ELISIONS

Clients inevitably tell lawyers partial accounts of their experience, feelings, and perspective. The boundaries of the relationship, the conditions of people's lives, the constraints upon the lawyer, and the audiences to whom the story matters will shape the narrative the client creates within the representation. While aware of these dynamics, lawyers need to remember the potential importance of the invisible aspects of narrative. What's missing from a story may matter as much as or more than what appears. Therefore, lawyers have to listen for narrative silence. Clients may suppress, omit, or delete events, feelings, relationships.[170] Finding what's not there is, of course, a problematic activity, although certainly familiar in other areas of lawyering, for example, fact investigation. The elements and structure of narrative provide disaggregated entry points for insight and inquiry; probing, charting, and projection offer ways to explore and expand an account to create a reintegrated narrative. Perhaps somewhat paradoxically, by listening for and inquiring about the elements and structure of narrative and by searching out ways to expand and situate its components, lawyers may also sense better what a client has omitted, features that mark holes in the story, situations that remain mysterious, dynamics that create instability in the story. Narrative charting may be particularly effective at revealing the missing pieces. Using narrative practices, lawyers can better identify client silences or elisions. For example, gaps or sudden shifts in time, missing characters, unexplained variations in emotional texture, a mood that seems in tension with events, odd or incongruous settings, all may serve as clues to what a client has left out, whether intentionally or unintentionally.

As lawyers attend to the dissonances within a component of a narrative or among its multiple parts, they can better locate specific absences, gaps, shifts, or ruptures that may be important to pursue. For example, a client may omit a major character, one who otherwise exerts significant power or evokes strong emotion, from a key action in the plot.[171] What accounts for the absence? Does the client have a reason for removing the person? Is the absence a product of the character's own motivations? Is someone else responsible? Exploring these questions can help a lawyer better locate and understand the dynamic driving the narrative, as well as a client's role within it.

Karen Davies and Mark Corbett may wonder at the conclusion of their meeting with Ms. Woods, as they begin the process of charting her narrative, who or what might be missing from her story. For example, Jerome's income from the hardware store is oddly absent. While Ms. Woods describes a lot about financial difficulties leading to the crisis with the house and her own contribution to the family income, she omits Jerome's role in the finances of the family; money he makes seems confined to the hardware store. Karen Davies and Mark Corbett have no way to know the reason for this hole in the story. Identifying it not only helps them plan for their next meeting with Ms. Woods, but also alerts them that the omission may signal a reason that Ms. Woods does not include this topic. Even though a silence may be difficult to identify early in the relationship because many factors can account for a missing piece of a story, lawyers may begin noting gaps in their own understanding of the account they have heard. If these persist, lawyers may decide to probe further to discover why clients seem repeatedly to skip over or avoid those areas.

In addition, silences and elisions may warn lawyers of areas that require great care in pursuing. Not knowing the reason for the silence, lawyers do not know whether they might need to decipher both the reason for and the content of the omission. A client may feel a need to protect both. Also, while the silence might mark a matter of great significance in the matter underlying the subject of representation, it may also be irrelevant. When lawyers do not know if the omission matters to the representation, they must proceed cautiously in their exploration as any inquiry might lie beyond the boundaries of their relationship with the client, however porous those boundaries may be. Simultaneously, they must remain aware that the client may have strong reasons, related or not to the matter of the representation, for maintaining silence. Thus, in pursuing what is not said, lawyers must proceed with heightened awareness of the dangers to a client's dignity, autonomy, privacy, or cultural understanding.[172]

The components of narrative yield many entry points for the lawyer to explore what is missing from the narrative as well as what is there. While the plot may be fraught with tension or fear for a particular client, discussion of the characters may feel possible. Or the reverse may be true. While a particular character may evoke panic, worry, or loathing, a client may be able to describe actions with great specificity. A client may be better able to talk about either with another person present or in a different context. Thus, lawyers have access to their narrative practices to elicit what the client has suppressed, while also remaining attentive to the dangers of exploring those aspects of the narrative most closely linked to a client's sense of self. Finally, even when a lawyer decides not to pierce a silence or fill in an elision, at least the lawyer remains aware of the gap as it may prove significant in the future.[173]

When silence persists, a lawyer's own imagination may serve as a technique for exploring the missing content, especially those silences that seem troubling or odd in some not always explicable way.[174] Using imagination, the lawyer can try to make sense of pieces of narrative that seem not to fit together. The lawyer remains aware that the imagined connections are likely to be wrong or the void filled incorrectly. The imaginative enterprise, however, can yield emotional connections or insights to the lawyer that perhaps create increased openness to the reasons for the suppressed accounts.

For example, if a client expresses great urgency about a matter or emphasizes its importance, but then, after not coming to a meeting or not answering a telephone call, offers no explanation or resists attempts to find out the reason, lawyers may try imagining why the client "failed" to attend or to answer the phone.[175] Similarly, Ms. Woods, after offering to get the refinancing papers from Jerome, even after Karen Davies and Mark Corbett have offered to contact him, may come to the next meeting without the documents. Her explanation for the lapse may be vague and she may give reassurances that she will get them right away, insisting that Mark Corbett and Karen Davies not assume this task. Mark Corbett and Karen Davies can then imagine why she might be reluctant to explain the absence of the papers, which she knows are critical to efforts to protect her house. They may imagine that she is scared of Jerome, that she does not want him to know she has lawyers, or even that he has taken the papers to a lawyer.

The lawyer's imagined reasons may not correspond to the client's actual reasons for not engaging with the lawyer. Mark Corbett and Karen Davies may be wrong in all their imagined explanations for Ms. Woods's reluctance not just to get the papers, but to explain why she has not. The imaginative effort, however, may open lawyers to hearing other reasons for clients' unresponsiveness, may provide a kind of metaphor for the lawyer of why the client remains silent. Possible extraneous dynamics in the client's life could have supplanted the matter of the representation; possible characters could have interfered with the client's efforts to seek representation; possible ambivalence about changing the status quo might have created anxiety; distrust of or shame about needing or seeking outside help may paralyze a client. While countless other possibilities exist,[176] the imaginative moment can expand the lawyer's insight, even if the particular metaphorical reason is wrong. This very openness to possible explanations takes lawyers out of their own reactions to the client's absence and helps keep lawyers from judging a client for a failure to engage.[177] If Mark Corbett and Karen Davies learn that Ms. Woods did not get the papers because Jerome had already gone to a lawyer to begin legal action to save the house and she felt confused about whether and how to proceed, their own efforts to imagine reasons for her disengagement may help them discuss with her possible reengagement.

6. SENSING GHOSTLY AUDIENCES

Clients may tell stories to lawyers with other listeners in mind. Even if a lawyer assures a client of the confidentiality of the conversation, a client might be imagining others hearing the story. The client might have told the story before to another person and that telling influences this one. The client might have been in other situations in which formal guarantees of confidentiality were violated regularly in practice. The client may be afraid of telling another and those fears might shape the telling. Clients' expectations of themselves might be shaped by the opinions of others who matter.[178] They might metaphorically bring those listeners into the conversation.[179]

In some situations, a lawyer may be able to anticipate a non-present listener. For example, when representing a juvenile, a lawyer may sense the role not just of parents but also of peers who exert force in the client's life. In a bankruptcy proceeding, a client may worry about others who do not even know of the debts amassed, let alone judge the client for those expenditures. Even aware of multiple possibilities, lawyers might not ever discover who these ghosts are, but they can at least know that others might be shaping a client's narrative. Narrative practices such as probing or imaginative projection might help the lawyer identify an invisible occupant, an other who occupies the room and has the power to shape the client's narrative. These insights may produce new entry points for conversation, for discovering more about another listener who matters to the client, even if not present. For example, Mark Corbett or Karen Davies might, when they know her better, be able to say to Ms. Woods, "It sounds as if you're trying to convince your sister that...." In some situations, these types of inquiries, more than questions about who is influencing an account, may provide clients space to reveal how another is part of the audience.

While clients have ghostly audiences, lawyers do, too. As they hear what a client says, lawyers might be wondering about how a court, opposing counsel, an adversary, or an ethics board might respond. They might already be recasting a client's story into a legal narrative that will fit with the movement of the case into the legal system.[180] They might be wondering about how others, not necessarily in the legal system—an expert, a colleague, an employer—might respond.[181] Banishing these ghosts is often not necessary and sometimes not desirable. As part of their job as listener and then as counselor, lawyers consider and analyze how others will hear a client's account.[182] Those audiences comprise an essential component of how lawyers will constitute narratives in their actions on behalf of the client in the world beyond the lawyer-client relationship. Within the relationship, clients often look to lawyers to help them understand how those audiences will respond to the narratives presented.

Aware of their own ghosts, lawyers can assess the impact on how they listen to a client's narrative. They may at moments choose to listen without these ghostly audiences, shunting them aside. For example, they may want to banish them for awhile when hearing the initial narratives of clients, particularly when a client wishes to proceed without invoking the legal system. When they listen, as they normally do, with these ghosts present, they may choose to alert a client to their presence. Lawyers routinely evoke their presence for clients when explaining how client accounts might be heard by judges or adversaries.[183] At times, they may even turn the ghosts into real-life figures as when a colleague might do a mock cross-examination in preparation for trial.

G. NARRATIVE PERSPECTIVES ON THE RELATIONSHIP BETWEEN LAWYERS AND CLIENTS

1. PROCESS AND CONTENT

Approaching the interactions between lawyers and clients as the ongoing construction of narratives implicates the process of interaction between lawyer and client and the content of clients' stories. As to process, narrative theory generates thinking about the dynamic between lawyers and clients as one of telling, hearing, and interpreting stories. In the conversational retelling, lawyers have another way to examine how their relationships with clients affect the ongoing reconstruction of stories by both clients and lawyers. But narrative theory also helps lawyers absorb, analyze, and expand the content of the narratives constructed through successive retellings.[184] Narrative theory provides entry points into the subject of the legal matter, tools for prompting insight and shaping inquiries, and processes for penetrating and pondering the content and dynamic of the story. With narrative analysis, lawyers expand and deepen their understanding of the content of clients' stories and see how the content is intertwined with the process of telling, hearing, and retelling those accounts. In using narrative understanding and adopting narrative practices, lawyers can reshape their relationships with clients and gain deeper understanding of the substance of matters for which clients seek help.[185]

2. DE–CENTERED CLIENTS AND CLIENT–CENTEREDNESS

Client-centered representation seems to presume a relatively stable client at the center of the process through which the lawyer guides the client. However, in their representation of clients, lawyers experience many clients as shifting. They may become frustrated by or angry with clients who do not know what they want, change their minds, disappear, alter an account of an event, or otherwise shift over time, in relationship to others or in different contexts. Because the intertwined activities of interviewing and counseling seem to presume a client who can and does participate in them, providing a center that anchors the lawyer's actions as the representation proceeds, lawyers may become dismayed and dis-gruntled when a client shifts. They may feel betrayed by the person around whom their effort, their emotion, and their zeal revolve. They may feel embarrassed if a client's shift occurs in a context, such as court, that is visible to others, especially adversaries, decision-makers, or others with whom they have interacted on the client's behalf. They may feel their credibility compromised, their judgment undercut, or their confidence undermined.

Narrative theory's perspective on the inevitability of change in clients' accounts provides an opportunity to re-examine how lawyers keep clients at the center through serious and meaningful engagement with them.[186] Each client who creates instability at the center of the relation-ship between lawyer and client highlights the importance of commitments to engaging with the client and to absorbing and honoring client accounts of experience. For us, these central characteristics of client-centeredness inform narrative practices. If the endings of a client's narrative keep changing—that is, if the client changes in projecting desire into the future—client-centeredness tells us to engage with the client to discover and understand the reasons for the shifts, to learn what might connect the different narrative trajectories. Engagement also demands that lawyers analyze how their actions, attitudes, and feelings about a client's narra-tive, as well as their own narratives to the client, have influenced the client's shifting accounts.[187] In response to lawyers, clients might have articulated a desire more clearly or forcefully than experienced.

With narrative theory, lawyers can see how engaging with a client's account involves listening, inquiring, and telling guided by narrative practices, as well as searching for different possible meanings of multiple narratives in a client's life. The process of disaggregating and reintegrating client accounts reveals for lawyers the dynamic and uncertain nature of client narrative. Different entry points expose different facets and different possible trajectories of a client's story. Helping clients figure out and articulate their desires requires that lawyers understand how fluid desire may be. Goals are rarely fixed things clients discover within themselves. Rather they emerge and re-form in and through interactions with the lawyer. In exchanging stories with lawyers at different times about how they want to resolve their problems, clients may expose many conflicting hopes, fears, and wishes that re-combine as the representation develops and they re-shape their desire.

The process of engagement is not only dynamic but uncertain. Since lawyers and clients necessarily go through change in the process of re-conceiving the end of the story—the desired outcome—lawyers must accept the uncertainty that accompanies learning what a client wants.[188] They may decide to alert a client to that uncertainty so that the client knows that it is acceptable to communicate evolving desire to the lawyer. Even as lawyers achieve enough clarity about client desire to have direction for moving on in the representation and taking action guided by how clients say they want to resolve their troubles, lawyers must concurrently anticipate that the desired outcome will change, sometimes as a result of the lawyer's actions or as the consequences of legal intervention take on increasing reality. Anticipating that clients will shift from a fixed center, lawyers can become increasingly comfortable with the fluidity that comes with engagement.

In addition to accepting the dynamic and uncertain character of clients' narratives, engaged client-centered lawyers may find in a narrative approach new ways to refrain from judging even as they probe, interpret, and challenge clients.[189] As lawyers work with the essential features of narrative, disaggregating them, maneuvering among them, and reintegrating them, they can gain understanding of how the content and trajectories of clients' stories are bound to change. For example, when clients do not answer phone calls or fail to show up at a hearing even when those activities are important or even necessary to what they have said they want to pursue, lawyers' narrative practices help them suspend judgment about the client's behavior and remain open to the changing trajectories of clients' stories. Not returning phone calls and missing hearings could be ways of rejecting a formerly articulated goal or of resisting an account influenced heavily by the lawyer that the client no longer embraces—as well as responses to other demands or needs in a client's life disconnected from the problem the client brought to the lawyer. Thus, narrative practices within engaged client-centeredness give lawyers a way to respond to a client whose center seems uncertain.

Even with these principles and practices of client-centeredness—engagement that seeks to explore with a client the dynamic, uncertain nature of experience and action and that anticipates and accepts the vicissitudes of clients' beliefs and behaviors—lawyers often need a client whose desires can guide the lawyer's decisions and actions. A lawyer with a client whose desire remains in flux may flounder. Thus, lawyers, especially novice ones, may be prone to identify something as a goal, even when that concept does not fit with a client's ways of thinking or acting. A lawyer may also in various ways seek to obtain a goal statement to which, for a variety of reasons, a client may reluctantly or ambiguously consent. While this statement may provide some comfort for the lawyer in moving on, this result may create a false sense of stability. The foundation for future action, although seemingly grounded in client desire, is actually insecure. Lawyers and clients may easily become frustrated, distanced, and suspicious within this scenario.

If instability in client accounts and client desires create recurring problems as lawyers seek to be client-centered, narrative theory provides practices that can help lawyers better engage with, anticipate, and respond to changes in their clients. As lawyers deploy narrative practices, they may see new ways to work with clients to shape a resolution to a problem—to tell the end of a story as yet unwritten—aware that the process will be filled with conflicts, fears, and disappointments, as well as understanding, hope, and fulfillment.

3. CO–CONSTRUCTION OF NARRATIVES: CONNECTION AND PERIL

Because, in the relationship between lawyers and clients, a client's narrative is necessarily constructed in conversation with the lawyer, the lawyer's behavior, responses, questions, attitudes, and narratives can all matter in the recurring accounts a client gives. While theories about lawyering alert lawyers to the importance of not imposing their own values, preferences, or judgments upon clients, seeing lawyers as part of clients' construction of a narrative provides a somewhat different perspective. Lawyers are not vessels receiving clients' accounts that emerge from their own understanding and knowledge. Lawyers are not transparent screens through which these accounts pass. Rapport and empathy are not just techniques to facilitate the movement of an account from clients to lawyers, to replicate as accurately as possible the pre-existing client story. Rather, connection achieved through rapport and empathy matter because they help shape a relationship between lawyers and clients in which significant aspects of clients' sense of self may be at stake.

When clients bring problems to lawyers, they may be in a process of change or transformation that goes beyond or underlies the resolution of the particular situation. In their narratives, people give shape to their place in that transformation. As clients narrate events in their lives, they may be casting and recasting their sense of themselves and others in the world, exploring possibilities and creating new realities. Although not part of all lawyer-client relationships, this process may be bound up with the events that bring clients to lawyers or with the interactions within that relationship. Clients in the midst of crisis may be at a critical moment of possible transition or transformation. The process of relating their stories to a lawyer and hearing the stories of the law may feel dangerous, while also important. A lawyer's promise of confidentiality may fail to reach many aspects of these dangers, including concerns that have little to do with or go beyond revelation to others of these matters.

As lawyers listen to clients' narratives within this process and recast those narratives in their responses and retelling, they can identify how client accounts may be important to clients' sense of themselves as situated in relationships, community, work, and the world, as well as in the lawyer-client relationship. In telling their stories, clients may be seeking from lawyers recognition of these parts of themselves. Therefore, lawyers' engagement with clients' narratives may matter beyond the account itself. Listening to and engaging with clients' stories can involve recognition and affirmation of clients' humanity and dignity. Lawyers' acceptance of and respect for clients as they present themselves in their stories convey that the telling of the story, even if never retold in public, marks a central moment in the relationship between client and lawyer.

Thus, the activity of working with clients as they construct their narratives is an intensely ethical project. Considering themselves as contributors to clients' narratives, lawyers have an additional way to approach client-centeredness. The quality and characteristics of a client's relationship with a lawyer enable the client to tell a different story because a listener has established a connection to the client that helps the narrative emerge. Lawyers' engagement with clients involves engagement with the story. With engagement comes the responsibility to remain aware of how lawyers' expectations or desires can affect clients' construction of their narratives, as well as acknowledgment of how clients' expectations or desires affect lawyers' construction of their narratives. With engagement comes the potential to help clients see more, express more, explore more within their narratives as a way of situating themselves consistent with the values they hold dear.

DISCUSSION QUESTIONS

1. Think about a time when someone you know described a problem to you, asking for your support, advice or help. Now analyze that person's story of the problem in terms of the elements of narrative analysis. Think about each element from the perspective of the storyteller. What was the setting of the story? Who were the characters and what motives did they have? What events occurred? Who moved the story forward (exercised agency)? Which elements of the story were filled with emotion?

2. Think about the same encounter. Now analyze the story in terms of the structure and dynamics of narrative. Think about the structure and dynamics from the perspective of the storyteller. What was the steady state? Did the story seem like a stock story? Did the storyteller present it as a stock story? How did the storyteller present time in the story? What was the beginning?

The end? Where did the story slow down and speed up? When was the account vivid and filled with details and when was the account sparse and vague? How did the storyteller characterize the trouble he or she felt? Did the storyteller want to reestablish the steady state that existed prior to the trouble or to create a new situation? What did the storyteller want to happen? What different alternatives for dealing with the problem came out of the conversation? Who suggested them? Did the storyteller make any decisions about how to approach the problem? Was there a theme or moral to the story?

3. Now think about how you listened to the story. What was it like to listen? How would you listen differently if you were thinking about the presentation of the problem as a story? Did you probe for more information? How did you choose the areas for probing? How did you organize the information you heard? Did you use your imagination to think more about anything you heard? Did the storyteller ever digress from what seemed to be the point of the story? Did the digressions reveal anything about the story? What was omitted from the story? What did you wonder about those omissions? Do you think the storyteller was thinking about anyone else hearing the story? Do you think the story was told differently to you than to others? How do you think your being the audience influenced how the problem was presented? Did you think about how you would recount the story to anyone else?

4. Did you engage in interpretation of the story as you heard it? Did you convey your thoughts? What did you say back? Can you analyze your response in terms of a story? Did your response affect the storyteller's approach to the problem? How? Why?

5. Does thinking about this encounter as mutual storytelling change your understanding of what happened?

---

1. Many disciplines use the terms narrative and storytelling in different ways with different meanings. While sometimes distinguished, either generally or for particular purposes, the two terms tend to be used interchangeably in much contemporary narrative analysis. Recognizing the complexity of defining these terms, Catherine Riessman, a major theorist of narrative and narrative methodology, provides a definition that works well for approaching the conversation between lawyers and clients: "In everyday oral storytelling, a speaker connects the meanings that the speaker wants listeners to take away from the story. Events perceived by the speaker as important are selected, organized, connected, and evaluated as meaningful for a particular audience." CATHERINE KOHLER RIESSMAN, NARRATIVE METHODS FOR THE HUMAN SCIENCES 3 (2008). Speakers link events and ideas into consequential patterns that shape a story.

2. People use stories/narratives not only to tell about their experiences, but also to listen to what others tell. People hear others' accounts of events as stories, but stories re-constructed through their own linkages.

3. *See* Erin Ryan, *The Discourse Beneath: Emotional Epistemology in Legal Deliberation and Negotiation,* 10 HARV. NEGOT. L. REV. 231 (2005). Ryan suggests that lawyers recognize and permit emotional involvement in order to have any control over its contribution.

4. For a discussion of how a lawyer's interpretation of the law will affect a client's feelings towards the law, see Chapter 8 ("Talking to Clients About the Law").

5. *See* Carolyn Grose, *'Wishin and Hopin and Thinkin and Prayin, Plannin and Dreamin':* *The Narrative Theor[ies] of Predatory Lending* 21 (2009) (unpublished article, *available at* http:// works.bepress.com/carolyn_grose/6) (explaining that there are several possible alternative narratives into which every story can be organized and that the formulation "depends on perspective, circumstances and interpretive frameworks").

6. A similar relationship arises between doctors and patients, and narrative theory has been studied extensively in this field. See RITA CHARON, NARRATIVE MEDICINE: HONORING THE STORIES OF ILLNESS (2006), in which Charon analyzes the relationship between patients and health care professionals through narrative. She defines narrative medicine as "medicine practiced with the narrative competence to recognize, absorb, interpret, and be moved by the stories of illness." *Id.* at vii. See also Katherine Young, *Narratives of Indeterminacy: Breaking the Medical Body into Its Discourses; Breaking the Discursive Body out of Postmodernism, in* NARRATOLOGIES: NEW PERSPECTIVES ON NARRATIVE ANALYSIS 197, 198 (David Herman ed., 1999) for an analysis of what she calls "joint productions" or "collaborative productions" in which the doctor helps the patient continue and elaborate her story.

7. *See generally* Lucie E. White, *Collaborative Lawyering in the Field? On Mapping the Paths from Rhetoric to Practice,* 1 CLINICAL L. REV. 157 (1994) (presenting a study from South Africa on the development of understanding between lawyers and clients).

8. See Leslie Espinoza, *Legal Narratives, Therapeutic Narratives: The Invisibility and Omnipresence of Race and Gender,* 95 MICH. L. REV. 901, 913–14 (1997), in which Espinoza emphasizes that recognizing flexibility in development of the story helps the client "own" the story while working together with the lawyer to shape the "legal story."

9. Animated by a view of law as constituted by narrative, Anthony Amsterdam and Jerome Bruner, in their book MINDING THE LAW, assimilate the vast sweep of narrative theory, attentive to its diverse and conflicting strands, to distill narrative concepts and approaches that help reveal the purposes behind and operation of the law in its many manifestations, including its practice by courts and by lawyers. We share with Amsterdam and Bruner their vision that law as practiced and experienced—and not just as stated in authoritative texts—is integral to understanding the meaning and theory of law. Narrative theory embraces the activities of lawyers and the meaning and operation of law for people (some of whom become clients) who, as part of the experience of their lives must deal with legal rules and processes, enter into the controversies assigned to the legal world, interpret the meaning of the law for their lives or perform daily practices dictated by the law. ANTHONY G. AMSTERDAM & JEROME BRUNER, MINDING THE LAW: HOW COURTS RELY ON STORYTELLING, AND HOW THEIR STORIES CHANGE THE WAYS WE UNDERSTAND THE LAW AND OURSELVES (2000). MINDING THE LAW marks only one moment for both authors in the development of narrative analysis that is applicable to the legal world. It draws together the prior work of both and creates a model of inquiry and analysis upon which they and others have expanded. *See also* Anthony G. Amsterdam, *Telling Stories and Stories About Them,* 1 CLIN. L. REV. 9, 11, 37 (1994); Anthony G. Amsterdam, Randy Hertz, Robin Walker–Sterling, *Introduction: Stories Told and Untold: Lawyering Theory Analyses of the First Rodney King Assault Trial,* 12 CLIN. L. REV. 1, 5 (2005).

10. Law "lives on narrative" not just in courts and legislatures, but within the stories clients and lawyers tell each other, the ways clients and lawyers listen to and think about those stories, the projection of those stories into possible worlds, and the repeated recasting of those stories in the conversations between lawyers and clients. AMSTERDAM & BRUNER, *supra* note 9, at 110.

11. For an example of a client using narrative to create an identity, see Catherine Kohler Riessman, *Strategic Uses of Narrative in the Presentation of Self and Illness: A Research Note,* 30 Soc. Sci. & Med. 1195 (1990), in which a divorced client with multiple sclerosis creates a masculine identity while recounting traditional emasculate behaviors.

12. See SUSAN J. BRISON, AFTERMATH: VIOLENCE AND THE REMAKING OF A SELF 26–28 (2002), in which Brison uses her own rape story to illustrate how narrative is necessary to provide a basis for empathy and enable "cultural attitudes and practices" that are different from the listener's own biases.

13. *See generally* JOHN M. CONLEY & WILLIAM M. O'BARR, JUST WORDS: LAW, LANGUAGE, & POWER 15–38 (1998) (analyzing how lawyers can re-shape client stories by asking pointed questions and using the power dynamics of the lawyer-client relationship to control the discourse); Binny Miller, *Give Them Back Their Lives,* 93 MICH. L. REV. 485, 503–04 (1994) (showing how lawyers can take care not to override the client's preferences with legal stories).

14. *See* Susan Bryant, *The Five Habits: Building Cross–Cultural Competence in Lawyers,* 8 CLINICAL L. REV. 33, 71–72 (2001) (teaching students practices to recognize their own biases and avoid making assumptions); *see also* JEAN KOH PETERS, REPRESENTING CHILDREN IN CHILD PROTECTIVE PROCEEDINGS: ETHICAL AND PRACTICAL DIMENSIONS 165–243 (Supp. 2000) (presenting a chapter on *The Five Habits*).

15. See Chapter 1 ("Introduction").

16. See Chapter 2 ("Connection Across Difference and Similarity"). The label for this stage is Introductions and Greetings.

17. See Chapter 2 for more on the importance of a lawyer's attitude or tone in his or her interactions with a client.

18. See Chapter 2 and Chapter 3 ("Engaged Client–Centered Counseling about Client Choices") for elaboration of a framework within theories of lawyering for helping a client make changes in her life that reflect what she wants. *See also* Bryant, *supra* note 14, at 70 (contending that, by gaining insight via narrative, lawyers can better translate between the legal system and a client's story).

19. *Cf.* Carolyn Grose, *'Once Upon a Time in a Land Far, Far Away . . .': Lawyers and Clients Telling Stories about Ethics (and Everything Else)*, 20 HASTINGS WOMEN'S L.J. 163–95 (2009) (probing a similar lawyer-client discussion that is plagued with ethical concerns seemingly incompatible with the client's desires).

20. See Chapter 2 ("Connection Across Difference and Similarity") (discussing recovery techniques lawyers can use in situations where they seem to have disrupted communication with a client, including providing an explanation for the disruption).

21. See Linda F. Smith, *Interviewing Clients: A Linguistic Comparison of the "Traditional" Interview and the "Client–Centered" Interview*, 1 CLINICAL L. REV. 541 (1995) for a discussion of the "participatory model" of client-attorney interaction, in which the attorney is encouraged to be an active listener and to encourage the client to develop a complete and accurate recalling of the events that led her to seek legal redress.

22. *See* Muneer I. Ahmad, *Interpreting Communities: Lawyering Across Language Difference*, 54 UCLA L. REV. 999, 1019–23 (2007) (discussing the ethical obligations of attorneys working across language barriers and the ways they can meet their obligations).

23. *See* Riessman, *supra* note 11, at 1197 (explaining that the environment and the relationship with the listener affect a client's choice about what to divulge because client stories are always and inevitably an edited version of reality).

24. *See* Ahmad, *supra* note 22, at 1019–23; *see also* PETERS, *supra* note 14; Bryant, *supra* note 14, at 64–78 (outlining habits lawyers should develop in order to increase their awareness of the effects of the participants).

25. Authors from different perspectives have addressed the power of law and lawyers to shape narratives within law. For example, *see* Christopher Gilkerson, *Poverty Law Narratives: The Critical Practice and Theory of Receiving and Translating Client Stories*, 43 HASTINGS L.J. 861 (1992) (criticizing traditional lawyering as not conducive to permitting the client to tell her story); Kim Lane Scheppele, *Foreword: Telling Stories*, 87 MICH. L. REV. 2073, 2094 (1989) (defining the boundaries and limits of storytelling in understanding legal theory). Narrative theorists within medicine have developed more nuanced approaches to how narrative can intersect with professional power. *See* CHARON, *supra* note 6, at 3–4 (asserting that narrative provides an avenue for medical practitioners to increase their consciousness, engagement, responsibility, and ethicality in diagnosing and treating patients).

26. From the multiplicity of approaches to narrative theory, Amsterdam and Bruner have distilled interconnected and interdependent components of narrative. AMSTERDAM & BRUNER, *supra* note 9, at 113–14; *see also* Amsterdam, Hertz & Walker–Sterling, *supra* note 9, at 5–9, 20–22.

27. *See* AMSTERDAM & BRUNER, *supra* note 9, 113 (a narrative "needs a *cast of human-like characters*, beings capable of *willing their own actions, forming intentions*") (emphasis in original).

28. Amsterdam and Bruner think that plot holds the elements together. *Id. at 113–14. See also* THOMAS M. LEITCH, WHAT STORIES ARE: NARRATIVE THEORY & INTERPRETATION 130–35 (1986) (calling plot "properly that aspect of narrative which displays the teleology of action, an image of human experience as a series of rational actions with a necessitous end"); PETER BROOKS, READING FOR THE PLOT: DESIGN AND INTENTION IN NARRATIVE (1984).

29. Since lawyers may impute a different meaning in hearing, different temporal frameworks may coexist within the evolving narratives of the relationship.

30. This structure comes from the one outlined in AMSTERDAM & BRUNER, *supra* note 9, at 113–14. For a similar structure, see William Labov & Joshua Waletzky, *Narrative Analysis: Oral Versions of Personal Experience,* in ESSAYS ON THE VERBAL AND VISUAL ARTS [PROCEEDINGS OF THE 1966 ANNUAL SPRING MEETING OF THE AMERICAN ETHNOLOGICAL SOCIETY] 12–44, reprinted in 7 *Journal of Narrative and Life History 3–38* (1997), which sets forth the components of plot as preamble, reversal or threatened reversal, action, restoration or replacement, and coda.

31. *See* Peggy Davis, *Contextual Legal Criticism: A Demonstration Exploring Hierarchy and Feminine Style*, 66 NYU L. REV. 1635, 1646 (1992) (explaining that lawyers use the steady state to orient themselves to the client's story and to identify the trouble that has brought the client to seek legal assistance).

32. See Chapter 2 ("Connection Across Difference and Similarity") arguing that a lawyer should understand the client's situation before he or she sought representation in order to understand better what the client is seeking.

33. *See* AMSTERDAM & BRUNER, *supra* note 9, at 113–14; Amsterdam, Hertz & Walker–Sterling, *supra* note 9, at 22.

34. *See* Chapter 9 ("Fast Talking: Lawyering Expertise and Its Impact on Interviewing and Counseling") (pointing out that although a narrative may have many different angles or elements, a lawyer will not have the time to address all of them).

35. As Kim Lane Scheppele emphasizes in analyzing the importance of storytelling, "the construction and selection of descriptions of events in the social world is not just the process of gathering up facts the way one might gather up stones on the beach. The process of making a bit of information, an insight, or a description of experience into a 'fact' is itself an important part of what it means to engage in the process of lawyering. . . ." Scheppele, *supra* note 25, at 2088; *see also* Amsterdam, Hertz & Walker–Sterling, *supra* note 9, at 31–32 (describing the difference between "hard core of material" and the "facts" of a story).

36. *See* Naomi Cahn, *Inconsistent Stories*, 81 GEO. L.J. 2475 (1993) (focusing on the client's freedom to develop her story as more important than an attorney's interpretation of the inconsistency); *see also* Riessman, *supra* note 11, at 1197 (arguing that interviewees make a choice about what to divulge when they tell their stories and this choice has meaning in itself); Scheppele, *supra* note 25, at 2097 (concluding that the first step to loosening restraints of traditional legal theory is to recognize that "the presence of different versions of a story does not automatically mean that someone is lying").

37. See Chapter 8 ("Talking to Clients About the Law") pointing out that stories are rarely told the same way twice.

38. *See* Cathy Lesser Mansfield, *Deconstructing Reconstructive Poverty Law: Practice-based Critique of the Storytelling Aspects of the Theoretics of Practice Movement*, 61 BROOK. L. REV. 889, 918 (1995) (emphasizing the need for lawyers to avoid interpreting the client's story until after the client has told the whole story and identified her goals).

39. For more on the dangers of boundedness in the narrative process, see Chapter 9 ("Fast Talking: Lawyering Expertise and Its Impact on Interviewing and Counseling").

40. *See* Bryant, *supra* note 14; Peters, *supra* note 14.

41. *See* Austin Sarat, *Exploring the Hidden Domains of Civil Justice: "Naming, Blaming, and Claiming" in Popular Culture*, 50 DePAUL L. REV. 425 (2000) (cautioning against attorney construction); CATHERINE KOHLER RIESSMAN, NARRATIVE ANALYSIS 8–22 (1993) (exploring the levels of narrative interpretation and awareness of representation).

42. *Cf.* Miller, *supra* note 13, at 499 (cautioning against overlooking the possibility that clients may have other goals for their case than winning the legal battle).

43. We follow the convention of using the names that Ms. Woods uses to identify others in her account.

44. For more concerning lawyer imposition on clients of legal understandings of client problems in the clinical literature, see Anthony V. Alfieri, *Reconstructive Poverty Law Practice: Learning Lessons of Client Narrative*, 100 YALE L.J. 2107 (1991); Christopher Gilkerson, *supra* note 25; Gerald Lopez, *Reconceiving Civil Rights Practice: Seven Weeks in the Life of a Rebellious Collaboration*, 77 Geo. L.J. 1603 (1989); Lucie White, *Subordination, Rhetorical Survival Skills, and Sunday Shoes: Notes on the Hearing of Mrs. G*, 38 BUFF. L. REV. 1 (1990); *see also* Toni Massaro, *Legal Storytelling: Empathy, Legal Storytelling, and the Rule of Law: New Words, Old Wounds?*, 87 MICH. L. REV. 2099 (1989) (cautioning that the traditional rule-of-law model, which trains legal personnel to "treat cases alike" and to define relevant similarities generally, is destructive).

45. See Chapter 2 ("Connection Across Difference and Similarity") for a discussion of using active listening to engender trust and develop rapport.

46. For example, generating alternatives about "things that might be useful in your situation"; deciding upon goals ("what you would like to have happen"); and identifying actions the lawyer can take to realize the goal ("do as much as possible to help make that happen").

47. See Chapter 9 ("Fast Talking: Lawyering Expertise and Its Impact on Interviewing and Counseling") (clarifying that the same kind of mistake can be made by an experienced lawyer as well as a novice lawyer since an experienced lawyer knows the standard narratives so well).

48. For an example highlighting the risks of making assumptions in lawyer-client relationships, see Chapter 2 ("Connection Across Difference and Similarity").

49. Mark Corbett and Karen Davies may be in a clinic identified as a domestic violence clinic so their own situation may help shape their expectations concerning Ms. Woods's situation.

50. *See* DAVID A. BINDER, ET AL., LAWYERS AS COUNSELORS: A CLIENT CENTERED APPROACH 86–111 (2d ed. 2004) (explaining that preliminary problem identification can help avoid premature diagnosis which might occur if the lawyer launches into detailed, typical questions immediately).

51. *See, e.g.,* Spencer Rand, *Creating My Client's Image: Is Case Theory Value Neutral in Public Benefits Cases?*, 28 WASH. U. J.L. & POL'Y 69 (2008) (discussing the importance of identifying what story the client is using as the "master narrative" and recognizing how this expected narrative affects how the client views her own situation).

52. Many have noted how this linkage has worked to create an expectation that a woman should seek a civil protection order or how the operation of the civil protection order system works to cast women as victims.

53. *See* Alfieri, *supra* note 44, at 2123 (arguing that pre-understanding, "a method of social construction that operates by applying a standard narrative to a client's story," is a problem that arises from traditional legal approaches).

54. BINDER ET AL., *supra* note 50, at 5.

55. *See* Miller, *supra* note 13, at 504 (arguing that clients must be given the chance to evaluate the non-legal consequences of a solution).

56. See Chapter 3 ("Engaged Client–Centered Counseling about Client Choices") explaining how clients, as the ultimate owners of their problems, deserve to be fully informed of the consequences and then permitted to make their own decisions. *See also* Corey S. Shdaimah, NEGOTIATING JUSTICE: PROGRESSIVE LAWYERING, LOW-INCOME CLIENTS, AND THE QUEST FOR SOCIAL CHANGE 68–96 (2009) (evaluating the tension that can emerge between client autonomy and a client's decision to seek an attorney's advice).

57. For a consideration of the tension that exists between becoming emotionally involved or remaining detached from a client's story, see Ryan, *supra* note 3, at 251. Ryan compares the need to keep emotions from impairing legal judgment with the potential costs that "clients who feel that their attorney is missing or ignoring the emotional impact of their dilemma may become dispirited."

58. For a discussion of how lawyers use a client's narrative silence to fit their case into a particular mold that is more likely to lead to a success for the lawyer, see Anthony V. Alfieri, *Welfare Stories*, in LAW STORIES: LAW, MEANING, AND VIOLENCE 36 (Gary Bellow and Martha Minow eds., 1996). See also Chapter 9 ("Fast Talking: Lawyering Expertise and Its Impact on Interviewing and Counseling") discussing further the warning against standard narratives and Chapter 8 ("Talking to Clients About the Law") explaining the dangers of trying to fit a client's narratives into a standard legal framework.

59. For more on how expert knowledge allows lawyers to distinguish between facts or events that are important for the client narrative and those that do not require further exploration, see Chapter 9 ("Fast Talking: Lawyering Expertise and Its Impact on Interviewing and Counseling").

60. *See* Katherine R. Kruse, *Fortress in the Sand: The Plural Values of Client–Centered Representation*, 12 CLINICAL L. REV. 369, 379 (2005–2006) (emphasizing the importance of being able to discern a client's story from a standard narrative).

61. John Conley and William O'Barr identify two types of clients, the rule-oriented client and the relational-oriented client, who might react to this situation differently. JOHN M. CONLEY & WILLIAM M. O'BARR, RULES VERSUS RELATIONSHIPS: THE ETHNOGRAPHY OF LEGAL DISCOURSE 58–61 (1990).

62. *See* Massaro, *supra* note 44, at 2101 (cautioning against traditional legal theory's tendency to treat similar cases alike).

63. For an explanation of how these tangents in the narrative may prove helpful to an attorney, see Catherine Kohler Riessman, *Beyond Reductionism: Narrative Genres in Divorce Accounts*, 1 J. NARRATIVE & LIFE HIST. 41 (1991). Riessman argues that narratives are "not necessarily organized around linear time, but contain flashbacks, flashforwards, circular time, and topic-centered discourse—a kind of time traveling where past experience and future possibilities are used to create present meaning." *Id.* at 45.

64. *See generally* Austin Sarat & William L. Felstiner, *Law and Social Relations: Vocabularies of Motive in Lawyer/Client Interaction*, 22 LAW & SOC'Y REV. 737 (1998) (analyzing vocabularies of motive in order to make sense out of people's actions and behaviors).

65. The question can be seen within lawyering theory as creating a transition to the next stage of the interview. For a discussion of the uses of open-ended questions in client interviews, see Chapter 2 ("Connection Across Difference and Similarity").

66. For more on the importance of open-ended questions when first meeting a client, see Chapter 9 ("Fast Talking: Lawyering Expertise and Its Impact on Interviewing and Counseling").

67. See Chapter 2 ("Connection Across Difference and Similarity") about how a lawyer should allow the client to describe her problem and related concerns at some length without at this early stage assuming too much about the facts or nature of the legal problem. *See also* Laurie Shanks, *Whose Story Is It Anyway? Guiding Students to Client–Centered Interviewing Through Storytelling*, 14 CLINICAL L. REV. 509, 532–33 (2008) (teaching exercises for students that can help clinic students encourage unencumbered client responses). *Cf.* J.A. Clark & E. Mishler, *Attending to Patients' Stories: Reframing the Clinical Task*, 14 SOC. HEALTH & ILLNESS, 344, 352 (1992) (encouraging physicians to use the information patients have provided to elicit more information, a method that is meant to act as an invitation to patients to tell stories).

68. *See* JEROME S. BRUNER, MAKING STORIES: LAW, LITERATURE, AND LIFE 63–88 (2003) (explaining that self-making is guided by cultural modes and the speaker's expectations of what the listener wants to hear); *see, e.g.,* BRISON, *supra* note 12, at 106 (explaining that, following her rape, she adapted her recounting of the event to the particular listener and what she thought that listener needed to know).

69. This is an example of how engaged client-centered lawyering does not need to take much more time than seemingly more routine approaches. See Chapter 9 ("Fast Talking: Lawyering Expertise and Its Impact on Interviewing and Counseling").

70. The reasons a client seeks out legal help may overlap with, but are often distinct from, the client's decisions about what he or she wants to achieve in the representation.

71. See CHARON, *supra* note 6, at 4, for a description of an analogous process of listening: "I had to follow the patient's narrative thread, identify the metaphors or images used in the telling, tolerate ambiguity and uncertainty as the story unfolded, identify the unspoken subtexts, and hear one story in light of others told by this teller. . . . I also had to be aware of my own response to what I heard, allowing myself to be personally moved to action on behalf of the patient. I was the interpreter of these accounts of events of illness that are, by definition, unruly and elusive."

72. See Chapter 6 ("Truth and Consequences") examining choices lawyers face in deciding about whether and how to pursue truth. See also Chapter 4 ("Interviewing and Counseling Atypical Clients") describing the importance of knowing what to pursue and how to pursue those matters when interviewing and counseling a client with an intellectual disability.

73. See Chapter 2 ("Connection Across Difference and Similarity") and Chapter 3 ("Engaged Client–Centered Counseling About Client Choices") for discussion of how a client-centered approach helps build trust and rapport. *Cf.* Rita Charon, *Narrative Medicine: A Model for Empathy, Reflection, Profession and Trust*, 286 J. AM. MED. ASS'N. 1897 (2001).

74. According to John M. Conley and William M. O'Barr, shifting perspectives in a story may serve to allow the "relevant party" to speak, revealing motives of the speaker, and to highlight important parts of the story. *See* CONLEY & O'BARR, *supra* note 61, at 39.

75. *See* Amsterdam, *supra* note 9, at 17–18.

76. See Chapter 2 ("Connection Across Difference and Similarity") discussing the importance of being aware of how a client sees himself and his relationship with others changing as a result of a particular legal outcome.

77. *See generally* AMSTERDAM & BRUNER, *supra* note 9, at 131–33 (exploring the historical and literary purposes of characters and the different types of characters that are traditionally found in narratives); THOMAS M. LEITCH, WHAT STORIES ARE: NARRATIVE THEORY AND INTERPRETATION 148–58 (1986) (presenting the literary theory of what a character is and how the character fits into the narrative).

78. Different cultures may constitute the role of others in a person's decisions in a variety of ways. A client may bring a cultural understanding that others are intrinsic to a decision-making process. Lawyers may be unaware of or inattentive to these dynamics as they listen to clients' stories. *See* Bryant, *supra* note 14, at 33. *Cf.* Rand, *supra* note 51, at 69 (positing that listening to how clients characterize other members of their social group can help reveal limitations that are imposed by a client's personal concern with social labels).

79. For a study of motive in lawyer-client relationships, see Sarat & Felstiner, *supra* note 64, in which divorce cases are used to examine how lawyers and clients attribute motive to define behaviors and make sense of the events that brought the client to the lawyer.

80. See Chapter 2 ("Connection Across Difference and Similarity") for a discussion of active listening as the process of hearing a client's message and reflecting it back.

81. *See* Espinoza, *supra* note 8, at 913–14 (arguing that, although the client should "own" her story, the client also needs the attorney to shape the account into a "legal story").

82. Until they enter the process of narrative probing. *E.g.,* Clark & Mishler, *supra* note 67, at 368.

83. See Chapter 2 ("Connection Across Difference and Similarity") encouraging a practice of allowing clients to give full descriptions of events before asking questions.

84. *See* Smith, *supra* note 21, at 543 (explaining that the participatory model of interviewing promotes client dignity); *see also* Chapter 9 ("Fast Talking: Lawyering Expertise and Its Impact on Interviewing and Counseling") (discussing the importance of allowing a client to tell his or her story even within a limited time-frame); Chapter 6 ("Truth and Consequences") (noting the importance of respecting the client by not assuming the client prefers self-interest to the truth).

85. See generally CONLEY & O'BARR, *supra* note 13, at 15–38, for a discussion how the power dynamics between lawyers and clients put lawyers in a position to shape the discourse by choosing the topic and asking pointed questions.

86. For an approach that attempts to refrain from directing the client's story, see Catherine Kohler Riessman, *When Gender is Not Enough: Women Interviewing Women,* 1 GENDER & SOC'Y 172, 176 (1987) (suggesting the use of non-lexical expressions to communicate understanding and encourage the narrator to continue, as well as questions for clarification that builds on the narrator's previous statement and prompts continued narrative).

87. *See, e.g.,* Ahmad, *supra* note 22 (exploring methods for dealing with cultural gaps in communication); *see also* Bryant, *supra* note 14, at 71–72; PETERS, *supra* note 14. See also Chapter 2 ("Connection Across Difference and Similarity") (highlighting how inconsistent statements should be explored because the reasons behind the inconsistencies might reflect client's goals or concerns); Chapter 4 ("Interviewing and Counseling Atypical Clients") (providing an example of how expectations may affect a client's account).

88. *See, e.g.,* BRISON, *supra* note 12, at 102 (describing a narrative as a social interaction "in which what gets told is shaped by the (perceived) interests of the listeners, by what the listeners want to know and also by what they cannot or will not hear").

89. See Chapter 8 ("Talking to Clients About the Law") for an analysis of how interpretation of the law matters in eliciting stories from clients.

90. See Chapter 6 ("Truth or Consequences") for discussion of the difficulties of seeking truth.

91. *See* Austin Sarat & William L.F. Felstiner, *Lawyers and Legal Consciousness: Law Talk in the Divorce Lawyer's Office,* 98 YALE L.J. 1663 (1989) (arguing that lawyers can help their clients by providing knowledge of the legal process, legal actors, and alternative solutions so that clients can make an informed decision about how to proceed).

92. *See* Shanks, *supra* note 67, at 532–33 (teaching lawyers to show clients what they are writing down and to explain the legal process going forward).

93. *Cf.* Riessman, *supra* note 63, at 46, for alternative forms of narrative that may be used. Riessman specifically explores three types: habitual narrative, hypothetical narrative, and approach-avoidance narrative.

94. For an argument that inconsistent stories are acceptable and important to narrative development, see Cahn, *supra* note 36, at 2501–04 (asserting that preservation of the client's voice is important to an attorney's interpretation of the story). *See also* Gilkerson, *supra* note 25 (asserting that, because clients are uncertain of their legal rights, they use their initial story as a tool to convince the lawyer of their rightness in the situation).

95. *See* Clark & Mishler, *supra* note 67, at 368 (defining good listening as a "joint effort" that develops the story through the listener's probing requests and acknowledgments).

96. *See* Espinoza, *supra* note 8, at 913–14 (emphasizing that clients' stories are not static but change as their lives continue and that attorneys need to recognize the importance of flexibility in developing the legal story).

97. For more about the interaction of client autonomy and attorney guidance, see generally SHDAIMAH, *supra* note 56, at 67–98 (analyzing tensions in goal of autonomy).

98. To learn skills for avoiding making assumptions that may be detrimental to understanding a client or a case, see Bryant, *supra* note 14, at 71–72; PETERS, *supra* note 14.

99. See Chapter 9 ("Fast Talking: Lawyering Expertise and Its Impact on Interviewing and Counseling") which stresses the importance of lawyers' being aware of how they influence different stages of their relationships with their clients.

100. *See, e.g.,* Riessman, *supra* note 11, at 1197 (recognizing that all stories are an edited version of reality).

101. See Chapter 3 ("Engaged Client–Centered Counseling About Client Choices") for an explanation of how engaged client-centered counseling does not simply accept a client's view without probing for an articulation of the client's rationale or challenging a client's assumptions.

102. For more on talking with a client about interpretations of the law at odds with the client's own perspective, see Chapter 8 ("Talking to Clients About the Law").

103. *Cf.* Clark & Mishler, *supra* note 67, at 352 (explaining how in medicine physicians use specific information the patient has presented to elicit more details about possibly important symptoms the patient has overlooked).

104. See Chapter 6 ("Truth and Consequences") for a full discussion of alternative approaches for working with clients when a lawyer believes a client is lying.

105. For a discussion of the limits of proceeding chronologically, see Riessman, *supra* note 86, at 173–183. *See also* Kristin M. Langellier & Eric E. Peterson, *Spinstorying: An Analysis of Women's Storytelling, in* PERFORMANCE, CULTURE, AND IDENTITY 157 (E. Fine & J. Speer eds. 1992) (presenting "kernel stories" that begin with the most significant part of the story as an alternative to a chronological structure).

106. For a consideration of why Karen Davies has the power to direct the conversation, see Conley & O'Barr, *supra* note 13, at 91. Analogous situations can also be found in medicine, in which patients cede to doctors the exclusive right to initiate and direct the conversation. *See* Young, *supra* note 6, at 198.

107. *See* RIESSMAN, *supra* note 41, at 3 (distinguishing the narrative approach of allowing a client to weave her or his own narrative from an approach that fractures a story into snippets of response that detract from the narrative meaning).

108. *See* Lucie White, *Seeking "The Faces of Otherness": A Response to Professors Sarat, Felstiner, and Cahn,* 77 CORNELL L. REV. 1499 (1992) (discussing Foucault's notion of the flows of power and applying it to the lawyer-client relationship).

109. *See* Ann Shalleck, *Theory and Experience in Constructing the Relationship Between Lawyer and Client: Representing Women Who Have Been Abused*, 64 TENN. L. REV. 1019, 1022–1027 (1997) (discussing victimization and agency in the representation of women who have been abused); BRISON, *supra* note 12, at 29–30 (identifying the dangers of generalizing about victimization); LISA A. GOODMAN & DEBORAH EPSTEIN, LISTENING TO BATTERED WOMEN 94 (2008) (discussing the importance of having control within the legal process).

110. *See* Chapter 2 ("Connection Across Difference and Similarity") (explaining how adding a client's emotions into a chronology of events transforms the account).

111. *See* Ryan, *supra* note 3, at 240, for a discussion of balancing emotion and reason. Ryan suggests that permitting emotional involvement is necessary for fully developed understanding. *See also* Kruse, *supra* note 60, at 377 (highlighting the importance of using the client's emotions in the act of decision-making); Chapter 9 ("Fast Talking: Lawyering Expertise and Its Impact on Interviewing and Counseling") (suggesting a technique for handling a client's emotions in the decision-making process).

112. *See, e.g.,* Riessman, *supra* note 63, at 41 (focusing on emotion as the organizing factor the client uses to justify why the divorce is necessary).

113. For more on the importance of emotions in a client's account, see Gary Bellow & Martha Minow, *Introduction: Rita's Case and Other Stories, in* LAW STORIES: LAW, MEANING, AND VIOLENCE 26 (Gary Bellow & Martha Minow, eds., 1996).

114. *See* AMSTERDAM & BRUNER, *supra* note 9, at 46 (describing a story's movement as going from "*an anterior steady state* (the prevalence or promise of a usual, expected, legitimate state of affairs) through some setback, reversal, or disruption (the Trouble)").

115. *See* Grose, *supra* note 19, at 180 (arguing that lawyers have to become familiar with "the multiple layers of the client's steady state" in order to fully grasp the client's reasons for seeking legal assistance).

116. *See* AMSTERDAM & BRUNER, *supra* note 9, at 121.

117. *See id.* at 117–18. *See also* Alfieri, *supra* note 44, at 2123 (calling this step "pre-understanding" and articulating a concern that applying standard narratives silences the voices of clients).

118. *Cf.* Rand, *supra* note 51, at 69, for a discussion of identifying master narratives in the welfare context.

119. *See* AMSTERDAM & BRUNER, *supra* note 9, at 121–22; Amsterdam, Hertz & Walker–Sterling, *supra* note 9, at 7.

120. *See, e.g.,* BRUNER, *supra* note 68, at 63–88 (presenting a theory that narratives are molded to create a self that the speaker thinks fits with cultural and the listener expectations); *cf.* BRISON, *supra* note 12, at 102 (describing her own post-rape experience that seemed to force her into one rigid version of her story).

121. *See* Amsterdam, *supra* note 9, at 23 n.78.

122. *See* AMSTERDAM & BRUNER, *supra* note 9, at 121.

123. See discussion *supra* pp. 153–57.

124. *See* AMSTERDAM & BRUNER, *supra* note 9, at 121–22; Amsterdam, Hertz & Walker–Sterling, *supra* note 9, at 16.

125. See Chapter 8 ("Talking to Clients About the Law") in which a lawyer, upon meeting with her client for the first time, "has already given shape to his story within the legal framework of child support and may have missed an entirely different story that Jeffries wants to tell."

126. For another example of an interaction between client and lawyer in which the lawyer interjects his own perspective on the situation in order to get the client to think more deeply about his decision, see Chapter 3 ("Engaged Client–Centered Counseling About Client Choices").

127. *See* Amsterdam, *supra* note 9, at 18.

128. *See* AMSTERDAM & BRUNER, *supra* note 9, at 122.

129. *See id.* at 124; Amsterdam, *supra* note 9, at 12.

130. *See* AMSTERDAM & BRUNER, *supra* note 9, at 124.

131. Narrative time is the pacing and spacing of an oral narrative that delineates particular moments. For example, in *Making Sense of Marital Violence: One Woman's Narrative, in* STORIED LIVES: THE CULTURAL POLITICS OF SELF-UNDERSTANDING 231, 239 (G. C. Rosenwald & R. L. Ochberg eds. 1992), Catherine Kohler Riessman explains how the woman's ellipses draw attention to the climax of the story, the final scene in which her husband rapes her, which led her to seek legal assistance.

132. *See* AMSTERDAM & BRUNER, *supra* note 9, at 124.

133. *See, e.g.,* Riessman, *supra* note 131, at 239 (asserting that the temporal structure chosen by the client can be used to give the story meaning, highlight specific facts, and draw attention to the climax).

134. For more about the various temporal structures the narrative could have taken, see RIESSMAN, *supra* note 41, at 17 (listing the three possible structures as chronological, consequential, and episodic). For a study of episodic storytelling, see Langellier & Peterson, *supra* note 105, at 162 (explaining that episodic, or kernel, stories lack a specific length, structure or climax).

135. *See* Davis, *supra* note 31, at 1643 (defining the trouble as the reason the client seeks legal redress).

136. *See* AMSTERDAM & BRUNER, *supra* note 9, at 130.

137. *See* Amsterdam, Hertz & Walker–Sterling, *supra* note 9, at 26.

138. *See, e.g.,* LEITCH, *supra* note 28, at 46 (comparing the role of the protagonist in a static story with the protagonist in a dynamic story).

139. *See, e.g.,* Trisha Greenhalgh, *Narrative Based Medicine in an Evidence Based World, in* NARRATIVE BASED MEDICINE: DIALOGUE AND DISCOURSE IN CLINICAL PRACTICE 318, 323–25 (T. Greenhalgh & B. Hurwitz eds., 1999) (arguing that doctors should interpret symptoms in light of the specific story of the individual patient in order to tailor a diagnosis).

140. See Chapter 3 ("Engaged Client–Centered Counseling About Client Choice") for how a lawyer explores a client's own efforts at solving a problem before moving on to other possibilities.

141. *See* AMSTERDAM & BRUNER, *supra* note 9, at 133 (recognizing that the "right ending" for some stories is restoration to a previous steady state, while for others it is a transformation to a new steady state).

142. See Chapter 3 ("Engaged Client–Centered Counseling About Client Choices") for how a lawyer uses a client's past efforts to remedy the problems as clues to identify possible solutions.

143. *See generally* AMSTERDAM & BRUNER, *supra* note 9, at 127–29 (discussing narrative teleology); LEITCH, *supra* note 28, at 42–62 (providing a literary explanation and analysis of teleology).

144. For a discussion of the importance of closure, or endings, to a narrative, see LEITCH, *supra* note 28, at 42–44, explaining that an entire narrative is defined by its ending and its trajectory towards that ending.

145. See Chapter 3 ("Engaged Client–Centered Counseling About Client Choices") for discussion of how lawyers identify what matters to a client in the future as part of framing different ways to proceed. See also Chapter 2 ("Connection Across Difference and Similarity") showing the importance of "hearing out your client's 'wildest dreams.' "

146. *See, e.g.,* AMSTERDAM & BRUNER, *supra* note 9, at 153–59 (comparing the use of the trajectory of the action to reach a desired result in Supreme Court opinions with classic tragedy structures).

147. See Chapter 3 ("Engaged Client–Centered Counseling About Client Choices") for an examination of the ways the consideration of alternatives reveals new aspects of a situation.

148. See Chapter 3 ("Engaged Client–Centered Counseling About Client Choices") for an examination of this process of strategic thinking.

149. *See, e.g.*, Grose, *supra* note 19, at 163 (exploring how narrative can help lawyers and clients develop alternatives for approaching a legal problem that avoid distortion of clients' wishes).

150. As lawyers work with clients, they may find the process of both engaging while remaining open to disengagement emotionally difficult, particularly when they disagree with clients' decisions or when clients unexpectedly or seemingly inexplicably extricate themselves from the lawyer-client relationship. See Chapter 3 ("Engaged Client–Centered Counseling About Client Choices") for a discussion of clients' hesitancies about the process of engagement. See also Chapter 7 ("Engaging in Moral Dialogue") for analysis of the particular challenges to client engagement created by a lawyer's decision to pursue moral dialogue as part of client decision-making.

151. *See* Sarat & Felstiner, *supra* note 64, at 740 (discussing how lawyers and clients create meaning from life events).

152. *See* Davis, *supra* note 31, at 1635 (examining how the coda allows a client to evaluate the meaning of the story for herself).

153. See Chapter 7 ("Engaging in Moral Dialogue") which explores the factors involved in engaging in discussion of values, as well as techniques that further productive discussions about difficult issues that may involve conflicts in values between lawyers and clients.

154. *See* Bryant, *supra* note 14, at 71–72 (suggesting how students can use narrative probing); *cf.* Clark & Mishler, *supra* note 67, at 368 (defining good listening as a "joint effort" that develops the story through the listener's probing requests and acknowledgments).

155. *See* Charon, *supra* note 73, at 1898–99 (teaching medical practitioners to chart their patients' stories and take the time to reflect back on the narrative before reaching any conclusions).

156. See Chapter 3 ("Engaged Client–Centered Counseling About Client Choices") for a discussion of the importance of a lawyer's attentiveness to the client's narrative.

157. As with all lawyer-client dialogue, this narrative construction is bounded by the parameters of the ethical rules. Discussion of ethical questions, like other matters in the representation, is susceptible to narrative analysis. *See* Grose, *supra* note 19, at 163.

158. See Chapter 6 ("Truth or Consequences") for a discussion of the parameters of pursuing truth.

159. See Chapter 3 ("Engaged Client–Centered Counseling About Clients Choices") explaining how honoring a client's choices and engaging in probing inquiry are not only consistent, but can reflect respect for the dignity of the client.

160. For alternative forms of narrative construction, see Reissman, *supra* note 63, at 46–63, discussing the use of habitual narratives, hypothetical narratives and approach-avoidance narratives.

161. For more information on trauma and memory lapses, see Bessel A. Van Der Kolk & Onno Van Der Hart, *The Intrusive Past: The Flexibility of Memory & the Engraving of Trauma*, *in* TRAUMA: EXPLORATIONS IN MEMORY 158 (Cathy Caruth ed., 1995).

162. *See* Charon, *supra* note 73, at 1898–99.

163. *See* Bryant, *supra* note 14, at 71–72 (examining assumptions in interviewing and suggesting solutions to avoid judging changes in the story).

164. *See* CHARON, *supra* note 6, at 187–89. Charon describes the process of creating this kind of chart of a visit with a patient: "I try my best to register the diction, the form, the images, the pace of speech. I pay attention—as I sit on the edge of my seat, absorbing what is being given—to metaphors, idioms, accompanying gestures, as well as plot and characters represented for me.... [My] notes are far more telling than they used to be—perhaps not systematically structured ... but filled now with levels of truth, evocative, alive to the presence of patients, and dutiful to the honor of having heard them out."

165. *See id.* at 155–74 (describing in detail the parallel chart). Charon defines the practice of parallel charting as "a method ... of encouraging health care professionals and students to write, in nontechnical language, about what they witness about their patients' experiences and what they themselves undergo in caring for the sick." *Id.* at 6, n.21.

166. Other difficult topics might also be explored this way. At some point, Mark Corbett and Karen Davies might ask Ms. Woods to imagine life in the future not in her house, either because they see a risk that they may not be able to stop a foreclosure or the options for sustaining the house are all too fraught with problems. They might also ask Ms. Woods to imagine having supports other than Laura or Jerome.

167. See Chapter 8 ("Talking to Clients About the Law") where a lawyer, using narrative, explains the legal options available to her incarcerated client, who is concerned about meeting his child support obligations while in jail. Mark Corbett and Karen Davies might use a similar approach.

168. See, e.g., Sarat & Felstiner, supra note 91, at 1671–76 (discussing the rules, both explicit and implicit, attorneys abide by in client interactions).

169. Cf. LEITCH, supra note 28, at 73–76 (analyzing the structure and meaning of narrative digressions in literature).

170. See Stefan H. Krieger, A Time to Keep Silent and a Time to Speak: The Functions of Silence in the Lawyering Process, 80 OR. L. REV. 199 (2001) (exploring the meanings of silence in speech, including the effects of structural relationships, power imbalances, and emotional dynamics); see also Riessman, supra note 41, at 12 (cautioning against deleting silences and nonlexicals in interpreting a client story because these choices have meaning).

171. The line from the Bob Dylan song, Lily, Rosemary and the Jack of Hearts, "The only person on the scene missing was the Jack of Hearts," captures this concept. BOB DYLAN, Lily, Rosemary and the Jack of Hearts, on BLOOD ON THE TRACKS (Columbia Records 1974).

172. See Ahmad, supra note 22, at 1063; Alfieri, supra note 58, at 36; Bryant, supra note 14, at 38.

173. For one context within which a lawyer might leave a silence but needs to be aware of a gap, see Chapter 6 ("Truth and Consequences") (noting that "in the imperfect world and nation in which we live, there may well be circumstances where the lawyer's full discovery of truth, and the subsequent ethical obligations incurred by such knowledge, will lead to results that she conscientiously sees as unjust").

174. See CHARON, supra note 6, at 5–6. Charon provides an account of using her imagination to open up insight about possible reasons for silence and to build connection that guides further inquiry. While her imaginative guesses at making sense of the silence were wrong, the narrative act of imagining a story to explain the silence acted as a "tool with which to get to the truth." Id. at 6. In addition, the imagined story "invested [Charon] in learning of [the patient's] true plight instead of blaming her or suspecting her of malingering." Id.

175. See Bryant, supra note 14, at 70–72 (analogizing this imaginative process with the process of parallel universe thinking).

176. See id. at 87 n.178.

177. See Chapter 2 ("Connection Across Difference and Similarity") and Chapter 3 ("Engaged Client–Centered Counseling About Client Choices") for discussion of the importance of not judging clients in the process of engagement.

178. See Chapter 3 ("Engaged Client–Centered Counseling About Client Choices") (illustrating how a client's sense of self is affected by others in the community).

179. For an example of a lawyer counseling an adolescent client concerned about her parents' reaction to her story, see Chapter 3 ("Interviewing and Counseling Atypical Clients").

180. See Chapter 8 ("Talking to Clients About the Law") (illustrating the importance of exploring the client's experience in deciding how to interpret the law and frame that experience within the categories of the law).

181. See Chapter 3 ("Engaged Client–Centered Counseling About Client Choices") (elaborating the idea that lawyers are affected in the decision-making process by what others in a profession will think).

182. See Chapter 8 ("Talking to Clients About the Law") in which a lawyer discusses with her client how different legal decision-makers are likely to interpret his story.

183. See Chapter 8 ("Talking to Clients About the Law") in which a lawyer explains to her client how judges in different counties respond to stories of non-support.

184. For a medical analogue that views doctors as "meaning-making vessels" for the patient, see CHARON, *supra* note 6, at 132. Charon analyzes how with narrative practices lawyers can hear and retell clients' stories in ways that achieve better understanding and provide help.

185. Continuing with the medical parallel, Charon argues that "narrative competence" assists in "recognize[ing] patients and diseases" and "convey[ing] knowledge and regard" and can lead to more humane, ethical, and effective care. *Id.* at vii.

186. See Chapter 3 ("Engaged Client–Centered Counseling About Client Choices") for a discussion of the centrality of engagement.

187. For more on the importance of self-reflection, see Chapter 2 ("Connection Across Difference and Similarity"). *See also* Kruse, *supra* note 60, at 377 (explaining that lawyers must make a conscious effort to examine the effects their attitudes and values have on their relationships with clients).

188. In the medical context, Charon identifies the inevitability of ambiguity and uncertainty. CHARON, *supra* note 6, at 4.

189. See Chapter 3 ("Engaged Client–Centered Counseling About Client Choices") for a full discussion of the complexity of the process.

CHAPTER 6

TRUTH AND CONSEQUENCES

■ ■ ■

INTRODUCTION

Consider the following excerpts from an initial interview, fortunately fictional, between a lawyer and a potential client in 2009. The lawyer, Michelle Washington, is a middle-class, white, legal services lawyer with many years of experience in immigration law. The person she is interviewing, Carlos Reyes, is a citizen of Colombia. He maintains that paramilitary gangs with links to the government persecuted him, along with many other Colombians, because of their role as trade union activists. Ms. Washington knows that if Mr. Reyes can persuade an asylum officer of the veracity of his account, he may be eligible for asylum in the United States. If, however, there are factors that permit or require denying him asylum, he may well be unable to remain in the United States.

After some preliminary ice-breaking conversation, the interview proceeds as follows (in English, which Mr. Reyes speaks fluently):

L1:   So, Mr. Reyes, I understand you are interested in applying for asylum.

C1:   That's right.

L2:   For me to understand your case and figure out whether we can help you, naturally I need to know the facts. Later on I'll need to get any documents you have that will help us make your case to the asylum officer, but for now I just want to hear in your own words what happened. Of course, everything you tell me is confidential. Why don't you tell me a bit about what happened to you in your home country that led to your wanting to seek asylum now?

[At this point, Mr. Reyes describes the ongoing violence against trade union activists in Colombia. As Ms. Washington listens, occasionally nodding or asking a brief follow-up question, he tells her about the many murders of union leaders, the absence of meaningful investigation by the authorities and the repeated threats to those brave enough to try to speak out in public against the killings. Washington then shifts the conversation's focus with the following question:]

227

L3:   Those are shocking events and certainly the kind of thing that asylum is meant to protect people from. Given what has been happening in Colombia, I really hope I can help you with your case. But you haven't told me very much yet about what happened to you as an individual during these terrible times; could you tell me more about that now?

C3:   Yes, of course. I joined a canning workers' union in 2007. The conditions in the plant were bad, really bad, and a lot of us joined up after an organizer named Enrique Marquez came to town. We went on strike in January 2008, and we were on strike for 3 months. Finally the owners gave in and we got a decent raise, and the night the contract was signed we had a big party. Enrique left late, walking off by himself. I wanted to accompany him, but he said, "No, Carlos, we've won. Tonight we won't worry."

[Mr. Reyes paused here and was obviously upset. After giving him time to take several deep breaths and getting him a glass of water, which he drank, Ms. Washington resumed:]

L4:   Did something happen to Enrique?

C4:   Yes ... We didn't know for a few days what had happened. He didn't show up for the union leadership meeting the next day, and we knew that wasn't like him at all, so we started searching. Of course we asked the police to help, and they laughed at us. It took us three days to find his body—stuffed in a sewer pipe. It had a note on it, just two words: "¿Quiere más?"—you know, "Want more?"

L5:   What happened next, Mr. Reyes?

C5:   Well, I just couldn't stand this. So I went to the local newspaper. In fact I sent letters to every big paper in the whole country. If they got in touch, I told them all about what had happened, and I told them to use my name and my picture, because I knew that people would be more likely to believe it and do something about it if the story came from someone with a name and a face they could look at.

L6:   That was very brave.

C6:   I didn't really feel brave, I was just outraged. Anyway, so then of course I got threats.

L7:   What sort of threats?

C7:   Death threats. Somebody would call me late at night and say "You're next." My windows got broken. That kind of thing. I'd expected it, and I wrote to the Mayor and the President for protection.

L8:   Did that help?

C8: No. I didn't really think it would, you know? But I was hoping things would eventually blow over. I thought I'd just be careful and I'd be okay. I was careful, too. I didn't go places alone, I bought a big dog for my house. Then I came home one evening, it wasn't even completely dark yet ... They'd killed the dog. And they stuck a note in his collar. The same words they'd left on Enrique: "¿Quiere más?"

L9: That's horrifying.

C9: Yes. They should never have killed that poor dog. But it made their point—I saw that there was no safety for me, and I knew I had to go. So I did. I left that house as soon as it was dark; I slipped out and went by back alleys to the house of a friend on the outskirts of town. He had a little shack you couldn't see from the road, and I stayed there for two nights trying to figure out what to do.

L10: Then did you leave the country?

C10: I wanted to, but it wasn't easy. First, I moved to another town where things weren't quite so crazy. And then I started trying to get out of the country, but it took me six months to find a way to do it. So I only got to the US a few months ago.

L11: Why did it take so long?

C11: Because I had to pay to get out. I couldn't exactly apply for a passport—that would have just told the people who wanted to kill me where I was. So I paid someone to get me across the border, and someone else to connect me to that guy, and someone else at the border when things seemed to be going wrong. I was lucky to manage it as soon as I did.

L12: How were you able to live during this time?

C12: Oh, well, that wasn't such a big problem. I found some people I knew, and they gave me a place to stay and enough to eat, and I returned the favor by helping them with whatever they needed doing.

L13: What kind of stuff was that?

C13: Mostly I drove a truck for them, making pickups and deliveries. It was mostly just regular stuff, I mean, nothing to worry about and not illegal, you know, or anything like that.

L14: I'm not sure I understand. Was some of the stuff you were carrying not what you call "regular stuff"?

C14: This is all confidential, right?

L15: Certainly.

C15:   Well, mostly it was just food, clothes, furniture—really all right, perfectly legal. But a couple of times the guy who owned the truck would ride in the truck with me and he'd say, "Okay, Carlos, tonight we'll have a special ride, huh?" I didn't like this at all, but I felt like I couldn't refuse to drive, because this man was helping me so much. So I tried to just laugh and go about the driving.

L16:   Did the truck owner ever tell you what was in the truck those times?

C16:   No.

L17:   So you really don't know what you might have been carrying then?

C17:   I know. I had to help unload it.

L18:   What was it?

C18:   It was . . . supplies for some people.

L19:   What kind of supplies?

[Mr. Reyes said nothing, and after a brief pause Ms. Washington went on:]

L20:   Please remember, Mr. Reyes, that what you tell me is confidential. But I do have to know the truth if I am going to represent you effectively. This is a crucial matter, Mr. Reyes, and if you don't feel you can tell me the truth, you need to understand that then I will not be able to take your case at all.

C20:   All right . . . all right. Anyway, it was just medicines, bandages, that kind of thing.

L21:   That doesn't sound like a problem. There's nothing wrong with delivering medical supplies, is there?

C21:   It was for the FARC.

L22:   I'm sorry?

C22:   You know, the rebels.

L23:   You brought supplies to the rebels? How many times?

C23:   Like I said, a couple.

L24:   I need to be clear. How many times, exactly?

C24:   Just a few times. Three or four times in the six months.

L25:   Three or four separate times? Not just a couple?

C25:   Yeah.

L26:   And who did you deliver them to?

C26:   He didn't say his name.

L27:   So how did you know he was from the FARC?

C27:   I just knew.

L28:   [Grimly] *How* did you "just know"?

C28:   He had their armband on. And he was armed.

L29:   So you delivered medical supplies to an armed guerrilla three or four times?

C29:   Yes. I told you, my friends asked me to do it. I had to. It was like returning all the favors they were doing for me. And I was afraid that if I didn't, maybe they'd decide not to take any more risk from hiding me—and then I'd have been back in as much danger as before.

L30:   Did you get paid extra for this favor?

C30:   They'd hand me a hundred dollars at the end of the trips. But I didn't think of it as pay.

[At these words, Ms. Washington stopped taking notes. She was silent for a minute, and then she said:]

L31:   Mr. Reyes, I wish what you've just told me had never happened. But since it did happen, I have to tell you that your transporting of supplies to the FARC may be an absolute bar to your getting asylum, and could mean you will wind up having to leave this country. I don't think that is fair, in fact I think it is very unfair, but it is what the law says. I'm not giving up at all, but this certainly makes things more difficult.

C31:   But does it have to come out at all?

L32:   Maybe not. You may not have to put any of this in the asylum application form you'll be filling out—that's a question we'll need to look at very carefully. But even if you don't have to put it in there, you may get asked the same kinds of questions I've just asked. And whatever you are asked, you'll need to answer if you want to get asylum, and then you'll have to tell the truth. And if you don't, and I'm representing you, I'll have to reveal the truth myself.

C32:   But you said it was all confidential.

Did Ms. Washington handle this interview appropriately? From one perspective, the answer is yes. She obviously needed to know what forms of persecution her potential client had suffered in order to assess his chances of convincing the U.S. asylum authorities that he should receive asylum. Her initial question (L12) about how Mr. Reyes survived during the six months he waited to get out of the country was a natural one, because she already knew that he had fled his town and his job. She naturally would have wanted to get a complete account of his experiences. When he surprised her by answering in a way that seemed to imply he had engaged in some activity that wasn't "regular" (C13), she had no alternative but to inquire further, because she knew that illegal activity in the home country could amount to a reason to deny asylum. His answers, moreover, never gave her any reason to stop inquiring, so she pressed on to the bitter end. When she learned, finally, that he had transported medicines to the rebels, she could tell him only what she did—that this information might be fatal to his case,[1] and that neither the client nor the lawyer could deny the facts if they became an issue in the case.[2]

From another perspective, the answer to the question of whether Ms. Washington handled this interview appropriately would be no. Ms. Washington did her best to win her client's confidence by employing the kinds of techniques lawyers should regularly use as a matter of good, standard interviewing: ice-breaking at the start, expressing her desire to help (L3), confirming that she shared his outrage at what happened (L3), personal attention and patience when her client became upset (after C3), and communicating empathy (L9) and admiration (L6). In addition, she repeatedly assured her client that what he told her was confidential, not only at the start of the interview (L2), but also when she and her client began discussing what turned out to be the deliveries to FARC (L15, L20). The third time she assured him of confidentiality (L20), Ms. Washington also reiterated that she needed the information in order to represent Mr. Reyes effectively. With all of these assurances to help her elicit answers, she asked questions that became decidedly more narrow and closed-ended, emphatic and insistent, even alarmed. It was only after her client grudgingly acknowledged the most damaging facts that Ms. Washington revealed two crucial points: first, the information she had just extracted (but which she had been aiming at for some time) was very damaging to the client's interests, and second, the client might be unable to keep this information secret, because if he was asked about it and tried to deny it, she would reveal it herself. In other words, only after telling the client that the information he shared with her would be confidential did Ms. Washington reveal how little that confidentiality was worth.

This dialogue raises a series of questions on interviewing ethics and skills, subjects which are the focus of this chapter. In the sections to come, we will consider the following issues:

First, is getting the whole truth always what lawyers should seek in interviewing? Should Ms. Washington have regarded it as her duty to pursue the facts about the medical supply deliveries?

Second, are lawyers who have elicited the truth either obliged or permitted to disclose it over the client's objection? Was Ms. Washington right that she could reveal what her client might want to keep hidden?

Third, what advice on confidentiality is consistent with the actual extent of lawyers' duty of disclosure? Should Ms. Washington have given the broad and repeated assurances of confidentiality that she did, and should she have announced the important qualification on these assurances—that she would have to reveal false testimony by her client—only deep into their meeting?

Fourth, what advice can lawyers give clients about the law that bears on the clients' situations without compromising the lawyers' obligations to truth? Here, could Ms. Washington have explained the legal significance of transporting medical supplies before (rather than after) asking the client about it?

Fifth, how skeptical should lawyers be about their clients' veracity? Here, for example, should Ms. Washington have accepted her client's half-truths (notably, his statement (C13) that he was mostly transporting "just regular stuff, I mean, nothing to worry about and not illegal, you know, or anything like that") as sufficient answers to her questions?

Sixth, when lawyers do need to press their clients for the truth, how should they do this? Was Ms. Washington justified in using the rather peremptory, demanding questions that she did?

We turn to these questions from a particular starting point. If the role of the engaged client-centered lawyer is first and foremost a helping one, it is because clients, as people, have a right to be helped. Without shutting our eyes for a moment to the realities of human frailty, we understand the proposition that clients have a right to be helped as implying at least a measure of respect for the clients, for their individual attributes or at any rate for the humanity they share with their attorneys. We believe that this respect implies a presumption—to be sure, a rebuttable presumption— that clients are, like their lawyers, people who have values and care about them, and who try, in the midst of the many complications of life, to understand and live by those commitments. Many clients, of course, have done things they regret, and some no doubt will do other things in the future that their lawyers will find dismaying, but to say this is only to say that people are indeed imperfect. Admittedly, some clients may be much worse than imperfect, may in fact disprove the presumption that they are people with values, and in a society governed by law, even these clients will enjoy the right to counsel. Nevertheless, we see the paradigmatic lawyer-client relationship as one between two honorable, or at least potentially honorable, people.

With that perspective in mind, we now turn to the questions we have posed. The answers we develop here are in some respects controversial;

indeed, we ourselves do not agree on some important elements of the arguments made here, and so this chapter will at times lay out quite contrasting possible approaches, from which ultimately you as a lawyer will need to choose. Our aim, ultimately, is not to convince you of the answers to these questions, so much as it is to demonstrate the complexity of the ethical issues embodied even in relatively straightforward lawyer-client encounters. Answering these questions—either as we do or in the different ways you may—requires lawyers to bring their practical decision-making and their reflective understanding of the very nature of the lawyering function into harmony. This is no small task.

A. IS TRUTH ALWAYS THE OBJECTIVE?

The fundamental purpose of interviewing is not to seek the truth; rather, it is to begin the work of effective representation of a client under the law. Ordinarily, however, it is in the client's interest for his lawyer to know the truth. A lawyer represents her client best when she knows all of the relevant circumstances. Only with this complete knowledge can a lawyer present the client's case or position in the most favorable light, avoid disastrous surprises, devise strategies to handle whatever weak points exist as well as they can be handled, and ensure that the eventual outcome of the case fits the client's actual wishes and interests as accurately as possible. For pragmatic and professional reasons, therefore, seeking the truth makes sense.

Can it be harmful for the lawyer to know the truth? Is there any downside to the lawyer's complete knowledge of the facts? Not if that knowledge imposes no constraints on the lawyer's freedom of action. For example, American lawyers take for granted that a lawyer may represent a criminal defendant who pleads "not guilty" and vigorously defend the case, even if the lawyer knows—from the client's own admissions and the lawyer's corroborating investigation—that the client is guilty as charged. The lawyer remains free to contest the charges no matter how fully she has become convinced of their validity.

In many other circumstances, however, it is conceivable that the lawyer might know too much. We discuss the obligations possessing that knowledge may impose in more detail in Part B. Here, it is enough to say that in all representations, lawyers are forbidden from making knowingly false statements of fact. In civil cases, they may not affirm or deny claims if they have no basis for doing so, may not knowingly introduce false evidence, and must correct evidence they have already offered if they come to know that it is false. Similar obligations apply to criminal prosecutors and *may* apply even to criminal defense attorneys. In short, knowledge may be empowering, but it may also be disempowering.

Of course, all of these constraints vanish if, as is sometimes argued, lawyers never know the truth or falsity of any proposition. Monroe Freedman and Abbe Smith call one version of this approach "the Roy

Cohn solution.''[3] Freedman & Smith, who question whether Cohn's solution "can properly be called an ethical one,''[4] quote Cohn as saying:

> Before a client could get three words out, any lawyer with half a brain would say, "You probably don't know whether you're guilty or not, because you don't know the elements of the crime you're charged with."

> [Then, to avoid hearing what I'm not supposed to hear, I ask the client:] "If someone was going to get up on the stand and lie about you, who would it be? And what would they lie about?" And if the client's got any brains, he'll know what I'm talking about.[5]

Freedman and Smith go on to explain:

> Under Cohn's solution, therefore, the lawyer has it both ways. For tactical purposes, he knows what he has to know. For purposes of any ethical obligation, however, he does not know either that the client is guilty or that the client is going to commit perjury when he denies the "lies" about him.[6]

Cohn seems to know, in all but name, exactly what he does not want to know. A more palatable approach might assert that only the jury can "know" the truth under our system of law. Yet another approach could invoke a modern, or post-modern, skepticism about the ascertainability of truth.

This is not a book about epistemology, and so we will not pursue the philosophical questions raised by these objections very far. We are quite certain, in any event, that there is much that lawyers are uncertain about. Perhaps, in the end, no one can be *absolutely* certain of anything. But if that is so, it does not follow that we can "know" nothing; rather, it follows that we must understand that when we say we "know" something, we are asserting something less than superhuman knowledge.

To respond instead by denying knowledge has two tremendous, and in our view fatal, disadvantages. The first is that it requires lawyers, who like everyone else no doubt believe that they "know" many things about many subjects, to profess utter lack of knowledge about matters they should be studying especially carefully, namely the facts of their cases. In other words, it requires lawyers to disclaim common sense.

The second disadvantage to disclaiming knowledge in this fashion is that it requires lawyers to assert that the many provisions in the professional codes of ethics which forbid lawyers from using or uttering knowing falsehoods are actually mere pretense, because they will never, ever have any bearing on lawyers' actual duties. We do not suggest that lawyers should casually assume they know the falsity of their clients' statements. On the contrary, we feel that the test for knowledge should be a demanding one, perhaps on the order of "beyond a reasonable doubt."[7] Precisely because such a test will not be satisfied easily, it fits with the lawyer's primary orientation as the representative and helper of her client (and fits especially well in the field of criminal defense where it is a truism that the defendant has the right to put the state to its proof). Nevertheless, lawyers must acknowledge that *sometimes* they know that they are hearing lies.

Can lawyers avoid seeking the truth? Even if knowledge exists and can be constraining, we would have no alternative but to seek it if we could not conceive of any other way to conduct an interview. Thus, it might be argued that, to the extent that interviews are concerned with the facts of the matter that has brought the client to the lawyer, there is nothing else lawyers can seek in interviews *except* the whole truth, for no other interviewing objective would be coherent. Clearly, lawyers do have other goals in interviewing besides learning the facts, such as the initiation of a positive relationship with their clients, and those goals might call for delicate decisions about when to seek particular aspects of the truth, perhaps even whether to seek it—yet truth might still be the touchstone of what the lawyer sought. But it is probably not true that the only coherent goal the lawyer could have, even simply with regard to the facts of the client's case, is to seek the truth. In criminal defense work, for example, the lawyer's goal could conceivably be the "collection of facts so that he can evaluate the extent to which inculpatory information is accessible to the government and usable to frame an indictment."[8] To achieve *this* goal, the lawyer must learn what the government knows and what it will have the legal ability to discover, but the lawyer does not necessarily have to learn the entire truth from the client's own mouth. Interviewing focused on this objective might start with an inquiry into everything the client knows about the state's case against him or her, and only then (if at all) ask for the client's explanation of the information thus assembled.

Scott Turow, a federal prosecutor and novelist, illustrates this mode of defense practice in his novel *Presumed Innocent*. In this novel, Rusty Sabich, a senior prosecutor, finds himself accused of murder and turns for his defense to his longtime adversary Sandy Stern. Stern takes the case. At one of their early meetings, the two of them discuss where the case stands, and Stern asks his client for a "thirty-second summation" of the prosecutor's opening argument to the jury. Before answering, Sabich reflects on why his lawyer has never simply asked him if he is the killer. One answer is that the lawyer fears Sabich will lie. Sabich observes:

> Thus it would be an act contrary to his professional acumen were Sandy Stern to commit himself to an unreserved faith in everything I say. Instead, he does not ask. The procedure has one further virtue. If I were to meet any new evidence by frontally contradicting what I had told Sandy in the past, legal ethics might require him to withhold me from the witness stand, where I almost certainly intend to go. Better to see everything the prosecution has, to be certain that my recollec- tion, as the lawyers put it, has been fully "refreshed," before Sandy inquires about my version. Caught in a system where the client is inclined to lie and the lawyer who seeks his client's confidence may not help him do that, Stern works in the small open spaces which

remain. Most of all, he desires to make an intelligent presentation. He does not wish to be misled, or to have his options curbed by rash declarations that prove to be untrue. As the trial approaches, he will need to know more. He may ask the question then; and I certainly will tell him the answer. For the time being, Stern has found, as usual, the most artful and indefinite means by which to probe.[9]

Criminal defense work, of course, differs from most other legal representation in a crucial way: the client does not have to testify or offer evidence against himself. Such strategic interviewing is harder to imagine in other legal contexts where the client is ultimately going to be subject to the probing of an adverse attorney or adjudicator. But even in these circumstances, it is possible to conceive of other interviewing objectives besides seeking "the truth, the whole truth, and nothing but the truth." The lawyer here might aim to learn those facts necessary to make out the client's case and to refute the likely contentions of the other side, but choose not to press her inquiries so far as to unearth damaging matters that the opposition most likely would overlook; if the lawyer could calibrate her inquiries to this goal, she could learn all she needs to in order to help her client, without learning additional information that would hurt his case.

Should lawyers seek the truth? Though lawyers clearly can seek something less than the truth, there are serious arguments against endorsing lawyers' doing so. The first problem is that this approach might well undermine effective representation of clients. We are skeptical about the ability of most lawyers, and most clients, to conduct carefully-structured dialogues with enough finesse to ensure that the lawyer learns what she must but does not hear what she would rather not. While we do not favor random probing for damaging information,[10] we believe that the lawyer is most likely to learn what she needs to know if she does not try to circumscribe her search for the facts. In the case with which this chapter begins, for example, the fact of Mr. Reyes's transporting medical supplies to FARC is deeply damaging, but there remain many possible factual inquiries that might help him to avoid being returned to Colombia.[11] It seems unlikely that Ms. Washington could easily explore these lines of potential defense or mitigation without also understanding what Mr. Reyes's legal problems are, and perhaps also unlikely that she would try to explore all these issues fully if she had not learned from her questioning that Mr. Reyes did have legal problems that needed to be dealt with.

To disregard the goal of truth with a client, moreover, may be deeply inconsistent with the presumption from which this chapter began—namely, that clients are worthy of respect as honorable people. Lawyers who are indifferent to the goal of truth with their clients may implicitly be assuming—normally, no doubt, without expressly discussing the point with the client themselves—that the clients are indifferent to honesty, or at least prefer self-interest to truth. This assumption denies clients the respect we believe they are due as human beings and is thus inconsistent with a basic foundation of the lawyer-client relationship.[12] Certainly many clients hesitate to speak candidly, whether for the many reasons that anyone may hesitate to confide in another or because they have specific worries about the legal consequences of telling the truth. We don't ask lawyers to ignore that reality, or to judge clients harshly for it. But it is one thing to understand how many considerations shape what a client says, and another to assume that honesty isn't one of them.[13]

We worry, also, that a relationship marked at its inception by avoidance of truth may grow worse rather than better over time (though it is also certainly true that a lawyer who probes too fast and too early may undercut the potential for building a relationship in which candor ultimately becomes possible). Clients who have avoided one truth with the lawyer's aid may avoid other truths as well, even against the lawyer's wishes. Lawyers who might seek, for example, to counsel their clients about ethical matters may find that their standing to do so has been impaired.

Even more fundamentally, such stratagems may be inconsistent with the function of lawyers in a just legal system. The rules of professional ethics, as we have already seen, impose obligations of candor on lawyers, and those obligations suggest that the lawyer's role, as our legal system has shaped it, has some connection to truth. Lawyers in an adversarial system, to be sure, are not bound to assist the tribunal in seeking the truth—that formulation has a more inquisitorial than adversarial flavor to it—but we as a society do not have lawyers *in order to* enable people to prevail on false claims. The Model Code of Professional Responsibility states the proposition, or truism, that members of our society are entitled to zealous representation "within the bounds of the law," so that everyone in our society will be able "to have his conduct judged and regulated in accordance with the law."[14] Nor do we protect attorney-client confidentiality *in order to* enable lawyer and client to cleverly skirt the truth in the privacy of the lawyer's office. On all these grounds, we might agree with Ms. Washington's desire to discern the truth.

In the face of these arguments, however, it may be somewhat startling to realize that the Model Rules of Professional Conduct, as well as the Model Code, do not explicitly state that the duty of the lawyer is to seek the truth from her client. The ABA has suggested that lawyers who avoid "knowledge" by "not questioning the client about the facts in the case . . . may be violating their duties under R[u]le 3.3 [to prevent and correct the use of false testimony] and their obligation to provide competent representation under Rule 1.1."[15] But these implications, plausible as they are, are not explicitly confirmed by the texts. Moreover, the *Restatement of the Law Governing Lawyers* also stops distinctly short of imposing such a duty. Instead, lawyers generally owe their clients "the competence and diligence normally exercised by lawyers in similar circumstances."[16] A comment explains that this duty requires lawyers to "perform tasks reasonably appropriate to the representation, including, where appropriate, inquiry into facts"—but this language does not specify the tenor of that inquiry.[17] As for the duty not to knowingly use false evidence, the

Restatement comments that "[a]ctual knowledge does not include un-known information, even if a reasonable lawyer would have discovered it through inquiry."[18] So, too, with the duty not to assist a client in action that the lawyer knows is criminal: "[A] lawyer is not required to make a particular kind of investigation in order to ascertain more certainly what the facts are, although it will often be prudent for the lawyer to do so."[19]

While other sources of law may impose greater obligations,[20] within the framework of the Restatement the main limit on competent, willed ignorance seems to be the doctrine of "conscious avoidance." Under this doctrine, a lawyer who deliberately avoids knowledge may be charged with having that knowledge.[21] As David Luban has pointed out, however, it is not necessarily the case that a person who avoids learning whether something is true or not actually knows that it *is* true.[22] Sandy Stern, in *Presumed Innocent*, may ultimately learn that Rusty Sabich is guilty, or that he is innocent. The view of the Restatement Reporter, Charles W. Wolfram, is consistent with this recognition; Wolfram writes that "the preferable rule is that proof of a lawyer's conscious disregard of facts is relevant evidence which, together with other evidence bearing on the question, may warrant a finding of actual knowledge."[23] Under this view, a lawyer who simply did not ask certain questions, but had no clear indication of what the answers to those questions would be, would seem to lack the "knowledge" upon which the Restatement places so much weight.

To say that lawyers are not legally obliged to seek the truth, however, provides no affirmative reason to depart from the arguments, founded in respect for clients and acknowledgment of the bounds of the law, that we have offered as reasons why lawyers ought to try to learn the truth. But affirmative reasons may exist. It might be argued, first, that even honor-able people, when caught within an unjust system, do not owe the operators of that system truth. We ourselves share this view. A Jew in Nazi Germany did not have an obligation to reveal his Jewishness to those who would kill him for it, even if he had to lie under oath in a court of law to keep the truth concealed.

The recognition that in some circumstances the injustice of a legal system justifies lying to oppose it immediately leads to the question of whether the American legal system is such a case. We are not in Nazi Germany.[24] Although American society and American law are far from perfect, perfection is not an attainable goal in life. The protections of constitutional rights and the rule of law in the United States, as well as the potential for democratic changes in unjust policies, provide strong justification for requiring lawyers—who have chosen to enter their profes-sion and taken an oath of fidelity to the law—to offer their clients representation only within the bounds of the law. The force of this justification is all the greater because while we believe that people in general do care about justice, we must also recognize that people often tend to view "what is just" as similar to "what they want." As soon as the principle that justice can override the bounds of law is admitted, both bad and good people, both victims and oppressors, will take advantage of it.

But this argument for fidelity to truth may not persuade you (and does not persuade all of us). We are not in Nazi Germany, but it is hardly self-evident that people in every country more benign than Nazi Germany are bound to live by the truth no matter what the harms their legal system may visit on them. The United States has a long and grim history of injustice and oppression, a history many (including all of us) would say continues to this day. In the field of immigration law in particular, many observers see profound and wrenching injustice being done to noncitizens on a daily basis (though there are also many observers who might sharply disagree with this assessment). It is up to each lawyer to judge her world, and to decide how just or unjust it is, and to assess her obligations to the law in that light. We can only add that ultimately this logic may lead lawyers to actions that are frankly unlawful; those choices may be morally justified, but legally perilous.[25]

It is not necessary, however, to follow this logic to such an extreme. In fact, as we have just seen, "the bounds of the law" are not as tight as might have been expected. Instead, it appears that they leave some room for lawyers to calibrate their inquiry into truth, through the questions they ask and do not ask and also, as we will see, through the advice they give about the limits on confidentiality for the clients' answers. If we lived in a perfectly just society, there might be no justification for the existence of such discretion. But in the imperfect world and nation in which we live, there may well be circumstances where the lawyer's full discovery of truth, and the subsequent ethical obligations incurred by such knowledge, will lead to results that she conscientiously sees as unjust. The lawyer who learns of a welfare client's petty fraud, for example, may be unable to press the client's claim for benefits essential to health or life. Exactly where justice ultimately lies in such a conflict between law's demands and equity's claims may be a profound philosophical problem, but the rules of professional ethics do not exist to resolve all such problems. Instead, within their boundaries, discretion remains for multiple, even differing moral perspectives. Put more concretely, the rules of professional duty leave no room for knowing violations, but they do leave some room for not knowing.[26] We will discuss how a lawyer who felt that justice called for such not-knowing at several points in this chapter, though our principal focus is on the obligations of lawyers who do not see such tension between the requirements of justice and the impact of truth.[27]

Had Ms. Washington believed that the denial of asylum to people who could not escape some brush with terrorists in a strife-filled society was profoundly unjust, she might have considered exercising this sort of discretion here. Before she asked Mr. Reyes what "[ir]regular" items he transported, however, she could not know his answer. For her to be sure that denial of asylum based on that answer would be unjust, she would have to hold the view that Mr. Reyes was entitled to asylum (assuming the other requirements of asylum law were satisfied) no matter what he was transporting. Would she maintain that view if the cargo had been, for instance, children enslaved into prostitution? If not, then her decision not to ask would have to factor in the possibility that she was becoming a party to injustice rather than justice. Additionally, she would need to believe that getting an answer to her question would be, as a tactical matter, more of a hindrance than a help. But here there is at least some possibility of arguing that Mr. Reyes's conduct did not render him ineligible for asylum (or another form of protection from removal), because it amounted neither to assistance in persecution nor to voluntary, material support for a terrorist organization.[28] She obviously would not want to learn this information for the first time during Mr. Reyes's asylum interview, when it would be too late to explore possible mitigating circumstances. Deciding what to do once she has the information may be difficult, but not asking requires her to make a similar decision in the dark. On these grounds, this particular case might not have been an appropriate one for the exercise of such discretion in the name of justice, and we suspect that similar considerations will frequently weigh against lawyers' choosing this course.

A second argument, however, might provide a further affirmative reason for the lawyer to shape her interviewing differently. The arguments about the justice or injustice of the law that we have just examined have treated the lawyer's assessment of the law as dispositive. Perhaps, however, it is the client whose assessment should be critical. The lawyer is forbidden by the rules of her profession to lie, but it is the client who must decide what he will tell the lawyer is the truth. We can imagine the client making that decision in a corrupt way, but we can also imagine clients—entitled to respect as honorable people—who might make their own judgment about the justice of the legal system, and might conclude that they should not offer up the facts that will lead to their suffering the system's injustice. Respect for clients might call for lawyers to put that choice in the clients' hands. In Chapter Eight, we lay out in detail an ethical and jurisprudential approach to the law that supports this conclusion. Concretely, here, the lawyer following this approach might fundamentally reshape the interview, so that the meeting would not be an occasion for her to seek from her client a candid account of what happened but instead would focus on educating the client about the law so that he could, if he so desired, shape what he said in light of the law's demands.

Needless to say, there are counterarguments to be considered here as well. It is doubtful, once again, whether clients generally can make these calculations soundly; a classic rationale for attorney-client privilege is precisely that it helps encourage clients to reveal facts that they believe would damage them, but that actually would help their case.[29] Moreover, the question of the justice or injustice of the legal system is no small question; clients might well seek their lawyers' advice about such a matter, or at the least lawyers might well believe they have knowledge and perspective that could help clients to grapple with this—and so the lawyer who seeks to leave the question of justice to the client may ultimately find herself shaping the client's view of the answer. In addition, some clients may not be honorable, and may dishonorably take advantage of the knowledge the lawyer imparts; in practice, lawyers who embrace this general approach may need to make fine judgments in the course of client meetings about what sort of people their clients are.

We lay out these arguments not to convince you that one approach is right and another is wrong, but precisely to make clear how profound the issues are that each lawyer must resolve in shaping her approach to learning the client's story. The remainder of this chapter largely seeks to work out the implications of a decision that the lawyer should generally seek the truth from her clients, though she should also honor her clients' right to know what the law is that affects their situation. But whether that decision is always the right one is an issue we do not decide, and instead present to you.

B.   HOW COMPLETE IS CONFIDENTIALITY?

Three times in the dialogue, Ms. Washington assures her client that what he tells her is confidential. Each of these assurances is unqualified. Perhaps she was right to speak in these terms,[30] but it is clear that she was not *accurate*. The truth is that what clients tell lawyers is not simply, and unqualifiedly, confidential. The exact contours of the limits on confidentiality vary from jurisdiction to jurisdiction, and you should always study the particular rules of the jurisdiction in which you are practicing, but we can briefly outline some of the leading restrictions.[31]

Our primary focus here is on the confidentiality protected by the codes of legal ethics. Confidentiality under the codes is a considerably broader notion than the attorney-client privilege. First of all, it prohibits, or purports to prohibit, all disclosures, not just those made in testimony (to which attorney-client privilege applies). Additionally, it protects from disclosure a much wider range of information. The difference in scope is reflected in DR 4–101 of the Model Code of Professional Responsibility, which explains that the ethics rule protects both "confidences" and "secrets."[32]

Confidences consist of "information protected by the attorney-client privilege under applicable law."[33] Wolfram offers the following "general encapsulation" of the scope of the privilege:

> (1) a person (client) who seeks legal advice or assistance (2) from a lawyer acting in behalf of the client, (3) for an indefinite time may invoke, and the lawyer must invoke in the client's behalf, an unqualified privilege not to testify (4) concerning the contents of a client communication (5) that was made by the client or by the client's communicative agent (6) in confidence (7) to the lawyer or the lawyer's confidential agent, (8) unless the client expressly or by implication waives the privilege.[34]

In addition to shielding such privileged information, DR 4–101 also protects "secrets"—"other information gained in the professional relationship that the client has requested be held inviolate or the disclosure of which would be embarrassing or would be likely to be detrimental to the client."[35] Model Rule 1.6 is, if anything, broader in scope than DR 4–101: the Model Rule protects "information relating to representation of a client"[36] and not just the various forms of "information gained in the professional relationship" encompassed in the Code's definition of "secrets." Broad as the protections under the Code and Rules are, however, they are also subject to profound limitations.

First, both the Model Code and the Model Rules authorize disclosure to prevent the client from committing future crimes.[37] The Model Code allows such disclosure in all cases,[38] while the Model Rules, once more resistant to disclosure on this score, now also permit it in a considerable range of situations.[39] Neither the Model Code nor the Model Rules ever requires disclosure on this basis,[40] but there are some states that do.[41] Moreover, the Model Rules may not just permit but require lawyers to carry out "noisy" withdrawals from representation—withdrawals accompanied by notification to adverse parties that the lawyer disavows prior assertions on the client's behalf—when the lawyer learns that those assertions were criminal or fraudulent and the client will not correct them.[42]

Second, both the Model Code and the Model Rules prohibit lawyers from making false statements of fact, or knowingly using false evidence, in the course of their representation of clients.[43] These duties quite clearly prevent lawyers in civil cases from offering testimony that they know to be false.[44] Just how far these duties reach in criminal cases may be debated, but the Model Rules plainly are meant to impose obligations in criminal as well as civil cases.[45]

Third, both the Model Code and the Model Rules also have provisions authorizing, and in fact requiring, disclosure to correct client perjury. The Model Code's provision contains an exception that seems to swallow the rule, so that under the Code, lawyers seemingly could report that their clients intended to commit perjury—as a future crime—but could not correct it after it occurred.[46] The Model Rules do not authorize disclosure of all future crimes as such, without more, but here there is more: perjury is "criminal or fraudulent conduct related to the proceeding," and Model Rule 3.3(b) requires lawyers to take "reasonable remedial measures, including, if necessary, disclosure to the tribunal," to prevent perjury from taking place or to remedy it if it has already happened.[47] This is what Ms. Washington threatens to do at the end of the dialogue (L32), and in those jurisdictions that follow the Model Rules, what she threatens might ultimately—if other "remedial measures" were unavailing—be no more than her duty.

Fourth, both the Model Code and the Model Rules permit lawyers to disclose confidential information when necessary to protect themselves against charges of misconduct.[48] It is notable that these charges need not be made by the erstwhile client; instead, the lawyer may disclose the client's confidential communications to demonstrate to a prosecutor, for example, that she (the lawyer) was not in league with the client in some improper scheme.[49] Moreover, a Model Rule comment indicates that the "charges" need not have ripened to the stage of litigation or prosecution; the lawyer may disclose information in order to prevent matters from ever reaching such a point.[50]

Fifth, lawyers may make disclosures if such disclosures are impliedly authorized as necessary to the representation.[51] If the lawyer believes that a particular matter must be disclosed in the course of representation in order to achieve the client's goals, for example, the lawyer may do so without explicit authorization. Although clients can certainly countermand such implicit authority, lawyers will frequently exercise this discretion in circumstances where clients will not be able to object until, from their point of view, it is already too late.[52]

Sixth, lawyers may make disclosures with the client's consent.[53] As a matter of theory, this is not an exception to client confidentiality at all, because no one questions that clients can waive confidentiality whenever they wish. But in practice, this may be an important limit on confidentiality, because lawyers have substantial power to press, or even coerce, their clients into giving such consent. The client whose lawyer threatens to withdraw from the case unless the client authorizes some disclosure, for example, may justly feel that the confidentiality of his communications is less than absolute.[54]

This is not a complete catalogue.[55] Moreover, no complete catalogue of the limitations the Model Code and Model Rules place on confidentiality is possible, for the laws of confidentiality and privilege are always subject to development and reconsideration, just as other laws are.[56] This proposition was vividly illustrated during the legal battles around the potential impeachment of President Clinton in the late 1990s, when the Office of the Independent Counsel, Kenneth Starr, vigorously litigated the dimensions of attorney-client privilege in the relationships between government attorneys and officials.[57] Given this inescapable uncertainty, it is impossible to fully and precisely describe the confidentiality of client communications. Even leaving that aside, it is clear that any reasonably comprehensive statement of the law of confidentiality must include a number of qualifications on the scope of confidentiality permitted by the laws and rules of ethics.

C. ADVISING THE CLIENT ABOUT CONFIDENTIALITY

It follows from what we have said in Part B that Ms. Washington's advice about confidentiality was incomplete and inaccurate. It does not necessarily follow that she should have said something different. To decide whether she should have chosen other words, we might begin by considering whether there are ways to make Ms. Washington's statement that "everything you tell me is confidential" more accurate without making radical changes to the basic approach she uses. Consider the following possibilities:

(a) "Everything you tell me is confidential as provided by law." That statement may be accurate, if "confidential as provided by law" actually means "confidential to the extent provided by law," but it is hopelessly obscure.

(b) "Everything you tell me is confidential to the extent provided by law." This statement avoids some of the ambiguity of the previous formulation, but the problem with this comment is that if the client really hears it he will know that he hasn't been told anything; whether his words are confidential at all depends on what "extent" of protection the law provides, and the lawyer hasn't actually said anything about that.

(c) "I want you to know that, of course, everything you tell me is confidential between us to the full extent provided by law." This statement, delivered with emphasis and a sincere expression, might lead the client to believe that he had just been assured of confidentiality, while at the same time the lawyer could accurately say that she had promised only what the law allowed. This gap between what is said and what is heard is not a virtue.

(d) "Everything you tell me about what has happened will be confidential between us." This statement reflects an important qualification on confidentiality—namely that the client's statements of criminal future intentions may not be confidential. As such, it is more accurate than the version in (a), which omitted this and all other qualifications. But the new formulation is still not accurate. It too omits the other qualifications,[58] and it might be taken to imply that nothing the client says about future intentions is confidential, when, in fact, information the client provides about his lawful future plans and actions *is* protected by confidentiality.

We could go on inventing and critiquing variations of these assurances. No statement will be perfect, for it is simply not possible to describe the rules on confidentiality completely, clearly, and accurately in one or two sentences. To progress further, we must first step back to recognize what purposes advice about confidentiality fulfills in a lawyer-client interview. Then we will be in a position to consider what kind of advice can best achieve those purposes.

One purpose of such advice is to tell the client about the law that governs his communications with the lawyer. So far, we have been using the performance of this function as the criterion for assessing Ms. Washington's advice and the variations on it. As a general proposition, one of the lawyer's responsibilities in the course of representing a client is to inform the client of the law bearing on his situation.[59] There is no reason why the lawyer's responsibilities on this score should not also include informing the client of the law bearing on the client's communications with the lawyer.[60]

The second purpose, however, is quite different. Assurances of confidentiality may be needed to encourage clients to tell the truth to their lawyers. Clients may be less likely to reveal damaging information—or helpful information that clients mistakenly think is damaging—if they do not believe their lawyers will keep what they said confidential. Clients, however, might not know or assume such confidentiality exists unless their lawyers explicitly tell them so. The lawyer's assurance of confidentiality may also serve as a way of winning the client's trust; if clients do not trust their lawyers, they surely will not communicate freely with them. It is worth remembering that lawyers can use reassurances of confidentiality strategically (which is not to say "improperly") by reminding clients of this protection at the very moments when clients are showing reluctance to speak.

Certainly, there are many reasons for clients to distrust, or simply to hesitate to confide in, their lawyers.[61] Aside from the intrinsic difficulty of discussing sensitive material with any stranger, lawyer-client relationships frequently present other, potentially significant barriers that need to be overcome. In the encounter between Ms. Washington and Mr. Reyes, for example, lawyer and client differ in ethnicity and nationality, though at least on paper the dialogue does not suggest that these differences divided them. The shock Ms. Washington seems to express in responding to the client's revelations suggests that they differ in social experience as well— that Ms. Washington has led a life guided by the law, while her potential client has lived in social worlds where law was less a guide and guarantee than an element of arbitrary power. There may be many other differences as well, both in our imagined dialogue and in actual lawyer-client relationships.[62] Such differences may actually be a source of strength in the relationship, and if they are instead a source of difficulty, we believe they usually can be dealt with—but they confirm the wisdom of shaping lawyers' interactions with their clients so as to build client trust as effectively as possible.

Both of these purposes of advice about confidentiality make sense. Each, however, is subject to important qualifications. Consider first the goal of informing the client of the law bearing on his situation—certainly, as a general proposition, an important objective. The lawyer's duty in this regard, however, is not to tell the client every legal consideration that could possibly bear on the client's situation, but rather to "explain . . . to the extent reasonably necessary to permit the client to make informed decisions regarding the representation."[63] There is little point in raising issues that are very unlikely to bear on a client's case. In fact, there is a good reason *not* to provide such extraneous information: the lawyer's job is to provide expert information in clear fashion to a layperson, not to turn that layperson into a lawyer. Too much information can confuse rather than enlighten.[64]

The goal of building client trust is also subject to qualification. Fred Zacharias has pointed out the paucity of "empirical research testing the benefits of strict confidentiality and the validity of its justifications."[65] As he observes, "[e]ven if a lawyer makes a good faith effort to explain the rules to clients, the clients are likely to remain confused at least as to details."[66] In any event it is hardly certain that a lawyer's assertion to clients that confidentiality is unqualified is central to most clients' willingness to speak frankly.[67] In addition, it is not clear that clients actually believe lawyers provide absolute confidentiality.[68] If distrust is endemic, arguably the best response is not false denial but rather a candid discussion, both of the possibility of clashes between lawyer and client and of the lawyer's ethical prerogatives and duties should such a clash arise.[69] We certainly do not endorse such dialogues as a routine step in initiating a lawyer-client relationship, but there is, again, little empirical evidence to support judgments either way.[70]

Moreover, these two functions—informing the client of the applicable law and encouraging truthful communication—if taken to extremes, plainly call for very different kinds of lawyer advice about confidentiality. To describe the law of confidentiality more or less fully might require pages of disclosures; Roy M. Sobelson has developed precisely such a detailed statement. Sobelson argues that "[b]ecause a truly accurate disclosure is so important, and likely to be fairly lengthy, to the extent possible it should be made in a written form, submitted to the client prior to the interview, complete with a space for the client to indicate his understanding of the terms."[71] His suggested form begins with the following admonition:

> NOTE: THIS DOCUMENT STATES IMPORTANT LEGAL RIGHTS. IT IS ESSENTIAL THAT YOU READ AND SIGN IT ALL BEFORE YOU CONFER WITH YOUR ATTORNEY. IF YOU HAVE QUESTIONS ABOUT IT, ASK THE ATTORNEY BEFORE YOU SIGN IT. YOUR SIGNATURE AT THE END WILL SIGNIFY YOUR UNDERSTANDING OF THE MATTERS STATED HERE.[72]

The form goes on to spell out the duty of confidentiality and then identifies five instances in which even confidential information isn't fully confidential (for example, when information must be revealed in discovery).[73] It continues by identifying five categories of information normally not covered by confidentiality at all (including the client's identity and statements made to obtain the lawyer's services in unlawful activity), points out four situations in which the lawyer may be "FORCED to reveal information" (including compliance with court orders, correction of client perjury, and prevention of future crimes by the client), and finally states the exceptions for lawyer self-defense and for suits to collect the fee the client owes the lawyer.[74] The form ends by saying: "IF YOU HAVE READ THE ABOVE DOCUMENT AND AGREE TO BE BOUND BY ITS TERMS, PLEASE SIGN BELOW."[75]

Ironically, even this form is not exhaustive; it does not, and cannot, spell out the details of the many confidentiality exceptions to which it refers. But it does seem safe to say that this form offers advice that, in many respects, most clients would not need (most clients, for example, probably have no reason to want to keep their own identity secret). In addition, this form may become a source of confusion and distraction at the very beginning of the lawyer-client relationship, a point at which other matters—above all, hearing the client's story and concerns—should take precedence. We believe that a client confronted with this elaborate set of limits on confidentiality will not be likely to emerge reassured about the privacy of his communications with his lawyer.

We suspect, finally, that requiring a client to focus on, and sign a form accepting, these limitations before any relationship has been established may imply to the client that the lawyer fears the client will soon run afoul of the limits on confidentiality. That implication is not consistent with our starting presumption that clients are entitled to respect, and some clients may well feel it as an affront.[76] The impact of such an initial encounter seems likely to make the subsequent relationship distant and cautious, rather than close and trusting.

On the other hand, advice that would be unqualifiedly reassuring might have to characterize confidentiality as absolute. Anthony Amsterdam, for example, has offered a very firmly worded model statement about confidentiality for use in criminal practice. He argues that in the early stages of the relationship between the lawyer and a criminal defendant, it is hard for the lawyer to demonstrate concretely that she deserves the client's trust. One of the few tools available to the lawyer, Amsterdam suggests, is an emphatic assurance of confidentiality. He proposes:

> Now, I am going to ask you to tell me some things about yourself and also about this charge they have against you. Before I do, I want you to know that everything you tell me is strictly private, just between you and me. Nothing you tell me goes to the police or to the District Attorney or to the judge or to anybody else. Nobody can make me tell them what you said to me, and I won't. Maybe you've heard about this thing that they call the attorney-client privilege. The law says that when a person is talking to [his] [her] lawyer, whatever [he] [she] tells the lawyer is confidential and secret between the two of them. This is because the law recognizes that the lawyer's obligation is to [his] [her] client and to nobody else; that the lawyer is supposed to be 100 per cent on the client's side; that the lawyer is only supposed to help [his] [her] client and never do anything—or tell anybody anything—that might hurt the client in any way. The District Attorney is the one who is supposed to represent the government in prosecuting cases; and the judge's job is to judge the cases. But the law wants to make sure that—even if everybody else is lined up against a defendant—there is one person who is not supposed to look out for the government but to be completely for the defendant. That is the defendant's lawyer. As your lawyer, I am completely for you. And I couldn't be completely for you if I were required to tell anybody else the things that you say to me in private. So you can trust me and tell me anything you want without worrying that I will ever pass it along to anyone else because I won't. I can't be ques-

tioned or forced to talk about what you tell me, even by a court, and I am not allowed to tell it to anyone else without your permission because I am 100 per cent on your side, and my job is to work for you and only for you; so everything we talk about stays just between us. Okay?[77]

We consider this example an impressive combination of giving advice about the law, presented in extremely clear language, while laying the building blocks of the relationship with the client. But the assurances this statement offers might go beyond what can be sustained. Certainly this is true if even criminal defense lawyers can be required to correct client perjury and are expected to "know" when perjury has been committed. It might be argued, and reasonably, that this advice is still not seriously inaccurate, because the chances that the lawyer will actually come to possess enough information to know that her client is lying are very slight.[78] We do not quarrel with a demanding test for knowledge, as we have already explained.[79] But even a demanding test will sometimes be satisfied, at least unless the lawyer is carefully shaping her questioning so as never to encounter inescapable knowledge. In any event, that is not the only difficulty with this statement.

A further problem is that the statement makes no mention of the situations in which a lawyer has discretion, though not an obligation, to reveal information. It might be argued that the lawyer can still promise all that this statement does, because even if the lawyer has the discretion to disclose information in various other circumstances, she is not bound to exercise her discretion that way. Strictly speaking, this argument is not correct, because the existence of such discretion means that it is not true that the lawyer is "not allowed to tell it to anyone else without your permission." That problem, however, could probably be overcome by some modest editing, and aside from that the lawyer who gives advice like this would do so in perfect good faith if she was herself committed, for example, never to use her discretion to (1) report future crimes of violence her client intends to commit; (2) reveal confidential information to defend herself against a charge of ineffective assistance of counsel; or (3) reveal confidential information to defend herself against a claim of conspiracy with her erstwhile client. We admire the zeal of criminal defense attorneys, and we understand the sympathy for those facing the power of the state and the terrible prospects of criminal punishment that can inspire some lawyers to make commitments as profound and far-reaching as these. But we suspect that even many criminal defense lawyers are not prepared to forswear such discretion altogether, and if they are not, they cannot uphold all that this statement says.[80] Moreover, the moral case for such absolute commitment to one's client is clearly weaker in most civil matters (though asylum cases, in which the client's life may be at stake if asylum is wrongly denied, may well be an exception).[81]

Because we know so little, empirically, about how clients respond to confidentiality statements, it is impossible to reach absolute conclusions about the best advice on confidentiality. We offer our own recommendations not as a settled model but as a basis for experimentation and further development. We suggest that the problems in this area can be addressed most effectively if we recognize that different kinds of advice are appropriate at different points in the lawyer-client relationship.[82] We suggest, in particular, that lawyers should distinguish between the advice they give at the start of the relationship and the advice they are prepared to give later on.

At the start of the relationship, we believe lawyers should presume that their clients are honest and well-intentioned enough to make it unlikely that any of the exceptions to confidentiality will come into play. Why should lawyers start from a presumption of client honesty and decent intentions? If all clients were honest and good, this presumption would be accurate (and unnecessary), but angels rarely seek legal representation.[83] It seems likely, in fact, that most clients, being human, find complete candor with their lawyers very difficult, and that many clients, again being human, harbor at least some ill intent towards others. Nonetheless, we think our presumption is the right one. We say this partly because we believe that many less-than-perfect clients will ultimately conform to this presumption in their dealings with their lawyer if they have the opportunity to develop a trusting relationship with her. More importantly, however, we see a presumption like this as fitting the fundamental characterization of the engaged client-centered lawyer's role, namely that the lawyer is a helper, who helps because she respects her clients.[84] The lawyer should not expect perfection, but she should not normally begin by expecting problems of the intensity that would bring the confidentiality exceptions into play.

Given that starting presumption, it would be possible to defend the lawyer's decision to provide unqualified assurances of confidentiality at the start of the relationship, on the lines of Ms. Washington's comments. After all, the argument goes, if clients won't encounter these exceptions, why mention them at all? But we think that this position is ultimately mistaken. It is, after all, *possible* that confidentiality exceptions will actually come to matter in any given case and while we have presumed that that possibility is not a likely one, we would not describe it as "remote." If there is a real chance that exceptions will ultimately affect the client's case, then a complete failure to mention that such exceptions exist entails a form of deception. To respect another person, we believe, involves assuming that the other person will benefit from knowledge and not be corrupted by it. Here, it is a fact that lawyer-client confidentiality is incomplete, and we do not think this should be denied. We are not altogether sure that it even can be denied; as we have already seen, there is modest empirical evidence indicating that clients do not believe lawyers honor confidentiality absolutely.[85]

Here and elsewhere in our analysis, timing is critical. While the dialogue at the beginning of this chapter goes from introductions to painful revelations in the space of a few pages, in reality lawyer-client interactions commonly occur in several meetings over a considerable period of time. In general, we believe that at the beginning of the relationship lawyers can rightly emphasize building trust more than complete disclosure; in later encounters, there will be more room, and sometimes there will be more need, for more painful and frank discussions. At the initial stage of the relationship, therefore, we recommend that the lawyer say something like this:

> For me to understand your case and figure out whether I can help you, I need to know the facts. The law realizes this and realizes that it is important for you to be able to speak to me fully and frankly. For that reason, ordinarily everything you tell me is confidential. That means I won't, and can't, repeat it without your consent. Now, you should know that this rule, like most rules, has some exceptions, and if it turns out to be necessary as we go along I will explain these to you in detail. But normally, as I've already said, what you tell me—even about things that may be embarrassing or even illegal—is confidential. That lets us talk frankly, which is what we need to do, and that's what I'd like to begin doing now.

This statement avoids asserting absolute confidentiality—the problem of the Amsterdam formulation.[86] It also avoids piling qualification on qualification—the problem of the Sobelson formulation.[87] Additionally, we believe, it offers a way to utilize the advice about confidentiality as a building block in the relationship, in the way that Amsterdam's formulation exemplifies, both by emphasizing the very substantial privacy lawyer and client do enjoy and by promising the lawyer's aid in clarifying any limits on privacy if understanding them becomes necessary. Finally, we believe this advice, by acknowledging but not belaboring the existence of exceptions to confidentiality, comports with the presumption of client honesty and decent intentions.

This advice also promotes the lawyer's search for truth in another way, namely by repeatedly emphasizing that the lawyer needs the client to be candid so that she can effectively represent him. We believe these statements are, in general, correct. Nevertheless this exhortation deserves a moment's examination, because we have already argued that *sometimes* a client would be better off if the lawyer did not know everything.[88] We believe it is appropriate not to raise this possibility at the start of the relationship, in part because it would be inconsistent with the presumption of client honesty to suggest at the beginning the possible value of dishonesty. More fundamentally, we do not think that it is ever appropriate to suggest to the client that he might be better off lying, because it is hard to see how such a suggestion could be made without directly increasing the chance of perjury. While we would avoid explicitly stating to a client that it is always in his interest to tell us everything—because that is not quite true—we endorse the kinds of statements in this advice about confidentiality, statements which make a similar, though not quite so blunt, argument.

The advice we have just suggested rests not only on the presumption of client honesty but also on the assumption that the lawyer in the particular case should be seeking the truth from her client. As we have already recognized, however, there are circumstances where a lawyer might conscientiously decide to skirt the truth in her encounters with her client.[89] The discretion to act in this way, as we have analyzed it, does not extend to avoiding explicit mention of facts that are staring the lawyer in the face—facts which, realistically, she already "knows"—but it does embrace techniques that limit the chance that the lawyer will ever come close to knowledge. One such technique might be a clear and pointed explanation of confidentiality exceptions early in the relationship. An immigration lawyer, for example, might say to her client:

> I want to understand what happened to you, and our conversations about what happened to you are confidential. But when you file your application, you will have to give the government information about many of the same things that you and I will be discussing, and what you tell me about these things you may have to tell the government too.

This statement is accurate as far as it goes (it is still, of course, far from a comprehensive discussion of confidentiality limits), and it does not invite the client to lie, but it certainly might encourage such behavior. At the same time, we share the view of Monroe Freedman and Abbe Smith that that this kind of advice at the start of a lawyer-client relationship may critically undermine the relationship itself.[90] This is a heavy price to pay and a further indication that conscientious lawyers should think long and hard before embarking on such a course.

If we adhere to the effort to seek the truth, however, we still do not suggest that lawyers should embrace the presumption of client honesty blindly. Their hopes may be disappointed, and when this happens, or seems likely to happen, the lawyers may have the obligation, or at least the discretion, to depart from confidentiality. Determining when a confidentiality qualification comes into play is inevitably a matter for judgment. We offer two general caveats. First, lawyers should be very reluctant to infer the existence of such problems from generalizations alone (for instance, an assumption that all criminal defendants lie[91]); instead, they should wait for developments in their particular case. Second, lawyers should not assume that the client's initially false, or implausible, story excludes him from the presumption of honesty; we presume that clients are capable of achieving honesty over time, not that they initially tell all. Indeed, the evolution of clients' own thoughts and feelings, and of their telling of their stories, is a theme of this book.

Nevertheless, the time may come when a confidentiality exception is in view. At this point, we believe the lawyer should explain the matter to the client by giving the client advice that explicitly calls to his attention whatever limits on confidentiality are being approached. Otherwise, the lawyer may not only betray the client but do so behind his back.[92]

We also believe, however, that the lawyer should aim to provide this supplemental advice about confidentiality *before* the breach of confidentiality becomes necessary. Doing so may, of course, teach the client to be more discreet and assist him in carrying out his plans without facing disclosure and obstruction—and perhaps selfishly protect the lawyer from facing a moral dilemma that needs to be faced. For example:

Client: I am so angry with my father about the way he's ruining our business that I just can't take it any more. I've just got to get my money out somehow. I think the only way I can do it is . . .

Lawyer: [Interrupting] I want you to understand that if you reveal information to me that indicates you are going to commit a crime I may have the right to reveal it to the authorities.

It may not really be possible to head off information this way, but in any case, we do not mean to suggest such a use of advice about confidentiality as a shield against knowledge. Indeed, this lawyer's crude intervention suggests that she is perilously near already "knowing" what she is trying not to hear. We recognize, however, that even if lawyers do not aim for this result, and do not aim their advice as this lawyer has, they may sometimes achieve the same result unintentionally. This we accept, in part because we believe lawyers should, in the words of the Model Code, "resolve reasonable doubts in favor of [their] client."[93] We also accept this risk because we see positive value in the lawyer-client conversations that such disclosures may trigger. Although we are very skeptical about the value of extensive dialogue regarding confidentiality limits at the start of the relationship, we think that lawyers' candid discussion of confidentiality exceptions—when they are really at issue in a particular case—may actually deepen the encounter between lawyer and client. We see such disclosure as potentially forming the starting point for the kind of "moral dialogue" between lawyer and client that may cause the client to refrain from the type of conduct that society needs disclosed and obstructed.[94]

Finally, we see such disclosure to head off client misconduct as consistent with Model Rule 1.4(a)(5). This provision obliges the lawyer who "knows that a client expects assistance not permitted by the Rules of Professional Conduct or other law" to "consult with the client about any relevant limitation on the lawyer's conduct."[95] As we have already indicated, we recommend disclosure not only when the lawyer anticipates being obliged to breach confidentiality, but also when she anticipates exercising an authorized discretion to do so. In both contexts, however, we see the lawyer as acting to prevent a rupture of the relationship before it becomes irrevocable. We hope for dialogues like this one:

Client: I am so angry with my father about the way he's ruining our business that I just can't take it any more. I've just got to get my money out somehow.

Lawyer: I think I understand how upsetting it must be to see what you've worked for being undermined. Have you thought about how you might be able to get your money out?

Client: I think the only way I can do it is to start fiddling the books.

Lawyer: Do you really think that fiddling the books will work?

Client: Yes! Yes, I do! I can do it, and no one will ever be the wiser.

Lawyer: I don't think you can really count on that.

Client: Why not? You're the only one who knows, and all you have to do is just not mention it in any of our documents.

Lawyer: Because fiddled books matter to people, and sooner or later those people come asking questions. Even if I could "just not mention it," if you get in trouble with the IRS, say, because some income turns up missing, or your bankers can't collect on a loan, and they come after you, well, they may come after me for information, and—remember when I told you at the start of our working together that there were some exceptions to lawyer-client confidentiality? Well, this is one.

Client: I can't believe I'm hearing this.

Lawyer: You don't have to like it, and for that matter I don't have to like it either. But it's the law. You can't be sure you'd get away with this idea, and that's one really good reason why you and I should try to figure out some better solution.

In this dialogue, the lawyer could have responded to the client's initial comment ("I've just got to get my money out somehow") with a warning about confidentiality meant to silence the client before he revealed anything he should not—as in the previous example. Instead, she responds with empathy and inquiry, in effect taking the position that she should continue to work on open terms with her client rather than warning him off. We think that was appropriate, because the lawyer did not yet have reason to believe that her client was contemplating illegal conduct. The result is that he does announce exactly that, and so her warning about confidentiality, when it comes, is too late to enable him to carry out his scheme without her knowledge. Her knowledge, however, remains quite limited; she does not probe for the details of her client's scheme, but instead, once she sees the direction of her client's thinking clearly, she almost at once tells him about the confidentiality issue. What she says about that issue is not very precise, and perhaps she should be faulted for this, but meanwhile she has continued to engage with her client, not primarily about legal ethics but about the core counseling question of whether his idea of "fiddling the books" will in fact accomplish his goal of getting his money out. That is the issue the two of them need to address, and in this perhaps idealized dialogue the lawyer's warning about confidentiality limits becomes a part of addressing it.

D. ADVICE ABOUT THE LAW

The encounter between Ms. Washington and her client might have turned out very differently if she had responded to the first hint of his deliveries to FARC (a hint that appears in C13 of the opening dialogue of this chapter) by explaining the relevant law. Perhaps the conversation would have proceeded like this:

L14*:   Mr. Reyes, this may be quite a sensitive matter for the government. You see, they don't much care if you broke some minor law in Colombia, say their truck registration laws, but they care a lot about some other matters.

C14*:   Sure, but like I told you, it was basically just regular stuff—and the truck was just old.

L15*:   Yes, I understand. But you should know that one thing the government cares a lot about is this. They feel that asylum is meant to protect people who've been treated really badly—and they don't want to give asylum to anyone who has been involved in treating other people badly himself. So I'm not sure who you might have been delivering to, or what you were delivering, but if you were involved somehow in persecution or terrorism, then your chances of getting asylum go way, way down.

C15*:   What if I didn't have any choice at all at the time?

L16*:   That might give us something to argue on your behalf, but even that wouldn't be good. This is something the U.S. has gotten really, really tough about.

C16*:   Well, that sounds completely unfair to me. But it doesn't matter, because I've never had anything to do with terrorists or anybody like that. It was just the opposite—sometimes we carried other union activists who were on the run from the paramilitaries.

The lawyer's role in this dialogue may actually be fairly guileless. The classic illustration of the use of legal advice to mold client testimony, however, features interviewing that is entirely strategic. In *Anatomy of a Murder*,[96] the defense attorney, Paul Biegler, has already heard his potential client, Lieutenant Manion, admit that he killed the dead man. As Biegler tells us:

> I had reached a point where a few wrong answers to a few right questions would leave me with a client—if I took his case—whose cause was legally defenseless. Either I stopped now and begged off and let some other lawyer worry over it or I asked him the few fatal questions and let him hang himself. Or else, like any smart lawyer, I went into the Lecture.[97]

Then Biegler explains "the Lecture":

The Lecture is an ancient device that lawyers use to coach their clients so that the client won't quite know he has been coached and his lawyer can still preserve the face-saving illusion that he hasn't done any coaching. For coaching clients, like robbing them, is not only frowned upon, it is downright unethical and bad, very bad. Hence the Lecture, an artful device as old as the law itself ....[98]

In this particular case, the Lecture consists of an explanation of the absolute necessity of presenting a plausible legal defense and the elimination, one by one, of all the available defenses except one—insanity. Lieutenant Manion takes the bait, and Biegler explains what an insanity claim is and how long someone acquitted on this basis might spend in a mental hospital. After one last enticement, in which Biegler appeals to his client's willingness to take a "calculated risk," Biegler is finished. He waits. His client utters the magic words: " 'Maybe,' he said, 'maybe I was insane.' "[99] After Manion manages, with some prompting, to provide suitable answers to the various questions entailed in this defense (for example, by "revealing" that he only assumes he killed the victim, because he can't remember the crucial moments), Biegler is satisfied that his client has a defense.[100]

Interviewing of this sort—deliberately guiding the client towards a story the lawyer does not suppose is true—has no place in a relationship in which the lawyer seeks to learn the truth in order to represent her clients within the law. But we cannot simply forbid lawyers to explain the law to their clients. On the contrary, lawyers are *supposed* to explain the law to their clients. In this context, we face an instance of a more general problem, namely the unfortunate truth that knowledge of the law may enable a client to violate it. Here, in *Anatomy of a Murder*, the particular violation at issue is, essentially, perjury (to say nothing of perhaps getting away with murder as a result).

This tension between truth-seeking and law-advising is acute. We assume that, as a general proposition, the lawyer cannot resolve it by failing to advise her client about the law, since she is clearly obliged to provide her client with that advice.[101] This general proposition has its limits.[102] We would not, for example, inform a perjurious client that one option available to him is to discharge us and find another lawyer to whom he can tell only his perjured story, nor—if the client raised this idea himself—would we inform him that he would probably be able to get away with this scheme (even if that were so). Advice to a client about the substantive legal rules affecting his case is, in general, far from such danger zones, but *Anatomy of a Murder* demonstrates that even this category of advice can be put to improper purposes.

How can this tension be addressed? In our discussion of advice about confidentiality earlier in this chapter, we suggested that at the beginning of the lawyer-client relationship the lawyer could rightly make very limited reference to the possibility of confidentiality exceptions, and instead could leave discussing the details of those until the need to do so emerged.[103] A somewhat similar approach to the timing of advice may here be well calculated to vindicate both the client's right to know the law and the lawyer's concern to learn the truth from her client. We might say, then, that the lawyer's first task in interviewing, including in interviewing that seeks to elicit the truth, is to hear the client's story as the client wishes to tell it. Her second task is to explore the details of the story the client has told, for example by getting the chronology clear and by looking for related points that the client has not initially mentioned.[104] If the lawyer can help the client to tell his story by proceeding on these lines, she does not need to explain the law to him yet.

This approach does not deny the client assistance in identifying relevant facts—though it does avoid marking those facts in advance as what the law seeks. In carrying out the familiar task of exploring the details of a client's account, the lawyer can and must look for facts that will sustain, or block, particular legal theories that might be relevant to the case. Even this may signal to the client what he should "remember." For example, a lawyer interviewing the victim of an automobile accident will surely want to know the client's physical symptoms; when she asks the client, "By the way, do you have any lower back pain?" the client may speedily invent some.[105] We think this risk is worth running, because without such specific and somewhat suggestive questions, important facts may never be discovered. But the client's need for guidance about what is relevant does not, at this point, require the lawyer to compound the leading effect of her questions by buttressing them with a description of the legal rules she is testing.

When all of this work is done, however, the process of interviewing and counseling the client is far from over. The client is entitled to know where he stands legally, and that will involve telling him what the facts he has laid out mean, and why. At this point, the client may offer new facts, though we do not assume that all clients will react this way. We do recognize, however, that clients—and people—rarely tell their story in exactly the same words, or with exactly the same details, twice. Lawyers always need to keep in mind that people remember, feel, assess, and report differently from one occasion to another, and being sensitive to those differences is an important part of working with a client. Here, somewhat artificially, we mean to break out from this general pattern one particular form of variation—the variation induced by the client's learning what is in his legal interest.[106]

Giving full weight to the impact of the client's new knowledge, perhaps we should say that the client will offer new "facts," to emphasize that these new claims may be false. But we do not assume that any new facts the clients do offer are necessarily false, even if they favor the client's story and contradict earlier accounts the client has given. (Contradiction is, of course, not inevitable; sometimes newly-reported facts may simply embellish the details already reported, and sometimes they may be inconsistent with the overall tenor of the earlier story but not directly contradict anything already said.) Memories are faulty and may actually be refreshed or restored over time. Even if the issue is not one of memory but of veracity, it may well be pointed out that clients sometimes lie out of a misunderstanding of the law and reveal the truth only when they are informed of the law's true provisions.[107] More generally, we should recognize that clients may not initially trust their lawyers and therefore may lie first, only to tell the truth later.

Another incident in the *Anatomy of a Murder* interview helps illuminate the lawyer's duty when a client's story changes. The defendant, Lieutenant Manion, having learned that killing his wife's rapist cannot be excused on grounds of provocation if the killing is only done when the rape is already some while in the past,[108] has an idea of his own for his defense:

> The Lieutenant's eyes narrowed and flickered ever so little. "Maybe," he began, and cleared his throat. "On second thought, maybe I *did* catch Quill in the act. I've never precisely told the police one way or the other." His eyes regarded me quietly, steadily.[109]

Biegler rejects this revision of the story, and certainly he has good reason to believe that Manion is lying. But he is not right simply because Manion's second story differs from his first. We recognize that by postponing the discussion of the law until after the basic interviewing is over, the lawyer following this approach may increase the chance that she will hear her client assert new facts whose veracity she will have some reason to doubt. Arguably, however, it is better for lawyers to take this risk and to evaluate their clients' claims with all the data at their disposal—including such features as the narrowing and flickering of the eyes—rather than invite the same possible fabrication to occur earlier on or deny the client, later, an understanding of the law under which he lives and will be judged.

We also recognize that by withholding this information until this stage, the lawyer will put those clients who do not understand the law at a disadvantage compared with veterans of the legal system who do understand it. The veterans will be able to produce either relevant truthful information at once, thereby avoiding later questions about their veracity, or false "information" instead, but again more credibly. If, however, the best way to reconcile truth-seeking and law-advising in general is to listen to the client's story first, and explain the law afterward, we would not be inclined to abandon this approach for all clients in order to give everyone the same opportunity to shape the facts to the law that repeat players enjoy.

Ms. Washington, in the version of the dialogue at the beginning of this chapter, pursues essentially the strategy we have just outlined. Here, the danger is not that the client will invent but that he will deny, and the danger is quite substantial, because it is evident and not surprising that the client already suspects that having made deliveries to the FARC could be a big legal problem for him. Ms. Washington does not initially know what the source of Mr. Reyes's anxiety is, but she soon begins to learn. Now her job, as she sees it, is to get past the client's resistance to telling the truth, and she accomplishes this by using various forms of pressure.[110] That job would surely be harder if she first verified the client's suspicions about the legal peril he faced by explaining exactly what the relevant law provided.

But it is difficult to escape the feeling that Mr. Reyes has essentially been tricked into revealing information that he would never have disclosed had he understood the law more clearly. Moreover, the approach we have just laid out, in which the lawyer offers no explicit guidance about the law until after the client has revealed this information, is not entirely consistent with the approach we suggested for discussions of confidentiality, in which we endorsed the lawyer's providing a degree of guidance about confidentiality limits at the very start, and then more as possible confidentiality danger zones emerged. All of this must be particularly troubling to lawyers—such as Ms. Washington herself (L31)—who would consider the denial of asylum to Mr. Reyes on the basis of the facts he has revealed to be a gross injustice. As we have seen repeatedly, the resolution of the tension between truth-seeking and law-advising may be different if the lawyer is exercising her discretion, within the rules of ethics, not to aim for the truth. Moreover, it is clearly Ms. Washington who has weighed the claims of truth and justice and decided that she must seek out the truth even at the risk of potential injustice; her client had no chance to reach his own judgment about this.

In this light, let us look again at the alternate dialogue with which this part began. Actually, this dialogue is quite a distance from Biegler's delicate dance of instruction to his client about what story to invent—and it is worth emphasizing that even from the perspective we are now developing we would consider the advice Biegler gives unacceptable because it too nearly approaches, if indeed it does not cross, the line to subornation of perjury. Ms. Washington, like Biegler, senses that there is a problem, but she knows very little about what that problem might be; she seems much further from deliberate avoidance of something she already virtually knows than Biegler does. Moreover, her guidance on the law is brief and straightforward; she does not offer a mini-course in what the wrong answers would be, as a predicate to asking for the right answer. She is engaged in giving her client important advice which may well affect what he will reveal, but she is not enmeshed in artifice.[111] Indeed, what she says about the law may even be seen as an effort to present the law to the client in terms of its underlying values, precisely so that the client can reach his own judgment about how his life and those values fit together— the role that Chapter Eight ("Talking to Clients About the Law") urges lawyers to perform.

It is possible to critique what Ms. Washington said even while accepting the basic point that she should have offered her client guidance of this sort. When she says to Mr. Reyes that "your chances of getting asylum go way, way down" (L15*), she is by no means being precise. A full, precise account of the law would take much longer, but the lawyer's job is to explain the law to the client clearly, rather than comprehensively.

Perhaps more important, a full account would have made clear that even if Mr. Reyes was "somehow" involved with persecution or terrorism, there were still a number of conceivable ways that he and Ms. Washington might have been able to make a successful case for his remaining in the United States. This comment, and her admonition that "[t]his is something the U.S. has gotten really, really tough about," are blunt, and somewhat loosely phrased, warnings that seem likely to block this line of discussion altogether even though the lawyer does not yet know if a careful assessment of the nuances of the facts might turn out in the client's favor, and even though the client might make a different choice about what to reveal if he knew the legal framework more completely. The lawyer engaged in offering anticipatory guidance about the law, in short, faces difficult questions about how to describe the law concisely and accurately—questions all the more difficult because the lawyer must give this advice without knowing what the facts actually are. The delicacy of this process is, indeed, a consideration weighing against undertaking it.[112]

In short, both of the approaches we have outlined—withholding advice about the law until after the client has told his story, and the opposite—have important virtues and serious problems. We ourselves would see Ms. Washington's advice in the alternate dialogue as within the bounds of ethical practice—and some of us would also see her approach in the opening dialogue as within those bounds.[113] But you should remember, as you reach your own judgment on this issue, that if both dialogues are realistic then the result of giving Mr. Reyes more information about the law earlier in the interview is, indeed, to lead him to lie to his lawyer. That may be the most just result, but it is not one that a lawyer should relish.

E. RESPECT AND INQUIRY

How skeptical should lawyers be of their clients' veracity? In the interview excerpt that begins this chapter, Ms. Washington does not set out to uncover the drug delivery problem. Her question about how Mr. Reyes lived during the six months he waited to get out of Colombia (L12) seems entirely explicable as part of an effort to get a complete account of the hardships he has suffered. But when the client responds with his quasi-admission of carrying some stuff that wasn't "regular," Ms. Washington pursues the issue and refuses to let go of it until she has extracted what turns out to be a potentially disastrous admission of bringing medical supplies to the FARC. Should she have let up earlier?

In many interviews—and to some extent in this one—the question of whether to press or not to press the client probably does not arise. Good interviewing entails hearing the client's story and eliciting relevant details he may have omitted or forgotten. To some extent, such interviewing inevitably tests the client's credibility, for such questioning reveals whether the client's original story and subsequent elaborations have the ring of truth. But questions of this sort would be necessary whether or not there was a client credibility issue, so they require no special justification in terms of the principle of respect for client honesty. If it is fair to say that Ms. Washington had heard her prospective client strongly hint that he had sometimes transported some sort of illegal goods (C13), she could hardly have omitted an inquiry into what these goods were; to realize that the client engaged in some sort of illegal conduct but not check what the conduct was would simply be incomplete. She might have prefaced that inquiry with more advice about the law and about confidentiality and its limits; but to simply leave this loose end unexamined would have been perilous for the client and for herself.

In many interviews, however, there are probably points at which the client offers information that might or might not be complete. Here, for example, when Ms. Washington presses Mr. Reyes to clarify what kind of "stuff" he was transporting (L14), he answers, "Well, mostly it was just food, clothes, furniture—really all right, perfectly legal." (C15). He doesn't stop there, and what he adds—a story of how the "special rides" operated—makes unmistakably clear that there was something very problematic about these rides. But suppose he had answered Ms. Washington's initial questions about his work (L12, followed by L13) by saying: "I drove a truck for them, making pick-ups and deliveries. We carried a bunch of stuff, mostly food and clothes, also some furniture." This answer could be complete and responsive. If that was how it sounded to the lawyer, and if there were no related loose ends that needed further inquiry as a matter of thorough, normal interviewing, then we believe that Ms. Washington would have no reason to press the matter further. She would not need to say, for example, "All that is no problem. But did you transport any goods for terrorists?" because she would have no reason to suspect that he did. Having no reason for such a question, in fact, she probably ought *not* to ask it, both because time is limited, and because random probing for impropriety is disrespectful to the client.[114]

In taking this position, we agree with Geoffrey Hazard and W. William Hodes, who argue in their Model Rules handbook, *The Law of Lawyering*, that normally a lawyer

> gives advice, negotiates, and helps consummate transactions on the basis of the facts presented to her by her client, not the facts that a thoroughgoing hostile investigation might reveal. Even where there is room for doubt about some of the details, a lawyer ordinarily demonstrates proper loyalty and zeal by giving a client the benefit of that doubt.[115]

We have already seen that the Model Code, the Model Rules and (half-heartedly) the Restatement offer support for this disposition in favor of believing what the client says.[116] Put differently, we might say that even though a lawyer should normally seek the truth from her client, she also has a duty to her client not to transmute that search into a search for *lies*.

As we have already recognized, however, there is a point at which the failure to recognize a fact becomes a "conscious avoidance" of knowledge one actually has, and by that point, the lawyer is acting improperly.[117] But it may be more important to recognize that there is surely a substantial area between the extremes of treating one's own client as an adversary or instead engaging in conscious avoidance of the truth. In this substantial area, we believe lawyers have discretion to inquire and generally should do so (again, perhaps with careful preliminary advice to the client about the law) when they feel they have significant grounds for uneasiness about their client's account. In other words, while we agree that lawyers should generally resolve doubts in favor of their clients, we do not believe that lawyers should passively accept whatever account their client gives so long as it is not proven beyond a reasonable doubt to be false. They should, in general, ask questions first and give the benefit of the doubt afterwards. To do so serves the goal of truth, and it also protects the client from the many perils involved in relying on a story that cannot withstand questioning.

Here we may differ from Professor Hodes, who has written that "the lawyer should trust the client all the way up to the point of *knowledge* that the client is up to no good."[118] One way to apply this proposition would be for the lawyer to shape every question she asks her client with a view not to eliciting the truth but to fostering the strongest possible story that the client can tell without triggering knowledge of its falsehood (though this approach may be far from what Professor Hodes is endorsing). We encourage lawyers to engage more deeply with what their client tells them, both in hearing the client's story and in counseling her on the choices she needs to make.

In the opening dialogue, Ms. Washington was probably operating in this zone of discretion almost from the moment the topic of the ir-"regular" shipments came up. The client's almost immediate request for reassurance about confidentiality signaled his own anxiety (C14), and the incomplete, but pregnant, answer he gave after receiving this reassurance would hardly have removed her doubts (C15). His response to her next question (C16)—telling her that the truck owner never told him what was in the truck—seems to offer a potential escape from the problem (namely, a defense of ignorance[119]), but the lawyer's follow-up (L17)—a leading question that tries to lock that defense in[120]—elicits the unwelcome news that Mr. Reyes *does* know what he was carrying. We think a failure to follow up further at this point would have approached or simply amounted to a deliberate avoidance of knowledge. In short, we believe Ms. Washington was justified in pursuing this matter, even though her focus on it surely implied at once that she did not fully accept her client's honesty or entirely accord him the respect an honest person would merit, and once she began, it would have been hard for her to stop.

Again, however, we should recognize that a lawyer who has decided to exercise the discretion she has to skirt the truth might handle the issues discussed in this Part quite differently. She might be slower to inquire about matters on which she is skeptical and correspondingly quicker to resolve doubts in her client's favor. If she did inquire, she might do so in a deliberately slanted way, hoping to elicit the answers she needs rather than those she fears. Such steps have many potential costs, but conscientious lawyers may sometimes believe these costs are less severe than the alternative of eliciting information whose discovery will lead to injustice.

F. TECHNIQUES FOR PURSUING THE TRUTH

We come now to the question of techniques for inquiry. When the lawyer believes she must press the client for the truth, how should she do it? In the opening dialogue, Ms. Washington employs several techniques. She reassures her client about confidentiality (more than she should have, as we have explained) (L15, L20). She asks her questions repeatedly, resisting her client's efforts to get her to accept half-answers (L13 & L14, L18 & L19, L23–L25, L27 & L28). She asks very specific questions (for example, "How many times?" (L23) and "How many times, exactly?" (L24)). Sometimes she uses closed-ended questions, calling for yes-or-no answers (L25, L30). She asks her questions emphatically when she feels her client is being particularly evasive (L24, L25, L28). Her approach to her client grows less friendly as the client continues to stall on admitting the full truth. When she begins these inquiries, she offers a little reassurance and even a hint of apology for her questions ("I'm not sure I understand. Was some of the stuff you were carrying not what you call 'regular stuff'?" (L14)), but by the end she is peppering her client with specific, probing questions. Near the end she adds sarcasm ("Did you get paid extra for this favor?" (L30)).

Broadly speaking, we approve of all these techniques in those cases where the lawyer rightly seeks to elicit the truth from her client. (Whether this was such a case is a different, and a debatable, question, as we've seen.) When the lawyer feels she must pursue the possibility that her client is lying or evading, she must reckon with the likelihood of client resistance, and her methods of overcoming that resistance may have to be firm or even aggressive. Ms. Washington certainly had ample reason to conclude that her client was being evasive. Moreover, while Ms. Washington was not gentle with her client, she also did not break faith with him. She used no tricks, offered no false promises (except for her unqualified assurances of confidentiality), and made no threats that she could not properly have carried out.[121]

While the kinds of techniques Ms. Washington uses are legitimate, we think she could have done a better job. She elicited the truth, but perhaps not the whole truth; the legal problems Mr. Reyes faced might have been mitigated in a number of ways, for example by more information about the pressure he felt to do the driving for his friend, and by evidence that he was himself deeply opposed to FARC's activities.[122] Ms. Washington hasn't forgotten that he may still have a case (hence her comment (L32) about the need to consider very carefully what he must say in the asylum application, and her assurance (L31) that she is "not giving up at all") but her interviewing focus seems to have shifted from exploring his case to demonstrating that he might not have one.[123]

Indeed, the implicit message she gives by stopping her note-taking and pausing at length before delivering the bad news at L31 seems at odds with what she says; she acts as if the case may be over when in fact her investigation has just begun. Had she avoided that unconscious shift in orientation, she might have learned more by using techniques that were somewhat less prosecutorial in style. Perhaps the confrontation with her client about the meaning of confidentiality would never have been necessary, if the two of them had completed their investigation and found a viable strategy to achieve Mr. Reyes's goals without pressing the bounds of truth.

We do not suggest that gentler approaches are always right, because they are not. They do, however, have a great virtue: they are less likely to disrupt the emotional relationship between lawyer and client. Sometimes, a gentler method may also be more effective; some clients may respond only to a lawyer whom they perceive as an ally and may shrink back from revelations to anyone who acts like something else. Additionally, we suspect that a practice of adopting aggressive approaches to one's own client may reflect, or promote, a disposition not to believe him, and we see that disposition as imperiling the lawyer's performance of her duty generally to resolve doubts in the client's favor. We think these considerations support a preference for ordinarily using gentler, less confrontational techniques first, rather than methods more characteristic of cross-examination or even interrogation. We do not believe, however, that any techniques consistent with good faith can be ruled out altogether. Instead, we believe that the lawyer should have a broad repertoire of techniques and choose from them in light of the situation before her. We offer here a brief catalogue of such techniques:

(a) *Testing the hypothesis that the client is lying*: Normal, basic interviewing elicits the client's story and then pursues various hypotheses guided by the lawyer's tentative legal theories.[124] If the issue in a particular case is whether the client can demonstrate that the contractor who built his garage was negligent, for instance, the lawyer would then ask the client about facts that would tend to demonstrate or disprove this theory (for example, how often did the client see the contractor actually on the site, supervising his employees?). Normally in such questioning, the lawyer is not directly seeking to test the hypothesis that the client is lying, but if need be, that can become a central part of the lawyer's focus.

Suppose, for example, that a defendant says he was beaten repeatedly by the police, and the lawyer is uneasy about the truth of this claim. She might reason that if the client really was beaten repeatedly, he should be able to tell a story of, for example, which rooms he was beaten in, by whom, and how many times. Certainly the client's memory of these details may be fuzzy, but if he can offer no details at all, there may be cause for doubting the client's allegations. Similarly, she might reason that an asylum client who says he was tortured during months of confinement in a prison known for its bad sanitation should be able to remember not just his torture but also either the abominable smell that would have assailed him constantly, or the daily routine of the prison; the client who remembers none of this may never have been imprisoned at all.[125] The lawyer should not put absolute faith in such inferences—indeed, the ones we've just mentioned may be deeply flawed—but she should evaluate them and, if she thinks they are plausible, even though not conclusive, she should not ignore them. Techniques such as these may be quite effective, both because they are not bluntly confrontational and because they approach the client's story from angles that a lying client might not anticipate.

(b) *Empathy and Reassurance*: As we've sought to demonstrate throughout this book, in general we believe that a positive relationship between lawyer and client improves communication between them. Broadly, a lawyer is more likely to hear the truth if the client trusts her to stay on his side and not to add her condemnation to the judgments of the client's adversaries or of society at large. This remains true even when the required communications become more painful. Building such a relationship is, of course, the function of interviewing and counseling tools, such as empathy.[126] Paying personal attention to the client's well-being can contribute to such trust.[127] Expressing approval of, or agreement with, the client's perspectives can also be helpful, though it has important pitfalls.[128] Providing clearly-phrased and sympathetically-reasoned explanations of why the lawyer feels the client is not telling the truth, and how falsehoods may damage the client's interests, may also be valuable. Techniques like these are important elements of ordinary interaction with clients, and they are no less important here.

(c) *Role-play and other techniques for client participation*: The techniques mentioned in the previous paragraph build connections between lawyer and client, but they share a common feature that is not necessarily a strength: all of them turn on what the lawyer says to the client. We are impressed with the potential of techniques that enable clients to say more, both as tools to affect clients' thinking and as ways to empower the clients in their own cases.[129] The lawyer might, for example, ask the client how he would respond to the client's own story if he were on the other side; this is close to the technique Rusty Sabich's lawyer uses in the excerpt quoted earlier.[130] The client might just articulate the arguments, or he might deliver them in role-playing the part of the prosecutor, for example, in an upcoming arraignment.[131] Alternatively, the client might be asked to play himself for an audience that he accepts as disinterested so that the client can experience, in the safety of the lawyer's office, the likely reaction to his performance. In all of these settings, clients who may be unable to come to grips with their situation in back-and-forth discussions with the lawyer may find deeper resources of performance and understanding.

(d) *Cross-examination and confrontation*: Many of the techniques Ms. Washington uses fall into this category. Techniques with the flavor of cross-examination include the use of narrow and leading questions; short, fast, and insistent series of questions; questions that confront the answerer with his own prior inconsistencies; and questions that confront the answerer with the inconsistent evidence of other sources.[132]

On a somewhat different dimension, questioners may seek to convey their skepticism and disbelief through the way they ask their questions and the way they connect to, or pull back from, the client. The lawyer might move back in her seat, stand up and pace, roll her eyes, or—a technique mentioned by Anthony Amsterdam—silently write extended notes while not looking at the client, in response to some remark she finds implausible.[133] In general, good interviewing normally includes feedback and encouragement as well as connection on many different levels with the client, but the lawyer may also need to turn off all these sources of reassurance and approval. More bluntly, the lawyer may say to the client, in so many words, "Don't bullshit me."

While we believe that techniques drawn from the realm of cross-examination do have a place in pursuing the truth with a client, we offer two caveats about their use. First, few witnesses welcome cross-examination, and few clients will feel warmer towards their lawyer as a result of experiencing cross-examination at her hands. The more direct the confrontation, in general, the greater the risk. Second, courtroom advocacy is aimed at convincing the finder of fact, but in the interview room there is no finder of fact except the lawyer and the client. Their task, if possible, is to come to a shared understanding about the case they will present to others. While a cross-examiner may be delighted to elicit evidence that can later be used to demonstrate the witness's falsity to the jury and may deliberately avoid putting that inference to the witness so as to avoid having the witness somehow defuse it, there is little point in such maneuvering with one's own client. The lawyer who discerns falsity will ultimately need to discuss it openly with her client.

(e) *Coercion*: We might hesitate to include "coercion" in a list of techniques that lawyers can use on their own clients.[134] No less an authority than the Supreme Court, however, has made it clear that coercion in the service of preventing client perjury can be the lawyer's duty. In *Nix v. Whiteside*,[135] the Supreme Court considered Whiteside's claim that his criminal defense lawyer breached his Sixth Amendment right to counsel by forcing him not to give testimony that would have supported his claim of killing in self-defense. According to the Court:

> Until shortly before trial, Whiteside consistently stated to Robinson [his attorney] that he had not actually seen a gun, but that he was convinced that Love [whom Whiteside had stabbed to death] had a gun in his hand. About a week before trial, during preparation for direct examination, Whiteside for the first time told Robinson . . . that he had seen something "metallic" in Love's hand. When asked about this, Whiteside responded:
>
>> "[I]n Howard Cook's case there was a gun. If I don't say I saw a gun, I'm dead."

Robinson told Whiteside that such testimony would be perjury and repeated that it was not necessary to prove that a gun was available but only that Whiteside reasonably believed that he was in danger. On Whiteside's insisting that he would testify that he saw "something metallic" Robinson told him, according to Robinson's testimony:

"[W]e could not allow him to [testify falsely] because that would be perjury, and as officers of the court we would be suborning perjury if we allowed him to do it; . . . I advised him that if he did do that it would be my duty to advise the Court of what he was doing and that I felt he was committing perjury; also, that I probably would be allowed to attempt to impeach that particular testimony."

Robinson also indicated that he would seek to withdraw from the representation if Whiteside insisted on committing perjury.[136]

Whiteside ultimately took the stand but omitted the testimony his lawyer felt would have been perjury.[137]

In short, Whiteside's lawyer threatened to inform the judge that he felt Whiteside was committing perjury, to attempt to impeach Whiteside's testimony himself, and if need be to seek to withdraw from the case, which was about to go to trial. Whiteside yielded to these threats and to his counsel's argument that the testimony he had in mind was unnecessary. All of this the Supreme Court approved:

Whether Robinson's conduct is seen as a successful attempt to dissuade his client from committing the crime of perjury, or whether seen as a "threat" to withdraw from representation and disclose the illegal scheme, Robinson's representation of Whiteside falls well within accepted standards of professional conduct and the range of reasonable professional conduct acceptable under [the Sixth Amendment] . . . .[138]

If such tactics are considered legitimate ones to use in the effort to dissuade perjury,[139] we infer that similar means can also be considered legitimate in trying to elicit the truth from the client in the first instance. We do not find this shocking. Seeking the truth from one's client is important and at times may be very difficult indeed. Nevertheless, we do not find tactics such as these desirable. They inevitably breed resentment on the client's part, and may poison the attorney-client relationship irreparably. They may also be used mistakenly. Although we are inclined to agree that Whiteside's lawyer knew his client was contemplating perjury, even in this case there is still some room for doubt. Finally, and most importantly, we do not assume that the difficulties of eliciting the truth are best resolved by coercion. Building a stronger and more trusting attorney-client relationship is surely preferable whenever it can be accomplished.

Conclusion

We have concluded with a discussion of techniques for eliciting the truth from reluctant clients. Many of these techniques are somewhat troubling to lawyers accustomed to the ethics of respect for clients and client-centeredness. We share that discomfort, and we do not list these techniques in order to recommend their frequent use. Instead, our hope is that the techniques of normal interviewing described elsewhere in our book, and the particular techniques of engaging with clients described earlier in this chapter, such as proper advice about confidentiality and proper discussion of the applicable law, will enable most lawyers and most clients to communicate effectively, and truthfully, without resort to more intrusive techniques. Nonetheless, difficult situations are among the situations lawyers face, and we should not shrink from understanding the techniques necessary to deal with them.

Questions

1. Do you agree that, in general, lawyers should seek the truth from their clients? Why or why not?

2. Though the chapter argues that there are strong reasons why lawyers should in general seek the truth from their clients, it also acknowledges that there have been nations that were so unjust that disobeying the rules of ethics within those countries' legal systems was morally justified. Do you think the United States today is such a country?

3. The chapter also takes the view that there are still serious injustices in American law and society, and that lawyers who represent clients experiencing these injustices have discretion, under the rules of ethics, to skirt the truth (though not to lie about it). Possible techniques for accomplishing this are sketched at several points in the chapter. Do you agree with this general position, and with the legitimacy of those techniques?

4. Even if you agree that in general lawyers should seek the truth from their clients, do you agree with the way Ms. Washington applied this principle? In particular, do you agree that when Mr. Reyes says that the "stuff" he was transporting was "mostly just regular stuff, I mean, nothing to worry about and not illegal, you know, or anything like that" (C13), his answer is so clearly incomplete that Ms. Washington rightly pressed for more information? Or should Ms. Reyes have accepted that answer as it stood? If you would resolve the basic ethical issues differently than the chapter does, how would your approach say Ms. Washington should have acted at this point?

5. Assuming that lawyers should in general seek the truth from their clients, how do you square that responsibility with lawyers' obligation to advise their clients about the law? In particular, do you think Ms. Washington was right not to explain the legal significance of making deliveries to the FARC until after she had questioned Mr. Reyes about exactly what he had done? If not, what should Ms. Washington have done, and why? And if you do not feel that lawyers should in general seek the truth from their clients, then how do you

feel Ms. Washington should have handled the issue of what to say about the law and when?

6.   In Chapter 5 ("Narrative Theory and Narrative Practice") we emphasize, in thinking about the lawyer's response to client narrative, how likely it is that the stories clients tell will change over time. Will questions focused on ascertaining truth tend to get in the way of questions meant to elicit clients' changing thoughts and feelings? How can lawyers fit a receptivity to clients' evolving narratives with a proper degree of attention to the truth of what happened?

---

1.   She was right on this point. Demonstrating that this is so requires a look at the complex provisions of United States immigration law. What we will find is that Reyes was in serious legal jeopardy and that a number of arguments in his favor still remained possible. Subject, certainly, to the need for further legal research, which a practitioner handling the case would clearly need to undertake we will examine Ms. Washington's decisions based on the assumption that these arguments were strong enough to deserve consideration. They seek to mitigate Reyes's conduct by demonstrating that it was minor in scope, and that it was undertaken under duress. They also seek to forestall his removal from the United States, even if he cannot obtain asylum, by demonstrating that he would face torture if he were returned to Colombia. All of these arguments, plainly, would require Ms. Washington to discuss the facts of Reyes's situation with him in more detail than she has so far.

Briefly, the two most serious possible obstacles to Reyes's remaining in the United States appear to be the "persecutor" and "material support to terrorism" bars. United States law bars from asylum anyone who has "ordered, incited, assisted, or otherwise participated in the persecution of any person on account of race, religion, nationality, membership in a particular social group, or political opinion." 8 U.S.C. § 1158(b)(2)(A)(i) (2006). Asylum is also generally barred for anyone who has engaged in terrorist activity, including "commit[ting] an act that the actor knows, or reasonably should know, affords material support . . . to a terrorist organization." *See* 8 U.S.C. §§ 1158(b)(2)(A)(v), 1182(a)(3)(B)(i)(I), 1182(a)(3)(B)(iv)(VI) (2006). *See generally* Won Kidane, *The Terrorism Exception to Asylum: Managing the Uncertainty in Status Determination*, 41 U. MICH. J.L. REF. 669 (2008). This is not the place for an extensive analysis of the activities of the FARC, the Revolutionary Armed Forces of Colombia, but it seems fair to say that both the "persecution" and "terrorism" statutes may apply to it, and it has been designated by the U.S. Department of State as a "foreign terrorist organization." *See* U.S. Department of State, Foreign Terrorist Organizations, *available at* http://www.state.gov/s/ct/rls/fs/37191.htm (last visited April 10, 2009).

If Reyes's delivery of medicines is viewed as either assistance or participation in FARC persecution, or as material support to FARC as a terrorist organization, he will be ineligible for asylum. Whether the particular actions Reyes took *will* be viewed as assistance, participation or support may depend on exactly what he did—how many times he brought supplies, and what they were. He may be able to argue that he did not himself take part in persecution, and that his delivery of medical supplies did not amount to "conduct that is 'active and ha[s] direct consequences for the victims,' " Weng v. Holder, 562 F.3d 510, 514 (2d Cir. 2009) and therefore was not "assistance" in persecution. Similarly, he might try to argue that the definition of "material support" in 8 U.S.C. § 1182(a)(3)(B)(iv)(VI) (2006), broad as it is, notably does not specifically include medical care or medical supplies, and therefore that his deliveries did not constitute material support for terrorism. If, nonetheless, he were found to have been sufficiently involved in persecution or terrorism, Reyes might still have a defense if he could show that his actions were under duress. Whether the facts as he stated them support that defense may be debated, but he may have more to reveal, and Ms. Washington would need to find out if that was so. Whether involuntary participation in prohibited acts is a bar to asylum is currently unsettled, by virtue of the Supreme Court's decision in Negusie v. Holder, 129 S. Ct. 1159 (2009).

If neither the persecutor nor the terrorist bar applies to Reyes, he might still be ineligible for asylum based on another prohibition, which bars asylum if "there are serious reasons for believing that the alien has committed a serious nonpolitical crime outside the United States" prior to entering the United States. 8 U.S.C. § 1158(b)(2)(A)(iii) (2006). Perhaps it could be argued, however, that if his deliveries of medical supplies did not constitute prohibited involvement in either persecution or terrorism, then they also did not constitute a serious crime of some other sort.

If Reyes is found ineligible for asylum on one of these grounds, he would not necessarily be required to leave the United States. To be sure, either involvement in persecution or commission of a serious nonpolitical crime would also preclude "withholding of removal," another form of immigration relief available to people who are victims of persecution in their home countries. *See* 8 U.S.C. §§ 1231(b)(3)(B)(i) & (iii) (2006). If, however, he were found to have provided material support to FARC, but not to have been involved in persecution, and if he could demonstrate that he provided that material support under duress, he would be eligible for special discretionary relief, dependent on the totality of circumstances, enabling him to remain in this country. *See* Melanie Nezer, *Inadmissibility for "Material Support" to Terrorism*, 2008 Emerging Issues 1438 (LexisNexis Expert Commentaries), at 4. Finally, an alien who is "more likely than not" to be tortured if returned to the country to which he or she has been ordered removed is eligible for "temporary deferral of removal" under 8 C.F.R. § 1208.17(a) (2008), pursuant to the Convention Against Torture and Cruel, Inhuman or Degrading Treatment or Punishment, Dec. 10, 1984, art. 3, S. Treaty Doc. No. 100–20, p. 20, 1465 U.N.T.S. 85, 114, to which the United States is a party. *See Negusie*, 129 S. Ct. at 1162.

2. The asylum application form, Form I–589 (as revised December 14, 2006), asks the applicant whether "you ... ever ordered, incited, assisted or otherwise participated in causing harm or suffering to any person because of his or her race, religion, nationality, membership in a particular social group or belief in a particular political opinion." (Part C, Question 3) It also asks whether "you ... [have] ever ... belonged to or been associated with any organizations or groups in your home country, such as, but not limited to ... military or paramilitary group ... [or] guerrilla organization" and then calls for a description of this involvement. (Part B, Question 3.A.) This form must be submitted under oath. (Part D) If a lawyer prepares the form, the lawyer must also "declare ... that the responses are based on all information of which I have knowledge, or which was provided to me by the applicant." (Part E) The lawyer is further required to declare her awareness that "knowing placement of false information" in the form may subject her to civil and criminal penalties.

Even if Mr. Reyes and Ms. Washington conclude that these questions can be answered "no"— on the ground that the assistance he provided to FARC did not constitute assistance in persecution or association with a paramilitary or guerrilla organization—the asylum interview may still examine the events Mr. Reyes has described. Still another question in Form I–589 asks the applicant for information about his "employment during the past five years," and it seems conceivable that an asylum officer would make the same inquiry into the nature of Mr. Reyes's work while he was in hiding that Ms. Washington did. Moreover, asylum officers have been instructed that "if the applicant lived in an area known for terrorist activity or civil unrest, it is generally appropriate to inquire into the applicant's level of contact with terrorists or terrorist organizations," to determine whether the "material support" bar applies. Jonathan Scharfen (Deputy Director, U.S. Citizenship and Immigration Services), *Processing the Discretionary Exemption to the Inadmissibility Ground for Providing Material Support to Certain Terrorist Organizations*, at 6 (May 24, 2007), *available at* www.uscis.gov/files/pressrelease/MaterialSupport_ 24May07.pdf (last visited June 25, 2009). These instructions go on to say that "the adjudicator must ask sufficient follow-up questions regarding the interaction with the possible terrorist organization to determine the nature of support the applicant rendered." *Id.* In addition, applicants hoping to receive discretionary relief based on duress, *see* Nezer, *supra* note 1, at 4 likely must satisfy the examining officer, as a threshold matter, that they have "fully disclosed, in all relevant applications and interviews with U.S. Government representatives and agents, the nature and circumstances of each provision of material support." U.S. Citizenship and Immigration Services, *Material Support Exemption Worksheet*, Part II ("Threshold Eligibility") (Rev. Date 5/11/2007), *available at* http://www.rcusa.org/index.php?page=refugee-waivers (last visited June 25, 2009). Then, if the matter went as far as a trial before an immigration judge, again these matters could be explored in testimony and cross-examination. Both at the asylum interview and in immigration court, finally, the lawyer would probably be bound by the rules governing candor to tribunals, discussed below at notes 43–47 and accompanying text. *See Ethical Issues for Immigration Lawyers*, in ETHICS IN A BRAVE NEW WORLD at 4, 10 (John L. Pinnix editor-in-chief, 2004–05 ed.) (updated by Hamel Vyas).

3. MONROE H. FREEDMAN & ABBE SMITH, UNDERSTANDING LAWYERS' ETHICS 169 (3rd ed. 2004). On Roy Cohn, a notorious and tormented figure, see Tom Wolfe, *Dangerous Obsessions* (Book Review), The New York Times, April 3, 1998, *available at* http://www.nytimes.com/1988/04/03/books/dangerous-obsessions.html?sec=&pagewanted=print (last visited June 25, 2009).

4. FREEDMAN & SMITH, *supra* note 3, at 169. While Freedman and Smith reject the Roy Cohn solution, they also generally reject the view that lawyers who do know uncomfortable truths about their clients are thereby limited in the steps they can take on their clients' behalf, *see id.* at 169–70. They might well disagree with many of the conclusions this chapter reaches.

5. *Id.* at 169 (quoting David Berreby, *On Trial: The Cohn/Dershowitz Debate*, Nat'l L.J., June 7, 1982, at 15).

6. FREEDMAN & SMITH, *supra* note 3, at 169.

7. For an overview of various standards that have been applied to this question, see DEBORAH L. RHODE & DAVID LUBAN, LEGAL ETHICS 329–31 (5th ed. 2009). The Restatement suggests a "firm factual basis" standard. RESTATEMENT OF THE LAW GOVERNING LAWYERS § 120 cmt. c (2000) [hereinafter RESTATEMENT].

8. KENNETH MANN, DEFENDING WHITE-COLLAR CRIME: A PORTRAIT OF ATTORNEYS AT WORK 38 (1985).

9. SCOTT TUROW, PRESUMED INNOCENT 156–57 (Warner Books 1987).

10. See *infra* note 114 and accompanying text.

11. See note 1, *supra*.

12. *Cf.* Robert F. Cochran, Jr., *Crime, Confession, and the Counselor-at-Law: Lessons from Dostoyevsky*, 35 HOUSTON L. REV. 327, 331 (1998) (arguing that "[l]awyers who prohibit client confession . . . ignore the possibility that the client might seek goals other than freedom, such as forgiveness, reconciliation, and a clear conscience; they ignore the possibility that the client might want to confess").

13. In Chapter 8 ("Talking to Clients About the Law") we will encounter a somewhat similar problem, in which the lawyer must decide whether to counsel her inmate client about child support law in a way that seeks to engage the client in a recognition of the just aspects of that law despite its currently arbitrary impact on him.

14. MODEL CODE OF PROF'L RESPONSIBILITY EC 7–1 (1983) [hereinafter MODEL CODE].

15. ABA Comm. on Ethics and Prof'l Responsibility, Formal Op. 87–353 n.9 (1987).

16. RESTATEMENT, *supra* note 7, § 52(1).

17. *Id.* cmt. c.

18. *Id.* § 120 cmt. c. In a similar vein, the Restatement posits that lawyers are generally not liable to non-clients for negligent misrepresentation, which might result from a factual inquiry not aimed at the truth. *Id.* § 56 cmt. f. Lawyers are also not liable for malicious prosecution if they act with "probable cause," *id.* § 57(2), and a comment declares: "Whether probable cause existed is determined on the basis of the facts known to the lawyer at the time." *Id.* cmt. d. The Reporter's Note refers to "the rule that probable cause is appraised on the basis of the information available to the lawyer, without any requirement of investigation," though citing one contrary decision, *Nelson v. Miller*, 607 P.2d 438, 448–49 (Kan. 1980).

19. RESTATEMENT, *supra* note 7, § 94 cmt. g.

20. For example, as the Restatement observes, procedural rules like Rule 11 of the Federal Rules of Civil Procedure typically require lawyers to undertake "an inquiry about facts and law that is reasonable in the circumstances." *Id.* § 110 cmt. c. Among these other sources of law may be provisions of the substantive criminal and civil law under which a lawyer might herself be found liable by reason of participation in a client scheme. On this issue, see GEOFFREY C. HAZARD, JR. & W. WILLIAM HODES, 1 THE LAW OF LAWYERING §§ 5.12 & 5.13 (3d ed. Supp. 2003).

21. *See, e.g.,* United States v. Cavin, 39 F.3d 1299, 1310 (5th Cir. 1994) (approving "deliberate ignorance" instruction "where the evidence shows (1) subjective awareness of a high probability of the existence of illegal conduct, and (2) purposeful contrivance to avoid learning of the illegal conduct"); Wyle v. R.J. Reynolds Indus., Inc., 709 F.2d 585, 590 (9th Cir. 1983) (similar).

22. *See* David Luban, *Contrived Ignorance*, 87 GEO. L.J. 957, 959, 961–62 & n.15 (1999).

23. RESTATEMENT, *supra* note 7, § 94 Reporter's Note on cmt. g. The Model Rules make clear that "[a] lawyer's knowledge that evidence is false . . . can be inferred from the circumstances," MODEL RULES OF PROFESSIONAL CONDUCT, R. 3.3 cmt. [8] (2009) [hereinafter MODEL RULES] (citing *id.*, R. 1.0(f)). "Thus," the comment continues, "although a lawyer should resolve doubts about the veracity of testimony or other evidence in favor of the client, the lawyer cannot ignore an obvious falsehood." *Id.*

24. Nor in apartheid South Africa. On the choices made by South African anti-apartheid lawyers to stay, or not stay, within the bounds of apartheid law, see Stephen Ellmann, *"To Live Outside the Law You Must Be Honest": Bram Fischer and the Meaning of Integrity*, 17 S. AFR. J. HUM. RTS. 451 (2001).

25. For a forceful argument in favor of lawyers' undertaking case-by-case assessment of the justice of the legal system, and deciding how and (in a sense) whether to obey the law in light of such assessments, see WILLIAM H. SIMON, THE PRACTICE OF JUSTICE: A THEORY OF LAWYERS' ETHICS (1998). We describe this choice in the text as resting on weighing the conflicting claims of morality and law; Simon takes a very broad view of the law and would characterize all of the relevant concerns as legal ones, some resting on enacted rules and some on immanent legal principles.

26. David Luban's insightful article develops a somewhat similar argument. *See* Luban, *supra* note 22, at 978–79.

27. See *infra* text accompanying notes 89–90 and notes 110–11, and text following note 120.

28. On these and other issues on which further factual investigation might have produced arguments on Mr. Reyes's behalf, see note 1 *supra*.

29. *See* F_REEDMAN & S_MITH, *supra* note 3, at 159–60.

30. See *infra* Part III for a discussion of this issue.

31. For a detailed analysis of all the limits on confidentiality, keyed to the relevant provisions of the Model Code of Professional Responsibility, see Roy M. Sobelson, *Lawyers, Clients and Assurances of Confidentiality: Lawyers Talking Without Speaking, Clients Hearing Without Listening*, 1 G_EO. J. L_EGAL E_THICS 703, 717–71 (1988). We have benefited from this discussion in the following pages. Our discussion, as you will see, refers both to the M_ODEL R_ULES OF P_ROFESSIONAL C_ONDUCT, *supra* note 23, and to their predecessor, the M_ODEL C_ODE OF P_ROFESSIONAL R_ESPONSIBILITY, *supra* note 14, as well as to the R_ESTATEMENT, *supra* note 7. Almost all jurisdictions have by now adopted the Model Rules, often with amendments, to govern the practice of law. S_TEPHEN G_ILLERS & R_OY D. S_IMON, R_EGULATION OF L_AWYERS: S_TATUTES AND S_TANDARDS 3 (2008).

32. M_ODEL C_ODE, *supra* note 14, DR 4–101(A).

33. *Id.*

34. C_HARLES W. W_OLFRAM, M_ODERN L_EGAL E_THICS § 6.3.1 at 251 (1986).

35. M_ODEL C_ODE, *supra* note 14, DR 4–101(A).

36. M_ODEL R_ULES, *supra* note 23, R. 1.6. The Restatement follows the Model Rules on this score. *See* R_ESTATEMENT, *supra* note 7, § 59 Reporter's Note on cmt. c.

37. A related doctrine in the law of attorney-client privilege, the "crime-fraud exception," makes clear that statements made by the client in the course of using the lawyer's services to further a crime or fraud are not privileged. *See* W_OLFRAM, *supra* note 34, § 6.4.10 at 279–82.

38. M_ODEL C_ODE, *supra* note 14, DR 4–101(C)(3).

39. M_ODEL R_ULES, *supra* note 23, R. 1.6(b) permits the lawyer to "reveal information relating to the representation of a client to the extent the lawyer reasonably believes necessary" for several purposes. The most relevant here are:

(1) to prevent reasonably certain death or substantial bodily harm; [and]

(2) to prevent the client from committing a crime or fraud that is reasonably certain to result in substantial injury to the financial interests or property of another and in furtherance of which the client has used or is using the lawyer's services.

The Restatement authorizes disclosure in circumstances similar to these. R_ESTATEMENT, *supra* note 7, §§ 66 & 67.

40. Both provisions are phrased permissively, as are the comparable Restatement sections. The comment to Rule 1.6 explicitly states that "[a] lawyer's decision not to disclose as permitted by paragraph (b) does not violate this Rule," though it adds that "[d]isclosure may be required . . . by other Rules," notably Rule 3.3. *Id.* R. 1.6 cmt. [15]. (We discuss Rule 3.3 *infra* at notes 44–48 and accompanying text.) To similar effect, *see* R_ESTATEMENT, *supra* note 7, §§ 66(3) & 67(4). Sobelson observes that footnote 16 to DR 4–101(C)(3) seems to suggest that disclosure could sometimes be obligatory, but he also comments that "[t]he exact persuasive force of a footnote is not clear." Sobelson, *supra* note 31, at 739 n.180; *see* M_ODEL C_ODE, *supra* note 14, Preamble n.1.

41. States imposing mandatory duties of disclosure with respect to some otherwise-confidential information include Arizona, Connecticut, Florida, Illinois, Nevada, New Jersey, North Dakota, Tennessee, Texas, Virginia, Washington, and Wisconsin. *See* G_ILLERS & S_IMON, *supra* note 31, at 87–93.

42. *See* M_ODEL R_ULES, *supra* note 23, R. 1.2 cmt. [10], R. 4.1 cmt. [3]; S_TEPHEN G_ILLERS, R_EGULATION OF L_AWYERS: P_ROBLEMS OF L_AW AND E_THICS 509–11 (8th ed. 2009); ABA Comm. on Ethics and Prof'l Responsibility, Formal Op. 92–366 (1992).

43. M_ODEL C_ODE, *supra* note 14, DR 7–102(A)(4) & (5); M_ODEL R_ULES, *supra* note 23, R. 3.3(a), 4.1; *see also* R_ESTATEMENT, *supra* note 7, § 120.

44. *See* M_ODEL R_ULES, *supra* note 23, R. 3.3 cmt. [7].

45. The comment to Rule 3.3 states: "The duties stated . . . apply to all lawyers, including defense counsel in criminal cases." *Id.* R. 3.3 cmt [7]. It goes on to acknowledge, however, that "some jurisdictions . . . have required counsel to present the accused as a witness or to give a narrative statement if the accused so desires, even if counsel knows that the testimony or statement will be false," and states that "[t]he obligation of the advocate under the Rules of Professional Conduct is subordinate to such requirements." *Id. See also* RESTATEMENT, *supra* note 7, § 120 cmt. i. (also maintaining that the rules against false testimony "generally govern defense counsel in criminal cases," while recognizing that criminal defendants pose special problems).

46. The provision in question is DR 7–102(B)(1), which begins by declaring that "[a] lawyer who receives information clearly establishing that ... [h]is client has, in the course of the representation, perpetrated a fraud upon a person or tribunal shall promptly call upon his client to rectify the same, and if his client refuses or is unable to do so, he shall reveal the fraud to the affected person or tribunal," and then—by virtue of a 1974 amendment—declares that this obligation does not apply "when the information is protected as a privileged communication." MODEL CODE, *supra* note 14, DR 7–102(B)(1). ABA Ethics Opinion 341 completed the evisceration of this disclosure duty by interpreting the words "privileged communication" here to include all confidential information under DR 4–101. ABA Comm. on Ethics and Prof'l Responsibility, Formal Op. 341 (1975); GILLERS, *supra* note 42, at 379–80. Gillers notes, however, that "[a] majority of jurisdictions rejected the 1974 amendment. Even more reject it today because they have the Model Rules." *Id.* at 380.

47. MODEL RULES, *supra* note 23, R. 3.3(b). Model Rules 3.3(a) and 3.3(b) both apply to conduct in a "tribunal," and, in the context of this chapter's dialogue, it is important to note that the asylum interview at least at first blush appears to be a "tribunal," defined in *id.*, R. 1.0(m) to include an "administrative agency or other body acting in an adjudicative capacity. A[n] ... administrative agency or other body acts in an adjudicative capacity when a neutral official, after the presentation of evidence or legal argument by a party or parties, will render a binding legal judgment directly affecting a party's interests in a particular matter." *See Ethical Issues for Immigration Lawyers, supra* note 2, at 10. Should this matter reach Immigration Court, the lawyer would be forbidden from "knowingly or with reckless disregard offering false evidence," 8 C.F.R. § 1003.102(c) (as amended through June 24, 2009), a duty more demanding than that of the Model Rules, which forbid only knowingly offering false evidence. MODEL RULES, *supra*, R. 3.3(a)(3). These duties may also apply to lawyers representing clients in asylum interviews. *See* 8 C.F.R. § 292.3(a) (as amended through June 24, 2009) (authorizing "[a]n adjudicatory official ... [to] impose disciplinary sanctions against any practitioner" for violation of 8 C.F.R. § 1003.102).

48. MODEL CODE, *supra* note 14, DR 4–101(C)(4); MODEL RULES, *supra* note 23, R. 1.6(b)(5).

49. *See* MODEL RULES, *supra* note 23, R. 1.6 cmt. [10].

50. *Id.* ("The lawyer's right to respond arises when an assertion of such complicity has been made."). The Restatement provision is similar, though a comment indicates that lawyers can only breach confidentiality on this basis "to defend against charges that imminently threaten the lawyer ... with serious consequences." RESTATEMENT, *supra* note 7, § 64 cmt. c.

51. *Id.* R. 1.6(a); *see also id.* R. 1.2(a). The Model Code contains a similar provision, but only in an Ethical Consideration. MODEL CODE, *supra* note 14, EC 4–2 (disclosure permitted "when necessary to perform [the lawyer's] professional employment"). The Restatement similarly permits disclosure of confidential information "when the lawyer reasonably believes that doing so will advance the interests of the client in the representation." RESTATEMENT, *supra* note 7, § 61.

52. Sobelson reasons that if a client attempted to restrict such disclosures so sharply that the lawyer could not competently handle the matter, the lawyer would be obliged to withdraw. Sobelson, *supra* note 31, at 726–27; *see* MODEL CODE, *supra* note 14, DR 2–110(B)(2) (requiring withdrawal if "continued employment will result in violation of Disciplinary Rule") & DR 6–101 (regarding "Failing to Act Competently"); MODEL RULES, *supra* note 23, R. 1.16(a)(1) (providing for mandatory withdrawal if "the representation will result in violation of the rules of professional conduct"), R. 1.2(c) ("A lawyer may limit the scope of the representation if the limitation is reasonable under the circumstances"), & R. 1.1 ("A lawyer shall provide competent representation to a client."). The Restatement, however, appears to take the view that a client's decision not to permit disclosures that the lawyer believes to be in the client's interest "is the client's definition of the client's interests ... which controls." RESTATEMENT, *supra* note 7, § 60 cmt. c(ii). In that case, withdrawal would not be mandatory, though it might still be permissible, under *id.* § 32(3)(f) (client insistence "on taking action that the lawyer considers ... imprudent").

53. MODEL CODE, *supra* note 14, DR 4–101(C)(1) (permitting disclosure "with the consent of the client or clients affected, but only after a full disclosure to them"); MODEL RULES, *supra* note 23, R. 1.6(a) (permitting disclosure if the client gives "informed consent," which under *id.*, R. 1.0(e) must be premised on the lawyer's having "communicated adequate information and an explanation about the material risks of and reasonably available alternatives to the proposed course of conduct"); *see also* RESTATEMENT, *supra* note 7, § 62.

54. The grounds on which lawyers can seek to withdraw from a case—and so the circumstances in which lawyers presumably can threaten their clients with this consequence—are quite numerous. *See* MODEL CODE, *supra* note 14, DR 2–110; MODEL RULES, *supra* note 23, R. 1.16; RESTATEMENT, *supra* note 7, § 32. On the lawyer's prerogative, if not responsibility, to discuss potential withdrawal with the client before carrying it out, see the discussion in Chapter 6 ("Engaging in Moral Dialogue") at notes 61–64.

55.   Some important information provided by clients to their lawyers—for example, the client's identity—is normally not treated as confidential at all. Sobelson, *supra* note 31, at 716. Even otherwise confidential information may also be revealed in circumstances besides those cited in the text, for example, when required by some law outside the ethics rules. MODEL CODE, *supra* note 14, DR 4–101(C)(2) (authorizing disclosure when "required by law"); MODEL RULES, *supra* note 23, R. 1.6(b)(6); *id.* R. 1.6 cmt. [12] ("Whether [other law] supersedes Rule 1.6 is a question of law beyond the scope of these Rules."); RESTATEMENT, *supra* note 7, § 63.

56.   For a recent list of possible "subjects of permissible breach of confidentiality," see Paul Rothstein, *"Anything You Say May Be Used Against You": A Proposed Seminar on the Lawyer's Duty to Warn of Confidentiality's Limits in Today's Post–Enron World*, 76 FORDHAM L. REV. 1745, 1754–61 (2007).

57.   *See, e.g., In re* Lindsey (Grand Jury Testimony), 158 F.3d 1263 (D.C. Cir., 1998), *cert. denied sub nom.* Office of the President v. Office of Indep. Counsel, 525 U.S. 996 (1998). For another example of the Independent Counsel's challenges to attorney-client privilege, this one unsuccessful, see Swidler & Berlin v. United States, 524 U.S. 399 (1998) (declining to allow attorney-client privilege to end with the death of the client).

58.   In some cases, moreover, what the client says about his past conduct may reveal that he is engaged in continuing criminality, in which case even information about past conduct may be subject to disclosure via the "future crime" exception. *See* Sobelson, *supra* note 31, at 749–52.

59.   MODEL CODE, *supra* note 14, EC 7–8 ("A lawyer should advise his client of the possible effect of each legal alternative."); MODEL RULES, *supra* note 23, R. 1.4(b) (requiring a lawyer to "explain a matter to the extent reasonably necessary to permit the client to make informed decisions regarding the representation"); RESTATEMENT, *supra* note 7, § 20(3) (incorporating the language of Model Rule 1.4(b)).

60.   Where the lawyer knows or should know that the client wants her to keep information confidential that she is legally obliged to reveal, under the Model Rules she is also obliged to explain this to the client. *See id.* R. 1.4(a)(5); R. 1.2 cmt. [13]; R. 1.6 cmt. [12]. A similar obligation could be inferred from the Restatement's general consultation duty, RESTATEMENT, § 20, and interestingly is explicitly imposed, if feasible, when the lawyer contemplates disclosure of confidential information to prevent harm to others. *Id.*, §§ 66(2) & 67(3).

61.   We explore many of the barriers to lawyer-client connection in Chapter 2 ("Connection Across Difference and Similarity").

62.   In our dialogue, one point on which lawyer and client do *not* differ is language. In reality, in immigration cases and elsewhere, language barriers may vastly complicate communication. *See generally* Muneer I. Ahmad, *Interpreting Communities: Lawyering Across Language Difference*, 54 UCLA L. REV. 999 (2007).

63.   MODEL RULES, *supra* note 23, R. 1.4(b). Additional duties of communication with clients are spelled out in *id.*, R. 1.4(a), but they do not change the point being made in the text.

64.   On the limits on the cognitive capacities of everyone—lawyers as well as clients—see Chapter 9 ("Fast Talking: Lawyering Expertise and Its Impact on Interviewing and Counseling").

65.   Fred C. Zacharias, *Rethinking Confidentiality*, 74 IOWA L. REV. 351, 353 (1989).

66.   *Id.* at 365.

67.   *See id.* at 386 (reporting on Zacharias's survey finding that only 15.1% of laypeople surveyed would withhold information "if the lawyer 'promised confidentiality except for specific types of information which he/she described in advance' "). *But cf. id.* at 395 (reporting survey evidence that confidentiality exceptions might deter 10–25% of clients from confiding in lawyers). To be sure, Zacharias' survey sample was not representative of the country as a whole, as he notes, *id.* at 379–80; *see* Lee A. Pizzimenti, *The Lawyer's Duty to Warn Clients About Limits on Confidentiality*, 39 CATH. U. L. REV. 441, 442 n.6 (1990).

68.   *See id.* at 394.

69.   *See* Robert A. Burt, *Conflict and Trust Between Attorney and Client*, 69 GEO. L.J. 1015, 1032–33 (1981).

70.   We do, however, see candid discussion of limits on confidentiality as valuable when those limits are really at issue in a particular case. *See infra* notes 90–95 and accompanying text.

71.   Sobelson, *supra* note 31, at 772.

72.   *Id.*

73.   *Id.* at 772–73.

74. *Id.* at 773.

75. *Id.* at 774.

76. We thank Tanina Rostain for pointing this out.

77. Anthony G. Amsterdam (Reporter), 1 Trial Manual for the Defense of Criminal Cases § 80 (4th ed. 1984) (Copyright 1984 the American Law Institute. Used with permission from American Law Institute–American Bar Association Commission on Continuing Professional Education).

78. Monroe Freedman and Abbe Smith see few instances where confidentiality should be breached, but because of the strong justification for those exceptions (for example, to save a life) and the great unlikelihood that they will actually have to be invoked, they would not inform clients of their existence. Freedman & Smith, *supra* note 3, at 171–72.

79. See *supra* note 7 and accompanying text.

80. To the extent that states have chosen to make some of the discretionary grounds for disclosure mandatory, *see* note 41 *supra*, of course, lawyers no longer have the discretion to choose nondisclosure.

81. For a provocative argument that the ethical considerations that should shape criminal defense are not so different from those applicable to other legal matters, see Simon, *supra* note 25, at 170–94.

82. Different kinds of advice may also be appropriate in different types of lawyer-client relationships. For example, experienced clients certainly may not need as much review of fundamentals as new entrants into the legal realm. Moreover, some matters on which lawyers are retained are so routine that no advice on confidentiality may be needed at all, or the chance of any qualifications on confidentiality ever becoming relevant may be so remote that all mention of these qualifications can be omitted. We do not, however, believe these exceptions are the rule.

83. *Cf.* The Federalist Papers # 51 (1788) (Alexander Hamilton or James Madison) ("If men were angels, no government would be necessary. If angels were to govern men, neither external nor internal controls on government would be necessary."), *available at* http://thomas.loc.gov/ home/histdox/fed_51.html (last visited June 26, 2009).

84. See *supra* text at page 233.

85. Zacharias, *supra* note 65, at 383.

86. See *supra* text accompanying note 77.

87. See *supra* notes 71–75 and accompanying text. In a thoughtful article, Lee A. Pizzimenti recognizes the danger of confusing clients by saying too much, but does call for more extensive initial discussion of the limits on confidentiality than we recommend. Pizzimenti, *supra* note 67, at 485–89.

88. See *supra* notes 3–7 and accompanying text.

89. See *supra* notes 25–28 and accompanying text.

90. Freedman & Smith, *supra* note 3, at 159–63.

91. Rusty Sabich, Scott Turow's prosecutor/murder defendant, eloquently voices this assumption. Turow, *supra* note 9, at 156.

92. We recognize that there may also be rare cases in which covert betrayal is in fact absolutely necessary and just—for example, where the lawyer discloses her client's intention to commit a murder and must do so in secret to avoid being murdered herself.

93. Model Code, *supra* note 14, EC 7–6. A Model Rules comment may go further, observing that "a lawyer should resolve doubts"—not "reasonable doubts"—"about the veracity of testimony or other evidence in favor of the client," though she "cannot ignore an obvious falsehood." Model Rules, *supra* note 23, R. 3.3 cmt. [8]. The Restatement, more faintly, comments that "[w]hen a lawyer's state of knowledge is relevant, in the absence of circumstances indicating otherwise, a lawyer may assume that a client will use the lawyer's counsel for proper purposes." Restatement, *supra* note 7, § 94 cmt. g. While we affirm the general proposition that lawyers should resolve doubts in their client's favor, we do not try here to measure exactly how strong their tilt in their clients' favor should be; it is enough to say, as we did earlier, that we favor a high standard, perhaps on the order of "reasonable doubt." See *supra* note 7 and accompanying text.

94. We discuss the proper contours of moral counseling in Chapter 7 ("Engaging in Moral Dialogue").

95. Model Rules, *supra* note 23, R. 1.4(a)(5). For related provisions, see *supra* note 60.

96. Robert Traver, Anatomy of a Murder (25th Anniversary ed. 1983).

97. *Id.* at 32.

98. *Id.* at 35.

99. *Id.* at 46.

100. *Id.* at 48–49.

101. See note 59 *supra*.

102. Both the Model Code and the Model Rules forbid lawyers from counseling or assisting their clients to commit at least some unlawful conduct. MODEL CODE, *supra* note 14, DR 7–102(A)(7) (prohibiting the lawyer from assisting "conduct that the lawyer knows to be illegal or fraudulent"); MODEL RULES, *supra* note 23, R. 1.2(d) (forbidding the lawyer from assisting in "conduct that the lawyer knows is criminal or fraudulent"). As Stephen Pepper emphasizes, however, the Model Rule, but not its Code counterpart, also declares that "a lawyer may discuss the legal consequences of any proposed course of conduct with a client." Stephen L. Pepper, *Counseling at the Limits of the Law: An Exercise in the Jurisprudence and Ethics of Lawyering*, 104 YALE L.J. 1545, 1587 (1995) (quoting Model Rule 1.2(d)). *Cf.* MODEL RULES, *supra*, R. 1.2 cmt. [9] (explaining that Rule 1.2(d) "does not preclude the lawyer from giving an honest opinion about the *actual* consequences that appear *likely* to result from a client's conduct" (emphasis added)).

Professor Pepper has argued that Rule 1.2(d) authorizes a lawyer to discuss the legal consequences of any course of action, including the practical likelihood or unlikelihood of sanctions, regardless of whether the result is in effect to encourage the client to violate the law. *Id.* at 1588–91. This reading of the Model Rule might be disputed, and Pepper notes that some commentators have taken different views, *see id.* at 1589 n.89; for its part, the Restatement, promulgated after Pepper's article was written, accepts that "[a]dvice about enforcement policy" is appropriate in some situations, but not "when the circumstances indicate that the lawyer thereby intended to counsel or assist the client's crime, fraud, or violation of a court order." RESTATEMENT, *supra* note 7, § 94 cmt. f. In any event, Pepper does not believe that lawyers *should* give any and all conceivable advice about law to their clients, regardless of the impact on the legal order. *See generally* Pepper, *supra*, at 1598–1610 (advocating a "rebuttable presumption that it is generally appropriate for the lawyer to educate the client concerning the law" and urging lawyers to consider the legal issues involved while also engaging the client in a discussion aimed at "assist[ing] the client as a person first and as a legal problem second").

103. See *supra* text accompanying notes 82–95.

104. This is, of course, a fundamental element in interviewing. See Chapter 2 ("Connection Across Difference and Similarity"), where we outline the basic frameworks of interviewing and counseling.

105. The lawyer portrayed by Denzel Washington asks a question like this, after accepting a rather weak personal injury claim, in the movie *Philadelphia* (Columbia Tristar 1993).

106. We discuss the ways that lawyers can attend to such changes in client narrative in Chapter 5 ("Narrative Theory and Narrative Practices").

107. *See* FREEDMAN & SMITH, *supra* note 3, at 160 (offering the example of a client who denied she had committed a killing, because she did not realize that the truthful account she later revealed would demonstrate that the killing was in self-defense).

108. TRAVER, *supra* note 96, at 37.

109. *Id.*

110. For a discussion of techniques for eliciting the truth, see Part F of this Chapter.

111. Other scholars have also disapproved of Biegler's guidance of his client in *Anatomy of a Murder*, but have nevertheless endorsed considerable guidance to clients about the law despite the recognition that this guidance might lead to clients' invention of facts. *See* HAZARD & HODES, *supra* note 20, at § 5.13. FREEDMAN & SMITH, *supra* note 3, at 211–14, suggest that Biegler's belief that he was inducing the client to tell a false story makes this case a unique one; in general, they believe "the lawyer can properly give the client relevant legal advice and ask leading questions that might help to draw out useful information that the client, consciously or unconsciously, might be withholding." *Id.* at 216.

112. While Ms. Washington may have made Mr. Reyes's situation look grimmer than it was, she might also be criticized for describing the law more benignly than she should have. If she felt, for example, that U.S. law on bars to asylum was deeply unfair—a sentiment she does express, in the main interview, at L31—she might have said so here. That in turn might have affected her client's assessment of the moral rights and wrongs involved in telling his story candidly.

113. The lawyer's resolution of the issue of how and when to give advice about the law may also shape her approach to a variety of other steps lawyers take to insure that their clients' testimony is as informed as possible. The Restatement considers the following forms of witness preparation appropriate, and we feel that all of these have a role with those witnesses who are clients as well:

[D]iscussing the role of the witness and effective courtroom demeanor; discussing the witness's recollection and probable testimony; revealing to the witness other testimony or evidence that will be presented and asking the witness to reconsider the witness's recollection or recounting of events in that light; discussing the applicability of law to the events in issue; reviewing the factual context into which the witness's observations or opinions will fit; reviewing documents or other physical evidence that may be introduced; and discussing probable lines of hostile cross-examination that the witness should be prepared to meet.

RESTATEMENT, *supra* note 7, § 116 cmt. b. The list may be uncontroversial, but lawyers will have important judgments to make about whether to use these techniques in ways that emphasize helping the client to articulate the truth or in ways that emphasize informing the client fully about the legal and evidentiary situation he is in. For an example of how to employ such tools with an emphasis on not distorting the truth—in this instance, by presenting another witness's account through "successive questions that reveal one bit at a time, taking care not to reveal any more than is needed to refresh [the witness's] memory"—see Richard C. Wydick, *The Ethics of Witness Coaching*, 17 CARDOZO L. REV. 1, 40–41 (1995).

It deserves emphasis, however, that preparing a client to testify is not the same as interviewing him (though there is certainly some overlap between the two tasks). Some steps that the Restatement also approves, such as "rehearsal of testimony" and "suggest[ing] choice of words that might be employed to make the witness's meaning clear," RESTATEMENT, *supra*, § 116 cmt. b, would ordinarily be quite out of place and inappropriate in an initial interview, when the client has not yet told his story—whether or not the lawyer feels she should offer legal guidance to the client in the process.

114. We would not, however, consider it "random probing" for her to ask her client, at some concluding point in the interview, whether there are any other problems in his case of which he is aware. Nor, of course, is it random probing to ask a question—for example, "Have you ever been engaged in drug trafficking?"—if the client will probably or definitely have to answer that same question from the other side. But the reason for asking the question in such a context is that someone else is going to ask it anyway, not that some aspect of the client's story independently would have called for further inquiry by his own lawyer. The time and manner of asking questions of this sort might also be different from the approach the lawyer takes to the core task of understanding what has happened to her client.

115. HAZARD & HODES, *supra* note 20, at § 1.23, at 1–45.

116. See *supra* note 93 and accompanying text.

117. See text and notes accompanying notes 20–23 *supra*; and, to similar effect, HAZARD & HODES, *supra* note 20, § 1.23 at 1–45 to 1–46.

118. W. William Hodes, *The Professional Duty to Horseshed Witnesses—Zealously, Within the Bounds of the Law*, 30 TEX. TECH L. REV. 1343, 1355 (1999).

119. We do not examine here whether a defense of ignorance would ultimately be persuasive in asylum proceedings.

120. Her question is not ferociously leading. She might have said, for example, "Now this is a very important point. You really don't know what you were carrying, do you, since you were never told?" But what the lawyer does ask is still a leading question, on a point that is far from clear when she asks about it. As such, her question does not fit well in an interview aimed at truth.

Even without resorting to leading questions, lawyers can influence their clients' answers by shading the questions they ask. Professor Wydick reports social scientific findings demonstrating that even slight variations in the phrasing of questions can influence the answers. Wydick, *supra* note 113, at 43. While we do not believe lawyers should ordinarily shape their questions so as to press the client in particular directions, we do not endorse "neutral" phrasing as completely as Wydick may. *See id.* Suppose, for example, that a client says, "I was in a terrible crash. This guy's car slammed into me." A thoroughly neutral, disengaged follow-up question might be, "Can you estimate the speed of the other car at the time of the accident?" But that question might imply that the lawyer does not accept the client's statement that he was in a "crash." The lawyer who wants her client to feel heard and believed needs to respond in the key in which the client has spoken: for example, "How fast was the car going when it crashed into you?" She may need to go on and ask a series of follow-up questions to appraise the client's basis for giving whatever estimate he gave, but her route to the truth should also be a route to a productive relationship with her client.

The lawyer's question at L21 is also leading, but again ineffectively so. Here her suggestion that "there's nothing wrong with delivering medical supplies" probably seems to the client just to miss the whole point, which he then explains (C21).

121. Her threat not to take the case if the client did not tell her the truth is certainly one she could have carried out, at least unless she were the "last lawyer in town." Lawyers have broad discretion to take or decline cases. *See* MODEL CODE, *supra* note 14, EC 2–26; MODEL RULES, *supra* note 23, R. 6.2 cmts. [1]–[2]; RESTATEMENT, *supra* note 7, § 14 cmt. b.

122. On the range of possibilities, see note 1 *supra*.

123. It is possible that in the end the information Ms. Washington uncovers will turn out to be fatal to his case. But most of the damaging information lawyers learn is probably not fatal, only damaging, and lawyers need to know it in order to mitigate the damage.

124. For a thoughtful articulation of ways that lawyers can formulate the hypotheses that will guide their questioning, see DAVID A. BINDER, PAUL BERGMAN, SUSAN C. PRICE, & PAUL R. TREMBLAY, LAWYERS AS COUNSELORS: A CLIENT-CENTERED APPROACH 153–66 (2d ed. 2004).

125. This example was suggested to one of us by an INS asylum supervisor.

126. We discuss the importance of empathy and other resources for building connection with clients in Chapter 2 ("Connection Across Difference and Similarity"). *See also* BINDER ET AL., *supra* note 124, at 27–28; THOMAS L. SHAFFER & JAMES R. ELKINS, LEGAL INTERVIEWING AND COUNSELING IN A NUTSHELL 65–72 (3d ed. 1997).

127. AMSTERDAM, *supra* note 77, §§ 77, 79, 88.

128. Stephen Ellmann, *Empathy and Approval*, 43 HASTINGS L.J. 991 (1992).

129. *See generally* Mary Marsh Zulack, *Rediscovering Client Decisionmaking: The Impact of Role-Playing*, 1 CLINICAL L. REV. 593, 598–99 (1995).

130. See *supra* text accompanying note 9. A related technique is for the lawyer to identify the problems in the client's story, but to do so in the role of the adversary—thereby somewhat increasing the chance that the client will not resent his own lawyer who is actually speaking, but the adversary whose words the lawyer imagines and delivers. Still another variation, one that might insulate the lawyer herself from the resentment that even a simulation could engender, is to have the adversary played by one of the lawyer's colleagues.

131. *See* Zulack, *supra* note 129, at 631 n.42.

132. For useful guidance on the techniques of cross-examination, see, e.g., MARILYN J. BERGER ET AL., TRIAL ADVOCACY: PLANNING, ANALYSIS AND STRATEGY 395–438 (2d ed. 2008).

133. AMSTERDAM, *supra* note 77, § 81.

134. As we will see later in this book, however, a lawyer contemplating withdrawal from a case because of moral disagreement with her client may also be justified in threatening that withdrawal and thus, to that extent, coercing her client. *See* Chapter 7 ("Engaging in Moral Dialogue").

135. 475 U.S. 157 (1986).

136. *Id.* at 160–61 (citation omitted; bracketed material and ellipsis on page 266 added).

137. *Id.* at 161–62.

138. *Id.* at 171.

139. A Model Rules comment on the lawyer's duty to disclose false testimony implicitly reinforces this point, observing that "unless it is clearly understood that the lawyer will act upon the duty to disclose the existence of false evidence, the client can simply reject the lawyer's advice to reveal the false evidence and insist that the lawyer keep silent. Thus the client could in effect coerce the lawyer into being a party to fraud on the court." MODEL RULES, *supra* note 23, R. 3.3 cmt. [11].

CHAPTER 7

ENGAGING IN MORAL DIALOGUE

■ ■ ■

We take for granted in this book that clients should make the key decisions in their cases. As we have emphasized repeatedly, however, that principle of client-centeredness does not mean that lawyers' role is simply to receive the client's decision and translate it into action. On the contrary, we see client-centered lawyers as *engaged* with their clients, offering the clients information, perspective, questions, even disagreements all meant to assist each client in reaching the best judgment he can.[1]

We have also considered, in some respects, the question of whether an engaged client-centered lawyer can rightly seek to *persuade* her client to make a choice against the client's stated inclinations. This is a question that can arise in many contexts. The most common may be situations where the lawyer believes the client's choice is unwise—and the classic example might be a criminal defendant's reluctance to accept a plea agreement based on a vain hope of winning acquittal at trial. Here the rationale for whatever intervention the lawyer undertakes is one that is at the heart of the lawyer's role—the protection of the client's own interests. No one doubts that lawyers should perform this role, within the limits of the law, though a lawyer who takes this rationale too far in her interactions with her clients may well slide from client-centered assistance to paternalistic interference. Where the lawyer seeking to protect the client's own best interests crosses the line between assistance and interference is an issue we encountered first in Chapter Two, and then examined further in Chapter Three.

In this chapter we examine the possibility of intervention for another reason—not the client's self-interest, at least not that self-interest exclusively, but the interests of others, or in other words the obligations of morality. The intervention we focus on here is more than discussion; engaged client-centeredness envisions *discussion* between lawyer and client on every matter relevant to the representation, and moral questions can certainly be relevant to a client's choice. Discussion is a powerful thing, and as we will note more than once in this chapter, the impact of such discussion may be profound. But our focus here is on the possibility that in some circumstances more than discussion is appropriate and justified. We focus here on situations where a lawyer might not only explore moral issues with a client, but also present—and not just present, but advocate—her own moral perspectives on the choices the client must make. In these cases, lawyers are relying on, or attempting to assert, a connection with their clients that is particularly intimate, or perhaps particularly intrusive. Whether to do so is a question, as we shall see, both of ethics and of skill; indeed, skill in this area is itself a matter of ethics. We begin, as we have in many chapters of this book, with an imagined dialogue, and in light of this dialogue focus first on whether and when moral advice is permissible and second on how it should be given when the lawyer does decide to give it.

A. A MORAL DIALOGUE

You have already encountered Richard Mathiesson and his client Bill Arnholtz in Chapter 2, but here we will imagine their interaction proceeding somewhat differently than it did there. Richard Mathiesson is a 50–year-old divorce lawyer, with 25 years of experience in the field. For several months he has been representing Bill Arnholtz, a 35–year-old engineer whose wife has left him for another man. They have quite a bit in common (both are white, Protestant and fairly well off) and as it happens, they have gotten along well, among other reasons because both are avid golfers and members of the same country club. It has been clear to Mathiesson for some time that the marriage is irretrievably over, and Arnholtz's wife has now filed for divorce. Her lawyer, another experienced practitioner in the midsize city in which they live, has contacted Mathiesson to begin negotiating the terms of the divorce, since both parties have told their respective lawyers (and each other) that they want to handle this process as amicably as possible. Although Arnholtz and Mathiesson have talked about what Arnholtz would like to see in a settlement, those conversations were more exploratory than concrete, and Mathiesson has now asked Arnholtz to come in so that they can talk these matters over in detail. Arnholtz arrives precisely on time, and Mathiesson comes out to the office reception area to meet him and bring him back to Mathiesson's office, where they'll have their meeting:

L1:   Bill, it's good to see you again. How have you been doing?

C1:   Oh, man, I've been terrible. I can't get to the golf course at all with this rain we've been having!

L2:   [As they enter Mathiesson's office] I know. It's a disaster. But otherwise are you okay?

C2:   Oh, I've been all right, I guess.

L3:   It's tough, huh?

C3:   It's really tough. I still can't believe she left me for that jerk, you know.

L4:   I understand.

C4:   And I'm like, lying awake at nights, re-running all the things we said to each other, and wondering how I could have missed the clues.

L5:   Bill, I think it's going to be hard for you to get anywhere with thoughts like those, you know . . .

C5:   Yeah, yeah, I know. I really know. My therapist says the same thing. But I can't help it. And when I'm not thinking about that I'm dreaming of having a chance to show this guy what a wreck he's made of my life—or maybe just to punch him out.

L6:   Well, Bill, I really do understand your wanting to punch this guy out, but [smiling] as your lawyer I can't advise you to take that course of action.

C6:   You know I'm not that kind of guy anyway.

L7:   I do know it, and I respect the way you've been doing everything you can to deal with this in the best and most adult way possible. These things are never fun, but I've felt good about working with you because you haven't ever made it worse than it had to be. I've had some clients who I just couldn't say that about . . . Which actually brings me to the business we need to do today, which is to talk about what you want to get in the separation agreement. Have you had a chance to think about that?

C7:   Yes, I have. I had a long talk with a good friend of mine, who's been through this himself, and that really helped me sort out what I wanted to do.

L8:   So: we've talked about the two basic issues that every divorcing couple with kids must deal with, and hopefully will deal with in a responsible way—money and custody—and you told me your initial feelings about both. Now that you've had a chance to think some more and to talk to your friend, what are your thoughts about these today?

C8:   Basically this: I don't want her to do this to me and then make a profit from it too.

L9:   I understand that feeling, Bill, but I'm not sure I know what you mean, concretely, as far as her not making a profit is concerned.

C9:   Well, you know all that law you told me about, that the courts see marriage as a partnership and basically say that each partner is entitled to an equal share of all the results of the partnership? Well, it seems to me that in a partnership if one partner is cheating on the other and the partnership breaks up, the cheater doesn't get half of what's left after the cheating. The cheater has to pay back the other partner, right?

L10: Bill, that is right—in commercial partnerships. But our state's law is very clear that what they call "marital fault"—the fact that one spouse or the other was a bad spouse and even was the cause of the divorce—isn't relevant to the settlement of the money issues in a divorce.

C10: Well, if you mean to tell me now that there's no alternative to a straight 50–50 split, why didn't you say so in the first place?

L11: Bill, I know you're upset, but that's not like you to jump to conclusions that way. That's not at all what I'm saying. What I am saying is that *if* this divorce goes to trial—and I know you've told me, very clearly, that you don't want that, because it would only make things harder for everyone—then it would be difficult for us to avoid a 50–50 split. From what you've told me, you and your wife both worked full-time or almost full-time, and you both contributed significantly to the joint income of the family ...

C11: I contributed twice as much as she did, you know that.

L12: Yes, I do, but her one-third would still be considered significant. Plus you both brought roughly the same assets to the marriage. And you have two kids, who have to be supported in whatever parent's home they live in.

C12: My friend says that if we settle out of court we can go quite a ways away from 50–50.

L13: Yes, that's right and I was about to talk about that. If we settle, as I know you want to—so that no one has to go through the expense and pain of a trial—then probably the judge will approve the agreement we make, even if it's not 50–50. The courts assume that, at least within a certain range, the divorcing couple knows best.

C13: So that's what I want to do. I want to settle, and I want the settlement to give my wife—I'm sorry, but this is how I feel—as little money as possible.

L14: Bill, you're entitled to feel that way, and you don't need to apologize to me for it. My job is to help you accomplish what you feel you want, as far as it can be accomplished.

C14: So how far can this be accomplished?

L15: Well, that depends first of all on who's going to have custody of the kids. Whoever has custody has to have enough money to support the kids, and the courts are pretty vigilant about that. The last time we spoke I thought you felt pretty clear that the kids would need to be primarily with their mother. Did I get that right?

C15: Yes. It has to be her, really. You know I travel 3 or 4 days a week for my job, and I have no one else to take care of them.

L16: So we have to include in our offer enough money for her to take care of the kids.

C16: Not from what my friend tells me.

L17: I'm not sure I see where you're going. What exactly did your friend tell you?

C17: He said that the way to make her back off on the money is to threaten to fight about custody.

L18: You mean, to tell her that we're going to press for custody even though you don't actually want custody?

C18: Yes, exactly.

L19: [Pause]

C19: Are you going to tell me there's something wrong with that? I don't see how there can be. If I'd broken my leg, and suffered $50,000 of damages, it wouldn't be wrong for me to start negotiating from $250,000, would it? I mean, doesn't that happen every day?

L20: Yes, that happens a lot, of course.

C20: And it's not as if I'd have no chance of getting custody if I did make a fight of it. I mean, she's had her problems as a mother, like I've told you, and if I had to I could always hire a nanny or an au pair or something to take care of them when I'm away.

L21: Tell me again what her problems as a mother were, would you?

C21: She had a nervous breakdown when our little one was a year old, and from then on she was in twice-a-week therapy. And for a while she had a drinking problem. I'm not saying she was a bad mom, not at all—and I'm not saying I was all that great a dad—but I could make a fight of it, don't you think?

L22: [Quietly] You could make a fight of it.

C22: And if I did, that would be pretty likely to make her want to come down on all the money issues, wouldn't it?

L23: Some people can be scared easier than others; I don't know how easily your wife would scare.

C23: Well, let's be frank. I know it would kill her to lose custody of the kids. I think she'll scare.

L24: Bill, there are a lot of things I could say to you about this. I'm not so sure she'll scare—remember, she has a lawyer too, and I do know that lawyer, and *she* doesn't scare very easily. And I know what threats lead to, and so do you—they lead to fury as much as fear. Hell hath no fury, Bill, hell hath no fury like this. She'll try to scare you back, and you'll maybe think of some other way to scare her even worse, and before you know it the two of you might even be in trial after all—maybe you won't get this divorce done for years.

C24: No, no, no, that wouldn't happen. I would never let it go so far.

L25: I wish I could share your confidence, but I've seen these things go from bad to worse more times than I like to think about. I know one couple who spent *eleven years* litigating their divorce. It became their drug, Bill, their addiction. By the time it was all over, there was nothing left to divide up—and the husband had a terminal illness. But maybe you will still settle it. Do you think the anger will go away? How long will your wife have to think about how you scared her into taking a bad money settlement, after this is over? Your kids are how old, 5 and 7?

C25: Yeah.

L26: So she'll have, oh, 15 years to think about this every day while she's trying to manage her life, and take care of the kids, on whatever you've agreed to let her have. She won't suffer in silence, Bill. What effect do you think that will have on how you and she deal with each other, and on your kids?

C26: All right, I hadn't thought about that. Maybe I need to give this some more thought.

L27: I really hope you will.

C27: But you're really coming on strong here, and I guess I want to make sure of one thing: if I come back and say, yes, this really is what I want to do, I know the risks and all and I've decided I can handle it, you will do it for me, won't you?

L28: Why don't we not cross that bridge till we come to it, Bill? There are some complicated issues of legal ethics here, frankly, and if we have to deal with them I'll explain them to you, but frankly, Bill, I don't think you're going to come back here and tell me that this is what you want to do. I have too much respect for the way you've handled yourself up till now to think that you're going to let the upset you're feeling affect your judgment this way.

C28: I don't get it. How can you say you respect me and at the same time not promise to help me do what I decide I want to do, as long as it's legal? I mean, if this is illegal I don't want any part of it, but it isn't, is it?

L29: No, Bill, I don't think it is. But it is something that a lot of lawyers just won't do, and I'll tell you why, so you don't think I'm speaking this way because I'm against you or anything like that. I have a lot of respect for you, Bill, and I think this conversation is just a bump in the road and that we'll look back on it someday and smile. The lawyers I'm thinking of—and I consider myself one of them, Bill, and I've been proud to work on your case because I think you're this sort of person yourself—we feel that even though in most negotiations and on most issues it's fair to play a very hard game of hardball, that isn't true when kids are at stake. Even if it would save you money, and you know I'm not at all sure it would, even then it would just be wrong. The parent who has custody of your kids needs a fair money settlement to take care of them, and even more important the kids need parents who aren't at each other's throats. If you go down this road, you risk harming your kids, and that's a risk I probably wouldn't be prepared to take on your behalf. I'm not deciding this for myself right now, because you might come back and show me some aspect of all this that I haven't thought about yet or understood properly, but right now, Bill, right now, my answer would be that I'd have to resign from your case if you insist on going this route.

C29:　Wow. I didn't think lawyers said things like that to their clients.

L30:　Well, they don't, usually. But sometimes they do, when what's at stake is something like children.

C30:　I guess I've got a lot of thinking to do. But you know that when I'm done thinking, I may be looking for another lawyer.

L31:　Yes, Bill, I understand that. I think we've worked well together up till now, and I'd like to continue with you, but if you want to get another lawyer, you certainly have that right, and I wouldn't stand in your way.

B.　THE MORALITY OF MORAL DIALOGUE

Should Mathiesson have had this conversation with his client at all? Obviously he needed to meet with Arnholtz in advance of the settlement negotiations. Otherwise, despite the apparently good relationship he had already established with his client, he could not have been sure that he was truly representing his client's wishes and he might have overlooked tactical options that only his client was aware of. The dialogue begins on these uncontroversial lines, but it does not long remain on this track. Quite soon, Arnholtz begins to voice sentiments that don't fit smoothly with the "adult" model that Mathiesson claims to have seen Arnholtz adhering to. Mathiesson seems uneasy with Arnholtz's stated desire to make his wife pay for her infidelity by insisting on as ungenerous a financial settlement as possible. While he avoids directly expressing this, and instead tries to focus Arnholtz on objective constraints on the extent to which he can achieve this desire, Arnholtz soon forces his lawyer's hand by proposing to threaten to seek custody as a bargaining chip aimed at forcing his wife to accept a bad financial agreement.

The custody threat strategy is not imaginary. One scholar, Scott Altman, found that as many as 20% of divorce negotiations in California featured some use of "pressure to trade custodial time for financial terms."[2] Both husbands and wives do this, but men, it seems, resort to it more often.[3] The same article reports that almost all lawyers surveyed about this practice said that when clients told them they wanted to proceed in this way, they (the lawyers) tried to dissuade the clients from doing so.[4] The dialogue at the beginning of this chapter is an example of what such a lawyer might say.

Dialogues like this one may be quite unusual in actual legal practice. As we will see, the professional codes of legal ethics in general do not mandate, though they do encourage, interactions of this sort.[5] How often lawyers find reason to be morally troubled by their clients' choices, and whether in those situations they intervene in any way are important empirical questions.[6] In many situations, lawyers who contemplate beginning such dialogues will hesitate because of their own fear of losing clients, including clients who can tarnish the lawyers' reputation or otherwise injure their business. Ideally, lawyers will rise above their own interests in such situations when they must—but "when they must" is far from "always," and we do not question that lawyers should consider their own well-being as well as the well-being of the people their clients seek to injure when they decide whether or not to begin such dialogues. We suspect that many lawyers faced with such dangers find ways to accomplish what they see as morally required through the process of counseling about the client's own self-interest, as shaped by legal requirements and predictable practical consequences—and (as we will explain in more detail later in this chapter) we do not quarrel with approaching moral concerns obliquely, by focusing on such practical considerations, when this tack is feasible and so long as the discussion of practical considerations is itself accurate.[7]

We also fully recognize that in many cases where lawyer and client may not be of one mind, the lawyer will not feel that the moral stakes justify the kind of intervention reflected in this chapter's dialogue. In many cases it may be perfectly legitimate for such lawyers to follow their clients' implicit lead and say nothing at all about morality. In other cases, lawyers might reject complete silence but see their role, quite appropriately, as limited to assisting clients to clarify their own thinking (by asking, for example, whether the clients have considered any moral issues that their plans might suggest). Lawyers might also offer moral comments that stick to suggesting to the client conclusions that might follow from the clients' own moral beliefs as the clients have already articulated them— rather than adding the lawyers' moral views as well. Both of these approaches, like the effort to achieve moral results by helping the client to better appraise his own self-interest, are natural applications of engaged client-centered lawyering.

We focus, however, on the possibility that sometimes more is appropriate as well. We seek to examine the justifications and the methods of conducting moral dialogues of the sort illustrated above—counseling conversations in which you invoke morality, rather than solely law or the client's pragmatic self-interest, in an effort to persuade a client to make a particular decision.[8] Few "moral dialogues" are exclusively about morality, and the dialogue with which this chapter begins is no exception. Mathiesson appeals to his client's self-interest (his desire not to go to trial, with all its attendant expense and suffering (L24)) and invokes legal requirements as well, such as the courts' insistence that the custodial parent have "enough money to support the kids." (L15) But Mathiesson also unmistakably invokes morality with his client, initially between the lines but in the end quite explicitly, telling Arnholtz that even if hardball negotiations affecting the children could save him money, "even then it would just be wrong." (L29).

There are powerful arguments both for and against such dialogues. The strongest argument in their favor is the most obvious: otherwise wrong will be done. The most compelling reason not to enter such dialogues is equally clear: you may violate the client's right to choose for himself. But neither of these arguments is as self-evidently valid as it might at first appear.

Take first the need to avoid wrong being done. What Mathiesson says to Arnholtz about the likely consequences of his vengeful strategy makes sense, and, whatever the moral rights and wrongs between divorcing spouses in this case or any other, there is no way to argue that the couple's young children deserve to be punished. Moreover, it is certainly reasonable to view Arnholtz's plan as not simply one individual's meanness to another, but as a direct exploitation, and intensification, of society's continued discrimination against women.

There is even more at stake when, as here, the client apparently wants the lawyer to execute the wrong on his behalf. (Some divorcing spouses apparently do their threatening in private, with the other spouse;[9] perhaps lawyers ought to expect this and ought to reach out affirmatively to try to dissuade their clients from acting this way, but in this context the lawyer's own responsibility is at least less direct.) Arnholtz not only wants to cause harm to his wife, but also to employ Mathiesson to do the job. Mathiesson, to be sure, has professional responsibilities to his clients, and lawyers' practice almost inevitably will require them sometimes to do harm to others for their clients' sake. But even if lawyers are, in general, morally justified in causing harm to others, within the bounds of the law, for their clients' benefit, it does not follow that they are obliged to do so in all cases. Lawyers remain people, and it is understandable, and we think desirable, that they draw lines between the harsh work they will do and the repellent work they won't.

But to say that "wrong will be done" is to assume that your view of what is right and wrong is correct, and it may not be. Lawyers have no monopoly on wisdom, and no immunity from bias, self-interest and limited perspective. Here, it is easy to share Mathiesson's disapproval of the custody threat tactic, which seems brutal and discriminatory. But it is not entirely obvious that what Arnholtz wants to do is improper. Custody and money are, it has been said, the two basic issues in every divorce of parents with children.[10] It is predictable that the two parents will have somewhat conflicting interests on each of these issues; even if both agree on who will be the custodial parent, for example, they may have many disagreements about matters such as visitation. It is hardly surprising that parents also trade concessions on one of these issues for gains on the other—what else would they bargain with?[11] It also appears, as mentioned earlier, that both husbands and wives use such tactics, so that it is not so obvious that Mr. Arnholtz is an example of patriarchy in microcosm.[12]

Moreover, there is always a danger—perhaps illustrated by this very dialogue—that the lawyer's focus on whether what the client wants is right or wrong will interfere with her ability to understand the client's thinking with sensitivity, or even to fully understand the facts of the case. Here, on the surface, it appears that Arnholtz is looking for a negotiation tactic. But perhaps he is in the process of re-thinking his own view of his spouse as a parent, and his own wishes on the issue of custody.[13] The facts, as we hear them in this dialogue, do not seem to rule out the possibility that the children would be better off in Arnholtz's custody— and if that is the case, then by overlooking this possibility Mathiesson may actually have harmed the children. At the least, it seems possible that Arnholtz could reasonably think his children would be better off with him. Arnholtz doesn't express that view in so many words anywhere in this dialogue, yet that may be the real point for Mathiesson to explore with his client. Perhaps if he had done so, he and Arnholtz would have come to a quite different understanding of the case and of the moral issues it presented, issues on which they might not have disagreed. We don't mean that all seeming moral gaps between lawyer and client are actually just differences of perception that can be resolved by more sensitive interviewing—but there is certainly a danger of the lawyer's missing the need for interviewing because of her anxiety about what she sees as a morally disturbing declaration by her client.

Why didn't Mathiesson treat Arnholtz's apparent change of heart as a reason for renewed interviewing rather than for moral persuasion? One plausible answer is that Mathiesson was too focused on insuring that he and his client did "the right thing" in the case. It was not wrong for Mathiesson to have this concern, but it is always a mistake for a lawyer to allow her own preoccupations to interfere with listening carefully to her client. As we emphasize in Chapter 5 ("Narrative Theory and Narrative Practice"), the client's story—and the client's own sense of himself—are not fixed in every detail, and a lawyer who expects her client to remain always as he first presented himself is bound for disappointment and difficulty. But we do not assume that Mathiesson made this mistake. At every juncture in a lawyer-client conversation, there are multiple paths open to the lawyer, and the lawyer must of necessity make choices among them. Here it may be that Mathiesson, who has been representing Arnholtz for some time, has a clearer understanding of Arnholtz' situation and Arnholtz' view of that situation than is entirely explicit in the dialogue. It is true that his memory on these points appears to be imperfect—he finds it necessary to ask his client to "[t]ell me again what her problems as a mother were, would you?" (L21)—but that may only reflect that he has thoroughly evaluated the situation some time ago and subsequently focused on other aspects of the case.

Understanding his client well, Mathiesson may judge that what he is hearing now is not new facts but new anger. With that in mind, he may decide that it would be a serious error for him to follow his client down this road by inviting Arnholtz to expand on his dissatisfactions with his wife's performance as a mother. To do that, Mathiesson might think, could propel Arnholtz towards even greater rage and towards decisions that might have irrevocable consequences. This perspective might not fully assure Mathiesson that there is no actual cause for concern about the mother's fitness—but it might lead him reasonably to think that that concern should be explored at some later, calmer moment. There is undoubtedly some measure of paternalism towards Arnholtz in such a decision—although there might also have been some degree of paternalism involved in the lawyer's pursuing the possibility that Arnholtz is actually moving towards a change of heart about custody when he himself has never said that. Conceivably there is even some measure of risk towards Arnholtz's children, if the later inquiries come too late to guide the final resolution of the case. But there are risks both in postponing further questioning and in undertaking it at once, and the lawyer must weigh what is in the client's best interest in light of her ongoing understanding of her client and his situation.

If it is difficult to determine whether moral dialogue is called for by the need to avoid wrong being done, however, it is also questionable whether moral dialogues always breach a client's right to choose. Talking morality with the client may be necessary, in fact, to avoid a different kind of implicit guidance that lawyers may otherwise inadvertently give their clients—a message that morality does not matter because, unlike tactics and strategy that promote the client's self-interests, morality goes unmentioned in the lawyer's office. If clients tend to defer to their lawyers, they may defer to the implicit exclusion of morality from legal business, though they might otherwise have been quite differently disposed.[14]

Nor is it self-evident that the client will consider discussion of morality an imposition, at least once he has had time to think the matter through. Here, for example, Arnholtz is, so far as we know, a reasonable person who has been deeply hurt by the collapse of his marriage; he is under stress but we have no reason to think of him as heartless or immoral. In fact, it appears from the dialogue that over the time they've worked together Arnholtz has given Mathiesson considerable reason to believe that the custody threat tactic is inconsistent with values Arnholtz himself holds dear. That background knowledge of his client gives Mathiesson reason to believe that Arnholtz is speaking now from anger rather than settled conviction, and that, as he says (L29), "this conversation is just a bump in the road." Even if Arnholtz had not previously discussed how he felt about the balance of his children's well-being against his own need for emotional vindication, Mathiesson would have had some basis for inferring that Arnholtz would value his children's happiness more highly—since that sentiment is one that so many people in our society would affirm. Indeed, if Mathiesson feels—as he has reason to—that he and his client share considerable common ground, then Mathiesson's own feeling that the children must come first is some evidence that Arnholtz may share that view.[15]

If we don't know what the client's reaction will be, we still have reason to err on the side of discussion, for it is a form of respect for another person to assume that he or she is a moral person who will want to address these issues.[16] A client who thinks through a moral issue for himself has achieved a special form of autonomy. So, too, a client who with the lawyer's help frees himself of anger or vengefulness or fear that are blunting his sensitivity to his own values has become more autonomous rather than less.

It follows that we should not assume that clients are insensitive to moral issues, or that they will consider a discussion of these issues an imposition. It is true, of course, that even a moral man or woman may well prefer to handle moral issues without outside "assistance," and indeed decent people, worthy of respect, will not always be of a mind to heed moral considerations. For these reasons, the lawyer's intervention may be initially unwelcome, but at least if the lawyer handles the discussion sensitively many clients faced with difficult moral choices may come to appreciate the lawyer's words. Many clients, yet not all; undoubtedly a client *may* feel imposed upon, and if he does, he may (but also may not) tell us. Still, he may feel quite the opposite. (Certainly we should not assume that a client feels imposed upon if he explicitly *invites* the lawyer to judge what he has in mind, as some clients probably will. At the same time, we should not assume that every invitation is equally sincere and equally voluntary.)

If the lawyer's decision to initiate moral dialogue is not always a form of coercion or undue influence, however, it certainly is sometimes. A lawyer's heavy-handed attempts to persuade a client to behave in a way the lawyer considers moral may overwhelm the client and reach the result the lawyer wants at the expense of the client's active and thoughtful decisionmaking on the matter. Even the fact that the client may come to feel grateful to the lawyer for the insight the lawyer's intervention produced is no guarantee of client self-determination, for that very gratitude may be part of what the lawyer has coerced or seduced the client into feeling. The line between persuasion and manipulation is never entirely clearcut, and the line between intense advocacy and browbeating can be equally ambiguous.

These lines are especially hazy when the advocate starts out with some form of special power over, or trust from, the person she seeks to convince. Very often, lawyers start such conversations in exactly this way.

In many cases, lawyers and clients do not see themselves as having equal status, because of differences on such matters as education, race, and class—and because, even when none of these demographic factors undercuts free and equal communication, the lawyer still often has the advantage of legal experience and a cooler head while the client faces all the perils that have brought him or her to the lawyer's office. Most troublingly, these various sources of lawyer power and influence over clients obviously suggest that lawyers sometimes will have the greatest success in influencing the decisions of poor, disadvantaged and upset people, while their richer, more determined clients will be most immune to persuasion. Rich clients, who by virtue of their social position probably have the greatest power over other people, may most need persuading, while poor clients may be most subject to it. Meanwhile, the danger that lawyers for powerful clients face may be that they will intervene too little rather than too much, out of a fear that raising a moral issue will cause them the loss of a client—as it may in this dialogue.

Aside from the risks of coercion and of misjudgment, there is a further danger in lawyers' undertaking moral dialogue with their clients: the risk of undercutting the attorney-client relationship. Mathiesson does not initially tell Arnholtz that he might simply refuse to assist Arnholtz with this scheme, but Arnholtz has good reason to become suspicious. Even if Mathiesson ultimately agreed to go along with Arnholtz' strategy, Arnholtz might still worry about Mathiesson's devotion to his cause. Arnholtz would know, after all, that he was employing Mathiesson to do something that he, Mathiesson, was uncomfortable with. Arnholtz might also simply feel uncomfortable with Mathiesson, however zealously Mathiesson proceeded, because Arnholtz might suspect that Mathiesson thought less of him because he had insisted on this harsh strategy. Suspicion and discomfort do not promote the careful discussion of difficult choices that lawyers and clients need to undertake, and the lawyer's injection of his own morality—even if it doesn't lead to an abrupt end to the relationship—may undercut its health from then on. Even if Arnholtz decides to follow Mathiesson's moral advice, moreover, the danger to the relationship is not erased, since Arnholtz's second thoughts, perhaps almost an inevitable prospect, may turn to anger against his persuasive attorney. Mathiesson, for his part, may find it harder to remain objective about the tactical choices ahead of them if he has launched them on a particular course based on his moral scruples.[17]

The moral calculus suggested by these cross-cutting arguments is not easy to resolve. The rules of professional ethics reflect this difficulty, and do not eliminate it. The Model Code tells us that "[a] lawyer should bring to bear the fullness of his [or her] experience" in counseling the client, but does so only in an Ethical Consideration rather than a Disciplinary Rule.[18] The Model Rules make clear that moral considerations are appropriate subjects for counseling, but stop short of requiring lawyers to address these considerations.[19] The Restatement of the Law Governing Lawyers is similar.[20] The Model Rules and the Restatement also authorize lawyers to withdraw from cases out of moral disagreement with their clients, and the Model Code authorizes this as well, though not as widely—but none of these rules compels lawyers to withdraw for these reasons so long as the lawyers are still able to vigorously represent their clients.[21]

The rules' hesitancy is not improper. What the rules do is, we think, what must be done—namely to leave the extent of moral counseling that lawyers undertake to be decided by each lawyer, and in each case. Moral dialogues are permitted, rather than mandated or forbidden, and so it is up to each lawyer to resolve the moral calculus. We ourselves have somewhat different responses to this problem, but we offer the following general guidelines that we hope will assist you in addressing it for yourselves. In theory, these factors might be taken as combining into a sliding scale, but we are hesitant to impose this mathematical model on the moral reflection lawyers will do; instead, we think that lawyers themselves need both to consider these factors and to judge how to weigh them together.[22]

The moral stakes: The case for a moral dialogue will be stronger the greater the moral wrong at stake. There is more reason to risk interfering with a client's autonomy or disrupting an effective lawyer-client relationship if the client has in mind to do great harm—to poison a child's relationship with a parent, say—than if she merely seeks some modest financial advantage—a tax benefit, for instance. Model Rule 1.6, as revised in 2003, reflects a similar calculus, allowing disclosure of confidential information to prevent "reasonably certain death or substantial bodily harm," or "to prevent the client from committing a crime or fraud that is reasonably certain to result in substantial injury to the financial interests or property of another," but not, in general, to prevent client actions with lesser consequences.[23]

The debatability of the issue: The clearer your conviction about what is morally required in the situation, the more willing you should be to intervene. Yet it is also true that the lawyer's own sense of certainty may bear no relation to the actual merits of her moral judgments—indeed, "it is much easier for us to believe that *others* have erred than it is to believe in *our own* errors regarding moral judgments"[24]—and so it is surely also right that the lawyer who contemplates intervening to challenge a client's decision should question her own certainties before trying to persuade her client of them.

We recognize the paradox implied by this guideline: a true dialogue is one in which both parties are open to change, but in the relatively infrequent cases where a lawyer following our guidelines would feel called upon to intervene morally, a lawyer convinced the issues are not debatable may be far from open to change. We must accept the probability of non-dialogic dialogues, and reckon it as one of the flaws of such interactions.

Does this prospect of one-sided dialogues mean that the lawyer who is firmly convinced that her client's plans are morally wrong has a conflict of interest with her client? If the lawyer's convictions are so strong that she simply cannot bring herself to carry out her client's lawful wishes, then her representation clearly is "materially limited," and in a way that seems impossible for a client to consent to.[25] But at the point of counseling that conflict has not yet been reached, for the client has not yet made his choice about what he would like the lawyer to do.[26] Is a lawyer with firm convictions unable to counsel her client without "material limitations," and therefore obliged to withdraw?[27] We would say that if the lawyer is so consumed by her own beliefs that she cannot listen carefully and offer advice thoughtfully, then she does indeed have a conflict of interest. But ordinarily we would not say that firm beliefs equate with inability to counsel. Rather, as a general matter, we would say that lawyers with firm beliefs are as qualified to counsel clients as lawyers without firm beliefs; lawyers' certainties and doubts undoubtedly shape their counseling, but there are no people, or lawyers, without certainties and doubts.

Suppose, instead, that the lawyer, on reflection, is not so sure of what is right. Lawyers are trained to persuade others of propositions that they themselves do not embrace, but there is no room for that sort of advocacy in a meeting with a client. The lawyer who is uncertain, however, need not be silent. She may want to initiate a more constrained dialogue in which she does not seek so much to persuade as truly to discuss. This form of dialogue would reflect her recognition that a moral issue is at stake but not assert a certainty about its resolution that she does not have.

The client's capacity:[28] The more able the client is to make an independent judgment, the more appropriate it is for you to urge your moral views. Ability to make an independent judgment is a multi-faceted and contextual matter—and it is not the same as the likelihood or unlikelihood of accepting the lawyer's advice. A client working with a lawyer whom he knows well as a friend and an equal may be very likely to accept the lawyer's advice, but out of justified trust rather than undue deference. More generally, clients who are able to understand the issues they face, both in terms of intelligence or experience and in terms of emotional composure, are more likely to make independent decisions than clients who are more confused or more upset. And some clients are surer of themselves and of their own capacity to make decisions than others, and these more confident clients are also those to whom the lawyer can speak most readily without fear of overreaching.

Some clients may expressly invite the lawyer to give her views, and that invitation can itself be a sign of client capacity. It is true that, in a different client, the request for the lawyer's views may be a warning sign of client dependence, but as a general proposition we feel that clients' requests for guidance should be taken seriously. Doing so in itself express- es the view that clients are ordinarily capable of making, and entitled to make, their own decisions, including the decision to request moral advice.

The presence of shared values: Lawyers and clients rarely have relationships so intense or so longstanding that the lawyer can "convert" the client. We mean "convert" partly in its religious sense—the law office normally is no place for a lawyer to press her religious views on a client, however much those views seem to the lawyer to embody moral truth.[29] We also mean the word "convert" more metaphorically: the lawyer is not likely to be able to alter the client's world view in some fundamental way, and it will rarely be fruitful or wise for her to try. It seems safe to say that lawyers and clients will make most progress together if they share a range of values and jointly explore their meaning.[30] When the lawyer moves from speaking in terms that she and the client can share, to attempting something more drastic, she will be in danger of doing too much—or accomplishing nothing at all.

We certainly do not consider "shared values" to be the equivalent of "shared demographics," but it is important to keep in mind, here as elsewhere, the potential impact of commonality and difference between the lawyer and client.[31] In the dialogue with which this chapter begins, the lawyer and client have a lot in common demographically: they are white, Protestant, male, professional, prosperous, and "avid golfers and members of the same country club" as well. The main demographic difference between them, so far as we know, is their age, and the age difference—Mathiesson is 15 years older than his client—is small enough that Mathiesson may well gain more from it in Arnholtz's likely respect for an older man's experience than he risks losing because of Arnholtz's sense of a generation gap. All of this may mean that in fact Mathiesson and Arnholtz really do share many values, and if so Mathiesson's moral appeals are more likely to be heard than if this were not the case. Even if their surface similarities conceal profound moral differences, the surface features may make Arnholtz more receptive to Mathiesson's appeals than he otherwise would be because he may imagine that they truly share more than they do. Lawyers and clients who seem to each other to share less will have to travel a greater distance towards common ground before a lawyer's moral intervention will be likely to be effective, or welcome.

Compatibility with the legal purposes of the relationship: Moral truth can be found in many places, but it is not the central concern of either lawyers or clients. There is more room for morality in some lawyer-client encounters than in others—more room in framing a will, perhaps, than in defending against a serious criminal charge, more room in longstanding relationships than in new, one-time-only ones—but still, in general, not the same room as in the confessional. Often, what clients want is not self-evidently good for the world. A guilty criminal defendant still probably wants to be free, even if he practices a religion that calls for wrongdoers to confess and atone. For a priest to urge this defendant to confess on moral grounds would not be bizarre, but the same suggestion from his lawyer likely would be. The scope of moral urging between lawyer and client needs to be constrained by the secular, pragmatic functions that seem to be the principal reason clients turn to lawyers in the first place.[32] We would not take this argument to its ultimate limit, which would say that moral discourse and legal counseling never intersect, but each lawyer must assess where the constraints of his role bar him from taking on some elements of another.

Lawyer self-interest: The goal of moral dialogue is to help clients to do the right thing. That goal may be compromised if the "right thing" as the lawyer sees it also happens to be what serves the lawyer's own self-interests best.[33] To take an obvious example, a lawyer might counsel settlement on moral grounds while also aware that his effective hourly fee would be higher if the case settled than if it went to trial. Or another lawyer might argue that particular tactics—custody threats, for example—were immoral, while knowing that she herself wanted to avoid a reputation for using unseemly (but legal) maneuvers. There is, moreover, a sense in which every action a lawyer might counsel on moral grounds serves the lawyer's self-interest. Even if a lawyer offers moral arguments to a client that undercut her own economic self-interest—say because she stands to earn a larger fee if the client persists in the course of action she is arguing against—we might still say that the lawyer's moral arguments fit with her self-interest in not being associated with immoral actions.

These concerns are important but should not be overstated. We do not suggest that lawyers are more prone to surrender to such temptation than other people are. Nor do we imagine that lawyers can ever be *perfectly* free of interests, moral or otherwise, that their clients do not share; to take one mundane example, lawyers who charge fees want to receive them, while their clients would probably prefer to be represented without charge. So we do not argue that the possibility of conflict of interest should silence lawyers' moral counseling—there are no perfect people available to counsel others, whether on moral grounds or merely practical ones.[34] Nor, as a general proposition, do we view lawyers with strong moral views as more potentially conflicted than lawyers without such views.[35]

We do suggest, however, that you should ask yourself whether your own concerns and needs may be distorting your views of the client's moral dilemma. If you sense such strong feelings at work, you need to make a judgment. If you sense that your reaction to your client's situation is being affected by some interest of your own that is reducing the integrity of your own thinking, you may need to refrain from pressing your views on the client, or even to withdraw from the case. If, on the other hand, you remain confident about your own judgment, even as you recognize the extent of your own self-interests at stake, silence may not be the answer; you may help your client best if you both state your views and disclose your own interests to the client so that the client can take them into account in making her own decision.

These six factors, as we have already said, do not add up in mathematical fashion. We believe, however, that these considerations rightly shape the decisions that lawyers must make about whether to engage in moral dialogue or not. They also rightly shape decisions about the intensity or intrusiveness of the dialogue to undertake, if such a conversation is undertaken at all. But even when the moral stakes are at their highest, it would be difficult to justify undertaking moral dialogue if it were impossible to conduct a dialogue that actually engaged with the client without coercing him.[36] We turn now, therefore, to a discussion of the elements of an appropriate moral dialogue.

C. THE METHODS OF MORAL DIALOGUE

In undertaking this examination, we will not focus on two polar cases. We offer no suggestions for the lawyer who believes the moral stakes are so high that they justify coercing or deceiving his client. Lawyers may occasionally find themselves in situations of this sort—trying to prevent a client from committing a homicide, for example—but if coercion or deception is really called for then the lawyer-client relationship has broken down already, in fact if not in name.[37] Nor, as we have already said, are we focusing here on the lawyer who decides to conduct a conversation about morality aiming not to persuade but, in the sense we developed in Chapter 3, to *engage* with the client about his choices. There are many cases where engagement rather than persuasion is appropriate, when the lawyer discerns that the client needs or wishes to think about morality but also believes that he or she should not try to persuade the client to adopt one view or another. We have already seen that discussions of this less pressured sort are indeed integral to engaged client-centered representation; moreover, we recognize that some lawyers evaluating our six factors may conclude that this discussion-without-persuasion is the only appropriate role for them to play with respect to morality. Our focus, however, is on those situations in which lawyers conclude that for reasons of morality they do wish to try to persuade their client to make a particular decision. When lawyers reach that conclusion, how should they go about acting on it? We set out our recommendations here, drawing on general principles of lawyer-client engagement, and subject, as always, to the lessons that practice will reveal.

1. THE MORAL DIALOGUE SHOULD BE AN INTEGRAL PART OF THE ATTORNEY–CLIENT RELATIONSHIP

Suppose that Mathiesson had handled his conversation with Arnholtz quite differently. After learning, unmistakably, that Arnholtz wanted to make a bluffing custody threat as a weapon to undercut his wife's financial demands, suppose that he had said:

> L19*: Well, Bill, this is of course your decision. I personally wouldn't feel this was the right thing to do, and we could talk about that if you like, but it's your call.

At first blush, it is hard to see what purpose this comment really serves—except, perhaps, to salve the lawyer's conscience. Mathiesson expresses his moral position, but without giving any reasons for it, and downgrades its significance by referring to it as his "personal[]" view. He stops short even of declaring that he would *like* to talk about it with the client. There may be clients who would accept even so delicate an offer of guidance as this.

There may even be clients who would only respond to an offer couched so carefully, but we think other gentle beginnings are likely to be at least as effective. Assuming, in any case, that this opening succeeds in initiating a conversation at all, it will be a conversation which began in a way that seems calculated to diminish the weight that the client accords to his lawyer's views.

The alternative to this self-effacing approach is to make the moral dialogue an integral part of the attorney-client relationship. Doing so is not a matter simply of more bluntness, but clear and unhesitating speech is certainly important. Thus it would be better for this lawyer to have said:

> L19†: Well, Bill, this is of course your decision. It happens to be one that I have real concerns about, and I want to explain those to you. First, ...

The point of this clear beginning is to convey the sense that the conversation the lawyer is initiating is not optional or ancillary to the work lawyer and client are doing together. For the lawyer who has decided that intervention is appropriate, this message accurately reflects his judgment of the importance of the dialogue he is initiating. It is true that the client may respond that this is none of the lawyer's business, but the client may do that at any point in the lawyer's interviewing and counseling. For the lawyer who undertakes a moral dialogue, the moral issues need discussion just as the facts and options do, and her manner and words should reflect this.[38]

It would be a bit odd, however, for the lawyer to suddenly announce an interest in morality after displaying indifference to it all along. In many attorney-client relationships, a lawyer simply committed to careful and empathetic listening would inevitably have encountered, and needed to respond to, the client's moral feelings, because those feelings would naturally have been part of what the client himself was thinking about and needed to discuss. At the same time, if moral considerations are truly an integral part of the lawyer's relationship with her client, then one might expect the lawyer to mention them at many points in the course of her dealings with the client—just as she would assure the client of her commitment to helping him, or remind him of the importance of frank discussion of the facts. Moreover, bringing morality into the conversation early on reinforces the message the lawyer may at some point have to deliver strongly, namely that morality actually *is* part of the work lawyer and client do together. Initial conversations about moral considerations also help the lawyer to get to know her client, and to evaluate both the appropriateness of serious moral dialogue and the methods by which it can effectively be conducted. Here, though we are evaluating only a single lawyer-client encounter, we can see hints in the dialogue that Mathiesson has in fact included morality in their past discussions, such as his observation (L8) that "we've talked about the two basic issues that every divorcing couple with kids must deal with, and hopefully will deal with in a responsible way."

References to morality need not be *labeled* as such. On the contrary, they are probably most effective if they are simply a part of the flow of conversation. Mathiesson applies this technique. At L7, he tells his client that he "respect[s] the way you've been doing everything you can to deal with this in the best and most adult way possible." A moment later, in the passage just quoted from L8, Mathiesson again alludes to morality without, we think, being "preachy." As this conversation heads towards a confrontation about morality, Mathiesson continues to try to invoke moral considerations. At L11, he reminds Arnholtz that "I know you've told me, very clearly, that you don't want [a trial], because it would only make things harder for everyone." Then, discussing how tough a financial settlement might be achievable, he says, "we have to include in our offer enough money for her to take care of the kids" (L16), a statement that seems to be presented as a legal proposition but surely has moral content as well.

While laying this groundwork for a moral discussion generally makes sense, it has serious pitfalls as well, and some of these too are evident from the dialogue between Mathiesson and Arnholtz. As a general proposition, lawyers need to present their clients with the real issues that the clients need to address, in as clear a way as possible. They do not advance these fundamental goals by raising red herrings or unnecessarily scaring or troubling their clients. It would be bizarre, for example, for a lawyer to routinely warn his client at the start of the relationship that there is a possibility the lawyer will find the client's wishes morally unacceptable and decide to withdraw. In the great majority of cases, this outcome is inconceivable, and it would be alarmist and provocative, rather than candid, to mention it. More generally, lawyers should not be discoursing on morality before that truly becomes an appropriate part of the relationship they have with their clients. This is not to say that morality plays no role in the developing conversations that take place between lawyer and client, for morality is a part of what clients weigh and the lawyer needs to understand the client's values as well as his interests or needs. Moreover, an engaged client-centered lawyer may well share her own views as part of building her connection with her client. But usually the references the lawyer will need to make to her own views will be modest, and more allusive than didactic. A reference to the satisfaction the lawyer has gotten in working out settlements that helped all members of a divorcing family to move on with their lives, for example, would be quite sufficient to initially "bookmark" the role of the lawyer's moral perspective.[39]

If they do more than this, lawyers risk appearing sanctimonious. Even more important, they may hem in their clients in ways that interfere with frank communication and potentially create a momentum leading them towards confrontation. Something like this may well have happened here. Since we are reading only a single dialogue, we obviously do not know whether Mathiesson overdid his discussion of morality before this session, and it is worth remembering that an overwrought client may react badly even to the most modest hints of potential disagreements. But when Arnholtz reacts to Mathiesson's seemingly straightforward discussion of state law on property division in divorce by saying (C10) "Well, if you mean to tell me now that there's no alternative to a straight 50–50 split, why didn't you say so in the first place?'', we have reason to believe that he has arrived in the office in a suspicious frame of mind. Arnholtz's sense that he has to apologize for feeling that his wife should receive as small a settlement as possible (C13) may be further evidence that a breach has already opened up between lawyer and client. In this light, Mathiesson's comments early in this session about his admiration for Arnholtz's "adult" approach to the divorce begin to sound like efforts to keep a straying client in line, rather than appropriate reminders of the background relevance of moral issues.

Perhaps the most challenging aspect of the suggestion that lawyers make moral dialogue an integral part of the lawyer-client relationship is the recognition that in a true dialogue both participants must speak and each party should be open to change. Any other approach would in effect assert that the lawyer has a monopoly on moral wisdom about a situation that the client rather than the lawyer must actually live through. Lawyers and clients certainly can have such conversations—we hope that engaged client-centered dialogues regularly embody this sort of shared exploration—but achieving this openness to the client's potentially contrary views in the midst of a conversation which seeks to persuade rather than just to explore is far from easy. After all, it is precisely in those relatively rare cases where lawyers feel most certain of their views that they will be most moved to intervene morally.

Ideally, lawyers who urge moral views with their clients will simultaneously feel sure enough of their convictions to act on them, and humble enough about their beliefs to be prepared to change them. Realistically, as we have already seen, moral dialogues may not always be dialogic.[40] Here, Mathiesson certainly does not silence his client, and we do not think that the pressure he brings to bear rises to the level of "undue influence,"[41] but it is striking that when the lawyer finally decides that he faces a moral issue on which he will intervene, he largely takes over "the floor" and speaks much more than his client does. (L24–L31). Moreover, while Mathiesson avoids declaring that he absolutely will not continue with the case if Arnholtz insists on his custody threat strategy (L29), he comes close to that, and the many signs of discomfort and resistance that he displays once the custody threat idea emerges suggest strongly that he will refuse to help his client down this road. He acknowledges the possibility that "you might come back and show me some aspect of all this that I haven't thought about yet or understood properly" (L29), but we—and, more importantly, his client—may doubt that he is actually open to changing his mind. We do not think that lawyers will inevitably monopolize the dialogue as much as Mathiesson does here, but we think that falling short of true openness to change is a persistent risk in moral dialogues.

2. LISTENING AND EMPATHY

Listening is important in every contact with a client, and moral dialogue is no exception. It is important for you to understand what the client actually wants to do, and to determine whether the client does have a moral basis for doing it. Moreover, here as elsewhere, your goal should not generally be to take the client through a series of highly focused and directive questions that allow the lawyer to dissect the client's thinking; rather, especially at the start, the client needs to be invited to speak and you need to make clear that you are listening. This is all the more important where, as is the case in a moral dialogue, you ultimately may not be prepared to offer the client *nonjudgmental* empathetic regard;[42] since you may well become judgmental, you need to do everything you can to still be otherwise empathetic and attentive.

Mathiesson wins the battle but loses the war as a listener. He learns—though not very quickly—that Arnholtz wants to threaten a custody battle, even though Arnholtz actually believes that his wife "has to" be the custodial parent and doesn't actually want custody. (L15–C18)[43] He also confirms that Arnholtz has a colorable legal claim for custody (L22), a recognition which surely contributes to his acknowledging that the strategy is a legal one.[44] (If it were not legal, then Mathiesson could oppose it on quite different, and more adamant, grounds.) After hearing Arnholtz's arguments for his own position (his partnership metaphor (C9), his assessment of who contributed more to the marriage financially (C11), his analogy to other hardball negotiating tactics (C19), and his belief that his wife will scare (C23)), moreover, Mathiesson can tell that his client has embraced this idea and a set of supporting arguments or rationalizations—many of which perhaps come from Arnholtz's friend. And, finally, Mathiesson can see, from Arnholtz's angry remarks (C10, C11, C19) and of course from his explicit questions and comments about whether Mathiesson will stick with the case even if Arnholtz sticks with his custody threat strategy (C27–C30), that Arnholtz has lost trust in him and found a more welcome adviser in the "friend" who suggested this tactic to him.

But part of the hostility Mathiesson encounters may have been triggered by his own failure to convey an empathetic understanding of his client's wishes. Instead, Mathiesson reacts in at least three distinctly unempathetic ways, which in the end suggest that he was engaged more in pressuring his client than in empathizing with him. First, he tries to convey an expectation that Arnholtz will stay on the "adult" path in this divorce. Some of his comments to this effect seem entirely benign, such as his gentle suggestion that Arnholtz should try not to lie awake re-running the breakdown of his marriage in his mind (L5). But Arnholtz hears these along with others whose purpose is more overtly directive, notably Mathiesson's comment that "I've felt good about working with you because you haven't ever made it [the divorce] worse than it had to be. I've had some clients who I just couldn't say that about… " (L7), and his later reminder to Arnholtz that "you've told me, very clearly, that you don't want [a trial], because it would only make things harder for everyone" (L11). Mathiesson seems to be trying to hold onto ground he has already won with his client, rather than focusing on his client's current feelings.

That Arnholtz gets this message is most evident at the end of the interview, when Mathiesson returns to this tack, saying that he has "too much respect for the way you've handled yourself up till now to think that you're going to let the upset you're feeling affect your judgment this way." (L28) Arnholtz responds by asking "[h]ow can you say you respect me...?" (C28).

Second, Mathiesson responds to the early hints that Arnholtz has a harsh strategy in mind in a notably analytic rather than embracing way. When Arnholtz says, dramatically but hardly cryptically, that "I don't want her to do this to me and then make a profit from it too," Mathiesson responds, "I understand that feeling, Bill, but I'm not sure I know what you mean, concretely, as far as her not making a profit is concerned." (C8–L9). The perfunctory claim of understanding here gives way at once to an effort to translate that feeling into dollars and cents. A more genuinely understanding response to the content of Arnholtz's remark, and one that would not have required exceptional insight on Mathiesson's part, would have been to say, "So you're feeling like the financial settlement here should make your wife pay for what she did to you?" Rather than help Arnholtz articulate his wishes, Mathiesson seems to be forcing him to do the work. The pattern continues in their next exchange, when Arnholtz makes a legal argument based on his understanding of partnership law and Mathiesson responds with more "law talk" of his own, launching them on a discussion of whether what Arnholtz wants is legally achievable (C9–L13).

Arnholtz finally brings them back to the issue—his desires, not the law—at C13, when he declares, with an apology, that he "want[s] the settlement to give my wife—I'm sorry, but this is how I feel—as little money as possible." Although Mathiesson responds to Arnholtz's apologetic declaration in C13 by saying "Bill, you're entitled to feel that way, and you don't need to apologize to me for it." (L14), in fact—as we will see in more detail in the discussion of "candor" below—he then tries to steer Arnholtz away from the custody threat strategy by saying, quite incorrectly, that their settlement offer would "*have to* include ... enough money" for Arnholtz's wife to take care of the kids (L16, emphasis added). When Arnholtz nevertheless begins to suggest the custody threat strategy, Mathiesson again makes him do the work of articulating it (L17: "I'm not sure I see where you're going. What exactly did your friend tell you?").

Third, Mathiesson reacts so negatively to Arnholtz's proposal, once it is finally on the table, as to suggest that he not only disagrees with his client's plan but is appalled by it. He spells the idea out in a way that makes it seem dishonest: "You mean, to tell her that we're going to press for custody even though you don't actually want custody?" (L18). When Arnholtz answers "Yes, exactly," Mathiesson's response is a pause so pregnant that Arnholtz rightly sees condemnation looming. (L19–C19). A moment later, Mathiesson concedes the strategy's viability, again with evident dismay (L22).

Mathiesson's responses may in part reflect his own passion on this subject—and we do not believe passion is out of place in moral dialogue.[45] But his responses also appear to embody a strategy, a strategy of sustained pressure meant to dissuade his client even before the lawyer actually offers a direct argument about the morality of the client's choice. The strategy fails here, and may in fact have worsened the ultimate confrontation between the two men. It would have been better, we think, had Mathiesson been more empathetic about his client's anger and need for revenge, and more willing to help his client articulate his desires in the form of a legal strategy. He might have responded to Arnholtz's intense reference to "what my friend tells me" (C16) by saying, for example,

> L17*: Bill, I'm not sure I'm going to agree with where you're going, but I think I understand the idea. You're hoping to find a way to force your wife to take a small financial settlement, right?

He might have continued by saying,

> L18*: I won't beat around the bush. The most common idea that people think about when they feel the way you do is threatening a custody fight. Is that what you have in mind?

There is a price to this approach, namely that it may reveal to the client an immoral tactic he hadn't yet thought of. But it hardly seems, at this point, that Arnholtz is unaware of this gambit. Had Mathiesson been more forthcoming and thus sustained his emotional alliance with the client further into the conversation, he might have been able to make a strong moral argument without putting the continuation of the lawyer-client relationship so completely at risk. As it is, his vigorous attempts at persuasion may have fallen on deaf ears. Having adopted a strategy of pressure that compromised his ability to be empathetic, he ultimately finds his relationship with his client in danger of becoming simply a clash of wills.

3. CANDOR

Obviously lawyers are not allowed to lie to their clients in their normal work with their clients. Plainly lawyers should not be allowed to conduct a "moral dialogue" through lies either. To do so would undercut both the trust that should sustain the lawyer-client relationship and the very premise—adherence to moral principle—that might justify the intervention entailed in a moral dialogue.

But it is not quite the case that lawyers are always required to be entirely candid with their clients. It seems clear that lawyers can legitimately feign more warmth towards a client than they actually feel, for example, or more confidence in the client's ability to handle an upcoming cross-examination. Such modest dissembling is part of establishing a workable and supportive relationship with the client, and thus in a sense is a facilitator of candor on the substantive issues that the lawyer and client will ultimately address, even if it is also, strictly speaking, a form of manipulation.[46] If, here, Mathiesson actually did not feel for Arnholtz the "respect" he claims he feels for "the way you've been doing everything you can to deal with this in the best and most adult way possible," (L7), his words might still be defended as a tactic for keeping Arnholtz's spirits up. If Mathiesson's purpose, however, was not to soothe his client's anguished feelings but to lead him to make the decisions Mathiesson preferred, then what he said would be a true breach of the duty of candor.

On occasion, lawyers are permitted another departure from complete candor. According to the Comment to Model Rule 1.4, "[i]n some circumstances, a lawyer may be justified in delaying transmission of information when the client would be likely to react imprudently to an immediate communication."[47] Mathiesson might have been relying on this authority when he told Arnholtz that "we have to include in our offer enough money for her to take care of the kids." (L16).

Was Mathiesson attempting to engage in "delayed transmission" of the information that a custody threat strategy was available? What he actually said went beyond delayed transmission, since it was in fact incorrect; as Mathiesson surely knew, even if Arnholtz never made a custody threat he was certainly free, legally and ethically, to begin the bargaining over money with a "lowball" proposal. But we might imagine that Mathiesson could have found some not-inaccurate way to avoid mentioning the lowball strategy, and so we can ask whether "delayed transmission" here would have been appropriate. It is possible that Mathiesson had been delaying transmission in previous meetings too; if Arnholtz felt that he had had to learn this important information from a friend because his lawyer had kept it secret, that would certainly explain his short temper in this session. (In Mathiesson's defense, it should be said that he did candidly acknowledge that Arnholtz could make a colorable argument for custody, and—no doubt in part for that very reason—that the custody threat would not be unlawful. (L22, L29).)

The Model Rules comment sheds little light on how long a lawyer can withhold information to save his client from imprudence, but does not appear to authorize withholding it forever on this ground. If Mathiesson hoped to do that, he was beyond the bounds of the rules of ethics.[48] Even if he was truly engaged only in temporary withholding, his conduct is very troublesome, not only because of the risk of backfire but also because, again, a moral dialogue should be based on a respect for the other party's capacity to make a moral decision. We think that Mathiesson's inaccurate and incomplete observation in L16 was a breach of that respect and should not have been uttered.[49]

Suppose, however, that Mathiesson had sensed that Arnholtz really did not want to wield the custody threat weapon, but that he (Arnholtz) was also desperately afraid that his wife would find some final way to take advantage of him. Suppose also that Mathiesson understood that Arnholtz's wife could make a custody threat herself—a threat to limit her husband's visitation time with the kids, for instance—in an effort to extract a particularly generous financial settlement.[50] If Mathiesson was confident, based on his contacts with the wife's lawyer, that the wife had no intention of trying this tactic, he might reasonably have decided not to mention the possibility to his client at all. There would be time enough to deal with it if the wife switched strategy, Mathiesson might have felt, and meanwhile his client would be so enraged by the hint of this possibility that he wouldn't be able to see straight, and so would abandon his own moral instincts out of rage. Here, remaining silent temporarily about the wife's possible maneuver might well be justified. Indeed, if the wife never did try this tactic, the lawyer might legitimately conclude that there was no occasion ever to mention it.

Perhaps the most important departure from complete candor in situations where morality is at stake, however, is a decision not to talk about morality at all. We suspect that in most circumstances where lawyers perceive a moral issue, they address this issue as a legal or practical problem. A manufacturer's seeming indifference to a defect in its products may be immoral, but the lawyer will discuss the public relations black eye it could generate, or the potential for tort liability. What the lawyer will not say is that she also believes the client's intended action is immoral. In other words, she will have a discussion about a moral issue in which she says nothing about morality. Plainly such discussions are not the explicit "moral dialogues" that we focus on in this chapter. It would not be surprising, however, if the client discerns in the nuances of such pragmatic talk the moral convictions the lawyer also holds, and it is also conceivable that the lawyer's appeals to self-interest actually enable the client to listen to the better angels of his or her nature without quite having to acknowledge doing so.

Is it ethical for the lawyer not to mention her moral concerns, given that she does have them and that, for her, they are important? If the lawyer says no more than the truth about the risks the client is running, we believe it is legitimate for her to say nothing about the moral issues that in her view are also important. Lawyers, after all, have an ethical discretion concerning whether or not to engage in moral dialogue with their client. If a lawyer believes that a full and appropriate discussion of legal rather than moral factors will cause the client to reject the option with moral costs, then the primary reason for moral dialogue—to prevent a moral wrong from happening—no longer applies. We think, in addition, that the lawyer's decision not to talk morality can be seen, in this context, as a relationship-building tactic rather than an effort to mislead. This may be especially the case if, as we suspect, the lawyer's moral sentiments appear "between the lines"; in a sense, such a conversation *is* a moral discussion, even though only tacitly, but without the potential for giving offense that explicit moral talk can have.[51] It is fair to say that in building a relationship by refraining from expressing her own moral views, the lawyer is building a relationship focused on assisting the client rather than on mutual openness—but that, we think, is no more than a statement that the lawyer-client relationship, though a humane, engaged, and even intimate one, is ordinarily a professional connection rather than a personal friendship.[52] If persuasion is an appropriate part of that professional relationship, then we accept persuasion by politic, but still honest, words.

But all of this rests on the assumption that the lawyer does not overstate the arguments from client self-interest that she employs. If she does overstate them in an effort to sway the client's judgment, she is engaged in deception. Even if she does not consciously distort her arguments in any way, moreover, there is always a possibility that her moral convictions will affect her assessment and presentation of the pragmatic arguments. There is no solution to this problem except the lawyer's conscientious examination of her own thinking. If she senses that she may be pulled too far by her own moral zeal, she may have to disclose her moralistic side to her client so that the client can weigh what she says in light of it; indeed, there is an argument that she should err on the side of disclosure since her own assessment of whether her judgment is being affected may itself be affected by the moral convictions she feels. In a case where her passions are irrevocably engaged, the lawyer may even have to withdraw. But in general we do not criticize the lawyer's fostering of moral good through discussions of the client's self-interest. After all, in a good society, just laws will tend to make it in the client's legal self-interest to act in morally right ways.

4. RESPECT

We have already criticized Mathiesson's conduct of this session for its seeming disrespect for his client. It is possible, and right, to respect the dignity of someone who is unable to make decisions for herself—a small child, for example, or an acutely schizophrenic mental patient. In relations between adults, however, and in particular between a lawyer and a competent client, however, respect should not merely recognize a common humanity but also acknowledge the client's prerogative and capacity to make decisions for herself. It arguably follows that the lawyer's intrusion on client decisionmaking should be as limited as possible under the circumstances.

Stating this proposition is much simpler than applying it. The rule of "intrusion as limited as possible" requires the lawyer to assess how much limitation *is* possible. That in turn requires the lawyer to assess how urgent the case for intervention is. The higher the stakes, the more urgent the need for a persuasive moral dialogue; the more disinclined to change his views the client is, the more intrusive the dialogue may have to be in order to be persuasive. Perhaps, in the end, it is more illuminating to say that the lawyer's intrusion should be limited to what is *proportional* to the situation.

The "intrusion as limited as possible" or "proportionality" standard also requires the lawyer to gauge the intrusiveness of different techniques. There is, however, no absolute scale of intrusiveness, and in fact the impact of a particular technique on a client may be very dependent on context. The lawyer who is a close friend of a client's may know that an appeal *from him* to the client's feelings about his children will trump any other consideration in the client's mind, because of the thoughts and feelings about their children that the two of them have shared over many years. The same appeal from a lawyer who knew the client only from this very case might fall on deaf ears.

Nevertheless, it is possible to identify, if not rules, at least signposts to help lawyers gauge the extent of their intrusion on clients' decision-making autonomy and so to weigh whether the moral issue at stake justifies one approach or another to conducting that dialogue. Certain conversations about morality are particularly unintrusive. Some, after all, are explicitly and competently *invited* by the client himself. Others, even if uninvited, do not entail any effort at persuasion at all. Thus a lawyer might ask a client if she has considered any possible moral concerns raised by her planned course of action. Somewhat more incisively, the lawyer might remind the client of the values she herself had earlier articulated, and ask her whether the course of action she has in mind fits with those values. A lawyer might also articulate his own view that, judged by the client's own values as the client has earlier stated them, a particular course of action seems improper. Or the lawyer might attempt more substantial, and in that sense more intrusive, transformation, by urging the client to accept a view of what is right that doesn't follow from what the client himself has already articulated; at this point, at least, the lawyer is engaged in the direct moral suasion that this chapter is assessing.[53]

Yet this first cut at calibration, though helpful, is not complete. What it largely leaves out is the manner in which the lawyer carries out the discussion. A conversation about the implications of the client's own stated values may turn out to be more intrusive than one that directly urges a change of heart, depending on how each is handled. Case law—not case law analyzing attorney-client interactions in particular, but contract law on "undue influence"—makes this clear.[54] Consider the *Odorizzi* case, in which school authorities approached a teacher who had just been released from jail following an arrest for homosexual activity and pressed him to resign.[55] The court found that the teacher was entitled to a trial on his claim that his resignation had been procured by undue influence, and observed that:

> [O]verpersuasion is generally accompanied by certain characteristics which tend to create a pattern. The pattern usually involves several of the following elements: (1) discussion of the transaction at an unusual or inappropriate time, (2) consummation of the transaction in an unusual place, (3) insistent demand that the business be finished at once, (4) extreme emphasis on untoward consequences of delay, (5) the use of multiple persuaders by the dominant side against a single servient party, (6) absence of third-party advisers to the servient party, (7) statements that there is no time to consult financial advisers or attorneys. If a number of these elements are simultaneously present, the persuasion may be characterized as excessive.[56]

Odorizzi's language does not transfer perfectly to the lawyer-client relationship, and we do not suggest it as a mechanical guideline. Indeed, there may be good reasons why, for example, a meeting must take place in an uncomfortable setting, such as a jail visiting area, or why delay is truly impossible. It might also be argued that a moral advocate could be justified in using methods of persuasion that go beyond what courts should permit a self-interested contracting party to employ—but we think the world has seen too much outrage from moral advocates to allow them this extra leeway. In any event, like the *Odorizzi* court, we do not presume undue influence from the presence of any one of these elements. But when techniques like these are deployed in the service of moral dialogue, the lawyer is on a dangerous path. Moral dialogue is always an exercise conducted on a slippery slope, and it is the lawyer's job to weigh scrupulously whether she is losing her balance.

5. PERSUASION

Persuasion is a field in itself. Law students and lawyers study it in connection with closing arguments and other trial tactics; in the context of negotiations and mediations; and in brief writing and oral argument. There is undoubtedly much to be learned from the general study of persuasion for the specific field of moral dialogue. To be sure, many tactics we accept as legitimate in other contexts would be out of bounds in the context of moral dialogue. A lawyer arguing a case to a judge on behalf of a client may offer arguments he himself does not believe should be accepted, or appeal to jurors' emotions in a way that he himself hopes will distract the jurors from focusing on the evidence in the case at hand. A negotiator may demand concessions simply on the basis of power. Insincere arguments are out of bounds in moral dialogue, and so are arguments or ploys meant to undercut instead of to enhance the client's ability to see a matter clearly. But many of the techniques that lawyers, or politicians, sometimes employ for merely strategic purposes nonetheless are potentially appropriate and helpful in the conduct of genuine moral dialogues.

Perhaps the most important point to remember is that persuasion is rarely dispassionate. These dialogues are not academic. Nor are moral decisions usually made by the pure exercise of analytic reason. Humans are emotional creatures, and emotion is part of our most fundamental choices.[57] Passion can be blinding, but trying to ignore or dismiss emotion is equally misguided. Instead, when lawyer and client discuss morality, they are inevitably discussing pressing issues about which they both probably feel strongly. In such discussions, it is not wrong for you, as the lawyer, to "come on strong." At the same time, it is wrong for you to be so overbearing that the decision the client makes is no longer meaningfully his own.

Here, when Mathiesson faces the custody threat issue head on, he does so in a generally appropriate—though certainly passionate—way. It is true that he focuses primarily on how unwise this strategy would be, rather than on morality as such (until the end, in L29), but his moral concerns about the children are evident (L26), and it is clear that Mathiesson in fact believes that this strategy is both unwise and immoral. His style of speech is clear, emphatic and blunt. He leaves his client no room for doubt about his (the lawyer's) position, or about how strongly he feels about this position, and he implies in a range of ways that what he is saying is self-evident. Thus he uses repetition ("Hell hath no fury, Bill, hell hath no fury like this" (L24)), and rhetorical questions, sometimes more than one at a time. ("Do you think the anger will go away? How long will your wife have to think about how you scared her into taking a bad money settlement, after this is over?" (L25)). He uses familiar phrases, which are not only attention-getting but also each invoke a host of folk wisdom (or folk assumptions)[58] about human behavior that the lawyer implicitly suggests his client would be foolish to ignore: "Hell hath no fury, Bill, hell hath no fury like this," (L24); and, a little later, "She won't suffer in silence, Bill." (L26). He is by turns rueful ("Hell hath no fury ..."), sarcastic ("She won't suffer in silence ..."), and impatient ("I know what threats lead to, and so do you ..." (L24)). He also employs alliterative, hopefully memorable language: threats, he says, "lead to fury as much as fear." (L24). He uses the metaphor of drug addiction to drive his point home even further. (L25). For a short stretch, probably two or three minutes, he also does almost all the talking, with his client offering one brief objection (C24) but otherwise carried along by the tide. (L24–L26).

He also tells, or at least sketches, a story. Here, as elsewhere, narrative can play an important role in effective communication.[59] The narrative Mathiesson traces is a vision of vengeance and feuding and the growing, implacable rage Arnholtz's wife will feel, a prospect that brings home the likely effects of Arnholtz' choice much more dramatically than, say, a reference to the statistics in the latest studies of divorce. Within that story he tells a more specific one, again trying to ensure that Arnholtz cannot ignore what he is saying: "I know one couple who spent *eleven years* litigating their divorce. By the time it was all over, there was nothing left to divide up—and the husband had a terminal illness." (L25). This story's reference to mortality is probably part of what it makes it effective; if Mathiesson had said that the fight caused the husband's illness, he would have been preposterous and laughable, but his outline of the bare facts of the situation lets Arnholtz speculate about this himself. Perhaps more important, this offhand reference to death helps remind Arnholtz that he has only one life to get right, an important consideration since this decision will, Mathiesson is urging, shape the next "oh, 15 years" (L26), during which his wife will be thinking every day about what Arnholtz did to her in this settlement.

In short, a bluntly phrased, emotionally loaded, near-monologue for several minutes is not excessive persuasion. To be sure, this is a judgment call, and reasonable lawyers might see Mathiesson as having gone too far even in these few minutes. Certainly the dialogue would have a different tinge if he had maintained this level of intensity for much longer. (As a practical matter, effective persuasion might well have required a longer conversation than our dialogue presents. In a longer conversation, however, we would have expected the emotional temperature to rise and fall, and the role of the client, overall, to be greater than it was in these few minutes here.)

In a range of other ways Mathiesson could have crossed the line into undue influence. The dialogue would certainly have been different if

Mathiesson had stepped out of the room and sent in an ally—Arnholtz's brother, for example—to join in the persuasive chorus. Had Mathiesson invented his vengeance narrative, or left out crucial parts of it, his conduct would also have been much harder to justify.[60] It would also have been a different and more troubling exchange if Mathiesson had gone beyond intensity to tears and shouts, or cries and whispers; this exchange is passionate but reasonably calm and that calm is an important part of what lawyers are supposed to bring to clients. For similar reasons this would have been a different conversation if Mathiesson had gone beyond vivid language ("It became their drug, Bill, their addiction." (L25)) to epithets or insults ("You'll be no better than a child-abuser, Bill."). We would also be much more disturbed if Mathiesson had made greater use of his emotional power vis-à-vis his client, for example by saying things like "I expected better of you" or "As a lawyer I feel your conduct is unacceptable"—though he does, as we have already noted, make some use of this sort of pressure early in the conversation and late, concluding with his comment (L29) that "I've been proud to work on your case because I think you're this sort of person. . . ." So, too, it would have been a much less appropriate conversation if Mathiesson had insisted that his client sign on the dotted line then and there. Mathiesson did put pressure on his client, and obviously meant to do exactly that. There was much more that he could have done, and did not do, however, and he appears to have avoided losing control on this admittedly slippery slope.

6. COERCION

In discussing "persuasion," we did not address the concluding exchanges of this dialogue, in which Arnholtz asks Mathiesson to assure him that he (Mathiesson) will accept Arnholtz's decision about the custody threat, whatever that decision turns out to be. Mathiesson responds first by saying that "[t]here are some complicated issues of legal ethics here, frankly," and telling Arnholtz that probably they'll never need to discuss these issues because "frankly, Bill, I don't think you're going to come back and tell me that this is what you want to do." (L28). These comments are somewhat disingenuous, as the repeated uses of "frankly" signal. Mathiesson no doubt understands very well that Arnholtz will not be happy to learn that Mathiesson is prepared to drop the case rather than do his client's bidding, but his effort to avoid revealing this possibility is itself provocative for Arnholtz. It would have been better to respond openly when Arnholtz first asked the question.

What Mathiesson finally says is, essentially, that he will "probably . . . . have to resign from your case if you insist on going this route." (L29). Having evaded the question once, Mathiesson now is candid; he makes clear that he does not view the custody threat strategy as illegal, but nevertheless says that he probably could not undertake it. Moreover, though we think that Mathiessen's moral concerns were largely evident throughout the conversation, it's at this point that he spells out for the first time that he would expect to object on moral grounds even if the strategy actually would save Arnholtz money. He does his best to make this message as palatable as possible—reiterating his respect for and fellowship with his client; restating the objections that he has already articulated concerning the custody threat strategy; and leaving room for the client to "come back and show me some aspect of all this that I haven't thought about yet or understood properly." Even so, Arnholtz is not assuaged. At the end of the conversation, it seems quite possible that the relationship between the two men has ruptured fatally, and that Arnholtz will never be back. Mathiesson affirms that he would like to continue as Arnholtz's lawyer but recognizes that "if you want to get another lawyer, you certainly have that right, and I wouldn't stand in your way." (L31).

As we have already seen, lawyers in some circumstances have the right to withdraw from cases because they are unwilling, for moral reasons, to assist the client even though what the client wants done is legal. Assuming that Mathiesson could have exercised this authority in this case,[61] it was obviously proper for him to answer Arnholtz' question accurately. Indeed, it is arguable that Mathiesson had a duty to volunteer this information, since it was certainly material to the decisions Arnholtz now had to make, both about the custody threat strategy and about his continued faith in his lawyer.[62] In this case, it seems possible that the effect of revealing this prospect was to weaken the persuasive impact of what Mathiesson had already said; if so, that was a price that had to be paid, at least when Arnholtz directly asked about Mathiesson's intentions.

In other cases, however, a threat to withdraw might have quite the opposite effect, adding to the persuasive reasoning the lawyer has put forward the frightening prospect, for the client, of being deprived of this lawyer or even (depending on the situation) deprived of all legal representation. It is plausible to see this threat, with such a client, as a form of coercion, and therefore we must ask the question of whether lawyers should employ this coercion as part of a moral dialogue. The answer is yes—under some circumstances.

At first impression, admittedly, threats appear to have no place in a dialogue premised on the idea that the client is a moral actor with whom the lawyer can reason about a moral choice.[63] It is odd to suggest, however, that the lawyer is ethically prohibited from employing information—the potential for his own withdrawal from the case—that he may simultaneously be ethically obliged to reveal. Moreover, the lawyer's intention to withdraw from the case is relevant to the client's judgment, quite aside from its significance as a threat, because it is a measure of the lawyer's moral conviction. The lawyer who is prepared to withdraw from a case is sacrificing the work, and the fee (if any) that the work would bring, and the lawyer's willingness to make such a sacrifice is itself a moral statement to the client.

But the threat itself may after all be relevant as well. The client contemplating a morally questionable act must consider not only its morality but also its feasibility, and a lawyer who is prepared to withdraw from the case rather than assist with such an act thereby makes it somewhat less feasible. Presumably lawyers who choose to withdraw from such cases do so in part to avoid being party to the immorality themselves but also in part with the hope that as a result the client will in fact find it more difficult to do what he wishes.[64] The difficulty the lawyer can cause for the client is tightly constrained by the rules of withdrawal, confidentiality and conflict of interest, but in the end some measure of power does remain. For those lawyers prepared to use it, this power is legitimate, and threatening to use it is legitimate as well.

Or, rather, the power and the threats to use it are legitimate in principle. Like other powers, this one can be abused. Possibly it was here. Mathiesson tells Arnholtz at the end of the dialogue (L29) that he is one of the lawyers who "feel that even though in most negotiations and on most issues it's fair to play a very hard game of hardball, that isn't true when kids are at stake." We do not know whether Mathiesson informed Arnholtz of this important limit on the work he was prepared to do for his client at the start of the relationship. Clearly, as a general matter, it is one thing to remind a client of a limit that the lawyer announced at the start of the relationship, before the client has made the decision to retain the lawyer, and another to spring this limit on the client late in the day. We argued earlier in this chapter that the lawyer need not elaborate on her moral views before a moral conflict ever comes into view,[65] but here Mathiesson surely could have predicted that his client might have a change of heart about his "adult" approach to the divorce. If Mathiesson did anticipate this, he did not have to trigger it by spelling out at the start exactly what he would and would not do in hypothetical circumstances later on, but he should have given Arnholtz a simple, general statement of the bounds he placed on his own practice.

There are other important constraints on the lawyer's use of the threat of withdrawal. It is again one thing to tell a client she must seek another lawyer if one is likely to be available, and quite another to say that to someone—a client of a legal aid office, for example—who cannot possibly find another attorney. It is also one thing to tell a client who is capable of undertaking the search that he will need to do so, and quite another to give this message to someone so distraught that he cannot take on this task. It is similarly one thing to withdraw from representing a client with whom the lawyer has a strictly professional, lawyerly relationship, and another to threaten to breach a relationship that has evolved into a more emotional, even more therapeutic, bond. In short, there may be many circumstances where the lawyer's responsibility to the client is such that she could not morally pull out of the case if her client rejected her moral guidance. In those cases, she need not reveal an intention to withdraw, and she must not assert one.

Though we do not endorse anything like routine use of the threat to withdraw, we recognize that it is startling to offer any support for such a step in the context of an effort to describe "engaged client-centeredness."[66] It is also sobering to remember that in this chapter's dialogue, by the time Mathiessen reaches this point, his client has gotten there too, and is clearly considering whether to fire Mathiessen. The prospect of using threats with a client is certainly not something to be welcomed, much less the prospect of losing a client the lawyer would like to continue representing. Yet in a sense we should not be surprised that these possibilities arise when lawyer and client challenge each other on such a difficult subject as morality. Engagement, even engagement on moral issues, does not normally entail "challenge" and in general we are confident that engaged client-centeredness is a path to strengthening lawyer-client relationships rather than jeopardizing them. But as with every engagement between people, there is a possibility of breakdown.

CONCLUSION

As we noted early in this chapter, dialogues of the kind we study here may be quite rare in legal practice—even if less fully articulated moral considerations infiltrate many lawyer-client encounters. Nevertheless, there will be cases where lawyers will have good reason to seriously consider initiating explicit moral dialogue of the kind this chapter examines. We hope that the guidelines we offer will help lawyers to decide when to undertake such conversations, and to shape conversations—when they do undertake them—that neither deny their clients the right to make their own decisions nor drive the clients away from the lawyers. At the same time, we hope that these guidelines assist lawyers who do undertake such conversations to do so successfully—to advocate their moral perspective persuasively and in a way that preserves their relationship with their clients.

QUESTIONS

We also hope that this discussion has prompted many questions in your own minds. Here are several issues that you may find particularly important to assess for yourselves:

1. If engaged client-centered lawyering, as we explicate it in this book, affirms the centrality of client autonomy, is moral dialogue—that is, dialogue in which the lawyer actively seeks to persuade the client to adopt the lawyer's moral perspective—consistent with our general approach to lawyering? Moral counseling, as we have sought to show in this chapter, offers both promise and threat to client autonomy. Should lawyers help clients reflect on moral issues, but not try to persuade them to take one view rather than another? Or can lawyers properly try to persuade their clients, but only so far? What techniques discussed in this chapter help you to draw the line in the right place?

2. If you conclude that moral dialogues of the type described in this chapter are not consistent with engaged client-centeredness, does that mean that moral dialogues are wrong or that engaged client-centeredness is?

3. How successful can moral dialogues actually be? Do you agree with this chapter's argument that lawyers cannot "convert" their clients? Do you think that lawyers can cause their clients to change to any extent? Do you think Mathiessen would have succeeded in persuading Arnholtz not to use the custody threat strategy?

4. Do you agree with this chapter's argument that the lawyer who believes she can achieve her moral goals without explicitly discussing morality can legitimately do so as long as what she does discuss (pragmatics and client self-interest) she discusses accurately? Is the lawyer's omission of any mention of her moral concerns a form of deception of her client? If so, is it justifiable under the rules of legal ethics?

5. Mathiesson does explicitly refer to morality in the end, but for much of what we have called a moral dialogue he does not invoke morality in so many words. For example, he calls the approach he endorses "adult" and "responsible," without saying that it's also "the moral way to handle this." Was that wise, because he was able to convey his moral convictions without spelling them out and sounding "preachy"? Or did his failure to use more extensively overt language of morality weaken the force of his arguments? Or breach his duty of candor to his client?

6. If moral dialogue is permissible, do you agree that dialogue that employs emotional tools of persuasion is also permissible? Isn't emotional argument irrational? If it is irrational, isn't it also manipulative?

7. If moral dialogue is permissible when a client might harm another person, is similar intervention permissible when a client might harm himself or herself? Would the factors laid out in this chapter to guide decisions to undertake moral dialogue also be useful guides to decisions to undertake dialogue meant to save the client from self-destructive choices? In thinking about this question, you should look back to our earlier discussions of counseling interventions with clients, in Chapters Two and Three.

8. If, as we've suggested, Mathiesson should have advised Arnholtz at the start of their relationship about the moral limits Mathiesson would adhere to, how should he have done this? What should he have said, so as to properly explain his position without (if possible) disrupting his relationship with his client?

9. Why didn't Mathiesson explore more deeply the issues Arnholtz raised about his wife's fitness to be the custodial parent? We explore some possible explanations in the chapter, but here we ask you to consider another: do you think he allowed his distaste for bare-knuckles custody litigation to diminish his attention to facts that might have made such litigation appropriate? If he did make such a mistake here, how could he—how could you—guard against such mistakes in the future?

---

1. We describe the counseling role of the engaged client-centered lawyer in detail in Chapter 3 ("Engaged Client–Centered Counseling About Client Choices").

2. Scott Altman, *Lurking in the Shadow*, 68 S. CAL. L. REV. 493, 503 (1995).

3. *Id*. at 501–02, 504.

4. *Id*. at 500 (54% of California family lawyers surveyed "responded that a client had suggested threatening [custody time] litigation to gain a favorable financial settlement in the last year. Nearly all of these lawyers (95%) tried to dissuade the client.") Altman's study does not tell us, however, whether these lawyers chose to do their dissuading by speaking to their clients in moral terms.

5. See *infra* text accompanying notes 18–21.

6. For one discussion, suggesting that relatively few large-firm lawyers encountered such moral problems, and that "professional training and experience" may "transform potentially troubling questions of values into matters of technique and strategy," see Robert L. Nelson, *Ideology, Practice, and Professional Autonomy: Social Values and Client Relationships in the Large Law Firm*, 37 STAN. L. REV. 503, 531–39 (1985).

7. See *infra* text accompanying notes 51–52.

8. A number of scholars have urged lawyers to undertake moral dialogue. *See, e.g.*, MONROE H. FREEDMAN & ABBE SMITH, UNDERSTANDING LAWYERS' ETHICS 53–55 (3d ed. 2004); DAVID LUBAN, LAWYERS AND JUSTICE: AN ETHICAL STUDY 160–74 (1988); Stephen Ellmann, *Lawyers and Clients*, 34 UCLA L. Rev. 717, 774–78 (1987); Charles Fried, *The Lawyer as Friend: The Moral Foundations of the Lawyer–Client Relation*, 85 YALE L.J. 1060, 1088 (1976); Peter Margulies, *"Who Are You to Tell Me That?" Attorney–Client Deliberation Regarding Nonlegal Issues and the Interests of Non-clients*, 68 N.C. L. REV. 213 (1990); Deborah L. Rhode, *Moral Counseling*, 75 FORDHAM L. REV. 1317 (2006). There appear, however, to have been few extended examinations of *how* such dialogues should be carried out. Thomas Shaffer and Robert F. Cochran, Jr., do address issues of technique thoughtfully and at length, in THOMAS L. SHAFFER & ROBERT F. COCHRAN, JR., LAWYERS, CLIENTS, AND MORAL RESPONSIBILITY 42–86 (2d ed. 2009). Other discussions of the skills issues, also thoughtful but relatively brief, include ROBERT M. BASTRESS & JOSEPH D. HARBAUGH, INTERVIEWING, COUNSELING, AND NEGOTIATING: SKILLS FOR EFFECTIVE REPRESENTATION 336–38 (1990) (reprinting excerpts from Robert M. Bastress, *Client-Centered Counseling and Moral Accountability of Lawyers*, 10 J. LEGAL PROF. 97 (1985); DAVID A. BINDER, PAUL BERGMAN, SUSAN C. PRICE, & PAUL R. TREMBLAY, LAWYERS AS COUNSELORS: A CLIENT-CENTERED APPROACH 391–93 (2d ed. 2004); ROBERT F. COCHRAN, JR., JOHN M.A. DIPIPPA, & MARTHA M. PETERS, THE COUNSELOR-AT-LAW: A COLLABORATIVE APPROACH TO CLIENT INTERVIEWING AND COUNSELING 185–90 (2d ed. 2006); STEFAN H. KRIEGER & RICHARD K. NEUMANN, JR., ESSENTIAL LAWYERING SKILLS: INTERVIEWING, COUNSELING, NEGOTIATION, AND PERSUASIVE FACT ANALYSIS 277–79 (3d ed. 2007); Stephen L. Pepper, *Lawyers' Ethics in the Gap Between Law and Justice*, 40 S. TEX. L. REV. 181, 202–04 (1999); *cf.* Robert D. Dinerstein, *Client-Centered Counseling: Reappraisal and Refinement*, 32 ARIZ. L. REV. 501, 561–65 (1990) (raising concerns about how non-domineering moral dialogues can be carried out).

9. *See* Altman, *supra* note 2, at 499–500.

10. *See* Robert H. Mnookin & Lewis Kornhauser, *Bargaining in the Shadow of the Law: The Case of Divorce*, 88 YALE L.J. 950, 963 (1979), *quoted in* Sally Burnett Sharp, *Fairness Standards and Separation Agreements: A Word of Caution on Contractual Freedom*, 132 U. PA. L. REV. 1399, 1437 (1984).

11. *See* In re Marriage of Lawrence, 642 P.2d 1043, 1049 (Mont. 1982) (for the court to "conclude that a separation is violative of public policy if one of the parties threatened a custody fight in order to gain in the property distribution . . . would not be based on any kind of a realistic understanding of preagreement negotiations").

12. Altman's data, from a survey of California family lawyers, suggest that both husbands and wives employ "pressure to trade custodial time for financial terms," though husbands, it seems, resort to it more often. *See* Altman, *supra* note 2, at 501–05.

13. *See* Katherine R. Kruse, *Fortress in the Sand: The Plural Values of Client–Centered Representation*, 12 CLIN. L. REV. 369, 436–37 (2006).

14. *See* Stephen L. Pepper, *Lawyers' Ethics in the Gap Between Law and Justice*, 40 S. TEX. L. REV. 181, 188–92 (1999).

15. There is, of course, peril in presuming too much commonality, a risk we examine in Chapter 2 ("Connection Across Difference and Similarity"); on the possibility that Mathiesson is in fact presuming too much here, see Kruse, *supra* note 13, at 436.

16. Fried, *supra* note 8, at 1088.

17. We have encountered similar tensions between lawyer and client before, in the encounter between a gay client and a lawyer whose church disapproves of homosexuality, discussed in Chapter 2.

18. MODEL CODE OF PROF'L RESPONSIBILITY EC 7–8 (1983) [hereinafter MODEL CODE].

19. MODEL RULES OF PROF'L CONDUCT Rule 2.1 (2009) [hereinafter MODEL RULES], provides:

> In representing a client, a lawyer shall exercise independent professional judgment and render candid advice. In rendering advice, a lawyer *may* refer not only to law but to other considerations such as moral, economic, social and political factors, that may be relevant to the client's situation.

(Emphasis added.) It is possible to read the comment to this Rule as declaring a duty to give moral advice in certain circumstances, notably when it observes that:

> Advice couched in narrow legal terms may be of little value to a client, especially where practical considerations, such as cost or effects on other people, are predominant. Purely technical legal advice, therefore, can sometimes be inadequate.

Id., cmt [2]. But the language of the Rule itself is permissive rather than mandatory.

20. RESTATEMENT OF THE LAW GOVERNING LAWYERS § 94(3) (2000) [hereinafter RESTATEMENT]:

> In counseling a client, a lawyer *may* address nonlegal aspects of a proposed course of conduct, including moral, reputational, economic, social, political, and business aspects.

(Emphasis added.) Under the Restatement such advice is required, if competent and diligent lawyers in similar circumstances would normally provide it. *See id.* cmt. h, citing *id.* § 52 ("The Standard of Care"). Hazard and Hodes view Model Rule 2.1 and Restatement § 94(3) as "more than merely permissive; both provisions should be read as active encouragement for lawyers to provide more broadly based and richer professional advice." GEOFFREY C. HAZARD, JR., & W. WILLIAM HODES, THE LAW OF LAWYERING at p. 23–6 (3d ed. Supp. 2002).

21. MODEL RULES, *supra* note 19, Rule 1.16(b)(4); MODEL CODE, *supra* note 18, DR 2–110(C)(1)(e); RESTATEMENT, *supra* note 20, § 32(3)(f).

22. For a similar set of factors, offered as guidelines for "overcoming the unequal power of the law office" in the context of moral dialogue, see SHAFFER & COCHRAN, *supra* note 8, at 54–57.

23. MODEL RULES, *supra* note 19, Rule 1.6(b)(1). For the history of the 2003 amendments, see STEPHEN GILLERS & ROY D. SIMON, REGULATION OF LAWYERS: STATUTES AND STANDARDS 2008 at 85–86. It is worth noting that if the conduct the client has in mind is not simply immoral but also criminal, the boundaries of legitimate counseling by the lawyer may be considerably broader than those analyzed here. This Chapter focuses on clients' choices among options that are legal, choices that competent clients are entitled to make. Competent clients are not entitled to choose to commit major crimes, and lawyers are not bound by the same duty to respect client competency in dissuading them.

24. Katherine R. Kruse, *Lawyers, Justice, and the Challenge of Moral Pluralism*, 90 MINN. L. REV. 389, 405 (2005).

25. *See* MODEL RULES, *supra* note 19, Rule 1.7(a)(2).

26. Whether a lawyer holding such views should inform the client of them at the start of the representation is a separate question, to which we return below. *See infra* text accompanying notes 38–39.

27. For the view that "moral conflict of interest" should be recognized as a form of conflict under existing ethics rules, and the observation that "the bar has been reluctant to fully embrace a moral conflict of interest standard," see Kruse, *supra* note 24, at 445 and *passim*.

28. We speak of "capacity" here in a broad sense, referring to the overall exercise of judgment by the client rather than to the possible impact of disabilities, cognitive or emotional, on the legal "capacity" of a client. As our discussion of atypical clients in Chapter 4 ("Interviewing and Counseling Atypical Clients") suggests, we view many clients with disabilities as having the legal capacity to make choices and direct their lawyers to implement those choices. At the same time, as we note in that Chapter, people with such disabilities can be especially susceptible to pressure and persuasion by others, including their lawyers. Certainly their attorneys need to take this susceptibility fully into account as they consider whether, and how, to engage in moral dialogue with them.

29. There may be times, however, when lawyers and clients who already share a religious background pray together in the lawyer's office; not all of us would seek shared understanding or encouragement this way, but the choices lawyers make on this score surely will vary in light of the role religion plays in each lawyer's life and culture. For sharply contrasting views on the proper role of religion in the law office, compare Thomas L. Shaffer, Jr., *The Practice of Law as Moral Discourse*, 55 NOTRE DAME LAW. 231 (1979), with Robert J. Condlin, *"What's Love Got to Do With It?"–"It's Not Like They're Your Friends for Christ's Sake": The Complicated Relationship Between Lawyer and Client*, 82 NEB. L. REV. 211 (2003).

30. More modestly, lawyers who may not fully share their clients' values may still be able to offer moral advice based explicitly on the client's values. The lawyer for a somewhat different Arnholtz might have said, "Given that you believe that seeking revenge is wrong, I wouldn't make that kind of threat in negotiations, because it won't actually help you—it'll just hurt her and that's really like seeking revenge." That advice may be less moral suasion than moral clarification, though a good deal of influence may be exerted in the process, or under the guise, of explanation.

31. We explore this issue in depth in Chapter 2.

32. John Leubsdorf and Stephen Pepper helped us understand these points.

33. A quite different threat to moral dialogue is the possibility that lawyers will consider them too risky to undertake, because of the risk of losing clients. We have already noted that some clients wield much more power over their lawyers than others do, and this reality means that some clients may be much better able to cut off their lawyers' moral entreaties than others are. Our focus in the text, however, is on those instances in which lawyers are prepared to undertake these dialogues.

34. A Model Rule comment on conflict of interest reminds us that "[t]he mere possibility of subsequent harm does not itself require disclosure and consent." MODEL RULES, *supra* note 19, Rule 1.7, cmt. [8].

35. See *supra* text accompanying notes 25–27.

36. Shaffer and Cochran define the issue similarly: "We have suggested that the lawyer as friend will (1) acknowledge, raise, and discuss moral issues with clients and (2) not impose the lawyer's morals on clients. We recognize that the challenge for lawyers will be to do both of these at the same time . . . ." SHAFFER & COCHRAN, *supra* note 8, at 65.

37. Homicide, of course, is not just a moral wrong but a criminal one as well. It is not easy to imagine situations of surpassing moral urgency that do not also involve illegal conduct. At the same time, it is not obvious that even in cases of potential homicide the lawyer ought to use deception or coercion. Some clients contemplating grave crimes remain open to sincere moral suasion. Others might pose such a danger to the lawyer herself that otherwise improper steps are justified.

38. The lawyer engaging in moral dialogue does not see that conversation as "optional," but it must be acknowledged that this conversation is not *mandatory* in quite the same sense as a discussion of the facts of the matter and the client's legal options. Without discussion of facts and legal choices, competent representation under the rules may simply be impossible; without discussion of morality, competent representation is probably still possible—just, in the lawyer's view, immoral. What is immoral may also be unacceptable, and the lawyer faced with an unacceptable task may seek to withdraw from the representation. But some lawyers may see the initiation of moral dialogue as necessary, while also believing that they can continue to represent a client who rejects their views or even refuses to join in the discussion.

39. There may be circumstances in which more than this "bookmarking" is called for, even early in the relationship. One of us has argued for "the necessity of identifying moral conflicts of interest at an early point in the representation, so as to avoid the harm that may come from identifying a conflict after a significant investment of time and expense." Kruse, *supra* note 24, at 454–55.

40. See *supra* text accompanying notes 24–27.

41. See *infra* text accompanying notes 54–56.

42. In the words of one clinical text, "Unless the client urges means or seeks ends that offend your values, the regard [you give to your client] should be unconditional and nonjudgmental." BASTRESS & HARBAUGH, *supra* note 8, at 130.

43. Or so Arnholtz's explicit comments indicate. As we've already seen, it is conceivable that Arnholtz was actually, perhaps not yet quite consciously, in the process of reassessing his views on who should have custody. *See supra* note 13 and accompanying text.

44. On the status of custody threats in legal ethics, see Altman, *supra* note 2, at 525–26.

45. See *infra* text accompanying note 57.

46. *See* Ellmann, *supra* note 8.

47. MODEL RULES, *supra* note 19, Rule 1.4, cmt. [7]. *See also* RESTATEMENT, *supra* note 20, § 20 cmt. c & d; § 24 cmt. c; & § 46 cmt. c, which together provide for a somewhat similar exception from disclosure.

48. Hazard and Hodes, who suggest that the "delayed transmission" comment "might be misunderstood and perhaps would have been better left unsaid," maintain that "[i]n particular, the Comment should not be interpreted to mean that a lawyer may withhold information simply because he fears the client will make an 'imprudent' decision *about the subject of the representation*, such as accepting an inadequate settlement offer." HAZARD & HODES, *supra* note 20, § 7.4 at pp. 7–8 to 7–9 (3d ed. Supp. 2003) (emphasis in the original). Mathieson's motive appears to be almost exactly what Hazard and Hodes would rule out. *See also* RONALD D. ROTUNDA & JOHN S. DZIENKOWSKI, PROFESSIONAL RESPONSIBILITY: A STUDENT'S GUIDE 140 (2008–09) (arguing that occasions for withholding information under Rule 1.4 are "rare" and saying that "[t]he lawyer should take reasonable efforts to find, rather promptly, a situation to make the disclosure under circumstances that can minimize the harm"). But for an argument implying that a lawyer might rightly, and permanently, withhold information from her client about a particular course of action, if the lawyer concludes that use of that course of action would lead to a breach of the purpose of the applicable law, see WILLIAM H. SIMON, THE PRACTICE OF JUSTICE: A THEORY OF LAWYERS' ETHICS 146–47 (1998).

49. We assume here that Mathiesson sincerely believes the other legal propositions he articulates, such as his statement that "the courts are pretty vigilant about" insuring that the custodial parent has enough money to support the children. (L15) If he is mistaken, of course, then he has failed (however inadvertently) to convey accurate information about the law to his client. Even if his other statements about the law were entirely accurate, moreover, in context they contributed to making his inaccurate assertion in L16 about what was needed in the bargaining offer seem more plausible, as a further look at this dialogue in Chapter 8 ("Talking to Clients About the Law") emphasizes.

What if Mathiesson sincerely believed everything he said about the law, but also recognized that some other family lawyers saw the law differently? (Family law is a contested area, and there might well be other lawyers, no less expert than Mathiesson, who might see this law as either less protective of mothers and children than he portrays it, or more hostile to the interests of fathers than he believes it is.) We do not believe that lawyers' duty to explain the law is a duty to explain all plausible views of the law, but as lawyers edit and summarize in order to provide clear and comprehensible advice they should be conscious of what they are *not* saying, and careful that their omissions are not disserving their clients. We discuss the challenges of talking to clients about the law in depth in Chapter 8.

50. Both spouses are capable of such maneuvers. See *supra* text accompanying note 3.

51. Krieger and Neumann endorse "appeal[ing] to the client's self-interest," and observe that, "In general, there is a limit to the number of times you can tell a client that the client is behaving immorally. With some clients, you will lose your credibility if you do it even once." KRIEGER & NEUMANN, *supra* note 8, at 278–79.

52. We have discussed the limits on lawyers' sharing their own lives with their clients in Chapter 2 ("Connection Across Difference and Similarity").

53. As we have already suggested, however, *see supra* text accompanying notes 29–31, even this level of persuasion will surely rest on some considerable overlap between what the client already believes and what the lawyer urges. Sharper transformations than that are the business of preachers or therapists rather than legal counselors.

54. *See* RESTATEMENT OF THE LAW OF CONTRACTS, SECOND, § 177 (undue influence) (1981). Comment (b) to this Section explains that "[t]he degree of persuasion that is unfair depends on a variety of circumstances. The ultimate question is whether the result was produced by means that seriously impaired the free and competent exercise of judgment."

55. Odorizzi v. Bloomfield School Dist., 246 Cal. App. 2d 123, 54 Cal. Rptr. 533 (1966) (cited in RESTATEMENT OF THE LAW OF CONTRACTS, SECOND, *supra* note 49, cmt. (b)).

56. 246 Cal. App. 2d at 133, 54 Cal. Rptr. at 541.

57. *See* ANTONIO DAMASIO, DESCARTES' ERROR: EMOTION, REASON, AND THE HUMAN BRAIN (1994). We return to the role of emotion in decisionmaking in Chapter 9 ("Fast Talking: Lawyering Expertise and Its Impact on Interviewing and Counseling").

58. On the significance of our "stock" of stories, characters, and theories to our actual understanding of much of what we experience in the world, see Gerald P. López, *Lay Lawyering*, 32 UCLA L. REV. 1, 5–9 (1984).

59. On the importance of storytelling, even implicit storytelling, to persuasion, see, e.g., Anthony G. Amsterdam, *Telling Stories and Stories About Them*, 1 CLIN. L. REV. 9 (1994); Anthony G. Amsterdam et al., *Stories Told and Untold: Lawyering Theory Analyses of the First Rodney King Assault Trial*, 12 CLIN. L. REV. 1 (2005). We look closely at the role of narrative in clients' communication with their lawyers in Chapter 5 ("Narrative Theory and Narrative Practice").

60. We agree with Steven J. Johansen, *This Is Not the Whole Truth: The Ethics of Telling Stories to Clients*, 38 ARIZ. ST. L.J. 961, 984–93 (2006), that there is a critical difference between such unacknowledged fictions and the incompleteness inherent in every story—and indeed in every argument.

61. *See* MODEL RULES, *supra* note 19, Rule 1.16(b)(4); MODEL CODE, *supra* note 18, DR 2–110(C)(1)(e). The central difference between the two sets of rules on this score is that the Model Code provision permits withdrawal on this basis only "in a matter not pending before a tribunal." *Id.* Both rules require withdrawing lawyers to take steps to protect their former clients' interests (MODEL RULES, *supra*, Rule 1.16(d); MODEL CODE, *supra*, DR 2–110(A)(2)), and both appear to recognize that a lawyer whom a court orders to continue on a case before it must continue (MODEL RULES, *supra*, Rule 1.16(c); MODEL CODE, *supra*, DR 2–110(A)(1)). Since Arnholtz's wife has filed for divorce, withdrawal based on moral disagreement would be impermissible in a Model Code jurisdiction, and would be permissible—but subject to potential override by the court hearing the case—in a Model Rules jurisdiction. (The vast majority of American state ethics codes are now based on the Model Rules, though often with important variations. *See* STEPHEN GILLERS & ROY D. SIMON, REGULATION OF LAWYERS—STATUTES AND STANDARDS 3 (2008).) The Restatement similarly permits withdrawal in response to "action that the lawyer considers repugnant or imprudent," again with the requirement that the lawyer take steps to protect the former client's interests. Under the Restatement, withdrawal is barred if a tribunal so orders or "if the harm that withdrawal would cause significantly exceeds the harm to the lawyer or others in not withdrawing." *See* RESTATEMENT, *supra* note 20, §§ 32(3)(e), (4) & (5), & § 33.

62. MODEL RULES, *supra* note 19, Rule 1.4(b) provides: "A lawyer shall explain a matter to the extent reasonably necessary to permit the client to make informed decisions regarding the representation." Hazard and Hodes maintain that "it would be improper to withdraw on this ground [repugnancy] without first explaining the lawyer's proposed course of action, so that the client would have a chance to reconsider, thus influencing the future course of the representation." HAZARD & HODES, *supra* note 20, § 20.9 at p. 20–21. The Restatement similarly endorses such "[c]onsultation with a client before withdrawal," and in fact a Restatement comment declares that "[t]he lawyer *must* consult with the client about the instruction, if withdrawal can be accomplished only with material adverse effect on the client ... and if it reasonably appears that reconsideration or other action by the client could, within a reasonable time, remove the basis for the withdrawal." RESTATEMENT, *supra* note 20, § 32 cmt. n.

63. In a related context, Steven Zeidman argues that criminal defense lawyers should not only express their views on whether their clients should plead guilty but should seek to persuade the clients of those views. But he also maintains that "because the accused makes the final decision, the attorney must strive to leave room for disagreement and must make sure that the client is aware that she will represent him zealously in any event." Steven Zeidman, *To Plead Or Not to Plead: Effective Assistance and Client–Centered Counseling*, 39 B.C. L. REV. 841, 897 (1998). But Zeidman is focusing on advice to clients about their own self-interest, and in the specially fraught context of criminal defense; for the reasons set out in the text, we think that the threat of withdrawal can be a legitimate element at least of some moral dialogues.

64. We do not question, of course, that each lawyer who withdraws must take reasonable steps to protect the client's interests. Even under the Restatement, however, a lawyer may withdraw because of the repugnance of the client's objectives despite the fact that doing so causes the client some measure of harm; withdrawal is barred "if the harm that withdrawal would cause *significantly exceeds* the harm to the lawyer or others in not withdrawing." RESTATEMENT, *supra* note 20, § 32(4) (emphasis added); *see* Hazard & Hodes, *supra* note 20, § 20.9 at p. 20–22. The "last lawyer in town" may have a duty to take, or keep, a morally repellent case, but other lawyers generally have more leeway.

65. See *supra* text following note 38.

66. This is not the first time, however, that we have found some space for coercion in the midst of engagement. As we argued in Chapter 6 ("Truth and Consequences"), there may be scope—limited scope—for such steps when a lawyer must press her client to tell her the truth about his case.

CHAPTER 8

TALKING TO CLIENTS ABOUT THE LAW

■ ■ ■

One of the most important things you will do as a lawyer is talk to your clients about the law: what the law allows, what it prohibits, and what it demands. Other chapters in this book offer strategies for engaged client-centered representation that ensure lawyers understand their clients' goals, values and objectives fully, such as establishing connection across difference and similarity, engaging with clients in assessing the clients' choices, and paying attention to the way clients narrate the stories of their lives and events. In this chapter, we turn to a different—yet equally important—question of how lawyers can engage clients in decision-making by making the law more accessible to their clients. Lawyers can—and often do—simply declare to their client a "bottom line" judgment about what the law allows, requires or prohibits. In this chapter, we explore how lawyers can engage more deeply in the process of legal explanation by giving clients insight into the law and the larger legal structures and systems that govern their lives and affairs. By doing so, lawyers can more effectively involve their clients in the process of developing the case theories the lawyers will use in advocacy. And, lawyers' more complete and contextualized explanations of the law can help put clients in the position to assess the legitimacy of the law and make informed decisions about the extent to which they value compliance with the structures of legal regulation that govern their affairs.

Discussions about the law are a place in legal counseling at which clients are particularly dependent on lawyers' judgments. After all, clients retain lawyers precisely because lawyers have the legal training and expertise that clients lack. Because of the asymmetry of knowledge and expertise, the way lawyers choose to explain the law implicates ethical issues of communication and allocation of decision making between lawyers and clients. Moreover, unlike judges' interpretive choices, which are public and reviewable, lawyers' interpretations of the law for their clients are carried out within the privacy and confidentiality of the lawyer-client relationship. Yet these interpretations come to define the reach of the law in the many cases that never come before a judge for decision. Because lawyers stand between the law and those whom the law governs, lawyer-client discussion about the law raise deeper jurisprudential questions about the role of lawyers in shaping the meaning and legitimacy of law.

To illustrate the ethical and jurisprudential dimensions of law talk, consider the following portion of an interview between client Devon Jeffries and lawyer Sandra Rossmueller. Jeffries is a prison inmate serving a 15–year sentence for delivery of a controlled substance. Rossmueller is a lawyer who works for the Legal Advocacy Project, a non-profit organization that provides legal services in a number of areas not covered by legal services corporation funding. She is in charge of a project providing family law assistance to state prison inmates. Because she works exclusively with prison inmates, she has gained a certain expertise in the way standard family law questions play out in the special circumstances of incarcerated parents.

L1:   Good afternoon, Mr. Jeffries, I'm Sandra Rossmueller. I'm here to talk to you about the request for legal assistance that you submitted to the Legal Advocacy Project. It looks like you have some concerns about your child support, and I am here to see whether there is anything we can do to help you.

C1:   I keep getting these notices saying how much child support money I owe. I didn't know anything about it until about six months ago. I know I can't pay it. Look at this! It says I owe $9,000. And every month I get a new notice. And the amount keeps going up.

L2:   It's frustrating to see that balance keep going up when you are stuck in here with no way to do anything about it.

C2:   Yeah. What are they thinking? I don't have this kind of money. I'm never going to have this kind of money. What do they want me to do? Rob a bank when I get out?

L3:   Let me see your statement for a minute. [Jeffries hands the statement to Rossmueller, who looks it over]. Okay, it says you owe $172.00 per month. That's a really common amount to owe in child support. Let me explain why. The law says that your child deserves to have a certain percentage of your income to support him ... or her. Do you have a son or a daughter?

C3:   I have a daughter. She's seven ... no, eight years old now. Her name is Natasha. I was in the hospital when she was born and her mother Tonya and me were together then.

L4:   OK, so the law says that Natasha deserves to have 17% of whatever money you make. That's because whoever she lives with ... Tonya?

C4:   Yeah. She lives with Tonya. We were living together for a couple of years after Natasha was born. But then Tonya got a new boyfriend. And then I got busted for dealing cocaine. And now, here I am in prison. Not earning any money.

L5:   Well, no matter what happens to you, Tonya is still spending money all the time for Natasha. Money for food. Money for rent. Money for clothes. All those things. Child support is your way to contribute to those expenses based on what you earn.

C5:   And I don't have a problem with that. Really. I always help Tonya out with Natasha. Always. Anytime she asked for this or for that, I have always gotten it for her.

L6:   That's great. And that's important. I am going to want to hear more about that in a minute. But first I want to explain where this $172.00 a month came from. $172.00 a month is 17% of minimum wage. I'm guessing that you weren't in court when this child support was ordered?

C6:   No, I wasn't in court for anything like that.

L7:   Well, usually for one child they will set child support at 17% of your monthly wages. But if they don't know how much money you make, they set it at 17% of minimum wage, because they assume that you could get a job that earns at least minimum wage.

C7:   How can they do that without even letting me know? I mean, they didn't even let me know! I could have been paying $172.00 a month when I was out. But how am I supposed to pay it now that I'm locked up?

L8:   I can't tell you everything that happened in your case without looking at your court file. For example, I can't tell you whether they went through the right steps to give you official notice of the court hearing when your child support was set. And if they didn't, we might have grounds to challenge the support order. But I can tell some things just by looking at your statement here. See this part? This is the date of the order. It looks like the child support order was entered about five years ago. And that would be . . .

C8:   . . . right around the time Tonya left me and hooked up with her new boyfriend.

L9:   Right. And I can also tell you something else that happened around that time.

C9:   What?

L10:   Tonya applied for public assistance. When a mother goes on public assistance, one of the things they do is refer the case to the child support enforcement agency. The child support enforcement agency tries to figure out who the father is and go into court to get a child support order. And if you signed an acknowledgment of paternity when you were in the hospital when Natasha was born . . .

C10:   I did. I know I did. I never had any issue with that. I knew I was Natasha's father. She even looks like me. You should see her. She's really something.

L11:   When was the last time you got to see your daughter?

C11:   She was up here last month. Tonya let her come up here with my Mama. Tonya's pretty tight with my Mama. And also with my Auntie. They all live right around each other.

L12:   You're lucky. Not too many guys in prison get to see their kids.

C12:   I know.

L13:   And it's really helpful for your child support situation that you and Tonya are on good terms with each other. I am going to want to hear more about your relationship with Tonya in a minute. But first I want to explain just a bit more about your child support award of $172.00 a month.

C13:   It just keeps going up and up.

L14:   I know it does. A motion to modify your child support order might be able to keep the $172.00 a month from going up and up. That is, if the court is willing to grant the motion.

C14:   Why wouldn't the court grant it? I'm not making minimum wage here in prison. I'm only making $35.00 a month. That's from working in the cafeteria. It might go up if I can get a different job. But the most would be about $60.00 a month. That's the top of the pay scale in here.

L15:   You're right that your actual income is way too low for you to be owing $172.00 a month. But sometimes the law allows child support to be based on what you *could be* earning instead of what you are *actually* earning. It's called imputed income. For example, suppose there's a doctor who makes good money— let's say $300,000 a year. The law says that he is going to owe 17% of $300,000.

C15:   Because that's what he makes.

L16:   Right, because that's his actual income. But suppose that now he's divorced. And he decides that he wants to enjoy his freedom. And he wants to fulfill the dream he always had of being a street artist. And he quits his job as a doctor and becomes a starving artist and spends his days selling his paintings on the sidewalk. And he's happy. But he's making next to nothing. The law says that he still owes his daughter 17% of $300,000. Why?

C16:   Because he's an idiot?

L17:   [Laughing] Well, sort of. It's because he still has the *potential* to earn $300,000 a year and he is making a *choice* not to make that much money. The idea behind the imputed income standard is that the choices you make about whether to have a job or what kind of job to have don't just affect you. They also affect your children. Even when you aren't living with your children, you still need to take their needs into account when you make important life choices. The imputed income standard is the reason they were able to set your child support at 17% of minimum wage. Because they figure everyone has the potential at least to get a minimum wage job, and that if you have kids you should be making the choice to earn what you can to support them.

C17:   But they know I'm in prison now. They're sending me these notices here in prison. They've got to know that I can't earn minimum wage anymore.

L18:   That's true. But the child support agency can't just change your child support order without going to a judge. And the judge has to look at why you are making less money than minimum wage. If the judge decides that your choice to earn less money is "voluntary and unreasonable," the judge may continue the child support order as it is.

C18:   That's just it, though. I didn't choose to go to prison. Nobody *chooses* to go to prison. The judge chooses to *send* you to prison. But you don't choose to *go* to prison.

L19:   I know—believe me, *I* know that. But some judges will look at the situation of someone in prison and say that you made the choice to commit a crime. And when you choose to commit a crime, you choose to do the time. I'm not saying it's right. I'm just saying that's the way some judges look at being in prison—as a voluntary choice.

C19:   So what can I do about it?

L20:   Well, think about it for a minute. There's another difference between you and the starving artist doctor. The doctor has the ability to give up the whole artist thing and go back to being a doctor. You don't have that ability. It's not like you can walk out of the front door of this prison and get a job at Mc-Donald's. When we impute income to the doctor, it's supposed to give him an incentive to start earning money at his highest earning potential again. You can't do anything about your income—at least not while you are locked up. We can make the argument that the imputed income standard doesn't really serve its purpose in your case.

C20:   What are my chances of winning that argument?

L21:   I hate to say this, but it depends. In this state, there's no bright line rule about whether prison counts as a change in circumstances. The judge has to decide the question on a case-by-case basis, taking into account the "totality of the circumstances." In some counties, courts almost always deny child support motions for prison inmates and in some counties the courts almost always grant them. The county you're from is what I would call "hit or miss." It's a big county with eight different family court judges, and our success on contested motions to modify child support depends a lot on the attitude of the judge in your case.

C21:   What about the $9,000 debt? Can I get at least get that taken off? Because I never even knew about this child support until now.

L22:   Like I said before, if they didn't give you proper notice, you may have an argument. But the requirements for proper notice are pretty low. And if they did give you proper notice—by publishing notice in a newspaper, for example—it can be very difficult. There's a federal law that says the court doesn't have the power to wipe out—to expunge—child support debt. Child support arrearages can only be expunged if the person you owe the money to is willing to forgive the debt.

C22:   I think Tonya would be willing to forgive me that. She knows I did what I could to help her when I was still out.

L23:   That's why I said before that it was important that you and Tonya are on good terms. And that's why it's important that you have been supporting her in other ways when she needed help with Natasha. But I can tell from looking at the statement that Tonya is not the only one you owe money to. Remember I said that Tonya was on public assistance when this order was entered? I can tell that because this line here shows that you owe about $4000.00 to the state for a couple of years. For the period of time she was on public assistance, you owe child support to the state and not to her.

C23:   Why? If she's on public assistance, isn't the state supposed to support her and Natasha?

L24:   Well, yes. You're exactly right. The state is supposed to be supporting Natasha when Tonya goes on public assistance. But child support debt is about paying back the person who supported your child during the time when you weren't paying support. When the state supports a parent with public assistance, the other parent owes child support to the state for that period of time.

C24:   Look, I don't mind owing Tonya and paying Tonya for the stuff that she's done for Natasha—and for what she's still doing every day for my daughter. But how am I going to have money to help Tonya if the state is coming after me to pay back their public assistance money? How is that fair?

L25:   It's not fair, really. Public assistance is barely enough to live on. Personally, I don't think it's really about helping families. It's about creating incentives to get people off public assistance as quickly as possible. Making fathers reimburse the state for public assistance by paying child support is part of that incentive. It's supposed to "send a message" to fathers that the state expects them to take primary responsibility for supporting their children. Personally, I don't agree with it. I think it's just awful public policy. It's based on punitive assumptions that parents in poverty are "bad dads." It's based on narrow ideas about what it means to be a "good dad." And public policy that's based on those assumptions just ends up placing additional burdens on families already struggling to raise their children in poverty.

C25:   [silence] Uh-huh.

L26:   Sorry, I get sort of worked up when I think about it. It makes me angry.

C26:   But how can you help *me*?

L27:   Depending on how things work out, there may be three ways for me to help you. I may be able to help you by making an argument in court that your child support order should be modified—that it is unfair to impute minimum wage income to you when you are incarcerated by the state and precluded from getting a minimum wage job. I may be able to convince Tonya to forgive her portion of your $9,000 child support debt. And I may be able to convince the child support enforcement agency attorneys to agree to modify your order of support and forgive the state's portion of your arrearage.

C27:   What do you need from me?

L28:   I want to be able to explain to the child support attorney why all the incentives that the law is supposed to create backfire in your case. To do that, I want to be able to show that you have been a good father to Natasha and helped out when you could. I want to be able to show that you and your family are strongly connected to your daughter and that you will be motivated to do everything you can to help her when you are released from prison. I want to show that when you get out, this debt is going to make it harder for you to get back on your feet and support your daughter in the long run.

C28:   Sounds good to me.

L29:   It does sound good. But it may not be easy. The biggest hurdle in your case is that—on paper—your lack of payment history before going to prison is going to look bad. It makes it look like you fit the stereotype of a "bad dad" who hasn't provided any care or taken any financial responsibility for his child. I want to be able to counteract that stereotype by showing all the ways that you *have* supported Natasha and Tonya—financial and otherwise—since Natasha was born. So, now that I've explained the law, I want to give you a chance to talk. I want to hear everything you remember about your relationship with Natasha before going to prison, starting with when you first learned that Tonya was pregnant. Can you tell me about that?

As you can see, the discussion of the law in this lawyer-client dialogue is really just an opening scene that sets the stage for the "problems and concerns" stage of an initial interview, in which Attorney Rossmueller will learn more about her client's story. We will leave the lawyer-client conversation at this point to examine in more detail the choices Attorney Rossmueller has made ib discussing the law with her client.

Does Rossmueller dive into the law too quickly?

Before turning to the ethical and jurisprudential dimentions of "law talk" itself, we will examine Rossmueller's choice to lay the legal framework before hearing her client's story more fully. As we said in Chapter 2 ("Connection Across Similarity and Difference"), it is crucially important for lawyers to spend time in an initial interview really listening to their clients—including allowing their clients to describe their situations as they see them—trying not to assume too much about the facts. Typically, it is only after asking open-ended questions designed to elicit the client's full narrative that the lawyer would begin to ask more targeted "fact development" questions to fill in gaps or pursue more information that is important to potential legal claims, legal defenses or legal constraints on clients' desired projects. Rossmueller's discussion of Jeffries' child support issues takes the steps in almost the opposite order. She begins by defining the problem for him, saying, "It looks like you have some concerns about your child support." (L1). She quickly moves to an analysis of the facts she can deduce about his case from the child support statement he has received and law defining the "imputed income" standard, eliciting closely targeted information about his relationship with his child, the child's mother, and his history of support for his child. It is only at the end of this discussion that attorney Rossmueller turns to the kind of open-ended questions that characterize the "problems and concerns" stage of interviewing that we discussed in Chapter 2.

Does Attorney Rossmueller's choice to dive into the specific legal issues regarding Jeffries' child support order violate basic tenets of an engaged client-centered interview by exercising too much influence and control over the story he tells her? As we reiterate throughout this book, there is no one "right" way to carry out an engaged client-centered relationship (although there may be some wrong ways to do it), and a lot depends on the context. Part of the context in this dialogue is that Rossmueller is an expert on prisoner child support representation, and many of her choices in this part of the dialogue reflect her expertise. As we discuss in more detail in Chapter 9 ("Fast Talking: Lawyering Expertise and its Impact on Interviewing and Counseling"), experts are able to organize and classify information as they hear it. This helps them focus in efficiently—almost intuitively—on the strongest arguments and most relevant information. The way Rossmueller maneuvers through Jeffries' legal options demonstrates her expertise. For example, rather than laying out all the possible options and consequences for him, she goes right to an assessment of three ways she thinks she can help him (L27); the best arguments in his favor based what he has told her so far and what she has deduced from the child support statement (L28); and the biggest obstacles to success (L29). In addition to drawing on her expertise, Rossmueller is conveying it to Jeffries, perhaps helping to build his confidence and trust in her. Her ability to seemingly divine information about Jeffries' life circumstances from the child support statement (L8, L10), and her demonstration of broad knowledge about how prisoner child support modifications are treated differently in different counties (L21), may help build connection with a pragmatist like Jeffries, who wants to know—as a bottom line—"But how can you help *me*?" (C26).

However, as we note in Chapter 9, the downside to expert listening is the tendency to miss information that falls outside the expert's schema for organizing information. A lawyer's tunnel vision on the "legally relevant" facts can cause the lawyer to "issue spot" the client rather than engage in what we have called in Chapter 2 "real listening," with the goal of understanding how the client's legal issues fit within the context of the client's unique values, priorities, goals and relationships. Rossmueller is clearly steering the interview, leaving little space for Jeffries's own perspective on his situation to emerge. In making the assumption that Jeffries is primarily concerned about his child support debt, Rossmueller has relied on a written request for legal assistance that Jeffries has mailed her from the prison. It may well be that he has other concerns—perhaps more pressing but also more personal—that he did not feel comfortable putting in writing and sending through a prison mail system. Although Rossmueller eventually gets to a point in the interview—at the end of this excerpt—where she is ready to sit back and listen to Jeffries' narrative of the history of his relationship with his daughter, she has already given shape to his story within the legal framework of child support and may have missed an entirely different story that Jeffries wants to tell. Even as an expert interviewer—and perhaps especially because she in an expert interviewer—Rossmueller would have done well to allow Jeffries a less constrained opportunity to tell his own story much earlier in the interview.

However, there are points within even this lawyer-directed portion of the initial interview at which Rossmueller signals that she is "really listening" to Devon Jeffries—not simply as a potential legal case—but as a person. When he responds to her initial query about his child support concerns with visible agitation, saying, "Look at this! It says I owe $9,000. And every month I get a new notice. And the amount keeps going up" (C1), Rossmueller counters with an "active listening" response, reflecting the emotions under the surface of his agitation, saying: "It's frustrating to see that balance keep going up when you are stuck in here with no way to do anything about it." (L2). Rossmueller also signals interest in Jeffries' own, unique story. In the midst of interpreting his child support statement, she asks whether he has a son or a daughter (L3)—a legally irrelevant fact, but one which helps her picture the human and interpersonal aspects within which his legal problem has arisen. She consistently refers to his daughter, Natasha, and Natasha's mother, Tonya, by name (e.g. L4, L5, L10). And, at a couple of points in the conversation, she tells Jeffries that what he is saying is important and that she will want to hear more about it "in a minute" (L6, L13). Of course, it is more than a minute before she reaches the end of this portion of the dialogue and begins to make good on the promise of hearing more. But by flagging these areas for further discussion, she lets Jeffries know that she is not merely brushing aside the details of his life, but simply deferring a fuller discussion until they have talked a bit more about the legal framework within which they will need to operate.

A. ETHICAL DIMENSIONS OF LAW TALK

The ethical dimensions of law talk arise from the lawyer's ethical responsibilities of reasonable communication and the asymmetry of lawyers' and clients' access to information about the law. As with many issues addressed in this book, the lawyer's choices about how to talk to clients about the law implicate deeper issues of the appropriate allocation of decision-making authority in representation. Accordingly, we explore not only how a lawyer's choices can pass minimal ethical standards, but how a lawyer can make choices that are consistent with and advance the principles of engaged client-centered representation. As we discuss in Chapter 3

("Engaged Client–Centered Counseling About Client Choices"), engaged client-centered representation rejects a lawyer-centered model of representation and emphasizes that clients should make the ultimate decisions in legal representation based on the clients' own goals, values and priorities; but also recognizes that questioning, probing, and sharing the lawyer's personal perspective may be an important part of the process of informed client decision-making.

Lawyers fulfill their ethical responsibilities and stay true to the principles of engaged client-centered representation by: (1) communicating clearly about what the law prohibits, allows and requires so that clients can make informed decisions about the representation; (2) refraining from encouraging clients to engage in criminal or fraudulent behavior, and (3) being vigilant about not hiding behind the law and their own legal expertise to avoid uncomfortable areas of disagreement with the client or to manipulate their clients for self-interested gain at their clients' expense.

1. EXPLAINING THE LAW

The most basic duty of communication is to translate the complexity of the lawyer's expert knowledge and understanding of the law into terms that make the law accessible to the client and assist the client's process of decision making. Lawyers owe their clients a duty to "explain a matter to the extent reasonably necessary to permit the client to make informed decisions regarding the representation."[1] This duty requires lawyers to translate legal concepts in ways that are simple enough to be understood by someone without legal training, while at the same time thorough and precise enough to be useful in making informed decisions regarding the legal representation.

Lawyers who are unable to strike the balance between legal technicality and simplicity may find themselves at one end of a scale or another. Lawyers who talk about the law in terms that are too technical for their clients to comprehend may lose their clients in a flurry of "legalese" that confounds rather than assists the client's decision making. On the other hand, lawyers who fall back on simplistic declarations of what the law requires or prohibits pre-empt meaningful client involvement in decisions about how the law might be shaped to fit the client's case.

Attorney Rossmueller uses several techniques to strike a balance between legal technicality and accessibility. For example, in explaining the law to her client, she several times refers to legal standards, such as a 17% child support guideline (L4; L6); the "imputed income standard" (L15); a "totality of the circumstances" test (L21); and a "federal law" that prohibits a court from expunging child support arrearages (L22). These legal standards come from diverse sources: state statutes, administrative rules, state case law, and federal regulation. Yet Rossmueller does not describe the sources of child support law in detail. She does not cite statutes, codes or cases by name, nor does she attempt to explain how the various sources of law interact to create the standards to which she refers.

Rather, she communicates the "bottom line" standard that emerges from a much more complex interaction of state, federal, statutory, administrative and case law.

Notice also that when she uses technical legal terms, attorney Rossmueller makes an effort to define the legal terminology for her client in more common language. At one point she provides a definition of "imputed income" for her client, saying, "Sometimes the law allows child support to be based on what you *could be* making instead of what you are *actually* making. It's called imputed income." (L15). Other times she doesn't define the legal term explicitly, but intersperses common phrases that help her client understand the meaning of the legal terms. For example, she uses the legal term "arrearage" interchangeably with the more common term "debt" saying, "Child support arrearages can only be changed if the person you owe the money to is willing to forgive the debt." (L22). She introduces the legal term "expunge" by juxtaposing it with the more common phrase "wipe out," saying "the court doesn't have the power to wipe out—to expunge—child support debt" (L22).

Remembering to define legal terminology in common terms is not easy. Lawyers are often so deeply immersed into legal culture that they forget their vocabulary itself can be inaccessible to non-lawyers. Clients may not always feel comfortable interrupting to ask questions or may not want to admit that they don't understand what a lawyer is saying. Lawyers need to be able to monitor themselves quite closely to include their client in the world of law on terms the client understands. This self-monitoring includes developing the ability to step outside yourself and hear what you are saying from your clients' point of view. It can also be accomplished by paying attention to your client's facial expressions and body language to see when the client is following what you are saying and when the client is getting lost. For example, one might question whether attorney Rossmueller has gone far enough in explaining the legal technical terms she uses. She seems to assume that her client is following the way she has implicitly defined some of the more technical terms like "expunge" or "arrearage" without more explanation. But, she never checks in with her client to make sure he understands what she is saying. And, she allows other legal terminology like "official notice" (L8); "bright-line rule," "totality of the circumstances," and "contested motions" (L21); and even "precluded" (L27) to slip into her conversation without further explanation.

Of course, a lawyer could also choose not to use technical legal terminology at all. Why not explain the client's situation entirely in non-legal terms like "debt" and "wipe out" and leave references to "arrearages" and "expungement" entirely out of the conversation? By mixing the technical legal terminology with more common phrases, attorney Rossmueller is educating her client about the vocabulary that will be used by child support enforcement attorneys and judges in the client's case. This education helps prepare him to understand and participate more fully in the representation. Devon Jeffries may be present for negotiation discussions or legal proceedings in which everyone else is using those terms. Rossmueller's introduction and explanation of the technical legal terms now will help him better understand what is going on in his case later, at times when it is more difficult for her to stop and explain them. Educating a client about legal terminology is a way of helping to include the client in the representation.

Perhaps the most interesting technique that attorney Rossmueller uses in explaining the law to her client is her invocation of a paradigm case or "stock story" to illustrate the imputed income standard. As Professor Gerald Lopez has explained, stock stories are paradigmatic stories that "capture various recurring forms of human interaction" with narratives that "embody our deepest human, social and political values."[2] When explaining the "imputed income" standard, Rossmueller tells a story about a fictional "stock character"—the "starving artist doctor"— who voluntarily chooses to abandon his medical career in favor of a free-spirited life as a street artist (L15–L17). Rossmueller uses this technique to help explain the assumptions that underlie the imputed income standard that "even when you aren't living with your children, you still need to take their needs into account when you make important life choices." (L17).

Later in the dialogue, Rossmueller uses the stock story of the starving artist doctor to explore legal arguments for why the court should not impute minimum wage income to Jeffries while he is in prison. She says, "When we impute income to him [the starving artist doctor], his child support debt is supposed to give him an incentive to go back to being a doctor. It's not like you can walk out of the front door of this prison and get a minimum wage job working at McDonald's" (L20). Devon Jeffries becomes engaged in comparing and contrasting his situation to the doctor in the stock story, disagreeing that he has made a choice to reduce his income, saying "nobody *chooses* to go to prison. The judge chooses to *send* you to prison. But you don't choose to *go* to prison" (C18). Rossmueller aligns herself with Jeffries in this view, though points out that not all judges will agree, saying "I know—believe me, *I* know ... I'm not saying it's right. I'm just saying that's the way some judges look at being in prison—as a voluntary choice" (L19).

Rosmueller's use of a "stock story" is accessible and engaging for many of the reasons that storytelling is a compelling form of legal advocacy. The story of the "starving artist doctor" captures the emotional core of the duty of support by putting concrete details onto the vague image of the "bad dad." The doctor in the story is portrayed as irresponsible and selfish, a man who puts his self-actualization over the needs of his children. And the imputed income law is portrayed as intervening appropriately into the doctor's life by creating an incentive for him to right the wrong created by his irresponsible and selfish choice. In short, the "stock story" illustrates the best and most just application of the imputed income standard. As such, it provides a framework against which Jeffries can tell his story and place himself in close or distant relationship from the quintessential "bad dad" that the law imagines.

2. ASSISTING CLIENT FRAUD

One of the most widely-discussed ethical issues concerning how lawyers talk to their clients about the law is the concern that lawyers will give their clients too much information. The fear—often illustrated by discussion of "the Lecture" in *Anatomy of a Murder*—is that clients will use knowledge of the law to fabricate facts that fit the best legal argument.[3] In the infamous exchange in *Anatomy of a Murder*, the client's criminal defense lawyer gives the client a laundry list of possible murder defenses, strongly suggesting to the client that the only way for the client to get off would be to mount an insanity defense. At the lawyer's prompting, the client ventures the suggestion that when he attacked the man who raped his wife, "maybe I was insane."

As we pointed out in Chapter 6 ("Truth and Consequences"), the lawyer in the *Anatomy of a Murder* scenario is strategically manipulating the story he hears from the client and subtly eliciting the client's cooperation in fabricating facts to fit a defense that the lawyer believes not to be true. As we said in Chapter 6, we believe this kind of interviewing crosses ethical boundaries. We also pointed out that one way to avoid that problem is by waiting until after the client has told the client's story in the client's own words before introducing information about the law that would lend legal significance to certain facts and "avoid marking those facts in advance as what the law seeks."

In her dialogue with Devon Jeffries, Attorney Rossmueller does just the opposite. Rather than withholding information about the law, she explains quite a few legal concepts up front. We end the dialogue just as Rossmueller is beginning the broader fact-gathering portion of the interview, in which she asks Jeffries to tell her the story of his relationship with his daughter Natasha and Natasha's mother, Tonya. (L29). Just prior to inviting Jeffries to tell her "everything you remember about your relationship with Natasha before going to prison, starting with when you first learned that Tonya was pregnant," Rossmueller lays out quite explicitly the legal strategy—or case theory—that she envisions pursuing in his case. She tells him that she wants to be able to counteract the assumption that he is a "bad dad" by "showing all the ways" that he has supported Natasha and Tonya since Natasha was born. (L28).

Does Attorney Rossmueller's explanation of the legal strategy she hopes to pursue in Jeffries's case run afoul of a lawyer's ethical responsibilities? We think that even this explicit discussion of what facts will be most favorable to her legal theory does not cross the line into assisting client fraud. However, it is worth noting how her conversation about the law is distinguishable from the lawyer in *Anatomy of a Murder*.

First, Attorney Rossmueller is seeking further details to elaborate the story that her client has already told her in fragments. She already knows that Devon Jeffries lived with his daughter's mother Tonya for a couple of years after Natasha was born. (C4). She also knows that his mother brings Natasha to visit him in prison, and from this fact has ascertained that he has maintained a relatively close relationship with Natasha compared to many prison inmates. (C11). Jeffries has also told Rossmueller that he always responded to Tonya's requests for help with expenses relating to Natasha's care and upbringing (C5), although he has been somewhat vague about the details of this support. It is on this foundation that Rossmueller has begun to build an initial case theory differentiating Jeffries from the "stereotype of a 'bad dad' who hasn't provided any care or taken any financial responsibility for his child." (L29).

Second, Jeffries's opportunity to fabricate information under the circumstances is limited. His memory of the support he provided Natasha in her early childhood may or may not be accurate. And the opportunity for him to exaggerate the extent of support her provided off the books is certainly present. However, the amount and frequency of support he remembers can be—and probably will be—either corroborated or contradicted by Tonya's memory of events. In such circumstances, there is little reason to withhold information about the law out of a fear that the client will use that information to manipulate the legal process.

Giving the client the outline of the case theory—the legal-factual story the lawyer wants to be able to tell in his case—can help the client participate more fully in the legal representation by encouraging him to elaborate the details that will bring his story to life and make his lawyer a more effective advocate.[4] As we discuss more fully in Chapter 5 ("Narrative Theory and Narrative Practices"), stories are rarely told the same way twice and almost always include a consciousness of audience that shapes the way the stories are told. There is no such thing as a pristine version of anyone's story unaffected by his reasons for telling it or his assumptions about what his audience wants to hear. The law defines the framework into which the client's story ultimately will be translated. If the lawyer "hides the ball" by not explaining the law until she assumes that the client has told his story "fully," the version of the story the client tells might miss important details that will bring his story to life and make his lawyer a more effective advocate within that legal framework.

3. HIDING BEHIND THE LAW

One of the most important functions of professional ethics is to provide a check on the self-interested behavior of the professional. And, discussions about the law are a place at which the lawyer's self-interest is at a particularly high risk of intruding into the lawyer-client relationship. Because of the asymmetry of knowledge and expertise between lawyers and clients, lawyers can use the law as a screen behind which to hide other kinds of interests, such as the lawyer's financial stake in the representation or the lawyer's interest in maintaining a reputation within the legal community. In a separate but somewhat related vein, it may be easier for the lawyer to use the law as an excuse not to take a particular course of action rather than confront a client about disagreements with the client over the course of action to pursue in the client's case. We discuss each of these ways of "hiding" behind the law.

The word "hide" sounds like it involves a deliberate attempt to mask some other concern—whether it be a financial, reputational, political or moral concern—behind a cloud of legal reasons. Commentary to the ABA Model Rules of Professional Conduct makes it clear that it is unethical for a lawyer to deliberately withhold or distort information about the law to serve the lawyer's own self-interest or convenience, or the interest or convenience of others.[5]

With regard to the lawyer's financial or reputational interests, it is fair to say that lawyers always have a self-interested stake in the legal representation based on how they are compensated for their services. However the lawyer gets paid—by the billable hour, contingent on the outcome, or on a flat fee or contract—the lawyer will have a financial interest in the how the representation proceeds. Hourly fees give the lawyer an interest in spending a lot of time on a case, especially if the client is a "deep pocket" with virtually unlimited resources to sink into legal representation. Consequently, a lawyer billing by the hour may have a financial interest in making an extravagant investment of time or resources in a task that produces only marginally better results for the client, and sophisticated corporate clients have increasingly relied on in-house counsel or independent auditors to monitor the reasonableness of their legal fees. But hourly fees are not alone. Contingent fees give lawyers an interest in maximizing outcomes with as little investment of time as possible, and are often subject to special ethical protection.[6] Flat fees or contracts give lawyers an interest in resolving the representation of each client as quickly as possible, providing an incentive to conclude or settle the matter whether or not the client has fully understood or bought into the terms of the settlement or agreement.

Because engaged client-centered representation resists a lawyer-centric approach to strategic decision-making and encourages collaboration between lawyers and clients, it also resists more subtle attempts by lawyers to deploy the authority of the lawyer's expertise to end discussion on matters of legal strategy. Moreover, the Model Rules of Professional Responsibility encourage consultation with clients over the means employed in representation especially on matters that involve the costs of litigation or the effects of particular means on others.[7] However, the law remains a kind of trump card the lawyer can play in lawyer-client conflicts over the nature or direction of representation. If the lawyer asserts that "the law does not allow" the client to do something or that "the case requires" certain motions, strategies or arguments, the client usually lacks the professional expertise or authority to disagree. And it is easy to fall into the trap of using the law as an excuse for avoiding a more difficult discussion with a client, even without meaning to deliberately deceive.

In this case, Attorney Rossmueller is a salaried employee of a non-profit organization providing legal assistance to prison inmates. It may seem that her self-interested motivations for manipulating the course of representation would be unsubstantial. Yet, they are still present. Her limited resources most likely require her to make choices about which cases to take and which to reject. She obviously believes that Devon Jeffries's case is worth taking, perhaps because the facts in his case both embody the stereotype of the "bad prison dad" and also challenge it. And, his child support order is from a county where arguments to modify child support for prison inmates are "hit or miss." Perhaps she sees in his case the potential to educate the judiciary in a "hit or miss" county by pushing against the stereotype with a relatively sympathetic case.

But what if the circumstances were different? Imagine that Rossmueller interviews a potential client with the same kind of facts as Devon Jeffries, but the client's child support order is from a county in which motions to modify child support by prison inmates are routinely denied? In such circumstances, Sandra Rossmueller might perceive it not to be worth her time to pursue the losing argument. She could explain honestly to the client that he has a legal argument—albeit a losing one—and that she simply cannot devote the time and resources of her program to filing a futile motion, however sympathetic. However, she might also be tempted to short-cut that explanation and avoid the discomfort of telling the client that his motion is not worth her time and effort by saying that however sympathetic the facts of his case, he has "no legal argument" to modify his child support.

The temptation to short-cut the discussion would be even stronger in a case where the facts presented by a potential client were less sympathetic. Imagine, for example, a potential client from the same "hit or miss" county as Devon Jeffries, but who better fits the stereotype of the "bad prison dad" that Rossmueller wants to counteract—someone without the history of non-monetary support and relationship with his child prior to coming to prison. Bringing a motion in that kind of case would be counterproductive to the larger mission of her prison legal assistance organization, because such a motion would tend to confirm the worst stereotypes about prison dads rather than implicitly challenge them. Rossmueller might be tempted to project her own views onto a fictitious judge by telling the client that he has "no legal argument" to modify his support, when what she really means is that he has an argument but that she is reluctant to make the legal argument for him because it would undercut her larger efforts at systemic reform.

This is not to say that Rossmueller must devote the limited resources of her legal services organization to taking cases that are almost certain to lose or that run counter to the larger mission of the organization. The problem arises in how Rossmueller chooses to explain her decision to the potential clients she turns away. If Rossmueller tells the potential clients that they have "no legal argument," she is giving them legal advice that is in fact inaccurate. Only truly sophisticated and well-connected clients are likely to venture a second opinion from another lawyer. And, in Rossmueller's case—where her organization may be the sole provider of free legal services to prison inmates—the potential clients she turns away may have no practical opportunity for a second opinion.

It is also worth noting that, if Rossmueller is motivated to take Jeffries's case primarily for political or legal reform purposes, she does not explain this to him directly, at least not in the excerpt of the dialogue we have seen. Yet, her motivations may well affect the way she weighs strategic decisions in the future. Although there is no apparent conflict between his objectives and her motivations, it seems most consistent with the collaborative goals of engaged client-centered representation for Jeffries to understand the reasons why Rossmueller in interested in representing him, from among the many prison inmates with child support debts whose cases she could take.

Lawyers may also be tempted to use the law to avoid moral disagreement with a course of action the client wants to pursue. In Chapter 7 ("Moral Dialogue"), we offered an example of a lawyer who morally disagreed with his client's proposal to use a claim of custody as a bargaining chip to extract a more favorable financial settlement in his divorce. That client was motivated in part by a desire to punish his wife for having an affair that ended their marriage. Eventually, the lawyer told the client that he and several other lawyers he knew simply wouldn't use child custody in a game of hardball negotiation because "it would just be wrong." However, as we noted, it took some probing from the client to force the lawyer to call "custody blackmail" what it was: a possible legal strategy that is so harmful to children that he morally objected to using it.

One of the ways the lawyer in that dialogue could have circumvented the moral dialogue would have been to put up the law as a screen behind which to hide the lawyer's moral opposition to the client's proposed tactic. At one point in the dialogue in Chapter 7, the lawyer uses the law in just this way. Let's look back at a portion of that dialogue to see how discussion of the morally objectionable "custody blackmail" tactic arose and the role that the lawyer's statements about the law played in that exchange:

*C12:   My friend says that if we settle out of court we can go quite a ways away from 50–50.

*L13:   Yes, that's right and I was about to talk about that. *If we settle*, as I know you want to—so that no one has to go through the expense and pain of a trial—*then probably the judge will approve the agreement we make, even if it's not 50–50. The courts assume that, at least within a certain range, the divorcing couple knows best*.

*C13:   So that's what I want to do. I want to settle, and I want the settlement to give my wife—I'm sorry, but this is how I feel—as little money as possible.

*L14:   Bill, you're entitled to feel that way, and you don't need to apologize to me for it. My job is to help you accomplish what you feel you want, as far as it can be accomplished.

*C14:   So how far can this be accomplished?

*L15:   Well, that depends first of all on who's going to have custody of the kids. ***Whoever has custody has to have enough money to support the kids, and the courts are pretty vigilant about that.*** The last time we spoke I thought you felt pretty clear that the kids would need to be primarily with their mother. Did I get that right?

*C15:   Yes. It has to be her, really. You know I travel 3 or 4 days a week for my job, and I have no one else to take care of them.

*L16:   ***So we have to include in our offer enough money for her to take care of the kids.***

*C16:   Not from what my friend tells me.

*L17:   I'm not sure I see where you're going. What exactly did your friend tell you?

*C17:   He said that the way to make her back off on the money is to threaten to fight about custody.

*L18:   You mean, to tell her that we're going to press for custody even though you don't actually want custody?

*C18:   Yes, exactly.

As we explained in Chapter 7, there is nothing wrong with a lawyer attempting to dissuade a client from taking a morally objectionable course of action for legal or pragmatic reasons, as long as the reasons given are accurate statements of the law. However, there is a real temptation for the lawyer to maneuver his statements of the law so that the law becomes a surrogate for the lawyer's unstated moral objections. The lawyer in this part of the dialogue is actively attempting to keep the conversation from going the direction the client wants to take it—to the "custody blackmail" tactic. And he uses the authority of law to help him.

In our discussion of candor in Chapter 7, we faulted the lawyer for making an inaccurate statement about negotiation strategy: "So we have to include in our offer enough money for her to take care of the kids." (*L16). As we said, that kind of inaccurate statement violated the respect that the lawyer owes the client and "should not have been uttered." Note how closely that inaccurate statement about negotiation strategy followed on the heels of the lawyer's legal assessment, "Whoever gets custody of the kids has to have enough money to support the kids, and the courts are pretty vigilant about that." (*L15). The statement that courts are "pretty vigilant" about child support is seemingly at odds with the lawyer's earlier statement that there is significant leeway in deviating from 50–50 divisions of property in divorce settlements because "courts assume, at least within a certain range, the divorcing couple knows best." (*L13).

Although nothing the lawyer says about the law in either statement is inaccurate, his overall discussion of the law is misleading in ways that might not be recognizable except to another lawyer. It is true that courts are vigilant in setting child support according to clear and sometimes mandatory guidelines based on a percentage of the non-custodial parent's income. When it comes to property division, the lawyer's earlier statement that the courts will allow significant leeway in approving settlements that deviate from a 50–50 split is also accurate. But child support and property division are two different aspects of a divorce settlement. By switching the topic from property division to child support, the lawyer has gravitated to a place in the law where children's needs are taken into account. His statement about the legal enforcement of child support law gives an aura of legal authority to his inaccurate statement that his client's settlement offer needs to include enough money to allow his wife to take care of the kids. The client in this case has enough sophistication—at least in the form of access to a friend who knows something about divorce law—to challenge his lawyer's statement. (*C16). And, the client eventually presses the lawyer to voice the lawyer's moral objection more directly and transparently.

Not all clients will be as persistent as the client in the Chapter 7 moral dialogue, and the risks to the lawyer of transparency are significant. When the lawyer in Chapter 7 eventually carries out the discussion of custody blackmail on moral rather than legal terms, the lawyer puts himself on a more level playing field with his client, losing the higher ground that legal expertise and authority provide. When he clarifies that it is not the law but he—the lawyer—standing in the client's way, he puts the representation at risk. Indeed, by the end of that dialogue, the client has told the lawyer that he needs to think about whether or not to continue the representation. It is precisely to avoid this kind of risk that lawyers may be tempted to hide moral objections behind the authority of law.

B. JURISPRUDENTIAL DIMENSIONS OF LAW TALK

When lawyers advise clients about what the law demands, prohibits and allows, lawyers are interpreting the law. By the end of the first year in law school, law students have usually internalized the lesson that law is neither simple nor determinate. In interpreting the law in a particular case, a judge must often choose among more than one possible answer about how the law should be applied, extended or modified. When lawyers explain the law to their clients, they are also called upon to make interpretive choices. Sometimes these choices are easy: for example, a one-year residency requirement for filing for divorce may be clear on its face and enforced with regularity. Other times, lawyers must make complicated judgments about how the client's situation fits within a web of interactive statutes, regulations, court decisions and informal practices that together make up "the law" that will affect the client's life affairs.

For example, a lawyer's statement to a client that "the law does not permit" a course of action may be shorthand for any number of other legal judgments. It may mean that the law does not on its face permit the client to take a certain course of action. It may mean that the law does not on its face permit it, even though the law could be interpreted to permit it. Or that the law may technically permit the client to take a certain course of action, but to do so would fly in the face of the intention behind the law. Or that the law in the lawyer's view ought to permit it, but that the judge in the client's jurisdiction is unlikely to see it that way. Or that the law prohibits a course of action, even though enforcement agencies are unlikely to require strict compliance with the law.

The interpretive choices that lawyers make in advising their clients about what "the law" demands, prohibits and allows play a role in creating law that is just as meaningful—though different—from the role legislators play when they enact statutes and from the role judges play when they adjudicate cases. Even though lawyers' interpretations of the law do not have precedential weight, their legal interpretations help determine the scope and meaning of law as law operates in the world.[8] Lawyers' advice to clients creates part of the web of "law in action" that exists beneath and within the shadow of the "law on the books." Most cases never reach litigation. In such cases, lawyers' interpretations of law may be the final word, at least for their clients, on what the law demands, prohibits or allows. The integrity and legitimacy of the "law in action" that lawyers create privately to guide their clients depends on lawyers making professionally responsible choices about how to interpret the law to their clients.

Recently, lawyers have come under fire for providing distorted and far-fetched interpretations of controlling law that have sanctioned socially harmful behavior. For example, the "creative and aggressive" legal interpretations of Enron lawyers have been faulted for helping to justify questionable accounting practices that eventually led to the collapse of the energy giant, drove up energy costs, and lined the pockets of speculators.[9] As one Enron executive described the prevailing attitude in the company toward legal constraints on accounting methods:

> Say you have a dog, but you need to create a duck on the financial statements. Fortunately, there are specific accounting rules for what constitutes a duck: yellow feet, white covering, orange beak. So you take the dog and paint its feet yellow and its fur white and you paste an orange plastic beak on its nose, and then you say to your accountants, "This is a duck! Don't you agree that it's a duck?" And the accountants say, "Yes, according to the rules, this is a duck."[10]

Similarly, following the 9/11 attacks, White House lawyers were encouraged to pursue "forward-leaning" interpretations of domestic and international that stretched the meaning of the laws against torture far beyond mainstream legal analysis.[11] When the "torture memos" produced by the Office of Legal Counsel to justify waterboarding and other degrading and painful interrogation tactics came to light, they set off a storm of controversy about the role that lawyers had played in sanctioning human rights violations. But the public repudiation of the questionable legal advice came too late to prevent the atrocities perpetrated by interrogators based on the legal authority the memos provided.

Because lawyers' interpretations of law in cases that never go to court help to define the reach and contour of law as it operates in the world, legal ethicists are beginning to see lawyers' advice to clients as a form of lawmaking that carries with it duties to the legal system. When lawyers twist the law out of shape to justify their clients' behavior, the damage is not limited to those who are financially or physically harmed by the clients' actions. Private exceptions and deviations from governing law erode the rule of law itself. Because lawyers have professional duties as officers of the legal system and as public citizens having special responsibility for the quality of justice,[12] the question arises of what duties lawyers have to uphold the law in their private communications with clients about the law. For example, is it proper for lawyers play the role of gatekeepers and enforcers of the law through the advice they give to their clients? Aren't clients entitled to information about the furthest reaches of plausible legal interpretation as well as advice about how they can avoid the enforcement of legal regulation? Such questions lead to even deeper questions of political and jurisprudential theory that have sparked vigorous debate among legal ethicists.[13]

The answers to these questions are far from settled. Some legal ethicists argue that, as custodians of the law, lawyers have a fiduciary duty to create a web of "law in action" that accurately reflects and supports the stability of the "law on the books."[14] However, the "law on the books" often fails to reflect the perspectives of racial minorities, sexual minorities, women, and people in poverty. Interpretations that require lawyers to hew closely to the "law on the books" when they advise clients run the risk of further silencing or ignoring the voices of those who lack power to influence the lawmaking process. Other legal ethicists have argued that when advising clients about the law—especially in situations that will never going to go to court and be corrected by an adversary process—lawyers should take on the responsibilities of judges to ensure that justice is done.[15] However, the delegation to lawyers of judgments about underlying principles of justice presents problems of its own. Lawyers who rely on their own judgments risk imposing their views of justice on clients who may disagree with them, but doing so under the mantle of legal authority and expertise.

Our view about how a lawyer should interpret the law is ultimately driven by the theory of lawyering that we embrace throughout this book: engaged client-centered representation. We view legitimate authority not as a property of law, but as a kind of respect that is accorded to law by those whom the law governs.[16] When viewed in this way, determining the "legitimacy of law" is not an essentially lawyer-centered activity. Although lawyers play an important role in the process, it is clients who ultimately confer legitimacy on the law—or not—based on the amount of respect they accord it. Yet clients do not make these judgments about legitimacy in a vacuum. As social scientists have demonstrated, the way individuals encounter the law in both formal processes like court hearings and informal processes like encounters with police officers, can affect the way they assess the legitimacy of the law and the legal system.[17] Conversations between lawyers and clients about the law are important informal encounters between the law and those it governs. Lawyers' portrayal of the law in these encounters can obscure or mystify law, explain law, defend law, or critically challenge law.[18] And, lawyers' choices about how to characterize the law to their clients can and will affect clients' assessments of law's legitimacy and their willingness to comply with legal directives.

From the engaged client-centered perspective we take in this book, we would measure lawyers' success in carrying out their duties to the legal system by how well their explanations of the law position their clients to assess both the force and the legitimacy of governing law and make informed decisions about compliance with the law. As Oliver Wendell Holmes famously wrote, "If you want to know the law and nothing else, you must look at it as a bad man, who cares only for the material consequences which such knowledge enables him to predict."[19] Looking at the law from the perspective of a Holmesian "bad man" who cares only about the constraints that law places on clients' actions, the lawyer's job is to employ legal knowledge and expertise to advise the client about the likelihood of enforcement of the law and the costs associated with violating it.

From the engaged client-centered approach we have been exploring in these chapters, we reject an approach to discussions of the law that begins and ends with the Holmesian "bad man" assumption that clients want nothing more than to avoid legal enforcement. To talk about the law in only such instrumentalist terms is objectionable from a client-centered perspective because it is disrespectful of clients. Such instrumentalist interpretation—without more—assumes that clients are interested only in competitively maximizing their wealth or freedom. It reduces clients to cardboard figures with narrow legal interests divorced from their other cares, commitments, relationships and loyalties. And, it overlooks, and may interfere with, a client's desire to participate in meaningful social cooperation through understanding the law and choosing to comply with it. Such instrumentalist interpretation of the law provides valuable information about the scope and reach of the law in the world, and this helps clients assess how much they can "get away" with. But it does little to assist clients in assessing whether they *want* to avoid legal regulation.

What must a lawyer do on a practical level to facilitate clients' assessments of law's legitimacy as well as its force? We believe that the function of engaging clients in assessing the legitimacy (or lack of legitimacy) of law is best served when lawyers find ways to explain the law in context. Law is created out of political forces and these forces are part of its context. But law is also created on the basis of principles or reasons that justify it as a means toward the greater public good. The strength, accuracy and validity of these justifying reasons define the relationship between law and justice. When a lawyer explains the reasons that best justify the law governing their clients' situations, lawyers invite their clients to assess the validity of those reasons and help position their clients to decide whether the "law on the books" is worthy of respect. Such explanations may in some cases help clients see the law as a reasonable constraint on their behavior designed to coordinate their interests with the interests of others. In other cases, such explanations may help clients see that the assumptions that underlie the law have little bearing in their circumstances and to decide that the law deserves little respect other than the fear of its enforcement.

Finally, consistent with our larger commitment to engaged client-centered representation, we believe that the lawyer's role is to facilitate the *client's* informed judgments and assessments about the law, rather than to impose the lawyer's assessments on the client or to proselytize the client to the lawyer's own view of how law relates to justice. We find it unavoidable that, in explaining the reasons behind the law, lawyers will engage their own understandings, perspectives and beliefs about law's legitimacy. As with the types of engagement discussed elsewhere in this book—such as the personal connection across difference and similarity we discuss in Chapter 2, the engagement in helping clients to make informed choices we discuss in Chapter 3, and the moral engagement we discuss in Chapter 7—we do not view lawyers' expression of their own opinions and attitudes as out-of-bounds. The key to a successful engaged client-centered dialogue is not lawyers' neutrality. Rather, it is in lawyers' self-reflective attention to the attitudes and assumptions they bring to the table and a foundational willingness to cede final decision-making to the client.

With these principles in mind, let's look back at the dialogue between Sandra Rossmueller and her client, Devon Jeffries, to see how Rossmueller uses information about the law to position Jeffries to decide how much authority and respect to accord the law. Rossmueller begins her explanation of child support law by employing a decidedly sympathetic account of its underlying purposes designed to engage Jeffries personally. For example, as Rossmueller explains the letter and purpose of the 17% child support standard, she repeatedly interrupts herself to apply it to Jeffries's situation. She says, "[t]he law says that your child deserves to have a certain percentage of your income to support him . . . or her. Do you have a son or a daughter?" (L3); and, "OK, so the law says that Natasha deserves to have 17% of whatever money you make. That's because whoever she lives with . . . Tonya?" (L4). Rossmueller then uses the personal information Jeffries offers to frame the purposes of child support law in sympathetic terms personal to him, saying, "Well, no matter what happens to you, Tonya is spending money all the time for Natasha. Money for food. Money for rent. Money for clothes. All those things. Child support is your way to contribute to those expenses based on what you earn." (L5).

By personalizing the purpose behind child support, Attorney Rossmueller moves Jeffries beyond thinking primarily about the effect of the child support debt on him to expressing continuity between his own values and the values reflected in the most sympathetic interpretation of child support law. At the beginning of the conversation, Jeffries is primarily concerned with how the child support debt will affect his life and future prospects. He says, "I don't have this kind of money. I'm never going to have this kind of money. What do they want me to do? Rob a bank when I get out?" (C2). After Rossmueller has explained the purpose of child support law, Jeffries agrees that he has "no problem" with paying Tonya back for the expenses she is incurring in raising Tonya while he is in prison. In fact, he volunteers that he would "always help Tonya out with Natasha." (C5). Rossmueller's explanation has facilitated his process of seeing some legitimacy in child support law—why it is worthy of his authority and respect.

Rossmueller and Jeffries have a more complex discussion about the purpose behind the imputed income standard. As you recall, to illustrate the imputed income standard, Rossmueller uses a hypothetical story about a "starving artist doctor" who foregoes his $300,000 annual income to follow his dream of being a street artist. The story of the "starving artist doctor" becomes an entry point for a discussion between Rossmueller and Jeffries about gaps between the assumptions that are built into the law and Jeffries's lived experience. Rossmueller uses the story to discuss the fact that some judges view the commission of a crime as a voluntary choice to forego potential income, not unlike the doctor's choice to be a street artist. (L19). She also uses the story to differentiate the "starving artist doctor," who "can make a choice to give up the whole artist thing and go back to being a doctor," from Devon Jeffries who can't "walk out of the front door of this prison and get a job at McDonald's." (L20).

At the heart of the "starving artist doctor" story is another decidedly sympathetic vision of the underlying principles at work in the imputed income standard. The starving artist doctor is not a real litigant. In fact, it is quite unlikely that such a person exists or would ever exist—a fact acknowledged when Jeffries jokes that the court would refuse to modify the doctor's income "because he's an idiot" (C16) and Rossmueller laughs in response (L17). The political reality—later acknowledged by Rossmueller—is that the imputed income standard is most often used in cases of parents in poverty who are chronically unemployed or underemployed. If such an eccentric character as the "starving artist doctor" existed, it is likely that he would have been able to structure his assets to allow him to pursue his dream of sidewalk artistry while still supporting his children. However, the "starving artist doctor" story does explain why it *would* be fair—in a just world—to impute income to a recalcitrant father based on his earning potential rather than his actual income. By extension, the differences between Jeffries and the "starving artist doctor" illustrate the ways in which the imputed income standard falls short of justice. The story thus becomes a way for Rossmueller and Jeffries to connect to the purposes of the law and at the same time to critique its legitimacy.

Rossmueller has the most difficulty communicating a sympathetic interpretation of the purposes of the law when it comes to the requirement that Jeffries pay child support to the state to reimburse the state for public assistance. Rossmueller gives purposive explanation a half-hearted try, saying "child support debt is about paying back the person who supported your child during the time when you weren't paying support. When the state supports a parent with public assistance, the other parent owes child support to the state for that period of time." (L24). However, she is quickly moved off this tack when Jeffries objects to the fairness of paying back the state for assistance money (C24); and Rossmueller goes into a tirade of her own about the unfairness of the law to families in poverty. (L25). Jeffries's next few responses pull her back to his case, by asking an ultimately instrumentalist question: "But how can you help *me*?" (C26).

In this exchange, Rossmueller has acknowledged explicitly that she believes the law is unfair and Jeffries has tacitly agreed. Although Jeffries does not seem to want to spend much time discussing the unfairness of the law, this does not mean that Rossmueller's expression of her views was unwelcome. To the contrary, it may have been an important way for Jeffries to see that she is at least politically aligned with him, even though the unfairness of the law may be more surprising and disappointing to someone with her privilege than it is to him. In response to Jeffries's instrumentalist queries, Rossmueller provides instrumentalist information about the law's likely enforcement. She acknowledges that success on "depends a lot on the attitude of the judge in your case." (L21). She later suggests that the better path to success in Jeffries's "hit or miss" county would be to attempt to persuade the child support attorney—a legal actor whose support for child support modification might wield more influence in the process than a good legal argument. (L27–L28).

Rossmueller's strategy for negotiating with the child support attorney capitalizes on the continuities revealed between Jeffries's values and the values in the law, and in demonstrating how the just purposes of the law fail in his case. She suggests using the sympathetic facts about Jeffries's case—his history of informal support off-the-books, his relatively connected relationship with his daughter, the likelihood of his continued support after his release—to set him apart from the "stereotype of a 'bad dad' who hasn't provided any care or taken any financial responsibility for his child." (L29). And, she suggests using the differences between Jeffries and the "starving artist doctor" to convince the child support attorney that "all the incentives that the law is supposed to create backfire in your case." (L28). The components of this legal strategy rest on matters that have come out in the discussion, such as how it is "unfair to impute minimum wage income to you when you are incarcerated by the state and precluded from getting a minimum wage job" (L26), and how it is "that when you get out, this debt is going to make it harder for you to get back on your feet and support your daughter in the long run." (L28).

Taken altogether, the dialogue between Rossmueller and Jeffries illustrates one way a lawyer can structure a discussion about the law that creates room for the client to understand the law sympathetically, assess it critically, and decide for himself whether to accord the law authority and respect. Rossmueller does not approach Jeffries with the assumption that her client's only interest will be to avoid enforcement of his child support debt. Indeed, she pushes back against his initial self-interested view with a personalized explanation of the purposes of child support law that help him situate his values in relation to the law and help him understand the potential for fairness and justice within existing child support doctrine. She uses devices like the "starving artist doctor" to explore how the assumptions built into the imputed income standard deviate from his life circumstances. And, she uses the fruits of this discussion to begin to build a case theory that both captures some of the unfairness of the law and is personalized to his situation. We do not believe that it is the only way that a lawyer can or should discuss the law. However, as with the other dialogues offered in this book, we hope that it provides useful fodder for discussion and critique.

DISCUSSION QUESTIONS

1. We have noted that in this dialogue, attorney Rossmueller "does not cite statutes, codes or cases by name, nor does she attempt to explain how the various sources of law interact to create the standards to which she refers. Rather, she communicates the "bottom line" standard that emerges from a much more complex interaction of state, federal, statutory, administrative and case law." Is this an appropriate level of generality for this case? Can you think of circumstances in which it would be necessary or appropriate for the attorney to share more details about the law with the client? Fewer details?

2. We have argued that despite laying out quite explicitly her legal case theory prior to asking her client to tell the story of his relationship with his daughter and ex-girlfriend, attorney Rossmueller did not run afoul of ethical constraints. Do you agree that there is no reason in this case to withhold information about the law up front? In what ways is this case similar or dissimilar to the lawyer-client dialogue in Chapter 6 between the immigration lawyer and her client seeking political asylum?

3. This dialogue between a lawyer and a client about the law purports to demonstrate "the way a lawyer can structure a discussion about the law that creates room for the client to understand the law sympathetically, assess it critically, and decide for himself whether to accord the law authority and respect." Do you agree that this dialogue achieves these objectives? Are they proper objectives for a lawyer to try to

achieve? Can you think of areas of law in which these objectives would be less appropriate? Inappropriate?

---

1. Model R. of Prof'l Conduct 1.4.

2. Gerald Lopez, *Lay Lawyering*, 32 UCLA L. REV. 1, 3–6 (1984).

3. This example is discussed at greater length in Chapter 6 ("Truth and Consequences").

4. *See* Binny Miller, *Give Them Back Their Lives: Recognizing Client Narrative in Case Theory*, 93 MICH. L. REV. 485 (1994).

5. Model R. of Prof'l Conduct 1.4, cmt. [7].

6. Model R. of Prof'l Conduct 1.5 places special restrictions on contingent fee agreements.

7. Model R. of Prof'l Conduct 1.2.

8. *See* DAVID LUBAN, *A Different Nightmare and a Different Dream*, *in* LEGAL ETHICS AND HUMAN DIGNITY.

9. W. Bradley Wendel, *Professionalism as Interpretation*, 99 N.W. U. L. REV. 1167, 1170–71 (2005).

10. *Id.* at 1171, citing BETHANY MCCLEAN & PETER ELKIND, THE SMARTEST GUYS IN THE ROOM: THE AMAZING RISE AND SCANDALOUS FALL OF ENRON 142–43 (2003) (quoting an unidentified Enron employee).

11. DAVID LUBAN, *The Torture Lawyers of Washington*, *in* LEGAL ETHICS AND HUMAN DIGNITY, at 172–73.

12. Model R. Prof'l Conduct, Preamble, par [1].

13. For contrasting views in this debate, see WILLIAM H. SIMON: THE PRACTICE OF JUSTICE: A THEORY OF LAWYERS' ETHICS (1998); Stephen L. Pepper, *Counseling at the Limits of the Law: An Exercise in the Jurisprudence and Ethics of Lawyering*, 104 YALE L.J. 1545 (1995).

14. W. Bradley Wendel, *Civil Obedience*, 104 COLUM. L. REV. 363 (2004).

15. WILLIAM H. SIMON: THE PRACTICE OF JUSTICE: A THEORY OF LAWYERS' ETHICS (1998).

16. Wendel, *Lawyers, Citizens and the Internal Point of View*, 75 FORDHAM L. REV. 1473, 1474–75 (2006) (differentiating the Holmesian "bad man" attitude from the "internal perspective" in which citizens view the laws as having normative force and thus providing reasons for acting).

17. TOM TYLER, WHY PEOPLE OBEY THE LAW (1990).

18. For an analysis of these issues with respect to the way divorce lawyers talk to their clients, see AUSTIN SARAT & WILLIAM L. F. FELSTINER, DIVORCE LAWYERS AND THEIR CLIENTS: POWER AND MEANING IN THE LEGAL PROCESS (1995).

19. Oliver Wendell Holmes, *The Path of the Law*, 10 HARV. L. REV. 457, 459 (1897).

CHAPTER 9

FAST TALKING: LAWYERING EXPERTISE
AND ITS IMPACT ON INTERVIEWING
AND COUNSELING

■ ■ ■

A. INTRODUCTION: THE MEANING OF "FAST TALKING"

We began this book with an imagined dialogue in which two law students struggled to cope with the challenges of beginning an interview with a potential client whom they had not met before. The students confronted a range of complexities, and they did so on the basis (we can assume) of only modest experience. Learning how to begin law practice is a crucial task—but it is not the end of lawyers' learning. In this chapter we will not ask how beginning law students should approach their first cases, but rather how expert lawyers handle the succession of cases and clients whom they seek to serve.

How do expert lawyers actually interview and counsel their clients? It isn't entirely clear that the answer to this question should matter. After all, a major impetus in the original development of client-centered models of practice was a sense that expert practitioners were not practicing right. The first generation of clinicians who articulated and embraced client-centeredness worried that their peers in the practicing bar were treating their clients badly–that they were inattentive, domineering and as a result insensitive to the clients' true needs and wishes. This critique surely was correct, at least for many of the lawyers to whom it was applied. These lawyers were no more indifferent to clients than their counterparts in many walks of life were, but also no less, and an era gradually more concerned with each person's voice has reshaped the norms of practice.

But by now there are also many lawyers in practice who were trained in the principles and guidelines of client-centered lawyering. Some of these lawyers may have put aside client-centeredness altogether, thinking that it is an academic ideal unconnected to the harsh realities of the world. Others, surely, remain client-centered in their aspirations, but understand that they must shape their practices in light of both those aspirations and the constraints of life after graduation.

Those constraints are real, and not necessarily to be deplored. Senior lawyers in elite private practice charge many hundreds of dollars per hour for their time; at those rates, efficiency must be a virtue. If we need not worry about clients prosperous enough to pay those rates at all, however, we certainly need to worry about the rest of the country, where legal needs very frequently go unmet and no one has time or money to burn. Lawyers, whether in private practice or public service, have to be efficient, or they sacrifice time and money belonging to their clients or to themselves. In the end, neither sacrifice can really be endured and so even client-centered lawyers must be searching for ways to honor their principles while practicing in an effective, economical way.

We suspect that, because skills texts and skills courses have not usually focused on this problem, our most client-centered graduates have had to carry out this search on their own. Perhaps they have even felt guilty about "cutting corners" in ways that their professors did not endorse. But efficient practice is not second-class practice, and client-centered lawyering should not be thought of as an exotic plant suitable only for clinics and exceptionally well-resourced law offices. Efficient client-centered practice is a proper topic for a textbook on interviewing and counseling, and it is our topic here.

In making it our topic, we do not reject the value of concentrating, as many (though by no means all) law school clinics do on teaching students how to practice in clinics where time is almost unlimited. Of course time is never completely unlimited, even in the smallest-caseload, most deliberately "slowed-down" clinics. Nor, in truth, does anyone ever aspire to examine *every* possibility in a situation; the number of possibilities is essentially infinite, or at any rate close enough to result in a "combinatorial explosion,"[1] and perhaps everyone acknowledges that there is some level of work that is too much. But in a broad sense clinicians have often chosen to put time constraints largely to one side in order to focus on the many other challenges involved in learning to be a lawyer. Adopting this approach gives students the opportunity to see practice at its most thorough, and there is value in that (though it is not the value of economy). Adopting this approach also in effect trades students' time and motivation for their lack of experience; by spending enough time, they may well be able to match their more experienced, but busier, counterparts in the matters they handle. We applaud all of this; our point, however, is that there is more to practice than what clinics often do, and that part of the task of law schools, and clinical texts, is to offer guidance for practicing lawyers who will face the fierce constraints of limited time and resources.[2]

Lawyers and law professors today have startlingly little systematic knowledge of the ways that today's client-centered lawyers interview and counsel their clients. Empirical work on this score is surely needed—

though we also do not assume that what well-intentioned lawyers are doing is necessarily what they should be doing; indeed, part of our goal here is to offer practicing lawyers models that avoid what may turn out to be common, though understandable, errors of practice. Proceeding without the lessons, both positive and negative, that comprehensive empirical study will surely provide, we believe it is still possible to draw inferences about the contours of practical client-centeredness. To do so, we need to consider more fully the dimensions of expert practice in general—what experts know, and how they use that knowledge to handle their work. From these sources we can grasp more of what expert client-centered lawyers are likely to be saying in their interviews and counseling sessions with clients.

Before we do so, however, we need to bring to the surface an issue of legal ethics implicit in this discussion. Resources are short, as we have already mentioned. Perhaps they are so short that it is impossible for the legal profession as it is constituted today to provide effective representation for everyone who needs it.[3] Perhaps, therefore, hard choices must be made about the quality of legal services to be provided to those who cannot pay for all they need. "Fast talking" might then be seen in a pejorative sense as the way lawyers operate when all they can provide to a client is the pretense of representation.

We will not disregard the argument for hard choices (we return to this issue in the concluding section of this chapter), but it is not our first concern. Instead, we mean to describe the role that fast talking—understood affirmatively as the ability of expert lawyers to engage with their clients well and quickly—plays in practice that is both effective and sensitive. Thus what we discuss here is *not* a prescription for second-class lawyering for those without the power and money to insist on more. Even lawyers for the most well-resourced clients will rely on expertise, not to undercut their clients but to serve them better. *Every* form of lawyering can be done more or less expertly. But for clients without such lavish resources, and for clients with few resources at all, what our profession ought to provide is lawyering that is competent, sensitive and effective. Lawyering of that quality is not "second-class," and our goal in this chapter is to begin to describe how actual lawyers may employ expertise to provide a level of representation that might at first blush seem unattainable under the real-world constraints of practice.

Finally, an important caveat: One way for lawyers to speed up their work would be for them to simply put aside their concern with their clients' emotional and social needs, indeed their overall wellbeing, and give up as well on the dream of building personally warm and respectful relationships with their clients. This is not our position. What we are writing about is not when to abandon engaged client-centeredness, but how to adhere to it when resources are tight. We seek to describe not any "fast talking" but *client-centered* fast talking.

1. WHO ACTUALLY DOES THE TALKING?

Our focus here is on the ways that lawyers themselves can accomplish this goal, but it is worth pausing for a moment to consider the ways that people other than lawyers may also contribute to it. Broadly speaking, these are methods of structuring law practice so as to reduce the demands on lawyers' time by redefining the work, or recruiting others to do it. For example, lawyers might "unbundle" the tasks of representation, and deliberately provide only selected, rather than comprehensive, services.[4] One scholar has observed that "[a]lthough little formal data exists, it is likely that hundreds of thousands of clients receive unbundled legal services via hotlines, *pro se* clinics, community education programs, and the provision of form pleadings."[5] Systems like these replace the lawyer's time with the client's—but unfortunately it seems likely that some, perhaps many, clients do not fare very well on their own.[6]

Within the context of traditional attorney-client relationships, lawyers may still save some of their own time by utilizing innovative methods of educating their clients about the legal issues they must resolve. As others have pointed out, after all, much of what lawyers do is educational. They help their clients to understand the legal situation they're in—the strengths and weaknesses of their legal claims, the consequences of one option or another, and even the nature of the attorney-client relationship itself, what client and lawyer can expect from each other. If lawyering is a form of pedagogy, then every tool of pedagogy may be useful to it. In particular, it may be possible for lawyers to save some scarce time for truly individualized work with clients if they can impart some of what clients need to learn by other means.

Examining this form of lawyer-client interaction is somewhat beyond the scope of a text focused on interviewing and counseling. But it is worth noting quickly some of the possible techniques. Lawyers may introduce clients to the process of legal representation through brochures or videos.[7] They may provide a range of information on websites.[8] These take time and effort to produce, of course, so it is not automatically the case that their net effect is to save lawyer time, nor (as teachers know) is it self-evident that such tools will work educationally—but they offer promise. So do documents that may be required as a matter of prudent and ethical practice anyway, such as retainer agreements—provided that these documents are carefully written to be not just legally sufficient but actually understandable; even then, they should function as part of a conversation rather than on their own.[9]

Perhaps most important, lawyers may shift some of the work of representation to paralegals.[10] If we can insure that paralegals interview and counsel clients well, both in terms of handling the relevant agenda items and of building a connection with the clients, then we can serve many more clients without having to find many more lawyers. Now this approach obviously involves many steps that are beyond the scope of a study of interviewing and counseling as such. Paralegals need training equal to the tasks they will be undertaking, and once trained they need supervision.

In addition, of course, the paralegal herself—if she is to contribute to the client-centered practice of law—must interview and counsel in a client-centered manner. If doing that takes a long time, the paralegal must invest that time; reliance on paralegals doesn't reduce the total time spent, but only the total *lawyer* time spent. If anything, reliance on paralegals should increase the total time spent, because now the paralegal will need to invest the time required to conduct the interview or counseling session, while the lawyer will also have to invest some time in supervising the paralegal.

Paralegals are no panacea. It will require careful thought for lawyers and their staff members to structure their work so that the paralegals' efforts actually enhance, rather than merely duplicating or even obstructing, the lawyer's impact. Moreover, the more prominent the paralegal's role, the more the lawyer's own interaction with the client will be reduced—and that in turn will add to the difficulties the lawyer faces in building his or her own meaningful connection with the client. Even when all these difficulties are resolved, additionally, there will surely be many interviews or counseling sessions that only the lawyer will have the expertise to undertake.

We do not dismiss any of these approaches to the crucial problem of providing efficient and sensitive legal services to clients. When all these steps are taken, however, lawyers' time will still be a scarce resource. Indeed, while saving lawyers' time, these techniques put responsibility for handling client concerns in the hands of people who may have many skills, but by definition lack lawyers' expertise: paralegals and clients themselves. Doing so makes sense, but it can only be successful if lawyers can both convey their expertise and (ideally, at least) in some way monitor the results. Neither of these tasks is simple. Without disregarding these techniques, therefore, we certainly need to look as well at how lawyers themselves can work quickly and well on behalf of clients. We turn now to the question of how expert practitioners can use their limited time to greatest advantage.

B. WHAT EXPERTS KNOW

Recent years have seen a wide flowering of studies of human expertise. What is it that experts have that novices do not? And, for our purposes, what do these expert abilities suggest about the nature of expert encounters with clients?

The broad answer is that experts are masters of the tasks of their occupation. Typically, and certainly in the case of lawyers, those tasks are of many types. A lawyer needs physical skills, such as the ability to project confidence or skepticism in the course of a trial or negotiation through body language or tone of voice. She needs interpersonal skills, including the ability to frame questions or offer suggestions while at the same time recognizing and taking into account her client's response to what she says. Certainly she needs extensive knowledge of the relevant law. The ideal lawyer, a Hercules of the bar, would be a master of all of these, though in reality no doubt every lawyer brings to his work a mixture of well-honed skills and some weaknesses.[11]

We focus in this section, however, on one particularly overarching skill: the ability to identify a client's problem and generate potential solutions to it. Without this skill, a lawyer's other assets may be of little use, and with this skill, she can employ those other abilities to greater effect. What is it, then, that experts bring to the task of problem-solving?

A central answer that expertise studies suggest is that experts possess extensive, well-organized knowledge of the domain in which they work, knowledge to which they have extremely quick access. The exact mechanisms are still not fully understood, and the account of expertise we offer here is a broad-brush one, but the main point is clear enough: where novices must struggle to identify and understand the significance of an almost infinite range of unfamiliar considerations, experts approach each case with a deeply practiced understanding of both what they need to learn and what they need to do once they've learned it.[12]

With this extensive reservoir of knowledge, experts are fast—very fast. Mark Aaronson comments that when a lawyer exercises judgment, "it sometimes can feel as though one is acting unreflectively." Aaronson maintains that the process is not unreflective, but if it is reflective it is not *deliberate*: it "entails applying knowledge that is in part already deeply internalized," and can take place "almost instan[tan]eously."[13] In some measure, in fact, expert judgment appears to be intuitive and even unconscious—like the feel of a familiar tool in one's hand.[14] Thus Ian Weinstein speaks of the "characteristically fast and unconscious" process of expert problem-solving.[15] One simulation study of legal interviewing found expert immigration attorneys focusing on the key issue within 5 minutes: "All the experts devoted the first minutes of the interview to asking a basic set of questions from which they were able to 'diagnose' the case."[16]

Let us pursue the nature of legal diagnosis further, by looking at the prototypical instance of "diagnosis": the work of doctors. As you'll see in the pages to come, we look often to evidence from the practice of medicine—though we also rely on expertise studies from a wide variety of other fields—and we should pause briefly to consider whether medicine does provide a useful analogy for lawyers. We believe it does. This is not because physicians' work is without flaws, for it is not; doctors are, no doubt, subject to the same range of human frailties as other people are—including lawyers. Nor is it because the tasks of doctors and lawyers are identical, for they are not. Doctors address a range of biological diversity, surely far greater than the number of "causes of action" available to lawyers—though perhaps not greater than the diversity of problems that clients bring to their attorneys. It might be said that the task of doctors is to accomplish the stunning intellectual feat of finding *the* diagnosis and *the* cure from amidst the tremendous range of possibilities, while the role of the lawyer is not primarily to achieve analytic feats but to maneuver through the social situations posed by adversaries, allies, clients, juries and judges. At the same time, doctors' role might be seen as framed by biology, whereas lawyers work with clients who are themselves to a large degree the definers of the problems they need addressed and the criteria for solving them—and whose definitions may change in the course of the representation. Whether these contrasting features make medical or law practice the more complicated field is an interesting question.

But these differences should not divert our attention from very substantial similarities. Broadly speaking, both professions encounter clients, must sort out complicated factual situations to determine the clients' problems, and must devise potential solutions to those problems and help the clients to decide which solutions to undertake. In addition, both professions operate under profound uncertainties. Surely this is true in law, where so much turns on the fallible and changing positions of the people involved in a matter, but it turns out to be true in medicine as well, where one scholar has commented that "[u]ncertainty creeps into medical practice through every pore."[17] Moreover, it is not actually true, at least in many cases, that medicine addresses only biology and can ignore the people whose biology is being treated; it is people who must live with their conditions and with the rigors of the treatments those conditions may need, and unless physicians and patients ally against a disease the course of treatment may be jeopardized.[18] Both professions also operate, at least very often, under serious time and cost constraints, which make it necessary for both doctors and lawyers to find ways to deliver their vital services quickly. There is, to be sure, much to say in criticism of these institutional constraints, for both professions, and we do not mean to justify or emulate uncaring or ineffective practice in either field. But it is striking that both professions have developed over recent decades an aspiration towards client- or patient-centered practice,[19] and we believe that the challenges facing doctors and lawyers who share this aspiration are related. Finally, and particularly importantly, the elements of doctors' actual practice of their profession have been studied in far greater empirical depth than lawyers' work has been.[20] We need to look to the evidence from the field of medicine because, ironically, we have so much less evidence (as distinguished from anecdote) in our own domain.

Certainly the studies of medical interviewing and diagnosis are striking. What we learn is that among physicians, whose standard encounters with patients apparently average 15 to 17 minutes,[21] the speed of initial inference is very high. It appears that "competent physicians begin generating hypotheses in the earliest moments of their encounters with patients" and *never* follow the "student-oriented approach" of "defer[ring] all hypotheses until the history taking and physical examination have been concluded."[22] One simulation study reports an expert's interview of a patient, an interview apparently well under 15 minutes in duration, in which the expert began with "19 exchanges to document the presenting problem fairly comprehensively . . . . Her questions are highly focused, and she is able to anticipate candidate findings with precision. . . . From this point on, she seems to know exactly what the problem is," and she arrives at the right diagnosis (of two related medical problems) based on making "only 16 findings" out of 76 possible ones in the case. The authors comment that this physician's interview "is an example of the effective use of predictive reasoning leading to efficient use of time, information, and other reasoning strategies to arrive at an accurate diagnosis."[23]

It is important to emphasize that, as this medical example reflects, experts' speed is not a matter of speaking more quickly than novices would but of reasoning more effectively. In routine cases, they do *not* examine all possible hypotheses looking for some way to achieve the client's goals—the step-by-step ends-means reasoning that might seem to be the key to effective development of case theory. They do not appear to brainstorm, because they are keying at once to the most promising explanations of the situation, not pursuing all possible alternatives.[24] Nor do experts try to discover all aspects of the facts of a situation—their strength is that they can learn more of what is important to learn, even if they in fact learn less in sheer quantity.[25]

How can experts do all this? The answer is not that they are smarter than non-experts. Everyone, expert or not, has roughly the same brain resources, and those resources are limited—apparently we cannot keep more than 5 to 10 items in our heads at a time.[26] Experts circumvent these limits, at least in part because they have organized their knowledge into libraries of patterns, so that they can work with entire patterns rather than with individual, disconnected items of information.[27] Thus chess masters consider "roughly the same number of [potential] moves" as novices do, but "seemed somehow to consider only relatively strong moves, while novices spent equal amounts of time exploring both weak and strong moves. Somehow, the masters seemed able simply to recognize the difference."[28]

To engage in this kind of reasoning without the knowledge base to support it is likely to be disastrous.[29] Even experts may leap to the wrong conclusion, as we shall see.[30] Novices, who do lack the knowledge base of experts, will do better to try to work through the possibilities more comprehensively—at least if time permits this effort, as it may in many clinics. But doing so is hard, precisely because of the cognitive limits we have already noted. More information can actually be worse than less.[31] As one appraisal of medical expertise put it, "being able to remember all the details is an adaptive strategy for chess and for medical students . . . but synthesizing all the details into a brief but coherent problem formulation, ignoring extraneous details, is a better description of medical experts"[32]—and, we think, of expert lawyers as well.

In emphasizing experts' speed—and the quality of the judgments made so speedily[33]—we do not mean to embrace unreflective intuition. There are moments, in expert judgment and in the thinking all of us do, when intuition works with remarkable power,[34] and there may well be at least some circumstances in which intuition by itself is the best guide to decisionmaking.[35] But experts do not, or should not, rely blindly on intuition; on the contrary, there is evidence that experts who confront unfamiliar situations take more time than novices do to grasp the true nature of what they face.[36] Even when experts are ready to bring their intuition to bear, moreover, we do not suggest that experts' intuitive judgments are conclusive by themselves.[37] Rather, we understand experts to function best when they use their remarkable capacities for intuitive insight to narrow the serious possibilities so dramatically that the work remaining is to test a very limited set of ideas rather than to explore, step-by-step, the field of possible ways to achieve a client's goals.[38] As a review of medical expertise describes the process of medical diagnosis:

> Although a physician may recognize a patient's problem within seconds or minutes, she then commonly goes through a more-or-less systematic search for additional data before she arrives at a conclusion, presumably based on the weighting of the features against internalized rules. Every so often, more likely for tough or unusual cases, the physician may well "go back to the basics" and reason things out from basic science principles.[39]

Expert thinking can, of course, go wrong. The intuitive pattern recognition that experts employ may be mistaken, and even when it is correct the lawyer hewing to long-established patterns may miss new possible moves that a fresher attorney would see. There are reasons why older lawyers' expertise gradually begins to be outmoded, and there are advantages to being young, hardworking and not fully informed about existing patterns of conduct.[40] Indeed, there are reasons never to be too confident of one's expertise, and we will return, at the end of this chapter, to the important question of how experts can reduce the danger that they will make mistakes.

Nevertheless, expertise is a goal that it is hard not to hold. As Ian Weinstein has commented, "We are all experts in a host of everyday domains."[41] Expert thinking appears simply to be the way that human beings characteristically think about matters with which they have become truly familiar.[42] As a practical matter, moreover, efficient handling of client problems is a virtue, and experts are those who can achieve this virtue most fully. Our concern, then, is with the ways that client-centered lawyers can employ their expertise—and with the steps they can take to save themselves from the dangers that expertise, with its intuitive insights and streamlined inquiries, can pose.

C. HOW EXPERTS (SHOULD) INTERVIEW AND COUNSEL CLIENTS

If what experts know is how to see a pattern, and likely the right pattern, fast, what does that mean for their interviewing? In particular, what does it mean for what might be called the stereotypical clinical interview, in which the lawyer listens to the client with the greatest of patience, assumes that whatever the client has to say is likely to be of some relevance, and explores as wide a range of theories and possibilities with the client as possible? And how does expertise reshape the paradigmatic clinical counseling session, in which the lawyer might set out to elicit the client's choice from among all potential courses of action, by helping the client to reach her own independent conclusion in light of a comprehensive review of each option's advantages and disadvantages?

1. LISTENING

It is a mistake to think of expert interviewing as easy or casual. It is neither. Only an expert can do it, because only an expert can bring to bear the extensive body of knowledge required to make the intuitive leaps of expertise correctly. But even experts cannot do expert interviewing inattentively. On the contrary, here, as in the first client meeting held by a new clinical student, listening is essential. The great danger in fast talking is of jumping to the wrong conclusion, and nothing makes that easier than to miss some essential element of the client's story.[43] A routine case of type A may be mistaken for one of type B. Or a case may appear routine, and suitable for fast work, when in fact it is so complex and unusual that the correct expert response is to recognize uncertainty and slow down.

There is, moreover, much more to listen to than "just the facts." We are describing engaged client-centered interviewing, founded in the belief that the client's legal problems have crucial personal implications that must be understood, and in the conviction that the lawyer-client relationship does not work effectively unless the lawyer builds a relationship of trust and respect with the client. Lawyers, expert or novice, need their clients' trust. Without this, the clients do not retain them, or after retaining them do not confide in them. Without candid client communication, the lawyer has little chance of learning whether the client's case actually is routine, or is instead one of the unusual cases that require special attention. Without confidence in the attorney, a client may not work faithfully with her lawyer and so whatever plans lawyer and client attempt to execute may run aground. And without trust, lawyer and client may not be able to engage with each other, and so the possibility that the client will be able to draw on that engagement to help reassess her situation and change her plans will be diminished.

In short, understanding the client's human concerns, and building a personal connection with the client, are a core part of the client-centered lawyer's work, whether that work is done fast or slow. As we suggest throughout this book, an especially critical part of this work, in turn, is a sensitivity to human difference. Lawyers need to be listening on all of these dimensions, and to be expert listeners in these areas they need a wealth of experience on all of these dimensions as well.

We do not mean to suggest that expert interviewing is impossibly hard—that experts somehow must approach each interview with superhuman concentration because they must gather, in abbreviated encounters, all the information that novices collect over much more prolonged meetings. Expert interviewing is *not* impossibly hard; indeed, it should be the case that expert interviewing is easier than novice interviewing, once expertise has been achieved, because the expert's extensive knowledge allows her to infer patterns—of legal fact or of human emotion—so much more effectively than a novice can. Where novices are overwhelmed by information and prone to miss critical statements a client makes, an expert is ready to hear them, provided that he or she is listening.

2. UNDERSTANDING THE CLIENT'S PROBLEM RIGHT AWAY

As we have just emphasized, lawyers who are prepared to make intuitive leaps based on their quick, patterned understanding of their clients' cases must take care not to misunderstand what the case is about. Of course, every lawyer needs to try to understand the outlines of a matter she is considering early rather than late. Unlike the novice lawyer who is prepared to do a comprehensive interview that traces and retraces the ground of the client's situation, and so potentially catches—eventually—some of what was missed early on, however, the expert lawyer aims not to go back. She needs to see the matter clearly the first time through, or at least see clearly that the matter is too complex to be handled as if it were routine.

The first stage of this process is to pay close attention to the client's opening words. Gay Gellhorn has cogently argued for the significance of these moments, which offer both critical indications of the client's actual concerns and a valuable opportunity to begin building a relationship with the client.[44] So, in general, expert lawyers, just like novices, need to begin with a very open question, such as "What brings you to my office?" or "How can I help you?"[45] The next question, moreover, may need to be another, equally open-ended inquiry, such as: "Is there anything else that you're concerned about?" Then, again just like novices, experts need to listen acutely to their clients' initial accounts of their problems; they need to give the clients an opportunity to tell their stories as they themselves experience them; and they need to provide the empathy and support that will help give the clients confidence in themselves and in their lawyer. While we strongly endorse encouraging the client to state his concerns, however, we do not recommend multiple repetitions of this sort of inquiry. Instead, we take it to be consistent with the need for efficiency for the lawyer to wrap up this stage when the client appears to have reached his own conclusion, perhaps with a comment like this:

> L: If there are other issues you're concerned about, please let me know about them as we go along. But right now I think I understand what's been happening, and I'd like to ask you some questions that will help us figure out what to do.

But it seems possible that the pressure of fast interviewing tends to lead professionals to cut off these opening client words much more quickly than they should. (Perhaps more accurately, time pressure may reinforce what is already an unfortunate tendency of many professionals to proceed in this fashion.) Medical studies have reported that although doctors do frequently ask their patients initial, open-ended questions to elicit their concerns, they typically interrupt or "redirect" the patients' answers within less than 30 seconds![46] Perhaps even more remarkably, these studies also reflect that when patients are allowed to complete their answers, stating all of the concerns that brought them to the physician, they do so within seconds, or at most minutes.[47] Similarly, Professor Linda Smith has studied a simulated legal interview in which the client "share[s] the essence of his problems in narrative story-telling fashion" and also "share[s] his attitude and goals, all in under 2½ minutes" at the start of the interview.[48]

It might be thought that eliciting all the patient's concerns immediately compromises the professional's goal of speed in the rest of the interview. On occasion, this may be true, and desirable—when what the expert elicits at the start is evidence that the case is too complicated to be handled as a matter of routine. But it is certainly possible that a client will present problems that are not too complex, but simply too numerous, for the expert to handle in the time available. If that is so, however, the task for the client-centered lawyer who simply does not have more time is not to avoid encountering this issue, but rather to make it a part of the respectful relationship she is forging with the client. In the context of "managed" medical care, it has been suggested that physicians work out with the patient—*negotiate* with him—the agenda for the session,[49] and in the end it is hard to see how any other technique would be consistent with respect for the client in these circumstances.[50]

3. BUILDING CONNECTION WITH THE CLIENT

Engaged client-centered lawyering emphasizes the importance of the lawyer's emotional connection to the client, a connection expressed in a variety of ways but above all through attentive, empathetic listening. We have already argued that listening is critical in fast interviewing as well as slow, and empathy is also important. It may be that the sheer accumulation of time spent together is a significant part of building attorney-client relationships, and if that is right then cutting that time—as we believe is inevitable—may somewhat cool those relationships. It is surely the case that a lawyer under time pressure cannot give her client one thing that clients may deeply appreciate, namely a collaborator who will listen very, very patiently to all that the client has to say. If that is true, however, it does not follow that the result must be attorney-client relationships that are distant and impersonal. Personal experience teaches that very close emotional connections are sometimes made in relatively short encounters, and we suspect the same can be true in lawyer-client relationships.

Again, the medical studies are instructive. It is important to acknowledge, of course, that doctor-patient relationships in this country often leave a lot to be desired in interpersonal terms—and that these shortcomings may affect not only patients' feelings but also their health—but this revelation is not news to physicians who seek to improve medical interviewing. What these physicians argue is that it is possible to use the techniques of client- or patient-centeredness very rapidly indeed. Even as modest a step as looking at the patient may make a difference in the physician's understanding of the other person's emotional state.[51] Moreover, as some writers emphasize, an empathetic response ("I can see how difficult this must be for you") takes next to no time.[52] Under time pressure, it may be easy to fall into expressions of empathy that palpably have no real emotional content, but that isn't inevitable. Indeed, physicians sometimes experience extremely intense moments with their patients in the midst of quite short encounters with them. For example, one study found, in interviews averaging from 11 to 21 minutes, that during such sessions a skilled clinician can see and open a window of connection, in which the patient's personal concerns become the focus of the interview, for a period that can last just a few minutes—and still be valuable.[53] The authors infer "that seasoned clinicians have learned through practice to employ brief but intense windows of opportunity to deal with their patients' concerns, and yet to remain time efficient. . . . [S]uch caring may not require extensive time if based on the trust developed in an ongoing patient-doctor relationship."[54]

Clients—like everyone else—evaluate people in context. It seems quite likely that clients whose lawyers have little time to spend with them resent this—as patients resent feeling rushed with their physicians.[55] It may be that lawyers will sometimes have to address this resentment explicitly. But it also seems possible that a client who understands that during their periods together his lawyer is truly focused on him will value the moments of mutual understanding despite, even because of, the constraints of time. To achieve that result, quickly, requires lawyers who are expert in understanding client feelings and in conveying that understanding—but these skills, too, are part of what client-centered lawyers' expertise encompasses. They are experts not only at reasoning but at entering into the intimacy of the lawyer-client relationship.

4. FOLLOWING UP ON THE CLIENT'S OPENING EXPRESSION OF CONCERNS

The task of finding the crucial facts, as the client knows them, may be the area in which experts will be able to save time best. A novice lawyer does not know what legal approaches she should undertake on a client's behalf. She needs to ask about everything, not because it is all important but because she does not know very well what is important and what isn't. Knowing what is important, however, is exactly what an expert does. It follows that expert lawyers will likely interview clients about fewer possibilities than novices; in other words, they will shorten the "fact exploration" stage of the interview.[56] They may even gather fewer facts, measured in sheer numbers, than novices would.

To take an example from outside the client interview context—and experts will likely save time in every aspect of case investigation, including but not limited to client interviews—an expert may see, for example, that a case could conceivably be made that the Volvo that injured the client suffered from defective brakes as a result of a design error. But she may also know, as a novice would not, that Volvo brakes do not have demonstrable design errors, and so she would put this theory aside right away. Or she might put the same theory aside simply because she realizes that it would be expensive to litigate, and when she hears that the car appeared to be speeding she quickly judges that the benefits of exploring the design defect theory are unlikely to outweigh the costs, including the costs involved in diminishing her focus on proving the speeding theory.[57]

She also will probably *not* try to think of all the ways that a particular fact might be proven. Her focus instead will be on those methods— probably just a few—that in her experience have proven the most promising in cases of this sort, and she will target her inquiries accordingly. We can imagine, to continue with our auto accident example, that a novice lawyer looking for evidence of speeding might carefully examine the possible lines of proof and come up with the following: (a) eyewitness observations of the car; (b) expert assessments of the evidence, for example for signs of the force of impact and for tire tracks; (c) judgments made by the police officers who arrived at the accident scene; (d) the client's own memories of the sight of the car and the sounds of its approach; (e) the possibility that the driver has a record of speeding offenses; (f) the possibility that the driver was ticketed at the scene of this accident itself. All of these would be plausibly relevant, and a complete, expert interview would certainly want to look into each possibility of which the client could have knowledge, including his recollections about eyewitnesses, police action at the scene, and the accident itself.

Suppose, however, that the accident takes place in a small town, and that the accident victim-client may well know some people who in turn know the driver personally. It would not be illogical to ask the client if he knows anyone who knows the driver, or might know the driver (based on shared workplace or other commonalities). It would then be possible for the lawyer to ask these other people if they are familiar with the driver's reputation as a safe or unsafe driver. But an expert lawyer might reject this line of inquiry altogether, on the ground that she can find out all that will readily be demonstrable in court about the driver's record by accessing a public, computerized database of driving offense convictions. (We admit that today's new lawyers might be quicker to go online than older lawyers, who may be far from technologically expert—a point that demonstrates that expertise has many aspects, and that the lawyer who wishes to remain an expert must continually be learning!)

Similarly, an expert lawyer might know that juries and judges in her jurisdiction almost always reject claims that a driver was speeding if the officer on the scene of the accident did not ticket the driver for that offense. A lawyer knowing that would ask about that possibility quite early on. If the answer was "no, he wasn't ticketed," she would likely ask little or nothing more about speeding (unless later investigation revealed that the client was mistaken, and the driver *had* been ticketed). In this and no doubt other ways, expert lawyers may learn less, but they learn more of what is essential. Learning less has a price, but it is, on balance, a price that experts rightly pay.

We can make these observations more general. Expert lawyers will *not* be comprehensive, if "comprehensive" means asking about *everything* connected to the case. They won't, for example, obtain a complete time line entailing everything the client can think of that has anything to do with the case. Nor will they pursue the elements of each of the possible legal theories bearing on the case. But they *will* focus very hard on those issues that they believe, based on their expert knowledge, are critical, and when they do so they may utilize all the techniques that novices of necessity employ in less focused ways, such as time lines, historical reconstruction, and generalizations.[58] So, for example, immigration lawyers may lock on to one theory, and put another, potentially viable, theory to one side—as the immigration lawyers in one simulation experiment actually did.[59]

We can expect one other important difference between the fact development questions of experts and those of novices. The questions experts ask, in addition to being better aimed, are more likely to be narrow and closed-ended. (Of course novices ask closed-ended questions too, and sometimes wisely—the difference we're pointing to is a relative rather than an absolute one.) Experts are not casting their net widely in hopes of picking up relevant information; they are predicting what facts are likely to be present and zeroing in on them. A novice who relies on closed-ended questions is likely to run into trouble, because she cannot predict well, but an expert can. Consider this dialogue, from a simulated interview by an expert physician:

> D [Doctor]: And I understand that you recently have been seen for a health problem. What did you notice that made you decide to seek help?

P [Patient]: Well, mostly I had an attack on the muscles of the leg about a month ago and at that time I couldn't stand or lift my leg—it was too weak.

D: This happened a month ago, and did it come on gradually or suddenly?

P: No, just suddenly.

D: Over a matter of hours or minutes or . . .?

P: Ahh, minutes.

D: Had you ever had any of this weakness before? . . . Or was this your very first time?

P: Well, it happened once before.[60]

In this series of exchanges, the physician begins with an open-ended question. As soon as she hears the patient's response, she focuses on the nature of onset, and then on prior history of the same problem. She is careful not to ask leading questions, but her questions are in no sense a continuation of a general inquiry into the patient's condition. We suspect that expert lawyers routinely use similarly focused questions as they interview their clients, because, again, they know what they need to find out.

Let us illustrate these thoughts with a concrete example from a legal interview. Suppose that a housing lawyer is interviewing a client who is facing eviction. Note, first, that the lawyer is not a lawyer in general practice; she is a "housing lawyer." Her focus will, inevitably, be on housing issues—though we do not suggest at all that she should be indifferent to matters going beyond housing law. After setting her client at ease, she begins the substance of the interview as we've suggested, by confirming the preliminary information already gathered by her staff, and then asking an open-ended question:

L1: I understand you're here because you're facing an eviction in 10 days and you'd like to stop it or at least delay it. Is that right?

C1: Yes, that's right.

L2: Are there any other legal problems you're having that you'd like to discuss as well?

C2: No. I mean I have a lot going on in my life, but this is what I've got to worry about right now.

L3: I understand. I think the best way for us to proceed, then, would be for you to tell me how your difficulties with your landlord started and then what happened along the way to right now.

[The client tells the story of what happened; the story he tells turns out to focus on his loss of a job a year ago, which led to his inability to pay the rent; the landlord allowed him to miss two months' payments, which the client was able to make up when he got another job. Then, one month ago, the client was laid off, and this time, although the client was able to assure the landlord, based on a letter from his employer, that he expected to be back at work within a few weeks, the landlord filed for eviction as soon as the client missed a month's rent. The lawyer suspects that the landlord sees possibilities of getting much higher rent from a new tenant in a neighborhood that is gentrifying, and also suspects that the landlord's own past practice might provide the client with an argument that the landlord's abrupt action is inconsistent with implied terms of the tenancy. But that argument, let us assume, is a hard one to win, and so she next turns to a possibly more promising line of inquiry:]

L4:   Let me ask you a few questions about other parts of this situation. First, how would you describe the general upkeep of the apartment?

C4:   Oh, it was terrible. The hot water hardly ever worked. There were rats. There was mildew. It was a lousy place, it still is a lousy place—but I need it because it's all I can find out there with rents the way they are.

L5:   I'm wondering if you ever complained to the landlord about these bad conditions in the apartment.

C5:   No. I just figured this was the best I could get.

L6:   Maybe you said something to the landlord about them on the phone

C6:   Nope, I don't think I ever did.

L7:   Did you ever consider making some kind of complaint to the landlord?

C7:   No, like I said, I didn't think I could get anything better.

From here, the lawyer turns to other topics. Notice what she did not ask: she never inquired into the details of what was wrong with the apartment. In that respect, the interview was much less than comprehensive. But she had (or so we may imagine) a very good reason for not doing so. If, in her jurisdiction, a defense against eviction based on bad conditions in the rental property cannot be made unless the renter at some point complained to the landlord about those conditions, then the key question she had to answer, once she knew there was a possible conditions claim, was not "how cold was the apartment" or "how bad were the rats" but "did the tenant complain"? On that question, the lawyer inquires not once but twice. And because she realizes there might be some special reason the client didn't complain—and that that reason, in turn, might point to either a legal argument or some fundamental aspect of the client's "story"—she goes on to ask whether the client had ever considered making a complaint. That question could have elicited the kind of special circumstances the lawyer was wondering about, but instead the client simply reiterates the point he's already made, that he expected no better for the rent he could afford. The lawyer has learned what had to be learned on this score, and now turns to other issues—as she must, because time is short. She risks not hearing some aspect of the client's story that might be important, but she has reduced that risk by her inquiries at the very beginning of the interview and now by her careful attention to the client's own account of what he did (and did not) do and why. (She might have reduced this risk still more by briefly explaining the legal significance of this point to the client.)[61] Again, she must judge which risks to take, since she cannot possibly ask *everything*.

5.　EXPERTISE AND COUNSELING

The classic model of client-centered counseling is a form of very careful brainstorming. The client's available options are elicited, and their pluses and minuses are identified and assembled, and the client is asked to make a decision.[62] If the client seems to be leaping to conclusions, the lawyer tries to slow him down; if he seems to be erring either in terms of self-interest or morality, the lawyer may try to intervene.

It is certainly possible to understand the expertise of the client-centered lawyer as an expertise in this very process. The experienced lawyer will handle the process more effectively, and probably more rapidly, even if she adheres to its guidelines completely. She will phrase options more clearly; she will ask questions that elicit the client's thinking more fully; she will hear what the client says more sensitively; and the net result should be that lawyer and client have fewer misunderstandings, cover issues more effectively, and conclude the decisionmaking process more successfully than would be the case with a novice attorney.

We suspect, however, that in important ways expert lawyers tend to depart from the most elaborate possible applications of this model when they confront the constraints of limited time and resources. We see two reasons for these departures. First, the classic model is clearly not meant, and never has been meant, to require lawyers and clients to examine every conceivable option, sub-option and variation a case might suggest. No one ever had time for that. Nor did anyone have the cognitive capacity; the same limitations on short-term memory that make expert pattern-memory such a powerful asset mean that neither lawyer nor client could keep all the details of many different options in mind at any one time.[63] The model always implied some measure of editing by the lawyer (and perhaps the client as well), to focus on the principal choices, and among them on the principal reasonably attractive choices, rather than on every possible course of action, however unpromising, or every modest variation on an option.[64] Expert lawyers should be able to do this editing better than novices, because they should understand the options better as well.

Second, experts would tend to depart from the extensive exploration called for by the model because they believe that in routine cases they largely know what needs to be done. This is not the same as asserting that experts are people who believe they know the single approach that will work for every routine case, and who then go to work to fit every routine client into this predetermined pattern. That vision, or critique, seems unfair, at least to lawyers who hold client-centered convictions.

An important part of what these lawyers likely believe they know is what the real choices are—and we think that in routine cases they are likely correct. We expect that engaged, expert client-centered lawyers, having interviewed the client with care—nothing we are saying is meant to endorse presuming the client's goals rather than actually learning them—and having a good idea of the best options for clients with the goals the particular client has expressed, will narrow the options the client considers in ways that the classic model does not appear to envision. They may suggest that some seemingly plausible options have such grave problems that a client will put them to one side. They may focus attention so much on particular options that others take a back seat. They may also present to the client only the pluses and minuses that experience has taught them turn out to matter to clients; doing so is another instance of omission of information, but that very omission of marginally relevant considerations helps the client to focus on the issues that are likely to make a difference.[65]

The real task for the client, such a lawyer may feel, is not to choose among options A through E—where C, D, and E are hard to execute and unlikely to succeed. Rather, the client's choice is between A and B, and the lawyer's job is to explain to the client that if he wants one set of goals, he should go with A, while if he wants another set of goals, he should choose B. The client's choice of goals is important, and the lawyer who gives advice of this sort has been, we would say, entirely client-centered in helping the client to focus his time and effort on the choice he really needs to make. But in the process the lawyer has put options C, D, and E to one side. Perhaps the lawyer will simply not mention them. In some circumstances, however, it will surely be better for the lawyer to mention these other options and briefly explain why they aren't really worth considering (or at least tell the client explicitly that other options do exist but that the lawyer feels it makes sense not to spend time on them). Mentioning what is going unexplored leaves room for the client to decide he wants more exploration, and so is a check on the danger that the expert may leap too quickly to conclusions—but too much discussion of what isn't central may confuse the client while costing scarce time.

We suspect, moreover, that the expert counselor will not always, perhaps not frequently, approach even options A and B by seeking to produce a comprehensive list of pros and cons and then asking the client to add them up and arrive at a decision. Some clients may make choices this way, and certainly a lawyer should assist a client who does think in this manner to do so as systematically as possible. But it appears that many people make decisions rather differently. Indeed, a wide literature now examines the ways people actually make choices, and many of the pathways that people turn out to follow are far from systematic, objective assessments of all available evidence. Some of these decisionmaking moves are far from ideal—at least in the context of the significant choices that are made in legal matters—and we will need to consider the impact of these weaknesses on both lawyers and clients.[66] But we will begin with two forms of decisionmaking that may actually be quite desirable (and probably often overlap in actual people's judgments), though they do not fit the model of comprehensive rational weighing.

First, clients may not be disposed to attempt an elaborate weighing process, and may instead employ "fast and frugal" decisionmaking heuristics.[67] Suppose, for instance, that a lawyer knows, from past experience, that a number of factors determine whether trial or settlement is the better choice in a medical malpractice case. These factors include severity of damages, clarity of causation, age of the plaintiff, reputation of the defendant, length of trial, expense of trial, and others. But of these factors, the lawyer believes the most important is severity of damages, and that in a particular client's case the "severity of damages" factor points towards settlement.

Does the lawyer really know this? Unfortunately, the answer is probably not; we collectively know much less than we need to about what factors lead to what outcomes in legal cases, or about what outcomes are ultimately best.[68] But we suspect most lawyers believe that they have valid, useful approaches available to guide many decisions. There is every reason for lawyers to seek to make these rules of practice as sound as possible, but we believe that there is also reason for lawyers to use the knowledge they have accumulated, as imperfect as it may be.

A "fast and frugal" decisionmaking heuristic called "Take the Best" would dictate that the decision should be based on looking to the relevant factors in order of their importance; if the most important factor points towards one decision, then that becomes the decision and the less important factors are never even consulted. (If the top factor is neutral, then "Take the Best" decisionmakers would turn to the second factor, and so on.)[69] Remarkably enough, it appears that when information is scarce and the interrelations between different bits of available information are obscure, decisionmaking of this sort can be not only quick but also comparable in accuracy to more elaborate techniques.[70] An expert lawyer, one who has a clear sense of which factors appear to be the most important, can advise a client accordingly, and many clients may—quite reasonably—choose to make their decisions based on such deliberative shortcuts.[71]

Second, many clients, perhaps the great majority, do not approach decisionmaking in an emotionally disengaged way. Instead, it appears that people in general approach decisions about their lives not as mathematical problems but as emotionally weighted judgments; without emotion, it seems, people cannot judge the meaning of choices for their lives.[72] Surely it is part of the lawyer's job to help clients make decisions under conditions as free of stress as possible,[73] but it would be a mistake to seek to induce clients to choose without emotion. Recognizing this reality, lawyers may need to counsel clients not so much by listing considerations as by helping the clients to feel their emotional weight. Thus a lawyer seeking to help a client to understand the weight of a particular factor in a decision (a factor that the client may ultimately employ in a "Take the Best" decisionmaking shortcut) may explain that weight by speaking in the framework of story, because people so often find emotional force in narrative.[74] For example, the lawyer might tell a story about the client who failed to consider factor X—not to push the client to be guided solely by factor X but to help the client to see his situation as vividly as possible. We suspect that a lawyer who can rely on experience with similar matters in the past and on practiced skill in finding an emotional basis for conveying that experience to the client can assist a client to get to the heart of the matter more quickly and more helpfully than a lawyer whose focus is on full, dispassionate elaboration of options and considerations.

But lawyers may do more than that as well. If we think of a physician meeting with a patient, we may draw some analogies. Where a choice involves major and subjective stakes, a physician may well take a very nondirective approach. But if, say, the question is what to do about a precancerous, localized skin condition, and if there is an approach that is customarily used by most physicians in dealing with this sort of problem, then the expert doctor may simply say, "You've got a small problem here, not dangerous as long as we take care of it. I think we should remove this growth, and we can do that right here; it'll only take 15 minutes, shouldn't have any lasting side-effects, and I have time to go ahead with it right now." Perhaps the patient will have hesitations, and if so the expert will answer the patient's questions and may step back and speak more comprehensively even without particular questions. (The doctor's advice we've just quoted may be a bit too brief, because it does not offer any invitation for the patient to express such concerns.) But if the patient feels confident in the expert's judgment, and the expert feels she knows what it makes sense to do, then it makes sense for both doctor and patient to proceed based on the doctor's explicit advice, delivered without any exploration of other possible alternatives.

We expect that there are many legal situations in which experts can and do make similar judgments, with their clients' explicit endorsement or tacit, but not unreasonable, acquiescence. Clients hire experts because they believe that experts know what to do. That belief may be mistaken, and certainly when a case isn't routine the lawyer should treat it with all the care it needs. That belief may also be a product of patterns of social domination which ought to be disrupted, and engaged client-centered practice does seek to support clients' taking ownership of the decisions affecting their own lives. But where lawyer and client reasonably conclude that the best use of their limited time together is for the lawyer to offer guidance of this sort, we would not see the lawyer's advice as a breach of client-centeredness; rather, we see it as client-centeredness-in-practice. And this is so even though it may well be that, with unlimited time and resources, a lawyer could do a less directive, and ultimately better, job for the client. It is not client-centered to ignore the existence of limits on time and resources. Rather, what is client-centered is to find ways to take as full account of client perceptions and client needs as possible, in the time available.

Will experts go further and attempt to guide their clients away from decisions the lawyers consider imprudent, on the ground that the lawyers are less subject to decisionmaking weaknesses than their clients are? Certainly lawyers can try to help their clients to reason as clearly as possible, though it does not appear to be easy to defuse the impact of at least some human decisionmaking traits.[75] Doing that openly and explicitly, as well as possible, is simply counseling. But should lawyers go further and try to push clients towards particular decisions, on the ground that the lawyers—unblinded by the clients' cognitive failings—rightly perceive these choices to be superior? There is some evidence, for example, that unadorned lawyer advice—advice given without an explanation, simply resting on the lawyer's authority as an expert—may sometimes be especially effective in shifting a client's choice in ways that seem to avoid the impact of decisionmaking flaws.[76] Should lawyers act accordingly?

We have considered the intensity of persuasion that might be appropriate in guiding a client away from a choice the lawyer believes is unwise elsewhere in this book,[77] but it is worth briefly returning to it in light of the literature on experts' cognitive skills. If experts really are expert, are they better decisionmakers than clients? To the extent that experts' training shields them from cognitive errors, the answer would be "yes." We should hope that lawyers are in fact less swayed by cognitive errors than their clients are, and in some respects this may be so,[78] but it seems quite clear that experts, including lawyers and judges, *are* prey to cognitive flaws too.[79] Similarly, while it is probably true that lawyers are usually less distressed by their clients' situations than the clients themselves are, it does not follow that lawyers approach cases free of emotion (even if that were thought to be desirable); more likely, lawyers are emotionally engaged too, but on different matters (for instance, their desire to handle cases in a way that wins them respect from their peers).[80] Moreover, the line between judgments founded on cognitive mistakes and judgments founded on clients' values is decidedly blurred, and lawyers (expert and otherwise) have no special prerogative to make value choices for their clients.[81]

On all these grounds, we do not view the teachings of the literature on human decisionmaking as supporting sheer imposition of lawyer authority, any more than older assumptions of lawyer superiority did.[82] At the same time, we recognize that lawyers influence clients with every word and gesture, and lawyers surely should choose words and gestures with an eye to shielding their clients from decisionmaking flaws as much as possible.[83] Ultimately, we suspect the answer to this important question of what to do about clients' decisionmaking weaknesses remains less a matter of asserting the superiority of one party to the lawyer-client relationship over the other than of building the connection between the two. Over the length of the relationship with their lawyer, as Ian Weinstein has thoughtfully illustrated, clients may reassess their own judgments, and so part of what lawyers can give clients is time, and calm, within which to think.[84] Lawyer and client also engage with each other, and their shared discussion will affect them both.[85] If lawyers focus more attention on actually understanding clients' values, moreover, their ability to engage with their clients, whether as helpers, colleagues, or guides, will surely be greater.[86] Time for client reflection and for lawyer-client engagement may be limited, but we encourage lawyers to use the time they have.

D. THE RISKS OF EXPERTISE—AND WHAT TO DO ABOUT THEM

After surveying the impressive cognitive skills experts bring to bear, and inferring the characteristics of expert legal practice that these skills support, it is unnerving to confront the evidence that experts do not actually make sound decisions. Unfortunately, there is quite a lot of evidence of exactly this. Richard Neumann notes that "[s]tudies have shown that there is little diagnostic consistency in the medical profession; exposed to the same data, physicians often reach wildly different conclusions."[87] Another study comments that research has "established that in many clinical prediction tasks experts were *less* accurate than simple formulas based on observable variables."[88] Experts in at least some fields may not even be much more accurate than novices; the same article reports that in a review of

> more than fifty comparisons of judgments by clinical psychologists and novices.... [t]he effect of training was not large ... but it existed in many studies [of using the MMPI to judge personality disorders]. Training, however, generally did *not* help in interpreting projective tests (drawings, Rorschach inkblots, and sentence-completion tests); using such tests, clinical psychologists probably are no more accurate than auto mechanics or insurance salesmen.[89]

How could this be? One answer is simply that experts are *people*. If human beings' decisionmaking is guided by heuristic shortcuts that often serve us well but sometimes distort our appreciation of the options and risks we face, then experts may suffer from the same defects, even though their databases are better than those of novices. We have already alluded to the burgeoning literature on human cognitive processes, and their startling weaknesses. People, it appears, tend to rely on the data most "available" to them—that is, most present in their minds—to guide their decisions, even if that data by no means captures broader conditions.[90] They also tend to employ what they view as "representative" prototypes and so discount the possibility of divergence from these patterns.[91] In addition, they are strikingly vulnerable to scaling and anchoring effects, in which, for instance, the same outcome looks much better if it is portrayed as a partial gain than if it is characterized as a partial loss.[92] Their judgments are integrally bound up with their emotions and moods, and these too can be sound or misleading guides.[93] They are subject to prejudices, conscious and unconscious. Perhaps most unnervingly, once people have formed opinions, even tentative ones, they tend to re-evaluate the evidence they've considered and build the case for the inclination they've adopted, and they discount evidence that doesn't fit their views.[94]

* * *

It might be hoped that experts would be immune to these weaknesses, by virtue of their ability to use the resources of hopefully-objective expert knowledge. Where expert knowledge is substantial, perhaps this is usually the case.[95] There may also be situations where experts' training specifically guards them against particular errors of judgment.[96] But in many cases, there is room for debate about what a situation is, and what response to it is required, and in those situations there is room for experts to make decisions in the same way that other people do. There is, in fact, quite a lot of evidence that experts are subject to the cognitive defects that everyone else experiences.[97] There is also evidence from medical practice suggesting that experts, like others in our society, do not always bridge the gaps of difference between themselves and their clients.[98] Indeed, some forms of expert work seem inextricably linked to the use of cognitive shortcuts and to the risks that flow from that use. One emergency room physician, for instance, has said of his field of practice that "[n]owhere in medicine is rationality more bounded by relatively poor access to information and with limited time to process it, all within a milieu renowned for its error-producing conditions. It is where heuristics dominate, and without them emergency departments would inexorably grind to a halt."[99]

It is important to add that the tasks experts deal with are actually *difficult*. In this light, it may not be too surprising to learn of studies of radiologists and pathologists revealing that these experts, when asked to examine the same x-ray or specimen on two separate occasions, disagree with their own prior judgments as much as 10–20% of the time.[100] Moreover, the stakes can be very high. It is also not entirely surprising, therefore, that physicians in one study (involving hypothetical cases of women facing potential risks of osteoporosis and of cancer resulting from estrogen treatment aimed at reducing the likelihood of osteoporosis) decided to prescribe estrogen considerably less often than their own stated judgments about the various risks and benefits would have called for. In part, this judgment may have reflected a heuristic mistake, the "over-weighting of small probabilities"—here, the very small risk of a very grave result, cancer. But in part it may also have reflected the physicians' anxiety not to be, themselves, the cause of cancer resulting from prescribing estrogen.[101] The choices for lawyers are not always so rushed, or so fateful, as those of some physicians, but they can be similar in both stakes and haste.

Moreover, it seems likely that the same features of expert knowledge that make experts so insightful and fast—their extremely well-organized databases of relevant knowledge, accessible through mental processes that are fast and even unconscious—also make experts prone to trusting their own expertise too far.[102] Every field has its own accumulated lore of knowledge, and Blasi observes that "prototypical solution methods ... acquire a life of their own, evolving in odd and unpredictable ways and becoming disconnected from the problems that spawned them, which may also have evolved."[103] Experts search problems incompletely and they may misunderstand them; once they've embraced the wrong framework they may not let loose.[104] It is worrying to learn that there is experimental evidence that people who have incentives to perform well, and who perceive themselves to be experts, may be more likely than other people to rely on their own intuition rather than on available, and more reliable, decision rules.[105] It is true, as we have already seen, that there is evidence that experts slow down when they realize they are dealing with a nonroutine case,[106] but now it must be added that sometimes experts may well be prone not to realize this when they should.

It may be that these strictures on expertise as a whole are overstated. It is also possible, of course, that legal expertise is not subject to the same failings as expertise in some other fields. But while it may currently be impossible to measure the impact of legal expertise, because legal matters are too multi-factored to permit comparisons to be definitively drawn across cases, it seems unlikely that lawyers (any more than doctors) have altogether escaped the cognitive limits that apparently plague their counterparts in some other fields.[107]

It might be tempting, in light of findings like these, to try to dispense with expertise altogether, but this simply seems impossible. Experience ineluctably breeds expertise. What does seem possible, and profoundly desirable, is to cultivate a form of expertise that checks the headlong, headstrong propensities of the experts we have focused on until now in favor of another form of expertise, which we might simply call judgment (or even wisdom). Clinicians such as Mark Aaronson and Richard Neumann have explored this demanding quality, one that at its most profound appears to call for a deep sensitivity, perhaps both intellectual and moral, to the particularities of complex situations, guided by the capacity for reflection-in-action—an intuitive application of accumulated understanding, not to reiterate routines but to creatively respond to challenge.[108] True wisdom, however, is not easy to attain, and we will be content here to seek a lesser goal—to try to identify ways that lawyers can simply reduce their likelihood of making mistakes.

Perhaps the path to such tempered expertise is through training that puts more of a premium on learning about problem-solving, even at the cost of slowing students' acquisition of specific expert schemas for handling particular issues.[109] The question of how law schools should design their programs so as to help students to begin acquiring the full range of professional skills and values needed for practice has long been a central concern of clinical legal education and is now, perhaps more than ever, a concern of legal education as a whole.[110] Our concern, however, is not primarily with educational strategy, important as that is, but with what experts can do, in practice, to avoid pre-judgment or mis-judgment and instead achieve judgment. Candidly, we know of no comprehensive solutions, and we view this as a crucial area for investigation.

Essentially, the task the expert must undertake is to step back from the very patterns she has mastered to ask whether a particular case fits the pattern she has found for it—and yet not give up the speed and insight that expert reasoning (at least at its best) generates. To say that a case does not fit a pattern, however, must mean more than that the case has its own special features. Every case has its own special features. Fitting a case to a pattern means focusing on the commonalities between the case and others, and rests on the judgment that the special features can safely be disregarded. Again, the task is to determine when the special features demand attention—or, to put it differently, the task is to take a "second look," not too long a look but long enough to catch the signs of uniqueness that were missed the first time around. We offer the following suggestions, and urge readers to employ them or to find others to meet this crucial need:

Steps the lawyer can take to monitor her own thinking:

- Simply pausing, at some point in the process, may make a difference; after the pause, the expert can ask himself, "Have I overestimated how much I know about this case?" Probably just intending to do this is not enough; to take time entails structuring one's practice to make some time available.[111]

- Consciously employing more deliberate reasoning strategies, such as brainstorming, on nagging features of a case may also be productive.[112]

- A single, key question may point the way to reassessment when it is needed, if the question is taken seriously. In a medical context, Jerome Groopman suggests asking, "What's the worst thing this could be?"[113] An analogous lawyer's question might be "What are the biggest pitfalls in this approach?" or perhaps (adding a question) "Is this the standard approach? Would other lawyers recommend different approaches, and why?" Still another might be, "What did I rule out right away?"—a question meant to prompt the lawyer to consider whether the roads not taken might need to be revisited. At the same time, it is crucial that the reassessment question not itself become a meaningless routine—and no formula can altogether avoid the risk of becoming formulaic. Even worse, perhaps, the "question" may turn into an "anchor" diverting the lawyer from the real nature of the case; the point of the question is to prompt reassessment but not to distort thinking.[114]

- Checklists—lists of issues to explore, or options to consider, or questions to ask—may prove surprisingly helpful if the items on the checklist are the result of careful analysis of the field of practice at issue, despite their obvious tendency to promote routinized, disengaged practice.[115]

Steps that the lawyer can take with her client:

- There may be questions that can be put to the client, in the course of interviews or counseling sessions, to give the client an opportunity to reconsider his understanding of the situation or his choices about it, or to enable the client to tell the lawyer that the lawyer's framework needs revising.[116] One such question might be an open-ended inquiry at the end of an interview: "Is there anything I've missed?" But this question itself, we suspect, is probably too unfocused and too late, because the momentum of the interview will by then have guided the client to stick with the focus that the lawyer has adopted. A better approach might start from the reality that the expert will likely have moved rapidly to embrace a theory of the case; the expert might say: "You know, as a lawyer it's my job to get a feel for a case so I can tell my client's story to the judge and the jury. But sometimes what I think I'm hearing just isn't the same as what my client is telling me. I'm seeing this case now as a story of [such-and-such]. Is that how it feels to you, or have I missed something that could be important to our handling this case right?"

- Rather than questions from the lawyer to the client, questions from the client to the lawyer may be critically important. But clients may hesitate to ask their lawyer questions; certainly patients often feel they have unasked questions about sessions with their doctors, and the danger exists that clients who don't speak up will not be heard.[117] For clients to ask, lawyers may first need to educate them about the importance and appropriateness of asking—so that client education, in this respect as in others, may be of critical importance. The client rights statements now required in every lawyer's office in New York are a simple example of this effort.[118] But clients need to know more than their rights, and in fact part of what classic client-centered interactions do is to guide the client towards an understanding that he should play a central role not only in describing the problems and prospects he faces but in deciding what to do about them. If time is short, this message may be diluted, but there is some indication that teaching medical patients how to deal with their doctors—another very rushed group of professionals—contributes to patients' progress, and it seems likely that the same will be true for lawyers' clients.[119] Time remains short, but if the clients know better how to use the time to interact successfully with their lawyer, their work together can potentially be more valuable.[120]

None of these steps is perfect. If questions like these radically slowed down the expert's handling of the case, they would frustrate much of what expertise promises in terms of efficiency. Yet if experts assume that in general such self-checks should not lead to fundamental reassessments, they are likely to let the self-checks themselves decline into mere routine. Client-centered lawyers (indeed, all lawyers) should share a concern to avoid these pitfalls, and to find standards of practice that offer more assurance of quality than expert intuitions may provide. In the medical profession, such concerns have led to efforts to develop data-based practice: to make readily available to physicians the kinds of objective data that may be needed as a challenge to their intuitive, but erroneous, habits of mind, and to make consulting such information a norm of good practice[121]—though it has also been argued that these tools themselves are potential pitfalls for the clinician who looks to them and not to the actual patient.[122]

We are very far from having such data-based standards to guide our work as lawyers, and the lack of such standards may well make the practice of individual, putatively "expert" lawyers even less consistent than it otherwise might be.[123] But even when we do have such standards, and all the more so now when we do not, we also need other people. Thus *steps the lawyer can take with her colleagues* amount to a third category of preventive measures. The expert is in danger of becoming locked in to her own sense of what is routine and predictable. What she needs is an alternative perspective—colleagues, in other words, whether within the firm or elsewhere. (The only difference, though it is an important one, is in the extent to which the lawyer can speak precisely about her cases while obeying the duty of confidentiality—but even a consultation that avoids using identifying details about a case can be illuminating.) We don't imagine lawyers can consult about every case: again, that would frustrate the speed that expertise permits. But they can be in the habit of consultation, or collegial discussion (in continuing legal education, and preferably in more personal and reflective contexts than those courses may always provide), and that habit may help them avoid other, more unfortunate routines. Expertise is, in large measure, a product of shared, community effort, and an expert will do well to continue that sharing.[124] Indeed, many of the steps we've identified as options for the lawyer alone, or for the lawyer with her client, may also be the basis for the discussions that lawyers can have with their colleagues. But it is important, albeit difficult, for the circle of trusted colleagues to embrace people holding genuinely diverse views; otherwise, there is every reason to expect shared discussion to reinforce rather than challenge heuristic preconceptions.[125]

CONCLUSION

In this chapter we have sought to demonstrate that lawyers' expertise in fact enables them to talk fast—to provide effective and client-centered representation without sacrificing efficiency. But we might ask, nonetheless, whether lawyers providing "effective" representation are providing ideal representation. The answer, in some circumstances, is no. This is not because more lawyering is always better lawyering; on the contrary, more lawyering may simply be over-lawyering. But it is possible to shape a practice that engages with clients and clients' needs in a deeper, more holistic way than the practice we have described in this chapter. In such a lawyer-client relationship, the lawyer's job would be to understand the client's legal problem completely, but not just to do that. She would also need to identify and understand the legal problems the client has that he did not mention, perhaps thought were irrelevant or had no hope of solving. She would need as well to understand the nonlegal ramifications of all these problems, or in other words to understand the client's life as well as his legal situation. And, finally, she would need to be ready to explore not only the solutions to these problems that the law might offer the client as an individual, but other approaches—from class actions in court to community organizing outside of it—that might be better suited to achieving real solutions.

We have the greatest respect for law practices that reach, or even approach, these ambitious aspirations.[126] Moreover, we believe that what we say here is in fact relevant even to such holistic and political lawyering. *Every* form of lawyering can be done more or less expertly. Every form of lawyering has its routine side—the community meeting, say, that resembles many prior meetings, just as one set of interrogatories may resemble many previous sets. And every lawyer has only so much time. Thus we aim to suggest approaches that are helpful to client-centered lawyers of every variety, and we suspect that such lawyers, whatever their particular practice mode, are in fact seeking ways to be both faithful to their clients and fast in their work.

But it is true that our principal focus has not been on these multifaceted forms of engagement with clients. Should lawyers limit the number of clients they represent, so that they can provide the people they do serve with representation of this quality? On the other hand, should lawyers accept for now the reality of insufficient resources and cut back their services so drastically that they can somehow provide something to every client in need? There are serious ethical arguments for and against either of these approaches and perhaps in certain circumstances each should be adopted—holistic representation to mark out the best that we can do, minimalist representation to mitigate intolerable suffering.

Our emphasis in this chapter, however, has been on understanding how expert lawyers carry out the regular work of lawyering—in representing clients who do not need extraordinary assistance, and should not receive ineffectual or insensitive aid. Many of these cases are routine—not in the sense that they are trivial, or easy, but in the sense that they can be handled satisfactorily in accordance with pre-existing patterns. (What proportion of cases is routine is certainly open to debate, and no doubt the answer depends to some extent on how much time and resource pressure the answerer sees as bearing on those who must handle these cases.[127]) Others are not routine at all, but their complexities respond to the masterful knowledge that the expert brings to her problem-solving. All this is the regular work of our profession, and to do this regular work well is an important thing.

For this work—and for every form of lawyering in which it is employed—we have emphasized that expertise is not a device for providing second-rate legal services to those who cannot pay for more. Rather, it is the way that we provide the best services that we can provide, under the constraints with which we work. Expertise, in the end, is simply what human beings achieve with effort and experience. If expertise is far from perfect, so after all are we. Expertise, properly guided, is the best that we can achieve—and we should do our best to achieve and employ it.

* * * * * * * * * * * * * *

QUESTIONS FOR STUDY AND DISCUSSION

1. This chapter argues that expert judgment is superior to novice judgment, in part because experts process information so quickly. But as we suggested in the Conclusion to this chapter, if experts can do many things fast, they can use that speed either to serve a few clients comprehensively and holistically, or to serve many clients in a more modest, though still "effective," way. Do you think that lawyers have an ethical obligation to choose one of these alternatives or the other, either pursuant to the Model Rules of Professional Conduct or as a matter of personal morality?

2. In Chapter 3, we explained our understanding of "engaged client-centered counseling," and illustrated what we were endorsing through an extended dialogue between a lawyer and the interim executive director of his client, a civil rights organization. Fred Jamison, the lawyer in that dialogue, is clearly a seasoned attorney. Is the meeting he has with Rev. McGill (the interim executive director) consistent with the picture of expert practice we have drawn in the present chapter? Could Jamison have worked more quickly than he did without sacrificing his ability to understand McGill's thoughts and concerns? Or is the meeting between Jamison and McGill an illustration of what experts ought to do when a case proves more complex than they anticipated? Or is it an illustration of an intensity of practice that even expert lawyers will often be unable to provide, because of the limitations of time and resources?

3. Sandra Rossmueller, the attorney who meets with Devon Jeffries in Chapter 8 ("Talking to Clients About the Law"), is also clearly an expert in the work she is doing. Look back at that interview too. Is Rossmueller's handling of this interview consistent with the description of expert practice we have offered here? Do you see ways that she is able to use her expertise to both inform and connect with her client quickly? Do you see differences between what she does and what the present chapter envisions?

4. Does the description of expertise in this chapter ring true to you? Think about professional tasks—such as studying for exams!—at which you may consider yourself expert. Can you describe what makes you an expert at these tasks? And how does your performance of them differ from what you'd expect of a novice given the same assignments?

5. How do you know when you're an expert? Scholars suggest that attaining expertise in many fields may require many years of practice and reflection.[128] But it is hard to imagine anyone waiting all those years until some magical point is reached at which he or she is an expert and can now safely use expert approaches. Expertise must develop and become part of a lawyer's work gradually. At the same time, it must always be tempting to cut corners by omitting some kinds of inquiry or research or discussion on the grounds that you firmly believe they aren't worth the time and effort involved. But when *do* you have an acceptable basis for this "firm belief," and how do you distinguish expert belief from novice over-confidence?

6. The chapter discusses ways that even truly expert judgment can go wrong, and suggests some possible steps to take to reduce this danger. But those steps likely are not perfect. Which of them look most promising to you? What else might you do to avoid making expert mistakes? And how much will those steps slow you down? If expertise requires its own precautions to reduce the danger of expert error, is expertise in the end really an asset?

---

1. Gary L. Blasi, *What Lawyers Know: Lawyering Expertise, Cognitive Science, and the Functions of Theory*, 45 J. LEGAL EDUC. 313, 334 (1995).

2. Ian Weinstein, *Lawyering in the State of Nature: Instinct and Automaticity in Legal Problem–Solving*, 23 VT. L. REV. 1, 17 (1998), comments that "many high volume, repetitive lawyering settings value speed.... Often ... a few episodes like this [i.e., lasting approximately half an hour] comprise all the focused problem solving that many cases receive in high volume practice settings," though he emphasizes that he "makes no normative claims about the appropriateness of valuing speed. There are clear dangers to valuing routine over creative solutions and suggesting that the result need only be good enough, or as good as the last case, although the volume of unmet legal needs poses a real pressure on poverty lawyers."

3. *See, e.g.*, Deborah L. Rhode, *Moral Counseling*, 75 FORDHAM L. REV. 1317, 1327 (2006) (discussing resources currently available for representation of indigent clients, and commenting that "[a]t these resource levels, triage is inevitable, and extensive counseling is more often an aspiration than an achievement").

4. For an overview of the potentials and problems of unbundling, see Mary Helen McNeal, *Unbundling and Law School Clinics: Where's the Pedagogy?*, 7 CLIN. L. REV. 341, 349–58 (2001).

5. *Id.* at 356.

6. *See id.* at 356–57.

7. For an illustration and discussion of the use of videotapes, in the course of an illuminating study of six law offices' practice methods, see Gary Neustadter, *When Lawyer and Client Meet: Observations of Interviewing and Counseling Behavior in the Consumer Bankruptcy Law Office*, 35 BUFF. L. REV. 177, 225–26, 242 (1986).

8. Lawyers can also answer client questions individually via e-mail or other forms of electronic communication, perhaps saving some time on a question-by-question basis—though it is hard to believe that the net impact of ready e-mail access for clients will be to save lawyer time! For an insightful exploration of the issues presented by lawyers' use of "computer-mediated communication," see Robert M. Bastress & Joseph D. Harbaugh, *Taking the Lawyer's Craft Into Virtual Space: Computer–Mediated Interviewing, Counseling, and Negotiating*, 10 CLIN. L. REV. 115 (2003).

9. So, for example, this language from a legal services retainer agreement, carefully reviewed by its drafters for readability, hopefully contributes to lawyer-client understanding: "A lawyer-client team works when each person tells the truth and cooperates with and trusts the other. Both [the agency] and I need to let the other know anything that happens that could affect my case. . . . [The agency] will use its best efforts, skill and judgment on my case. It cannot and does not guarantee how my case will turn out." For a more extended illustration of a "plain language" retainer agreement, see Alex J. Hurder, *Negotiating the Lawyer–Client Relationship: A Search for Equality and Collaboration*, 44 BUFF. L. REV. 71, 89–90 n.105 (1996).

10. Weinstein, *supra* note 2, at 17 n.81, mentions a number of practice settings that "offer fertile ground for the private practitioner who can organize and manage a large non-lawyer staff and handle a large number of relatively small cases."

11. One study of the elements of decision-making expertise concluded by observing "how difficult it would be for any one person to consistently demonstrate excellence in resolving every one of the cardinal issues for any class of decision problem. This makes one suspect that true, across-the-board decision-making expertise is exceedingly rare." J. Frank Yates & Michael D. Tschirhart, *Decision-Making Expertise*, in THE CAMBRIDGE HANDBOOK OF EXPERTISE AND EXPERT PERFORMANCE 421, 435 (K. Anders Ericsson et al., eds., 2006). (This volume is cited hereafter as HANDBOOK.)

12. *See, e.g.*, Vimla L. Patel, David A. Evans & David R. Kaufman, *A Cognitive Framework for Doctor–Patient Interaction*, in COGNITIVE SCIENCE IN MEDICINE 257, 262 (David A. Evans & Vimla L. Patel eds., 1988) [hereinafter Patel, Evans & Kaufman, *A Cognitive Framework*] (inferring "that physicians have a rich network of knowledge linking disorders within a category and that their knowledge is indexed by a large number of patterns of features that facilitate rapid discrimination among alternative interpretations of cues"); Jennifer Wiley, *Expertise As Mental Set: The Effects of Domain Knowledge in Creative Problem Solving*, 26 MEMORY & COGNITION 716, 716 (1998) (expert knowledge is organized "in a way that is accessible, proceduralized, integrated, and principled . . . . The proceduralization of an expert's knowledge base tends to allow for quick and easy access to memory and possible solution paths").

13. Mark Neal Aaronson, *We Ask You to Consider: Learning About Practical Judgment in Lawyering*, 4 CLIN. L. REV. 247, 289 & n.107 (1998).

14. Anna T. Ciancolo et al., *Tacit Knowledge, Practical Intelligence, and Expertise*, in HANDBOOK, *supra* note 11, at 613, 615 (citing observations by Michael Polanyi). We'll consider below the important question of whether experts' speed and automaticity interfere with their ability to adjust to unfamiliar, nonroutine problems. See *infra* text at notes 102–106.

15. Weinstein, *supra* note 2, at 6; *see* Paul J. Feltovich et al., *Studies of Expertise from Psychological Perspectives*, in HANDBOOK, *supra* note 11, at 41, 53 ("automaticity is central to the development of expertise").

16. Fernando Colon-Navarro, *Thinking Like a Lawyer: Expert-Novice Differences in Simulated Client Interviews*, 21 J. LEGAL PROF. 107, 132 (1996).

17. David M. Eddy, *Variations in Physician Practice: The Role of Uncertainty*, in PROFESSIONAL JUDGMENT: A READER IN CLINICAL DECISION MAKING 45, 45 (Jack Dowie & Arthur Elstein eds., 1988) [hereafter cited as PROFESSIONAL JUDGMENT]. Eddy later comments that "[t]he final decision about how to manage a patient . . . . would be an extremely hard task for a research team; there is no hope that it could occur with any precision in the head of a busy clinician." *Id.* at 54.

18. *See* Albert R. Martin & Thomas J. Coates, *A Clinician's Guide to Helping Patients Change Behavior*, 146 WESTERN J. MED. 751, 751 (1987):

Physicians possess great understanding of disease, but treatment and prevention frequently rely on patients' ability and willingness to implement medical and life-style changes. Adherence to a prescribed regimen of medication occurs only 50% to 70% of the time, and only 5% to 30% of patients comply with preventive measures such as quitting smoking, losing weight or changing diet.

19. *See generally* DEBRA L. ROTER & JUDITH A. HALL, DOCTORS TALKING WITH PATIENTS/PATIENTS TALKING WITH DOCTORS: IMPROVING COMMUNICATION IN MEDICAL VISITS (2d ed. 2006).

20. *See* Linda F. Smith, *Client-Lawyer Talk: Lessons from Other Disciplines*, 13 CLIN. L. REV. 505, 514 (2006) ("over 7000 titles considering the doctor-patient consultation").

21. Richard M. Frankel, Diane S. Morse, Anthony Suchman & Howard B. Beckman, *Can I Really Improve My Listening Skills with Only 15 Minutes to See My Patients?*, 5 HMO PRACTICE 114, 114 (1991) ("According to the National Ambulatory Medical Care Survey (NAMCS) the average length of all office-based visits is 16.1 minutes, while nearly 70% are 15 minutes or less"). More recent data indicate that average visits to general practitioners last 17 minutes, and that "the average medical visit has increased between one and two minutes in duration over the past decade." ROTER & HALL, *supra* note 19, at 111, 112 (citing David Mechanic, Donna D. McAlpine, & Marsha Rosenthal, *Are Patients' Office Visits with Physicians Getting Shorter?*, 344 N. ENG. J. MED. 198 (2001)).

22.   Hilliard Jason, *Foreword*, in ARTHUR S. ELSTEIN, LEE S. SHULMAN & SARAH A. SPRAFKA, MEDICAL PROBLEM SOLVING: AN ANALYSIS OF CLINICAL REASONING ix (1978); *see also* Robert M. Hamm, *Clinical Intuition and Clinical Analysis: Expertise and the Cognitive Continuum*, in PROFESSIONAL JUDG-MENT, *supra* note 17, at 78, 79.

23.   Patel, Evans & Kaufman, *A Cognitive Framework*, *supra* note 12, at 291–92. My estimate of the interview's length is based on the total number of doctor-patient exchanges for this expert, labeled E_2, which is given as 71, *id.* at 288, compared to the 125 exchanges used by another physician, who accomplished that in 15 minutes, *see id.* at 299, 301. The total number of possible findings in the case, 76, is reported at *id.* at 279.

24.   Thus Kaufman and Patel find in another study that medical residents in a simulated diagnostic interview generated more "negative findings" than experts did, and observe:

> The comparably large number of negative findings is suggestive of the fact that this group had difficulty accounting for the myriad of problems the patient was presenting with and could not develop a coherent problem representation. The generation of numerous negative findings would also indicate that these subjects were considering multiple hypotheses and were attempt-ing to rule-out as many as possible.... The experts develop a coherent representation of the distinctive pattern of findings and elicit fewer negative findings because they do not perceive as great a need to rule out competing diagnoses.

David R. Kaufman & Vimla L. Patel, *The Nature of Expertise in the Clinical Interview: Interactive Medical Problem Solving*, in THE TENTH ANNUAL CONFERENCE OF THE COGNITIVE SCIENCE SOCIETY 461, 463–64 (August 17–19, 1988, Montreal, Quebec, Canada) [hereinafter Kaufman & Patel, *The Nature of Expertise*]. Moreover, the experts generated more findings per question/answer ex-change than the other groups, indicating "that the experts are more efficient in identifying cues in the patient data and ask the appropriate questions which lead to the generation of findings." *Id.* at 464. *But cf.* Colon–Navarro, *supra* note 16, at 127 (legal interview simulation study in which experts and novices apparently did not differ significantly in the number of facts found).

25.   Feltovich et al., *supra* note 15, at 55 ("Expertise ... involves learning which information is most useful and which is tangential or superfluous").

26.   Vimla L. Patel, José F. Arocha & David R. Kaufman, *A Primer on Aspects of Cognition for Medical Informatics*, 8 J. AM. MED. INFORM. ASSOC. 324, 328 (2001).

27.   Experts may also have developed such well-marked cognitive pathways that they can supplement the limited resources of short-term memory by tapping directly into long-term memory as well. Feltovich et al., *supra* note 15, at 50, 54–59.

28.   Blasi, *supra* note 1, at 335. Apparently novices see individual pieces and relations between them; experts see the pattern of the whole. Moreover, Blasi observes, "there is ample evidence that experts in many domains possess the same sort of ability to perceive and recall patterns ... observed in chess masters." *Id.* at 343.

29.   "Forward reasoning," the intuitive insight that some characterize as the core of expert medical clinical thinking, "is almost certain to produce erroneous results when knowledge is inadequate." Vimla L. Patel, Guy J. Groen & Geoffrey R. Norman, *Effects of Conventional and Problem–Based Medical Curricula on Problem Solving*, 66 ACAD. MED. 380, 381 (1991) [hereinafter Patel et al., *Curricula*]. There is evidence, however, that novices *do* follow the same investigative strategy as experts—"generating a set of hypotheses or problem formulations based on very limited data ... and using these formulations to guide subsequent data selection," Jack Dowie & Arthur Elstein, *Introduction*, in PROFESSIONAL JUDGMENT, *supra* note 17, at 12.

30.   See *infra* text accompanying notes 87–107.

31.   Arthur Elstein and Georges Bordage have observed that "the more data collected, the less likely it is that all will be used." Arthur S. Elstein & Georges Bordage, *Psychology of Clinical Reasoning*, in PROFESSIONAL JUDGMENT, *supra* note 17, at 109, 114. "While in no way minimizing the importance of thoroughness," *id.*, the authors comment that "[t]he interpretive process can be adversely affected by collecting too much data, for the sheer volume of facts may impair the clinician's ability to sort out and focus upon the relevant variables." *Id.* at 118. Similarly, Patel, Arocha & Kaufman have observed that "hypothesis-driven reasoning is slower and may make heavy demands on working memory, because of the need to keep track of such things as goals and hypotheses.... Hypothesis-driven reasoning is a type of 'weak' method, i.e. a strategy that is used when the problem solver either lacks knowledge about the domain or is highly uncertain about the solution." Patel, Arocha & Kaufman, *supra* note 26, at 339. (For a more positive characteriza-tion of "hypothetico-deductive" reasoning, however, emphasizing its integral part in expert thinking about "unfamiliar, difficult or complex" questions, see Howard S. Barrows, Problem-Based Learning Applied to Medical Education 12 (rev. ed. 2000).)

32. Geoff Norman et al., *Expertise in Medicine and Surgery*, in Handbook, *supra* note 11, at 339, 341.

33. Peter A. Frensch & Robert J. Sternberg, *Expertise and Intelligent Thinking: When Is It Worse to Know Better?*, 5 Advances in the Psychology of Human Intelligence 157, 159 (Robert J. Sternberg ed., 1989) ("speed and quality of performance might be and, in fact, have been empirically demonstrated to be significantly correlated in most studies on expertise").

34. The power of intuition is the subject of Malcolm Gladwell's well-known book, Blink: The Power of Thinking Without Thinking (2005). The physician Jerome Groopman, in his book How Doctors Think (2007), also recognizes the power of intuition, though he insists on the necessity for systematic thought as well. He describes a case in which an endocrinologist shook a patient's hand and, from the feel of his hand, at once "made the diagnosis that had eluded all the other doctors." *Id.* at 204.

35. *See* Karel G. Ross, Jennifer L. Shafer, & Gary Klein, *Professional Judgments and "Naturalistic Decision Making,"* in Handbook, *supra* note 11, at 403 (on the superiority of intuitive decision making as compared with analytical processes when experts must act "in the context of time pressure, uncertainty, ill-defined goals, and high personal stakes," as for instance in military action). Gladwell urges that in situations where "a flash of insight" is needed, requiring people to articulate the reasons for their choices can block the necessary intuitive leaps. Gladwell, *supra* note 34, at 119–22.

36. *See* Blasi, *supra* note 1, at 344–45; Michelene T.H. Chi, *Two Approaches to the Study of Experts' Characteristics*, in Handbook, *supra* note 11, at 21, 23; Mica R. Endsley, *Expertise and Situation Awareness*, in Handbook, *supra* note 11, at 633, 649 ("experts spend considerable effort at the task of situation assessment"); Frensch & Sternberg, *supra* note 33, at 161–62; Feltovich et al., *supra* note 15, at 44. Two scholars have observed that "[f]lexibility and adaptability to the task environment are salient expert characteristics; they do not hesitate to change paths—to reframe the problem—if that seems indicated, and they are quick to recognize a new problem as a variant of a familiar type." Dowie & Elstein, *supra* note 29, at 13. Another scholar has made the point vividly: "[P]ut an unfamiliar or troublesome problem in front of the experienced physician and you will see metacognition and the hypothetico-deductive process in full bloom," Barrows, *supra* note 31, at 18. On this account, what experts do when they recognize unfamiliarity is to return to this "weak," *see supra* note 31, but more searching, method of inquiry, putting aside at least for a time the speed, or short cuts, of forward reasoning. As we will see later, however, experts' flexibility has its limits.

37. There are sharp critiques of the power of intuitive judgment, at least in contexts requiring complex analytical judgments. *See* Robyn M. Dawes, *You Can't Systematize Human Judgment: Dyslexia*, in Professional Judgment, *supra* note 17, at 150 (on the superiority of regression equations to intuitive clinical judgment); Hamm, *supra* note 22, at 81–82 ("Intuitive thought involves rapid, unconscious data processing that combines the available information by 'averaging' it, has low consistency, and is moderately accurate.... Analysis, the other end of the cognitive continuum, has the opposite features: Analytic thought is slow, conscious, and consistent; it is usually quite accurate (though it occasionally produces large errors); and it is quite likely to combine information using organizing principles that are more complicated than simple 'averaging'.").

38. *Cf.* Steven A. Sloman, *Two Systems of Reasoning*, in Heuristics and Biases: The Psychology of Intuitive Judgment 379, 382–83 (Thomas Gilovich, Dale Griffin, & Daniel Kahneman eds., 2002) [hereafter cited as Heuristics] (suggesting that people have two reasoning systems, one associative and intuitive, the other rule-based and deliberative, and that "the common mode of operation of the two systems is clearly interactive," though their results do not always agree).

39. Norman et al., *supra* note 32, at 346.

40. *See id.* at 348–49.

41. Weinstein, *supra* note 2, at 25.

42. "[T]he road from novice to expert is a continuous one," as two psychologists argue, in Patrick Shafto & John D. Coley, *Development of Categorization and Reasoning in the Natural World: Novices to Experts, Naive Similarity to Ecological Knowledge*, 29 J. Exp. Psych: Learning, Memory, & Cognition 641, 648 (2003).

43. For examples of such errors, see Mary Marsh Zulack, *Rediscovering Client Decisionmaking: The Impact of Role-Playing*, 1 Clin. L. Rev. 593, 636–37 n.54 (1995); see also *infra* note 104.

44. *See* Gay Gellhorn, *Law and Language: An Empirically-Based Model for the Opening Moments of Client Interviews*, 4 Clin. L. Rev. 321 (1998).

45. It is worth mentioning here the question of *who* asks these open-ended questions and hears the client's telling of her own story. Our focus here is on lawyers' direct interaction with clients, but as we have already mentioned, lawyers may in fact rely on paralegals (or others, such as secretaries) to undertake much of the office's contact with clients. *See supra* text accompanying note 10. Indeed, the question of who undertakes a given part of the needed work with the client arises at many points in the relationship, from the beginning of the first interview through the closing of the case. At every stage, the lawyer designing her office systems must weigh the ability of assistants to work effectively with clients along with the possible costs involved in reducing the lawyer's own engagement with the people she represents. More prosaically, lawyers and their staffs will need to address the challenges involved in coordinating their roles—for example, building from the paralegal's initial questions, or the screening form filled out by the secretary, to the lawyer's later follow-ups.

46. Howard B. Beckman & Richard M. Frankel, *The Effect of Physician Behavior on the Collection of Data*, 101 ANNALS INTERNAL MED. 692, 694 (1984) ("Characteristically, after a brief period of time (mean, 18 seconds), and most often after the expression of a single stated concern, the physicians in our study took control of the visit by asking increasingly specific, closed-ended questions that effectively halted the spontaneous flow of information from the patient"); Kim Marvel, Ronald M. Epstein, Kristine Flowers & Howard B. Beckman, *Soliciting the Patient's Agenda: Have We Improved?*, 281 J. AM. MED. ASS'N 283, 285 (1999) (follow-up study finding that "[t]he mean time available to patients to initially express their concerns before the first physician redirection was 23.1 seconds").

47. *See id*. at 286 ("patients who initiated 1 or more concerns and were given the opportunity to complete their concerns used an average of only 32 seconds"). In Beckman & Frankel's earlier study, "most completed statements took less than 60 seconds and none took longer than 150 seconds." Beckman & Frankel, *supra* note 46, at 695. Beckman and his colleagues also suggest, plausibly, that when patients don't get to state their concerns at the start, they are more likely to inject them later on. *See* Marvel et al., *supra* note 46, at 285; H.B. Beckman, R.M. Frankel, & J. Darnley, *Soliciting the Patients [sic] Complete Agenda: A Relationship to the Distribution of Concerns*, 33 CLINICAL RES. 714A (1985) (abstract submitted to The Society for Research and Education in Primary Care Internal Medicine, Washington, D.C., May 3 and 4, 1985).

48. Linda F. Smith, *Was It Good for You Too? Conversation Analysis of Two Interviews*, 96 KY. L.J. 579, 599 (2007–08).

49. *See* Geoffrey H. Gordon, Laurence Baker & Wendy Levinson, *Physician-Patient Communication in Managed Care*, 163 WEST. J. MED. 527, 527 (1995) ("Once all of a patient's concerns and requests are aired, a realistic agenda for the visit can usually be consensually negotiated.").

50. *See* Hurder, *supra* note 9, at 92 (suggesting that "[t]he agenda of the lawyer-client conference might itself be a subject of negotiation as the client might have interests in how the conference is conducted"). There are other circumstances, however, where the lawyer may have to take control of the agenda, and drastically narrow it, in order to accomplish work that cannot be postponed. The lawyer interviewing her client in the holding cell immediately before his bail hearing will often have to tell the client that their discussion must focus on some issues, those bearing on bail, and not others, and that other issues will have to be the subject of another conversation. Hurder gives a similar example from the context of seeking an emergency order of protection against domestic violence. *Id*. at 95.

51. Roter and Hall cite a study finding that "physicians who gazed frequently at the patient were more successful in recognizing psychological distress." ROTER & HALL, *supra* note 19, at 123.

52. *See* Frankel et al., *supra* note 21, at 116 (commenting that responding empathetically "adds negligible time to the interview") & 117 (noting a recent study finding "that physicians who used active listening took, on average, one minute longer to complete their visits than physicians who used traditional biomedically oriented interviewing techniques"); Dale A. Matthews, Anthony L. Suchman, & William T. Branch, *Making 'Connexions': Enhancing the Therapeutic Potential of Patient-Clinician Relationships*, 118 ANN. INTERNAL MED. 973, 974 (1993); Moira Stewart, Judith Belle Brown, & W. Wayne Weston, *Patient-Centred Interviewing Part III: Five Provocative Questions*, 35 CAN. FAM. PHYSICIAN 159, 160 (1989) (summarizing their study, which found that interviews scored as least patient-centered in terms of eliciting feelings [receiving a score of 1 on a 4-point scale] took an average of 7.8 minutes; those scored "2" lasted 9.8 minutes; those scored "3" took 12.0 minutes and those scored "4" 10.4 minutes, and concluding "that physicians who are struggling with the patient-centred concepts, but not fully utilizing and integrating them, engage in longer interviews compared to doctors who have mastered the approach, or doctors who have very low scores on patient-centredness").

53. William T. Branch & Tariq K. Malik, *Using 'Windows of Opportunities' in Brief Interviews to Understand Patients' Concerns*, 269 J. AM. MED. ASS'N 1667 (1993).

54. *Id.* at 1668. For an account of a remarkable creation of "connexion" between a doctor and patient—in which a doctor's simple statement that "I'm beginning to understand how hard it is to be you" produced a moment in which "it felt like we [doctor and patient] were joined, both parts of some larger whole; it was very peaceful and reassuring, even loving"—see Matthews et al., *supra* note 52, at 976.

55. *See* Gordon et al., *supra* note 49, at 529 (illustrating the frustration of a patient facing new limits on her care under an HMO's plan, and suggesting a number of responses, including dealing "explicitly" with "[t]he patient's ability to trust her new physician").

56. See element 5 of our outline of interviewing, in Chapter 2 ("Connection Across Difference and Similarity").

57. This example is suggested by one offered by Marilyn Berger and her co-authors. For a recent version, see MARILYN J. BERGER, JOHN B. MITCHELL, RONALD H. CLARK, & MONIQUE C.M. LEAHY, PRETRIAL ADVOCACY: PLANNING, ANALYSIS & STRATEGY 21–22 (2d ed. 2007).

58. On these and other techniques of factual investigation, see DAVID A. BINDER, PAUL BERGMAN, SUSAN C. PRICE, & PAUL R. TREMBLAY, LAWYERS AS COUNSELORS: A CLIENT-CENTERED APPROACH 114–19, 153–66 (2d ed. 2004). Interestingly, Professor Binder and his co-authors indicate that certain techniques they describe are not to be used always and everywhere, but "only if it seems helpful to do so," *id.* at 116 (breaking time-line "clumps" into their component events), 157 & n.11 (reminding readers that "[y]ou need not ritualistically develop alternative factual propositions for every element in every cause of action").

59. Colon-Navarro, *supra* note 16, at 129–32 (expert attorneys did spend some minutes "developing 'the fallback' position of political asylum," but not as much time as the novices spent on this claim; "to the experts, the fact that the client was from El Salvador made the probability of an asylum petition very unlikely to succeed, as the political situation is such that the requisite 'proof' of reasonable fear of persecution is very rare").

60. Patel, Evans & Kaufman, *A Cognitive Framework*, *supra* note 12, at 293.

61. We look closely at lawyers' advice to their clients about the law in both Chapters 6 ("Truth and Consequences") and 8 ("Talking to Clients About the Law").

62. See steps 5 through 7 of our counseling outline in Chapter 2.

63. Techniques such as written lists, and making time for clients' reflection about them, certainly can to some extent offer a way around short-term memory limits. But even with these tools, a truly comprehensive collection of options and considerations would likely be overwhelming.

64. There is also evidence "that the deliberation of large consideration sets [i.e., multiple options] can do more than simply waste time. It can also exact significant psychological costs, such as turmoil over the possibility of failing to pick the very best alternative." Yates & Tschirhart, *supra* note 11, at 431. In fact, in consumer choice settings, people presented with too many alternatives are apparently less likely to choose *any* of them than they would if they had fewer options. *See* Sheena S. Iyengar & Mark R. Lepper, *When Choice Is Demotivating: Can One Desire Too Much of a Good Thing?*, 79 J. PERSONALITY & SOC. PSYCHOL. 995 (2000); Jennifer Senior, *Dark Thoughts on Happiness*, NEW YORK, July 17, 2006, at 26, 32.

65. To use a medical analogy, suppose that past experience (or even scientific study) has shown that only tiny proportions of patients contemplating a particular surgery are dissuaded by some side effects, while certain other side effects affect many people's choices. It might well make sense to talk with the patient only about the side effects that seem to matter, in the hope that he will really come to grips with those, rather than risk losing these concerns in the midst of a longer, more complete list. "*What is worth knowing*" guides "*what is worth saying*, in order to make best use of individuals' limited attention." Baruch Fischhoff, *Heuristics and Biases in Application*, in HEURISTICS, *supra* note 38, at 730, 744–46.

66. *See infra* text accompanying notes 90–107.

67. *See* Gerd Gigerenzer, Jean Czerlinski, & Laura Martignon, *How Good Are Fast and Frugal Heuristics?*, in HEURISTICS, *supra* note 38, at 559.

68. Ian Weinstein, *Don't Believe Everything You Think: Cognitive Bias in Legal Decision Making*, 9 CLIN. L. REV. 783, 811 (2003).

69. Gigerenzer et al., *supra* note 67, at 563.

70. *Id.* at 574.

71. This choice logically entails both a choice of decisionmaking method and an application of that method, but we do not assume that either of these choices will be made based on elaborate weighing, or even that they will be distinct in clients' minds; the entire process, we imagine, will be "fast and frugal."

72. *See* ANTONIO DAMASIO, DESCARTES' ERROR: EMOTION, REASON, AND THE HUMAN BRAIN (Penguin Book 2005) (1994). Damasio suggests that "gut feelings"—more formally, "somatic markers"—are generated by emotions and "connected, by learning, to predicted future outcomes of certain scenarios." In the process of choice, "[s]omatic markers do not deliberate for us. They assist the deliberation by highlighting some options (either dangerous or favorable) .... [T]he number of scenarios under scrutiny is immense, and my idea is that somatic markers (or something like them) assist the process of sifting through such a wealth of detail—in effect, reduce the need for sifting because they provide an automated detection of the scenario components which are more likely to be relevant," and which then can become the subject of conscious deliberation. *Id.* at 174–75.

73. "Numerous studies have shown that acute stress narrows the scope of attention," Yates & Tschirhart, *supra* note 11, at 432, and the more our attention is occupied the fewer mental resources we can bring to bear on decisionmaking.

74. We explore the impact and meaning of narrative in chapter 5 ("Narrative Theory and Narrative Practice"), though our focus there is on the lawyer's hearing the client's narrative rather than on her counseling the client by using narratives of her own.

75. *See, e.g.,* Baruch Fischhoff, *DeBiasing,* in JUDGMENT UNDER UNCERTAINTY: HEURISTICS AND BIASES 422 (Daniel Kahneman, Paul Slovic, & Amos Tversky eds., 1982) (reviewing studies of efforts to reduce "hindsight bias" and "overconfidence").

76. *See* Russell Korobkin & Chris Guthrie, *Psychology, Economics, and Settlement: A New Look at the Role of the Lawyer,* 76 TEX. L. REV. 77, 113–21 (1997).

77. See the analysis of the dialogue between attorney Richard Mathiesson and his client Bill Arnholtz in Chapter 2, and the extended discussion of a somewhat different dialogue between Mathiesson and Arnholtz in Chapter 7 ("Engaging in Moral Dialogue"), as well as the consideration of occasions for intervention in client decisionmaking in Chapter 3 ("Engaged Client–Centered Counseling About Client Choices").

78. *See* Korobkin & Guthrie, *supra* note 76, at 137 ("Our experimental results support the hypothesis that lawyers, on average, evaluate litigation options differently than litigants, with lawyers' evaluations more likely to be consistent with the expected value analysis presumed by economic models of litigation."); Weinstein, *supra* note 68, at 819–21.

79. For a study arguing that lawyers are unlikely to realize or to control for the fact that they are susceptible to the same sorts of cognitive biases as their clients (in particular, the "self-serving bias" which leads people on opposite sides of disputes to assess the facts in the light most favorable to their own interests), see Linda Babcock, George Loewenstein, & Samuel Issacharoff, *Creating Convergence: Debiasing Biased Litigants,* 22 L. & SOC. INQUIRY 913, 921 (1997). There is also striking evidence of the problematic impact of cognitive heuristics or shortcuts on judges. *See* Chris Guthrie, Jeffrey Rachlinski, & Andrew J. Wistrich, *Blinking on the Bench: How Judges Decide Cases,* 93 CORNELL L. REV. 1, 19–29 (2007). On the susceptibility of experts in other fields to cognitive weaknesses, see *infra* text accompanying notes 90–107.

80. We have emphasized elsewhere in this book, particularly in Chapters 2 and 7, the ways that lawyers' emotions and values may sway their handling of interactions with their clients.

81. *See* Korobkin & Guthrie, *supra* note 76, at 131–36. Korobkin and Guthrie do not view every case as ambiguous, however, and they also raise the question of whether lawyers might have a duty to the legal system to dissuade clients from using it "as a forum for the fulfillment of psychological aspirations," however rational such use might be from the point of view of individual clients. *Id.* at 141.

82. Similarly, Korobkin & Guthrie disclaim the use of lawyer advice-without-explanation, despite its potential impact, mentioned in the text accompanying note 76 *supra.* They call for "an interactive counseling process" in which lawyers may ultimately "volunteer advice, but such advice should be accompanied by an explicit description of the considerations underlying the advice and an explanation of the considerations that suggest the client might not want to alter his analysis despite the lawyer's urging." *Id.* at 136; *see also* John M.A. DiPippa, *How Prospect Theory Can Improve Legal Counseling,* 24 U. ARK. LITTLE ROCK L. REV. 81, 104–15 (2001).

83. Lawyers might, for instance, recognize the persuasive impact of familiar examples on people's thinking, and respond in kind, by "meet[ing] ill chosen persuasive details [from clients] with better selected persuasive details." Weinstein, *supra* note 68, at 827.

84. *Id.* at 817 ("Patience should be the first line of defense.").

85. The intensity of the counseling encounters between engaged client-centered lawyers and clients is a central theme of Chapter 3 of this book.

86. For a discussion of an unnerving study suggesting how little attending physicians knew their patients' values despite often having been acquainted with the patients for over six months, see Yates & Tschirhart, *supra* note 11, at 434.

87. Richard K. Neumann, Jr., *Donald Schön, The Reflective Practitioner, and the Comparative Failures of Legal Education*, 6 CLIN. L. REV. 401, 412 (2000). Groopman reports autopsy data indicating that diagnoses are wrong some 10–15% of the time. GROOPMAN, *supra* note 34, at 24, 276. A medical educator, Ronald A. Arky, has observed that "[a] RAND study revealed that the appropriate treatment is given in only 50 percent of visits to general physicians." Ronald A. Arky, *Shattuck Lecture: The Family Business—To Educate*, 354 N. ENG. J. MED. 1922, 1926 (2006).

88. Colin F. Camerer & Eric J. Johnson, *The Process-Performance Paradox in Expert Judgment: How Can Experts Know So Much and Predict So Badly?*, in TOWARD A GENERAL THEORY OF EXPERTISE: PROSPECTS AND LIMITS at 195, 196 (K. Anders Ericsson & Jacqui Smith eds., 1991).

89. *Id.* at 200 (describing findings in Howard N. Garb, *Clinical Judgment, Clinical Training, and Professional Experience*, 105 PSYCH. BULL. 387 (1989)).

90. *See* Amos Tversky & Daniel Kahneman, *Judgment Under Uncertainty: Heuristics and Biases*, in JUDGMENT UNDER UNCERTAINTY: HEURISTICS AND BIASES, *supra* note 75, at 3, 11–14.

91. *See id.* at 4–11; Amos Tversky & Daniel Kahneman, *Extensional Versus Intuitive Reasoning: The Conjunction Fallacy in Probability Judgment*, in HEURISTICS, *supra* note 38, at 19.

92. *See* Tversky & Kahneman, *supra* note 90, at 14–18. *But cf.* Robert J. Condlin, *Legal Bargaining Theory's New "Prospecting" Aganda: It May Be Social Science, But Is It News?*, University of Maryland School of Law, Legal Studies Research Paper No. 2009–4, available at http://ssrn.com/abstract=1336683, at 6 n.31 (noting that the "heuristics and biases" literature, or "Prospect Theory," "does not lack for skeptics and critics both in the social sciences and in law"); *id.* at 8 n.36 (commenting that "the concept of anchoring" may have been "abandoned, or at least downgraded").

93. Paul Slovic et al., *The Affect Heuristic*, in HEURISTICS, *supra* note 38, at 397, 398 comment that "[a]lthough analysis is certainly important in some decision-making circumstances, reliance on affect and emotion is a quicker, easier, and more efficient way to navigate in a complex, uncertain, and sometimes dangerous world." As they explain, "[u]sing an overall, readily available affective impression can be far easier—more efficient—than weighing the pros and cons or retrieving from memory many relevant examples, especially when the required judgment or decision is complex or mental resources are limited." *Id.* at 400. But this "experiential thinking," *id.* at 416, is also "frightening in its dependency upon context and experience, allowing us to be led astray or manipulated—inadvertently or intentionally—silently and invisibly." *Id.* at 420.

On the impact of mood, see Norman Schwarz, *Feelings as Information: Moods Influence Judgments and Processing Strategies*, in HEURISTICS, *supra* note 38, at 534. As to whether the impact of mood in decisionmaking promotes good or bad decisions, Schwarz observes that "[t]he 'problem' is not that attending to the information provided by our feelings interferes with what would otherwise be a rational judgment process, but that we may misread feelings that are due to an unrelated source as our response to the current situation or the target at hand." *Id.* at 547.

94. In medicine, for example, the necessity of focusing on quickly-shaped hypotheses saves vital time and effort, but "as a problem solver works with a particular set of hypotheses, psychological commitment takes place and it becomes more difficult to restructure the problem." Dowie & Elstein, *supra* note 29, at 19. Moreover, these scholars continue, "[t]he most common error in processing data is to interpret data which should be non-contributory to a particular hypothesis, and which might even suggest that an alternative be considered, as consistent with hypotheses already under consideration. The data best remembered tend to be those that fit the hypotheses generated. Where findings are distorted in recall, it is generally in the direction of making the facts more consistent with typical clinical patterns. Positive findings tend to be overemphasized and negative findings discounted and there is a tendency to seek information that would confirm a hypothesis rather than the information that would permit testing of two or more competing hypotheses." *Id.* at 20.

95. Professor Condlin observes that "experienced actors generally are less susceptible than novices to heuristics and biases of imperfect rationality." Conlin, *supra* note 92, at 23. Indeed, "[m]any studies have found that when experts perform in their domain in their natural context, bias is alleviated and experts yield good judgments." Ross et al., *supra* note 35, at 405. If the "knowledge" experts have is actually mistaken, however, then their mastery of it may not be so helpful. That may be the lesson of the studies of interpretations of psychological interpretive tests, mentioned in the text accompanying note *supra*.

96. One often-cited instance is weather forecasting—as imperfect a science as this still is. *See* Derek J. Koehler, Lyle Brenner, & Dale Griffin, *The Calibration of Expert Judgment: Heuristics and Biases Beyond the Laboratory*, in HEURISTICS, *supra* note 38, at 686, 701.

97. *See* Max Henrion & Baruch Fischhoff, *Assessing Uncertainty in Physical Constants*, in HEURISTICS, *supra* note 38, at 666 (physics); Werner F.M. De Bondt & Richard H. Thaler, *Do Analysts Overreact?*, in HEURISTICS, *supra* note 38, at 678 (securities analysts).

98. On the impact of race in medical care, see, e.g., Jersey Chen et al., *Racial Differences in The Use of Cardiac Catheterization after Acute Myocardial Infarction*, 344 N. ENG. J. MED. 1443 (2001) (African–American patients receive cardiac catheterization less frequently than whites, regardless of the race of the doctor); Lisa Cooper–Patrick et al., *Race, Gender, and Partnership in the Patient–Physician Relationship*, 282 J. AM. MED. ASS'N 583, 583 (1999) (finding that "African American patients rated their visits as significantly less participatory than whites" and that "[p]atients in race-concordant relationships with their physicians [i.e., where patient and doctor were of the same race] rated their visits as significantly more participatory than patients in race-discordant relationships"); J. Hector Pope et al., *Missed Diagnoses of Acute Cardiac Ischemia in* *the Emergency Department*, 342 N. ENG. J. MED 1163 (2000) (although overall errors were few, African-Americans were two to four times more at risk of "being sent home" than were whites).

99. Pat Croskerry, *The Importance of Cognitive Errors in Diagnosis and Strategies to Minimize Them*, 78 ACAD. MED. 775, 776 (2003) (footnote omitted).

100. Eddy, *supra* note 17, at 48.

101. Arthur S. Elstein et al., *Comparison of Physicians' Decisions Regarding Estrogen Replacement Therapy for Menopausal Women and Decisions Derived From a Decision Analytic Model*, in PROFESSIONAL JUDGMENT, *supra* note 17, at 298, 314.

102. So, for example, Frensch & Sternberg, *supra* note 33, at 164, suggest that "[a] highly structured and complex knowledge system that contains many procedures will be relatively inflexible. Thus, the very same cognitive mechanisms that are thought to be underlying experts' sometimes amazingly superior performances on familiar tasks will also hinder their performances when situational or task demands change." *See also* Paul J. Feltovich, Rand J. Spiro & Richard L. Coulson, *Issues of Expert Flexibility in Contexts Characterized by Complexity and Change*, in EXPERTISE IN CONTEXT: HUMAN AND MACHINE 125 (Paul J. Feltovich, Kenneth M. Ford, & Robert R. Hoffman eds., 1997); Ahmad Hashem, Michelene T.H. Chi, & Charles P. Friedman, *Medical Errors as a Result of Specialization*, 36 J. BIOMEDICAL INFORMATICS 61, 68 (2003); Kevin W. Eva, Lee R. Brooks, & Geoffrey R. Norman, *Does "Shortness of Breath" = "Dyspnea"? The Biasing Effect of Feature Instantiation in Medical Diagnosis*, 76 ACAD. MED. S11, S13 (2001).

103. Blasi, *supra* note 1, at 396.

104. For a striking example of an expert who goes wrong right from the start of a simulated interview, see Patel, Evans, & Kaufman, *A Cognitive Framework*, *supra* note 12, at 292–97. The patient told the physician that his "first major" complaint, or difference from his normal condition, was "a weakness in the legs," and Patel and her colleagues comment that "[a]fter determining the time of onset [of this weakness], the expert completely neglects the presenting complaint." The physician instead asked about other issues, and "focused exclusively on the signs and symptoms of the common disorder, *hyperthyroidism*, while failing to recognize the rare disorder of *hypokalemic periodic paralysis*." The authors conclude that "[i]t was clear from the outset that this [incomplete diagnosis] was the only hypothesis that [the physician] had considered and that he used a predictive reasoning strategy before having gathered sufficient information via diagnostic reasoning." *Id. See also* Wiley, *supra* note 12; Stefan Krieger, *Domain Knowledge and the Teaching of Creative Problem-Solving*, 11 CLIN. L. REV. 149, 175–76 (2004).

105. Hal R. Arkes et al., *Factors Influencing the Use of a Decision Rule in a Probabilistic Task*, in PROFESSIONAL JUDGMENT, *supra* note 17, at 163, 177–78. The authors of this study suggest that medical diagnosis would exemplify such a situation, *id.* at 177, and the same might well be true of legal practice.

106. *See supra* note 36.

107. For a thoughtful exploration of the cognitive limits on both clients and lawyers, *see* Weinstein, *supra* note 68.

108. *See* Aaronson, *supra* note 13, at 256–79; Neumann, *supra* note 87, at 404–12.

109. *Cf.* Croskerry, *supra* note 99, at 779 (suggesting "[training] for a reflective approach to problem solving: stepping back from the immediate problem to examine and reflect on the thinking process"). Or perhaps the right pedagogical course is the opposite, to give students more of a foundation in detailed study of legal doctrine and conventional legal practice norms so that they have a grounding for their own early efforts at independent problem-solving. *Cf.* Patel et al., *supra* note 29; Krieger, *supra* note 104.

110. *See* WILLIAM M. SULLIVAN ET AL., EDUCATING LAWYERS: PREPARATION FOR THE PROFESSION OF LAW (2007); ROY STUCKEY ET AL., BEST PRACTICES FOR LEGAL EDUCATION: A VISION AND A ROAD MAP (2007), *available at* http://www.cleaweb.org/documents/bestpractices/best_practices-full.pdf.

111. So Guthrie et al., *supra* note 79, at 35–36, propose to do for judges. Wiley suggests that pausing is most likely to be useful when the misleading prejudgment is not deeply ingrained— unfortunately not necessarily the case, it seems, with expert knowledge. *See* Wiley, *supra* note 12, at 727. Feltovich et al., *supra* note 102, at 137 urge experts to "adopt[] a personal epistemology, or worldview about knowledge and its application . . . , that recognizes that what is to be learned can be messy, irregular, and exceptional." They encourage an "active inclination to see things many ways, to explain in many ways, to use in many ways, to connect in many ways." *Id.* at 138.

112. Wiley suggests that when experts seek to overcome their mistaken "fixation" on a given solution, they may need to engage in "massed effort," in which by sheer persistence they may exhaust the possibilities they were initially disposed to embrace, and so free their thinking to focus elsewhere. Wiley, *supra* note 12, at 727.

113. GROOPMAN, *supra* note 34, at 75; *see also id.* at 263. "Several studies have found that asking people to consider the possibility that the opposite hypothesis is true is sufficient to undo the bias of one-sided thinking." Timothy D. Wilson et al., *Mental Contamination and the Debiasing Problem*, in HEURISTICS, *supra* note 38, at 185, 197; *see* Babcock, Loewenstein, & Issacharoff, *supra* note 79, at 916. Notably, simply reminding people that cognitive biases exist does not suffice. *See id.* at 916, 921 (citing an earlier study in which "[d]isputants who were informed of the bias expected their bargaining counterpart to exhibit the bias but seemed to think that they themselves were immune").

114. Thus Croskerry notes, as a potentially risky "cognitive disposition to respond," the possibility that "clinicians may (consciously or otherwise) deliberately inflate the likelihood of disease, such as in the strategy of "rule out worst-case scenario" to avoid missing a rare but significant diagnosis." Croskerry, *supra* note 99, at 777.

115. On the value of checklists, see Atul Gawande, *The Checklist*, THE NEW YORKER, Dec. 10, 2007, at 86; Guthrie et al., *supra* note 79, at 40–42.

116. Cochran, DiPippa & Peters suggest a framework-changing approach when they advise that "[t]he lawyer and the client should review the decision once the client has made his choice. This review allows the client to look at the chosen option in isolation from all of the others." ROBERT F. COCHRAN, JR., JOHN M.A. DiPIPPA & MARTHA M. PETERS, THE COUNSELOR-AT-LAW: A COLLABORATIVE APPROACH TO CLIENT INTERVIEWING AND COUNSELING 158 (2nd ed. 2006).

117. In a study from the 1970s, Carl Hosticka found that when legal aid clients were "persistent"—reflected in "interruption, changing the subject, continuing the topic without regard to interventions by the lawyers" and not answering the lawyers' questions—their lawyers considered them "hostile" but "[l]awyers worked harder for clients who were perceived as hostile and who persisted in trying to contact the lawyer." Carl J. Hosticka, *We Don't Care About What Happened, We Only Care About What Is Going to Happen: Lawyer–Client Negotiations of Reality*, 26 SOC. PROBLEMS 599, 607 (1979).

118. *See* Statement of Client's Rights, N.Y. COMP. CODES R. & REGS tit. 22, § 1210.1 (2009), *available at* http://mycourts.gov/attorneysclientsrights.shtml.

119. Jennifer Wright Oliver, Richard L. Kravitz, Sherrie H. Kaplan, & Frederick J. Meyers, *Individualized Patient Education and Coaching to Improve Pain Control Among Cancer Outpatients*, 19 J. CLIN. ONCOLOGY 2206 (2001); *cf.* Gordon et al., *supra* note 49, at 530 (recommending programs "to educate and coach patients in the management of common health problems" as well as explanations for patients, in the managed care "plan," of such issues as "what to expect regarding time with a physician").

120. *See* GROOPMAN, *supra* note 34, at 260–69. Groopman's call is noteworthy because only about 6 percent of the time in patients' encounters with doctors "is taken up by patients asking questions. This is particularly troubling," Roter and Hall write, "because many studies have demonstrated that patients often have questions they would like to ask but do not." ROTER & HALL, *supra* note 19, at 121. For Roter and Hall's recommendations on "empowering patients to be actively engaged in their health," see *id.* at 169–73.

121. *See* Neumann, *supra* note 87, at 420.

122. GROOPMAN, *supra* note 34, at 5–6.

123. *Cf.* Robert S. Wigton et al., *How Physicians Use Clinical Information in Diagnosing Pulmonary Embolism: An Application of Conjoint Analysis*, in PROFESSIONAL JUDGMENT, *supra* note 17, at 131, 144–48 (finding, in a clinical situation "when there is no clear guidance about the best use of diagnostic information," that there is "a considerable variability in diagnostic information use which does not appear to decrease with increasing experience" and seeking to explain why experience apparently does *not* generate consensus).

124. *Cf.* Guthrie et al., *supra* note 79, at 38–40 (on "training and feedback" for judges). Wiley comments that "[o]utside of highly controlled experimental contexts, it seems quite plausible that the successful solution of previously unsolved problems could depend on a combination of these two mechanisms—that is, both the fading of irrelevant associations and *the exposure to relevant cues*." Wiley, *supra* note 12, at 728 (emphasis added). "Relevant cues"—or, one might say, helpful hints—are just what trusted colleagues can provide.

125. *See* David Schkade, Cass R. Sunstein, & Reed Hastie, *What Happened on Deliberation Day?*, 95 CAL. L. REV. 915 (2007) (on the unnerving tendency for "deliberation among like-minded people [to] produce[] *ideological amplification*—an amplification of preexisting tendencies, in which group discussion leads to greater extremism," *id.* at 917).

126. *See generally* Gary Bellow, *Turning Solutions into Problems: The Legal Aid Experience*, NLADA Bʀɪᴇғᴄᴀsᴇ 106 (Aug. 1977).

127. Stefan Krieger has commented that "both legal and medical problems can span the spectrum from minimally to very ill-structured." Krieger, *supra* note 104, at 156. Donald Schön, whose understanding of expert judgment emphasizes its creativity rather than its routine speed, observed that "[A]ll doctors will tell you that some percentage of the patients that come into the office are not in the book.... (Doctors do vary about what this percentage is: I have never heard it lower than thirty percent or higher than eighty percent, but I have heard it put at eighty percent by someone whom I regard as a very good doctor.) In some fields ... the frequency of uniqueness is even greater. The psychiatrist Erik Erikson once said the patient is a universe of one, and very good architects say that each site is unique." Donald A. Schön, *Educating the Reflective Legal Practitioner*, 2 Cʟɪɴ. L. Rᴇᴠ. 231, 239 (1995). Richard Neumann, who quotes this passage in Neumann, *supra* note 87, at 406, includes among Schön's key insights the judgment that "[m]ost of professional work starts in confusion, and the professional usually cannot develop certainty." *Id.* at 405.

128. One scholar has observed that "the most compelling evidence for the role of vast experience in expertise comes from investigators who have shown that, even for the most talented individuals, ten years of experience in a domain (ten-year rule) is necessary to become an expert ... and to win at an international level." K. Anders Ericsson, *The Influence of Experience and Deliberate Practice on the Development of Superior Expert Performance*, in Hᴀɴᴅʙᴏᴏᴋ, *supra* note 11, at 683, 689.

AFTERWORD

You have joined us on a long and complex journey. We end with the hope that you now feel that the familiar steps of interviewing and counseling have a new clarity and resonance.

As you've seen, each word of a meeting between lawyer and client reflects choices: by the client certainly, but also by the lawyer. How far will you share facts about yourself as part of building connection with a client? How will you respond if the client takes offense at something you have said? Can you build connections with clients from whom you feel very different, or provide objective advice to clients with whom you feel very similar? How can you offer your own thoughts and insights about the decisions the client must make without taking those decisions away from the client? Can you engage successfully with clients who may be outside of the mainstream of clients with whom you have dealt? Can you hear the story your client may want to tell but hasn't voiced? Will you ask your client to tell you the truth, and will you assure him of confidentiality in the process? Will you broach issues of morality with your client, or urge your client to take action based on these concerns, and how far will you be prepared to defer to her views of what morality requires? What will you tell your client about the law, and how will you respond to what your client says in return? And how will you do all of this, as a practical matter, with your first client, and your hundredth?

We have offered answers, or frameworks for answers, to most of these questions. But we end with this—we are all, lawyers as well as our counterparts in other professions, still learning how people flourish, and how one person can best help another to flourish. We are exploring the dynamics of human thought and feeling, and we are, every day, moving forward into new social structures which we, collectively, will shape as we go along and which will, in turn, shape us. What shall we do, in the midst of such promise and such uncertainty? We must act based on what we know—for we have no alternative–but we have a great deal still to understand. Above all we hope this book encourages you to join in discovering more about how lawyers can do their vital work.

Lawyers and clients have been meeting together for many hundreds of years. Much of what we do today no doubt reflects the accumulated wisdom, and mistakes, of all those past generations. It is our task—and our opportunity—to examine the practices we have inherited, to grasp fully the lessons they teach, and to continue to learn how we can work better, in each meeting to come.

*

INDEX

References are to Pages

References are to Pages

†